Praise for
The Greatest Words Ever Spoken

"There is power in the Word of Christ! *The Greatest Words Ever Spoken* will help you experience His power like never before!"
—JOSH D. McDOWELL, author and speaker

"If you've ever wanted to understand Jesus' heart, listen to what He said. Using all the recorded words of Jesus, this book makes it easy."
—GARY D. CHAPMAN, PhD, best-selling author
of *The Five Love Languages* and *Love as a Way of Life*

"The greatest words ever spoken were delivered by the greatest man who ever lived: Jesus Christ. Steven Scott has done us a wonderful favor by organizing these life-transforming truths by topic."
—JAMES ROBISON, founder and president
of LIFE Outreach International

"In *The Greatest Words Ever Spoken,* you, dear reader, will come to know the very essence of who Jesus is—and how His heart seeks after you."
—JANET PARSHALL, radio host of *Janet Parshall's America!*

"I love being able to see Jesus' statements on a single topic arranged one right after the other. This is a helpful tool not only for study but also for personal devotions."
—DR. HENRY CLOUD, best-selling author of *The Secret Things of God* and coauthor of *Boundaries*

"Packed with every word Jesus spoke and grouped by topic, this book should be a constant companion to your Bible."
—DR. DAVID JEREMIAH, founder of Turning Point Ministries, best-selling author of *Captured by Grace*

"*The Greatest Words Ever Spoken* makes it possible for anyone to have instant access to everything Christ taught on virtually any subject. *Amazing!*"
—ROY BLUNT, member U.S. House of Representatives

THE GREATEST
WORDS
EVER SPOKEN

THE GREAT WORDS EVER SPOKEN

EVERYTHING JESUS SAID ABOUT YOU, YOUR LIFE, AND EVERYTHING ELSE

STEVEN K. SCOTT

WATERBROOK
PRESS

The author has made every effort to ensure the accuracy of the stories and anecdotes in this book. In
some instances, names and identifying details have been changed to protect the privacy of the person
or persons involved.

ISBN 978-1-4000-7463-1
ISBN 978-0-307-44612-1 (electronic)

Copyright © 2008 by Steve Scott

Published in the United States by WaterBrook Multnomah, an imprint of the Crown Publishing
Group, a division of Random House Inc., New York.

WATERBROOK and its deer colophon are registered trademarks of Random House Inc.

The Library of Congress cataloged the hardcover edition as follows:
Scott, Steve, 1948–
    The greatest words ever spoken : everything Jesus said about you, your life, and everything else /
Steve Scott ; foreword by Gary Smalley. — 1st ed.
        p. cm.
    ISBN 978-1-4000-7462-4
    1. Jesus Christ—Words. I. Title.
BT306.S43 2008
232.9'54—dc22

2008025021

Printed in the United States of America
2010—Trade Paperback Edition

10 9 8 7 6 5 4 3

SPECIAL SALES
Most WaterBrook Multnomah books are available in special quantity discounts when purchased in
bulk by corporations, organizations, and special interest groups. Custom imprinting or excerpting can
also be done to fit special needs. For information, please e-mail SpecialMarkets@WaterBrookPress.com
or call 1-800-603-7051.

CONTENTS

FOREWORD

AN IMPORTANT WORD FROM GARY SMALLEY

Steve Scott has been one of my best friends for more than thirty years. He coauthored and published my first two books, which enabled me to launch my ministry in 1979. Eight years later Steve produced and distributed our *Hidden Keys to Loving Relationships* video series, which helped millions of couples throughout the world improve their marriages.

Since I have known him, Steve has undertaken scores of projects. The companies he has created with his business partners have blessed the lives of millions of people. He also has authored a number of international bestsellers on personal achievement. But two years ago he told me about something that he considered the most important project of his life. He said he was gathering all the statements of Jesus Christ and organizing them by topic.

At the time Steve had already organized all the Lord's statements from the gospels of John and Mark, but he hadn't yet started Luke and Matthew. I asked about his publisher, and his answer surprised me. "Gary, I don't even know if I'm going to publish it… I'm doing this one for *me*."

Steve told me that based on his reading of John 8:31-32 and Matthew 7:21-25, he wanted the words of Christ to form the concrete foundation of his beliefs on every subject and issue of life and to do that he needed to put *everything* the Lord said on every subject into an easily accessible format. Once he had the foundation of Christ's words on any given subject, he could then build everything else pertaining to that subject *securely* upon the foundation of Christ's teachings.

I asked if I could look at what he had so far, and he pulled out his manuscript. I quickly found a topic that meant a lot to me, and as I read the Lord's words, I was overcome with emotion. I looked at Steve and said, "This is the most powerful thing I have ever read." You see, even though I had read every one of the verses on that subject dozens of times throughout my life, I had *never* read them *together*. The authority, clarity, and power of all the Lord's teachings on that subject impacted me in a way that the piecemeal reading never had. My heart was melted by an intense love that I felt from the Lord.

As I read one particular topic, it was like each statement Jesus made penetrated deeper and deeper and deeper into my soul. I've never felt anything as powerful. This is what the disciples must have felt as He intimately answered their greatest questions.

Steve told me he had felt the same kind of impact. He said that bringing all of Christ's statements together on a given subject was like bringing all the individual pieces of a jigsaw puzzle together. Separately, every piece has color, meaning, and beauty…but you never see the full picture until the pieces are brought together. Steve then said something I'll never forget: "Gary, it's like having a personal appointment with the Lord, where you can ask Him about anything you want, and He then tells you *everything* He taught about that subject when He was on earth. You say, 'Lord, tell me about forgiveness,' and He then tells you *everything* He taught on forgiveness."

I told Steve he had to get this book published—and promised that I would promote it all over the world. He later told me that my encouragement was timed perfectly, because his efforts to categorize the Lord's statements had been the hardest thing he had ever done, and he had been on the verge of quitting.

I have now had the completed manuscript for several months, and it's everything I hoped it would be, and more. It's not only perfect for study; it's wonderful for your devotional time as well. You prayerfully ask questions that are on your heart, and Jesus gives the answers. And because most of the verses are quoted from the New International Version (and a few from the New King James Version and the New American Standard Bible), it's just as readable for children as it is for adults. This book is going to be my Christmas gift to each of my children, their spouses, and their children, because I'm convinced that each one of them should have their own copy.

And here's something I *wasn't* expecting. Steve divided all the topics into nine general categories that make up the nine chapters of the book. He has written short chapter introductions that are extremely enlightening and compelling to *non-Christians*. Steve said he did this so he could give the book to his skeptical friends who have no interest in church or religion. His goal is to enable them to take a fresh look at the person of Christ, judging Him not on what anyone else has said or done but solely on what Christ said. So many people have misconceptions about Jesus that when they simply read what He said, those misconceptions are eliminated.

Jesus has made incredible promises to every man and woman, boy and girl who would learn His words and follow them. *The Greatest Words Ever Spoken* provides us with the perfect tool to do just that. With more than nineteen hundred statements of the Lord organized into more than two hundred topics, it's a treasure chest of answers, promises, inspiration, encouragement, love, faith, and power for living that *no* Christian home should be without. My prayer is that you and your family will use it as a tool to become even more intimate with the Lord Jesus Christ. I also pray that you will use it to place His incomparable words into the hands of the non-Christians whom God brings across your path.

ACKNOWLEDGMENTS

Thank you, Ryan Scott, for giving your dad the perfect title for this book. Not only was it better than the one I had thought of; it is truly the only title that sufficiently describes the incomparable words of the Lord Jesus Christ.

I can't begin to express my gratitude to Michael Palgon, deputy publisher of the Doubleday Broadway Publishing Group, and my Doubleday editor, Roger Scholl, for their incredible support of my vision for this book. Without *your* vision this book would never have been distributed beyond my own family.

I am so very grateful to Ron Lee, my brilliant editor at WaterBrook. Ron, you have made this book so much better than my original manuscript. You amaze me!

Carol Bartley and the copyeditors did such a wonderful job of catching all the things I missed. They came up with wonderful ways to make this book so much better for you, the reader.

I am grateful to Michael Smalley and the Logos Project for your vision for developing church curriculum to help bring *The Greatest Words Ever Spoken* to the pulpits and Sunday schools of churches throughout the world.

THE GREATEST WORDS
EVER SPOKEN

I know men; and I tell you that Jesus Christ is not a man....
Between Him and whoever else in the world,
there is no possible term of comparison.
—NAPOLEON BONAPARTE

"The greatest words ever spoken." How could such a claim be made about any collection of statements? With all the life-changing words spoken by so many great men and women throughout history, how could the words of one person rise above all the others?

To qualify as the greatest words ever spoken, they would have to reveal incredible truths that would otherwise go undiscovered. They would have to bring extraordinary, perhaps even near-miraculous benefit to the hearts, minds, and lives of those who read them. Certainly, to qualify as the greatest words ever spoken, they would have to produce life-altering changes not just for a few people but for millions. They would have to impart hope to those in despair, joy to those whose hearts are broken, and peace that subdues even the most paralyzing fears.

To earn the ranking of the greatest words ever spoken, the words would have to exert enough power to transform a hateful heart into a loving one, a mind driven by greed into one overflowing with generosity, a life ruled by arrogance into one that is driven by the desire to serve others. And if they were truly the greatest words ever spoken, they would have the power to give sight to the blind, deliverance to the captive, forgiveness to the wrongdoer, and life to the dead. If anyone's words could accomplish these things, they would certainly rise above all other words in history. They would deserve to be called the greatest words ever spoken.

These words exist; they have been spoken and recorded. And, yes, they *have* accomplished remarkable, miraculous results. The greatest words ever spoken are the words of Jesus of Nazareth, who claimed to be the Son of the living God.

The If-Then Statement That Can Change Your Life

If Jesus is who He claimed to be, then everything He said must be fully, absolutely true. If He is the Son of God, He would never speak in error. Think of the implications. First, if Jesus' words are absolute truth, they are the standard by which all other purported truths must be measured. Second, everything Jesus said about you, your life, and your circumstances is true. His words describe your life and reveal your immediate and long-term future. To succeed in life, to understand yourself, and to gain wisdom about your present and your future, you need to learn everything Jesus said about you. In that way you will discover what He wants for you and from you.

And then there are the promises Jesus made. If you choose to follow Him, then all of his 108 promises are promises you can count on—promises that will produce peace in a troubled heart, joy in the midst of tragedy, success in place of failure, and most important, a glorified life that lasts for eternity.

And this leads to the most important question you will ever face. *Is* Jesus of Nazareth the person He claimed to be, or was He a mere man?

Napoleon Bonaparte, the emperor of France and one of the greatest military geniuses who ever lived, concluded that Jesus was no mere man. Once when Napoleon was discussing various emperors and their empires with his most trusted advisors, the name of Jesus came up. To the surprise of his generals, Napoleon exclaimed:

> I know men; and I tell you that Jesus Christ is not a man. Superficial minds see a resemblance between Christ and the founders of empires, and the gods of other religions. That resemblance does not exist.... Everything

in Christ astonishes me. His spirit overawes me, and His will confounds me. Between Him and whoever else in the world, there is no possible term of comparison. He is truly a being by Himself. His ideas and sentiments, the truth which He announces, His manner of convincing, are not explained either by human organization or by the nature of things… The nearer I approach, the more carefully I examine, everything is above me—everything remains grand, of a grandeur which overpowers.… One can absolutely find nowhere, but in Him alone, the imitation or the example of His life… I search in vain in history to find the similar to Jesus Christ… Neither history, nor humanity, nor the ages, nor nature, offer me anything with which I am able to compare it or explain it. Here everything is extraordinary.[i]

Jesus of Nazareth

What did Napoleon know that some of us do not? He was a student of history and a student of men, and he had diligently studied the life and words of Christ. In light of this, he believed that no one in history could compare to Jesus of Nazareth. Think about it: how could one man from an obscure village in the Middle East have changed so many millions of lives as well as the course of history? If ever a man should have been overlooked by history, it was Jesus.

Consider the facts:

Jesus was born to a peasant couple in a village in the middle of nowhere. He lived in a country occupied by foreign conquerors. His only means of transportation was His legs.

He was a carpenter until He turned thirty, and only then did He begin to teach and speak in public. For three short years He proclaimed His message, mostly in small villages.

After being falsely accused and then convicted in a rigged trial, He was sentenced to death by an official who believed Him to be innocent. He died the death of a criminal and was executed on a cross between two convicted criminals. Only His mother and a few of His close followers were present at His execution. The rest of His disciples had fled, hiding from the mob and the Roman officials.

It was only after Jesus rose from the dead and appeared to His followers that His disciples were transformed from distraught cowards into confident, fearless believers and preachers of Jesus' message. But they had no means to spread His story and teachings to a mass audience. There were no radios, televisions, or printing presses. In fact, paper as we know it had not yet been invented. Every papyrus scroll had to be painstakingly written by hand. The only way to make a copy was to read the original and laboriously copy it word by word.

In first-century Palestine, the thought that Jesus' life might make a significant impact on anyone beyond the Judean countryside was laughable. Any history of this itinerant rabbi who appeared in public for only three years should have been lost—either burned or buried—in the rubble when Jerusalem was destroyed by the Roman legions less than forty years after Jesus walked the earth. Against such a background, you can begin to understand the miracle of His life and words. Jesus' short earthly life—far from being lost to the generations who have followed—became the focal point of history.

How could one man's life impact humanity to a greater extent than any other person or any series of events in history? As you read *The Greatest Words Ever Spoken,* you will get to know this man who changed everything...forever. Jesus did it all, not with money, armies, science, or politics, but with the witness of His life and the power of His words. His life and the miracles He performed attracted the attention of the crowds, but it was what He *said* that melted their hearts and transformed their lives. The apostle John said, "The Word became flesh and made his dwelling among us. We have seen his glory, the glory of the One and Only, who came from the Father, full of grace and truth" (John 1:14).

The Tragedy of the Information Age

Today we have more information about everything than any past generation had, yet most people know less of what Jesus said. Countless people are so unaware of first-century history that they are swayed by baseless myths perpetuated by works of fiction such as *The Da Vinci Code.* Many Christians have built their beliefs and values on the words of Bible teachers, authors, and television and radio preachers rather than on the words of Christ. As wonderful as the words of preachers and writers may be, they can't begin to compare in wonder and power to the pure, undiluted words of Jesus Christ. After all,

He alone claimed to be the embodiment of all truth when He said, "I am the way and the truth and the life" (John 14:6). He made incredible promises to those who would build their lives on His words.

It's important to realize that Jesus did not make these promises to people who followed the words of any other teacher, prophet, or leader. The words of Jesus stand alone in truth, power, and authority. For example, He promised, "If you *abide* in My word, then you are truly disciples of Mine; and you shall know the truth, and the truth shall make you free" (John 8:31-32, NASB). And that was just the beginning. Here are a few of the many promises Jesus made to those who choose to abide in His Word:

- You will receive eternal life.
- Your desires will be fulfilled in answer to your prayers.
- God the Father, Jesus, and the Holy Spirit will be your constant companions, both with you and within you.
- You will receive a level of peace and joy, direct from God, that is otherwise unattainable.
- You will impact the lives of others in ways that can't be achieved strictly by human effort.
- You will be loved by God in a unique way.
- You will avoid God's ultimate judgment.
- You will see miracles in your life that others can't understand or explain.
- You will learn eternal truths that will set you free from all that holds you captive.

Jesus Was *Not* a Religious Leader!

Jesus Christ did not come to earth to start a new religion. In fact, He leveled His harshest criticisms at the religious leaders of His day. He accused them of not knowing God and said they had used religion to bind people to a life of misery, frustration, and failure. He claimed they were blind and had blinded the "spiritual eyes" of their followers (see Matthew 15:13-14; 23:13-24).

When He described Himself, Jesus claimed that He had come from God and that His mission was to reveal who God was and what God wanted. Most important, Jesus claimed that He could lead anyone into an intimate relationship with the only true God and that in doing so He would lead them into eternal life. In His final prayer before His crucifixion, Jesus stated, "Now this is eternal life: that they may know you, the only true God, and Jesus Christ, whom you have sent" (John 17:3).

Think about getting to know the God who created the universe. What would it be like to know Him on a first-name basis—or, even better, to know Him so intimately that you could call Him your best friend, even your dad? Imagine what it would be like if you could consistently experience His presence and a level of peace and joy that no adversity could vanquish. That's exactly what will happen as you begin to focus on the words of Christ.

The words of Jesus have changed the course of history by changing millions of lives, one life at a time. His words were first believed by those who witnessed His miracles. He turned water into wine and caused the blind to receive their sight, the lame to walk, and the dead to rise. Fortunately for us, He promised even greater blessings to those in later generations who would believe in Him without seeing Him in person. For two thousand years Jesus has kept that promise. He extends the same promise to you. As you begin to store up His words in your mind and heart, you will discover their life-changing power in ways you never thought possible.

The Life Issues That Jesus Addressed

In this book you will find every word of Jesus that is recorded in the New Testament, organized in more than two hundred topics. This will enable you to read everything Jesus said without the interruption of commentary, transitional scenes, and details about the activities of the people who surrounded Him. As you read this book, you can immerse yourself in Jesus' *words*. You can reflect on every statement He made about things that are important to you. You'll see everything the Lord said on such subjects as prayer, faith, eternal life, fear, your life priorities, His incredible promises, and the claims He made about Himself.

Because Jesus' words are organized by topic, you can easily grasp the breadth of what He said on each one. In a matter of minutes, you can read everything He said about a topic, which will help you gain a deeper understanding of His teachings. People who have read Jesus' words as they are organized in this book say they gained a depth of wisdom and experienced a life-changing power far greater than they could have imagined.

The two hundred-plus topics have been grouped into nine chapters, each addressing a general category. At the beginning of every chapter, I added a few thoughts about the topics addressed in that chapter. The chapters are:

1. The Greatest Words Ever Spoken About Jesus
2. The Greatest Words Ever Spoken About God the Father
3. The Greatest Words Ever Spoken About the Holy Spirit
4. The Greatest Words Ever Spoken About Eternity
5. The Greatest Words Ever Spoken to Jesus' Followers
6. The Greatest Words Ever Spoken About Humanity
7. The Greatest Words Ever Spoken About God Reaching Out to Us
8. The Greatest Words Ever Spoken About How to Know God
9. The Greatest Words Ever Spoken About Personal Relationships

The Only Foundation That Is Truly Secure

Jesus made a number of incredible promises to men and women who learn, embrace, and follow His words. He said we should base all our values, beliefs, and behaviors on the foundation of His words. Unfortunately, most of us base our lives on a mixture of things we've learned from every source we've been exposed to. As a result, the foundation of our beliefs is a combination of truth and falsehood, including contradictory information and false assumptions. My hope is that as you study the words of Christ, any weaknesses in your current foundation will be revealed, and you will replace them with the undiluted, indestructible concrete of Jesus' words. May He bless you in your pursuit of intimacy with God and the eternal truths revealed by His incomparable words.

How to Get the Most Out of This Book

This is not a book you will read cover to cover in a few sittings. You won't find even one of the chapters to be a quick read. Instead, this book is a resource you can use for the rest of your life. The two hundred-plus topics offer great variety. If you're seeking an answer to a specific question, a quick reading of Jesus' words on that topic will meet that need. If you're wrestling with an important decision, the wisdom and inspiration you seek can be found by reading His words on the appropriate topics. At the same time, a focused study of a topic can provide a rock-solid foundation for your faith. It will deepen your love for God and will provide an anchor in the greatest trials of life.

This book can easily be adapted to the need of the moment. Depending on the topic and how you approach it, the spiritual meal can range from a quick-energy bar to an entire buffet. Because the wisdom offered on each topic comes solely from the undiluted statements of Christ, their breadth, depth, and power are enlightening, faith building, and life changing.

Here are two suggestions that will help you get the most out of reading this book.

Use It as a Quick Reference

Whenever you are studying a biblical subject, considering a spiritual question, or seeking guidance for a decision, the first question you should ask is "What did Jesus say?" His words will provide the foundation for all your values, beliefs, and doctrines.

To locate a topic, check the book's table of contents, which lists the nine general categories (one per chapter) and the specific topics within each of the nine categories. You can also go to the back of the book and search the two hundred-plus topics in alphabetical order. Once located, each topic includes every direct statement Christ made on that topic and most of the implied references. Because context is so important, the verses surrounding the key points are usually provided.

As you begin to read Jesus' statements, underline the key points. For example, in chapter 5 under the heading "The Promises of Christ," you will find more than one hundred promises that Jesus made to His followers. Here is one of the crucial promises Jesus made:

> Most assuredly, I say to you, <u>he who hears My word and believes in Him</u> <u>who sent Me</u> **has everlasting life, and shall not come into judgment,** but has passed from death into life. Most assuredly, I say to you, the hour is coming, and now is, when the dead will hear the voice of the Son of God; and those who hear will live. (John 5:24–25, NKJV)

In this promise, I underlined the condition to be met so the promise can be fulfilled. The condition is you must hear (follow) Christ's words and truly believe in the God who sent Him. The promised benefits, set in boldface type, are you'll receive eternal life and you won't be subject to God's judgment.

When you underline or highlight the key points of every statement of Jesus as you study them, something wonderful happens. Each statement becomes like a piece of a jigsaw puzzle. As you read all of Christ's statements on a given topic and underline or highlight the key points, you'll see the pieces of the puzzle come together to create a clear picture of what He is teaching. Any other Bible verses you read on that subject will serve as additional pieces for the picture.

Use It for Topical Studies for You and Your Family

One of the greatest values of this book is that it will enable you to quickly and effectively study any subject that Christ spoke about. Individuals, couples, and families can select topics to study during morning or evening devotions, in-depth individual Bible studies, or group Bible studies. I suggest going through the table of contents and placing a check by the topics that interest you the most. One of my friends asked his wife and his children to put their initials beside each topic they wanted to study. This helped them prioritize the subjects they wanted to study first. They decided not only to study the topics individually but to use that list for selecting topics for family devotions.

As you study the words of Christ, you will receive the benefits He promised in John 16:13 and John 14:26. The Holy Spirit will guide you into all truth, He will tell you things to come, and He will glorify Christ. Jesus also promises that the Holy Spirit will teach you all things and bring to your remembrance all the things that Christ has spoken to you.

You will notice that most of the Scripture sections begin with verses from the gospel of John, followed by verses from Matthew, Mark, Luke, and sometimes Acts, 1 or 2 Corinthians, or Revelation, in that order. I begin the topical sections with verses from John because his gospel is more direct and more intimate. John referred to himself as "the disciple...Jesus loved" (John 21:20). John's account of Jesus' life conveys an unmistakable warmth and a sense of immediacy. Reading his gospel is like receiving an invitation from an old friend. I hope you will accept his invitation as you read Jesus' words addressing various subjects in this book.

Jesus' greatest promises were made to those who will hear His words and do them. His words will provide abundant light and perfect wisdom for any decision you face and all the power you will need to overcome any adversity. But the promises He makes and the power He offers will never be known by those who refuse to hear His words. In my forty-three years of discovering and relying on His words, I have experienced miraculous outcomes in every area of my life. What His words have done for me, I know they will also do for you. May you learn their meaning and experience their power as never before.

I

THE GREATEST WORDS EVER SPOKEN ABOUT JESUS

What Christ Tells Us About Himself

No theologian or historian would dispute the fact that Jesus was the single most influential figure ever to walk the earth. His actions, words, and miracles changed the course of history. He inspired entire societies to incorporate compassion and mercy into their cultures. He redefined the standards of morality. He not only changed the course of nations; He brought an unexplainable measure of purpose, peace, and joy into the lives of hundreds of millions of individuals.

Only God Could Beat These Impossible Odds

In His brief life, Jesus fulfilled hundreds of Old Testament prophecies describing the birth, life, and death of the Jewish Messiah. Mathematics professors Peter W. Stoner and Dr. Robert C. Newman calculated the statistical probability of one person fulfilling just forty-eight of these detailed prophecies. The odds turned out to be 1 in 10^{157}. That's a 1 in 10,000,000,000,000,000,000, 000,000,000,000,000,000,000,000,000,000,000,000,000,000,000,000,000, 000,000,000,000,000,000,000,000,000,000,000,000,000,000,000,000,000, 000,000,000,000,000,000,000,000,000,000,000,000 chance.[ii]

To put it in perspective, let's say you built a wooden box so big that the solar system would fit inside it. Then you filled that box with silver BBs and placed just one copper BB in the box. The chances of anyone reaching into the box and picking out the copper BB on the first try would be trillions of times *more likely* than the odds of one person fulfilling all the prophecies that Jesus fulfilled. No occurrence in history or physical science has been verified with a higher degree of statistical certainty than the fact that Jesus is exactly who He claimed to be—the Messiah, the Son of the living God.

Since His death and resurrection, more words have been written about Jesus Christ than about any person or event in history. But more important than the words written about Him are the words that Jesus spoke about Himself. Who was Jesus, and where did He come from? What was His mission, and what is He accomplishing now, and what will He do in the future? What are His plans for your life, your future, and the future of the world? What is His relationship with God, and what kind of relationship does Jesus want to have with His followers?

And most important, how are His words relevant to each of us and our families right now? These are just a few of the questions Jesus answers in the twenty topics in this chapter.

One of my favorite sections in this chapter is "The Claims Jesus Made About Himself." Here we see more than 170 amazing claims Jesus made about Himself. If you or I made even a couple of these claims about ourselves, we would be committed to a mental institution. And yet, those who heard Him firsthand marveled at His teachings.

Why? First, Jesus spoke with a level of confidence and authority that we can't even imagine. Second, He backed up His seemingly preposterous claims with actions that proved the claims to be absolutely true. For example, He not only claimed that He could raise people from the dead, but He revived a corpse that had been rotting in a tomb. And He did it in front of eyewitnesses (John 11:38-44). Jesus also claimed He was going to be executed, buried for three days, and then rise from the dead. This claim was so preposterous His disciples didn't believe it—until He appeared in their midst after His resurrection.

Jesus made other incredible claims. He said He was the Light of the World and the embodiment of eternal truth. He claimed to be the only path by which men and women could enter into an eternal relationship with God. He claimed to be in perfect unity with God the Father and the only One who had ever seen God. He claimed to be the only begotten Son of the Eternal

God. He claimed that He was present at the beginning of time and that at the end of time He will be the One to judge every person who has ever lived. He even claimed that all authority in heaven and on earth had been given to Him. He claimed that He could grant eternal life to anyone who would follow Him.

And these are only 10 of His more than 170 claims.

The power of these claims has convinced many of the world's most brilliant atheists to become devout believers in God and followers of Christ. One such man was the former chairman of the literature departments of Oxford and Cambridge; another was one of America's most celebrated historians; and a third was a leading nuclear physicist, a man who earned eight doctorates.

In addition to chairing departments at two of the world's most prestigious universities, atheist-turned-Christian C. S. Lewis became one of the world's, and Christianity's, greatest novelists. Historian Lew Wallace, another atheist-turned-Christian, destroyed his anti-Christian manuscript titled *The Myth of Christianity* and replaced it with the most celebrated historical novel of all time, *Ben Hur: A Tale of the Christ.* And Dr. Charles Payne, a nuclear physicist with eight doctorates and also an atheist-turned-Christian, gave up his efforts to scientifically disprove Christianity and instead began proclaiming the scientific evidence for the existence of God and the divinity of Christ.

As you read this chapter, you'll find the statements Jesus made about His second coming and the signs of the times surrounding His return. As you read His statements on these topics, you'll gain a better perspective of what's happening in the Middle East and, more important, a basis for tremendous hope and confidence that we are the first generation in which His prophecies of His second coming are being fulfilled. As you read the statements under "Jesus' Relationship with God the Father," you will gain a deeper understanding of the relationship and fellowship that has always existed between these Persons of the Trinity.

Finally, near the end of this chapter, you will read Jesus' words spoken in parables, metaphors, and allegories. These stories reveal the depth of God's love and forgiveness and a number of eternal mysteries. If you have ever questioned your worth as a person or how much God loves you, Christ's statements and illustrations will resolve those questions. May His words speak with revelation and power to the depths of your soul.

The Claims Jesus Made About Himself

This is the single most important subject Jesus spoke about, because the authority for everything He did and everything else He said is built on this foundation. Jesus made more than 170 claims that no one else in history could have authoritatively made. In some cases a single statement reveals multiple claims. Apply any of these to someone else in history, and neither their lives nor their accomplishments would support even one of these claims. Yet, every one of the claims fits comfortably with Jesus. Here again, He made His claims using direct statements, implied statements, and metaphors. His claims were also made by His acceptance of what others said about Him. Who else could claim to be both a king and a servant, the Son of God and the Son of Man, the Beginning and the End, the Light of the World, the Living Water who gives eternal life, and the total fulfillment of the law and all righteousness? Who else could offer to provide *eternal life* and not be looked upon as a lunatic or an outright fraud? In this section you will see both the ultimate in humility and the ultimate in majesty. You will experience a level of gratitude as you realize that this glorious Person knows you better than any other. And in spite of His majesty, He intimately loves you more than you have ever been loved by anyone.[iii]

JOHN 3:10-13 "You are Israel's teacher," said Jesus, "and do you not understand these things? [11]I tell you the truth,

we speak of what we know, and we testify to what we have seen, but still you people do not accept our testimony. [12]I have spoken to you of earthly things and you do not believe; how then will you believe if I speak of heavenly things? [13]No one has ever gone into heaven except the one who came from heaven—the Son of Man."

JOHN 3:16-17 "For God so loved the world that he gave his one and only Son, that whoever believes in him shall not perish but have eternal life. [17]For God did not send his Son into the world to condemn the world, but to save the world through him."

JOHN 4:7-10, 13-14 When a Samaritan woman came to draw water, Jesus said to her, "Will you give me a drink?" [8](His disciples had gone into the town to buy food.) [9]The Samaritan woman said to him, "You are a Jew and I am a Samaritan woman. How can you ask me for a drink?" (For Jews do not associate with Samaritans.) [10]Jesus answered her, "If you knew the gift of God and who it is that asks you for a drink, you would have asked him and he would have given you living water." [13]Jesus answered, "Everyone who drinks this water will be thirsty again, [14]but whoever drinks the water I give him will never thirst. Indeed, the water I give him will become in him a spring of water welling up to eternal life."

JOHN 4:25-26 The woman said, "I know that Messiah" (called Christ) "is coming. When he comes, he will explain everything to us." [26]Then Jesus declared, "I who speak to you am he."

JOHN 5:20 "For the Father loves the Son and shows him all he does. Yes, to your amazement he will show him even greater things than these."

JOHN 5:21-23 "For just as the Father raises the dead and gives them life, even so the Son gives life to whom he is pleased to give it. [22]Moreover, the Father judges no one, but has entrusted all judgment to the Son, [23]that all may honor the Son just as they honor the Father. He who does not honor the Son does not honor the Father, who sent him."

JOHN 5:26-27 "For as the Father has life in himself, so he has granted the Son to have life in himself. [27]And he has given him authority to judge because he is the Son of Man."

JOHN 6:27 "Do not work for food that spoils, but for food that endures to eternal life, which the Son of Man will give you. On him God the Father has placed his seal of approval."

JOHN 6:33 "For the bread of God is he who comes down from heaven and gives life to the world."

JOHN 6:35 Then Jesus declared, "I am the bread of life. He who comes to me will never go hungry, and he who believes in me will never be thirsty."

JOHN 6:37-40 "All that the Father gives me will come to me, and whoever comes to me I will never drive away. [38]For I have come down from heaven not to do my will but to do the will of him who sent me. [39]And this is the will of him who sent me, that I shall lose none of all that he has given me, but raise them up at the last day. [40]For my Father's will is that everyone who looks to the Son and believes in him shall have eternal life, and I will raise him up at the last day."

JOHN 6:43-44 "Stop grumbling among yourselves," Jesus answered. [44]"No one can come to me unless the Father who sent me draws him, and I will raise him up at the last day."

JOHN 6:46-47 "No one has seen the Father except the one who is from God; only he has seen the Father. [47]I tell you the truth, he who believes has everlasting life."

JOHN 6:48-51 "I am the bread of life. [49]Your forefathers ate the manna in the desert, yet they died. [50]But here is the bread that comes down from heaven, which a man may eat and not die. [51]I am the living bread that came down from heaven. If anyone eats of this bread, he will live forever. This bread is my flesh, which I will give for the life of the world."

JOHN 6:53-56 Jesus said to them, "I tell you the truth, unless you eat the flesh of the Son of Man and drink his blood, you have no life in you. [54]Whoever eats my flesh and drinks my blood has eternal life, and I will raise him up at the last day. [55]For my flesh is real food and my blood is real drink. [56]Whoever eats my flesh and drinks my blood remains in me, and I in him."

JOHN 6:57-58 "Just as the living Father sent me and I live because of the Father, so the one who feeds on me will live because of me. [58]This is the bread that came down from heaven. Your forefathers ate manna and died, but he who feeds on this bread will live forever."

JOHN 6:63 "The Spirit gives life; the flesh counts for nothing. The words I have spoken to you are spirit and they are life."

JOHN 7:16 Jesus answered, "My teaching is not my own. It comes from him who sent me."

JOHN 7:28 Then Jesus, still teaching in the temple courts, cried out, "Yes, you know me, and you know where I am from. I am not here on my own, but he who sent me is true...."

JOHN 7:38-39 "Whoever believes in me, as the Scripture has said, streams of living water will flow from within him." [39]By this he meant the Spirit, whom those who believed in him were later to receive. Up to that time the Spirit had not been given, since Jesus had not yet been glorified.

JOHN 8:12 When Jesus spoke again to the people, he said, "I am the light of the world. Whoever follows me will never walk in darkness, but will have the light of life."

JOHN 8:23-24 But he continued, "You are from below; I am from above. You are of this world; I am not of this world. [24]I told you that you would die in your sins; if you do not believe that I am the one I claim to be, you will indeed die in your sins."

JOHN 8:38 "I am telling you what I have seen in the Father's presence...."

JOHN 8:42 Jesus said to them, "If God were your Father, you would love me, for I came from God and now am here. I have not come on my own; but he sent me."

JOHN 8:49-50 "I am not possessed by a demon," said Jesus, "but I honor my Father and you dishonor me. [50]I am not seeking glory for myself; but there is one who seeks it, and he is the judge."

JOHN 8:51 "I tell you the truth, if anyone keeps my word, he will never see death."

JOHN 8:54-56 Jesus replied, "If I glorify myself, my glory means nothing.

My Father, whom you claim as your God, is the one who glorifies me. [55]Though you do not know him, I know him. If I said I did not, I would be a liar like you, but I do know him and keep his word. [56]Your father Abraham rejoiced at the thought of seeing my day; he saw it and was glad."

JOHN 8:58 "I tell you the truth," Jesus answered, "before Abraham was born, I am!"

JOHN 9:4-5 "As long as it is day, we must do the work of him who sent me. Night is coming, when no one can work. [5]While I am in the world, I am the light of the world."

JOHN 9:35-37 Jesus heard that they had thrown him [a man healed of blindness] out, and when he found him, he said, "Do you believe in the Son of Man?" [36]"Who is he, sir?" the man asked. "Tell me so that I may believe in him." [37]Jesus said, "You have now seen him; in fact, he is the one speaking with you."

JOHN 10:7-9 Therefore Jesus said again, "I tell you the truth, I am the gate for the sheep. [8]All who ever came before me were thieves and robbers, but the sheep did not listen to them. [9]I am the gate; whoever enters through me will be saved. He will come in and go out, and find pasture."

JOHN 10:10 "The thief comes only to steal and kill and destroy; I have come that they may have life, and have it to the full."

JOHN 10:14-15 "I am the good shepherd; I know my sheep and my sheep know me— [15]just as the Father knows me and I know the Father—and I lay down my life for the sheep."

JOHN 10:17-18 "The reason my Father loves me is that I lay down my life—only to take it up again. [18]No one takes it from me, but I lay it down of my own accord. I have authority to lay it down and authority to take it up again. This command I received from my Father."

JOHN 10:27-29 "My sheep listen to my voice; I know them, and they follow me. [28]I give them eternal life, and they shall never perish; no one can snatch them out of my hand. [29]My Father, who has given them to me, is greater than all; no one can snatch them out of my Father's hand."

JOHN 10:30-31 "I and the Father are one." [31]Again the Jews picked up stones to stone him.

JOHN 10:34-36 Jesus answered them, "Is it not written in your Law, 'I have said you are gods'? [35]If he called them 'gods,' to whom the word of God came—and the Scripture cannot be broken—[36]what about the one whom the Father set apart as his very own and sent into the world? Why then do you accuse me of blasphemy because I said, 'I am God's Son'?"

JOHN 11:25-26 Jesus said to her [Martha], "I am the resurrection and the life. He who believes in me will live, even though he dies; [26]and whoever lives and believes in me will never die. Do you believe this?"

JOHN 12:48-50 "There is a judge for the one who rejects me and does not accept my words; that very word which I spoke will condemn him at the last day. [49]For I did not speak of my own accord, but the Father who sent me commanded me what to say and how to say it. [50]I

know that his command leads to eternal life. So whatever I say is just what the Father has told me to say."

JOHN 14:1-4 "Do not let your hearts be troubled. Trust in God; trust also in me. [2]In my Father's house are many rooms; if it were not so, I would have told you. I am going there to prepare a place for you. [3]And if I go and prepare a place for you, I will come back and take you to be with me that you also may be where I am. [4]You know the way to the place where I am going."

JOHN 14:6 Jesus answered, "I am the way and the truth and the life. No one comes to the Father except through me."

JOHN 14:9-11 Jesus answered: "Don't you know me, Philip, even after I have been among you such a long time? Anyone who has seen me has seen the Father. How can you say, 'Show us the Father'? [10]Don't you believe that I am in the Father, and that the Father is in me? The words I say to you are not just my own. Rather, it is the Father, living in me, who is doing his work. [11]Believe me when I say that I am in the Father and the Father is in me; or at least believe on the evidence of the miracles themselves."

JOHN 14:12-14 "I tell you the truth, anyone who has faith in me will do what I have been doing. He will do even greater things than these, because I am going to the Father. [13]And I will do whatever you ask in my name, so that the Son may bring glory to the Father. [14]You may ask me for anything in my name, and I will do it."

JOHN 14:16-17 "And I will ask the Father, and he will give you another Counselor to be with you forever— [17]the

Spirit of truth. The world cannot accept him, because it neither sees him nor knows him. But you know him, for he lives with you and will be in you."

JOHN 14:19-21 "Before long, the world will not see me anymore, but you will see me. Because I live, you also will live. 20On that day you will realize that I am in my Father, and you are in me, and I am in you. 21Whoever has my commands and obeys them, he is the one who loves me. He who loves me will be loved by my Father, and I too will love him and show myself to him."

JOHN 14:23-24 Jesus replied, "If anyone loves me, he will obey my teaching. My Father will love him, and we will come to him and make our home with him. 24He who does not love me will not obey my teaching. These words you hear are not my own; they belong to the Father who sent me."

JOHN 14:26 "But the Counselor, the Holy Spirit, whom the Father will send in my name, will teach you all things and will remind you of everything I have said to you."

JOHN 14:27 "Peace I leave with you; my peace I give you. I do not give to you as the world gives. Do not let your hearts be troubled and do not be afraid."

JOHN 15:1-8 "I am the true vine, and my Father is the gardener. 2He cuts off every branch in me that bears no fruit, while every branch that does bear fruit he prunes so that it will be even more fruitful. 3You are already clean because of the word I have spoken to you. 4Remain in me, and I will remain in you. No branch can bear fruit by itself; it must remain in the vine. Neither can you bear fruit unless you remain in me. 5I am the vine; you are the branches. If a man remains in me and I in him, he will bear much fruit; apart from me you can do nothing. 6If anyone does not remain in me, he is like a branch that is thrown away and withers; such branches are picked up, thrown into the fire and burned. 7If you remain in me and my words remain in you, ask whatever you wish, and it will be given you. 8This is to my Father's glory, that you bear much fruit, showing yourselves to be my disciples."

JOHN 15:9-11 "As the Father has loved me, so have I loved you. Now remain in my love. 10If you obey my commands, you will remain in my love, just as I have obeyed my Father's commands and remain in his love. 11I have told you this so that my joy may be in you and that your joy may be complete."

JOHN 15:16 "You did not choose me, but I chose you and appointed you to go and bear fruit—fruit that will last. Then the Father will give you whatever you ask in my name."

JOHN 15:23-24 "He who hates me hates my Father as well. 24If I had not done among them what no one else did, they would not be guilty of sin. But now they have seen these miracles, and yet they have hated both me and my Father."

JOHN 15:26 "When the Counselor comes, whom I will send to you from the Father, the Spirit of truth who goes out from the Father, he will testify about me."

JOHN 16:5-6 "Now I am going to him who sent me, yet none of you asks me, 'Where are you going?' 6Because I have said these things, you are filled with grief."

JOHN 16:14-15 "He will bring glory to me by taking from what is mine and making it known to you. ¹⁵All that belongs to the Father is mine. That is why I said the Spirit will take from what is mine and make it known to you."

JOHN 16:26-28 "In that day you will ask in my name. I am not saying that I will ask the Father on your behalf. ²⁷No, the Father himself loves you because you have loved me and have believed that I came from God. ²⁸I came from the Father and entered the world; now I am leaving the world and going back to the Father."

JOHN 17:2-4 "For you [God the Father] granted him [Christ] authority over all people that he might give eternal life to all those you have given him. ³Now this is eternal life: that they may know you, the only true God, and Jesus Christ, whom you have sent. ⁴I have brought you glory on earth by completing the work you gave me to do."

JOHN 17:5 "And now, Father, glorify me in your presence with the glory I had with you before the world began."

JOHN 18:36 Jesus said, "My kingdom is not of this world. If it were, my servants would fight to prevent my arrest by the Jews. But now my kingdom is from another place."

JOHN 18:37 "You are a king, then!" said Pilate. Jesus answered, "You are right in saying I am a king. In fact, for this reason I was born, and for this I came into the world, to testify to the truth. Everyone on the side of truth listens to me."

JOHN 19:11 Jesus answered, "You [Pilate] would have no power over me if it were not given to you from above. There-fore the one who handed me over to you is guilty of a greater sin."

MATTHEW 5:17 "Do not think that I have come to abolish the Law or the Prophets; I have not come to abolish them but to fulfill them."

MATTHEW 11:27 "All things have been committed to me by my Father. No one knows the Son except the Father, and no one knows the Father except the Son and those to whom the Son chooses to reveal him."

MATTHEW 11:28-30 "Come to me, all you who are weary and burdened, and I will give you rest. ²⁹Take my yoke upon you and learn from me, for I am gentle and humble in heart, and you will find rest for your souls. ³⁰For my yoke is easy and my burden is light."

MATTHEW 12:6-8 "I tell you that one greater than the temple is here. ⁷If you had known what these words mean, 'I desire mercy, not sacrifice,' you would not have condemned the innocent. ⁸For the Son of Man is Lord of the Sabbath."

MATTHEW 12:40 "For as Jonah was three days and three nights in the belly of a huge fish, so the Son of Man will be three days and three nights in the heart of the earth."

MATTHEW 16:16-17 Simon Peter answered, "You are the Christ, the Son of the living God." ¹⁷Jesus replied, "Blessed are you, Simon son of Jonah, for this was not revealed to you by man, but by my Father in heaven."

MATTHEW 16:24-27 Then Jesus said to his disciples, "If anyone would come after me, he must deny himself and take up his cross and follow me. ²⁵For whoever wants to save his life will lose it, but whoever loses his life for me will find it. ²⁶What good will it be for a man if he gains the whole world, yet forfeits his soul? Or what can a man give in exchange for his soul? ²⁷For the Son of Man is going to come in his Father's glory with his angels, and then he will reward each person according to what he has done."

MATTHEW 19:28 Jesus said to them [the disciples], "I tell you the truth, at the renewal of all things, when the Son of Man sits on his glorious throne, you who have followed me will also sit on twelve thrones, judging the twelve tribes of Israel."

MATTHEW 20:28 "…the Son of Man did not come to be served, but to serve, and to give his life as a ransom for many." (See also Mark 10:45.)

MATTHEW 23:8-10 "But you are not to be called 'Rabbi,' for you have only one Master and you are all brothers. ⁹And do not call anyone on earth 'father,' for you have one Father, and he is in heaven. ¹⁰Nor are you to be called 'teacher,' for you have one Teacher, the Christ."

MATTHEW 23:37-39 "O Jerusalem, Jerusalem, you who kill the prophets and stone those sent to you, how often I have longed to gather your children together, as a hen gathers her chicks under her wings, but you were not willing. ³⁸Look, your house is left to you desolate. ³⁹For I tell you, you will not see me again until you say, 'Blessed is he who comes in the name of the Lord.'" (See also Luke 13:34-35.)

MATTHEW 24:30 "At that time the sign of the Son of Man will appear in the sky, and all the nations of the earth will

mourn. They will see the Son of Man coming on the clouds of the sky, with power and great glory."

MATTHEW 25:31-34, 41 "When the Son of Man comes in his glory, and all the angels with him, he will sit on his throne in heavenly glory. ³²All the nations will be gathered before him, and he will separate the people one from another as a shepherd separates the sheep from the goats. ³³He will put the sheep on his right and the goats on his left. ³⁴Then the King will say to those on his right, 'Come, you who are blessed by my Father; take your inheritance, the kingdom prepared for you since the creation of the world.' ⁴¹Then he will say to those on his left, 'Depart from me, you who are cursed, into the eternal fire prepared for the devil and his angels.'"

MATTHEW 26:31-32 Then Jesus told them [the disciples], "This very night you will all fall away on account of me, for it is written: 'I will strike the shepherd, and the sheep of the flock will be scattered.' ³²But after I have risen, I will go ahead of you into Galilee." (See also Mark 14:27-28.)

MATTHEW 26:53-54 "Do you think I cannot call on my Father, and he will at once put at my disposal more than twelve legions of angels? ⁵⁴But how then would the Scriptures be fulfilled that say it must happen in this way?"

MATTHEW 26:63-64 But Jesus remained silent. The high priest said to him, "I charge you under oath by the living God: Tell us if you are the Christ, the Son of God." ⁶⁴"Yes, it is as you say," Jesus replied. "But I say to all of you: In the future you will see the Son of Man sitting at the right hand of the Mighty One and coming on the clouds of heaven."

MATTHEW 28:18-20 Then Jesus came to them [the eleven disciples] and said, "All authority in heaven and on earth has been given to me. [19]Therefore go and make disciples of all nations, baptizing them in the name of the Father and of the Son and of the Holy Spirit, [20]and teaching them to obey everything I have commanded you. And surely I am with you always, to the very end of the age."

MARK 2:10 "...the Son of Man has authority on earth to forgive sins...."

MARK 2:17 On hearing this, Jesus said to them, "It is not the healthy who need a doctor, but the sick. I have not come to call the righteous, but sinners."

MARK 2:27-28 Then he said to them, "The Sabbath was made for man, not man for the Sabbath. [28]So the Son of Man is Lord even of the Sabbath."

MARK 13:26-27 "At that time men will see the Son of Man coming in clouds with great power and glory. [27]And he will send his angels and gather his elect from the four winds, from the ends of the earth to the ends of the heavens."

MARK 14:61-62 But Jesus remained silent and gave no answer. Again the high priest asked him, "Are you the Christ, the Son of the Blessed One?" [62]"I am," said Jesus. "And you will see the Son of Man sitting at the right hand of the Mighty One and coming on the clouds of heaven."

MARK 15:2 "Are you the king of the Jews?" asked Pilate. "Yes, it is as you say," Jesus replied.

LUKE 6:5 Then Jesus said to them, "The Son of Man is Lord of the Sabbath."

LUKE 10:22 "All things have been committed to me by my Father. No one knows who the Son is except the Father, and no one knows who the Father is except the Son and those to whom the Son chooses to reveal him."

LUKE 11:32 "The men of Nineveh will stand up at the judgment with this generation and condemn it; for they repented at the preaching of Jonah, and now one greater than Jonah is here."

LUKE 13:31, 33 At that time some Pharisees came to Jesus and said to him, "Leave this place and go somewhere else. Herod wants to kill you." [33][Jesus replied,] "In any case, I must keep going today and tomorrow and the next day—for surely no prophet can die outside Jerusalem!"

LUKE 21:25-27 "There will be signs in the sun, moon and stars. On the earth, nations will be in anguish and perplexity at the roaring and tossing of the sea. [26]Men will faint from terror, apprehensive of what is coming on the world, for the heavenly bodies will be shaken. [27]At that time they will see the Son of Man coming in a cloud with power and great glory."

LUKE 22:67-70 "If you are the Christ," they [chief priests and teachers of the law] said, "tell us." Jesus answered, "If I tell you, you will not believe me, [68]and if I asked you, you would not answer. [69]But from now on, the Son of Man will be seated at the right hand of the mighty God." [70]They all asked, "Are you then the Son of God?" He replied, "You are right in saying I am."

LUKE 24:25-27 He said to them [two people on the road to Emmaus], "How foolish you are, and how slow of heart to believe all that the prophets have spoken! [26]Did not the Christ have to suffer these things and then enter his glory?" [27]And beginning with Moses and all the Prophets, he explained to them what was said in all the Scriptures concerning himself.

LUKE 24:49 "I am going to send you what my Father has promised; but stay in the city until you have been clothed with power from on high."

REVELATION 1:8 "I am the Alpha and the Omega," says the Lord God, "who is, and who was, and who is to come, the Almighty."

REVELATION 22:13 "I am the Alpha and the Omega, the First and the Last, the Beginning and the End."

Fulfilled Prophecy

JOHN 15:24-25 "If I had not done among them what no one else did, they would not be guilty of sin. But now they have seen these miracles, and yet they have hated both me and my Father. [25]But this is to fulfill what is written in their Law: 'They hated me without reason.'"

LUKE 24:44 He said to them [the disciples], "This is what I told you while I was still with you: Everything must be fulfilled that is written about me in the Law of Moses, the Prophets and the Psalms."

LUKE 24:46-49 He told them, "This is what is written: The Christ will suffer and rise from the dead on the third day, [47]and repentance and forgiveness of sins will be preached in his name to all nations, beginning at Jerusalem. [48]You are witnesses of these things. [49]I am going to send you what my Father has promised; but stay in the city until you have been clothed with power from on high."

Jesus' Blood

JOHN 6:53-58 Jesus said to them, "I tell you the truth, unless you eat the flesh of the Son of Man and drink his blood, you have no life in you. [54]Whoever eats my flesh and drinks my blood has eternal life, and I will raise him up at the last day. [55]For my flesh is real food and my blood is real drink. [56]Whoever eats my flesh and drinks my blood remains in me, and I in him. [57]Just as the living Father sent me and I live because of the Father, so the one who feeds on me will live because of me. [58]This is the bread that came down from heaven. Your forefathers ate manna and died, but he who feeds on this bread will live forever."

MATTHEW 26:26-29 While they were eating, Jesus took bread, gave thanks and broke it, and gave it to his disciples, saying, "Take and eat; this is my body." [27]Then he took the cup, gave thanks and offered it to them, saying, "Drink from it, all of you. [28]This is my blood of the covenant, which is poured out for many for the forgiveness of sins. [29]I tell you, I will not drink of this fruit of the vine from now on until that day when I drink it anew with you in my Father's kingdom."

MARK 14:23-24 Then he took the cup, gave thanks and offered it to them, and they all drank from it. [24]"This is my blood of the covenant, which is poured out for many," he said to them.

LUKE 22:20 In the same way, after the supper he took the cup, saying, "This cup is the new covenant in my blood, which is poured out for you."

I CORINTHIANS 11:25 In the same way, after supper he took the cup, saying, "This cup is the new covenant in my blood; do this, whenever you drink it, in remembrance of me."

Jesus, the Bread of God and the Bread of Life

JOHN 6:32-33 Jesus said to them, "I tell you the truth, it is not Moses who has given you the bread from heaven, but it is my Father who gives you the true bread from heaven. [33]For the bread of God is he who comes down from heaven and gives life to the world."

JOHN 6:48-51 "I am the bread of life. [49]Your forefathers ate the manna in the desert, yet they died. [50]But here is the bread that comes down from heaven, which a man may eat and not die. [51]I am the living bread that came down from heaven. If anyone eats of this bread, he will live forever. This bread is my flesh, which I will give for the life of the world."

JOHN 6:53-58, 61-64 Jesus said to them, "I tell you the truth, unless you eat the flesh of the Son of Man and drink his blood, you have no life in you. [54]Whoever eats my flesh and drinks my blood has eternal life, and I will raise him up at the last day. [55]For my flesh is real food and my blood is real drink. [56]Whoever eats my

flesh and drinks my blood remains in me, and I in him. [57]Just as the living Father sent me and I live because of the Father, so the one who feeds on me will live because of me. [58]This is the bread that came down from heaven. Your forefathers ate manna and died, but he who feeds on this bread will live forever." [61]Aware that his disciples were grumbling about this, Jesus said to them, "Does this offend you? [62]What if you see the Son of Man ascend to where he was before! [63]The Spirit gives life; the flesh counts for nothing. The words I have spoken to you are spirit and they are life. [64]Yet there are some of you who do not believe." For Jesus had known from the beginning which of them did not believe and who would betray him.

Jesus' Death, Resurrection, and Second Coming

JOHN 3:14-15 "Just as Moses lifted up the snake in the desert, so the Son of Man must be lifted up, [15]that everyone who believes in him may have eternal life."

JOHN 10:17-18 "The reason my Father loves me is that I lay down my life—only to take it up again. [18]No one takes it from me, but I lay it down of my own accord. I have authority to lay it down and authority to take it up again. This command I received from my Father."

JOHN 13:36 Simon Peter asked him, "Lord, where are you going?" Jesus replied, "Where I am going, you cannot follow now, but you will follow later."

JOHN 14:1-4 "Do not let your hearts be troubled. Trust in God; trust also in me. [2]In my Father's house are many rooms; if it were not so, I would have told you. I am going there to prepare a place for you. [3]And if I go and prepare a place for you, I will come back and take you to be with me that you also may be where I am. [4]You know the way to the place where I am going."

JOHN 14:18-19 "I will not leave you as orphans; I will come to you. [19]Before long, the world will not see me anymore, but you will see me. Because I live, you also will live."

JOHN 14:27-29 "Peace I leave with you; my peace I give you. I do not give to you as the world gives. Do not let your hearts be troubled and do not be afraid. [28]You heard me say, 'I am going away and I am coming back to you.' If you loved me, you would be glad that I am going to the Father, for the Father is greater than I. [29]I have told you now before it happens, so that when it does happen you will believe."

JOHN 16:5-6 "Now I am going to him who sent me, yet none of you asks me, 'Where are you going?' [6]Because I have said these things, you are filled with grief."

JOHN 16:16 "In a little while you will see me no more, and then after a little while you will see me."

JOHN 16:20-22 "I tell you the truth, you will weep and mourn while the world rejoices. You will grieve, but your grief will turn to joy. [21]A woman giving birth to a child has pain because her time has come; but when her baby is born she forgets the anguish because of her joy that a child is born into the world. [22]So with you: Now

is your time of grief, but I will see you again and you will rejoice, and no one will take away your joy."

JOHN 16:28 "I came from the Father and entered the world; now I am leaving the world and going back to the Father."

JOHN 20:13-16 They asked her [Mary], "Woman, why are you crying?" "They have taken my Lord away," she said, "and I don't know where they have put him." [14]At this, she turned around and saw Jesus standing there, but she did not realize that it was Jesus. [15]"Woman," he said, "why are you crying? Who is it you are looking for?" Thinking he was the gardener, she said, "Sir, if you have carried him away, tell me where you have put him, and I will get him." [16]Jesus said to her, "Mary." She turned toward him and cried out in Aramaic, "Rabboni!" (which means Teacher).

JOHN 20:19-20 On the evening of that first day of the week, when the disciples were together, with the doors locked for fear of the Jews, Jesus came and stood among them and said, "Peace be with you!" [20]After he said this, he showed them his hands and side. The disciples were overjoyed when they saw the Lord.

JOHN 21:4-6, 9-12 Early in the morning, Jesus stood on the shore, but the disciples did not realize that it was Jesus. [5]He called out to them, "Friends, haven't you any fish?" "No," they answered. [6]He said, "Throw your net on the right side of the boat and you will find some." When they did, they were unable to haul the net in because of the large number of fish. [9]When they landed, they saw a fire of burning coals there with fish on it, and some bread. [10]Jesus said to them, "Bring some of the fish you have just caught." [11]Simon Peter climbed aboard and dragged the net ashore. It was full of large fish, 153, but even with so many the net was not torn. [12]Jesus said to them, "Come and have breakfast." None of the disciples dared ask him, "Who are you?" They knew it was the Lord.

MATTHEW 10:16-23 "I am sending you out like sheep among wolves. Therefore be as shrewd as snakes and as innocent as doves. [17]Be on your guard against men; they will hand you over to the local councils and flog you in their synagogues. [18]On my account you will be brought before governors and kings as witnesses to them and to the Gentiles. [19]But when they arrest you, do not worry about what to say or how to say it. At that time you will be given what to say, [20]for it will not be you speaking, but the Spirit of your Father speaking through you. [21]Brother will betray brother to death, and a father his child; children will rebel against their parents and have them put to death. [22]All men will hate you because of me, but he who stands firm to the end will be saved. [23]When you are persecuted in one place, flee to another. I tell you the truth, you will not finish going through the cities of Israel before the Son of Man comes."

MATTHEW 12:39-40 He answered, "A wicked and adulterous generation asks for a miraculous sign! But none will be given it except the sign of the prophet Jonah. [40]For as Jonah was three days and three nights in the belly of a huge fish, so the Son of Man will be three days and three nights in the heart of the earth."

MATTHEW 16:27-28 "For the Son of Man is going to come in his Father's glory with his angels, and then he will reward each person according to what he has done. [28]I tell you the truth, some who are standing here will not taste death before they see the Son of Man coming in his kingdom."

MATTHEW 17:9 As they were coming down the mountain [of Transfiguration], Jesus instructed them, "Don't tell anyone what you have seen, until the Son of Man has been raised from the dead."

MATTHEW 17:11-12 Jesus replied, "To be sure, Elijah comes and will restore all things. [12]But I tell you, Elijah has already come, and they did not recognize him, but have done to him everything they wished. In the same way the Son of Man is going to suffer at their hands."

MATTHEW 17:22-23 When they came together in Galilee, he said to them, "The Son of Man is going to be betrayed into the hands of men. [23]They will kill him, and on the third day he will be raised to life." And the disciples were filled with grief. (See also Mark 9:31.)

MATTHEW 21:33-40 "Listen to another parable: There was a landowner who planted a vineyard. He put a wall around it, dug a winepress in it and built a watchtower. Then he rented the vineyard to some farmers and went away on a journey. [34]When the harvest time approached, he sent his servants to the tenants to collect his fruit. [35]The tenants seized his servants; they beat one, killed another, and stoned a third. [36]Then he sent other servants to them, more than the first time, and the tenants treated them the same way. [37]Last of all, he sent his son to them. 'They will respect my son,' he said. ³⁸But when the tenants saw the son, they said to each other, 'This is the heir. Come, let's kill him and take his inheritance.' ³⁹So they took him and threw him out of the vineyard and killed him. ⁴⁰Therefore, when the owner of the vineyard comes, what will he do to those tenants?"

MATTHEW 21:42 Jesus said to them, "Have you never read in the Scriptures: 'The stone the builders rejected has become the capstone; the Lord has done this, and it is marvelous in our eyes'?"

MATTHEW 24:3-29 As Jesus was sitting on the Mount of Olives, the disciples came to him privately. "Tell us," they said, "when will this happen, and what will be the sign of your coming and of the end of the age?" ⁴Jesus answered: "Watch out that no one deceives you. ⁵For many will come in my name, claiming, 'I am the Christ,' and will deceive many. ⁶You will hear of wars and rumors of wars, but see to it that you are not alarmed. Such things must happen, but the end is still to come. ⁷Nation will rise against nation, and kingdom against kingdom. There will be famines and earthquakes in various places. ⁸All these are the beginning of birth pains. ⁹Then you will be handed over to be persecuted and put to death, and you will be hated by all nations because of me. ¹⁰At that time many will turn away from the faith and will betray and hate each other, ¹¹and many false prophets will appear and deceive many people. ¹²Because of the increase of wickedness, the love of most will grow cold, ¹³but he who stands firm to the end will be saved. ¹⁴And this gospel

of the kingdom will be preached in the whole world as a testimony to all nations, and then the end will come. ¹⁵So when you see standing in the holy place 'the abomination that causes desolation,' spoken of through the prophet Daniel—let the reader understand— ¹⁶then let those who are in Judea flee to the mountains. ¹⁷Let no one on the roof of his house go down to take anything out of the house. ¹⁸Let no one in the field go back to get his cloak. ¹⁹How dreadful it will be in those days for pregnant women and nursing mothers! ²⁰Pray that your flight will not take place in winter or on the Sabbath. ²¹For then there will be great distress, unequaled from the beginning of the world until now—and never to be equaled again. ²²If those days had not been cut short, no one would survive, but for the sake of the elect those days will be shortened. ²³At that time if anyone says to you, 'Look, here is the Christ!' or, 'There he is!' do not believe it. ²⁴For false Christs and false prophets will appear and perform great signs and miracles to deceive even the elect—if that were possible. ²⁵See, I have told you ahead of time. ²⁶So if anyone tells you, 'There he is, out in the desert,' do not go out; or, 'Here he is, in the inner rooms,' do not believe it. ²⁷For as lightning that comes from the east is visible even in the west, so will be the coming of the Son of Man. ²⁸Wherever there is a carcass, there the vultures will gather. ²⁹Immediately after the distress of those days 'the sun will be darkened, and the moon will not give its light; the stars will fall from the sky, and the heavenly bodies will be shaken.'" (See also Luke 21:8-28.)

MATTHEW 24:32-35 "Now learn this lesson from the fig tree: As soon as its twigs get tender and its leaves come out, you know that summer is near. [33]Even so, when you see all these things, you know that it is near, right at the door. [34]I tell you the truth, this generation will certainly not pass away until all these things have happened. [35]Heaven and earth will pass away, but my words will never pass away."

MATTHEW 25:1-13 "At that time the kingdom of heaven will be like ten virgins who took their lamps and went out to meet the bridegroom. [2]Five of them were foolish and five were wise. [3]The foolish ones took their lamps but did not take any oil with them. [4]The wise, however, took oil in jars along with their lamps. [5]The bridegroom was a long time in coming, and they all became drowsy and fell asleep. [6]At midnight the cry rang out: 'Here's the bridegroom! Come out to meet him!' [7]Then all the virgins woke up and trimmed their lamps. [8]The foolish ones said to the wise, 'Give us some of your oil; our lamps are going out.' [9]'No,' they replied, 'there may not be enough for both us and you. Instead, go to those who sell oil and buy some for yourselves.' [10]But while they were on their way to buy the oil, the bridegroom arrived. The virgins who were ready went in with him to the wedding banquet. And the door was shut. [11]Later the others also came. 'Sir! Sir!' they said. 'Open the door for us!' [12]But he replied, 'I tell you the truth, I don't know you.' [13]Therefore keep watch, because you do not know the day or the hour."

MATTHEW 25:31-46 "When the Son of Man comes in his glory, and all the angels with him, he will sit on his throne in heavenly glory. [32]All the nations will be gathered before him, and he will separate the people one from another as a shepherd separates the sheep from the goats. [33]He will put the sheep on his right and the goats on his left. [34]Then the King will say to those on his right, 'Come, you who are blessed by my Father; take your inheritance, the kingdom prepared for you since the creation of the world. [35]For I was hungry and you gave me something to eat, I was thirsty and you gave me something to drink, I was a stranger and you invited me in, [36]I needed clothes and you clothed me, I was sick and you looked after me, I was in prison and you came to visit me.' [37]Then the righteous will answer him, 'Lord, when did we see you hungry and feed you, or thirsty and give you something to drink? [38]When did we see you a stranger and invite you in, or needing clothes and clothe you? [39]When did we see you sick or in prison and go to visit you?' [40]The King will reply, 'I tell you the truth, whatever you did for one of the least of these brothers of mine, you did for me.' [41]Then he will say to those on his left, 'Depart from me, you who are cursed, into the eternal fire prepared for the devil and his angels. [42]For I was hungry and you gave me nothing to eat, I was thirsty and you gave me nothing to drink, [43]I was a stranger and you did not invite me in, I needed clothes and you did not clothe me, I was sick and in prison and you did not look after me.' [44]They also will answer, 'Lord, when did we see you hungry or thirsty or a stranger or needing clothes or sick or in prison, and did not help you?' [45]He will reply, 'I tell you the truth, whatever you did not do for one of the least of these, you did not do for me.' [46]Then they will go away to eternal punishment, but the righteous to eternal life."

MATTHEW 26:1-4 When Jesus had finished saying all these things, he said to his disciples, [2]"As you know, the Passover is two days away—and the Son of Man will be handed over to be crucified." [3]Then the chief priests and the elders of the people assembled in the palace of the high priest, whose name was Caiaphas, [4]and they plotted to arrest Jesus in some sly way and kill him.

MATTHEW 26:26-28 While they were eating, Jesus took bread, gave thanks and broke it, and gave it to his disciples, saying, "Take and eat; this is my body." [27]Then he took the cup, gave thanks and offered it to them, saying, "Drink from it, all of you. [28]This is my blood of the covenant, which is poured out for many for the forgiveness of sins."

MATTHEW 26:39 Going a little farther, he fell with his face to the ground and prayed, "My Father, if it is possible, may this cup be taken from me. Yet not as I will, but as you will."

MATTHEW 26:52-54 "Put your sword back in its place," Jesus said to him [Peter], "for all who draw the sword will die by the sword. [53]Do you think I cannot call on my Father, and he will at once put at my disposal more than twelve legions of angels? [54]But how then would the Scriptures be fulfilled that say it must happen in this way?"

MATTHEW 26:64 "...I say to all of you: In the future you will see the Son of Man sitting at the right hand of the Mighty One and coming on the clouds of heaven."

MARK 2:20 "But the time will come when the bridegroom will be taken from them, and on that day they will fast."

MARK 8:31 He then began to teach them [the disciples] that the Son of Man must suffer many things and be rejected by the elders, chief priests and teachers of the law, and that he must be killed and after three days rise again. (See also Matthew 16:21.)

MARK 8:38 "If anyone is ashamed of me and my words in this adulterous and sinful generation, the Son of Man will be ashamed of him when he comes in his Father's glory with the holy angels."

MARK 9:1 And he said to them, "I tell you the truth, some who are standing here will not taste death before they see the kingdom of God come with power."

MARK 10:33-34 "We are going up to Jerusalem," he said, "and the Son of Man will be betrayed to the chief priests and teachers of the law. They will condemn him to death and will hand him over to the Gentiles, [34]who will mock him and spit on him, flog him and kill him. Three days later he will rise."

MARK 13:3-27 As Jesus was sitting on the Mount of Olives opposite the temple, Peter, James, John and Andrew asked him privately, [4]"Tell us, when will these things happen? And what will be the sign that they are all about to be fulfilled?" [5]Jesus said to them: "Watch out that no one deceives you. [6]Many will come in my name, claiming, 'I am he,' and will deceive many. [7]When you hear of wars and rumors of wars, do not be alarmed. Such things must happen, but the end is still to come. [8]Nation will rise against nation, and kingdom against kingdom. There will be earthquakes in various places, and famines. These are the beginning of birth pains. [9]You must be on your guard. You will be handed over to the local councils and flogged in the synagogues. On account of me you will stand before governors and kings as witnesses to them. [10]And the gospel must first be preached to all nations. [11]Whenever you are arrested and brought to trial, do not worry beforehand about what to say. Just say whatever is given you at the time, for it is not you speaking, but the Holy Spirit. [12]Brother will betray brother to death, and a father his child. Children will rebel against their parents and have them put to death. [13]All men will hate you because of me, but he who stands firm to the end will be saved. [14]When you see 'the abomination that causes desolation' standing where it does not belong—let the reader understand—then let those who are in Judea flee to the mountains. [15]Let no one on the roof of his house go down or enter the house to take anything out. [16]Let no one in the field go back to get his cloak. [17]How dreadful it will be in those days for pregnant women and nursing mothers! [18]Pray that this will not take place in winter, [19]because those will be days of distress unequaled from the beginning, when God created the world, until now—and never to be equaled again. [20]If the Lord had not cut short those days, no one would survive. But for the sake of the elect, whom he has chosen, he has shortened them. [21]At that time if

anyone says to you, 'Look, here is the Christ!' or, 'Look, there he is!' do not believe it. [22]For false Christs and false prophets will appear and perform signs and miracles to deceive the elect—if that were possible. [23]So be on your guard; I have told you everything ahead of time. [24]But in those days, following that distress, 'the sun will be darkened, and the moon will not give its light; [25]the stars will fall from the sky, and the heavenly bodies will be shaken.' [26]At that time men will see the Son of Man coming in clouds with great power and glory. [27]And he will send his angels and gather his elect from the four winds, from the ends of the earth to the ends of the heavens."

MARK 13:28-37 "Now learn this lesson from the fig tree: As soon as its twigs get tender and its leaves come out, you know that summer is near. [29]Even so, when you see these things happening, you know that it is near, right at the door. [30]I tell you the truth, this generation will certainly not pass away until all these things have happened. [31]Heaven and earth will pass away, but my words will never pass away. [32]No one knows about that day or hour, not even the angels in heaven, nor the Son, but only the Father. [33]Be on guard! Be alert! You do not know when that time will come. [34]It's like a man going away: He leaves his house and puts his servants in charge, each with his assigned task, and tells the one at the door to keep watch. [35]Therefore keep watch because you do not know when the owner of the house will come back—whether in the evening, or at midnight, or when the rooster crows, or at dawn. [36]If he comes suddenly, do not let him find you sleeping. ³⁷What I say to you, I say to everyone: 'Watch!' "

MARK 14:22-25 While they were eating, Jesus took bread, gave thanks and broke it, and gave it to his disciples, saying, "Take it; this is my body." ²³Then he took the cup, gave thanks and offered it to them, and they all drank from it. ²⁴"This is my blood of the covenant, which is poured out for many," he said to them. ²⁵"I tell you the truth, I will not drink again of the fruit of the vine until that day when I drink it anew in the kingdom of God."

MARK 14:27-28 "You will all fall away," Jesus told them [the disciples], "for it is written: 'I will strike the shepherd, and the sheep will be scattered.' ²⁸But after I have risen, I will go ahead of you into Galilee."

MARK 14:61-62 But Jesus remained silent and gave no answer. Again the high priest asked him, "Are you the Christ, the Son of the Blessed One?" ⁶²"I am," said Jesus. "And you will see the Son of Man sitting at the right hand of the Mighty One and coming on the clouds of heaven."

LUKE 5:34-35 Jesus answered, "Can you make the guests of the bridegroom fast while he is with them? ³⁵But the time will come when the bridegroom will be taken from them; in those days they will fast."

LUKE 9:21-22 Jesus strictly warned them not to tell this to anyone. ²²And he said, "The Son of Man must suffer many things and be rejected by the elders, chief priests and teachers of the law, and he must be killed and on the third day be raised to life."

LUKE 9:44 "Listen carefully to what I am about to tell you: The Son of Man is going to be betrayed into the hands of men."

LUKE 12:35-40 "Be dressed ready for service and keep your lamps burning, ³⁶like men waiting for their master to return from a wedding banquet, so that when he comes and knocks they can immediately open the door for him. ³⁷It will be good for those servants whose master finds them watching when he comes. I tell you the truth, he will dress himself to serve, will have them recline at the table and will come and wait on them. ³⁸It will be good for those servants whose master finds them ready, even if he comes in the second or third watch of the night. ³⁹But understand this: If the owner of the house had known at what hour the thief was coming, he would not have let his house be broken into. ⁴⁰You also must be ready, because the Son of Man will come at an hour when you do not expect him."

LUKE 12:42-53 The Lord answered, "Who then is the faithful and wise manager, whom the master puts in charge of his servants to give them their food allowance at the proper time? ⁴³It will be good for that servant whom the master finds doing so when he returns. ⁴⁴I tell you the truth, he will put him in charge of all his possessions. ⁴⁵But suppose the servant says to himself, 'My master is taking a long time in coming,' and he then begins to beat the menservants and maidservants and to eat and drink and get drunk. ⁴⁶The master of that servant will come on a day when he does not expect him and at an hour he is not aware of. He will cut him to pieces and assign him a place with the unbelievers. [47]That servant who knows his master's will and does not get ready or does not do what his master wants will be beaten with many blows. [48]But the one who does not know and does things deserving punishment will be beaten with few blows. From everyone who has been given much, much will be demanded; and from the one who has been entrusted with much, much more will be asked. [49]I have come to bring fire on the earth, and how I wish it were already kindled! [50]But I have a baptism to undergo, and how distressed I am until it is completed! [51]Do you think I came to bring peace on earth? No, I tell you, but division. [52]From now on there will be five in one family divided against each other, three against two and two against three. [53]They will be divided, father against son and son against father, mother against daughter and daughter against mother, mother-in-law against daughter-in-law and daughter-in-law against mother-in-law."

LUKE 17:22-30 Then he said to his disciples, "The time is coming when you will long to see one of the days of the Son of Man, but you will not see it. [23]Men will tell you, 'There he is!' or 'Here he is!' Do not go running off after them. [24]For the Son of Man in his day will be like the lightning, which flashes and lights up the sky from one end to the other. [25]But first he must suffer many things and be rejected by this generation. [26]Just as it was in the days of Noah, so also will it be in the days of the Son of Man. [27]People were eating, drinking, marrying and being given in marriage up to the day Noah entered the ark. Then the flood came and destroyed them all. [28]It was the same in the days of Lot. People were eating and drinking, buying and selling, planting and building. [29]But the day Lot left Sodom, fire and sulfur rained down from heaven and destroyed them all. [30]It will be just like this on the day the Son of Man is revealed."

LUKE 17:30-35, 37 "It will be just like this on the day the Son of Man is revealed. [31]On that day no one who is on the roof of his house, with his goods inside, should go down to get them. Likewise, no one in the field should go back for anything. [32]Remember Lot's wife! [33]Whoever tries to keep his life will lose it, and whoever loses his life will preserve it. [34]I tell you, on that night two people will be in one bed; one will be taken and the other left. [35]Two women will be grinding grain together; one will be taken and the other left." [37]"Where, Lord?" they asked. He replied, "Where there is a dead body, there the vultures will gather."

LUKE 18:1-8 Then Jesus told his disciples a parable to show them that they should always pray and not give up. [2]He said: "In a certain town there was a judge who neither feared God nor cared about men. [3]And there was a widow in that town who kept coming to him with the plea, 'Grant me justice against my adversary.' [4]For some time he refused. But finally he said to himself, 'Even though I don't fear God or care about men, [5]yet because this widow keeps bothering me, I will see that she gets justice, so that she won't eventually wear me out with her coming!'" [6]And the Lord said, "Listen to what the unjust judge says. [7]And will not God bring about justice for his chosen ones, who cry out to him day and night? Will he keep putting them off? [8]I tell you, he will see that they get justice, and quickly. However, when the Son of Man comes, will he find faith on the earth?"

LUKE 18:31-33 Jesus took the Twelve aside and told them, "We are going up to Jerusalem, and everything that is written by the prophets about the Son of Man will be fulfilled. [32]He will be handed over to the Gentiles. They will mock him, insult him, spit on him, flog him and kill him. [33]On the third day he will rise again."

LUKE 21:29-36 He told them this parable: "Look at the fig tree and all the trees. [30]When they sprout leaves, you can see for yourselves and know that summer is near. [31]Even so, when you see these things happening, you know that the kingdom of God is near. [32]I tell you the truth, this generation will certainly not pass away until all these things have happened. [33]Heaven and earth will pass away, but my words will never pass away. [34]Be careful, or your hearts will be weighed down with dissipation, drunkenness and the anxieties of life, and that day will close on you unexpectedly like a trap. [35]For it will come upon all those who live on the face of the whole earth. [36]Be always on the watch, and pray that you may be able to escape all that is about to happen, and that you may be able to stand before the Son of Man."

LUKE 22:17-18 After taking the cup, he gave thanks and said, "Take this and divide it among you. [18]For I tell you I will not drink again of the fruit of the vine until the kingdom of God comes."

LUKE 22:19 And he took bread, gave thanks and broke it, and gave it to them [the apostles], saying, "This is my body given for you; do this in remembrance of me."

1 CORINTHIANS 11:23-26 For I received from the Lord what I also passed on to you: The Lord Jesus, on the night he was betrayed, took bread, [24]and when he had given thanks, he broke it and said, "This is my body, which is for you; do this in remembrance of me." [25]In the same way, after supper he took the cup, saying, "This cup is the new covenant in my blood; do this, whenever you drink it, in remembrance of me." [26]For whenever you eat this bread and drink this cup, you proclaim the Lord's death until he comes.

REVELATION 1:10-11, 17-20 On the Lord's Day I [John] was in the Spirit, and I heard behind me a loud voice like a trumpet, [11]which said: "Write on a scroll what you see and send it to the seven churches: to Ephesus, Smyrna, Pergamum, Thyatira, Sardis, Philadelphia and Laodicea." [17]When I saw him, I fell at his feet as though dead. Then he placed his right hand on me and said: "Do not be afraid. I am the First and the Last. [18]I am the Living One; I was dead, and behold I am alive for ever and ever! And I hold the keys of death and Hades. [19]Write, therefore, what you have seen, what is now and what will take place later. [20]The mystery of the seven stars that you saw in my right hand and of the seven golden lampstands is this: The seven stars are the angels of the seven churches, and the seven lampstands are the seven churches."

REVELATION 3:1-2, 12 "...These are the words of him who holds the seven spirits of God and the seven stars. I know your deeds; you have a reputation of being alive, but you are dead. [2]Wake up! Strengthen what remains and is about to die, for I have not found your deeds complete in the sight of my God. [12]Him who overcomes I will make a pillar in the temple of my God. Never again will he leave it. I will write on him the name of my God and the name of the city of my God, the new Jerusalem, which is coming down out of heaven from my God; and I will also write on him my new name."

REVELATION 16:15 "Behold, I come like a thief! Blessed is he who stays awake and keeps his clothes with him, so that he may not go naked and be shamefully exposed."

REVELATION 22:7 "Behold, I am coming soon! Blessed is he who keeps the words of the prophecy in this book."

REVELATION 22:12 "Behold, I am coming soon! My reward is with me, and I will give to everyone according to what he has done."

REVELATION 22:20 He who testifies to these things says, "Yes, I am coming soon." Amen. Come, Lord Jesus.

Jesus' Eternal Existence

JOHN 3:10-13 "You are Israel's teacher," said Jesus, "and do you not understand these things? [11]I tell you the truth, we speak of what we know, and we testify to what we have seen, but still you

people do not accept our testimony. [12]I have spoken to you of earthly things and you do not believe; how then will you believe if I speak of heavenly things? [13]No one has ever gone into heaven except the one who came from heaven—the Son of Man."

JOHN 6:38 "For I have come down from heaven not to do my will but to do the will of him who sent me."

JOHN 6:41-42 At this the Jews began to grumble about him because he said, "I am the bread that came down from heaven." [42]They said, "Is this not Jesus, the son of Joseph, whose father and mother we know? How can he now say, 'I came down from heaven'?"

JOHN 6:46 "No one has seen the Father except the one who is from God; only he has seen the Father."

JOHN 7:33-34 Jesus said, "I am with you for only a short time, and then I go to the one who sent me. [34]You will look for me, but you will not find me; and where I am, you cannot come."

JOHN 8:21, 23-24 Once more Jesus said to them, "I am going away, and you will look for me, and you will die in your sin. Where I go, you cannot come." [23]But he continued, "You are from below; I am from above. You are of this world; I am not of this world. [24]I told you that you would die in your sins; if you do not believe that I am the one I claim to be, you will indeed die in your sins."

JOHN 8:42 Jesus said to them, "If God were your Father, you would love me, for I came from God and now am here. I have not come on my own; but he sent me."

JOHN 8:54-56 Jesus replied, "If I glorify myself, my glory means nothing. My Father, whom you claim as your God, is the one who glorifies me. [55]Though you do not know him, I know him. If I said I did not, I would be a liar like you, but I do know him and keep his word. [56]Your father Abraham rejoiced at the thought of seeing my day; he saw it and was glad."

JOHN 8:58 "I tell you the truth," Jesus answered, "before Abraham was born, I am!"

JOHN 16:27-28 "No, the Father himself loves you because you have loved me and have believed that I came from God. [28]I came from the Father and entered the world; now I am leaving the world and going back to the Father."

JOHN 17:4-5 "I have brought you glory on earth by completing the work you gave me to do. [5]And now, Father, glorify me in your presence with the glory I had with you before the world began."

JOHN 17:20-24 "...I pray also for those who will believe in me through their message, [21]that all of them may be one, Father, just as you are in me and I am in you. May they also be in us so that the world may believe that you have sent me. [22]I have given them the glory that you gave me, that they may be one as we are one: [23]I in them and you in me. May they be brought to complete unity to let the world know that you sent me and have loved them even as you have loved me. [24]Father, I want those you have given me to be with me where I am, and to see my glory, the glory you have given me because you loved me before the creation of the world."

REVELATION 1:8 "I am the Alpha and the Omega," says the Lord God, "who is, and who was, and who is to come, the Almighty."

REVELATION 22:13 "I am the Alpha and the Omega, the First and the Last, the Beginning and the End."

REVELATION 22:15-16 "Outside are the dogs, those who practice magic arts, the sexually immoral, the murderers, the idolaters and everyone who loves and practices falsehood. [16]I, Jesus, have sent my angel to give you this testimony for the churches. I am the Root and the Off-spring of David, and the bright Morning Star."

Jesus' Identity

In Jesus' statements about His identity, He reveals who He is and where He came from. He does this in a number of ways—with direct statements, implied statements, and metaphors. Sometimes He identifies Himself by simply accepting the superlative statements of others. And in one instance, by allowing a man to *worship* Him, Jesus identified Himself as God (see John 9:38). Jesus' identity is also revealed through His willingness to engage in divine actions and to identify with traits and a level of authority that previously had been associated only with God the Father. Examples of this are Jesus' claims that He is able to forgive sins and that He existed before time began (see Matthew 9:2-5; John 8:58). Jesus' un-equivocal statements in this section alone separate Him from every person who has ever lived.

JOHN 1:35-43 The next day John was there again with two of his disciples. [36]When he saw Jesus passing by, he said, "Look, the Lamb of God!" [37]When the two disciples heard him say this, they followed Jesus. [38]Turning around, Jesus saw them following and asked, "What do you want?" They said, "Rabbi" (which means Teacher), "where are you staying?" [39]"Come," he replied, "and you will see." So they went and saw where he was staying, and spent that day with him. It was about the tenth hour. [40]Andrew, Simon Peter's brother, was one of the two who heard what John had said and who had followed Jesus. [41]The first thing Andrew did was to find his brother Simon and tell him, "We have found the Messiah" (that is, the Christ). [42]And he brought him to Jesus. Jesus looked at him and said, "You are Simon son of John. You will be called Cephas" (which, when translated, is Peter). [43]The next day Jesus decided to leave for Galilee. Finding Philip, he said to him, "Follow me."

JOHN 1:47-51 When Jesus saw Nathanael approaching, he said of him, "Here is a true Israelite, in whom there is nothing false." [48]"How do you know me?" Nathanael asked. Jesus answered, "I saw you while you were still under the fig tree before Philip called you." [49]Then Nathanael declared, "Rabbi, you are the Son of God; you are the King of Israel." [50]Jesus said, "You believe because I told you I saw you under the fig tree. You shall see greater things than that." [51]He then added, "I tell you the truth, you shall see heaven open, and the angels of God ascending and descending on the Son of Man."

JOHN 2:14-19 In the temple courts he found men selling cattle, sheep and doves, and others sitting at tables exchanging money. [15]So he made a whip out of cords, and drove all from the temple area, both sheep and cattle; he scattered the coins of the money changers and overturned their tables. [16]To those who sold doves he said, "Get these out of here! How dare you turn my Father's house into a market!" [17]His disciples remembered that it is written: "Zeal for your house will consume me." [18]Then the Jews demanded of him, "What miraculous sign can you show us to prove your authority to do all this?" [19]Jesus answered them, "Destroy this temple, and I will raise it again in three days."

JOHN 3:10-13 "You are Israel's teacher," said Jesus, "and do you not understand these things? [11]I tell you the truth, we speak of what we know, and we testify to what we have seen, but still you people do not accept our testimony. [12]I have spoken to you of earthly things and you do not believe; how then will you believe if I speak of heavenly things? [13]No one has ever gone into heaven except the one who came from heaven—the Son of Man."

JOHN 4:7-10, 26 When a Samaritan woman came to draw water, Jesus said to her, "Will you give me a drink?" [8](His disciples had gone into the town to buy food.) [9]The Samaritan woman said to him, "You are a Jew and I am a Samaritan woman. How can you ask me for a drink?" (For Jews do not associate with Samaritans.) [10]Jesus answered her, "If you knew the gift of God and who it is that asks you for a drink, you would have asked him and he would have given you living water." [26]Then Jesus declared, "I who speak to you am he [the Messiah]."

JOHN 5:16-17 So, because Jesus was doing these things on the Sabbath, the Jews persecuted him. [17]Jesus said to them, "My Father is always at his work to this very day, and I, too, am working."

JOHN 6:37-40 "All that the Father gives me will come to me, and whoever comes to me I will never drive away. [38]For I have come down from heaven not to do my will but to do the will of him who sent me. [39]And this is the will of him who sent me, that I shall lose none of all that he has given me, but raise them up at the last day. [40]For my Father's will is that everyone who looks to the Son and believes in him shall have eternal life, and I will raise him up at the last day."

JOHN 6:41-42 At this the Jews began to grumble about him because he said, "I am the bread that came down from heaven." [42]They said, "Is this not Jesus, the son of Joseph, whose father and mother we know? How can he now say, 'I came down from heaven'?"

JOHN 6:44-45 "No one can come to me unless the Father who sent me draws him, and I will raise him up at the last day. [45]It is written in the Prophets: 'They will all be taught by God.' Everyone who listens to the Father and learns from him comes to me."

JOHN 6:46 "No one has seen the Father except the one who is from God; only he has seen the Father."

JOHN 6:66-71 From this time many of his disciples turned back and no longer followed him. [67]"You do not want to leave too, do you?" Jesus asked the Twelve. [68]Simon Peter answered him, "Lord, to whom shall we go? You have the words of eternal life. [69]We believe and know that you are the Holy One of God." [70]Then Jesus replied, "Have I not chosen you, the Twelve? Yet one of you is a devil!" [71](He meant Judas, the son of Simon Iscariot, who, though one of the Twelve, was later to betray him.)

JOHN 7:33-34 Jesus said, "I am with you for only a short time, and then I go to the one who sent me. [34]You will look for me, but you will not find me; and where I am, you cannot come."

JOHN 8:58 "I tell you the truth," Jesus answered, "before Abraham was born, I am!"

JOHN 9:35-38 Jesus heard that they had thrown him [a man healed of blindness] out, and when he found him, he said, "Do you believe in the Son of Man?" [36]"Who is he, sir?" the man asked. "Tell me so that I may believe in him." [37]Jesus said, "You have now seen him; in fact, he is the one speaking with you." [38]Then the man said, "Lord, I believe!" And he worshiped him.

JOHN 10:30 "I and the Father are one."

JOHN 12:34 The crowd spoke up, "We have heard from the Law that the Christ will remain forever, so how can you say, 'The Son of Man must be lifted up'? Who is this 'Son of Man'?"

JOHN 16:17-18 Some of his disciples said to one another, "What does he mean by saying, 'In a little while you will see me no more, and then after a little while you will see me,' and 'Because I am going to the Father'?" [18]They kept asking, "What does he mean by 'a little while'? We don't understand what he is saying."

JOHN 18:3-9 So Judas came to the grove, guiding a detachment of soldiers and some officials from the chief priests and Pharisees. They were carrying torches, lanterns and weapons. [4]Jesus, knowing all that was going to happen to him, went out and asked them, "Who is it you want?" [5]"Jesus of Nazareth," they replied. "I am he," Jesus said. (And Judas the traitor was standing there with them.) [6]When Jesus said, "I am he," they drew back and fell to the ground. [7]Again he asked them, "Who is it you want?" And they said, "Jesus of Nazareth." [8]"I told you that I am he," Jesus answered. "If you are looking for me, then let these men go." [9]This happened so that the words he had spoken would be fulfilled: "I have not lost one of those you gave me."

JOHN 18:33-34 Pilate then went back inside the palace, summoned Jesus and asked him, "Are you the king of the Jews?" [34]"Is that your own idea," Jesus asked, "or did others talk to you about me?"

MATTHEW 9:2, 4-5 Some men brought to him a paralytic, lying on a mat. When Jesus saw their faith, he said to the paralytic, "Take heart, son; your sins are forgiven." [4]Knowing their thoughts, Jesus said, "Why do you entertain evil thoughts in your hearts? [5]Which is easier: to say, 'Your sins are forgiven,' or to say, 'Get up and walk'?"

MATTHEW 12:6-8 "I tell you that one greater than the temple is here. [7]If you had known what these words mean, 'I

desire mercy, not sacrifice,' you would not have condemned the innocent. [8]For the Son of Man is Lord of the Sabbath." (See also Luke 6:5.)

MATTHEW 12:40 "For as Jonah was three days and three nights in the belly of a huge fish, so the Son of Man will be three days and three nights in the heart of the earth."

MATTHEW 16:13-17 When Jesus came to the region of Caesarea Philippi, he asked his disciples, "Who do people say the Son of Man is?" [14]They replied, "Some say John the Baptist; others say Elijah; and still others, Jeremiah or one of the prophets." [15]"But what about you?" he asked. "Who do you say I am?" [16]Simon Peter answered, "You are the Christ, the Son of the living God." [17]Jesus replied, "Blessed are you, Simon son of Jonah, for this was not revealed to you by man, but by my Father in heaven."

MATTHEW 16:27-28 "For the Son of Man is going to come in his Father's glory with his angels, and then he will reward each person according to what he has done. [28]I tell you the truth, some who are standing here will not taste death before they see the Son of Man coming in his kingdom."

MATTHEW 17:1-8 After six days Jesus took with him Peter, James and John the brother of James, and led them up a high mountain by themselves. [2]There he was transfigured before them. His face shone like the sun, and his clothes became as white as the light. [3]Just then there appeared before them Moses and Elijah, talking with Jesus. [4]Peter said to Jesus, "Lord, it is good for us to be here. If you wish, I will put up three shelters—one for you, one for Moses and one for Elijah." [5]While he was still speaking, a bright cloud enveloped them, and a voice from the cloud said, "This is my Son, whom I love; with him I am well pleased. Listen to him!" [6]When the disciples heard this, they fell facedown to the ground, terrified. [7]But Jesus came and touched them. "Get up," he said. "Don't be afraid." [8]When they looked up, they saw no one except Jesus.

MATTHEW 17:9 As they were coming down the mountain [of Transfiguration], Jesus instructed them, "Don't tell anyone what you have seen, until the Son of Man has been raised from the dead."

MATTHEW 19:28 Jesus said to them [the disciples], "I tell you the truth, at the renewal of all things, when the Son of Man sits on his glorious throne, you who have followed me will also sit on twelve thrones, judging the twelve tribes of Israel."

MATTHEW 21:2-3 ..."Go to the village ahead of you, and at once you will find a donkey tied there, with her colt by her. Untie them and bring them to me. [3]If anyone says anything to you, tell him that the Lord needs them, and he will send them right away." (See also Mark 11:1-3; Luke 19:29-31.)

MATTHEW 21:13 "It is written," he said to them, " 'My house will be called a house of prayer,' but you are making it a 'den of robbers.' "

MATTHEW 21:23-27 Jesus entered the temple courts, and, while he was teaching, the chief priests and the elders of the people came to him. "By what author-ity are you doing these things?" they asked. "And who gave you this authority?" [24]Jesus replied, "I will also ask you one question. If you answer me, I will tell you by what authority I am doing these things. [25]John's baptism—where did it come from? Was it from heaven, or from men?" They discussed it among themselves and said, "If we say, 'From heaven,' he will ask, 'Then why didn't you believe him?' [26]But if we say, 'From men'—we are afraid of the people, for they all hold that John was a prophet." [27]So they answered Jesus, "We don't know." Then he said, "Neither will I tell you by what authority I am doing these things." (See also Mark 11:27-33; Luke 20:1-8.)

MATTHEW 21:42-44 Jesus said to them, "Have you never read in the Scriptures: 'The stone the builders rejected has become the capstone; the Lord has done this, and it is marvelous in our eyes'? [43]Therefore I tell you that the kingdom of God will be taken away from you and given to a people who will produce its fruit. [44]He who falls on this stone will be broken to pieces, but he on whom it falls will be crushed."

MATTHEW 22:41-45 While the Pharisees were gathered together, Jesus asked them, [42]"What do you think about the Christ? Whose son is he?" "The son of David," they replied. [43]He said to them, "How is it then that David, speaking by the Spirit, calls him 'Lord'? For he says, [44]'The Lord said to my Lord: "Sit at my right hand until I put your enemies under your feet."' [45]If then David calls him 'Lord,' how can he be his son?"

MATTHEW 23:8-12 "But you are

not to be called 'Rabbi,' for you have only one Master and you are all brothers. [9]And do not call anyone on earth 'father,' for you have one Father, and he is in heaven. [10]Nor are you to be called 'teacher,' for you have one Teacher, the Christ. [11]The greatest among you will be your servant. [12]For whoever exalts himself will be humbled, and whoever humbles himself will be exalted."

MATTHEW 23:37-39 "O Jerusalem, Jerusalem, you who kill the prophets and stone those sent to you, how often I have longed to gather your children together, as a hen gathers her chicks under her wings, but you were not willing. [38]Look, your house is left to you desolate. [39]For I tell you, you will not see me again until you say, 'Blessed is he who comes in the name of the Lord.'"

MATTHEW 26:17-25 On the first day of the Feast of Unleavened Bread, the disciples came to Jesus and asked, "Where do you want us to make preparations for you to eat the Passover?" [18]He replied, "Go into the city to a certain man and tell him, 'The Teacher says: My appointed time is near. I am going to celebrate the Passover with my disciples at your house.'" [19]So the disciples did as Jesus had directed them and prepared the Passover. [20]When evening came, Jesus was reclining at the table with the Twelve. [21]And while they were eating, he said, "I tell you the truth, one of you will betray me." [22]They were very sad and began to say to him one after the other, "Surely not I, Lord?" [23]Jesus replied, "The one who has dipped his hand into the bowl with me will betray me. [24]The Son of Man will go just as it is

written about him. But woe to that man who betrays the Son of Man! It would be better for him if he had not been born." [25]Then Judas, the one who would betray him, said, "Surely not I, Rabbi?" Jesus answered, "Yes, it is you."

MATTHEW 26:63-64 But Jesus remained silent. The high priest said to him, "I charge you under oath by the living God: Tell us if you are the Christ, the Son of God." [64]"Yes, it is as you say," Jesus replied. "But I say to all of you: In the future you will see the Son of Man sitting at the right hand of the Mighty One and coming on the clouds of heaven."

MATTHEW 27:11 Meanwhile Jesus stood before the governor, and the governor asked him, "Are you the king of the Jews?" "Yes, it is as you say," Jesus replied. (See also Mark 15:2; Luke 23:3.)

MATTHEW 28:18-20 Then Jesus came to them [the eleven disciples] and said, "All authority in heaven and on earth has been given to me. [19]Therefore go and make disciples of all nations, baptizing them in the name of the Father and of the Son and of the Holy Spirit, [20]and teaching them to obey everything I have commanded you. And surely I am with you always, to the very end of the age."

MARK 8:27-29 Jesus and his disciples went on to the villages around Caesarea Philippi. On the way he asked them, "Who do people say I am?" [28]They replied, "Some say John the Baptist; others say Elijah; and still others, one of the prophets." [29]"But what about you?" he asked. "Who do you say I am?" Peter answered, "You are the Christ."

MARK 12:35-37 While Jesus was teaching in the temple courts, he asked, "How is it that the teachers of the law say that the Christ is the son of David? [36]David himself, speaking by the Holy Spirit, declared: 'The Lord said to my Lord: "Sit at my right hand until I put your enemies under your feet."' [37]David himself calls him 'Lord.' How then can he be his son?" The large crowd listened to him with delight.

MARK 14:17-21 When evening came, Jesus arrived with the Twelve. [18]While they were reclining at the table eating, he said, "I tell you the truth, one of you will betray me—one who is eating with me." [19]They were saddened, and one by one they said to him, "Surely not I?" [20]"It is one of the Twelve," he replied, "one who dips bread into the bowl with me. [21]The Son of Man will go just as it is written about him. But woe to that man who betrays the Son of Man! It would be better for him if he had not been born."

MARK 14:61-62 But Jesus remained silent and gave no answer. Again the high priest asked him, "Are you the Christ, the Son of the Blessed One?" [62]"I am," said Jesus. "And you will see the Son of Man sitting at the right hand of the Mighty One and coming on the clouds of heaven."

LUKE 7:24-27 After John's messengers left, Jesus began to speak to the crowd about John: "What did you go out into the desert to see? A reed swayed by the wind? [25]If not, what did you go out to see? A man dressed in fine clothes? No, those who wear expensive clothes and indulge in luxury are in palaces. [26]But what did you go out to see? A prophet? Yes, I tell you, and more than a prophet. [27]This is the one about whom it is written: 'I will send my messenger ahead of you, who will prepare your way before you.'" (See also Matthew 11:7-10.)

LUKE 8:22-25 One day Jesus said to his disciples, "Let's go over to the other side of the lake." So they got into a boat and set out. [23]As they sailed, he fell asleep. A squall came down on the lake, so that the boat was being swamped, and they were in great danger. [24]The disciples went and woke him, saying, "Master, Master, we're going to drown!" He got up and rebuked the wind and the raging waters; the storm subsided, and all was calm. [25]"Where is your faith?" he asked his disciples. In fear and amazement they asked one another, "Who is this? He commands even the winds and the water, and they obey him." (See also Matthew 8:23-27; Mark 4:35-41.)

LUKE 9:18-20 Once when Jesus was praying in private and his disciples were with him, he asked them, "Who do the crowds say I am?" [19]They replied, "Some say John the Baptist; others say Elijah; and still others, that one of the prophets of long ago has come back to life." [20]"But what about you?" he asked. "Who do you say I am?" Peter answered, "The Christ of God."

LUKE 9:57-58 As they were walking along the road, a man said to him, "I will follow you wherever you go." [58]Jesus replied, "Foxes have holes and birds of the air have nests, but the Son of Man has no place to lay his head."

LUKE 17:30-35, 37 "It will be just

like this on the day the Son of Man is revealed. [31]On that day no one who is on the roof of his house, with his goods inside, should go down to get them. Likewise, no one in the field should go back for anything. [32]Remember Lot's wife! [33]Whoever tries to keep his life will lose it, and whoever loses his life will preserve it. [34]I tell you, on that night two people will be in one bed; one will be taken and the other left. [35]Two women will be grinding grain together; one will be taken and the other left." [37]"Where, Lord?" they asked. He replied, "Where there is a dead body, there the vultures will gather."

LUKE 19:37-40 When he came near the place where the road goes down the Mount of Olives, the whole crowd of disciples began joyfully to praise God in loud voices for all the miracles they had seen: [38]"Blessed is the king who comes in the name of the Lord!" "Peace in heaven and glory in the highest!" [39]Some of the Pharisees in the crowd said to Jesus, "Teacher, rebuke your disciples!" [40]"I tell you," he replied, "if they keep quiet, the stones will cry out."

LUKE 20:41-44 Then Jesus said to them, "How is it that they say the Christ is the Son of David? [42]David himself declares in the Book of Psalms: 'The Lord said to my Lord: "Sit at my right hand [43]until I make your enemies a footstool for your feet."' [44]David calls him 'Lord.' How then can he be his son?"

LUKE 22:20-22 In the same way, after the supper he took the cup, saying, "This cup is the new covenant in my blood, which is poured out for you. [21]But the hand of him who is going to betray me is with mine on the table. [22]The Son of Man will go as it has been decreed, but woe to that man who betrays him."

LUKE 22:35-38 Then Jesus asked them, "When I sent you without purse, bag or sandals, did you lack anything?" "Nothing," they answered. [36]He said to them, "But now if you have a purse, take it, and also a bag; and if you don't have a sword, sell your cloak and buy one. [37]It is written: 'And he was numbered with the transgressors'; and I tell you that this must be fulfilled in me. Yes, what is written about me is reaching its fulfillment." [38]The disciples said, "See, Lord, here are two swords." "That is enough," he replied.

LUKE 22:47-51 While he was still speaking a crowd came up, and the man who was called Judas, one of the Twelve, was leading them. He approached Jesus to kiss him, [48]but Jesus asked him, "Judas, are you betraying the Son of Man with a kiss?" [49]When Jesus' followers saw what was going to happen, they said, "Lord, should we strike with our swords?" [50]And one of them struck the servant of the high priest, cutting off his right ear. [51]But Jesus answered, "No more of this!" And he touched the man's ear and healed him.

LUKE 22:67-70 "If you are the Christ," they [chief priests and teachers of the law] said, "tell us." Jesus answered, "If I tell you, you will not believe me, [68]and if I asked you, you would not answer. [69]But from now on, the Son of Man will be seated at the right hand of the mighty God." [70]They all asked, "Are you then the Son of God?" He replied, "You are right in saying I am."

LUKE 24:15-27 As they talked and discussed these things with each other, Jesus himself came up and walked along with them; [16]but they were kept from recognizing him. [17]He asked them, "What are you discussing together as you walk along?" They stood still, their faces downcast. [18]One of them, named Cleopas, asked him, "Are you only a visitor to Jerusalem and do not know the things that have happened there in these days?" [19]"What things?" he asked. "About Jesus of Nazareth," they replied. "He was a prophet, powerful in word and deed before God and all the people. [20]The chief priests and our rulers handed him over to be sentenced to death, and they crucified him; [21]but we had hoped that he was the one who was going to redeem Israel. And what is more, it is the third day since all this took place. [22]In addition, some of our women amazed us. They went to the tomb early this morning [23]but didn't find his body. They came and told us that they had seen a vision of angels, who said he was alive. [24]Then some of our companions went to the tomb and found it just as the women had said, but him they did not see." [25]He said to them, "How foolish you are, and how slow of heart to believe all that the prophets have spoken! [26]Did not the Christ have to suffer these things and then enter his glory?" [27]And beginning with Moses and all the Prophets, he explained to them what was said in all the Scriptures concerning himself.

LUKE 24:44 He said to them, "This is what I told you while I was still with you: Everything must be fulfilled that is written about me in the Law of Moses, the Prophets and the Psalms."

REVELATION 22:13 "I am the Alpha and the Omega, the First and the Last, the Beginning and the End."

Jesus' Lordship

JOHN 5:21-23 "For just as the Father raises the dead and gives them life, even so the Son gives life to whom he is pleased to give it. [22]Moreover, the Father judges no one, but has entrusted all judgment to the Son, [23]that all may honor the Son just as they honor the Father. He who does not honor the Son does not honor the Father, who sent him."

JOHN 8:31-32 Then Jesus said to those Jews who believed Him, "If you abide in My word, you are My disciples indeed. [32]And you shall know the truth, and the truth shall make you free." (NKJV)

JOHN 10:27-30 "My sheep listen to my voice; I know them, and they follow me. [28]I give them eternal life, and they shall never perish; no one can snatch them out of my hand. [29]My Father, who has given them to me, is greater than all; no one can snatch them out of my Father's hand. [30]I and the Father are one."

JOHN 12:25-26 "The man who loves his life will lose it, while the man who hates his life in this world will keep it for eternal life. [26]Whoever serves me must follow me; and where I am, my servant also will be. My Father will honor the one who serves me."

JOHN 14:15 "If you love me, you will obey what I command."

JOHN 14:23-24 Jesus replied, "If anyone loves me, he will obey my teaching. My Father will love him, and we will come to him and make our home with him. [24]He who does not love me will not obey my teaching. These words you hear are not my own; they belong to the Father who sent me."

MATTHEW 7:21-27 "Not everyone who says to Me, 'Lord, Lord,' shall enter the kingdom of heaven, but he who does the will of My Father in heaven. [22]Many will say to Me in that day, 'Lord, Lord, have we not prophesied in Your name, cast out demons in Your name, and done many wonders in Your name?' [23]And then I will declare to them, 'I never knew you; depart from Me, you who practice lawlessness!' [24]Therefore whoever hears these sayings of Mine, and does them, I will liken him to a wise man who built his house on the rock: [25]and the rain descended, the floods came, and the winds blew and beat on that house; and it did not fall, for it was founded on the rock. [26]But everyone who hears these sayings of Mine, and does not do them, will be like a foolish man who built his house on the sand: [27]and the rain descended, the floods came, and the winds blew and beat on that house; and it fell. And great was its fall." (NKJV)

MATTHEW 10:34-39 "Do not suppose that I have come to bring peace to the earth. I did not come to bring peace, but a sword. [35]For I have come to turn 'a man against his father, a daughter against her mother, a daughter-in-law against her mother-in-law— [36]a man's enemies will be the members of his own household.' [37]Anyone who loves his father or mother more than me is not worthy of me; anyone who loves his son or daughter more than me is not worthy of me; [38]and anyone who does not take his cross and follow me is not worthy of me. [39]Whoever finds his life will lose it, and whoever loses his life for my sake will find it."

MATTHEW 16:23-27 Jesus turned and said to Peter, "Get behind me, Satan! You are a stumbling block to me; you do not have in mind the things of God, but the things of men." [24]Then Jesus said to his disciples, "If anyone would come after me, he must deny himself and take up his cross and follow me. [25]For whoever wants to save his life will lose it, but whoever loses his life for me will find it. [26]What good will it be for a man if he gains the whole world, yet forfeits his soul? Or what can a man give in exchange for his soul? [27]For the Son of Man is going to come in his Father's glory with his angels, and then he will reward each person according to what he has done."

MATTHEW 19:21, 23-26 Jesus answered, "If you want to be perfect, go, sell your possessions and give to the poor, and you will have treasure in heaven. Then come, follow me." [23]Then Jesus said to his disciples, "I tell you the truth, it is hard for a rich man to enter the kingdom of heaven. [24]Again I tell you, it is easier for a camel to go through the eye of a needle than for a rich man to enter the kingdom of God." [25]When the disciples heard this, they were greatly astonished and asked, "Who then can be saved?" [26]Jesus looked at them and said, "With man this is impossible, but with God all things are possible."

MARK 8:34-38 Then he called the crowd to him along with his disciples and said: "If anyone would come after me, he must deny himself and take up his cross and follow me. [35]For whoever wants to save his life will lose it, but whoever loses his life for me and for the gospel will save it. [36]What good is it for a man to gain the whole world, yet forfeit his soul? [37]Or what can a man give in exchange for his soul? [38]If anyone is ashamed of me and my words in this adulterous and sinful generation, the Son of Man will be ashamed of him when he comes in his Father's glory with the holy angels."

LUKE 6:46-49 "Why do you call me, 'Lord, Lord,' and do not do what I say? [47]I will show you what he is like who comes to me and hears my words and puts them into practice. [48]He is like a man building a house, who dug down deep and laid the foundation on rock. When a flood came, the torrent struck that house but could not shake it, because it was well built. [49]But the one who hears my words and does not put them into practice is like a man who built a house on the ground without a foundation. The moment the torrent struck that house, it collapsed and its destruction was complete."

LUKE 9:23-26 Then he said to them all: "If anyone would come after me, he must deny himself and take up his cross daily and follow me. [24]For whoever wants to save his life will lose it, but whoever loses his life for me will save it. [25]What good is it for a man to gain the whole world, and yet lose or forfeit his very self? [26]If anyone is ashamed of me and my words, the Son of Man will be ashamed

of him when he comes in his glory and in the glory of the Father and of the holy angels."

REVELATION 1:10-11, 17-20 On the Lord's Day I [John] was in the Spirit, and I heard behind me a loud voice like a trumpet, [11]which said: "Write on a scroll what you see and send it to the seven churches: to Ephesus, Smyrna, Pergamum, Thyatira, Sardis, Philadelphia and Laodicea." [17]When I saw him, I fell at his feet as though dead. Then he placed his right hand on me and said: "Do not be afraid. I am the First and the Last. [18]I am the Living One; I was dead, and behold I am alive for ever and ever! And I hold the keys of death and Hades. [19]Write, therefore, what you have seen, what is now and what will take place later. [20]The mystery of the seven stars that you saw in my right hand and of the seven golden lampstands is this: The seven stars are the angels of the seven churches, and the seven lampstands are the seven churches."

Jesus' Love

JOHN 10:10-17 "The thief comes only to steal and kill and destroy; I have come that they may have life, and have it to the full. [11]I am the good shepherd. The good shepherd lays down his life for the sheep. [12]The hired hand is not the shepherd who owns the sheep. So when he sees the wolf coming, he abandons the sheep and runs away. Then the wolf attacks the flock and scatters it. [13]The man runs away because he is a hired hand and cares nothing for the sheep. [14]I am the good shepherd; I know my sheep and my sheep know me— [15]just as the Father knows me and I know the Father—and I lay down my life for the sheep. [16]I have other sheep that are not of this sheep pen. I must bring them also. They too will listen to my voice, and there shall be one flock and one shepherd. [17]The reason my Father loves me is that I lay down my life—only to take it up again."

JOHN 11:33-35 When Jesus saw her weeping, and the Jews who had come along with her also weeping, he was deeply moved in spirit and troubled. [34]"Where have you laid him?" he asked. "Come and see, Lord," they replied. [35]Jesus wept.

JOHN 13:34 "A new command I give you: Love one another. As I have loved you, so you must love one another."

JOHN 14:1-4 "Do not let your hearts be troubled. Trust in God; trust also in me. [2]In my Father's house are many rooms; if it were not so, I would have told you. I am going there to prepare a place for you. [3]And if I go and prepare a place for you, I will come back and take you to be with me that you also may be where I am. [4]You know the way to the place where I am going."

JOHN 14:21 "Whoever has my commands and obeys them, he is the one who loves me. He who loves me will be loved by my Father, and I too will love him and show myself to him."

JOHN 14:23-24 Jesus replied, "If anyone loves me, he will obey my teaching. My Father will love him, and we will come to him and make our home with him. [24]He who does not love me will not obey my teaching. These words you hear

are not my own; they belong to the Father who sent me."

JOHN 15:9-15 "As the Father has loved me, so have I loved you. Now remain in my love. [10]If you obey my commands, you will remain in my love, just as I have obeyed my Father's commands and remain in his love. [11]I have told you this so that my joy may be in you and that your joy may be complete. [12]My command is this: Love each other as I have loved you. [13]Greater love has no one than this, that he lay down his life for his friends. [14]You are my friends if you do what I command. [15]I no longer call you servants, because a servant does not know his master's business. Instead, I have called you friends, for everything that I learned from my Father I have made known to you."

MATTHEW 18:10, 12-14 "See that you do not look down on one of these little ones. For I tell you that their angels in heaven always see the face of my Father in heaven. [12]What do you think? If a man owns a hundred sheep, and one of them wanders away, will he not leave the ninety-nine on the hills and go to look for the one that wandered off? [13]And if he finds it, I tell you the truth, he is happier about that one sheep than about the ninety-nine that did not wander off. [14]In the same way your Father in heaven is not willing that any of these little ones should be lost."

MATTHEW 23:37 "O Jerusalem, Jerusalem, you who kill the prophets and stone those sent to you, how often I have longed to gather your children together, as a hen gathers her chicks under her wings, but you were not willing."

LUKE 15:4-10 "Suppose one of you has a hundred sheep and loses one of them. Does he not leave the ninety-nine in the open country and go after the lost sheep until he finds it? [5]And when he finds it, he joyfully puts it on his shoulders [6]and goes home. Then he calls his friends and neighbors together and says, 'Rejoice with me; I have found my lost sheep.' [7]I tell you that in the same way there will be more rejoicing in heaven over one sinner who repents than over ninety-nine righteous persons who do not need to repent. [8]Or suppose a woman has ten silver coins and loses one. Does she not light a lamp, sweep the house and search carefully until she finds it? [9]And when she finds it, she calls her friends and neighbors together and says, 'Rejoice with me; I have found my lost coin.' [10]In the same way, I tell you, there is rejoicing in the presence of the angels of God over one sinner who repents."

Jesus' Missions

In this section Jesus identifies twenty-six different missions that He set out to achieve when He came to earth. Unlike you and me, Jesus was not self-serving in His missions. Every mission He undertook was related to serving God and serving you and me. Like His identity and His claims, His mission on earth set Him apart from every other person who has ever lived. We see Jesus' incomparable love for His Father as well as for you and me. His missions were as broad as living a perfectly righteous life by fulfilling all points of the moral laws of God, and redeeming mankind. The missions were as visible as healing the sick and raising the dead, and as invisible as setting captives free. They were as humble as preaching the gospel and as lofty as glorifying God. If we desire to experience an intimate relationship with Jesus, discovering and embracing His missions will be key to fulfilling that desire.

JOHN 3:14-17 "Just as Moses lifted up the snake in the desert, so the Son of Man must be lifted up, [15]that everyone who believes in him may have eternal life. [16]For God so loved the world that he gave his one and only Son, that whoever believes in him shall not perish but have eternal life. [17]For God did not send his Son into the world to condemn the world, but to save the world through him."

JOHN 4:31-34 Meanwhile his disciples urged him, "Rabbi, eat something." [32]But he said to them, "I have food to eat that you know nothing about." [33]Then his disciples said to each other, "Could someone have brought him food?" [34]"My food," said Jesus, "is to do the will of him who sent me and to finish his work."

JOHN 5:21-22 "For just as the Father raises the dead and gives them life, even so the Son gives life to whom he is pleased to give it. [22]Moreover, the Father judges no one, but has entrusted all judgment to the Son."

JOHN 5:30 "By myself I can do nothing; I judge only as I hear, and my judgment is just, for I seek not to please myself but him who sent me."

JOHN 6:38-40 "For I have come down from heaven not to do my will but to do the will of him who sent me. [39]And this is the will of him who sent me, that I shall lose none of all that he has given me, but raise them up at the last day. [40]For my Father's will is that everyone who looks to the Son and believes in him shall have eternal life, and I will raise him up at the last day."

JOHN 6:44-45 "No one can come to me unless the Father who sent me draws him, and I will raise him up at the last day. [45]It is written in the Prophets: 'They will all be taught by God.' Everyone who listens to the Father and learns from him comes to me."

JOHN 6:48-51 "I am the bread of life. [49]Your forefathers ate the manna in the desert, yet they died. [50]But here is the bread that comes down from heaven, which a man may eat and not die. [51]I am the living bread that came down from heaven. If anyone eats of this bread, he will live forever. This bread is my flesh, which I will give for the life of the world."

JOHN 7:16-19 Jesus answered, "My teaching is not my own. It comes from him who sent me. [17]If anyone chooses to do God's will, he will find out whether my teaching comes from God or whether I speak on my own. [18]He who speaks on his own does so to gain honor for himself, but he who works for the honor of the one who sent him is a man of truth; there is nothing false about him. [19]Has not Moses given you the law? Yet not one of you keeps the law. Why are you trying to kill me?"

JOHN 8:14-18 Jesus answered, "Even if I testify on my own behalf, my testimony is valid, for I know where I came from and where I am going. But you have

no idea where I come from or where I am going. [15]You judge by human standards; I pass judgment on no one. [16]But if I do judge, my decisions are right, because I am not alone. I stand with the Father, who sent me. [17]In your own Law it is written that the testimony of two men is valid. [18]I am one who testifies for myself; my other witness is the Father, who sent me."

JOHN 8:28-29 So Jesus said, "When you have lifted up the Son of Man, then you will know that I am the one I claim to be and that I do nothing on my own but speak just what the Father has taught me. [29]The one who sent me is with me; he has not left me alone, for I always do what pleases him."

JOHN 8:49-50 "I am not possessed by a demon," said Jesus, "but I honor my Father and you dishonor me. [50]I am not seeking glory for myself; but there is one who seeks it, and he is the judge."

JOHN 9:3-7 "Neither this man nor his parents sinned," said Jesus, "but this [being born blind] happened so that the work of God might be displayed in his life. [4]As long as it is day, we must do the work of him who sent me. Night is coming, when no one can work. [5]While I am in the world, I am the light of the world." [6]Having said this, he spit on the ground, made some mud with the saliva, and put it on the man's eyes. [7]"Go," he told him, "wash in the Pool of Siloam" (this word means Sent). So the man went and washed, and came home seeing.

JOHN 9:39 Jesus said, "For judgment I have come into this world, so that the blind will see and those who see will become blind."

JOHN 10:10-11 "The thief comes only to steal and kill and destroy; I have come that they may have life, and have it to the full. [11]I am the good shepherd. The good shepherd lays down his life for the sheep."

JOHN 10:14-16 "I am the good shepherd; I know my sheep and my sheep know me— [15]just as the Father knows me and I know the Father—and I lay down my life for the sheep. [16]I have other sheep that are not of this sheep pen. I must bring them also. They too will listen to my voice, and there shall be one flock and one shepherd."

JOHN 10:17-18 "The reason my Father loves me is that I lay down my life—only to take it up again. [18]No one takes it from me, but I lay it down of my own accord. I have authority to lay it down and authority to take it up again. This command I received from my Father."

JOHN 10:27-30 "My sheep listen to my voice; I know them, and they follow me. [28]I give them eternal life, and they shall never perish; no one can snatch them out of my hand. [29]My Father, who has given them to me, is greater than all; no one can snatch them out of my Father's hand. [30]I and the Father are one."

JOHN 12:23-24 Jesus replied, "The hour has come for the Son of Man to be glorified. [24]I tell you the truth, unless a kernel of wheat falls to the ground and dies, it remains only a single seed. But if it dies, it produces many seeds."

JOHN 12:27-28 "Now my heart is troubled, and what shall I say? 'Father, save me from this hour'? No, it was for this very reason I came to this hour. [28]Father, glorify your name!" Then a voice came from heaven, "I have glorified it, and will glorify it again."

JOHN 12:47-50 "As for the person who hears my words but does not keep them, I do not judge him. For I did not come to judge the world, but to save it. [48]There is a judge for the one who rejects me and does not accept my words; that very word which I spoke will condemn him at the last day. [49]For I did not speak of my own accord, but the Father who sent me commanded me what to say and how to say it. [50]I know that his command leads to eternal life. So whatever I say is just what the Father has told me to say."

JOHN 14:2-4 "In my Father's house are many rooms; if it were not so, I would have told you. I am going there to prepare a place for you. [3]And if I go and prepare a place for you, I will come back and take you to be with me that you also may be where I am. [4]You know the way to the place where I am going."

JOHN 17:2-4 "For you [God the Father] granted him [Christ] authority over all people that he might give eternal life to all those you have given him. [3]Now this is eternal life: that they may know you, the only true God, and Jesus Christ, whom you have sent. [4]I have brought you glory on earth by completing the work you gave me to do."

JOHN 17:13-14 "I am coming to you [God the Father] now, but I say these things while I am still in the world, so that they may have the full measure of my joy within them. [14]I have given them your word and the world has hated them, for they are not of the world any more than I am of the world."

JOHN 17:17-19 "Sanctify them by the truth; your word is truth. ¹⁸As you sent me into the world, I have sent them into the world. ¹⁹For them I sanctify myself, that they too may be truly sanctified."

JOHN 17:24-26 "Father, I want those you have given me to be with me where I am, and to see my glory, the glory you have given me because you loved me before the creation of the world. ²⁵Righteous Father, though the world does not know you, I know you, and they know that you have sent me. ²⁶I have made you known to them, and will continue to make you known in order that the love you have for me may be in them and that I myself may be in them."

JOHN 18:11 Jesus commanded Peter, "Put your sword away! Shall I not drink the cup the Father has given me?"

JOHN 18:36 Jesus said, "My kingdom is not of this world. If it were, my servants would fight to prevent my arrest by the Jews. But now my kingdom is from another place."

JOHN 18:37 "You are a king, then!" said Pilate. Jesus answered, "You are right in saying I am a king. In fact, for this reason I was born, and for this I came into the world, to testify to the truth. Everyone on the side of truth listens to me."

JOHN 19:11 Jesus answered, "You [Pilate] would have no power over me if it were not given to you from above.…"

JOHN 20:17 Jesus said, "Do not hold on to me, for I have not yet returned to the Father. Go instead to my brothers and tell them, 'I am returning to my Father and your Father, to my God and your God.'…"

MATTHEW 5:17 "Do not think that I have come to abolish the Law or the Prophets; I have not come to abolish them but to fulfill them."

MATTHEW 9:6 "But so that you may know that the Son of Man has authority on earth to forgive sins.…" Then he said to the paralytic, "Get up, take your mat and go home."

MATTHEW 9:12-13 On hearing this, Jesus said, "It is not the healthy who need a doctor, but the sick. ¹³But go and learn what this means: 'I desire mercy, not sacrifice.' For I have not come to call the righteous, but sinners."

MATTHEW 11:27 "All things have been committed to me by my Father. No one knows the Son except the Father, and no one knows the Father except the Son and those to whom the Son chooses to reveal him."

MATTHEW 15:24-28 He answered, "I was sent only to the lost sheep of Israel." ²⁵The woman came and knelt before him. "Lord, help me!" she said. ²⁶He replied, "It is not right to take the children's bread and toss it to their dogs." ²⁷"Yes, Lord," she said, "but even the dogs eat the crumbs that fall from their masters' table." ²⁸Then Jesus answered, "Woman, you have great faith! Your request is granted." And her daughter was healed from that very hour.

MATTHEW 16:27 "For the Son of Man is going to come in his Father's glory with his angels, and then he will reward each person according to what he has done."

MATTHEW 18:12-14 "What do you think? If a man owns a hundred sheep, and one of them wanders away, will he not leave the ninety-nine on the hills and go to look for the one that wandered off? [13]And if he finds it, I tell you the truth, he is happier about that one sheep than about the ninety-nine that did not wander off. [14]In the same way your Father in heaven is not willing that any of these little ones should be lost."

MATTHEW 20:25-28 Jesus called them [the disciples] together and said, "You know that the rulers of the Gentiles lord it over them, and their high officials exercise authority over them. [26]Not so with you. Instead, whoever wants to become great among you must be your servant, [27]and whoever wants to be first must be your slave— [28]just as the Son of Man did not come to be served, but to serve, and to give his life as a ransom for many."

MATTHEW 21:42 Jesus said to them, "Have you never read in the Scriptures: 'The stone the builders rejected has become the capstone; the Lord has done this, and it is marvelous in our eyes'?"

MATTHEW 26:39 Going a little farther, he fell with his face to the ground and prayed, "My Father, if it is possible, may this cup be taken from me. Yet not as I will, but as you will."

MATTHEW 26:52-54 "Put your sword back in its place," Jesus said to him [Peter], "for all who draw the sword will die by the sword. [53]Do you think I cannot call on my Father, and he will at once put at my disposal more than twelve legions of angels? [54]But how then would the Scriptures be fulfilled that say it must happen in this way?"

MATTHEW 26:64 "...I say to all of you: In the future you will see the Son of Man sitting at the right hand of the Mighty One and coming on the clouds of heaven."

MARK 1:38 Jesus replied, "Let us go somewhere else—to the nearby villages—so I can preach there also. That is why I have come."

MARK 2:10 "...the Son of Man has authority on earth to forgive sins...."

MARK 2:17 On hearing this, Jesus said to them, "It is not the healthy who need a doctor, but the sick. I have not come to call the righteous, but sinners."

MARK 10:45 "For even the Son of Man did not come to be served, but to serve, and to give his life as a ransom for many."

LUKE 2:49 "Why were you searching for me?" he asked. "Didn't you know I had to be in my Father's house?"

LUKE 4:18-21 "The Spirit of the Lord is on me, because he has anointed me to preach good news to the poor. He has sent me to proclaim freedom for the prisoners and recovery of sight for the blind, to release the oppressed, [19]to proclaim the year of the Lord's favor." [20]Then he rolled up the scroll, gave it back to the attendant and sat down. The eyes of everyone in the synagogue were fastened on him, [21]and he began by saying to them, "Today this scripture is fulfilled in your hearing."

LUKE 4:43 But he said, "I must preach the good news of the kingdom of God to the other towns also, because that is why I was sent."

LUKE 5:31-32 Jesus answered them, "It is not the healthy who need a doctor, but the sick. [32]I have not come to call the righteous, but sinners to repentance."

LUKE 9:55-56 But He turned and rebuked them, and said, "You do not know what manner of spirit you are of. [56]For the Son of Man did not come to destroy men's lives but to save them." And they went to another village. (NKJV)

LUKE 12:49-53 "I have come to bring fire on the earth, and how I wish it were already kindled! [50]But I have a baptism to undergo, and how distressed I am until it is completed! [51]Do you think I came to bring peace on earth? No, I tell you, but division. [52]From now on there will be five in one family divided against each other, three against two and two against three. [53]They will be divided, father against son and son against father, mother against daughter and daughter against mother, mother-in-law against daughter-in-law and daughter-in-law against mother-in-law."

LUKE 19:9-10 Jesus said to him [Zacchaeus], "Today salvation has come to this house, because this man, too, is a son of Abraham. [10]For the Son of Man came to seek and to save what was lost."

LUKE 22:69 "But from now on, the Son of Man will be seated at the right hand of the mighty God."

Jesus' Name—Its Power and Meaning

JOHN 3:16-18 "For God so loved the world that he gave his one and only Son, that whoever believes in him shall not perish but have eternal life. [17]For God did not send his Son into the world to condemn the world, but to save the world through him. [18]Whoever believes in him is not condemned, but whoever does not believe stands condemned already because he has not believed in the name of God's one and only Son."

JOHN 14:13-14 "And I will do whatever you ask in my name, so that the Son may bring glory to the Father. [14]You may ask me for anything in my name, and I will do it."

JOHN 14:26 "But the Counselor, the Holy Spirit, whom the Father will send in my name, will teach you all things and will remind you of everything I have said to you."

JOHN 15:16 "You did not choose me, but I chose you and appointed you to go and bear fruit—fruit that will last. Then the Father will give you whatever you ask in my name."

JOHN 16:23-27 "In that day you will no longer ask me anything. I tell you the truth, my Father will give you whatever you ask in my name. [24]Until now you have not asked for anything in my name. Ask and you will receive, and your joy will be complete. [25]Though I have been speaking figuratively, a time is coming when I will no longer use this kind of language but will tell you plainly about my Father. [26]In that day you will ask in my name. I am not saying that I will ask the Father on your behalf. [27]No, the Father himself loves you because you have loved me and have believed that I came from God."

JOHN 17:11-12 "I will remain in the world no longer, but they are still in the world, and I am coming to you. Holy

Father, protect them by the power of your name—the name you gave me—so that they may be one as we are one. [12]While I was with them, I protected them and kept them safe by that name you gave me. None has been lost except the one doomed to destruction so that Scripture would be fulfilled."

MATTHEW 7:21-23 "Not everyone who says to Me, 'Lord, Lord,' shall enter the kingdom of heaven, but he who does the will of My Father in heaven. [22]Many will say to Me in that day, 'Lord, Lord, have we not prophesied in Your name, cast out demons in Your name, and done many wonders in Your name?' [23]And then I will declare to them, 'I never knew you; depart from Me, you who practice lawlessness!' " (NKJV)

MATTHEW 18:5 "And whoever welcomes a little child like this in my name welcomes me."

MATTHEW 18:18-20 "I tell you the truth, whatever you bind on earth will be bound in heaven, and whatever you loose on earth will be loosed in heaven. [19]Again, I tell you that if two of you on earth agree about anything you ask for, it will be done for you by my Father in heaven. [20]For where two or three come together in my name, there am I with them."

MATTHEW 24:4-5 Jesus answered: "Watch out that no one deceives you. [5]For many will come in my name, claiming, 'I am the Christ,' and will deceive many."

MATTHEW 28:18-20 Then Jesus came to them [the eleven disciples] and said, "All authority in heaven and on earth has been given to me. [19]Therefore go and make disciples of all nations, baptizing them in the name of the Father and of the Son and of the Holy Spirit, [20]and teaching them to obey everything I have commanded you. And surely I am with you always, to the very end of the age."

MARK 9:35-37 Sitting down, Jesus called the Twelve and said, "If anyone wants to be first, he must be the very last, and the servant of all." [36]He took a little child and had him stand among them. Taking him in his arms, he said to them, [37]"Whoever welcomes one of these little children in my name welcomes me; and whoever welcomes me does not welcome me but the one who sent me."

MARK 9:38-41 "Teacher," said John, "we saw a man driving out demons in your name and we told him to stop, because he was not one of us." [39]"Do not stop him," Jesus said. "No one who does a miracle in my name can in the next moment say anything bad about me, [40]for whoever is not against us is for us. [41]I tell you the truth, anyone who gives you a cup of water in my name because you belong to Christ will certainly not lose his reward." (See also Luke 9:49-50.)

MARK 13:5-6 Jesus said to them [Peter, James, John, Andrew]: "Watch out that no one deceives you. [6]Many will come in my name, claiming, 'I am he,' and will deceive many."

MARK 16:17-18 "And these signs will accompany those who believe: In my name they will drive out demons; they will speak in new tongues; [18]they will pick up snakes with their hands; and when they drink deadly poison, it will not hurt them at all; they will place their hands on sick people, and they will get well."[iv]

LUKE 21:8 He replied: "Watch out that you are not deceived. For many will come in my name, claiming, 'I am he,' and, 'The time is near.' Do not follow them."

ACTS 9:15-16 But the Lord said to Ananias, "Go! This man [Saul, renamed Paul] is my chosen instrument to carry my name before the Gentiles and their kings and before the people of Israel. [16]I will show him how much he must suffer for my name."

REVELATION 2:13 "I know where you live—where Satan has his throne. Yet you remain true to my name. You did not renounce your faith in me, even in the days of Antipas, my faithful witness, who was put to death in your city—where Satan lives."

REVELATION 3:8 "I know your deeds. See, I have placed before you an open door that no one can shut. I know that you have little strength, yet you have kept my word and have not denied my name."

Jesus' Prayers

JOHN 11:41-43 So they [Lazarus's friends] took away the stone. Then Jesus looked up and said, "Father, I thank you that you have heard me. [42]I knew that you always hear me, but I said this for the benefit of the people standing here, that they may believe that you sent me." [43]When he had said this, Jesus called in a loud voice, "Lazarus, come out!"

JOHN 12:27-28 "Now my heart is troubled, and what shall I say? 'Father, save me from this hour'? No, it was for this very reason I came to this hour. [28]Father, glorify your name!" Then a voice came from heaven, "I have glorified it, and will glorify it again."

JOHN 17:1-26 After Jesus said this, he looked toward heaven and prayed: "Father, the time has come. Glorify your Son, that your Son may glorify you. [2]For you granted him authority over all people that he might give eternal life to all those you have given him. [3]Now this is eternal life: that they may know you, the only true God, and Jesus Christ, whom you have sent. [4]I have brought you glory on earth by completing the work you gave me to do. [5]And now, Father, glorify me in your presence with the glory I had with you before the world began. [6]I have revealed you to those whom you gave me out of the world. They were yours; you gave them to me and they have obeyed your word. [7]Now they know that everything you have given me comes from you. [8]For I gave them the words you gave me and they accepted them. They knew with certainty that I came from you, and they believed that you sent me. [9]I pray for them. I am not praying for the world, but for those you have given me, for they are yours. [10]All I have is yours, and all you have is mine. And glory has come to me through them. [11]I will remain in the world no longer, but they are still in the world, and I am coming to you. Holy Father, protect them by the power of your name—the name you gave me—so that they may be one as we are one. [12]While I was with them, I protected them and kept them safe by that name you gave me. None has been lost except the one doomed to destruction so that Scripture would be fulfilled. [13]I am coming to you now, but I say these things while I am still in the world, so that they may have the full measure of my joy within them. [14]I have given them your word and the world has hated them, for they are not of the world any more than I am of the world. [15]My prayer is not that you take them out of the world but that you protect them from the evil one. [16]They are not of the world, even as I am not of it. [17]Sanctify them by the truth; your word is truth. [18]As you sent me into the world, I have sent them into the world. [19]For them I sanctify myself, that they too may be truly sanctified. [20]My prayer is not for them alone. I pray also for those who will believe in me through their message, [21]that all of them may be one, Father, just as you are in me and I am in you. May they also be in us so that the world may believe that you have sent me. [22]I have given them the glory that you gave me, that they may be one as we are one: [23]I in them and you in me. May they be brought to complete unity to let the world know that you sent me and have loved them even as you have loved me. [24]Father, I want those you have given me to be with me where I am, and to see my glory, the glory you have given me because you loved me before the creation of the world. [25]Righteous Father, though the world does not know you, I know you, and they know that you have sent me. [26]I have made you known to them, and will continue to make you known in order that the love you have for me may be in them and that I myself may be in them."

MATTHEW 6:8-13 "Do not be like them [pagans], for your Father knows what you need before you ask him. [9]This, then, is how you should pray: 'Our Father in heaven, hallowed be your name, [10]your kingdom come, your will be done on earth as it is in heaven. [11]Give us today our daily bread. [12]Forgive us our debts, as we also have forgiven our debtors. [13]And lead us not into temptation, but deliver us from the evil one.'" (See also Luke 11:2-4.)

MATTHEW 11:25-26 At that time Jesus said, "I praise you, Father, Lord of heaven and earth, because you have hidden these things from the wise and learned, and revealed them to little children. [26]Yes, Father, for this was your good pleasure."

MATTHEW 26:39 Going a little farther, he fell with his face to the ground and prayed, "My Father, if it is possible, may this cup be taken from me. Yet not as I will, but as you will."

MATTHEW 27:46 About the ninth hour Jesus cried out in a loud voice, *"Eloi, Eloi, lama sabachthani?"*—which means, "My God, my God, why have you forsaken me?" (See also Mark 15:34.)

LUKE 10:21 At that time Jesus, full of joy through the Holy Spirit, said, "I praise you, Father, Lord of heaven and earth, because you have hidden these things from the wise and learned, and revealed them to little children. Yes, Father, for this was your good pleasure."

LUKE 22:42 "Father, if you are willing, take this cup from me; yet not my will, but yours be done."

LUKE 23:34 Jesus said, "Father, forgive them, for they do not know what they are doing." And they divided up his clothes by casting lots.

LUKE 23:46 Jesus called out with a loud voice, "Father, into your hands I commit my spirit." When he had said this, he breathed his last.

Jesus' Relationship with God the Father

Because Jesus is a coequal, coeternal member of the Trinity, it is easy to almost gloss over or even miss the extraordinary significance of His relationship with God the Father. In doing so it is easy for us to diminish the role of the Father in Jesus' life and in ours. We are quick to quote John 5:23: "He who does not honor the Son, does not honor the Father." But the converse of this verse is also true: he who does not honor the Father does not honor the Son. As you look at the Lord's statements in this section, you will discover the eternal, incredibly rich relationship that exists between Jesus and God the Father. Jesus told the woman at the well that the Father *seeks* worshipers who will worship *Him* in spirit and in *truth*. We cannot worship the Father in spirit or in truth unless we see Him for who He really is and understand His relationship with the Son.

JOHN 5:19-20 Jesus gave them this answer: "I tell you the truth, the Son can do nothing by himself; he can do only what he sees his Father doing, because whatever the Father does the Son also does. 20For the Father loves the Son and shows him all he does. Yes, to your amaze-

ment he will show him even greater things than these."

JOHN 5:22-23, 26-27 "Moreover, the Father judges no one, but has entrusted all judgment to the Son, 23that all may honor the Son just as they honor the Father. He who does not honor the Son does not honor the Father, who sent him. 26For as the Father has life in himself, so he has granted the Son to have life in himself. 27And he has given him authority to judge because he is the Son of Man."

JOHN 5:36 "I have testimony weightier than that of John. For the very work that the Father has given me to finish, and which I am doing, testifies that the Father has sent me."

JOHN 5:43 "I have come in my Father's name, and you do not accept me; but if someone else comes in his own name, you will accept him."

JOHN 6:27 "Do not work for food that spoils, but for food that endures to eternal life, which the Son of Man will give you. On him God the Father has placed his seal of approval."

JOHN 6:37-40 "All that the Father gives me will come to me, and whoever comes to me I will never drive away. 38For I have come down from heaven not to do my will but to do the will of him who sent me. 39And this is the will of him who sent me, that I shall lose none of all that he has given me, but raise them up at the last day. 40For my Father's will is that everyone who looks to the Son and believes in him shall have eternal life, and I will raise him up at the last day."

JOHN 6:44 "No one can come to me unless the Father who sent me draws him, and I will raise him up at the last day."

JOHN 6:46 "No one has seen the Father except the one who is from God; only he has seen the Father."

JOHN 6:57 "Just as the living Father sent me and I live because of the Father, so the one who feeds on me will live because of me."

JOHN 7:16-19 Jesus answered, "My teaching is not my own. It comes from him who sent me. [17]If anyone chooses to do God's will, he will find out whether my teaching comes from God or whether I speak on my own. [18]He who speaks on his own does so to gain honor for himself, but he who works for the honor of the one who sent him is a man of truth; there is nothing false about him. [19]Has not Moses given you the law? Yet not one of you keeps the law. Why are you trying to kill me?"

JOHN 7:28 Then Jesus, still teaching in the temple courts, cried out, "Yes, you know me, and you know where I am from. I am not here on my own, but he who sent me is true...."

JOHN 8:16 "But if I do judge, my decisions are right, because I am not alone. I stand with the Father, who sent me."

JOHN 8:25-26 "Who are you?" they asked. "Just what I have been claiming all along," Jesus replied. [26]"I have much to say in judgment of you. But he who sent me is reliable, and what I have heard from him I tell the world."

JOHN 8:28-29 So Jesus said, "When you have lifted up the Son of Man, then you will know that I am the one I claim to be and that I do nothing on my own but

speak just what the Father has taught me. [29]The one who sent me is with me; he has not left me alone, for I always do what pleases him."

JOHN 8:54-55 Jesus replied, "If I glorify myself, my glory means nothing. My Father, whom you claim as your God, is the one who glorifies me. [55]Though you do not know him, I know him. If I said I did not, I would be a liar like you, but I do know him and keep his word."

JOHN 10:15 "...the Father knows me and I know the Father—and I lay down my life for the sheep."

JOHN 10:17-18 "The reason my Father loves me is that I lay down my life—only to take it up again. [18]No one takes it from me, but I lay it down of my own accord. I have authority to lay it down and authority to take it up again. This command I received from my Father."

JOHN 10:30-32 "I and the Father are one." [31]Again the Jews picked up stones to stone him, [32]but Jesus said to them, "I have shown you many great miracles from the Father. For which of these do you stone me?"

JOHN 10:35-36 "If he [the psalmist] called them 'gods,' to whom the word of God came—and the Scripture cannot be broken— [36]what about the one whom the Father set apart as his very own and sent into the world? Why then do you accuse me of blasphemy because I said, 'I am God's Son'?"

JOHN 10:37-38 "Do not believe me unless I do what my Father does. [38]But if I do it, even though you do not believe me, believe the miracles, that you may know and understand that the Father is in me, and I in the Father."

JOHN 12:27-28 "Now my heart is troubled, and what shall I say? 'Father, save me from this hour'? No, it was for this very reason I came to this hour. [28]Father, glorify your name!" Then a voice came from heaven, "I have glorified it, and will glorify it again."

JOHN 12:44-45 Then Jesus cried out, "When a man believes in me, he does not believe in me only, but in the one who sent me. [45]When he looks at me, he sees the one who sent me."

JOHN 12:49-50 "For I did not speak of my own accord, but the Father who sent me commanded me what to say and how to say it. [50]I know that his command leads to eternal life. So whatever I say is just what the Father has told me to say."

JOHN 13:31-33 When he [Judas] was gone, Jesus said, "Now is the Son of Man glorified and God is glorified in him. [32]If God is glorified in him, God will glorify the Son in himself, and will glorify him at once. [33]My children, I will be with you only a little longer. You will look for me, and just as I told the Jews, so I tell you now: Where I am going, you cannot come."

JOHN 14:1-2 "Do not let your hearts be troubled. Trust in God; trust also in me. [2]In my Father's house are many rooms; if it were not so, I would have told you. I am going there to prepare a place for you."

JOHN 14:7 "If you really knew me, you would know my Father as well. From now on, you do know him and have seen him."

JOHN 14:9-11 Jesus answered: "Don't you know me, Philip, even after I have been among you such a long time? Anyone who has seen me has seen the Father. How can you say, 'Show us the Father'? [10]Don't you believe that I am in the Father, and that the Father is in me? The words I say to you are not just my own. Rather, it is the Father, living in me, who is doing his work. [11]Believe me when I say that I am in the Father and the Father is in me; or at least believe on the evidence of the miracles themselves."

JOHN 14:16-18 "And I will ask the Father, and he will give you another Counselor to be with you forever— [17]the Spirit of truth. The world cannot accept him, because it neither sees him nor knows him. But you know him, for he lives with you and will be in you. [18]I will not leave you as orphans; I will come to you."

JOHN 14:20 "On that day you will realize that I am in my Father, and you are in me, and I am in you."

JOHN 14:23-24 Jesus replied, "If anyone loves me, he will obey my teaching. My Father will love him, and we will come to him and make our home with him. [24]He who does not love me will not obey my teaching. These words you hear are not my own; they belong to the Father who sent me."

JOHN 14:28 "You heard me say, 'I am going away and I am coming back to you.' If you loved me, you would be glad that I am going to the Father, for the Father is greater than I."

JOHN 14:31 "…the world must learn that I love the Father and that I do exactly what my Father has commanded me…."

JOHN 15:1-2 "I am the true vine, and my Father is the gardener. [2]He cuts off every branch in me that bears no fruit, while every branch that does bear fruit he prunes so that it will be even more fruitful."

JOHN 15:9-10 "As the Father has loved me, so have I loved you. Now remain in my love. [10]If you obey my commands, you will remain in my love, just as I have obeyed my Father's commands and remain in his love."

JOHN 15:15 "I no longer call you servants, because a servant does not know his master's business. Instead, I have called you friends, for everything that I learned from my Father I have made known to you."

JOHN 15:23-24 "He who hates me hates my Father as well. [24]If I had not done among them what no one else did, they would not be guilty of sin. But now they have seen these miracles, and yet they have hated both me and my Father."

JOHN 16:14-15 "He will bring glory to me by taking from what is mine and making it known to you. [15]All that belongs to the Father is mine. That is why I said the Spirit will take from what is mine and make it known to you."

JOHN 16:32 "But a time is coming, and has come, when you will be scattered, each to his own home. You will leave me all alone. Yet I am not alone, for my Father is with me."

JOHN 17:1-4 After Jesus said this, he looked toward heaven and prayed: "Father, the time has come. Glorify your Son, that your Son may glorify you. [2]For you granted him authority over all people that he might give eternal life to all those you have given him. [3]Now this is eternal life: that they may know you, the only true God, and Jesus Christ, whom you have sent. [4]I have brought you glory on earth by completing the work you gave me to do."

JOHN 17:6-12 "I have revealed you to those whom you gave me out of the world. They were yours; you gave them to me and they have obeyed your word. [7]Now they know that everything you have given me comes from you. [8]For I gave them the words you gave me and they accepted them. They knew with certainty that I came from you, and they believed that you sent me. [9]I pray for them. I am not praying for the world, but for those you have given me, for they are yours. [10]All I have is yours, and all you have is mine. And glory has come to me through them. [11]I will remain in the world no longer, but they are still in the world, and I am coming to you. Holy Father, protect them by the power of your name—the name you gave me—so that they may be one as we are one. [12]While I was with them, I protected them and kept them safe by that name you gave me. None has been lost except the one doomed to destruction so that Scripture would be fulfilled."

JOHN 17:20-26 "My prayer is not for them [the disciples] alone. I pray also for those who will believe in me through their message, [21]that all of them may be one, Father, just as you are in me and I am in you. May they also be in us so that the world may believe that you have sent me. [22]I have given them the glory that you gave me, that they may be one as we are one: [23]I in them and you in me. May they be brought to complete unity to let the world know that you sent me and have loved them even as you have loved me. [24]Father, I want those you have given me to be with me where I am, and to see my glory, the glory you have given me because you loved me before the creation of the world. [25]Righteous Father, though the world does not know you, I know you, and they know that you have sent me. [26]I have made you known to them, and will continue to make you known in order that the love you have for me may be in them and that I myself may be in them."

JOHN 20:17 Jesus said, "Do not hold on to me, for I have not yet returned to the Father. Go instead to my brothers and tell them, 'I am returning to my Father and your Father, to my God and your God.'"

MATTHEW 11:25-27 At that time Jesus said, "I praise you, Father, Lord of heaven and earth, because you have hidden these things from the wise and learned, and revealed them to little children. [26]Yes, Father, for this was your good pleasure. [27]All things have been committed to me by my Father. No one knows the Son except the Father, and no one knows the Father except the Son and those to whom the Son chooses to reveal him."

MATTHEW 16:27 "For the Son of Man is going to come in his Father's glory with his angels, and then he will reward each person according to what he has done."

MATTHEW 25:34 "Then the King

will say to those on his right, 'Come, you who are blessed by my Father; take your inheritance, the kingdom prepared for you since the creation of the world.'"

MARK 8:36-38 "What good is it for a man to gain the whole world, yet forfeit his soul? [37]Or what can a man give in exchange for his soul? [38]If anyone is ashamed of me and my words in this adulterous and sinful generation, the Son of Man will be ashamed of him when he comes in his Father's glory with the holy angels."

MARK 9:35, 37 Sitting down, Jesus called the Twelve and said, "If anyone wants to be first, he must be the very last, and the servant of all. [37]Whoever welcomes one of these little children in my name welcomes me; and whoever welcomes me does not welcome me but the one who sent me."

LUKE 2:49 "Why were you searching for me?" he asked. "Didn't you know I had to be in my Father's house?"

LUKE 10:21-22 At that time Jesus, full of joy through the Holy Spirit, said, "I praise you, Father, Lord of heaven and earth, because you have hidden these things from the wise and learned, and revealed them to little children. Yes, Father, for this was your good pleasure. [22]All things have been committed to me by my Father. No one knows who the Son is except the Father, and no one knows who the Father is except the Son and those to whom the Son chooses to reveal him."

LUKE 22:28-30 "You are those who have stood by me in my trials. [29]And I confer on you a kingdom, just as my

Father conferred one on me, [30]so that you may eat and drink at my table in my kingdom and sit on thrones, judging the twelve tribes of Israel."

LUKE 22:42 "Father, if you are willing, take this cup from me; yet not my will, but yours be done."

LUKE 23:44, 46 It was now about the sixth hour, and darkness came over the whole land until the ninth hour. [46]Jesus called out with a loud voice, "Father, into your hands I commit my spirit." When he had said this, he breathed his last.

Jesus' Righteousness

JOHN 2:14-19 In the temple courts he found men selling cattle, sheep and doves, and others sitting at tables exchanging money. [15]So he made a whip out of cords, and drove all from the temple area, both sheep and cattle; he scattered the coins of the money changers and overturned their tables. [16]To those who sold doves he said, "Get these out of here! How dare you turn my Father's house into a market!" [17]His disciples remembered that it is written: "Zeal for your house will consume me." [18]Then the Jews demanded of him, "What miraculous sign can you show us to prove your authority to do all this?" [19]Jesus answered them, "Destroy this temple, and I will raise it again in three days."

JOHN 7:18-19 "He who speaks on his own does so to gain honor for himself, but he who works for the honor of the one who sent him is a man of truth; there is nothing false about him. [19]Has not

Moses given you the law? Yet not one of you keeps the law. Why are you trying to kill me?"

MATTHEW 3:15 Jesus replied, "Let it be so now; it is proper for us to do this to fulfill all righteousness." Then John consented [to Jesus' baptism].

MARK 11:15-17 On reaching Jerusalem, Jesus entered the temple area and began driving out those who were buying and selling there. He overturned the tables of the money changers and the benches of those selling doves, [16]and would not allow anyone to carry merchandise through the temple courts. [17]And as he taught them, he said, "Is it not written: 'My house will be called a house of prayer for all nations'? But you have made it 'a den of robbers.'" (See also Matthew 21:12-13; Luke 19:45-46.)

Jesus' Suffering and Death

JOHN 10:17-18 "The reason my Father loves me is that I lay down my life—only to take it up again. [18]No one takes it from me, but I lay it down of my own accord. I have authority to lay it down and authority to take it up again. This command I received from my Father."

JOHN 12:23-33 Jesus replied, "The hour has come for the Son of Man to be glorified. [24]I tell you the truth, unless a kernel of wheat falls to the ground and dies, it remains only a single seed. But if it dies, it produces many seeds. [25]The man who loves his life will lose it, while the man who hates his life in this world will keep it for eternal life. [26]Whoever serves me must follow me; and where I am, my servant also will be. My Father will honor the one who serves me. ^{27}Now my heart is troubled, and what shall I say? 'Father, save me from this hour'? No, it was for this very reason I came to this hour. ^{28}Father, glorify your name!" Then a voice came from heaven, "I have glorified it, and will glorify it again." ^{29}The crowd that was there and heard it said it had thundered; others said an angel had spoken to him. ^{30}Jesus said, "This voice was for your benefit, not mine. ^{31}Now is the time for judgment on this world; now the prince of this world will be driven out. ^{32}But I, when I am lifted up from the earth, will draw all men to myself." ^{33}He said this to show the kind of death he was going to die.

MATTHEW 20:18-19 "We are going up to Jerusalem, and the Son of Man will be betrayed to the chief priests and the teachers of the law. They will condemn him to death ^{19}and will turn him over to the Gentiles to be mocked and flogged and crucified. On the third day he will be raised to life!"

MARK 9:12-13 Jesus replied, "To be sure, Elijah does come first, and restores all things. Why then is it written that the Son of Man must suffer much and be rejected? ^{13}But I tell you, Elijah has come, and they have done to him everything they wished, just as it is written about him."

LUKE 17:22-25 Then he said to his disciples, "The time is coming when you will long to see one of the days of the Son of Man, but you will not see it. ^{23}Men will tell you, 'There he is!' or 'Here he is!' Do

not go running off after them. ^{24}For the Son of Man in his day will be like the lightning, which flashes and lights up the sky from one end to the other. ^{25}But first he must suffer many things and be rejected by this generation."

Jesus' Teaching on Miracles and Seeking Miraculous Signs

JOHN 4:48 "Unless you people see miraculous signs and wonders," Jesus told him, "you will never believe."

JOHN 14:12 "I tell you the truth, anyone who has faith in me will do what I have been doing. He will do even greater things than these, because I am going to the Father."

MATTHEW 16:2-4 He replied, "When evening comes, you say, 'It will be fair weather, for the sky is red,' ^{3}and in the morning, 'Today it will be stormy, for the sky is red and overcast.' You know how to interpret the appearance of the sky, but you cannot interpret the signs of the times. ^{4}A wicked and adulterous generation looks for a miraculous sign, but none will be given it except the sign of Jonah." Jesus then left them and went away.

MATTHEW 16:8-11 Aware of their [the disciples'] discussion, Jesus asked, "You of little faith, why are you talking among yourselves about having no bread? ^{9}Do you still not understand? Don't you remember the five loaves for the five thousand, and how many basketfuls you gathered? ^{10}Or the seven loaves for the four thousand, and how many basketfuls you gathered? [11]How is it you don't understand that I was not talking to you about bread? But be on your guard against the yeast of the Pharisees and Sadducees."

MARK 8:12 He sighed deeply and said, "Why does this generation ask for a miraculous sign? I tell you the truth, no sign will be given to it."

MARK 8:17-21 Aware of their discussion, Jesus asked them: "Why are you talking about having no bread? Do you still not see or understand? Are your hearts hardened? [18]Do you have eyes but fail to see, and ears but fail to hear? And don't you remember? [19]When I broke the five loaves for the five thousand, how many basketfuls of pieces did you pick up?" "Twelve," they replied. [20]"And when I broke the seven loaves for the four thousand, how many basketfuls of pieces did you pick up?" They answered, "Seven." [21]He said to them, "Do you still not understand?"

LUKE 4:23-24 Jesus said to them [people in the synagogue], "Surely you will quote this proverb to me: 'Physician, heal yourself! Do here in your hometown what we have heard that you did in Capernaum.' [24]I tell you the truth," he continued, "no prophet is accepted in his hometown."

LUKE 12:54-56 He said to the crowd: "When you see a cloud rising in the west, immediately you say, 'It's going to rain,' and it does. [55]And when the south wind blows, you say, 'It's going to be hot,' and it is. [56]Hypocrites! You know how to interpret the appearance of the earth and the sky. How is it that you don't know how to interpret this present time?

Jesus' Words, Their Role and Power

JOHN 6:63 "The Spirit gives life; the flesh counts for nothing. The words I have spoken to you are spirit and they are life."

JOHN 8:31-32 Then Jesus said to those Jews who believed Him, "If you abide in My word, you are My disciples indeed. [32]And you shall know the truth, and the truth shall make you free." (NKJV)

JOHN 8:37-38 "I know you are Abraham's descendants. Yet you are ready to kill me, because you have no room for my word. [38]I am telling you what I have seen in the Father's presence, and you do what you have heard from your father."

JOHN 8:51 "I tell you the truth, if anyone keeps my word, he will never see death."

JOHN 12:47-50 "As for the person who hears my words but does not keep them, I do not judge him. For I did not come to judge the world, but to save it. [48]There is a judge for the one who rejects me and does not accept my words; that very word which I spoke will condemn him at the last day. [49]For I did not speak of my own accord, but the Father who sent me commanded me what to say and how to say it. [50]I know that his command leads to eternal life. So whatever I say is just what the Father has told me to say."

JOHN 14:10-11 "Don't you believe that I am in the Father, and that the Father is in me? The words I say to you are not just my own. Rather, it is the Father, living in me, who is doing his work. [11]Believe me when I say that I am in the Father and the Father is in me; or at least believe on the evidence of the miracles themselves."

JOHN 14:23-26 Jesus replied, "If anyone loves me, he will obey my teaching. My Father will love him, and we will come to him and make our home with him. ²⁴He who does not love me will not obey my teaching. These words you hear are not my own; they belong to the Father who sent me. ²⁵All this I have spoken while still with you. ²⁶But the Counselor, the Holy Spirit, whom the Father will send in my name, will teach you all things and will remind you of everything I have said to you."

JOHN 15:3-4 "You are already clean because of the word I have spoken to you. ⁴Remain in me, and I will remain in you. No branch can bear fruit by itself; it must remain in the vine. Neither can you bear fruit unless you remain in me."

JOHN 15:7-8 "If you remain in me and my words remain in you, ask whatever you wish, and it will be given you. ⁸This is to my Father's glory, that you bear much fruit, showing yourselves to be my disciples."

JOHN 15:10-11 "If you obey my commands, you will remain in my love, just as I have obeyed my Father's commands and remain in his love. ¹¹I have told you this so that my joy may be in you and that your joy may be complete."

MATTHEW 7:21-27 "Not everyone who says to Me, 'Lord, Lord,' shall enter the kingdom of heaven, but he who does the will of My Father in heaven. ²²Many will say to Me in that day, 'Lord, Lord, have we not prophesied in Your name, cast out demons in Your name, and done many wonders in Your name?' ²³And then I will declare to them, 'I never knew you; depart from Me, you who practice lawlessness!' ²⁴Therefore whoever hears these sayings of Mine, and does them, I will liken him to a wise man who built his house on the rock: ²⁵and the rain descended, the floods came, and the winds blew and beat on that house; and it did not fall, for it was founded on the rock. ²⁶But everyone who hears these sayings of Mine, and does not do them, will be like a foolish man who built his house on the sand: ²⁷and the rain descended, the floods came, and the winds blew and beat on that house; and it fell. And great was its fall." (NKJV)

MATTHEW 16:24-26 Then Jesus said to his disciples, "If anyone would come after me, he must deny himself and take up his cross and follow me. ²⁵For whoever wants to save his life will lose it, but whoever loses his life for me will find it. ²⁶What good will it be for a man if he gains the whole world, yet forfeits his soul? Or what can a man give in exchange for his soul?"

MATTHEW 24:34-35 "I tell you the truth, this generation will certainly not pass away until all these things have happened. ³⁵Heaven and earth will pass away, but my words will never pass away." (See also Mark 13:30-31; Luke 21:32-33.)

MARK 4:13-20 Then Jesus said to them [the disciples], "Don't you understand this parable? How then will you understand any parable? ¹⁴The farmer sows the word. ¹⁵Some people are like seed along the path, where the word is sown. As soon as they hear it, Satan comes and takes away the word that was sown in them. [16]Others, like seed sown on rocky places, hear the word and at once receive it with joy. [17]But since they have no root, they last only a short time. When trouble or persecution comes because of the word, they quickly fall away. [18]Still others, like seed sown among thorns, hear the word; [19]but the worries of this life, the deceitfulness of wealth and the desires for other things come in and choke the word, making it unfruitful. [20]Others, like seed sown on good soil, hear the word, accept it, and produce a crop—thirty, sixty or even a hundred times what was sown."

MARK 8:34-38 Then he called the crowd to him along with his disciples and said: "If anyone would come after me, he must deny himself and take up his cross and follow me. [35]For whoever wants to save his life will lose it, but whoever loses his life for me and for the gospel will save it. [36]What good is it for a man to gain the whole world, yet forfeit his soul? [37]Or what can a man give in exchange for his soul? [38]If anyone is ashamed of me and my words in this adulterous and sinful generation, the Son of Man will be ashamed of him when he comes in his Father's glory with the holy angels."

LUKE 6:46-49 "Why do you call me, 'Lord, Lord,' and do not do what I say? [47]I will show you what he is like who comes to me and hears my words and puts them into practice. [48]He is like a man building a house, who dug down deep and laid the foundation on rock. When a flood came, the torrent struck that house but could not shake it, because it was well built. [49]But the one who hears my words and does not put them into practice is like

a man who built a house on the ground without a foundation. The moment the torrent struck that house, it collapsed and its destruction was complete."

LUKE 9:23-26 Then he said to them all: "If anyone would come after me, he must deny himself and take up his cross daily and follow me. [24]For whoever wants to save his life will lose it, but whoever loses his life for me will save it. [25]What good is it for a man to gain the whole world, and yet lose or forfeit his very self? [26]If anyone is ashamed of me and my words, the Son of Man will be ashamed of him when he comes in his glory and in the glory of the Father and of the holy angels."

Jesus' Words from the Cross

JOHN 19:26-27 When Jesus saw his mother there, and the disciple whom he loved standing nearby, he said to his mother, "Dear woman, here is your son," [27]and to the disciple, "Here is your mother." From that time on, this disciple took her into his home.

JOHN 19:28-30 Later, knowing that all was now completed, and so that the Scripture would be fulfilled, Jesus said, "I am thirsty." [29]A jar of wine vinegar was there, so they soaked a sponge in it, put the sponge on a stalk of the hyssop plant, and lifted it to Jesus' lips. [30]When he had received the drink, Jesus said, "It is finished." With that, he bowed his head and gave up his spirit.

MATTHEW 27:45-46 From the sixth hour until the ninth hour darkness came over all the land. [46]About the ninth hour Jesus cried out in a loud voice, *"Eloi,*

Eloi, lama sabachthani?"—which means, "My God, my God, why have you forsaken me?" (See also Mark 15:33-34.)

LUKE 23:34 Jesus said, "Father, forgive them, for they do not know what they are doing." And they divided up his clothes by casting lots.

LUKE 23:42-43 Then he [a criminal crucified with Jesus] said, "Jesus, remember me when you come into your kingdom." [43]Jesus answered him, "I tell you the truth, today you will be with me in paradise."

LUKE 23:46 Jesus called out with a loud voice, "Father, into your hands I commit my spirit." When he had said this, he breathed his last.

Jesus' Words in Parables, Metaphors, and Allegories

Jesus often used stories to powerfully and vividly communicate the central points of His message. He told parables to tangibly illustrate the magnificent intangible truths of God's kingdom. His stories made such concepts as redemption, sin and righteousness, eternal life, God's relationship with His people, and the type of commitment and obedience that God seeks from His people more easily understood. And in at least one instance, Jesus referred to a recent event to teach about sin and repentance (see Luke 13:1-5). This section includes nearly all the allegories, stories, and parables that Jesus told. They address a multitude of subjects, so don't try to find a common thematic thread. Instead, as you read Jesus' parables and simple allegories, allow the Holy Spirit to open your mental, emotional, and spiritual eyes. Ask Him to deliver His teachings in all of their cinematic power to the depths of your soul. If you do, your understanding will increase and your love and commitment to the Lord will grow deeper than you can imagine.

JOHN 3:8 "The wind blows wherever it pleases. You hear its sound, but you cannot tell where it comes from or where it is going. So it is with everyone born of the Spirit."

JOHN 3:19-21 "This is the verdict: Light has come into the world, but men loved darkness instead of light because their deeds were evil. [20]Everyone who does evil hates the light, and will not come into the light for fear that his deeds will be exposed. [21]But whoever lives by the truth comes into the light, so that it may be seen plainly that what he has done has been done through God."

JOHN 4:13-14 Jesus answered, "Everyone who drinks this water will be thirsty again, [14]but whoever drinks the water I give him will never thirst. Indeed, the water I give him will become in him a spring of water welling up to eternal life."

JOHN 6:27 "Do not work for food that spoils, but for food that endures to eternal life, which the Son of Man will give you. On him God the Father has placed his seal of approval."

JOHN 6:32-33 Jesus said to them, "I tell you the truth, it is not Moses who has given you the bread from heaven, but it is my Father who gives you the true bread from heaven. [33]For the bread of God is he who comes down from heaven and gives life to the world."

JOHN 6:35 Then Jesus declared, "I am the bread of life. He who comes to me will never go hungry, and he who believes in me will never be thirsty."

JOHN 6:48-51 "I am the bread of life. [49]Your forefathers ate the manna in the desert, yet they died. [50]But here is the bread that comes down from heaven, which a man may eat and not die. [51]I am the living bread that came down from heaven. If anyone eats of this bread, he will live forever. This bread is my flesh, which I will give for the life of the world."

JOHN 6:53-58 Jesus said to them, "I tell you the truth, unless you eat the flesh of the Son of Man and drink his blood, you have no life in you. [54]Whoever eats my flesh and drinks my blood has eternal life, and I will raise him up at the last day. [55]For my flesh is real food and my blood is real drink. [56]Whoever eats my flesh and drinks my blood remains in me, and I in him. [57]Just as the living Father sent me and I live because of the Father, so the one who feeds on me will live because of me. [58]This is the bread that came down from heaven. Your forefathers ate manna and died, but he who feeds on this bread will live forever."

JOHN 7:37-38 On the last and greatest day of the Feast, Jesus stood and said in a loud voice, "If anyone is thirsty, let him come to me and drink. [38]Whoever believes in me, as the Scripture has said, streams of living water will flow from within him."

JOHN 8:12 When Jesus spoke again to the people, he said, "I am the light of the world. Whoever follows me will never walk in darkness, but will have the light of life."

JOHN 10:1-5 "I tell you the truth, the man who does not enter the sheep pen by the gate, but climbs in by some other way, is a thief and a robber. [2]The man who enters by the gate is the shepherd of his sheep. [3]The watchman opens the gate for him, and the sheep listen to his voice. He calls his own sheep by name and leads them out. [4]When he has brought out all his own, he goes on ahead of them, and his sheep follow him because they know his voice. [5]But they will never follow a stranger; in fact, they will run away from him because they do not recognize a stranger's voice."

JOHN 10:7-16 Therefore Jesus said again, "I tell you the truth, I am the gate for the sheep. [8]All who ever came before me were thieves and robbers, but the sheep did not listen to them. [9]I am the gate; whoever enters through me will be saved. He will come in and go out, and find pasture. [10]The thief comes only to steal and kill and destroy; I have come that they may have life, and have it to the full. [11]I am the good shepherd. The good shepherd lays down his life for the sheep. [12]The hired hand is not the shepherd who owns the sheep. So when he sees the wolf coming, he abandons the sheep and runs away. Then the wolf attacks the flock and scatters it. [13]The man runs away because he is a hired hand and cares nothing for the sheep. [14]I am the good shepherd; I know my sheep and my sheep know me— [15]just as the Father knows me and I know the Father—and I lay down my life for the sheep. [16]I have other sheep that are not of this sheep pen. I must bring them also. They too will listen to my voice, and there shall be one flock and one shepherd."

JOHN 10:25-30 Jesus answered, "I did tell you, but you do not believe. The miracles I do in my Father's name speak for me, [26]but you do not believe because you are not my sheep. [27]My sheep listen to my voice; I know them, and they follow me. [28]I give them eternal life, and they shall never perish; no one can snatch them out of my hand. [29]My Father, who has given them to me, is greater than all; no one can snatch them out of my Father's hand. [30]I and the Father are one."

JOHN 11:7-10 Then he said to his disciples, "Let us go back to Judea." [8]"But Rabbi," they said, "a short while ago the Jews tried to stone you, and yet you are going back there?" [9]Jesus answered, "Are there not twelve hours of daylight? A man who walks by day will not stumble, for he sees by this world's light. [10]It is when he walks by night that he stumbles, for he has no light."

JOHN 12:35-36 Then Jesus told them, "You are going to have the light just a little while longer. Walk while you have the light, before darkness overtakes you. The man who walks in the dark does not know where he is going. [36]Put your trust in the light while you have it, so that you may become sons of light."...

JOHN 14:1-2 "Do not let your hearts be troubled. Trust in God; trust also in me. [2]In my Father's house are many rooms; if it were not so, I would have told

you. I am going there to prepare a place for you."

JOHN 15:1-8 "I am the true vine, and my Father is the gardener. [2]He cuts off every branch in me that bears no fruit, while every branch that does bear fruit he prunes so that it will be even more fruitful. [3]You are already clean because of the word I have spoken to you. [4]Remain in me, and I will remain in you. No branch can bear fruit by itself; it must remain in the vine. Neither can you bear fruit unless you remain in me. [5]I am the vine; you are the branches. If a man remains in me and I in him, he will bear much fruit; apart from me you can do nothing. [6]If anyone does not remain in me, he is like a branch that is thrown away and withers; such branches are picked up, thrown into the fire and burned. [7]If you remain in me and my words remain in you, ask whatever you wish, and it will be given you. [8]This is to my Father's glory, that you bear much fruit, showing yourselves to be my disciples."

JOHN 16:21-22 "A woman giving birth to a child has pain because her time has come; but when her baby is born she forgets the anguish because of her joy that a child is born into the world. [22]So with you: Now is your time of grief, but I will see you again and you will rejoice, and no one will take away your joy."

MATTHEW 5:15-16 "Neither do people light a lamp and put it under a bowl. Instead they put it on its stand, and it gives light to everyone in the house. [16]In the same way, let your light shine before men, that they may see your good deeds and praise your Father in heaven."

MATTHEW 6:22-23 "The eye is the lamp of the body. If your eyes are good, your whole body will be full of light. 23But if your eyes are bad, your whole body will be full of darkness. If then the light within you is darkness, how great is that darkness!"

MATTHEW 7:3-5 "Why do you look at the speck of sawdust in your brother's eye and pay no attention to the plank in your own eye? 4How can you say to your brother, 'Let me take the speck out of your eye,' when all the time there is a plank in your own eye? 5You hypocrite, first take the plank out of your own eye, and then you will see clearly to remove the speck from your brother's eye." (See also Luke 6:41-42.)

MATTHEW 7:6 "Do not give dogs what is sacred; do not throw your pearls to pigs. If you do, they may trample them under their feet, and then turn and tear you to pieces."

MATTHEW 7:15-20 "Watch out for false prophets. They come to you in sheep's clothing, but inwardly they are ferocious wolves. 16By their fruit you will recognize them. Do people pick grapes from thornbushes, or figs from thistles? 17Likewise every good tree bears good fruit, but a bad tree bears bad fruit. 18A good tree cannot bear bad fruit, and a bad tree cannot bear good fruit. 19Every tree that does not bear good fruit is cut down and thrown into the fire. 20Thus, by their fruit you will recognize them."

MATTHEW 7:24-27 "Therefore whoever hears these sayings of Mine, and does them, I will liken him to a wise man who built his house on the rock: 25and the rain descended, the floods came, and the winds blew and beat on that house; and it did not fall, for it was founded on the rock. 26But everyone who hears these sayings of Mine, and does not do them, will be like a foolish man who built his house on the sand: 27and the rain descended, the floods came, and the winds blew and beat on that house; and it fell. And great was its fall." (NKJV)

MATTHEW 9:15-17 Jesus answered, "How can the guests of the bridegroom mourn while he is with them? The time will come when the bridegroom will be taken from them; then they will fast. 16No one sews a patch of unshrunk cloth on an old garment, for the patch will pull away from the garment, making the tear worse. 17Neither do men pour new wine into old wineskins. If they do, the skins will burst, the wine will run out and the wineskins will be ruined. No, they pour new wine into new wineskins, and both are preserved."

MATTHEW 13:3-15 Then he told them many things in parables, saying: "A farmer went out to sow his seed. 4As he was scattering the seed, some fell along the path, and the birds came and ate it up. 5Some fell on rocky places, where it did not have much soil. It sprang up quickly, because the soil was shallow. 6But when the sun came up, the plants were scorched, and they withered because they had no root. 7Other seed fell among thorns, which grew up and choked the plants. 8Still other seed fell on good soil, where it produced a crop—a hundred, sixty or thirty times what was sown. 9He who has ears, let him hear." 10The disciples came to him and asked, "Why do you speak to the people in parables?" [11]He replied, "The knowledge of the secrets of the kingdom of heaven has been given to you, but not to them. [12]Whoever has will be given more, and he will have an abundance. Whoever does not have, even what he has will be taken from him. [13]This is why I speak to them in parables: Though seeing, they do not see; though hearing, they do not hear or understand. [14]In them is fulfilled the prophecy of Isaiah: 'You will be ever hearing but never understanding; you will be ever seeing but never perceiving. [15]For this people's heart has become calloused; they hardly hear with their ears, and they have closed their eyes. Otherwise they might see with their eyes, hear with their ears, understand with their hearts and turn, and I would heal them.' "

MATTHEW 13:18-23 "Listen then to what the parable of the sower means: [19]When anyone hears the message about the kingdom and does not understand it, the evil one comes and snatches away what was sown in his heart. This is the seed sown along the path. [20]The one who received the seed that fell on rocky places is the man who hears the word and at once receives it with joy. [21]But since he has no root, he lasts only a short time. When trouble or persecution comes because of the word, he quickly falls away. [22]The one who received the seed that fell among the thorns is the man who hears the word, but the worries of this life and the deceitfulness of wealth choke it, making it unfruitful. [23]But the one who received the seed that fell on good soil is the man who hears the word and understands it. He produces a crop, yielding a hundred, sixty or thirty times what was sown."

MATTHEW 13:24-30 Jesus told them another parable: "The kingdom of heaven is like a man who sowed good seed in his field. [25]But while everyone was sleeping, his enemy came and sowed weeds among the wheat, and went away. [26]When the wheat sprouted and formed heads, then the weeds also appeared. [27]The owner's servants came to him and said, 'Sir, didn't you sow good seed in your field? Where then did the weeds come from?' [28]'An enemy did this,' he replied. The servants asked him, 'Do you want us to go and pull them up?' [29]'No,' he answered, 'because while you are pulling the weeds, you may root up the wheat with them. [30]Let both grow together until the harvest. At that time I will tell the harvesters: First collect the weeds and tie them in bundles to be burned; then gather the wheat and bring it into my barn.' "

MATTHEW 13:31-32 He told them another parable: "The kingdom of heaven is like a mustard seed, which a man took and planted in his field. [32]Though it is the smallest of all your seeds, yet when it grows, it is the largest of garden plants and becomes a tree, so that the birds of the air come and perch in its branches." (See also Luke 13:18-19.)

MATTHEW 13:33 He told them still another parable: "The kingdom of heaven is like yeast that a woman took and mixed into a large amount of flour until it worked all through the dough." (See also Luke 13:20-21.)

MATTHEW 13:37-43 He answered, "The one who sowed the good seed is the

Son of Man. [38]The field is the world, and the good seed stands for the sons of the kingdom. The weeds are the sons of the evil one, [39]and the enemy who sows them is the devil. The harvest is the end of the age, and the harvesters are angels. [40]As the weeds are pulled up and burned in the fire, so it will be at the end of the age. [41]The Son of Man will send out his angels, and they will weed out of his kingdom everything that causes sin and all who do evil. [42]They will throw them into the fiery furnace, where there will be weeping and gnashing of teeth. [43]Then the righteous will shine like the sun in the kingdom of their Father. He who has ears, let him hear."

MATTHEW 13:44-46 "The kingdom of heaven is like treasure hidden in a field. When a man found it, he hid it again, and then in his joy went and sold all he had and bought that field. [45]Again, the kingdom of heaven is like a merchant looking for fine pearls. [46]When he found one of great value, he went away and sold everything he had and bought it."

MATTHEW 13:47-50 "Once again, the kingdom of heaven is like a net that was let down into the lake and caught all kinds of fish. [48]When it was full, the fishermen pulled it up on the shore. Then they sat down and collected the good fish in baskets, but threw the bad away. [49]This is how it will be at the end of the age. The angels will come and separate the wicked from the righteous [50]and throw them into the fiery furnace, where there will be weeping and gnashing of teeth."

MATTHEW 13:51-52 "Have you understood all these things?" Jesus asked. "Yes," they replied. [52]He said to them, "Therefore every teacher of the law who has been instructed about the kingdom of heaven is like the owner of a house who brings out of his storeroom new treasures as well as old."

MATTHEW 17:25-27 ...When Peter came into the house, Jesus was the first to speak. "What do you think, Simon?" he asked. "From whom do the kings of the earth collect duty and taxes— from their own sons or from others?" [26]"From others," Peter answered. "Then the sons are exempt," Jesus said to him. [27]"But so that we may not offend them, go to the lake and throw out your line. Take the first fish you catch; open its mouth and you will find a four-drachma coin. Take it and give it to them for my tax and yours."

MATTHEW 18:10, 12-14 "See that you do not look down on one of these little ones. For I tell you that their angels in heaven always see the face of my Father in heaven. [12]What do you think? If a man owns a hundred sheep, and one of them wanders away, will he not leave the ninety-nine on the hills and go to look for the one that wandered off? [13]And if he finds it, I tell you the truth, he is happier about that one sheep than about the ninety-nine that did not wander off. [14]In the same way your Father in heaven is not willing that any of these little ones should be lost."

MATTHEW 18:21-35 Then Peter came to Jesus and asked, "Lord, how many times shall I forgive my brother when he sins against me? Up to seven times?" [22]Jesus answered, "I tell you, not seven times, but seventy-seven times.

[23]Therefore, the kingdom of heaven is like a king who wanted to settle accounts with his servants. [24]As he began the settlement, a man who owed him ten thousand talents was brought to him. [25]Since he was not able to pay, the master ordered that he and his wife and his children and all that he had be sold to repay the debt. [26]The servant fell on his knees before him. 'Be patient with me,' he begged, 'and I will pay back everything.' [27]The servant's master took pity on him, canceled the debt and let him go. [28]But when that servant went out, he found one of his fellow servants who owed him a hundred denarii. He grabbed him and began to choke him. 'Pay back what you owe me!' he demanded. [29]His fellow servant fell to his knees and begged him, 'Be patient with me, and I will pay you back.' [30]But he refused. Instead, he went off and had the man thrown into prison until he could pay the debt. [31]When the other servants saw what had happened, they were greatly distressed and went and told their master everything that had happened. [32]Then the master called the servant in. 'You wicked servant,' he said, 'I canceled all that debt of yours because you begged me to. [33]Shouldn't you have had mercy on your fellow servant just as I had on you?' [34]In anger his master turned him over to the jailers to be tortured, until he should pay back all he owed. [35]This is how my heavenly Father will treat each of you unless you forgive your brother from your heart."

MATTHEW 19:23-26 Then Jesus said to his disciples, "I tell you the truth, it is hard for a rich man to enter the kingdom of heaven. [24]Again I tell you, it is easier for a camel to go through the eye of a needle than for a rich man to enter the kingdom of God." [25]When the disciples heard this, they were greatly astonished and asked, "Who then can be saved?" [26]Jesus looked at them and said, "With man this is impossible, but with God all things are possible."

MATTHEW 20:1-16 "For the kingdom of heaven is like a landowner who went out early in the morning to hire men to work in his vineyard. [2]He agreed to pay them a denarius for the day and sent them into his vineyard. [3]About the third hour he went out and saw others standing in the marketplace doing nothing. [4]He told them, 'You also go and work in my vineyard, and I will pay you whatever is right.' [5]So they went. He went out again about the sixth hour and the ninth hour and did the same thing. [6]About the eleventh hour he went out and found still others standing around. He asked them, 'Why have you been standing here all day long doing nothing?' [7]'Because no one has hired us,' they answered. He said to them, 'You also go and work in my vineyard.' [8]When evening came, the owner of the vineyard said to his foreman, 'Call the workers and pay them their wages, beginning with the last ones hired and going on to the first.' [9]The workers who were hired about the eleventh hour came and each received a denarius. [10]So when those came who were hired first, they expected to receive more. But each one of them also received a denarius. [11]When they received it, they began to grumble against the landowner. [12]'These men who were hired last worked only one hour,' they said, 'and you have made them equal to us who have borne the burden of the work and the heat of the day.' [13]But he answered one of them, 'Friend, I am not being unfair to you. Didn't you agree to work for a denarius? [14]Take your pay and go. I want to give the man who was hired last the same as I gave you. [15]Don't I have the right to do what I want with my own money? Or are you envious because I am generous?' [16]So the last will be first, and the first will be last."

MATTHEW 21:28-32 "What do you think? There was a man who had two sons. He went to the first and said, 'Son, go and work today in the vineyard.' [29]'I will not,' he answered, but later he changed his mind and went. [30]Then the father went to the other son and said the same thing. He answered, 'I will, sir,' but he did not go. [31]Which of the two did what his father wanted?" "The first," they answered. Jesus said to them, "I tell you the truth, the tax collectors and the prostitutes are entering the kingdom of God ahead of you. [32]For John came to you to show you the way of righteousness, and you did not believe him, but the tax collectors and the prostitutes did. And even after you saw this, you did not repent and believe him."

MATTHEW 21:33-40 "Listen to another parable: There was a landowner who planted a vineyard. He put a wall around it, dug a winepress in it and built a watchtower. Then he rented the vineyard to some farmers and went away on a journey. [34]When the harvest time approached, he sent his servants to the tenants to collect his fruit. [35]The tenants

seized his servants; they beat one, killed another, and stoned a third. [36]Then he sent other servants to them, more than the first time, and the tenants treated them the same way. [37]Last of all, he sent his son to them. 'They will respect my son,' he said. [38]But when the tenants saw the son, they said to each other, 'This is the heir. Come, let's kill him and take his inheritance.' [39]So they took him and threw him out of the vineyard and killed him. [40]Therefore, when the owner of the vineyard comes, what will he do to those tenants?"

MATTHEW 21:42-44 Jesus said to them, "Have you never read in the Scriptures: 'The stone the builders rejected has become the capstone; the Lord has done this, and it is marvelous in our eyes'? [43]Therefore I tell you that the kingdom of God will be taken away from you and given to a people who will produce its fruit. [44]He who falls on this stone will be broken to pieces, but he on whom it falls will be crushed."

MATTHEW 22:1-14 Jesus spoke to them again in parables, saying: [2]"The kingdom of heaven is like a king who prepared a wedding banquet for his son. [3]He sent his servants to those who had been invited to the banquet to tell them to come, but they refused to come. [4]Then he sent some more servants and said, 'Tell those who have been invited that I have prepared my dinner: My oxen and fattened cattle have been butchered, and everything is ready. Come to the wedding banquet.' [5]But they paid no attention and went off—one to his field, another to his business. [6]The rest seized his servants, mistreated them and killed them. [7]The king was enraged. He sent his army and destroyed those murderers and burned their city. [8]Then he said to his servants, 'The wedding banquet is ready, but those I invited did not deserve to come. [9]Go to the street corners and invite to the banquet anyone you find.' [10]So the servants went out into the streets and gathered all the people they could find, both good and bad, and the wedding hall was filled with guests. [11]But when the king came in to see the guests, he noticed a man there who was not wearing wedding clothes. [12]'Friend,' he asked, 'how did you get in here without wedding clothes?' The man was speechless. [13]Then the king told the attendants, 'Tie him hand and foot, and throw him outside, into the darkness, where there will be weeping and gnashing of teeth.' [14]For many are invited, but few are chosen."

MATTHEW 24:32-34 "Now learn this lesson from the fig tree: As soon as its twigs get tender and its leaves come out, you know that summer is near. [33]Even so, when you see all these things, you know that it is near, right at the door. [34]I tell you the truth, this generation will certainly not pass away until all these things have happened."

MATTHEW 24:36-44 "No one knows about that day or hour, not even the angels in heaven, nor the Son, but only the Father. [37]As it was in the days of Noah, so it will be at the coming of the Son of Man. [38]For in the days before the flood, people were eating and drinking, marrying and giving in marriage, up to the day Noah entered the ark; [39]and they knew nothing about what would happen until the flood came and took them all away. That is how it will be at the coming of the Son of Man. [40]Two men will be in the field; one will be taken and the other left. [41]Two women will be grinding with a hand mill; one will be taken and the other left. [42]Therefore keep watch, because you do not know on what day your Lord will come. [43]But understand this: If the owner of the house had known at what time of night the thief was coming, he would have kept watch and would not have let his house be broken into. [44]So you also must be ready, because the Son of Man will come at an hour when you do not expect him."

MATTHEW 24:45-51 "Who then is the faithful and wise servant, whom the master has put in charge of the servants in his household to give them their food at the proper time? [46]It will be good for that servant whose master finds him doing so when he returns. [47]I tell you the truth, he will put him in charge of all his possessions. [48]But suppose that servant is wicked and says to himself, 'My master is staying away a long time,' [49]and he then begins to beat his fellow servants and to eat and drink with drunkards. [50]The master of that servant will come on a day when he does not expect him and at an hour he is not aware of. [51]He will cut him to pieces and assign him a place with the hypocrites, where there will be weeping and gnashing of teeth." (See also Luke 12:42-46.)

MATTHEW 25:1-13 "At that time the kingdom of heaven will be like ten virgins who took their lamps and went out to meet the bridegroom. [2]Five of them were foolish and five were wise. [3]The foolish ones took their lamps but did not take any oil with them. [4]The wise, however, took oil in jars along with their lamps. [5]The bridegroom was a long time in coming, and they all became drowsy and fell asleep. [6]At midnight the cry rang out: 'Here's the bridegroom! Come out to meet him!' [7]Then all the virgins woke up and trimmed their lamps. [8]The foolish ones said to the wise, 'Give us some of your oil; our lamps are going out.' [9]'No,' they replied, 'there may not be enough for both us and you. Instead, go to those who sell oil and buy some for yourselves.' [10]But while they were on their way to buy the oil, the bridegroom arrived. The virgins who were ready went in with him to the wedding banquet. And the door was shut. [11]Later the others also came. 'Sir! Sir!' they said. 'Open the door for us!' [12]But he replied, 'I tell you the truth, I don't know you.' [13]Therefore keep watch, because you do not know the day or the hour."

MATTHEW 25:14-30 "Again, it will be like a man going on a journey, who called his servants and entrusted his property to them. [15]To one he gave five talents of money, to another two talents, and to another one talent, each according to his ability. Then he went on his journey. [16]The man who had received the five talents went at once and put his money to work and gained five more. [17]So also, the one with the two talents gained two more. [18]But the man who had received the one talent went off, dug a hole in the ground and hid his master's money. [19]After a long time the master of those servants returned and settled accounts with them. [20]The man who had received the five talents brought the other five. 'Master,' he said, 'you entrusted me with five talents. See, I have gained five more.' [21]His master replied, 'Well done, good and faithful servant! You have been faithful with a few things; I will put you in charge of many things. Come and share your master's happiness!' [22]The man with the two talents also came. 'Master,' he said, 'you entrusted me with two talents; see, I have gained two more.' [23]His master replied, 'Well done, good and faithful servant! You have been faithful with a few things; I will put you in charge of many things. Come and share your master's happiness!' [24]Then the man who had received the one talent came. 'Master,' he said, 'I knew that you are a hard man, harvesting where you have not sown and gathering where you have not scattered seed. [25]So I was afraid and went out and hid your talent in the ground. See, here is what belongs to you.' [26]His master replied, 'You wicked, lazy servant! So you knew that I harvest where I have not sown and gather where I have not scattered seed? [27]Well then, you should have put my money on deposit with the bankers, so that when I returned I would have received it back with interest. [28]Take the talent from him and give it to the one who has the ten talents. [29]For everyone who has will be given more, and he will have an abundance. Whoever does not have, even what he has will be taken from him. [30]And throw that worthless servant outside, into the darkness, where there will be weeping and gnashing of teeth.'"

MATTHEW 25:31-46 "When the Son of Man comes in his glory, and all the angels with him, he will sit on his throne in heavenly glory. [32]All the nations will be gathered before him, and he will separate the people one from another as a shepherd separates the sheep from the goats. [33]He will put the sheep on his right and the goats on his left. [34]Then the King will say to those on his right, 'Come, you who are blessed by my Father; take your inheritance, the kingdom prepared for you since the creation of the world. [35]For I was hungry and you gave me something to eat, I was thirsty and you gave me something to drink, I was a stranger and you invited me in, [36]I needed clothes and you clothed me, I was sick and you looked after me, I was in prison and you came to visit me.' [37]Then the righteous will answer him, 'Lord, when did we see you hungry and feed you, or thirsty and give you something to drink? [38]When did we see you a stranger and invite you in, or needing clothes and clothe you? [39]When did we see you sick or in prison and go to visit you?' [40]The King will reply, 'I tell you the truth, whatever you did for one of the least of these brothers of mine, you did for me.' [41]Then he will say to those on his left, 'Depart from me, you who are cursed, into the eternal fire prepared for the devil and his angels. [42]For I was hungry and you gave me nothing to eat, I was thirsty and you gave me nothing to drink, [43]I was a stranger and you did not invite me in, I needed clothes and you did not clothe me, I was sick and in prison and you did not look after me.' [44]They also will answer, 'Lord, when did we see you hungry or thirsty or a stranger or needing clothes or sick or in prison, and did not help you?' [45]He will reply, 'I tell you the truth, whatever you did not do for one of the least of these, you did not do for me.' [46]Then they will go away to eternal punishment, but the righteous to eternal life."

MARK 4:3-20 "Listen! A farmer went out to sow his seed. [4]As he was scattering the seed, some fell along the path, and the birds came and ate it up. [5]Some fell on rocky places, where it did not have much soil. It sprang up quickly, because the soil was shallow. [6]But when the sun came up, the plants were scorched, and they withered because they had no root. [7]Other seed fell among thorns, which grew up and choked the plants, so that they did not bear grain. [8]Still other seed fell on good soil. It came up, grew and produced a crop, multiplying thirty, sixty, or even a hundred times." [9]Then Jesus said, "He who has ears to hear, let him hear." [10]When he was alone, the Twelve and the others around him asked him about the parables. [11]He told them, "The secret of the kingdom of God has been given to you. But to those on the outside everything is said in parables [12]so that, 'they may be ever seeing but never perceiving, and ever hearing but never understanding; otherwise they might turn and be forgiven!' " [13]Then Jesus said to them, "Don't you understand this parable? How then will you understand any parable? [14]The farmer sows the word. [15]Some people are like seed along the path, where the word is sown. As soon as they hear it, Satan comes and takes away the word that was sown in them. [16]Others, like seed sown on rocky places, hear the word and at once receive it with joy. [17]But since they have no root, they last only a short time. When trouble or persecution comes because of the word, they quickly fall away. [18]Still others, like seed sown among thorns, hear the word; [19]but the worries of this life, the deceitfulness of wealth and the desires for other things come in and choke the word, making it unfruitful. [20]Others, like seed sown on good soil, hear the word, accept it, and produce a crop—thirty, sixty or even a hundred times what was sown."

MARK 4:21-23 He said to them, "Do you bring in a lamp to put it under a bowl or a bed? Instead, don't you put it on its stand? [22]For whatever is hidden is meant to be disclosed, and whatever is concealed is meant to be brought out into the open. [23]If anyone has ears to hear, let him hear."

MARK 10:23-27 Jesus looked around and said to his disciples, "How hard it is for the rich to enter the kingdom of God!" [24]The disciples were amazed at his words. But Jesus said again, "Children, how hard it is to enter the kingdom of God! [25]It is easier for a camel to go through the eye of a needle than for a rich man to enter the kingdom of God." [26]The disciples were even more amazed, and said to each other, "Who then can be saved?" [27]Jesus looked at them and said, "With man this is impossible, but not with God; all things are possible with God."

MARK 12:1-9 He then began to speak to them in parables: "A man planted a vineyard. He put a wall around it, dug a pit for the winepress and built a watch-tower. Then he rented the vineyard to some farmers and went away on a journey. [2]At harvest time he sent a servant to the tenants to collect from them some of the fruit of the vineyard. [3]But they seized him, beat him and sent him away empty-handed. [4]Then he sent another servant to them; they struck this man on the head and treated him shamefully. [5]He sent still another, and that one they killed. He sent many others; some of them they beat, others they killed. [6]He had one left to send, a son, whom he loved. He sent him last of all, saying, 'They will respect my son.' [7]But the tenants said to one another, 'This is the heir. Come, let's kill him, and the inheritance will be ours.' [8]So they took him and killed him, and threw him out of the vineyard. [9]What then will the owner of the vineyard do? He will come and kill those tenants and give the vineyard to others."

MARK 12:14-17 They came to him and said, "Teacher, we know you are a man of integrity. You aren't swayed by men, because you pay no attention to who they are; but you teach the way of God in accordance with the truth. Is it right to pay taxes to Caesar or not? [15]Should we pay or shouldn't we?" But Jesus knew their hypocrisy. "Why are you trying to trap me?" he asked. "Bring me a denarius and let me look at it." [16]They brought the coin, and he asked them, "Whose portrait is this? And whose inscription?" "Caesar's," they replied. [17]Then Jesus said to them, "Give to Caesar what is Caesar's and to God what is God's."... (See also Matthew 22:16-21; Luke 20:21-25.)

MARK 13:28-31 "Now learn this lesson from the fig tree: As soon as its twigs get tender and its leaves come out, you know that summer is near. ²⁹Even so, when you see these things happening, you know that it is near, right at the door. ³⁰I tell you the truth, this generation will certainly not pass away until all these things have happened. ³¹Heaven and earth will pass away, but my words will never pass away."

LUKE 6:39-40 He also told them this parable: "Can a blind man lead a blind man? Will they not both fall into a pit? ⁴⁰A student is not above his teacher, but everyone who is fully trained will be like his teacher."

LUKE 6:43-45 "No good tree bears bad fruit, nor does a bad tree bear good fruit. ⁴⁴Each tree is recognized by its own fruit. People do not pick figs from thornbushes, or grapes from briers. ⁴⁵The good man brings good things out of the good stored up in his heart, and the evil man brings evil things out of the evil stored up in his heart. For out of the overflow of his heart his mouth speaks."

LUKE 6:47-49 "I will show you what he is like who comes to me and hears my words and puts them into practice. ⁴⁸He is like a man building a house, who dug down deep and laid the foundation on rock. When a flood came, the torrent struck that house but could not shake it, because it was well built. ⁴⁹But the one who hears my words and does not put them into practice is like a man who built a house on the ground without a foundation. The moment the torrent struck that house, it collapsed and its destruction was complete."

LUKE 8:4-15 While a large crowd was gathering and people were coming to Jesus from town after town, he told this parable: ⁵"A farmer went out to sow his seed. As he was scattering the seed, some fell along the path; it was trampled on, and the birds of the air ate it up. ⁶Some fell on rock, and when it came up, the plants withered because they had no moisture. ⁷Other seed fell among thorns, which grew up with it and choked the plants. ⁸Still other seed fell on good soil. It came up and yielded a crop, a hundred times more than was sown." When he said this, he called out, "He who has ears to hear, let him hear." ⁹His disciples asked him what this parable meant. ¹⁰He said, "The knowledge of the secrets of the kingdom of God has been given to you, but to others I speak in parables, so that, 'though seeing, they may not see; though hearing, they may not understand.' ¹¹This is the meaning of the parable: The seed is the word of God. ¹²Those along the path are the ones who hear, and then the devil comes and takes away the word from their hearts, so that they may not believe and be saved. ¹³Those on the rock are the ones who receive the word with joy when they hear it, but they have no root. They believe for a while, but in the time of testing they fall away. ¹⁴The seed that fell among thorns stands for those who hear, but as they go on their way they are choked by life's worries, riches and pleasures, and they do not mature. ¹⁵But the seed on good soil stands for those with a noble and good heart, who hear the word, retain it, and by persevering produce a crop."

LUKE 8:16-18 "No one lights a lamp and hides it in a jar or puts it under a bed.

Instead, he puts it on a stand, so that those who come in can see the light. [17]For there is nothing hidden that will not be disclosed, and nothing concealed that will not be known or brought out into the open. [18]Therefore consider carefully how you listen. Whoever has will be given more; whoever does not have, even what he thinks he has will be taken from him."

LUKE 10:29-37 But he [an expert in the law] wanted to justify himself, so he asked Jesus, "And who is my neighbor?" [30]In reply Jesus said: "A man was going down from Jerusalem to Jericho, when he fell into the hands of robbers. They stripped him of his clothes, beat him and went away, leaving him half dead. [31]A priest happened to be going down the same road, and when he saw the man, he passed by on the other side. [32]So too, a Levite, when he came to the place and saw him, passed by on the other side. [33]But a Samaritan, as he traveled, came where the man was; and when he saw him, he took pity on him. [34]He went to him and bandaged his wounds, pouring on oil and wine. Then he put the man on his own donkey, took him to an inn and took care of him. [35]The next day he took out two silver coins and gave them to the innkeeper. 'Look after him,' he said, 'and when I return, I will reimburse you for any extra expense you may have.' [36]Which of these three do you think was a neighbor to the man who fell into the hands of robbers?" [37]The expert in the law replied, "The one who had mercy on him." Jesus told him, "Go and do likewise."

LUKE 11:5-13 Then he said to them, "Suppose one of you has a friend, and he goes to him at midnight and says, 'Friend, lend me three loaves of bread, [6]because a friend of mine on a journey has come to me, and I have nothing to set before him.' [7]Then the one inside answers, 'Don't bother me. The door is already locked, and my children are with me in bed. I can't get up and give you anything.' [8]I tell you, though he will not get up and give him the bread because he is his friend, yet because of the man's boldness he will get up and give him as much as he needs. [9]So I say to you: Ask and it will be given to you; seek and you will find; knock and the door will be opened to you. [10]For everyone who asks receives; he who seeks finds; and to him who knocks, the door will be opened. [11]Which of you fathers, if your son asks for a fish, will give him a snake instead? [12]Or if he asks for an egg, will give him a scorpion? [13]If you then, though you are evil, know how to give good gifts to your children, how much more will your Father in heaven give the Holy Spirit to those who ask him!" (See also Matthew 7:7-11.)

LUKE 11:33-36 "No one lights a lamp and puts it in a place where it will be hidden, or under a bowl. Instead he puts it on its stand, so that those who come in may see the light. [34]Your eye is the lamp of your body. When your eyes are good, your whole body also is full of light. But when they are bad, your body also is full of darkness. [35]See to it, then, that the light within you is not darkness. [36]Therefore, if your whole body is full of light, and no part of it dark, it will be completely lighted, as when the light of a lamp shines on you."

LUKE 12:4-7 "I tell you, my friends,

do not be afraid of those who kill the body and after that can do no more. [5]But I will show you whom you should fear: Fear him who, after the killing of the body, has power to throw you into hell. Yes, I tell you, fear him. [6]Are not five sparrows sold for two pennies? Yet not one of them is forgotten by God. [7]Indeed, the very hairs of your head are all numbered. Don't be afraid; you are worth more than many sparrows."

LUKE 12:15-21 Then he said to them, "Watch out! Be on your guard against all kinds of greed; a man's life does not consist in the abundance of his possessions." [16]And he told them this parable: "The ground of a certain rich man produced a good crop. [17]He thought to himself, 'What shall I do? I have no place to store my crops.' [18]Then he said, 'This is what I'll do. I will tear down my barns and build bigger ones, and there I will store all my grain and my goods. [19]And I'll say to myself, "You have plenty of good things laid up for many years. Take life easy; eat, drink and be merry." ' [20]But God said to him, 'You fool! This very night your life will be demanded from you. Then who will get what you have prepared for yourself?' [21]This is how it will be with anyone who stores up things for himself but is not rich toward God."

LUKE 12:35-40 "Be dressed ready for service and keep your lamps burning, [36]like men waiting for their master to return from a wedding banquet, so that when he comes and knocks they can immediately open the door for him. [37]It will be good for those servants whose master finds them watching when he comes. I

tell you the truth, he will dress himself to serve, will have them recline at the table and will come and wait on them. [38]It will be good for those servants whose master finds them ready, even if he comes in the second or third watch of the night. [39]But understand this: If the owner of the house had known at what hour the thief was coming, he would not have let his house be broken into. [40]You also must be ready, because the Son of Man will come at an hour when you do not expect him."

LUKE 13:6-9 Then he told this parable: "A man had a fig tree, planted in his vineyard, and he went to look for fruit on it, but did not find any. [7]So he said to the man who took care of the vineyard, 'For three years now I've been coming to look for fruit on this fig tree and haven't found any. Cut it down! Why should it use up the soil?' [8]'Sir,' the man replied, 'leave it alone for one more year, and I'll dig around it and fertilize it. [9]If it bears fruit next year, fine! If not, then cut it down.' "

LUKE 13:24-27 "Make every effort to enter through the narrow door, because many, I tell you, will try to enter and will not be able to. [25]Once the owner of the house gets up and closes the door, you will stand outside knocking and pleading, 'Sir, open the door for us.' But he will answer, 'I don't know you or where you come from.' [26]Then you will say, 'We ate and drank with you, and you taught in our streets.' [27]But he will reply, 'I don't know you or where you come from. Away from me, all you evildoers!' "

LUKE 14:4-5 But they [Pharisees and experts in the law] remained silent. So taking hold of the man, he healed him and sent him away. [5]Then he asked them, "If one of you has a son or an ox that falls into a well on the Sabbath day, will you not immediately pull him out?"

LUKE 14:8-11 "When someone invites you to a wedding feast, do not take the place of honor, for a person more distinguished than you may have been invited. [9]If so, the host who invited both of you will come and say to you, 'Give this man your seat.' Then, humiliated, you will have to take the least important place. [10]But when you are invited, take the lowest place, so that when your host comes, he will say to you, 'Friend, move up to a better place.' Then you will be honored in the presence of all your fellow guests. [11]For everyone who exalts himself will be humbled, and he who humbles himself will be exalted."

LUKE 14:12-14 Then Jesus said to his host, "When you give a luncheon or dinner, do not invite your friends, your brothers or relatives, or your rich neighbors; if you do, they may invite you back and so you will be repaid. [13]But when you give a banquet, invite the poor, the crippled, the lame, the blind, [14]and you will be blessed. Although they cannot repay you, you will be repaid at the resurrection of the righteous."

LUKE 14:15-24 When one of those at the table with him heard this, he said to Jesus, "Blessed is the man who will eat at the feast in the kingdom of God." [16]Jesus replied: "A certain man was preparing a great banquet and invited many guests. [17]At the time of the banquet he sent his servant to tell those who had been invited, 'Come, for everything is now ready.' [18]But

they all alike began to make excuses. The first said, 'I have just bought a field, and I must go and see it. Please excuse me.' [19]Another said, 'I have just bought five yoke of oxen, and I'm on my way to try them out. Please excuse me.' [20]Still another said, 'I just got married, so I can't come.' [21]The servant came back and reported this to his master. Then the owner of the house became angry and ordered his servant, 'Go out quickly into the streets and alleys of the town and bring in the poor, the crippled, the blind and the lame.' [22]'Sir,' the servant said, 'what you ordered has been done, but there is still room.' [23]Then the master told his servant, 'Go out to the roads and country lanes and make them come in, so that my house will be full. [24]I tell you, not one of those men who were invited will get a taste of my banquet.'"

LUKE 14:25-35 Large crowds were traveling with Jesus, and turning to them he said: [26]"If anyone comes to me and does not hate his father and mother, his wife and children, his brothers and sisters—yes, even his own life—he cannot be my disciple. [27]And anyone who does not carry his cross and follow me cannot be my disciple. [28]Suppose one of you wants to build a tower. Will he not first sit down and estimate the cost to see if he has enough money to complete it? [29]For if he lays the foundation and is not able to finish it, everyone who sees it will ridicule him, [30]saying, 'This fellow began to build and was not able to finish.' [31]Or suppose a king is about to go to war against another king. Will he not first sit down and consider whether he is able with ten thousand men to oppose the one coming against him with twenty thousand? [32]If he is not able, he will send a delegation while the other is still a long way off and will ask for terms of peace. [33]In the same way, any of you who does not give up everything he has cannot be my disciple. [34]Salt is good, but if it loses its saltiness, how can it be made salty again? [35]It is fit neither for the soil nor for the manure pile; it is thrown out. He who has ears to hear, let him hear."

LUKE 15:4-7 "Suppose one of you has a hundred sheep and loses one of them. Does he not leave the ninety-nine in the open country and go after the lost sheep until he finds it? [5]And when he finds it, he joyfully puts it on his shoulders [6]and goes home. Then he calls his friends and neighbors together and says, 'Rejoice with me; I have found my lost sheep.' [7]I tell you that in the same way there will be more rejoicing in heaven over one sinner who repents than over ninety-nine righteous persons who do not need to repent."

LUKE 15:8-10 "Or suppose a woman has ten silver coins and loses one. Does she not light a lamp, sweep the house and search carefully until she finds it? [9]And when she finds it, she calls her friends and neighbors together and says, 'Rejoice with me; I have found my lost coin.' [10]In the same way, I tell you, there is rejoicing in the presence of the angels of God over one sinner who repents."

LUKE 15:11-32 Jesus continued: "There was a man who had two sons. [12]The younger one said to his father, 'Father, give me my share of the estate.' So he divided his property between them.

[13]Not long after that, the younger son got together all he had, set off for a distant country and there squandered his wealth in wild living. [14]After he had spent everything, there was a severe famine in that whole country, and he began to be in need. [15]So he went and hired himself out to a citizen of that country, who sent him to his fields to feed pigs. [16]He longed to fill his stomach with the pods that the pigs were eating, but no one gave him anything. [17]When he came to his senses, he said, 'How many of my father's hired men have food to spare, and here I am starving to death! [18]I will set out and go back to my father and say to him: Father, I have sinned against heaven and against you. [19]I am no longer worthy to be called your son; make me like one of your hired men.' [20]So he got up and went to his father. But while he was still a long way off, his father saw him and was filled with compassion for him; he ran to his son, threw his arms around him and kissed him. [21]The son said to him, 'Father, I have sinned against heaven and against you. I am no longer worthy to be called your son.' [22]But the father said to his servants, 'Quick! Bring the best robe and put it on him. Put a ring on his finger and sandals on his feet. [23]Bring the fattened calf and kill it. Let's have a feast and celebrate. [24]For this son of mine was dead and is alive again; he was lost and is found.' So they began to celebrate. [25]Meanwhile, the older son was in the field. When he came near the house, he heard music and dancing. [26]So he called one of the servants and asked him what was going on. [27]'Your brother has come,' he replied, 'and your father has

killed the fattened calf because he has him back safe and sound.' [28]The older brother became angry and refused to go in. So his father went out and pleaded with him. [29]But he answered his father, 'Look! All these years I've been slaving for you and never disobeyed your orders. Yet you never gave me even a young goat so I could celebrate with my friends. [30]But when this son of yours who has squandered your property with prostitutes comes home, you kill the fattened calf for him!' [31]'My son,' the father said, 'you are always with me, and everything I have is yours. [32]But we had to celebrate and be glad, because this brother of yours was dead and is alive again; he was lost and is found.' "

LUKE 16:1-13 Jesus told his disciples: "There was a rich man whose manager was accused of wasting his possessions. [2]So he called him in and asked him, 'What is this I hear about you? Give an account of your management, because you cannot be manager any longer.' [3]The manager said to himself, 'What shall I do now? My master is taking away my job. I'm not strong enough to dig, and I'm ashamed to beg— [4]I know what I'll do so that, when I lose my job here, people will welcome me into their houses.' [5]So he called in each one of his master's debtors. He asked the first, 'How much do you owe my master?' [6]'Eight hundred gallons of olive oil,' he replied. The manager told him, 'Take your bill, sit down quickly, and make it four hundred.' [7]Then he asked the second, 'And how much do you owe?' 'A thousand bushels of wheat,' he replied. He told him, 'Take your bill and make it

eight hundred.' [8]The master commended the dishonest manager because he had acted shrewdly. For the people of this world are more shrewd in dealing with their own kind than are the people of the light. [9]I tell you, use worldly wealth to gain friends for yourselves, so that when it is gone, you will be welcomed into eternal dwellings. [10]Whoever can be trusted with very little can also be trusted with much, and whoever is dishonest with very little will also be dishonest with much. [11]So if you have not been trustworthy in handling worldly wealth, who will trust you with true riches? [12]And if you have not been trustworthy with someone else's property, who will give you property of your own? [13]No servant can serve two masters. Either he will hate the one and love the other, or he will be devoted to the one and despise the other. You cannot serve both God and Money."

LUKE 16:19-31 "There was a rich man who was dressed in purple and fine linen and lived in luxury every day. [20]At his gate was laid a beggar named Lazarus, covered with sores [21]and longing to eat what fell from the rich man's table. Even the dogs came and licked his sores. [22]The time came when the beggar died and the angels carried him to Abraham's side. The rich man also died and was buried. [23]In hell, where he was in torment, he looked up and saw Abraham far away, with Lazarus by his side. [24]So he called to him, 'Father Abraham, have pity on me and send Lazarus to dip the tip of his finger in water and cool my tongue, because I am in agony in this fire.' [25]But Abraham replied, 'Son, remember that in your lifetime you received your good things, while Lazarus received bad things, but now he is comforted here and you are in agony. [26]And besides all this, between us and you a great chasm has been fixed, so that those who want to go from here to you cannot, nor can anyone cross over from there to us.' [27]He answered, 'Then I beg you, father, send Lazarus to my father's house, [28]for I have five brothers. Let him warn them, so that they will not also come to this place of torment.' [29]Abraham replied, 'They have Moses and the Prophets; let them listen to them.' [30]'No, father Abraham,' he said, 'but if someone from the dead goes to them, they will repent.' [31]He said to him, 'If they do not listen to Moses and the Prophets, they will not be convinced even if someone rises from the dead.' "

LUKE 18:1-8 Then Jesus told his disciples a parable to show them that they should always pray and not give up. [2]He said: "In a certain town there was a judge who neither feared God nor cared about men. [3]And there was a widow in that town who kept coming to him with the plea, 'Grant me justice against my adversary.' [4]For some time he refused. But finally he said to himself, 'Even though I don't fear God or care about men, [5]yet because this widow keeps bothering me, I will see that she gets justice, so that she won't eventually wear me out with her coming!' " [6]And the Lord said, "Listen to what the unjust judge says. [7]And will not God bring about justice for his chosen ones, who cry out to him day and night? Will he keep putting them off? [8]I tell you, he will see that they get justice, and

quickly. However, when the Son of Man comes, will he find faith on the earth?"

LUKE 18:9-14 To some who were confident of their own righteousness and looked down on everybody else, Jesus told this parable: [10]"Two men went up to the temple to pray, one a Pharisee and the other a tax collector. [11]The Pharisee stood up and prayed about himself: 'God, I thank you that I am not like other men—robbers, evildoers, adulterers—or even like this tax collector. [12]I fast twice a week and give a tenth of all I get.' [13]But the tax collector stood at a distance. He would not even look up to heaven, but beat his breast and said, 'God, have mercy on me, a sinner.' [14]I tell you that this man, rather than the other, went home justified before God. For everyone who exalts himself will be humbled, and he who humbles himself will be exalted."

LUKE 18:24-27 Jesus looked at him [a rich ruler] and said, "How hard it is for the rich to enter the kingdom of God! [25]Indeed, it is easier for a camel to go through the eye of a needle than for a rich man to enter the kingdom of God." [26]Those who heard this asked, "Who then can be saved?" [27]Jesus replied, "What is impossible with men is possible with God."

LUKE 19:12-27 He said: "A man of noble birth went to a distant country to have himself appointed king and then to return. [13]So he called ten of his servants and gave them ten minas. 'Put this money to work,' he said, 'until I come back.' [14]But his subjects hated him and sent a delegation after him to say, 'We don't want this man to be our king.' [15]He was made king, however, and returned home. Then he sent for the servants to whom he had given the money, in order to find out what they had gained with it. [16]The first one came and said, 'Sir, your mina has earned ten more.' [17]'Well done, my good servant!' his master replied. 'Because you have been trustworthy in a very small matter, take charge of ten cities.' [18]The second came and said, 'Sir, your mina has earned five more.' [19]His master answered, 'You take charge of five cities.' [20]Then another servant came and said, 'Sir, here is your mina; I have kept it laid away in a piece of cloth. [21]I was afraid of you, because you are a hard man. You take out what you did not put in and reap what you did not sow.' [22]His master replied, 'I will judge you by your own words, you wicked servant! You knew, did you, that I am a hard man, taking out what I did not put in, and reaping what I did not sow? [23]Why then didn't you put my money on deposit, so that when I came back, I could have collected it with interest?' [24]Then he said to those standing by, 'Take his mina away from him and give it to the one who has ten minas.' [25]'Sir,' they said, 'he already has ten!' [26]He replied, 'I tell you that to everyone who has, more will be given, but as for the one who has nothing, even what he has will be taken away. [27]But those enemies of mine who did not want me to be king over them—bring them here and kill them in front of me.' "

LUKE 20:9-18 He went on to tell the people this parable: "A man planted a vineyard, rented it to some farmers and went away for a long time. [10]At harvest time he sent a servant to the tenants so they would give him some of the fruit of the vineyard. But the tenants beat him and sent him away empty-handed. [11]He sent another servant, but that one also they beat and treated shamefully and sent away empty-handed. [12]He sent still a third, and they wounded him and threw him out. [13]Then the owner of the vineyard said, 'What shall I do? I will send my son, whom I love; perhaps they will respect him.' [14]But when the tenants saw him, they talked the matter over. 'This is the heir,' they said. 'Let's kill him, and the inheritance will be ours.' [15]So they threw him out of the vineyard and killed him. What then will the owner of the vineyard do to them? [16]He will come and kill those tenants and give the vineyard to others." When the people heard this, they said, "May this never be!" [17]Jesus looked directly at them and asked, "Then what is the meaning of that which is written: 'The stone the builders rejected has become the capstone'? [18]Everyone who falls on that stone will be broken to pieces, but he on whom it falls will be crushed."

Jesus' Works

JOHN 4:31-34 Meanwhile his disciples urged him, "Rabbi, eat something." [32]But he said to them, "I have food to eat that you know nothing about." [33]Then his disciples said to each other, "Could someone have brought him food?" [34]"My food," said Jesus, "is to do the will of him who sent me and to finish his work."

JOHN 5:36 "I have testimony weightier than that of John. For the very work that the Father has given me to finish, and which I am doing, testifies that the Father has sent me."

JOHN 9:3-7 "Neither this man nor his parents sinned," said Jesus, "but this [being born blind] happened so that the work of God might be displayed in his life. [4]As long as it is day, we must do the work of him who sent me. Night is coming, when no one can work. [5]While I am in the world, I am the light of the world." [6]Having said this, he spit on the ground, made some mud with the saliva, and put it on the man's eyes. [7]"Go," he told him, "wash in the Pool of Siloam" (this word means Sent). So the man went and washed, and came home seeing.

JOHN 10:25 Jesus answered, "I did tell you, but you do not believe. The miracles I do in my Father's name speak for me."

JOHN 10:32 …Jesus said to them, "I have shown you many great miracles from the Father. For which of these do you stone me?"

JOHN 10:37-38 "Do not believe me unless I do what my Father does. [38]But if I do it, even though you do not believe me, believe the miracles, that you may know and understand that the Father is in me, and I in the Father."

JOHN 14:10-11 "Don't you believe that I am in the Father, and that the Father is in me? The words I say to you are not just my own. Rather, it is the Father,

living in me, who is doing his work. [11]Believe me when I say that I am in the Father and the Father is in me; or at least believe on the evidence of the miracles themselves."

JOHN 15:23-25 "He who hates me hates my Father as well. [24]If I had not done among them what no one else did, they would not be guilty of sin. But now they have seen these miracles, and yet they have hated both me and my Father. [25]But this is to fulfill what is written in their Law: 'They hated me without reason.'"

JOHN 17:4-5 "I have brought you glory on earth by completing the work you gave me to do. [5]And now, Father, glorify me in your presence with the glory I had with you before the world began."

MATTHEW 11:21-24 "Woe to you, Korazin! Woe to you, Bethsaida! If the miracles that were performed in you had been performed in Tyre and Sidon, they would have repented long ago in sackcloth and ashes. [22]But I tell you, it will be more bearable for Tyre and Sidon on the day of judgment than for you. [23]And you, Capernaum, will you be lifted up to the skies? No, you will go down to the depths. If the miracles that were performed in you had been performed in Sodom, it would have remained to this day. [24]But I tell you that it will be more bearable for Sodom on the day of judgment than for you."

2

THE GREATEST WORDS
EVER SPOKEN ABOUT
GOD THE FATHER

What Christ Tells Us About His Father in Heaven

From the beginning of human history, in every culture and civilization, men and women have pondered the existence of a god or gods. Most created their own gods, forming them from metal or carving them out of wood or stone. Most cultures believed in many gods, and they created rituals and religions to try to please and appease their gods. But the Hebrews believed in the existence of one eternal, almighty God. Beside Him, there were no others.

And then there are agnostics and people who arrogantly proclaim themselves to be atheists. Agnostics hold the position that they simply do not *know* if God exists. Atheists, on the other hand, claim intellectual superiority over all others, saying they know there is no God. For example, a popular liberal political satirist recently stated, "Have you ever noticed that all of the intelligent people are atheists?"[v] Trying to appear intelligent himself, he had instead made one of the most ignorant statements imaginable. Does he think men like George Washington, Benjamin Franklin, Thomas Jefferson, and Abraham Lincoln were idiots? Does he think Thomas Edison, Henry Ford, John D. Rockefeller, Albert Schweitzer, Albert Einstein, Wernher von Braun (creator of America's space program), and thousands of other scientists and physicians who had a strong belief in God were all unintelligent? Or how about J. R. R. Tolkien, the Oxford professor whose genius gave us the Lord of the Rings trilogy, as well as his simple yet brilliant proof of Christ's deity? Using the claims of Christ, he transformed his fellow professor C. S. Lewis (Oxford's most articulate atheist) into one of the world's most passionate Christian apologists.

I have never met anyone who has made a thorough, intellectually honest investigation into the life and words of Jesus Christ who has not come away convinced that Christ was who He said He was. In fact, every doubter I have known or read about—including some of the world's most brilliant—who has studied Jesus' words has become a follower of Christ. This includes C. S. Lewis, General Lew Wallace, and Dr. Charles Payne. Two of these men attempted to prove Christianity was nothing more than a myth, but each became a believer in God and a devout follower of Christ. That is the inherent power in the words of Jesus.

If God Exists, What Does He Want?

If we believe God exists, then the two most important questions in life are "What is He like?" and "What does He want?" Is He the terrifying god that so many cultures in the past sacrificed their own people to? Or is He a New Age, Santa Claus–type god who loves and accepts everybody and who places no demands or expectations on us?

Jesus answered these questions and every question we could ask about God. His answers were not skewed by presumption, prejudice, or cultural tradition. He answered out of His perfect, experiential knowledge. He knew God more intimately than anyone has ever known a member of his family. From that experiential knowledge, Jesus revealed the perfect truth about God the Father—the first Person of the Trinity. Jesus proclaimed that there is only *one* true God and that Jesus is the only One who has ever seen and known God. Jesus called Him both God and His Heavenly Father. Jesus claimed that the Father Himself had sent Him to earth on a messianic mission. He claimed that everything He—Christ—said and did while He was on that mission emanated directly from God. In fact, Jesus proclaimed that He was in *perfect unity* with the Father, that the Father was in Him, and that He was in the Father. In fact, Jesus said those who saw and heard Him had actually seen and heard God the Father.

In this chapter you will encounter everything Jesus said about God, His nature, His Spirit, His fatherhood, and His character. You'll discover firsthand what Jesus revealed about His relationship with God and what God desires in His relationship with you and me. You'll discover what Jesus said about God's love and goodness, His Word, and His works. You'll discover what you can do to honor and glorify God. And last but not least, you'll learn what Jesus revealed to be God's desires and will.

We all have preconceptions about God. We assume we know what He wants or offers to us. Unfortunately, many of our assumptions and conclusions are unfounded. In this chapter you can read the truth about God, based on the *facts* of Christ's knowledge. He is the only One in history who could reveal every important facet of God.

In John 14:9 Jesus stated, "Anyone who has seen me has seen the Father." Together with Jesus' words about God, Jesus' life and works provide a perfect revelation of God the Father. If you want to know what God thinks and feels, how He acts and works, what grieves Him and what pleases Him, all you have to do is read the words and observe the behavior of Jesus Christ.

God's Character

JOHN 3:16 "For God so loved the world that he gave his one and only Son, that whoever believes in him shall not perish but have eternal life."

JOHN 7:28-29 Then Jesus, still teaching in the temple courts, cried out, "Yes, you know me, and you know where I am from. I am not here on my own, but he who sent me is true. You do not know him, ²⁹but I know him because I am from him and he sent me."

MATTHEW 6:26 "Look at the birds of the air; they do not sow or reap or store away in barns, and yet your heavenly Father feeds them. Are you not much more valuable than they?"

MATTHEW 7:7-11 "Ask and it will be given to you; seek and you will find; knock and the door will be opened to you.

⁸For everyone who asks receives; he who seeks finds; and to him who knocks, the door will be opened. ⁹Which of you, if his son asks for bread, will give him a stone? ¹⁰Or if he asks for a fish, will give him a snake? ¹¹If you, then, though you are evil, know how to give good gifts to your children, how much more will your Father in heaven give good gifts to those who ask him!"

LUKE 6:35-36 "But love your enemies, do good to them, and lend to them without expecting to get anything back. Then your reward will be great, and you will be sons of the Most High, because he is kind to the ungrateful and wicked. ³⁶Be merciful, just as your Father is merciful."

LUKE 11:9-13 "So I say to you: Ask and it will be given to you; seek and you will find; knock and the door will be opened to you. ¹⁰For everyone who asks receives; he who seeks finds; and to him who knocks, the door will be opened. [11]Which of you fathers, if your son asks for a fish, will give him a snake instead? [12]Or if he asks for an egg, will give him a scorpion? [13]If you then, though you are evil, know how to give good gifts to your children, how much more will your Father in heaven give the Holy Spirit to those who ask him!"

LUKE 12:4-7 "I tell you, my friends, do not be afraid of those who kill the body and after that can do no more. [5]But I will show you whom you should fear: Fear him who, after the killing of the body, has power to throw you into hell. Yes, I tell you, fear him. [6]Are not five sparrows sold for two pennies? Yet not one of them is forgotten by God. [7]Indeed, the very hairs of your head are all numbered. Don't be afraid; you are worth more than many sparrows."

LUKE 12:22-32 Then Jesus said to his disciples: "Therefore I tell you, do not worry about your life, what you will eat; or about your body, what you will wear. [23]Life is more than food, and the body more than clothes. [24]Consider the ravens: They do not sow or reap, they have no storeroom or barn; yet God feeds them. And how much more valuable you are than birds! [25]Who of you by worrying can add a single hour to his life? [26]Since you cannot do this very little thing, why do you worry about the rest? [27]Consider how the lilies grow. They do not labor or spin. Yet I tell you, not even Solomon in all his splendor was dressed like one of these. [28]If that is how God clothes the grass of the field, which is here today, and tomorrow is thrown into the fire, how much more will he clothe you, O you of little faith! [29]And do not set your heart on what you will eat or drink; do not worry about it. [30]For the pagan world runs after all such things, and your Father knows that you need them. [31]But seek his kingdom, and these things will be given to you as well. [32]Do not be afraid, little flock, for your Father has been pleased to give you the kingdom."

LUKE 18:19 "Why do you call me good?" Jesus answered. "No one is good—except God alone."

God's Desires

JOHN 4:23 "Yet a time is coming and has now come when the true worshipers will worship the Father in spirit and truth, for they are the kind of worshipers the Father seeks."

JOHN 5:22-23 "Moreover, the Father judges no one, but has entrusted all judgment to the Son, [23]that all may honor the Son just as they honor the Father. He who does not honor the Son does not honor the Father, who sent him."

JOHN 8:42 Jesus said to them, "If God were your Father, you would love me, for I came from God and now am here. I have not come on my own; but he sent me."

JOHN 12:26 "Whoever serves me must follow me; and where I am, my servant also will be. My Father will honor the one who serves me."

JOHN 14:23 Jesus replied, "If anyone loves me, he will obey my teaching. My

Father will love him, and we will come to him and make our home with him."

MATTHEW 6:1-4 "Be careful not to do your 'acts of righteousness' before men, to be seen by them. If you do, you will have no reward from your Father in heaven. [2]So when you give to the needy, do not announce it with trumpets, as the hypocrites do in the synagogues and on the streets, to be honored by men. I tell you the truth, they have received their reward in full. [3]But when you give to the needy, do not let your left hand know what your right hand is doing, [4]so that your giving may be in secret. Then your Father, who sees what is done in secret, will reward you."

MATTHEW 6:5-7 "And when you pray, do not be like the hypocrites, for they love to pray standing in the synagogues and on the street corners to be seen by men. I tell you the truth, they have received their reward in full. [6]But when you pray, go into your room, close the door and pray to your Father, who is unseen. Then your Father, who sees what is done in secret, will reward you. [7]And when you pray, do not keep on babbling like pagans, for they think they will be heard because of their many words."

MATTHEW 6:31-33 "So do not worry, saying, 'What shall we eat?' or 'What shall we drink?' or 'What shall we wear?' [32]For the pagans run after all these things, and your heavenly Father knows that you need them. [33]But seek first his kingdom and his righteousness, and all these things will be given to you as well." (See also Luke 12:29-31.)

MATTHEW 7:7-11 "Ask and it will be given to you; seek and you will find; knock and the door will be opened to you. [8]For everyone who asks receives; he who seeks finds; and to him who knocks, the door will be opened. [9]Which of you, if his son asks for bread, will give him a stone? [10]Or if he asks for a fish, will give him a snake? [11]If you, then, though you are evil, know how to give good gifts to your children, how much more will your Father in heaven give good gifts to those who ask him!"

MATTHEW 7:12 "So in everything, do to others what you would have them do to you, for this sums up the Law and the Prophets."

MATTHEW 18:12-14 "What do you think? If a man owns a hundred sheep, and one of them wanders away, will he not leave the ninety-nine on the hills and go to look for the one that wandered off? [13]And if he finds it, I tell you the truth, he is happier about that one sheep than about the ninety-nine that did not wander off. [14]In the same way your Father in heaven is not willing that any of these little ones should be lost."

MATTHEW 18:19 "Again, I tell you that if two of you on earth agree about anything you ask for, it will be done for you by my Father in heaven."

MATTHEW 19:17 "Why do you ask me about what is good?" Jesus replied. "There is only One who is good. If you want to enter life, obey the commandments."

MATTHEW 19:18-21 ...Jesus replied, "'Do not murder, do not commit adultery, do not steal, do not give false testimony, honor your father and mother,' and 'love your neighbor as yourself.'" [20]"All these I have kept," the young man said. "What do I still lack?" [21]Jesus answered, "If you want to be perfect, go, sell your possessions and give to the poor, and you will have treasure in heaven. Then come, follow me."

LUKE 11:9-13 "So I say to you: Ask and it will be given to you; seek and you will find; knock and the door will be opened to you. [10]For everyone who asks receives; he who seeks finds; and to him who knocks, the door will be opened. [11]Which of you fathers, if your son asks for a fish, will give him a snake instead? [12]Or if he asks for an egg, will give him a scorpion? [13]If you then, though you are evil, know how to give good gifts to your children, how much more will your Father in heaven give the Holy Spirit to those who ask him!"

LUKE 15:4-7 "Suppose one of you has a hundred sheep and loses one of them. Does he not leave the ninety-nine in the open country and go after the lost sheep until he finds it? [5]And when he finds it, he joyfully puts it on his shoulders [6]and goes home. Then he calls his friends and neighbors together and says, 'Rejoice with me; I have found my lost sheep.' [7]I tell you that in the same way there will be more rejoicing in heaven over one sinner who repents than over ninety-nine righteous persons who do not need to repent."

LUKE 22:37 "It is written: 'And he was numbered with the transgressors'; and I tell you that this must be fulfilled in me.

Yes, what is written about me is reaching its fulfillment."

God the Father

Jesus spoke more words about God the Father and His intimate relationship with the Father than He did about any other subject. As you prayerfully read these verses, notice the love and adoration the Son has for the Father. Notice Jesus' perfect obedience and His driving desire to serve, please, and glorify His Heavenly Father. Amazingly, this is the truest picture of the kind of relationship God desires to have with us. And through the terrible and glorious atoning sacrifice of Jesus on Calvary, we too can have an intimate, fulfilling relationship with our Heavenly Father.

JOHN 5:19-20 Jesus gave them this answer: "I tell you the truth, the Son can do nothing by himself; he can do only what he sees his Father doing, because whatever the Father does the Son also does. [20]For the Father loves the Son and shows him all he does. Yes, to your amazement he will show him even greater things than these."

JOHN 5:22-23 "Moreover, the Father judges no one, but has entrusted all judgment to the Son, [23]that all may honor the Son just as they honor the Father. He who does not honor the Son does not honor the Father, who sent him."

JOHN 5:26-27 "For as the Father has life in himself, so he has granted the Son to have life in himself. [27]And he has given him authority to judge because he is the Son of Man."

JOHN 5:37-38 "And the Father who sent me has himself testified concerning me. You have never heard his voice nor seen his form, [38]nor does his word dwell in you, for you do not believe the one he sent."

JOHN 6:37-40 "All that the Father gives me will come to me, and whoever comes to me I will never drive away. [38]For I have come down from heaven not to do my will but to do the will of him who sent me. [39]And this is the will of him who sent me, that I shall lose none of all that he has given me, but raise them up at the last day. [40]For my Father's will is that everyone who looks to the Son and believes in him shall have eternal life, and I will raise him up at the last day."

JOHN 6:44 "No one can come to me unless the Father who sent me draws him, and I will raise him up at the last day."

JOHN 6:46 "No one has seen the Father except the one who is from God; only he has seen the Father."

JOHN 7:16-19 Jesus answered, "My teaching is not my own. It comes from him who sent me. [17]If anyone chooses to do God's will, he will find out whether my teaching comes from God or whether I speak on my own. [18]He who speaks on his own does so to gain honor for himself, but he who works for the honor of the one who sent him is a man of truth; there is nothing false about him. [19]Has not Moses given you the law? Yet not one of you keeps the law. Why are you trying to kill me?"

JOHN 8:25-26 "Who are you?" they asked. "Just what I have been claiming all along," Jesus replied. [26]"I have much to say in judgment of you. But he who sent me is reliable, and what I have heard from him I tell the world."

JOHN 8:28-29 So Jesus said, "When you have lifted up the Son of Man, then you will know that I am the one I claim to be and that I do nothing on my own but speak just what the Father has taught me. [29]The one who sent me is with me; he has not left me alone, for I always do what pleases him."

JOHN 8:54 Jesus replied, "If I glorify myself, my glory means nothing. My Father, whom you claim as your God, is the one who glorifies me."

JOHN 10:17 "The reason my Father loves me is that I lay down my life—only to take it up again."

JOHN 10:30 "I and the Father are one."

JOHN 10:37-38 "Do not believe me unless I do what my Father does. [38]But if I do it, even though you do not believe me, believe the miracles, that you may know and understand that the Father is in me, and I in the Father."

JOHN 12:44-45 Then Jesus cried out, "When a man believes in me, he does not believe in me only, but in the one who sent me. [45]When he looks at me, he sees the one who sent me."

JOHN 12:49-50 "For I did not speak of my own accord, but the Father who sent me commanded me what to say and how to say it. [50]I know that his command leads to eternal life. So whatever I say is just what the Father has told me to say."

JOHN 14:1-2 "Do not let your hearts be troubled. Trust in God; trust also in me. ²In my Father's house are many rooms; if it were not so, I would have told you. I am going there to prepare a place for you."

JOHN 14:7 "If you really knew me, you would know my Father as well. From now on, you do know him and have seen him."

JOHN 14:10-11 "Don't you believe that I am in the Father, and that the Father is in me? The words I say to you are not just my own. Rather, it is the Father, living in me, who is doing his work. ¹¹Believe me when I say that I am in the Father and the Father is in me; or at least believe on the evidence of the miracles themselves."

JOHN 14:20 "On that day you will realize that I am in my Father, and you are in me, and I am in you."

JOHN 14:23 Jesus replied, "If anyone loves me, he will obey my teaching. My Father will love him, and we will come to him and make our home with him."

JOHN 14:28 "You heard me say, 'I am going away and I am coming back to you.' If you loved me, you would be glad that I am going to the Father, for the Father is greater than I."

JOHN 15:1-2 "I am the true vine, and my Father is the gardener. ²He cuts off every branch in me that bears no fruit, while every branch that does bear fruit he prunes so that it will be even more fruitful."

JOHN 15:9-10 "As the Father has loved me, so have I loved you. Now remain in my love. ¹⁰If you obey my commands, you will remain in my love, just as I have obeyed my Father's commands and remain in his love."

JOHN 15:23-24 "He who hates me hates my Father as well. ²⁴If I had not done among them what no one else did, they would not be guilty of sin. But now they have seen these miracles, and yet they have hated both me and my Father."

JOHN 16:32 "But a time is coming, and has come, when you will be scattered, each to his own home. You will leave me all alone. Yet I am not alone, for my Father is with me."

JOHN 17:1-4 After Jesus said this, he looked toward heaven and prayed: "Father, the time has come. Glorify your Son, that your Son may glorify you. ²For you granted him authority over all people that he might give eternal life to all those you have given him. ³Now this is eternal life: that they may know you, the only true God, and Jesus Christ, whom you have sent. ⁴I have brought you glory on earth by completing the work you gave me to do."

JOHN 17:6 "I have revealed you [God] to those whom you gave me out of the world. They were yours; you gave them to me and they have obeyed your word."

JOHN 17:9-11 "I pray for them [the disciples]. I am not praying for the world, but for those you have given me, for they are yours. ¹⁰All I have is yours, and all you have is mine. And glory has come to me through them. ¹¹I will remain in the world no longer, but they are still in the world, and I am coming to you. Holy Father, protect them by the power of your name—the name you gave me—so that they may be one as we are one."

JOHN 17:20-23 "My prayer is not for them [the disciples] alone. I pray also for those who will believe in me through their message, [21]that all of them may be one, Father, just as you are in me and I am in you. May they also be in us so that the world may believe that you have sent me. [22]I have given them the glory that you gave me, that they may be one as we are one: [23]I in them and you in me. May they be brought to complete unity to let the world know that you sent me and have loved them even as you have loved me."

JOHN 20:17 Jesus said, "Do not hold on to me, for I have not yet returned to the Father. Go instead to my brothers and tell them, 'I am returning to my Father and your Father, to my God and your God.'"

MATTHEW 5:8-9 "Blessed are the pure in heart, for they will see God. [9]Blessed are the peacemakers, for they will be called sons of God."

MATTHEW 5:44-48 "But I tell you: Love your enemies and pray for those who persecute you, [45]that you may be sons of your Father in heaven. He causes his sun to rise on the evil and the good, and sends rain on the righteous and the unrighteous. [46]If you love those who love you, what reward will you get? Are not even the tax collectors doing that? [47]And if you greet only your brothers, what are you doing more than others? Do not even pagans do that? [48]Be perfect, therefore, as your heavenly Father is perfect."

MATTHEW 6:3-4 "But when you give to the needy, do not let your left hand know what your right hand is doing, [4]so that your giving may be in secret. Then your Father, who sees what is done in secret, will reward you."

MATTHEW 6:6-8 "But when you pray, go into your room, close the door and pray to your Father, who is unseen. Then your Father, who sees what is done in secret, will reward you. [7]And when you pray, do not keep on babbling like pagans, for they think they will be heard because of their many words. [8]Do not be like them, for your Father knows what you need before you ask him."

MATTHEW 6:14-15 "For if you forgive men when they sin against you, your heavenly Father will also forgive you. [15]But if you do not forgive men their sins, your Father will not forgive your sins."

MATTHEW 6:17-18 "But when you fast, put oil on your head and wash your face, [18]so that it will not be obvious to men that you are fasting, but only to your Father, who is unseen; and your Father, who sees what is done in secret, will reward you."

MATTHEW 7:7-11 "Ask and it will be given to you; seek and you will find; knock and the door will be opened to you. [8]For everyone who asks receives; he who seeks finds; and to him who knocks, the door will be opened. [9]Which of you, if his son asks for bread, will give him a stone? [10]Or if he asks for a fish, will give him a snake? [11]If you, then, though you are evil, know how to give good gifts to your children, how much more will your

Father in heaven give good gifts to those who ask him!"

MATTHEW 10:19-20 "But when they arrest you, do not worry about what to say or how to say it. At that time you will be given what to say, [20]for it will not be you speaking, but the Spirit of your Father speaking through you."

MATTHEW 11:25-26 At that time Jesus said, "I praise you, Father, Lord of heaven and earth, because you have hidden these things from the wise and learned, and revealed them to little children. [26]Yes, Father, for this was your good pleasure."

MATTHEW 11:27 "All things have been committed to me by my Father. No one knows the Son except the Father, and no one knows the Father except the Son and those to whom the Son chooses to reveal him."

MATTHEW 18:10, 12-14 "See that you do not look down on one of these little ones. For I tell you that their angels in heaven always see the face of my Father in heaven. [12]What do you think? If a man owns a hundred sheep, and one of them wanders away, will he not leave the ninety-nine on the hills and go to look for the one that wandered off? [13]And if he finds it, I tell you the truth, he is happier about that one sheep than about the ninety-nine that did not wander off. [14]In the same way your Father in heaven is not willing that any of these little ones should be lost."

MATTHEW 19:17 "Why do you ask me about what is good?" Jesus replied. "There is only One who is good. If you want to enter life, obey the commandments."

MATTHEW 25:34 "Then the King will say to those on his right, 'Come, you who are blessed by my Father; take your inheritance, the kingdom prepared for you since the creation of the world.'"

MARK 11:22-25 "Have faith in God," Jesus answered. [23]"I tell you the truth, if anyone says to this mountain, 'Go, throw yourself into the sea,' and does not doubt in his heart but believes that what he says will happen, it will be done for him. [24]Therefore I tell you, whatever you ask for in prayer, believe that you have received it, and it will be yours. [25]And when you stand praying, if you hold anything against anyone, forgive him, so that your Father in heaven may forgive you your sins."

LUKE 11:2-4 He said to them, "When you pray, say: 'Father, hallowed be your name, your kingdom come. [3]Give us each day our daily bread. [4]Forgive us our sins, for we also forgive everyone who sins against us. And lead us not into temptation.'"

LUKE 11:9-13 "So I say to you: Ask and it will be given to you; seek and you will find; knock and the door will be opened to you. [10]For everyone who asks receives; he who seeks finds; and to him who knocks, the door will be opened. [11]Which of you fathers, if your son asks for a fish, will give him a snake instead? [12]Or if he asks for an egg, will give him a scorpion? [13]If you then, though you are evil, know how to give good gifts to your children, how much more will your

Father in heaven give the Holy Spirit to those who ask him!"

God's Glory

JOHN 8:54-55 Jesus replied, "If I glorify myself, my glory means nothing. My Father, whom you claim as your God, is the one who glorifies me. 55Though you do not know him, I know him. If I said I did not, I would be a liar like you, but I do know him and keep his word."

JOHN 11:4 When he heard this [Lazarus was sick], Jesus said, "This sickness will not end in death. No, it is for God's glory so that God's Son may be glorified through it."

JOHN 11:40 Then Jesus said, "Did I not tell you that if you believed, you would see the glory of God?"

JOHN 12:23-24 Jesus replied, "The hour has come for the Son of Man to be glorified. 24I tell you the truth, unless a kernel of wheat falls to the ground and dies, it remains only a single seed. But if it dies, it produces many seeds."

JOHN 13:31-33 When he [Judas] was gone, Jesus said, "Now is the Son of Man glorified and God is glorified in him. 32If God is glorified in him, God will glorify the Son in himself, and will glorify him at once. 33My children, I will be with you only a little longer. You will look for me, and just as I told the Jews, so I tell you now: Where I am going, you cannot come."

JOHN 15:5-8 "I am the vine; you are the branches. If a man remains in me and I in him, he will bear much fruit; apart

from me you can do nothing. 6If anyone does not remain in me, he is like a branch that is thrown away and withers; such branches are picked up, thrown into the fire and burned. 7If you remain in me and my words remain in you, ask whatever you wish, and it will be given you. 8This is to my Father's glory, that you bear much fruit, showing yourselves to be my disciples."

JOHN 17:9-10 "I pray for them [the disciples]. I am not praying for the world, but for those you have given me, for they are yours. 10All I have is yours, and all you have is mine. And glory has come to me through them."

JOHN 17:22-23 "I have given them the glory that you [God] gave me, that they may be one as we are one: 23I in them and you in me. May they be brought to complete unity to let the world know that you sent me and have loved them even as you have loved me."

JOHN 17:24 "Father, I want those you have given me to be with me where I am, and to see my glory, the glory you have given me because you loved me before the creation of the world."

MATTHEW 16:27 "For the Son of Man is going to come in his Father's glory with his angels, and then he will reward each person according to what he has done."

God's Goodness

JOHN 3:16-17 "For God so loved the world that he gave his one and only Son, that whoever believes in him shall not perish but have eternal life. [17]For God did not send his Son into the world to condemn the world, but to save the world through him."

JOHN 6:37-39 "All that the Father gives me will come to me, and whoever comes to me I will never drive away. [38]For I have come down from heaven not to do my will but to do the will of him who sent me. [39]And this is the will of him who sent me, that I shall lose none of all that he has given me, but raise them up at the last day."

JOHN 10:27-29 "My sheep listen to my voice; I know them, and they follow me. [28]I give them eternal life, and they shall never perish; no one can snatch them out of my hand. [29]My Father, who has given them to me, is greater than all; no one can snatch them out of my Father's hand."

JOHN 14:21 "Whoever has my commands and obeys them, he is the one who loves me. He who loves me will be loved by my Father, and I too will love him and show myself to him."

JOHN 14:23 Jesus replied, "If anyone loves me, he will obey my teaching. My Father will love him, and we will come to him and make our home with him."

JOHN 16:27 "No, the Father himself loves you because you have loved me and have believed that I came from God."

JOHN 17:23 "I in them and you in me. May they be brought to complete unity to let the world know that you sent me and have loved them even as you have loved me."

MATTHEW 6:25-33 "Therefore I tell you, do not worry about your life, what you will eat or drink; or about your body, what you will wear. Is not life more important than food, and the body more important than clothes? [26]Look at the birds of the air; they do not sow or reap or store away in barns, and yet your heavenly Father feeds them. Are you not much more valuable than they? [27]Who of you by worrying can add a single hour to his life? [28]And why do you worry about clothes? See how the lilies of the field grow. They do not labor or spin. [29]Yet I tell you that not even Solomon in all his splendor was dressed like one of these. [30]If that is how God clothes the grass of the field, which is here today and tomorrow is thrown into the fire, will he not much more clothe you, O you of little faith? [31]So do not worry, saying, 'What shall we eat?' or 'What shall we drink?' or 'What shall we wear?' [32]For the pagans run after all these things, and your heavenly Father knows that you need them. [33]But seek first his kingdom and his righteousness, and all these things will be given to you as well."

MATTHEW 7:7-11 "Ask and it will be given to you; seek and you will find; knock and the door will be opened to you. [8]For everyone who asks receives; he who seeks finds; and to him who knocks, the door will be opened. [9]Which of you, if his son asks for bread, will give him a stone? [10]Or if he asks for a fish, will give him a snake? [11]If you, then, though you are evil, know how to give good gifts to your children, how much more will your Father in heaven give good gifts to those who ask him!"

MATTHEW 10:27-31 "What I tell you in the dark, speak in the daylight;

what is whispered in your ear, proclaim from the roofs. [28]Do not be afraid of those who kill the body but cannot kill the soul. Rather, be afraid of the One who can destroy both soul and body in hell. [29]Are not two sparrows sold for a penny? Yet not one of them will fall to the ground apart from the will of your Father. [30]And even the very hairs of your head are all numbered. [31]So don't be afraid; you are worth more than many sparrows."

MARK 10:18 "Why do you call me good?" Jesus answered. "No one is good—except God alone."

God's Love

JOHN 3:16-17 "For God so loved the world that he gave his one and only Son, that whoever believes in him shall not perish but have eternal life. [17]For God did not send his Son into the world to condemn the world, but to save the world through him."

JOHN 5:42-44 "…I know you. I know that you do not have the love of God in your hearts. [43]I have come in my Father's name, and you do not accept me; but if someone else comes in his own name, you will accept him. [44]How can you believe if you accept praise from one another, yet make no effort to obtain the praise that comes from the only God?"

JOHN 14:21 "Whoever has my commands and obeys them, he is the one who loves me. He who loves me will be loved by my Father, and I too will love him and show myself to him."

JOHN 14:23 Jesus replied, "If anyone loves me, he will obey my teaching. My Father will love him, and we will come to him and make our home with him."

JOHN 15:9-10 "As the Father has loved me, so have I loved you. Now remain in my love. [10]If you obey my commands, you will remain in my love, just as I have obeyed my Father's commands and remain in his love."

JOHN 16:26-27 "In that day you will ask in my name. I am not saying that I will ask the Father on your behalf. [27]No, the Father himself loves you because you have loved me and have believed that I came from God."

JOHN 17:22-26 "I have given them the glory that you [God] gave me, that they may be one as we are one: [23]I in them and you in me. May they be brought to complete unity to let the world know that you sent me and have loved them even as you have loved me. [24]Father, I want those you have given me to be with me where I am, and to see my glory, the glory you have given me because you loved me before the creation of the world. [25]Righteous Father, though the world does not know you, I know you, and they know that you have sent me. [26]I have made you known to them, and will continue to make you known in order that the love you have for me may be in them and that I myself may be in them."

MATTHEW 6:6 "But when you pray, go into your room, close the door and pray to your Father, who is unseen. Then your Father, who sees what is done in secret, will reward you."

MATTHEW 6:30-33 "If that is how God clothes the grass of the field, which is here today and tomorrow is thrown into the fire, will he not much more clothe you, O you of little faith? [31]So do not worry, saying, 'What shall we eat?' or 'What shall we drink?' or 'What shall we wear?' [32]For the pagans run after all these things, and your heavenly Father knows that you need them. [33]But seek first his kingdom and his righteousness, and all these things will be given to you as well." (See also Luke 12:28-31.)

MATTHEW 18:12-14 "What do you think? If a man owns a hundred sheep, and one of them wanders away, will he not leave the ninety-nine on the hills and go to look for the one that wandered off? [13]And if he finds it, I tell you the truth, he is happier about that one sheep than about the ninety-nine that did not wander off. [14]In the same way your Father in heaven is not willing that any of these little ones should be lost."

MARK 5:19 Jesus did not let him [the man freed of demons go with him], but said, "Go home to your family and tell them how much the Lord has done for you, and how he has had mercy on you." (See also Luke 8:38-39.)

MARK 12:30 "Love the Lord your God with all your heart and with all your soul and with all your mind and with all your strength." (See also Matthew 22:37.)

LUKE 15:7 "I tell you that in the same way there will be more rejoicing in heaven over one sinner who repents than over ninety-nine righteous persons who do not need to repent."

LUKE 15:11-32 Jesus continued: "There was a man who had two sons. [12]The younger one said to his father, 'Father, give me my share of the estate.' So he divided his property between them. [13]Not long after that, the younger son got together all he had, set off for a distant country and there squandered his wealth in wild living. [14]After he had spent everything, there was a severe famine in that whole country, and he began to be in need. [15]So he went and hired himself out to a citizen of that country, who sent him to his fields to feed pigs. [16]He longed to fill his stomach with the pods that the pigs were eating, but no one gave him anything. [17]When he came to his senses, he said, 'How many of my father's hired men have food to spare, and here I am starving to death! [18]I will set out and go back to my father and say to him: Father, I have sinned against heaven and against you. [19]I am no longer worthy to be called your son; make me like one of your hired men.' [20]So he got up and went to his father. But while he was still a long way off, his father saw him and was filled with compassion for him; he ran to his son, threw his arms around him and kissed him. [21]The son said to him, 'Father, I have sinned against heaven and against you. I am no longer worthy to be called your son.' [22]But the father said to his servants, 'Quick! Bring the best robe and put it on him. Put a ring on his finger and sandals on his feet. [23]Bring the fattened calf and kill it. Let's have a feast and celebrate. [24]For this son of mine was dead and is alive again; he was lost and is found.' So they began to celebrate. [25]Meanwhile, the older son was in the field. When he came near the house, he heard music and dancing. [26]So he called one of the servants and asked him what was going on. [27]'Your brother has come,' he replied, 'and your father has killed the fattened calf because he has him back safe and sound.' ²⁸The older brother became angry and refused to go in. So his father went out and pleaded with him. ²⁹But he answered his father, 'Look! All these years I've been slaving for you and never disobeyed your orders. Yet you never gave me even a young goat so I could celebrate with my friends. ³⁰But when this son of yours who has squandered your property with prostitutes comes home, you kill the fattened calf for him!' ³¹'My son,' the father said, 'you are always with me, and everything I have is yours. ³²But we had to celebrate and be glad, because this brother of yours was dead and is alive again; he was lost and is found.' "

God's Mercy

JOHN 3:16-17 "For God so loved the world that he gave his one and only Son, that whoever believes in him shall not perish but have eternal life. ¹⁷For God did not send his Son into the world to condemn the world, but to save the world through him."

MATTHEW 6:13-14 " 'And lead us not into temptation, but deliver us from the evil one.' ¹⁴For if you forgive men when they sin against you, your heavenly Father will also forgive you."

MATTHEW 6:26-33 "Look at the birds of the air; they do not sow or reap or store away in barns, and yet your heavenly Father feeds them. Are you not much more valuable than they? ²⁷Who of you by worrying can add a single hour to his life? ²⁸And why do you worry about clothes? See how the lilies of the field grow. They do not labor or spin. ²⁹Yet I tell you that not even Solomon in all his splendor was dressed like one of these. ³⁰If that is how God clothes the grass of the field, which is here today and tomorrow is thrown into the fire, will he not much more clothe you, O you of little faith? ³¹So do not worry, saying, 'What shall we eat?' or 'What shall we drink?' or 'What shall we wear?' ³²For the pagans run after all these things, and your heavenly Father knows that you need them. ³³But seek first his kingdom and his righteousness, and all these things will be given to you as well." (See also Luke 12:24-31.)

MATTHEW 7:7-11 "Ask and it will be given to you; seek and you will find; knock and the door will be opened to you. ⁸For everyone who asks receives; he who seeks finds; and to him who knocks, the door will be opened. ⁹Which of you, if his son asks for bread, will give him a stone? ¹⁰Or if he asks for a fish, will give him a snake? ¹¹If you, then, though you are evil, know how to give good gifts to your children, how much more will your Father in heaven give good gifts to those who ask him!" (See also Luke 11:9-13.)

MATTHEW 20:1-16 "For the kingdom of heaven is like a landowner who went out early in the morning to hire men to work in his vineyard. ²He agreed to pay them a denarius for the day and sent them into his vineyard. ³About the third hour he went out and saw others standing in the marketplace doing nothing. ⁴He told them, 'You also go and work in my vineyard, and I will pay you whatever is right.'

⁵So they went. He went out again about the sixth hour and the ninth hour and did the same thing. ⁶About the eleventh hour he went out and found still others standing around. He asked them, 'Why have you been standing here all day long doing nothing?' ⁷'Because no one has hired us,' they answered. He said to them, 'You also go and work in my vineyard.' ⁸When evening came, the owner of the vineyard said to his foreman, 'Call the workers and pay them their wages, beginning with the last ones hired and going on to the first.' ⁹The workers who were hired about the eleventh hour came and each received a denarius. ¹⁰So when those came who were hired first, they expected to receive more. But each one of them also received a denarius. ¹¹When they received it, they began to grumble against the landowner. ¹²'These men who were hired last worked only one hour,' they said, 'and you have made them equal to us who have borne the burden of the work and the heat of the day.' ¹³But he answered one of them, 'Friend, I am not being unfair to you. Didn't you agree to work for a denarius? ¹⁴Take your pay and go. I want to give the man who was hired last the same as I gave you. ¹⁵Don't I have the right to do what I want with my own money? Or are you envious because I am generous?' ¹⁶So the last will be first, and the first will be last."

MARK 5:19 Jesus…said [to the man freed of demons], "Go home to your family and tell them how much the Lord has done for you, and how he has had mercy on you."

LUKE 6:35-36 "But love your ene-mies, do good to them, and lend to them without expecting to get anything back. Then your reward will be great, and you will be sons of the Most High, because he is kind to the ungrateful and wicked. ³⁶Be merciful, just as your Father is merciful."

LUKE 8:39 "Return home and tell how much God has done for you." So the man [freed of demons] went away and told all over town how much Jesus had done for him.

God's Nature

JOHN 3:16-17 "For God so loved the world that he gave his one and only Son, that whoever believes in him shall not perish but have eternal life. ¹⁷For God did not send his Son into the world to condemn the world, but to save the world through him."

JOHN 4:24 "God is spirit, and his worshipers must worship in spirit and in truth."

JOHN 6:46 "No one has seen the Father except the one who is from God; only he has seen the Father."

MATTHEW 6:26-33 "Look at the birds of the air; they do not sow or reap or store away in barns, and yet your heavenly Father feeds them. Are you not much more valuable than they? ²⁷Who of you by worrying can add a single hour to his life? ²⁸And why do you worry about clothes? See how the lilies of the field grow. They do not labor or spin. ²⁹Yet I tell you that not even Solomon in all his splendor was dressed like one of these. ³⁰If that is how God clothes the grass of the field, which is here today and tomorrow is thrown into the fire, will he not much more clothe you, O you of little faith? [31]So do not worry, saying, 'What shall we eat?' or 'What shall we drink?' or 'What shall we wear?' [32]For the pagans run after all these things, and your heavenly Father knows that you need them. [33]But seek first his kingdom and his righteousness, and all these things will be given to you as well." (See also Luke 12:24-31.)

MATTHEW 7:7-11 "Ask and it will be given to you; seek and you will find; knock and the door will be opened to you. [8]For everyone who asks receives; he who seeks finds; and to him who knocks, the door will be opened. [9]Which of you, if his son asks for bread, will give him a stone? [10]Or if he asks for a fish, will give him a snake? [11]If you, then, though you are evil, know how to give good gifts to your children, how much more will your Father in heaven give good gifts to those who ask him!" (See also Luke 11:9-13.)

MARK 10:18 "Why do you call me good?" Jesus answered. "No one is good— except God alone."

LUKE 6:35-36 "But love your enemies, do good to them, and lend to them without expecting to get anything back. Then your reward will be great, and you will be sons of the Most High, because he is kind to the ungrateful and wicked. [36]Be merciful, just as your Father is merciful."

God's Sovereignty

JOHN 10:27-30 "My sheep listen to my voice; I know them, and they follow me. [28]I give them eternal life, and they shall never perish; no one can snatch them out of my hand. [29]My Father, who has given them to me, is greater than all; no one can snatch them out of my Father's hand. [30]I and the Father are one."

JOHN 15:16 "You did not choose me, but I chose you and appointed you to go and bear fruit—fruit that will last. Then the Father will give you whatever you ask in my name."

JOHN 19:11 Jesus answered, "You [Pilate] would have no power over me if it were not given to you from above. Therefore the one who handed me over to you is guilty of a greater sin."

MATTHEW 10:27-31 "What I tell you in the dark, speak in the daylight; what is whispered in your ear, proclaim from the roofs. [28]Do not be afraid of those who kill the body but cannot kill the soul. Rather, be afraid of the One who can destroy both soul and body in hell. [29]Are not two sparrows sold for a penny? Yet not one of them will fall to the ground apart from the will of your Father. [30]And even the very hairs of your head are all numbered. [31]So don't be afraid; you are worth more than many sparrows."

MATTHEW 11:25-26 At that time Jesus said, "I praise you, Father, Lord of heaven and earth, because you have hidden these things from the wise and learned, and revealed them to little children. [26]Yes, Father, for this was your good pleasure."

MATTHEW 11:27 "All things have been committed to me by my Father. No one knows the Son except the Father, and no one knows the Father except the Son and those to whom the Son chooses to reveal him."

MATTHEW 20:1-16 "For the kingdom of heaven is like a landowner who went out early in the morning to hire men to work in his vineyard. [2]He agreed to pay them a denarius for the day and sent them into his vineyard. [3]About the third hour he went out and saw others standing in the marketplace doing nothing. [4]He told them, 'You also go and work in my vineyard, and I will pay you whatever is right.' [5]So they went. He went out again about the sixth hour and the ninth hour and did the same thing. [6]About the eleventh hour he went out and found still others standing around. He asked them, 'Why have you been standing here all day long doing nothing?' [7]'Because no one has hired us,' they answered. He said to them, 'You also go and work in my vineyard.' [8]When evening came, the owner of the vineyard said to his foreman, 'Call the workers and pay them their wages, beginning with the last ones hired and going on to the first.' [9]The workers who were hired about the eleventh hour came and each received a denarius. [10]So when those came who were hired first, they expected to receive more. But each one of them also received a denarius. [11]When they received it, they began to grumble against the landowner. [12]'These men who were hired last worked only one hour,' they said, 'and you have made them equal to us who have borne the burden of the work and the heat of the day.' [13]But he answered one of them, 'Friend, I am not being unfair to you. Didn't you agree to work for a denarius? [14]Take your pay and go. I want to give the man who was hired last the same as I gave you. [15]Don't I have the right to do what I want with my own money? Or are you envious because I am generous?' [16]So the last will be first, and the first will be last."

MATTHEW 20:20-23 Then the mother of Zebedee's sons [James and John] came to Jesus with her sons and, kneeling down, asked a favor of him. [21]"What is it you want?" he asked. She said, "Grant that one of these two sons of mine may sit at your right and the other at your left in your kingdom." [22]"You don't know what you are asking," Jesus said to them. "Can you drink the cup I am going to drink?" "We can," they answered. [23]Jesus said to them, "You will indeed drink from my cup, but to sit at my right or left is not for me to grant. These places belong to those for whom they have been prepared by my Father."

MARK 10:35-40 Then James and John, the sons of Zebedee, came to him. "Teacher," they said, "we want you to do for us whatever we ask." [36]"What do you want me to do for you?" he asked. [37]They replied, "Let one of us sit at your right and the other at your left in your glory." [38]"You don't know what you are asking," Jesus said. "Can you drink the cup I drink or be baptized with the baptism I am baptized with?" [39]"We can," they answered. Jesus said to them, "You will drink the cup I drink and be baptized with the baptism I am baptized with, [40]but to sit at my right or left is not for me to grant. These places belong to those for whom they have been prepared."

LUKE 12:22-32 Then Jesus said to his disciples: "Therefore I tell you, do not worry about your life, what you will eat; or about your body, what you will wear.

[23]Life is more than food, and the body more than clothes. [24]Consider the ravens: They do not sow or reap, they have no storeroom or barn; yet God feeds them. And how much more valuable you are than birds! [25]Who of you by worrying can add a single hour to his life? [26]Since you cannot do this very little thing, why do you worry about the rest? [27]Consider how the lilies grow. They do not labor or spin. Yet I tell you, not even Solomon in all his splendor was dressed like one of these. [28]If that is how God clothes the grass of the field, which is here today, and tomorrow is thrown into the fire, how much more will he clothe you, O you of little faith! [29]And do not set your heart on what you will eat or drink; do not worry about it. [30]For the pagan world runs after all such things, and your Father knows that you need them. [31]But seek his kingdom, and these things will be given to you as well. [32]Do not be afraid, little flock, for your Father has been pleased to give you the kingdom."

ACTS 10:11-15 He saw heaven opened and something like a large sheet being let down to earth by its four corners. [12]It contained all kinds of four-footed animals, as well as reptiles of the earth and birds of the air. [13]Then a voice told him, "Get up, Peter. Kill and eat." [14]"Surely not, Lord!" Peter replied. "I have never eaten anything impure or unclean." [15]The voice spoke to him a second time, "Do not call anything impure that God has made clean."

2 CORINTHIANS 12:7-9 To keep me [Paul] from becoming conceited because of these surpassingly great revela-tions, there was given me a thorn in my flesh, a messenger of Satan, to torment me. [8]Three times I pleaded with the Lord to take it away from me. [9]But he said to me, "My grace is sufficient for you, for my power is made perfect in weakness." Therefore I will boast all the more gladly about my weaknesses, so that Christ's power may rest on me.

REVELATION 4:1-2 After this I [John] looked, and there before me was a door standing open in heaven. And the voice I had first heard speaking to me like a trumpet said, "Come up here, and I will show you what must take place after this." [2]At once I was in the Spirit, and there before me was a throne in heaven with someone sitting on it.

God's Spirit

JOHN 4:21-24 Jesus declared, "Be-lieve me, woman, a time is coming when you will worship the Father neither on this mountain nor in Jerusalem. [22]You Samaritans worship what you do not know; we worship what we do know, for salvation is from the Jews. [23]Yet a time is coming and has now come when the true worshipers will worship the Father in spirit and truth, for they are the kind of worshipers the Father seeks. [24]God is spirit, and his worshipers must worship in spirit and in truth."

MATTHEW 10:19-20 "But when they arrest you, do not worry about what to say or how to say it. At that time you will be given what to say, [20]for it will not be you speaking, but the Spirit of your Father speaking through you."

MATTHEW 12:25-32 Jesus knew their [the Pharisees'] thoughts and said to them, "Every kingdom divided against itself will be ruined, and every city or household divided against itself will not stand. ²⁶If Satan drives out Satan, he is divided against himself. How then can his kingdom stand? ²⁷And if I drive out demons by Beelzebub, by whom do your people drive them out? So then, they will be your judges. ²⁸But if I drive out demons by the Spirit of God, then the kingdom of God has come upon you. ²⁹Or again, how can anyone enter a strong man's house and carry off his possessions unless he first ties up the strong man? Then he can rob his house. ³⁰He who is not with me is against me, and he who does not gather with me scatters. ³¹And so I tell you, every sin and blasphemy will be forgiven men, but the blasphemy against the Spirit will not be forgiven. ³²Anyone who speaks a word against the Son of Man will be forgiven, but anyone who speaks against the Holy Spirit will not be forgiven, either in this age or in the age to come."

LUKE 4:18-19 "The Spirit of the Lord is on me, because he has anointed me to preach good news to the poor. He has sent me to proclaim freedom for the prisoners and recovery of sight for the blind, to release the oppressed, ¹⁹to proclaim the year of the Lord's favor."

God's Will

JOHN 6:37-40 "All that the Father gives me will come to me, and whoever comes to me I will never drive away. ³⁸For I have come down from heaven not to do my will but to do the will of him who sent me. ³⁹And this is the will of him who sent me, that I shall lose none of all that he has given me, but raise them up at the last day. ⁴⁰For my Father's will is that everyone who looks to the Son and believes in him shall have eternal life, and I will raise him up at the last day."

JOHN 6:43 "Stop grumbling among yourselves," Jesus answered. ⁴⁴"No one can come to me unless the Father who sent me draws him, and I will raise him up at the last day."

JOHN 6:65 He went on to say, "This is why I told you that no one can come to me unless the Father has enabled him."

MATTHEW 6:9-10 "This, then, is how you should pray: 'Our Father in heaven, hallowed be your name, ¹⁰your kingdom come, your will be done on earth as it is in heaven.'"

MATTHEW 10:29-31 "Are not two sparrows sold for a penny? Yet not one of them will fall to the ground apart from the will of your Father. ³⁰And even the very hairs of your head are all numbered. ³¹So don't be afraid; you are worth more than many sparrows."

MATTHEW 12:49-50 Pointing to his disciples, he said, "Here are my mother and my brothers. ⁵⁰For whoever does the will of my Father in heaven is my brother and sister and mother."

MATTHEW 18:10, 12-14 "See that you do not look down on one of these little ones. For I tell you that their angels in heaven always see the face of my Father in heaven. ¹²What do you think? If a man owns a hundred sheep, and one of them wanders away, will he not leave the ninety-nine on the hills and go to look for the one that wandered off? [13]And if he finds it, I tell you the truth, he is happier about that one sheep than about the ninety-nine that did not wander off. [14]In the same way your Father in heaven is not willing that any of these little ones should be lost."

MATTHEW 20:20-23 Then the mother of Zebedee's sons [James and John] came to Jesus with her sons and, kneeling down, asked a favor of him. [21]"What is it you want?" he asked. She said, "Grant that one of these two sons of mine may sit at your right and the other at your left in your kingdom." [22]"You don't know what you are asking," Jesus said to them. "Can you drink the cup I am going to drink?" "We can," they answered. [23]Jesus said to them, "You will indeed drink from my cup, but to sit at my right or left is not for me to grant. These places belong to those for whom they have been prepared by my Father."

MATTHEW 26:39 Going a little farther, he fell with his face to the ground and prayed, "My Father, if it is possible, may this cup be taken from me. Yet not as I will, but as you will."

MATTHEW 26:42-46 He went away a second time and prayed, "My Father, if it is not possible for this cup to be taken away unless I drink it, may your will be done." [43]When he came back, he again found them sleeping, because their eyes were heavy. [44]So he left them and went away once more and prayed the third time, saying the same thing. [45]Then he returned to the disciples and said to them, "Are you still sleeping and resting?

Look, the hour is near, and the Son of Man is betrayed into the hands of sinners. [46]Rise, let us go! Here comes my betrayer!" (See also Mark 14:39-42.)

MARK 3:33-35 "Who are my mother and my brothers?" he [Jesus] asked. [34]Then he looked at those seated in a circle around him and said, "Here are my mother and my brothers! [35]Whoever does God's will is my brother and sister and mother."

MARK 10:35-40 Then James and John, the sons of Zebedee, came to him. "Teacher," they said, "we want you to do for us whatever we ask." [36]"What do you want me to do for you?" he asked. [37]They replied, "Let one of us sit at your right and the other at your left in your glory." [38]"You don't know what you are asking," Jesus said. "Can you drink the cup I drink or be baptized with the baptism I am baptized with?" [39]"We can," they answered. Jesus said to them, "You will drink the cup I drink and be baptized with the baptism I am baptized with, [40]but to sit at my right or left is not for me to grant. These places belong to those for whom they have been prepared."

MARK 14:36 "*Abba,* Father," he said, "everything is possible for you. Take this cup from me. Yet not what I will, but what you will."

LUKE 22:42 "Father, if you are willing, take this cup from me; yet not my will, but yours be done."

ACTS 23:11 The following night the Lord stood near Paul and said, "Take courage! As you have testified about me in Jerusalem, so you must also testify in Rome."

God's Word

JOHN 12:47-50 "As for the person who hears my words but does not keep them, I do not judge him. For I did not come to judge the world, but to save it. [48]There is a judge for the one who rejects me and does not accept my words; that very word which I spoke will condemn him at the last day. [49]For I did not speak of my own accord, but the Father who sent me commanded me what to say and how to say it. [50]I know that his command leads to eternal life. So whatever I say is just what the Father has told me to say."

JOHN 14:10-11 "Don't you believe that I am in the Father, and that the Father is in me? The words I say to you are not just my own. Rather, it is the Father, living in me, who is doing his work. [11]Believe me when I say that I am in the Father and the Father is in me; or at least believe on the evidence of the miracles themselves."

JOHN 14:23-26 Jesus replied, "If anyone loves me, he will obey my teaching. My Father will love him, and we will come to him and make our home with him. [24]He who does not love me will not obey my teaching. These words you hear are not my own; they belong to the Father who sent me. [25]All this I have spoken while still with you. [26]But the Counselor, the Holy Spirit, whom the Father will send in my name, will teach you all things and will remind you of everything I have said to you."

JOHN 15:9-11 "As the Father has loved me, so have I loved you. Now remain in my love. [10]If you obey my commands, you will remain in my love, just as I have obeyed my Father's commands and remain in his love. [11]I have told you this so that my joy may be in you and that your joy may be complete."

JOHN 17:13-17 "I am coming to you [God the Father] now, but I say these things while I am still in the world, so that they may have the full measure of my joy within them. [14]I have given them your word and the world has hated them, for they are not of the world any more than I am of the world. [15]My prayer is not that you take them out of the world but that you protect them from the evil one. [16]They are not of the world, even as I am not of it. [17]Sanctify them by the truth; your word is truth."

MATTHEW 4:4 Jesus answered, "It is written: 'Man does not live on bread alone, but on every word that comes from the mouth of God.'" (See also Luke 4:4.)

MATTHEW 4:7 Jesus answered him [the devil], "It is also written: 'Do not put the Lord your God to the test.'" (See also Luke 4:12.)

MATTHEW 4:10 Jesus said to him, "Away from me, Satan! For it is written: 'Worship the Lord your God, and serve him only.'" (See also Luke 4:8.)

MARK 4:13-20 Then Jesus said to them [the disciples], "Don't you understand this parable? How then will you understand any parable? [14]The farmer sows the word. [15]Some people are like seed along the path, where the word is sown. As soon as they hear it, Satan comes and takes away the word that was sown in them. [16]Others, like seed sown on rocky places, hear the word and at once receive it with joy. [17]But since they have no root, they last only a short time. When trouble or persecution comes because of the word, they quickly fall away. [18]Still others, like seed sown among thorns, hear the word; [19]but the worries of this life, the deceitfulness of wealth and the desires for other things come in and choke the word, making it unfruitful. [20]Others, like seed sown on good soil, hear the word, accept it, and produce a crop—thirty, sixty or even a hundred times what was sown."

MARK 7:6-13 He replied, "Isaiah was right when he prophesied about you hypocrites; as it is written: 'These people honor me with their lips, but their hearts are far from me. [7]They worship me in vain; their teachings are but rules taught by men.' [8]You have let go of the commands of God and are holding on to the traditions of men." [9]And he said to them: "You have a fine way of setting aside the commands of God in order to observe your own traditions! [10]For Moses said, 'Honor your father and your mother,' and, 'Anyone who curses his father or mother must be put to death.' [11]But you say that if a man says to his father or mother: 'Whatever help you might otherwise have received from me is Corban' (that is, a gift devoted to God), [12]then you no longer let him do anything for his father or mother. [13]Thus you nullify the word of God by your tradition that you have handed down. And you do many things like that."

LUKE 8:21 He replied, "My mother and brothers are those who hear God's word and put it into practice."

LUKE 11:28 He replied, "Blessed rather are those who hear the word of God and obey it."

God's Works

JOHN 6:28-29 Then they asked him, "What must we do to do the works God requires?" [29]Jesus answered, "The work of God is this: to believe in the one he has sent."

JOHN 9:3-7 "Neither this man nor his parents sinned," said Jesus, "but this [being born blind] happened so that the work of God might be displayed in his life. [4]As long as it is day, we must do the work of him who sent me. Night is coming, when no one can work. [5]While I am in the world, I am the light of the world." [6]Having said this, he spit on the ground, made some mud with the saliva, and put it on the man's eyes. [7]"Go," he told him, "wash in the Pool of Siloam" (this word means Sent). So the man went and washed, and came home seeing.

JOHN 10:32 …Jesus said to them, "I have shown you many great miracles from the Father. For which of these do you stone me?"

JOHN 10:37-38 "Do not believe me unless I do what my Father does. [38]But if I do it, even though you do not believe me, believe the miracles, that you may know and understand that the Father is in me, and I in the Father."

JOHN 14:10-11 "Don't you believe that I am in the Father, and that the Father is in me? The words I say to you are not just my own. Rather, it is the Father, living in me, who is doing his work.

[11]Believe me when I say that I am in the Father and the Father is in me; or at least believe on the evidence of the miracles themselves."

MATTHEW 19:26 Jesus looked at them and said, "With man this [being saved] is impossible, but with God all things are possible."

Loving God, Loving Christ
(See also "Loving Christ," p. 280.)

MARK 12:28-30 One of the teachers of the law came and heard them [Jesus and Sadducees] debating. Noticing that Jesus had given them a good answer, he asked him, "Of all the commandments, which is the most important?" [29]"The most important one," answered Jesus, "is this: 'Hear, O Israel, the Lord our God, the Lord is one. [30]Love the Lord your God with all your heart and with all your soul and with all your mind and with all your strength.' "

LUKE 7:40-48 Jesus answered him, "Simon, I have something to tell you." "Tell me, teacher," he said. [41]"Two men owed money to a certain moneylender. One owed him five hundred denarii, and the other fifty. [42]Neither of them had the money to pay him back, so he canceled the debts of both. Now which of them will love him more?" [43]Simon replied, "I suppose the one who had the bigger debt canceled." "You have judged correctly," Jesus said. [44]Then he turned toward the woman and said to Simon, "Do you see this woman? I came into your house. You did not give me any water for my feet, but she wet my feet with her tears and wiped

them with her hair. [45]You did not give me a kiss, but this woman, from the time I entered, has not stopped kissing my feet. [46]You did not put oil on my head, but she has poured perfume on my feet. [47]Therefore, I tell you, her many sins have been forgiven—for she loved much. But he who has been forgiven little loves little." [48]Then Jesus said to her, "Your sins are forgiven."

Reverence for God

JOHN 4:23-24 "Yet a time is coming and has now come when the true worshipers will worship the Father in spirit and truth, for they are the kind of worshipers the Father seeks. [24]God is spirit, and his worshipers must worship in spirit and in truth."

JOHN 5:22-23 "Moreover, the Father judges no one, but has entrusted all judgment to the Son, [23]that all may honor the Son just as they honor the Father. He who does not honor the Son does not honor the Father, who sent him."

MATTHEW 23:6-12 "[T]hey love the place of honor at banquets and the most important seats in the synagogues; [7]they love to be greeted in the marketplaces and to have men call them 'Rabbi.' [8]But you are not to be called 'Rabbi,' for you have only one Master and you are all brothers. [9]And do not call anyone on earth 'father,' for you have one Father, and he is in heaven. [10]Nor are you to be called 'teacher,' for you have one Teacher, the Christ. [11]The greatest among you will be your servant. [12]For whoever exalts himself will be humbled, and whoever humbles himself will be exalted."

MARK 7:6-8 He replied, "Isaiah was right when he prophesied about you hypocrites; as it is written: 'These people honor me with their lips, but their hearts are far from me. [7]They worship me in vain; their teachings are but rules taught by men.' [8]You have let go of the commands of God and are holding on to the traditions of men." [The opposite of true reverence for God.]

will be humbled; and whoever humbles himself will be exalted."

Mark 7:6-8 He replied, "Isaiah was right when he prophesied about you hypocrites; as it is written: 'These people honor me with their lips, but their hearts are far from me. They worship me in vain; their teachings are but rules taught by men.' You have let go of the commands of God and are holding on to the traditions of men'." [The opposite of true reverence for God.]

though born with a heart, mind, body, and soul—was born spiritually dead (1 Corinthians 15:22; Ephesians 2:1–5). In John 3:3–8, Jesus tells Nicodemus that the only way a person can enter the kingdom of God is by being born again, or born from above. Every person must receive a spiritual birth, and in John 3:6 Jesus declares that this birth must come from the Holy Spirit.

3

THE GREATEST WORDS
EVER SPOKEN ABOUT
THE HOLY SPIRIT

What Christ Tells Us About the Third Person of the Trinity

If you could have any new car in the world, what would you choose? Now, imagine there's a knock on your front door. You go to the door and find a smiling automobile dealer pointing to that particular car, now parked in your driveway with a big ribbon tied around it. He hands you the keys and says it's yours, free and clear. As you scream with excitement, the auto dealer mentions there is good news and bad news. The good news is that this car has a brand-new kind of engine that will power it faster than any car on the planet, and it can travel more than 100,000 miles on a single tank of its unique and remarkable fuel. The bad news is, the required fuel is a refined plutonium pellet that sells for a little over $25 million, and your car was delivered without the pellet. As wonderful as the car and its nuclear-powered engine might be, it's worthless to you. Without the fuel it will never leave your driveway.

The greatest gift ever given to you and me is a gift from God: the atoning sacrifice of His only begotten Son. This gift was free to us, yet it cost our Heavenly Father and the Lord Jesus Christ *everything*. As you'll discover in chapter 4 of this book, the only requirement to receive the greatest gift is to be born a second time, a birth that Jesus described as a spiritual birth. The Bible teaches that when the first man and woman sinned, the spirit they had been endowed with from God died. From that point on, all of humanity—

though born with a heart, mind, body, and soul—was born spiritually dead (1 Corinthians 15:22; Ephesians 2:1-5). In John 3:3-8, Jesus tells Nicodemus that the only way a person can enter the kingdom of God is by being born again, or born from above. Every person must receive a spiritual birth, and in John 3:6 Jesus declares that this birth must come from the Holy Spirit.

But our spiritual birth is just the beginning of our new relationship with God. After being born again, we need to grow spiritually. And our spiritual growth is dependent on the priceless fuel that God gives us to empower our spirit to follow Christ in every aspect of our behavior. Amazingly, this priceless fuel is the outworking of the third Person of the Trinity, the Holy Spirit. Without His ministry to us and His presence within us, we would be powerless to become what God wants us to be, to live the way He wants us to live, to achieve what He wants us to achieve, and to influence others the way He wants us to influence them.

Jesus revealed in John 14:17 that although the Holy Spirit had been present with the disciples, there would be a time when He would actually be "in" them. The Holy Spirit came later, on the day of Pentecost, to indwell the believers (see Acts 2:1-17).

Although we can live what the world would consider a perfectly normal (although self-centered) life without the empowering presence of the Holy Spirit, we can *not* produce any eternal or truly spiritual fruit unless He dwells within us. Equally important, we cannot be the person God desires us to be. On the other hand, when the Holy Spirit indwells us and we yield our will to His guidance, He will produce all the spiritual fruit that God desires to be produced within us and through us.

As you will see in the statements of Jesus quoted in this chapter, during the Last Supper, Jesus identified ten roles the Holy Spirit would perform in His ministry to believers (see John 14-16). Jesus said the Holy Spirit will

- teach us all things and guide us into all truth,
- cause us to remember everything Christ said to us,
- be a testifying witness of Christ (to us and through us),
- be our Helper and Comforter,
- convict unbelievers of their sin,
- reveal the righteousness of Christ,
- reveal the condemning judgment of God,

- reveal future events to believers,
- empower believers with spiritual power,
- enable believers to be powerful witnesses for Christ.

During His ministry on earth, Jesus could be in only one place at one time. The Holy Spirit, on the other hand, can be in all places at the same time. As the third Person of the Trinity, He is coequal and coeternal with God the Father and God the Son.

In John 14:17, Jesus tells the disciples that on a particular day the Holy Spirit, who has been "with you," will be "*in*" you." Jesus said, "On that day you will realize that I am in my Father, and you are in me, and I am in you" (John 14:20). In other words, beginning at Pentecost, God the Father and God the Son would indwell the spirit of believers by the Holy Spirit, making the spirits of the believers alive and entering into a union with their spirit. The Holy Spirit comes to live within the spirit of every true, born-again child of God.

Walking in the Holy Spirit

Years later the apostle Paul recorded aspects of the Holy Spirit's ministry to the church as a whole and to individual believers in particular (see Romans 12 and 1 Corinthians 12). In Galatians 5:22-23, Paul revealed the fruit that the Holy Spirit produces in the life of each believer, namely, love, joy, peace, patience, kindness, goodness, faithfulness, gentleness, and self-control. It is impossible for our human nature to produce any of these. But it is natural for the Holy Spirit to produce all of these in the life of a believer, because each one is inherent in Him. And yet a daily battle rages between the natural outworking of our own nature (see Galatians 5:19-21) and our spirit, which longs to yield to the Holy Spirit. In a single sentence Paul revealed the only way we can overcome the power of our own nature: "So I say, live by the Spirit, and you will not gratify the desires of the sinful nature" (Galatians 5:16).

Unfortunately, many believers have focused so intently on the gifts of the Spirit that they have lost sight of the fruit of the Spirit and the Holy Spirit's other vital ministries. The words of Christ form the perfect foundation upon which our beliefs must rest. Interestingly, the first role or ministry of the Holy Spirit that the Lord revealed was that "He will teach you all things, and bring to your remembrance all things that I have said to you" (John 14:26, NKJV).

The Holy Spirit and His Ministry

JOHN 3:5-8 Jesus answered, "I tell you the truth, no one can enter the kingdom of God unless he is born of water and the Spirit. [6]Flesh gives birth to flesh, but the Spirit gives birth to spirit. [7]You should not be surprised at my saying, 'You must be born again.' [8]The wind blows wherever it pleases. You hear its sound, but you cannot tell where it comes from or where it is going. So it is with everyone born of the Spirit."

JOHN 14:15-16 "If you love me, you will obey what I command. [16]And I will ask the Father, and he will give you another Counselor to be with you forever."

JOHN 14:26 "But the Counselor, the Holy Spirit, whom the Father will send in my name, will teach you all things and will remind you of everything I have said to you."

JOHN 15:26 "When the Counselor comes, whom I will send to you from the Father, the Spirit of truth who goes out from the Father, he will testify about me. [27]And you also must testify, for you have been with me from the beginning."

JOHN 16:6-11 "Because I have said these things, you are filled with grief. [7]But I tell you the truth: It is for your good that I am going away. Unless I go away, the Counselor will not come to you; but if I go, I will send him to you. [8]When he comes, he will convict the world of guilt in regard to sin and righteousness and judgment: [9]in regard to sin, because men do not believe in me; [10]in regard to righteousness, because I am going to the Father, where you can see me no longer; [11]and in regard to judgment, because the prince of this world now stands condemned."

JOHN 16:12-15 "I have much more to say to you, more than you can now bear. [13]But when he, the Spirit of truth, comes, he will guide you into all truth. He will not speak on his own; he will speak only what he hears, and he will tell you what is yet to come. [14]He will bring glory to me by taking from what is mine and making it known to you. [15]All that belongs to the Father is mine. That is why I said the Spirit will take from what is mine and make it known to you."

JOHN 16:20, 22-23 "I tell you the truth, you will weep and mourn while the world rejoices. You will grieve, but your grief will turn to joy. [22]So with you: Now is your time of grief, but I will see you again and you will rejoice, and no one will take away your joy. [23]In that day you will no longer ask me anything. I tell you the truth, my Father will give you whatever you ask in my name."

MATTHEW 10:19-20 "But when they arrest you, do not worry about what to say or how to say it. At that time you will be given what to say, [20]for it will not be you speaking, but the Spirit of your Father speaking through you."

MATTHEW 28:18-20 Then Jesus came to them [the eleven disciples] and said, "All authority in heaven and on earth has been given to me. [19]Therefore go and make disciples of all nations, baptizing them in the name of the Father and of the Son and of the Holy Spirit, [20]and teaching them to obey everything I have commanded you. And surely I am with you always, to the very end of the age."

MARK 13:11 "Whenever you are arrested and brought to trial, do not worry beforehand about what to say. Just say whatever is given you at the time, for it is not you speaking, but the Holy Spirit."

LUKE 4:18-19 "The Spirit of the Lord is on me, because he has anointed me to preach good news to the poor. He has sent me to proclaim freedom for the prisoners and recovery of sight for the blind, to release the oppressed, 19to proclaim the year of the Lord's favor."

LUKE 11:5-13 Then he said to them, "Suppose one of you has a friend, and he goes to him at midnight and says, 'Friend, lend me three loaves of bread, 6because a friend of mine on a journey has come to me, and I have nothing to set before him.' 7Then the one inside answers, 'Don't bother me. The door is already locked, and my children are with me in bed. I can't get up and give you anything.' 8I tell you, though he will not get up and give him the bread because he is his friend, yet because of the man's boldness he will get up and give him as much as he needs. 9So I say to you: Ask and it will be given to you; seek and you will find; knock and the door will be opened to you. 10For everyone who asks receives; he who seeks finds; and to him who knocks, the door will be opened. 11Which of you fathers, if your son asks for a fish, will give him a snake instead? 12Or if he asks for an egg, will give him a scorpion? 13If you then, though you are evil, know how to give good gifts to your children, how much more will your Father in heaven give the Holy Spirit to those who ask him!"

LUKE 12:8-12 "I tell you, whoever acknowledges me before men, the Son of Man will also acknowledge him before the angels of God. 9But he who disowns me before men will be disowned before the angels of God. 10And everyone who speaks a word against the Son of Man will be forgiven, but anyone who blasphemes against the Holy Spirit will not be forgiven. 11When you are brought before synagogues, rulers and authorities, do not worry about how you will defend yourselves or what you will say, 12for the Holy Spirit will teach you at that time what you should say."

ACTS 1:4-5 On one occasion, while he was eating with them [the apostles], he gave them this command: "Do not leave Jerusalem, but wait for the gift my Father promised, which you have heard me speak about. 5For John baptized with water, but in a few days you will be baptized with the Holy Spirit." (See also Acts 11:16.)

ACTS 1:8 "But you will receive power when the Holy Spirit comes on you; and you will be my witnesses in Jerusalem, and in all Judea and Samaria, and to the ends of the earth."

4

THE GREATEST WORDS
EVER SPOKEN
ABOUT ETERNITY

Life After Death, Heaven and Hell, Forgiveness,
and Other Crucial Eternal Matters

In this chapter we'll look at what Jesus said about the most important issues any of us will ever face. When Jesus talked about eternity, He revealed the absolutes that will determine your destiny and the destiny of your loved ones. Will you spend eternity in the incomprehensible joy of God's presence or the devastating emptiness of His absence? No matter what your religious beliefs are, this is the one matter about which you don't want to be surprised.

In the gospel of Matthew, Jesus gives us a partial picture of what such a surprise will look like for those who don't know Him in the way He wants to be known. In Matthew 7:21-23, He states, "Not everyone who says to Me, 'Lord, Lord,' shall enter the kingdom of heaven, but he who does the will of My Father in heaven. Many will say to Me in that day, 'Lord, Lord, have we not prophesied in Your name, cast out demons in Your name, and done many wonders in Your name?' And then I will declare to them, 'I never knew you; depart from Me, you who practice lawlessness!'" (NKJV). What a terrible shock for those who seem to be followers of Christ. Can you imagine the despair a person will experience upon hearing Jesus say these words? There will be no second chances. That will be *it*...for eternity!

That's the bad news. The good news is, if you know what Jesus said about eternal issues and act upon His words, you needn't worry about experiencing such a disaster. In fact, Jesus goes on to say, "Therefore whoever hears these sayings of Mine, and does them, I will liken him to a wise man who built his house on the rock: and the rain descended, the floods came, and the winds blew and beat on that house; and it did not fall, for it was founded on the rock" (Matthew 7:24-25, NKJV). It doesn't matter what everyone else says or thinks; the only thing that matters is what Jesus said.

In today's culture most people live as if their behavior will have no significant consequences. Even though the majority of us acknowledge that God exists, most of us live as if He doesn't. Some people, of course, believe that life simply ends at the grave. But most believe in a Santa Claus–type God who will never hold them accountable. They grab for everything they can get as fast as they can get it, regardless of the long-term consequences. They focus their lives on their own needs and desires.

Believing there are no consequences for what people say or do may seem like a utopian existence to some. In his song "Imagine," John Lennon described what he thought would be a perfect world—one with no religion, no heaven, and no hell. Although such hopes allowed him to do whatever he wanted during his brief life, that philosophy cannot provide true joy on earth or an eternity spent with God in the afterlife.

The Dangerous Myth of No Consequences

Those who live as if there are no eternal consequences will, in fact, face four devastating consequences.

First, they will go through life experiencing only superficial happiness—happiness that is little more than skin deep. They will always be chasing the next new thing, whether it's more money, a firmer, sexier body, or a new relationship that promises more excitement than the one they're in now. No matter what they have, they'll never be content. I've worked with some of the world's most beautiful models and actresses. The truth is, not one of them was satisfied with her looks. I've worked with some of America's wealthiest businesspeople and have seen them robbed of happiness because of personal failures with their families or their never-ending greed for money or power.

I've also known scores of people who have yet to achieve their dreams and mistakenly think that when they get a new house, new car, new job, new spouse, or fatter bank account, they'll finally be happy. In each case unless they change their ways, they'll reach the end of their lives unhappy and unfulfilled.

Second, they will find it easy to blame God when tragedy strikes—whether an accident or a terminal illness or a catastrophic event such as September 11. They instantly think, *If God does exist, how could He let such a terrible thing happen?* They have never spent significant time investigating the life and words of Christ, which He makes clear will be the sole basis upon which our eternal destiny rests.

Third, they will never personally experience intimate knowledge of the most loving and caring Being in the universe. When you look at what God did to save us, you begin to fathom the depth of His love. Not one of us would willingly sacrifice the life of our child to save the life of someone who hates us or whose values and beliefs are totally opposed to our own. But that is exactly what God did when He sent Jesus to the cross. And it's but a tiny glimpse of the unfathomable love that God has for each of us. Those who never know Him or His love will miss out on the greatest relationship they could ever experience.

Fourth, the greatest tragedy is that those who do not follow Jesus' words will spend eternity separated from God and His love. According to Jesus, they will spend eternity in misery. The best news of all is that Jesus wants to give each of us the gift of eternal life, perhaps even more than we want to receive it. That will become obvious as you study His words in this chapter. You'll read everything that Jesus said about the spiritual birth that is necessary to enter the kingdom of God. You'll read the greatest words ever spoken about eternal life and salvation, the resurrection of the dead, heaven, and the forgiveness of even one's most devastating failures and wrongdoings. Throughout this chapter you will find the words of Jesus on the subjects of angels, demons, deliverance, and Satan and his nature.

My hope and prayer is that as you read the powerful words of our Savior on these eternal issues, your eyes will be opened as never before. I believe your heart will be melted by the light and the righteousness and the love of Christ.

Angels

JOHN 1:51 He then added, "I tell you the truth, you shall see heaven open, and the angels of God ascending and descending on the Son of Man."

MATTHEW 13:37-43 He answered, "The one who sowed the good seed is the Son of Man. ³⁸The field is the world, and the good seed stands for the sons of the kingdom. The weeds are the sons of the evil one, ³⁹and the enemy who sows them is the devil. The harvest is the end of the age, and the harvesters are angels. ⁴⁰As the weeds are pulled up and burned in the fire, so it will be at the end of the age. ⁴¹The Son of Man will send out his angels, and they will weed out of his kingdom everything that causes sin and all who do evil. ⁴²They will throw them into the fiery furnace, where there will be weeping and gnashing of teeth. ⁴³Then the righteous will shine like the sun in the kingdom of their Father. He who has ears, let him hear."

MATTHEW 16:24-27 Then Jesus said to his disciples, "If anyone would come after me, he must deny himself and take up his cross and follow me. ²⁵For whoever wants to save his life will lose it, but whoever loses his life for me will find it. ²⁶What good will it be for a man if he gains the whole world, yet forfeits his soul? Or what can a man give in exchange for his soul? ²⁷For the Son of Man is going to come in his Father's glory with his angels, and then he will reward each person according to what he has done."

MATTHEW 18:10 "See that you do not look down on one of these little ones. For I tell you that their angels in heaven always see the face of my Father in heaven."

MATTHEW 22:30 "At the resurrection people will neither marry nor be given in marriage; they will be like the angels in heaven."

MATTHEW 24:31 "And he will send his angels with a loud trumpet call, and they will gather his elect from the four winds, from one end of the heavens to the other."

MATTHEW 25:31-32 "When the Son of Man comes in his glory, and all the angels with him, he will sit on his throne in heavenly glory. ³²All the nations will be gathered before him, and he will separate the people one from another as a shepherd separates the sheep from the goats."

MATTHEW 26:52-54 "Put your sword back in its place," Jesus said to him [Peter], "for all who draw the sword will die by the sword. ⁵³Do you think I cannot call on my Father, and he will at once put at my disposal more than twelve legions of angels? ⁵⁴But how then would the Scriptures be fulfilled that say it must happen in this way?"

MARK 8:38 "If anyone is ashamed of me and my words in this adulterous and sinful generation, the Son of Man will be ashamed of him when he comes in his Father's glory with the holy angels."

MARK 12:25 "When the dead rise, they will neither marry nor be given in marriage; they will be like the angels in heaven."

MARK 13:24-27 "But in those days, following that distress, 'the sun will be darkened, and the moon will not give its light; ²⁵the stars will fall from the sky, and the heavenly bodies will be shaken.' [26]At that time men will see the Son of Man coming in clouds with great power and glory. [27]And he will send his angels and gather his elect from the four winds, from the ends of the earth to the ends of the heavens."

LUKE 15:10 "In the same way, I tell you, there is rejoicing in the presence of the angels of God over one sinner who repents."

LUKE 20:35-36 "But those who are considered worthy of taking part in that age and in the resurrection from the dead will neither marry nor be given in marriage, [36]and they can no longer die; for they are like the angels. They are God's children, since they are children of the resurrection."

Atonement

JOHN 3:14-17 "Just as Moses lifted up the snake in the desert, so the Son of Man must be lifted up, [15]that everyone who believes in him may have eternal life. [16]For God so loved the world that he gave his one and only Son, that whoever believes in him shall not perish but have eternal life. [17]For God did not send his Son into the world to condemn the world, but to save the world through him."

MATTHEW 20:28 "...the Son of Man did not come to be served, but to serve, and to give his life as a ransom for many." (See also Mark 10:45.)

LUKE 9:62 Jesus replied, "No one who puts his hand to the plow and looks back is fit for service in the kingdom of God."

LUKE 22:19-20 And he took bread, gave thanks and broke it, and gave it to them [the apostles], saying, "This is my body given for you; do this in remembrance of me." [20]In the same way, after the supper he took the cup, saying, "This cup is the new covenant in my blood, which is poured out for you."

Death

JOHN 3:14-16 "Just as Moses lifted up the snake in the desert, so the Son of Man must be lifted up, [15]that everyone who believes in him may have eternal life. [16]For God so loved the world that he gave his one and only Son, that whoever believes in him shall not perish but have eternal life."

JOHN 5:24-25 "I tell you the truth, whoever hears my word and believes him who sent me has eternal life and will not be condemned; he has crossed over from death to life. [25]I tell you the truth, a time is coming and has now come when the dead will hear the voice of the Son of God and those who hear will live."

JOHN 6:47-51 "I tell you the truth, he who believes has everlasting life. [48]I am the bread of life. [49]Your forefathers ate the manna in the desert, yet they died. [50]But here is the bread that comes down from heaven, which a man may eat and not die. [51]I am the living bread that came down from heaven. If anyone eats of this bread, he will live forever. This bread is my flesh, which I will give for the life of the world."

JOHN 8:51 "I tell you the truth, if anyone keeps my word, he will never see death."

JOHN 11:25-26 Jesus said to her [Martha], "I am the resurrection and the life. He who believes in me will live, even though he dies; [26]and whoever lives and believes in me will never die. Do you believe this?"

MATTHEW 7:13-14 "Enter through the narrow gate. For wide is the gate and broad is the road that leads to destruction, and many enter through it. [14]But small is the gate and narrow the road that leads to life, and only a few find it."

MATTHEW 10:28 "Do not be afraid of those who kill the body but cannot kill the soul. Rather, be afraid of the One who can destroy both soul and body in hell."

MATTHEW 25:29-30 "For everyone who has will be given more, and he will have an abundance. Whoever does not have, even what he has will be taken from him. [30]And throw that worthless servant outside, into the darkness, where there will be weeping and gnashing of teeth."

MATTHEW 25:41 "Then he will say to those on his left, 'Depart from me, you who are cursed, into the eternal fire prepared for the devil and his angels.'"

MATTHEW 25:45-46 "He will reply, 'I tell you the truth, whatever you did not do for one of the least of these, you did not do for me.' [46]Then they will go away to eternal punishment, but the righteous to eternal life."

MARK 9:42-43, 45, 47-48 "And if anyone causes one of these little ones who believe in me to sin, it would be better for him to be thrown into the sea with a large millstone tied around his neck. [43]If your hand causes you to sin, cut it off. It is better for you to enter life maimed than with two hands to go into hell, where the fire never goes out. [45]And if your foot causes you to sin, cut it off. It is better for you to enter life crippled than to have two feet and be thrown into hell. [47]And if your eye causes you to sin, pluck it out. It is better for you to enter the kingdom of God with one eye than to have two eyes and be thrown into hell, [48]where 'their worm does not die, and the fire is not quenched.'"

LUKE 12:16-21 And he told them this parable: "The ground of a certain rich man produced a good crop. [17]He thought to himself, 'What shall I do? I have no place to store my crops.' [18]Then he said, 'This is what I'll do. I will tear down my barns and build bigger ones, and there I will store all my grain and my goods. [19]And I'll say to myself, "You have plenty of good things laid up for many years. Take life easy; eat, drink and be merry."' [20]But God said to him, 'You fool! This very night your life will be demanded from you. Then who will get what you have prepared for yourself?' [21]This is how it will be with anyone who stores up things for himself but is not rich toward God."

LUKE 13:2-5 Jesus answered, "Do you think that these Galileans were worse sinners than all the other Galileans because they suffered this way? [3]I tell you, no! But unless you repent, you too will all perish. [4]Or those eighteen who died when the tower in Siloam fell on them—do you think they were more guilty than all the others living in Jerusalem? [5]I tell you, no! But unless you repent, you too will all perish."

LUKE 16:19-31 "There was a rich man who was dressed in purple and fine linen and lived in luxury every day. ²⁰At his gate was laid a beggar named Lazarus, covered with sores ²¹and longing to eat what fell from the rich man's table. Even the dogs came and licked his sores. ²²The time came when the beggar died and the angels carried him to Abraham's side. The rich man also died and was buried. ²³In hell, where he was in torment, he looked up and saw Abraham far away, with Lazarus by his side. ²⁴So he called to him, 'Father Abraham, have pity on me and send Lazarus to dip the tip of his finger in water and cool my tongue, because I am in agony in this fire.' ²⁵But Abraham replied, 'Son, remember that in your lifetime you received your good things, while Lazarus received bad things, but now he is comforted here and you are in agony. ²⁶And besides all this, between us and you a great chasm has been fixed, so that those who want to go from here to you cannot, nor can anyone cross over from there to us.' ²⁷He answered, 'Then I beg you, father, send Lazarus to my father's house, ²⁸for I have five brothers. Let him warn them, so that they will not also come to this place of torment.' ²⁹Abraham replied, 'They have Moses and the Prophets; let them listen to them.' ³⁰'No, father Abraham,' he said, 'but if someone from the dead goes to them, they will repent.' ³¹He said to him, 'If they do not listen to Moses and the Prophets, they will not be convinced even if someone rises from the dead.'"

LUKE 20:35-36 "But those who are considered worthy of taking part in that age and in the resurrection from the dead will neither marry nor be given in marriage, ³⁶and they can no longer die; for they are like the angels. They are God's children, since they are children of the resurrection."

LUKE 23:43 Jesus answered him [a criminal crucified with Jesus], "I tell you the truth, today you will be with me in paradise."

Deliverance

MATTHEW 6:9-13 "This, then, is how you should pray: 'Our Father in heaven, hallowed be your name, ¹⁰your kingdom come, your will be done on earth as it is in heaven. ¹¹Give us today our daily bread. ¹²Forgive us our debts, as we also have forgiven our debtors. ¹³And lead us not into temptation, but deliver us from the evil one.'"

MATTHEW 7:22-23 "Many will say to Me in that day, 'Lord, Lord, have we not prophesied in Your name, cast out demons in Your name, and done many wonders in Your name?' ²³And then I will declare to them, 'I never knew you; depart from Me, you who practice lawlessness!'" (NKJV)

MATTHEW 8:28-32 When he arrived at the other side in the region of the Gadarenes, two demon-possessed men coming from the tombs met him. They were so violent that no one could pass that way. ²⁹"What do you want with us, Son of God?" they shouted. "Have you come here to torture us before the appointed time?" ³⁰Some distance from them a large herd of pigs was feeding. ³¹The demons begged Jesus, "If you drive us out, send us into the herd of pigs." ³²He said to them, "Go!" So they came out and went into the pigs, and the whole herd rushed down the steep bank into the lake and died in the water.

MATTHEW 12:25-29 Jesus knew their [the Pharisees'] thoughts and said to them, "Every kingdom divided against itself will be ruined, and every city or household divided against itself will not stand. 26If Satan drives out Satan, he is divided against himself. How then can his kingdom stand? 27And if I drive out demons by Beelzebub, by whom do your people drive them out? So then, they will be your judges. 28But if I drive out demons by the Spirit of God, then the kingdom of God has come upon you. 29Or again, how can anyone enter a strong man's house and carry off his possessions unless he first ties up the strong man? Then he can rob his house."

MATTHEW 15:22-28 A Canaanite woman from that vicinity came to him, crying out, "Lord, Son of David, have mercy on me! My daughter is suffering terribly from demon-possession." 23Jesus did not answer a word. So his disciples came to him and urged him, "Send her away, for she keeps crying out after us." 24He answered, "I was sent only to the lost sheep of Israel." 25The woman came and knelt before him. "Lord, help me!" she said. 26He replied, "It is not right to take the children's bread and toss it to their dogs." 27"Yes, Lord," she said, "but even the dogs eat the crumbs that fall from their masters' table." 28Then Jesus answered, "Woman, you have great faith! Your request is granted." And her daughter was healed from that very hour.

MATTHEW 17:14-20 And when they had come to the multitude, a man came to Him, kneeling down to Him and saying, 15"Lord, have mercy on my son, for he is an epileptic and suffers severely; for he often falls into the fire and often into the water. 16So I brought him to Your disciples, but they could not cure him." 17Then Jesus answered and said, "O faithless and perverse generation, how long shall I be with you? How long shall I bear with you? Bring him here to Me." 18And Jesus rebuked the demon, and it came out of him; and the child was cured from that very hour. 19Then the disciples came to Jesus privately and said, "Why could we not cast it out?" 20So Jesus said to them, "Because of your unbelief; for assuredly, I say to you, if you have faith as a mustard seed, you will say to this mountain, 'Move from here to there,' and it will move; and nothing will be impossible for you." (NKJV)

MARK 1:23-26 Just then a man in their synagogue who was possessed by an evil spirit cried out, 24"What do you want with us, Jesus of Nazareth? Have you come to destroy us? I know who you are—the Holy One of God!" 25"Be quiet!" said Jesus sternly. "Come out of him!" 26The evil spirit shook the man violently and came out of him with a shriek.

MARK 5:1-19 They went across the lake to the region of the Gerasenes. 2When Jesus got out of the boat, a man with an evil spirit came from the tombs to meet him. 3This man lived in the tombs, and no one could bind him any more, not even with a chain. 4For he had often been chained hand and foot, but he tore the chains apart and broke the irons on his feet. No one was strong enough to subdue him. 5Night and day among the tombs and in the hills he would cry out and cut himself with stones. ⁶When he saw Jesus from a distance, he ran and fell on his knees in front of him. ⁷He shouted at the top of his voice, "What do you want with me, Jesus, Son of the Most High God? Swear to God that you won't torture me!" ⁸For Jesus had said to him, "Come out of this man, you evil spirit!" ⁹Then Jesus asked him, "What is your name?" "My name is Legion," he replied, "for we are many." ¹⁰And he begged Jesus again and again not to send them out of the area. ¹¹A large herd of pigs was feeding on the nearby hillside. ¹²The demons begged Jesus, "Send us among the pigs; allow us to go into them." ¹³He gave them permission, and the evil spirits came out and went into the pigs. The herd, about two thousand in number, rushed down the steep bank into the lake and were drowned. ¹⁴Those tending the pigs ran off and reported this in the town and countryside, and the people went out to see what had happened. ¹⁵When they came to Jesus, they saw the man who had been possessed by the legion of demons, sitting there, dressed and in his right mind; and they were afraid. ¹⁶Those who had seen it told the people what had happened to the demon-possessed man—and told about the pigs as well. ¹⁷Then the people began to plead with Jesus to leave their region. ¹⁸As Jesus was getting into the boat, the man who had been demon-possessed begged to go with him. ¹⁹Jesus did not let him, but said, "Go home to your family and tell them how much the Lord has done for you, and how he has had mercy on you."

MARK 7:25-29 In fact, as soon as she heard about him, a woman whose little daughter was possessed by an evil spirit came and fell at his feet. ²⁶The woman was a Greek, born in Syrian Phoenicia. She begged Jesus to drive the demon out of her daughter. ²⁷"First let the children eat all they want," he told her, "for it is not right to take the children's bread and toss it to their dogs." ²⁸"Yes, Lord," she replied, "but even the dogs under the table eat the children's crumbs." ²⁹Then he told her, "For such a reply, you may go; the demon has left your daughter."

MARK 9:14-29 And when He came to the disciples, He saw a great multitude around them, and scribes disputing with them. ¹⁵Immediately, when they saw Him, all the people were greatly amazed, and running to Him, greeted Him. ¹⁶And He asked the scribes, "What are you discussing with them?" ¹⁷Then one of the crowd answered and said, "Teacher, I brought You my son, who has a mute spirit. ¹⁸And wherever it seizes him, it throws him down; he foams at the mouth, gnashes his teeth, and becomes rigid. So I spoke to Your disciples, that they should cast it out, but they could not." ¹⁹He answered him and said, "O faithless generation, how long shall I be with you? How long shall I bear with you? Bring him to Me." ²⁰Then they brought him to Him. And when he saw Him, immediately the spirit convulsed him, and he fell on the ground and wallowed, foaming at the mouth. ²¹So He asked his father, "How long has this been happening to him?" And he said, "From childhood. ²²And often he has thrown him both into the fire and into the water to destroy him. But if You can do anything, have compassion on us and help us." [23]Jesus said to him, "If you can believe, all things are possible to him who believes." [24]Immediately the father of the child cried out and said with tears, "Lord, I believe; help my unbelief!" [25]When Jesus saw that the people came running together, He rebuked the unclean spirit, saying to it, "Deaf and dumb spirit, I command you, come out of him, and enter him no more!" [26]Then the spirit cried out, convulsed him greatly, and came out of him. And he became as one dead, so that many said, "He is dead." [27]But Jesus took him by the hand and lifted him up, and he arose. [28]And when He had come into the house, His disciples asked Him privately, "Why could we not cast it out?" [29]So He said to them, "This kind can come out by nothing but prayer and fasting." (NKJV)

MARK 16:17 "And these signs will accompany those who believe: In my name they will drive out demons; they will speak in new tongues."[vi]

LUKE 4:18-21 "The Spirit of the Lord is on me, because he has anointed me to preach good news to the poor. He has sent me to proclaim freedom for the prisoners and recovery of sight for the blind, to release the oppressed, [19]to proclaim the year of the Lord's favor." [20]Then he rolled up the scroll, gave it back to the attendant and sat down. The eyes of everyone in the synagogue were fastened on him, [21]and he began by saying to them, "Today this scripture is fulfilled in your hearing."

LUKE 4:33-35 In the synagogue there was a man possessed by a demon, an evil spirit. He cried out at the top of his voice, [34]"Ha! What do you want with us, Jesus of Nazareth? Have you come to destroy us? I know who you are—the Holy One of God!" [35]"Be quiet!" Jesus said sternly. "Come out of him!" Then the demon threw the man down before them all and came out without injuring him.

LUKE 8:26-39 They sailed to the region of the Gerasenes, which is across the lake from Galilee. [27]When Jesus stepped ashore, he was met by a demon-possessed man from the town. For a long time this man had not worn clothes or lived in a house, but had lived in the tombs. [28]When he saw Jesus, he cried out and fell at his feet, shouting at the top of his voice, "What do you want with me, Jesus, Son of the Most High God? I beg you, don't torture me!" [29]For Jesus had commanded the evil spirit to come out of the man. Many times it had seized him, and though he was chained hand and foot and kept under guard, he had broken his chains and had been driven by the demon into solitary places. [30]Jesus asked him, "What is your name?" "Legion," he replied, because many demons had gone into him. [31]And they begged him repeatedly not to order them to go into the Abyss. [32]A large herd of pigs was feeding there on the hillside. The demons begged Jesus to let them go into them, and he gave them permission. [33]When the demons came out of the man, they went into the pigs, and the herd rushed down the steep bank into the lake and was drowned. [34]When those tending the pigs saw what had happened, they ran off and reported this in the town and countryside, [35]and the people went out to see what had happened. When they came to Jesus, they found the man from whom the demons had gone out, sitting at Jesus' feet, dressed and in his right mind; and they were afraid. [36]Those who had seen it told the people how the demon-possessed man had been cured. [37]Then all the people of the region of the Gerasenes asked Jesus to leave them, because they were overcome with fear. So he got into the boat and left. [38]The man from whom the demons had gone out begged to go with him, but Jesus sent him away, saying, [39]"Return home and tell how much God has done for you." So the man went away and told all over town how much Jesus had done for him.

LUKE 9:37-42 The next day, when they came down from the mountain, a large crowd met him. [38]A man in the crowd called out, "Teacher, I beg you to look at my son, for he is my only child. [39]A spirit seizes him and he suddenly screams; it throws him into convulsions so that he foams at the mouth. It scarcely ever leaves him and is destroying him. [40]I begged your disciples to drive it out, but they could not." [41]"O unbelieving and perverse generation," Jesus replied, "how long shall I stay with you and put up with you? Bring your son here." [42]Even while the boy was coming, the demon threw him to the ground in a convulsion. But Jesus rebuked the evil spirit, healed the boy and gave him back to his father.

LUKE 10:17-20 The seventy-two returned with joy and said, "Lord, even the demons submit to us in your name." [18]He replied, "I saw Satan fall like lightning from heaven. [19]I have given you authority to trample on snakes and scorpions and to overcome all the power of the enemy; nothing will harm you. [20]However, do not rejoice that the spirits submit to you, but rejoice that your names are written in heaven."

Demons

MATTHEW 7:22-23 "Many will say to Me in that day, 'Lord, Lord, have we not prophesied in Your name, cast out demons in Your name, and done many wonders in Your name?' [23]And then I will declare to them, 'I never knew you; depart from Me, you who practice lawlessness!'" (NKJV)

MATTHEW 8:28-32 When he arrived at the other side in the region of the Gadarenes, two demon-possessed men coming from the tombs met him. They were so violent that no one could pass that way. [29]"What do you want with us, Son of God?" they shouted. "Have you come here to torture us before the appointed time?" [30]Some distance from them a large herd of pigs was feeding. [31]The demons begged Jesus, "If you drive us out, send us into the herd of pigs." [32]He said to them, "Go!" So they came out and went into the pigs, and the whole herd rushed down the steep bank into the lake and died in the water.

MATTHEW 10:5-10 These twelve Jesus sent out with the following instructions: "Do not go among the Gentiles or enter any town of the Samaritans. [6]Go rather to the lost sheep of Israel. [7]As you go, preach this message: 'The kingdom of heaven is near.' [8]Heal the sick, raise the dead, cleanse those who have leprosy, drive out demons. Freely you have received, freely give. [9]Do not take along any gold or silver or copper in your belts; [10]take no bag for the journey, or extra tunic, or sandals or a staff; for the worker is worth his keep."

MATTHEW 12:25-30 Jesus knew their [the Pharisees'] thoughts and said to them, "Every kingdom divided against itself will be ruined, and every city or household divided against itself will not stand. [26]If Satan drives out Satan, he is divided against himself. How then can his kingdom stand? [27]And if I drive out demons by Beelzebub, by whom do your people drive them out? So then, they will be your judges. [28]But if I drive out demons by the Spirit of God, then the kingdom of God has come upon you. [29]Or again, how can anyone enter a strong man's house and carry off his possessions unless he first ties up the strong man? Then he can rob his house. [30]He who is not with me is against me, and he who does not gather with me scatters."

MATTHEW 12:43-45 "When an evil spirit comes out of a man, it goes through arid places seeking rest and does not find it. [44]Then it says, 'I will return to the house I left.' When it arrives, it finds the house unoccupied, swept clean and put in order. [45]Then it goes and takes with it seven other spirits more wicked than itself, and they go in and live there. And the final condition of that man is worse than the first. That is how it will be with this wicked generation."

MATTHEW 15:22-28 A Canaanite woman from that vicinity came to him, crying out, "Lord, Son of David, have mercy on me! My daughter is suffering terribly from demon-possession." [23]Jesus did not answer a word. So his disciples came to him and urged him, "Send her away, for she keeps crying out after us." [24]He answered, "I was sent only to the lost sheep of Israel." [25]The woman came and knelt before him. "Lord, help me!" she said. [26]He replied, "It is not right to take the children's bread and toss it to their dogs." [27]"Yes, Lord," she said, "but even the dogs eat the crumbs that fall from their masters' table." [28]Then Jesus answered, "Woman, you have great faith! Your request is granted." And her daughter was healed from that very hour.

MATTHEW 17:14-20 And when they had come to the multitude, a man came to Him, kneeling down to Him and saying, [15]"Lord, have mercy on my son, for he is an epileptic and suffers severely; for he often falls into the fire and often into the water. [16]So I brought him to Your disciples, but they could not cure him." [17]Then Jesus answered and said, "O faithless and perverse generation, how long shall I be with you? How long shall I bear with you? Bring him here to Me." [18]And Jesus rebuked the demon, and it came out of him; and the child was cured from that very hour. [19]Then the disciples came to Jesus privately and said, "Why could we not cast it out?" [20]So Jesus said to them, "Because of your unbelief; for assuredly, I say to you, if you have faith as a mustard seed, you will say to this mountain, 'Move from here to there,' and it will move; and nothing will be impossible for you." (NKJV)

MARK 1:23-26 Just then a man in their synagogue who was possessed by an evil spirit cried out, [24]"What do you want with us, Jesus of Nazareth? Have you come to destroy us? I know who you are—the Holy One of God!" [25]"Be quiet!" said Jesus sternly. "Come out of him!" [26]The evil spirit shook the man violently and came out of him with a shriek.

MARK 5:1-19 They went across the lake to the region of the Gerasenes. [2]When Jesus got out of the boat, a man with an evil spirit came from the tombs to meet him. [3]This man lived in the tombs, and no one could bind him any more, not even with a chain. [4]For he had often been chained hand and foot, but he tore the chains apart and broke the irons on his feet. No one was strong enough to subdue him. [5]Night and day among the tombs and in the hills he would cry out and cut himself with stones. [6]When he saw Jesus from a distance, he ran and fell on his knees in front of him. [7]He shouted at the top of his voice, "What do you want with me, Jesus, Son of the Most High God? Swear to God that you won't torture me!" [8]For Jesus had said to him, "Come out of this man, you evil spirit!" [9]Then Jesus asked him, "What is your name?" "My name is Legion," he replied, "for we are many." [10]And he begged Jesus again and again not to send them out of the area. [11]A large herd of pigs was feeding on the nearby hillside. [12]The demons begged Jesus, "Send us among the pigs; allow us to go into them." [13]He gave them permission, and the evil spirits came out and went into the pigs. The herd, about two thousand in number, rushed down the steep bank into the lake and were drowned. [14]Those tending the pigs ran off and reported this in the town and countryside, and the people went out to see what had happened. [15]When they came to Jesus, they saw the man who had been possessed by the legion of demons, sitting there, dressed and in his right mind; and they were afraid. [16]Those who had seen it told the people what had happened to the demon-possessed man—and told about the pigs as well. [17]Then the people began to plead with Jesus to leave their region. [18]As Jesus was getting into the boat, the man who had been demon-possessed begged to go with him. [19]Jesus did not let him, but said, "Go home to your family and tell them how much the Lord has done for you, and how he has had mercy on you."

MARK 7:25-29 In fact, as soon as she heard about him, a woman whose little daughter was possessed by an evil spirit came and fell at his feet. [26]The woman was a Greek, born in Syrian Phoenicia. She begged Jesus to drive the demon out of her daughter. [27]"First let the children eat all they want," he told her, "for it is not right to take the children's bread and toss it to their dogs." [28]"Yes, Lord," she replied, "but even the dogs under the table eat the children's crumbs." [29]Then he told her, "For such a reply, you may go; the demon has left your daughter."

MARK 9:14-29 And when He came to the disciples, He saw a great multitude around them, and scribes disputing with them. [15]Immediately, when they saw Him, all the people were greatly amazed, and running to Him, greeted Him. [16]And He asked the scribes, "What are you discussing with them?" [17]Then one of the crowd answered and said, "Teacher, I brought You my son, who has a mute spirit. [18]And wherever it seizes him, it throws him down; he foams at the mouth, gnashes his teeth, and becomes rigid. So I spoke to Your disciples, that they should cast it out, but they could not." [19]He answered him and said, "O faithless generation, how long shall I be with you? How long shall I bear with you? Bring him to Me." [20]Then they brought him to Him. And when he saw Him, immediately the spirit convulsed him, and he fell on the ground and wallowed, foaming at the mouth. [21]So He asked his father, "How long has this been happening to him?" And he said, "From childhood. [22]And often he has thrown him both into the fire and into the water to destroy him. But if You can do anything, have compassion on us and help us." [23]Jesus said to him, "If you can believe, all things are possible to him who believes." [24]Immediately the father of the child cried out and said with tears, "Lord, I believe; help my unbelief!" [25]When Jesus saw that the people came running together, He rebuked the unclean spirit, saying to it, "Deaf and dumb spirit, I command you, come out of him, and enter him no more!" [26]Then the spirit cried out, convulsed him greatly, and came out of him. And he became as one dead, so that many said, "He is dead." [27]But Jesus took him by the hand and lifted him up, and he arose. [28]And when He had come into the house, His disciples asked Him privately, "Why could we not cast it out?" [29]So He said to them, "This kind can come out by nothing but prayer and fasting." (NKJV)

LUKE 4:33-35 In the synagogue there was a man possessed by a demon, an evil spirit. He cried out at the top of his voice, [34]"Ha! What do you want with us, Jesus of Nazareth? Have you come to destroy us? I know who you are—the Holy One of God!" [35]"Be quiet!" Jesus said sternly. "Come out of him!" Then the demon threw the man down before them all and came out without injuring him.

LUKE 8:26-39 They sailed to the region of the Gerasenes, which is across the lake from Galilee. [27]When Jesus stepped ashore, he was met by a demon-possessed man from the town. For a long time this man had not worn clothes or lived in a house, but had lived in the tombs. [28]When he saw Jesus, he cried out and fell at his feet, shouting at the top of his voice, "What do you want with me, Jesus, Son of the Most High God? I beg you, don't torture me!" [29]For Jesus had commanded the evil spirit to come out of the man. Many times it had seized him, and though he was chained hand and foot and kept under guard, he had broken his chains and had been driven by the demon into solitary places. [30]Jesus asked him, "What is your name?" "Legion," he replied, because many demons had gone into him. [31]And they begged him repeatedly not to order them to go into the Abyss. [32]A large herd of pigs was feeding there on the hillside. The demons begged Jesus to let them go into them, and he gave them permission. [33]When the demons came out of the man, they went into the pigs, and the herd rushed down the steep bank into the lake and was drowned. [34]When those tending the pigs saw what had happened, they ran off and reported this in the town and countryside, [35]and the people went out to see what had happened. When they came to Jesus, they found the man from whom the demons had gone out, sitting at Jesus' feet, dressed and in his right mind; and they were afraid. [36]Those who had seen it told the people how the demon-possessed man had been cured. [37]Then all the people of the region of the Gerasenes asked Jesus to leave them, because they were overcome with fear. So he got into the boat and left. [38]The man from whom the demons had gone out begged to go with him, but Jesus sent him away, saying, [39]"Return home and tell how much God has done for you." So the man went away and told all over town how much Jesus had done for him.

LUKE 9:37-42 The next day, when they came down from the mountain, a large crowd met him. [38]A man in the crowd called out, "Teacher, I beg you to look at my son, for he is my only child. [39]A spirit seizes him and he suddenly screams; it throws him into convulsions so that he foams at the mouth. It scarcely ever leaves him and is destroying him. [40]I begged your disciples to drive it out, but they could not." [41]"O unbelieving and perverse generation," Jesus replied, "how long shall I stay with you and put up with you? Bring your son here." [42]Even while the boy was coming, the demon threw him to the ground in a convulsion. But Jesus rebuked the evil spirit, healed the boy and gave him back to his father.

LUKE 10:17-20 The seventy-two returned with joy and said, "Lord, even the demons submit to us in your name." [18]He replied, "I saw Satan fall like lightning from heaven. [19]I have given you authority to trample on snakes and scorpions and to overcome all the power of the enemy; nothing will harm you. [20]However, do not rejoice that the spirits submit to you, but rejoice that your names are written in heaven."

LUKE 11:17-22 Jesus knew their thoughts and said to them: "Any kingdom divided against itself will be ruined, and a house divided against itself will fall. [18]If Satan is divided against himself, how can his kingdom stand? I say this because you claim that I drive out demons by Beelzebub. [19]Now if I drive out demons by Beelzebub, by whom do your followers drive them out? So then, they will be your judges. [20]But if I drive out demons by the finger of God, then the kingdom of God has come to you. [21]When a strong man, fully armed, guards his own house, his possessions are safe. [22]But when someone stronger attacks and overpowers him, he takes away the armor in which the man trusted and divides up the spoils."

LUKE 11:24-26 "When an evil spirit comes out of a man, it goes through arid places seeking rest and does not find it. Then it says, 'I will return to the house I left.' [25]When it arrives, it finds the house swept clean and put in order. [26]Then it goes and takes seven other spirits more wicked than itself, and they go in and live there. And the final condition of that man is worse than the first."

LUKE 13:10-13 On a Sabbath Jesus was teaching in one of the synagogues, [11]and a woman was there who had been crippled by a spirit for eighteen years. She was bent over and could not straighten up at all. [12]When Jesus saw her, he called her forward and said to her, "Woman, you are set free from your infirmity." [13]Then he put his hands on her, and immediately she straightened up and praised God.

LUKE 13:31-32 At that time some Pharisees came to Jesus and said to him, "Leave this place and go somewhere else. Herod wants to kill you." [32]He replied, "Go tell that fox [Herod], 'I will drive out demons and heal people today and tomorrow, and on the third day I will reach my goal.'"

Eternal Life (Salvation)

In this section we find the most important words any of us will ever read—the absolute truth about what it takes to receive eternal life, from the lips of the God who will decide who enters heaven and who does not. He alone has determined the ultimate criteria. No higher authority and no greater light or clarity is revealed anywhere than here in our Savior's words. As you read His words, you will see that receiving the gift of eternal life is as simple as believing in Christ and being born again. But you'll also discover that His definition of *believe* and our modern-day definition are quite different. Jesus equates believing with *doing* what He tells us to do. This is one topic that you should take notes on as you read the words of Jesus. Underline the words and passages that stand out to you. Write down the insights you receive. It is crucial that what you believe about eternal life be rooted in the rock-solid revelation of Christ's words.

JOHN 3:3-8 In reply Jesus declared, "I tell you the truth, no one can see the kingdom of God unless he is born again." [4]"How can a man be born when he is old?" Nicodemus asked. "Surely he cannot enter a second time into his mother's womb to be born!" [5]Jesus answered, "I tell you the truth, no one can enter the kingdom of God unless he is born of water and the Spirit. [6]Flesh gives birth to flesh, but the Spirit gives birth to spirit. [7]You should not be surprised at my saying, 'You must be born again.' [8]The wind blows wherever it pleases. You hear its sound, but you cannot tell where it comes from or where it is going. So it is with everyone born of the Spirit."

JOHN 3:14-18 "Just as Moses lifted up the snake in the desert, so the Son of Man must be lifted up, [15]that everyone who believes in him may have eternal life. [16]For God so loved the world that he gave his one and only Son, that whoever believes in him shall not perish but have eternal life. [17]For God did not send his Son into the world to condemn the world, but to save the world through him. [18]Whoever believes in him is not condemned, but whoever does not believe stands condemned already because he has not believed in the name of God's one and only Son."

JOHN 5:21-23 "For just as the Father raises the dead and gives them life, even so the Son gives life to whom he is pleased to give it. [22]Moreover, the Father judges no one, but has entrusted all judgment to the Son, [23]that all may honor the Son just as they honor the Father. He who does not honor the Son does not honor the Father, who sent him."

JOHN 5:24-25 "I tell you the truth, whoever hears my word and believes him who sent me has eternal life and will not be condemned; he has crossed over from death to life. [25]I tell you the truth, a time is coming and has now come when the dead will hear the voice of the Son of God and those who hear will live."

JOHN 5:28-29 "Do not be amazed at this, for a time is coming when all who are in their graves will hear his voice [29]and come out—those who have done good will rise to live, and those who have done evil will rise to be condemned."

JOHN 5:31-35 "If I testify about myself, my testimony is not valid. [32]There is another who testifies in my favor, and I know that his testimony about me is valid. [33]You have sent to John and he has testified to the truth. [34]Not that I accept human testimony; but I mention it that you may be saved. [35]John was a lamp that burned and gave light, and you chose for a time to enjoy his light."

JOHN 5:39-40 "You diligently study the Scriptures because you think that by them you possess eternal life. These are the Scriptures that testify about me, [40]yet you refuse to come to me to have life."

JOHN 6:27 "Do not work for food

that spoils, but for food that endures to eternal life, which the Son of Man will give you. On him God the Father has placed his seal of approval."

JOHN 6:37-40 "All that the Father gives me will come to me, and whoever comes to me I will never drive away. [38]For I have come down from heaven not to do my will but to do the will of him who sent me. [39]And this is the will of him who sent me, that I shall lose none of all that he has given me, but raise them up at the last day. [40]For my Father's will is that everyone who looks to the Son and believes in him shall have eternal life, and I will raise him up at the last day."

JOHN 6:44-51 "No one can come to me unless the Father who sent me draws him, and I will raise him up at the last day. [45]It is written in the Prophets: 'They will all be taught by God.' Everyone who listens to the Father and learns from him comes to me. [46]No one has seen the Father except the one who is from God; only he has seen the Father. [47]I tell you the truth, he who believes has everlasting life. [48]I am the bread of life. [49]Your forefathers ate the manna in the desert, yet they died. [50]But here is the bread that comes down from heaven, which a man may eat and not die. [51]I am the living bread that came down from heaven. If anyone eats of this bread, he will live forever. This bread is my flesh, which I will give for the life of the world."

JOHN 6:53-58 Jesus said to them, "I tell you the truth, unless you eat the flesh of the Son of Man and drink his blood, you have no life in you. [54]Whoever eats my flesh and drinks my blood has eternal life, and I will raise him up at the last day. [55]For my flesh is real food and my blood is real drink. [56]Whoever eats my flesh and drinks my blood remains in me, and I in him. [57]Just as the living Father sent me and I live because of the Father, so the one who feeds on me will live because of me. [58]This is the bread that came down from heaven. Your forefathers ate manna and died, but he who feeds on this bread will live forever."

JOHN 8:51 "I tell you the truth, if anyone keeps my word, he will never see death."

JOHN 10:7-9 Therefore Jesus said again, "I tell you the truth, I am the gate for the sheep. [8]All who ever came before me were thieves and robbers, but the sheep did not listen to them. [9]I am the gate; whoever enters through me will be saved. He will come in and go out, and find pasture."

JOHN 10:27-29 "My sheep listen to my voice; I know them, and they follow me. [28]I give them eternal life, and they shall never perish; no one can snatch them out of my hand. [29]My Father, who has given them to me, is greater than all; no one can snatch them out of my Father's hand."

JOHN 11:25-26 Jesus said to her [Martha], "I am the resurrection and the life. He who believes in me will live, even though he dies; [26]and whoever lives and believes in me will never die. Do you believe this?"

JOHN 12:49-50 "For I did not speak of my own accord, but the Father who sent me commanded me what to say and how to say it. [50]I know that his command leads to eternal life. So whatever I say is just what the Father has told me to say."

JOHN 14:1-4 "Do not let your hearts be troubled. Trust in God; trust also in me. [2]In my Father's house are many rooms; if it were not so, I would have told you. I am going there to prepare a place for you. [3]And if I go and prepare a place for you, I will come back and take you to be with me that you also may be where I am. [4]You know the way to the place where I am going."

JOHN 14:6 Jesus answered, "I am the way and the truth and the life. No one comes to the Father except through me."

JOHN 17:2-3 "For you [God the Father] granted him [Christ] authority over all people that he might give eternal life to all those you have given him. [3]Now this is eternal life: that they may know you, the only true God, and Jesus Christ, whom you have sent."

MATTHEW 5:19-20 "Anyone who breaks one of the least of these commandments and teaches others to do the same will be called least in the kingdom of heaven, but whoever practices and teaches these commands will be called great in the kingdom of heaven. [20]For I tell you that unless your righteousness surpasses that of the Pharisees and the teachers of the law, you will certainly not enter the kingdom of heaven."

MATTHEW 7:13-14 "Enter through the narrow gate. For wide is the gate and broad is the road that leads to destruction, and many enter through it. [14]But small is the gate and narrow the road that leads to life, and only a few find it."

MATTHEW 7:21-23 "Not everyone who says to Me, 'Lord, Lord,' shall enter the kingdom of heaven, but he who does the will of My Father in heaven. [22]Many will say to Me in that day, 'Lord, Lord, have we not prophesied in Your name, cast out demons in Your name, and done many wonders in Your name?' [23]And then I will declare to them, 'I never knew you; depart from Me, you who practice lawlessness!' " (NKJV)

MATTHEW 7:24-27 "Therefore whoever hears these sayings of Mine, and does them, I will liken him to a wise man who built his house on the rock: [25]and the rain descended, the floods came, and the winds blew and beat on that house; and it did not fall, for it was founded on the rock. [26]But everyone who hears these sayings of Mine, and does not do them, will be like a foolish man who built his house on the sand: [27]and the rain descended, the floods came, and the winds blew and beat on that house; and it fell. And great was its fall." (NKJV) (See also Luke 6:47-49.)

MATTHEW 8:10-12 When Jesus heard this [the centurion's testimony], he was astonished and said to those following him, "I tell you the truth, I have not found anyone in Israel with such great faith. [11]I say to you that many will come from the east and the west, and will take their places at the feast with Abraham, Isaac and Jacob in the kingdom of heaven. [12]But the subjects of the kingdom will be thrown outside, into the darkness, where there will be weeping and gnashing of teeth."

MATTHEW 13:18-23 "Listen then to what the parable of the sower means: [19]When anyone hears the message about the kingdom and does not understand it, the evil one comes and snatches away what was sown in his heart. This is the seed sown along the path. [20]The one who received the seed that fell on rocky places is the man who hears the word and at once receives it with joy. [21]But since he has no root, he lasts only a short time. When trouble or persecution comes because of the word, he quickly falls away. [22]The one who received the seed that fell among the thorns is the man who hears the word, but the worries of this life and the deceitfulness of wealth choke it, making it unfruitful. [23]But the one who received the seed that fell on good soil is the man who hears the word and understands it. He produces a crop, yielding a hundred, sixty or thirty times what was sown."

MATTHEW 18:2-4 He called a little child and had him stand among them. [3]And he said: "I tell you the truth, unless you change and become like little children, you will never enter the kingdom of heaven. [4]Therefore, whoever humbles himself like this child is the greatest in the kingdom of heaven."

MATTHEW 18:5-7 "And whoever welcomes a little child like this in my name welcomes me. [6]But if anyone causes one of these little ones who believe in me to sin, it would be better for him to have a large millstone hung around his neck and to be drowned in the depths of the sea. [7]Woe to the world because of the things that cause people to sin! Such things must come, but woe to the man through whom they come!"

MATTHEW 18:10, 12-14 "See that you do not look down on one of these little ones. For I tell you that their angels in heaven always see the face of my Father in heaven. [12]What do you think? If a man owns a hundred sheep, and one of them wanders away, will he not leave the ninety-nine on the hills and go to look for the one that wandered off? [13]And if he finds it, I tell you the truth, he is happier about that one sheep than about the ninety-nine that did not wander off. [14]In the same way your Father in heaven is not willing that any of these little ones should be lost."

MATTHEW 19:17-21 "Why do you ask me about what is good?" Jesus replied. "There is only One who is good. If you want to enter life, obey the commandments." [18]"Which ones?" the man inquired. Jesus replied, " 'Do not murder, do not commit adultery, do not steal, do not give false testimony, [19]honor your father and mother,' and 'love your neighbor as yourself.' " [20]"All these I have kept," the young man said. "What do I still lack?" [21]Jesus answered, "If you want to be perfect, go, sell your possessions and give to the poor, and you will have treasure in heaven. Then come, follow me."

MATTHEW 19:23-26 Then Jesus said to his disciples, "I tell you the truth, it is hard for a rich man to enter the kingdom of heaven. [24]Again I tell you, it is easier for a camel to go through the eye of a needle than for a rich man to enter the kingdom of God." [25]When the disciples heard this, they were greatly astonished and asked, "Who then can be saved?" [26]Jesus looked at them and said, "With man this is impossible, but with God all things are possible."

MATTHEW 19:28-30 Jesus said to them [the disciples], "I tell you the truth, at the renewal of all things, when the Son of Man sits on his glorious throne, you who have followed me will also sit on twelve thrones, judging the twelve tribes of Israel. [29]And everyone who has left houses or brothers or sisters or father or mother or children or fields for my sake will receive a hundred times as much and will inherit eternal life. [30]But many who are first will be last, and many who are last will be first."

MATTHEW 21:28-32 "What do you think? There was a man who had two sons. He went to the first and said, 'Son, go and work today in the vineyard.' [29]'I will not,' he answered, but later he changed his mind and went. [30]Then the father went to the other son and said the same thing. He answered, 'I will, sir,' but he did not go. [31]Which of the two did what his father wanted?" "The first," they answered. Jesus said to them, "I tell you the truth, the tax collectors and the prostitutes are entering the kingdom of God ahead of you. [32]For John came to you to show you the way of righteousness, and you did not believe him, but the tax collectors and the prostitutes did. And even after you saw this, you did not repent and believe him."

MATTHEW 22:1-14 Jesus spoke to them again in parables, saying: [2]"The kingdom of heaven is like a king who prepared a wedding banquet for his son. [3]He sent his servants to those who had been invited to the banquet to tell them to come, but they refused to come. [4]Then he sent some more servants and said, 'Tell those who have been invited that I have prepared my dinner: My oxen and fattened cattle have been butchered, and everything is ready. Come to the wedding banquet.' [5]But they paid no attention and went off—one to his field, another to his business. [6]The rest seized his servants, mistreated them and killed them. [7]The king was enraged. He sent his army and destroyed those murderers and burned their city. [8]Then he said to his servants, 'The wedding banquet is ready, but those I invited did not deserve to come. [9]Go to the street corners and invite to the banquet anyone you find.' [10]So the servants went out into the streets and gathered all the people they could find, both good and bad, and the wedding hall was filled with guests. [11]But when the king came in to see the guests, he noticed a man there who was not wearing wedding clothes. [12]'Friend,' he asked, 'how did you get in here without wedding clothes?' The man was speechless. [13]Then the king told the attendants, 'Tie him hand and foot, and throw him outside, into the darkness, where there will be weeping and gnashing of teeth.' [14]For many are invited, but few are chosen."

MATTHEW 24:9-13 "Then you will be handed over to be persecuted and put to death, and you will be hated by all nations because of me. [10]At that time many will turn away from the faith and will betray and hate each other, [11]and many false prophets will appear and deceive many people. [12]Because of the increase of wickedness, the love of most will grow cold, [13]but he who stands firm to the end will be saved."

MATTHEW 25:31-46 "When the Son of Man comes in his glory, and all the angels with him, he will sit on his throne in heavenly glory. [32]All the nations will be gathered before him, and he will separate the people one from another as a shepherd separates the sheep from the goats. [33]He will put the sheep on his right and the goats on his left. [34]Then the King will say to those on his right, 'Come, you who are blessed by my Father; take your inheritance, the kingdom prepared for you since the creation of the world. [35]For I was hungry and you gave me something to eat, I was thirsty and you gave me something to drink, I was a stranger and you invited me in, [36]I needed clothes and you clothed me, I was sick and you looked after me, I was in prison and you came to visit me.' [37]Then the righteous will answer him, 'Lord, when did we see you hungry and feed you, or thirsty and give you something to drink? [38]When did we see you a stranger and invite you in, or needing clothes and clothe you? [39]When did we see you sick or in prison and go to visit you?' [40]The King will reply, 'I tell you the truth, whatever you did for one of the least of these brothers of mine, you did for me.' [41]Then he will say to those on his left, 'Depart from me, you who are cursed, into the eternal fire prepared for the devil and his angels. [42]For I was hungry and you gave me nothing to eat, I was thirsty and you gave me nothing to drink, [43]I was a stranger and you did not invite me in, I needed clothes and you did not clothe me, I was sick and in prison and you did not look after me.' [44]They also will answer, 'Lord, when did we see you hungry or thirsty or a stranger or needing clothes or sick or in prison, and did not help you?' [45]He will reply, 'I tell you the truth, whatever you did not do for one of the least of these, you did not do for me.' [46]Then they will go away to eternal punishment, but the righteous to eternal life."

MARK 4:13-20 Then Jesus said to them [the disciples], "Don't you understand this parable? How then will you understand any parable? [14]The farmer sows the word. [15]Some people are like seed along the path, where the word is sown. As soon as they hear it, Satan comes and takes away the word that was sown in them. [16]Others, like seed sown on rocky places, hear the word and at once receive it with joy. [17]But since they have no root, they last only a short time. When trouble or persecution comes because of the word, they quickly fall away. [18]Still others, like seed sown among thorns, hear the word; [19]but the worries of this life, the deceitfulness of wealth and the desires for other things come in and choke the word, making it unfruitful. [20]Others, like seed sown on good soil, hear the word, accept it, and produce a crop—thirty, sixty or even a hundred times what was sown."

MARK 10:17-25 As Jesus started on his way, a man ran up to him and fell on his knees before him. "Good teacher," he asked, "what must I do to inherit eternal life?" [18]"Why do you call me good?" Jesus answered. "No one is good—except God alone. [19]You know the commandments: 'Do not murder, do not commit adultery, do not steal, do not give false testimony, do not defraud, honor your father and mother.'" [20]"Teacher," he declared, "all

these I have kept since I was a boy." [21]Jesus looked at him and loved him. "One thing you lack," he said. "Go, sell everything you have and give to the poor, and you will have treasure in heaven. Then come, follow me." [22]At this the man's face fell. He went away sad, because he had great wealth. [23]Jesus looked around and said to his disciples, "How hard it is for the rich to enter the kingdom of God!" [24]The disciples were amazed at his words. But Jesus said again, "Children, how hard it is to enter the kingdom of God! [25]It is easier for a camel to go through the eye of a needle than for a rich man to enter the kingdom of God."

MARK 16:15-16 He said to them [the Eleven], "Go into all the world and preach the good news to all creation. [16]Whoever believes and is baptized will be saved, but whoever does not believe will be condemned."[vii]

LUKE 7:41-50 "Two men owed money to a certain moneylender. One owed him five hundred denarii, and the other fifty. [42]Neither of them had the money to pay him back, so he canceled the debts of both. Now which of them will love him more?" [43]Simon replied, "I suppose the one who had the bigger debt canceled." "You have judged correctly," Jesus said. [44]Then he turned toward the woman and said to Simon, "Do you see this woman? I came into your house. You did not give me any water for my feet, but she wet my feet with her tears and wiped them with her hair. [45]You did not give me a kiss, but this woman, from the time I entered, has not stopped kissing my feet. [46]You did not put oil on my head, but she has poured perfume on my feet. [47]Therefore, I tell you, her many sins have been forgiven—for she loved much. But he who has been forgiven little loves little." [48]Then Jesus said to her, "Your sins are forgiven." [49]The other guests began to say among themselves, "Who is this who even forgives sins?" [50]Jesus said to the woman, "Your faith has saved you; go in peace."

LUKE 10:17-20 The seventy-two returned with joy and said, "Lord, even the demons submit to us in your name." [18]He replied, "I saw Satan fall like lightning from heaven. [19]I have given you authority to trample on snakes and scorpions and to overcome all the power of the enemy; nothing will harm you. [20]However, do not rejoice that the spirits submit to you, but rejoice that your names are written in heaven."

LUKE 10:25-28 On one occasion an expert in the law stood up to test Jesus. "Teacher," he asked, "what must I do to inherit eternal life?" [26]"What is written in the Law?" he replied. "How do you read it?" [27]He answered: " 'Love the Lord your God with all your heart and with all your soul and with all your strength and with all your mind'; and, 'Love your neighbor as yourself.'" [28]"You have answered correctly," Jesus replied. "Do this and you will live."

LUKE 13:2-5 Jesus answered, "Do you think that these Galileans were worse sinners than all the other Galileans because they suffered this way? [3]I tell you, no! But unless you repent, you too will all perish. [4]Or those eighteen who died when the tower in Siloam fell on them—do you think they were more guilty than all the others living in Jerusalem? [5]I tell you, no! But unless you repent, you too will all perish."

LUKE 13:23-30 Someone asked him, "Lord, are only a few people going to be saved?" He said to them, [24]"Make every effort to enter through the narrow door, because many, I tell you, will try to enter and will not be able to. [25]Once the owner of the house gets up and closes the door, you will stand outside knocking and pleading, 'Sir, open the door for us.' But he will answer, 'I don't know you or where you come from.' [26]Then you will say, 'We ate and drank with you, and you taught in our streets.' [27]But he will reply, 'I don't know you or where you come from. Away from me, all you evildoers!' [28]There will be weeping there, and gnashing of teeth, when you see Abraham, Isaac and Jacob and all the prophets in the kingdom of God, but you yourselves thrown out. [29]People will come from east and west and north and south, and will take their places at the feast in the kingdom of God. [30]Indeed there are those who are last who will be first, and first who will be last."

LUKE 14:16-24 Jesus replied: "A certain man was preparing a great banquet and invited many guests. [17]At the time of the banquet he sent his servant to tell those who had been invited, 'Come, for everything is now ready.' [18]But they all alike began to make excuses. The first said, 'I have just bought a field, and I must go and see it. Please excuse me.' [19]Another said, 'I have just bought five yoke of oxen, and I'm on my way to try them out. Please excuse me.' [20]Still another said, 'I just got married, so I can't come.' [21]The servant came back and reported this to his master. Then the owner of the house became angry and ordered his servant, 'Go out quickly into the streets and alleys of the town and bring in the poor, the crippled, the blind and the lame.' [22]'Sir,' the servant said, 'what you ordered has been done, but there is still room.' [23]Then the master told his servant, 'Go out to the roads and country lanes and make them come in, so that my house will be full. [24]I tell you, not one of those men who were invited will get a taste of my banquet.'"

Luke 18:16-17 But Jesus called the children to him and said, "Let the little children come to me, and do not hinder them, for the kingdom of God belongs to such as these. [17]I tell you the truth, anyone who will not receive the kingdom of God like a little child will never enter it."

Luke 18:18-27 A certain ruler asked him, "Good teacher, what must I do to inherit eternal life?" [19]"Why do you call me good?" Jesus answered. "No one is good—except God alone. [20]You know the commandments: 'Do not commit adultery, do not murder, do not steal, do not give false testimony, honor your father and mother.'" [21]"All these I have kept since I was a boy," he said. [22]When Jesus heard this, he said to him, "You still lack one thing. Sell everything you have and give to the poor, and you will have treasure in heaven. Then come, follow me." [23]When he heard this, he became very sad, because he was a man of great wealth. [24]Jesus looked at him and said, "How hard it is for the rich to enter the kingdom of God! [25]Indeed, it is easier for a camel to go through the eye of a needle than

for a rich man to enter the kingdom of God." [26]Those who heard this asked, "Who then can be saved?" [27]Jesus replied, "What is impossible with men is possible with God."

Luke 19:5, 9-10 When Jesus reached the spot, he looked up and said to him, "Zacchaeus, come down immediately. I must stay at your house today." [9]Jesus said to him, "Today salvation has come to this house, because this man, too, is a son of Abraham. [10]For the Son of Man came to seek and to save what was lost."

Luke 23:42-43 Then he [a criminal crucified with Jesus] said, "Jesus, remember me when you come into your kingdom." [43]Jesus answered him, "I tell you the truth, today you will be with me in paradise."

Forgiveness of Sins
(See also pages 253 and 481.)

Matthew 6:9-15 "This, then, is how you should pray: 'Our Father in heaven, hallowed be your name, [10]your kingdom come, your will be done on earth as it is in heaven. [11]Give us today our daily bread. [12]Forgive us our debts, as we also have forgiven our debtors. [13]And lead us not into temptation, but deliver us from the evil one.' [14]For if you forgive men when they sin against you, your heavenly Father will also forgive you. [15]But if you do not forgive men their sins, your Father will not forgive your sins." (See also Luke 11:2-4.)

Matthew 9:5-6 "Which is easier: to say, 'Your sins are forgiven,' or to say, 'Get up and walk'? [6]But so that you may know that the Son of Man has authority on earth to forgive sins...." Then he said to the paralytic, "Get up, take your mat and go home." (See also Mark 2:9-11; Luke 5:23-24.)

MATTHEW 26:26-29 While they were eating, Jesus took bread, gave thanks and broke it, and gave it to his disciples, saying, "Take and eat; this is my body." [27]Then he took the cup, gave thanks and offered it to them, saying, "Drink from it, all of you. [28]This is my blood of the covenant, which is poured out for many for the forgiveness of sins. [29]I tell you, I will not drink of this fruit of the vine from now on until that day when I drink it anew with you in my Father's kingdom."

MARK 11:25 "And when you stand praying, if you hold anything against anyone, forgive him, so that your Father in heaven may forgive you your sins."

LUKE 7:44-48 Then he turned toward the woman and said to Simon, "Do you see this woman? I came into your house. You did not give me any water for my feet, but she wet my feet with her tears and wiped them with her hair. [45]You did not give me a kiss, but this woman, from the time I entered, has not stopped kissing my feet. [46]You did not put oil on my head, but she has poured perfume on my feet. [47]Therefore, I tell you, her many sins have been forgiven—for she loved much. But he who has been forgiven little loves little." [48]Then Jesus said to her, "Your sins are forgiven."

LUKE 24:46-47 He told them, "This is what is written: The Christ will suffer and rise from the dead on the third day, [47]and repentance and forgiveness of sins will be preached in his name to all nations, beginning at Jerusalem."

Heaven

Closely linked to questions about eternity and eternal life are questions about the reality of heaven. In this section you will find the most important words ever spoken about heaven. Jesus left heaven to come to earth, so His words on the subject merit your full attention. As you read Jesus' words, take notes on the insights you receive, and underline anything that stands out to you.

JOHN 3:10-13 "You are Israel's teacher," said Jesus, "and do you not understand these things? [11]I tell you the truth, we speak of what we know, and we testify to what we have seen, but still you people do not accept our testimony. [12]I have spoken to you of earthly things and you do not believe; how then will you believe if I speak of heavenly things? [13]No one has ever gone into heaven except the one who came from heaven—the Son of Man."

JOHN 6:32-33 Jesus said to them, "I tell you the truth, it is not Moses who has given you the bread from heaven, but it is my Father who gives you the true bread from heaven. [33]For the bread of God is he who comes down from heaven and gives life to the world."

JOHN 6:48-51 "I am the bread of life. [49]Your forefathers ate the manna in the desert, yet they died. [50]But here is the bread that comes down from heaven, which a man may eat and not die. [51]I am the living bread that came down from heaven. If anyone eats of this bread, he will live forever. This bread is my flesh, which I will give for the life of the world."

JOHN 6:57-58 "Just as the living Father sent me and I live because of the Father, so the one who feeds on me will live because of me. [58]This is the bread that came down from heaven. Your forefathers ate manna and died, but he who feeds on this bread will live forever."

JOHN 14:2-4 "In my Father's house are many rooms; if it were not so, I would have told you. I am going there to prepare a place for you. [3]And if I go and prepare a place for you, I will come back and take you to be with me that you also may be where I am. [4]You know the way to the place where I am going."

MATTHEW 4:17 From that time on Jesus began to preach, "Repent, for the kingdom of heaven is near."

MATTHEW 5:3 "Blessed are the poor in spirit, for theirs is the kingdom of heaven."

MATTHEW 5:10 "Blessed are those who are persecuted because of righteousness, for theirs is the kingdom of heaven."

MATTHEW 5:19-20 "Anyone who breaks one of the least of these commandments and teaches others to do the same will be called least in the kingdom of heaven, but whoever practices and teaches these commands will be called great in the kingdom of heaven. [20]For I tell you that unless your righteousness surpasses that of the Pharisees and the teachers of the law, you will certainly not enter the kingdom of heaven."

MATTHEW 6:9-10 "This, then, is how you should pray: 'Our Father in heaven, hallowed be your name, [10]your kingdom come, your will be done on earth as it is in heaven.'"

MATTHEW 7:21 "Not everyone who says to Me, 'Lord, Lord,' shall enter the kingdom of heaven, but he who does the will of My Father in heaven." (NKJV)

MATTHEW 10:6-7 "Go rather to the lost sheep of Israel. [7]As you go, preach this message: 'The kingdom of heaven is near.'"

MATTHEW 11:11 "I tell you the truth: Among those born of women there has not risen anyone greater than John the Baptist; yet he who is least in the kingdom of heaven is greater than he."

MATTHEW 13:31-32 He told them another parable: "The kingdom of heaven is like a mustard seed, which a man took and planted in his field. [32]Though it is the smallest of all your seeds, yet when it grows, it is the largest of garden plants and becomes a tree, so that the birds of the air come and perch in its branches."

MATTHEW 13:33 He told them still another parable: "The kingdom of heaven is like yeast that a woman took and mixed into a large amount of flour until it worked all through the dough."

MATTHEW 13:44-46 "The kingdom of heaven is like treasure hidden in a field. When a man found it, he hid it again, and then in his joy went and sold all he had and bought that field. [45]Again, the kingdom of heaven is like a merchant looking for fine pearls. [46]When he found one of great value, he went away and sold everything he had and bought it."

MATTHEW 13:47-50 "Once again, the kingdom of heaven is like a net that was let down into the lake and caught all kinds of fish. [48]When it was full, the fishermen pulled it up on the shore. Then they sat down and collected the good fish in baskets, but threw the bad away. [49]This is how it will be at the end of the age. The angels will come and separate the wicked from the righteous [50]and throw them into the fiery furnace, where there will be weeping and gnashing of teeth."

MATTHEW 13:51-52 "Have you understood all these things?" Jesus asked. "Yes," they replied. [52]He said to them, "Therefore every teacher of the law who has been instructed about the kingdom of heaven is like the owner of a house who brings out of his storeroom new treasures as well as old."

MATTHEW 16:17-19 Jesus replied, "Blessed are you, Simon son of Jonah, for this was not revealed to you by man, but by my Father in heaven. [18]And I tell you that you are Peter, and on this rock I will build my church, and the gates of Hades will not overcome it. [19]I will give you the keys of the kingdom of heaven; whatever you bind on earth will be bound in heaven, and whatever you loose on earth will be loosed in heaven."

MATTHEW 18:2-4 He called a little child and had him stand among them. [3]And he said: "I tell you the truth, unless you change and become like little children, you will never enter the kingdom of heaven. [4]Therefore, whoever humbles himself like this child is the greatest in the kingdom of heaven."

MATTHEW 19:11-12 Jesus replied, "Not everyone can accept this word [on divorce], but only those to whom it has been given. [12]For some are eunuchs because they were born that way; others were made that way by men; and others have renounced marriage because of the kingdom of heaven. The one who can accept this should accept it."

MATTHEW 19:14 Jesus said, "Let the little children come to me, and do not hinder them, for the kingdom of heaven belongs to such as these."

MATTHEW 19:21 Jesus answered, "If you want to be perfect, go, sell your possessions and give to the poor, and you will have treasure in heaven. Then come, follow me."

MATTHEW 19:23-26 Then Jesus said to his disciples, "I tell you the truth, it is hard for a rich man to enter the kingdom of heaven. [24]Again I tell you, it is easier for a camel to go through the eye of a needle than for a rich man to enter the kingdom of God." [25]When the disciples heard this, they were greatly astonished and asked, "Who then can be saved?" [26]Jesus looked at them and said, "With man this is impossible, but with God all things are possible."

MATTHEW 20:1-16 "For the kingdom of heaven is like a landowner who went out early in the morning to hire men to work in his vineyard. [2]He agreed to pay them a denarius for the day and sent them into his vineyard. [3]About the third hour he went out and saw others standing in the marketplace doing nothing. [4]He told them, 'You also go and work in my vineyard, and I will pay you whatever is right.' [5]So they went. He went out again about the sixth hour and the ninth hour and did the same thing. [6]About the eleventh hour he went out and found still others standing around. He asked them, 'Why have you been standing here all day long doing nothing?' [7]'Because no one has hired us,' they answered. He said to them, 'You also go and work in my vineyard.' [8]When evening came, the owner of the vineyard said to his foreman, 'Call the workers and pay them their wages, beginning with the last ones hired and going on to the first.' [9]The workers who were hired about the eleventh hour came and each received a denarius. [10]So when those came who were hired first, they expected to receive more. But each one of them also received a denarius. [11]When they received it, they began to grumble against the landowner. [12]'These men who were hired last worked only one hour,' they said, 'and you have made them equal to us who have borne the burden of the work and the heat of the day.' [13]But he answered one of them, 'Friend, I am not being unfair to you. Didn't you agree to work for a denarius? [14]Take your pay and go. I want to give the man who was hired last the same as I gave you. [15]Don't I have the right to do what I want with my own money? Or are you envious because I am generous?' [16]So the last will be first, and the first will be last."

MATTHEW 22:1-14 Jesus spoke to them again in parables, saying: [2]"The kingdom of heaven is like a king who prepared a wedding banquet for his son. [3]He sent his servants to those who had been invited to the banquet to tell them to come, but they refused to come. [4]Then he sent some more servants and said, 'Tell those who have been invited that I have prepared my dinner: My oxen and fattened cattle have been butchered, and

everything is ready. Come to the wedding banquet.' [5]But they paid no attention and went off—one to his field, another to his business. [6]The rest seized his servants, mistreated them and killed them. [7]The king was enraged. He sent his army and destroyed those murderers and burned their city. [8]Then he said to his servants, 'The wedding banquet is ready, but those I invited did not deserve to come. [9]Go to the street corners and invite to the banquet anyone you find.' [10]So the servants went out into the streets and gathered all the people they could find, both good and bad, and the wedding hall was filled with guests. [11]But when the king came in to see the guests, he noticed a man there who was not wearing wedding clothes. [12]'Friend,' he asked, 'how did you get in here without wedding clothes?' The man was speechless. [13]Then the king told the attendants, 'Tie him hand and foot, and throw him outside, into the darkness, where there will be weeping and gnashing of teeth.' [14]For many are invited, but few are chosen."

MATTHEW 22:29-32 Jesus replied, "You are in error because you do not know the Scriptures or the power of God. [30]At the resurrection people will neither marry nor be given in marriage; they will be like the angels in heaven. [31]But about the resurrection of the dead—have you not read what God said to you, [32]'I am the God of Abraham, the God of Isaac, and the God of Jacob'? He is not the God of the dead but of the living."

MATTHEW 25:1-13 "At that time the kingdom of heaven will be like ten virgins who took their lamps and went out to meet the bridegroom. [2]Five of them were foolish and five were wise. [3]The foolish ones took their lamps but did not take any oil with them. [4]The wise, however, took oil in jars along with their lamps. [5]The bridegroom was a long time in coming, and they all became drowsy and fell asleep. [6]At midnight the cry rang out: 'Here's the bridegroom! Come out to meet him!' [7]Then all the virgins woke up and trimmed their lamps. [8]The foolish ones said to the wise, 'Give us some of your oil; our lamps are going out.' [9]'No,' they replied, 'there may not be enough for both us and you. Instead, go to those who sell oil and buy some for yourselves.' [10]But while they were on their way to buy the oil, the bridegroom arrived. The virgins who were ready went in with him to the wedding banquet. And the door was shut. [11]Later the others also came. 'Sir! Sir!' they said. 'Open the door for us!' [12]But he replied, 'I tell you the truth, I don't know you.' [13]Therefore keep watch, because you do not know the day or the hour."

MATTHEW 25:14-30 "Again, it will be like a man going on a journey, who called his servants and entrusted his property to them. [15]To one he gave five talents of money, to another two talents, and to another one talent, each according to his ability. Then he went on his journey. [16]The man who had received the five talents went at once and put his money to work and gained five more. [17]So also, the one with the two talents gained two more. [18]But the man who had received the one talent went off, dug a hole in the ground and hid his master's money. [19]After a long time the master of those servants returned and settled accounts with them. [20]The man who had received the five talents brought the other five. 'Master,' he said, 'you entrusted me with five talents. See, I have gained five more.' [21]His master replied, 'Well done, good and faithful servant! You have been faithful with a few things; I will put you in charge of many things. Come and share your master's happiness!' [22]The man with the two talents also came. 'Master,' he said, 'you entrusted me with two talents; see, I have gained two more.' [23]His master replied, 'Well done, good and faithful servant! You have been faithful with a few things; I will put you in charge of many things. Come and share your master's happiness!' [24]Then the man who had received the one talent came. 'Master,' he said, 'I knew that you are a hard man, harvesting where you have not sown and gathering where you have not scattered seed. [25]So I was afraid and went out and hid your talent in the ground. See, here is what belongs to you.' [26]His master replied, 'You wicked, lazy servant! So you knew that I harvest where I have not sown and gather where I have not scattered seed? [27]Well then, you should have put my money on deposit with the bankers, so that when I returned I would have received it back with interest. [28]Take the talent from him and give it to the one who has the ten talents. [29]For everyone who has will be given more, and he will have an abundance. Whoever does not have, even what he has will be taken from him. [30]And throw that worthless servant outside, into the darkness, where there will be weeping and gnashing of teeth.'"

MATTHEW 25:31-36, 41-46 "When the Son of Man comes in his glory, and all the angels with him, he will sit on his throne in heavenly glory. [32]All the nations will be gathered before him, and he will separate the people one from another as a shepherd separates the sheep from the goats. [33]He will put the sheep on his right and the goats on his left. [34]Then the King will say to those on his right, 'Come, you who are blessed by my Father; take your inheritance, the kingdom prepared for you since the creation of the world. [35]For I was hungry and you gave me something to eat, I was thirsty and you gave me something to drink, I was a stranger and you invited me in, [36]I needed clothes and you clothed me, I was sick and you looked after me, I was in prison and you came to visit me.' [41]Then he will say to those on his left, 'Depart from me, you who are cursed, into the eternal fire prepared for the devil and his angels. [42]For I was hungry and you gave me nothing to eat, I was thirsty and you gave me nothing to drink, [43]I was a stranger and you did not invite me in, I needed clothes and you did not clothe me, I was sick and in prison and you did not look after me.' [44]They also will answer, 'Lord, when did we see you hungry or thirsty or a stranger or needing clothes or sick or in prison, and did not help you?' [45]He will reply, 'I tell you the truth, whatever you did not do for one of the least of these, you did not do for me.' [46]Then they will go away to eternal punishment, but the righteous to eternal life."

MARK 12:24-27 Jesus replied, "Are you not in error because you do not know the Scriptures or the power of God? [25]When the dead rise, they will neither marry nor be given in marriage; they will be like the angels in heaven. [26]Now about the dead rising—have you not read in the book of Moses, in the account of the bush, how God said to him, 'I am the God of Abraham, the God of Isaac, and the God of Jacob'? [27]He is not the God of the dead, but of the living. You are badly mistaken!"

LUKE 10:17-20 The seventy-two returned with joy and said, "Lord, even the demons submit to us in your name." [18]He replied, "I saw Satan fall like lightning from heaven. [19]I have given you authority to trample on snakes and scorpions and to overcome all the power of the enemy; nothing will harm you. [20]However, do not rejoice that the spirits submit to you, but rejoice that your names are written in heaven."

LUKE 15:7-10 "I tell you that in the same way there will be more rejoicing in heaven over one sinner who repents than over ninety-nine righteous persons who do not need to repent. [8]Or suppose a woman has ten silver coins and loses one. Does she not light a lamp, sweep the house and search carefully until she finds it? [9]And when she finds it, she calls her friends and neighbors together and says, 'Rejoice with me; I have found my lost coin.' [10]In the same way, I tell you, there is rejoicing in the presence of the angels of God over one sinner who repents."

LUKE 16:19-31 "There was a rich man who was dressed in purple and fine linen and lived in luxury every day. [20]At his gate was laid a beggar named Lazarus, covered with sores [21]and longing to eat what fell from the rich man's table. Even the dogs came and licked his sores. [22]The time came when the beggar died and the angels carried him to Abraham's side. The rich man also died and was buried. [23]In hell, where he was in torment, he looked up and saw Abraham far away, with Lazarus by his side. [24]So he called to him, 'Father Abraham, have pity on me and send Lazarus to dip the tip of his finger in water and cool my tongue, because I am in agony in this fire.' [25]But Abraham replied, 'Son, remember that in your lifetime you received your good things, while Lazarus received bad things, but now he is comforted here and you are in agony. [26]And besides all this, between us and you a great chasm has been fixed, so that those who want to go from here to you cannot, nor can anyone cross over from there to us.' [27]He answered, 'Then I beg you, father, send Lazarus to my father's house, [28]for I have five brothers. Let him warn them, so that they will not also come to this place of torment.' [29]Abraham replied, 'They have Moses and the Prophets; let them listen to them.' [30]'No, father Abraham,' he said, 'but if someone from the dead goes to them, they will repent.' [31]He said to him, 'If they do not listen to Moses and the Prophets, they will not be convinced even if someone rises from the dead.'"

LUKE 19:12-27 He said: "A man of noble birth went to a distant country to have himself appointed king and then to return. [13]So he called ten of his servants and gave them ten minas. 'Put this money to work,' he said, 'until I come back.' [14]But his subjects hated him and sent a delegation after him to say, 'We don't want this man to be our king.' [15]He was made king, however, and returned home.

Then he sent for the servants to whom he had given the money, in order to find out what they had gained with it. [16]The first one came and said, 'Sir, your mina has earned ten more.' [17]'Well done, my good servant!' his master replied. 'Because you have been trustworthy in a very small matter, take charge of ten cities.' [18]The second came and said, 'Sir, your mina has earned five more.' [19]His master answered, 'You take charge of five cities.' [20]Then another servant came and said, 'Sir, here is your mina; I have kept it laid away in a piece of cloth. [21]I was afraid of you, because you are a hard man. You take out what you did not put in and reap what you did not sow.' [22]His master replied, 'I will judge you by your own words, you wicked servant! You knew, did you, that I am a hard man, taking out what I did not put in, and reaping what I did not sow? [23]Why then didn't you put my money on deposit, so that when I came back, I could have collected it with interest?' [24]Then he said to those standing by, 'Take his mina away from him and give it to the one who has ten minas.' [25]'Sir,' they said, 'he already has ten!' [26]He replied, 'I tell you that to everyone who has, more will be given, but as for the one who has nothing, even what he has will be taken away. [27]But those enemies of mine who did not want me to be king over them—bring them here and kill them in front of me.'"

LUKE 20:34-37 Jesus replied, "The people of this age marry and are given in marriage. [35]But those who are considered worthy of taking part in that age and in the resurrection from the dead will neither marry nor be given in marriage, [36]and they can no longer die; for they are like the angels. They are God's children, since they are children of the resurrection. [37]But in the account of the bush, even Moses showed that the dead rise, for he calls the Lord "the God of Abraham, and the God of Isaac, and the God of Jacob.'"

The Judgment, Hell, and Eternal Punishment

"If God is a God of love, how could He ever condemn anyone to eternal punishment?" I've heard this question hundreds of times. The answer is simple: God is also a God of righteousness and justice. As much as we would like Him to be Santa Claus, He is not. His justice demands eternal punishment for those who do not live according to the righteous laws that reflect His nature. The good news is, His love has provided a perfect substitute sacrifice upon which all His judgment was poured. By believing in God's Son and following Him, anyone can avoid God's judgment. Why? Because Jesus received all of God's punishment for the sins *we* have committed. In 2 Corinthians 5:21, the apostle Paul wrote: "For He made Him who knew no sin to be sin for us, that we might become the righteousness of God in Him" (NKJV). Jesus makes it clear that ultimate judgment will take place. But He makes it equally clear that those who truly believe in Him will avoid this judgment, because their sins have already been paid for with His atoning sacrifice.

JOHN 3:18-21 "Whoever believes in him [Christ] is not condemned, but who-ever does not believe stands condemned already because he has not believed in the name of God's one and only Son. [19]This is the verdict: Light has come into the world, but men loved darkness instead of light because their deeds were evil. [20]Everyone who does evil hates the light, and will not come into the light for fear that his deeds will be exposed. [21]But whoever lives by the truth comes into the light, so that it may be seen plainly that what he has done has been done through God."

JOHN 5:21-22 "For just as the Father raises the dead and gives them life, even so the Son gives life to whom he is pleased to give it. [22]Moreover, the Father judges no one, but has entrusted all judgment to the Son."

JOHN 5:24-29 "I tell you the truth, whoever hears my word and believes him who sent me has eternal life and will not be condemned; he has crossed over from death to life. [25]I tell you the truth, a time is coming and has now come when the dead will hear the voice of the Son of God and those who hear will live. [26]For as the Father has life in himself, so he has granted the Son to have life in himself. [27]And he has given him authority to judge because he is the Son of Man. [28]Do not be amazed at this, for a time is coming when all who are in their graves will hear his voice [29]and come out—those who have done good will rise to live, and those who have done evil will rise to be condemned."

JOHN 5:45-47 "But do not think I will accuse you before the Father. Your accuser is Moses, on whom your hopes are set. [46]If you believed Moses, you would believe me, for he wrote about me. [47]But since you do not believe what he wrote, how are you going to believe what I say?"

JOHN 8:14-16 Jesus answered, "Even if I testify on my own behalf, my testimony is valid, for I know where I came from and where I am going. But you have no idea where I come from or where I am going. [15]You judge by human standards; I pass judgment on no one. [16]But if I do judge, my decisions are right, because I am not alone. I stand with the Father, who sent me."

JOHN 8:49-51 "I am not possessed by a demon," said Jesus, "but I honor my Father and you dishonor me. [50]I am not seeking glory for myself; but there is one who seeks it, and he is the judge. [51]I tell you the truth, if anyone keeps my word, he will never see death."

JOHN 9:39 Jesus said, "For judgment I have come into this world, so that the blind will see and those who see will become blind."

JOHN 12:31-32 "Now is the time for judgment on this world; now the prince of this world will be driven out. [32]But I, when I am lifted up from the earth, will draw all men to myself."

JOHN 12:47-50 "As for the person who hears my words but does not keep them, I do not judge him. For I did not come to judge the world, but to save it. [48]There is a judge for the one who rejects me and does not accept my words; that very word which I spoke will condemn him at the last day. [49]For I did not speak of my own accord, but the Father who sent me commanded me what to say and how to say it. [50]I know that his command leads to eternal life. So whatever I say is just what the Father has told me to say."

JOHN 15:22 "If I had not come and spoken to them, they would not be guilty of sin. Now, however, they have no excuse for their sin."

JOHN 15:24-25 "If I had not done among them what no one else did, they would not be guilty of sin. But now they have seen these miracles, and yet they have hated both me and my Father. [25]But this is to fulfill what is written in their Law: 'They hated me without reason.' "

JOHN 16:8-11 "When he [the Holy Spirit] comes, he will convict the world of guilt in regard to sin and righteousness and judgment: [9]in regard to sin, because men do not believe in me; [10]in regard to righteousness, because I am going to the Father, where you can see me no longer; [11]and in regard to judgment, because the prince of this world now stands condemned."

MATTHEW 5:21-22 "You have heard that it was said to the people long ago, 'Do not murder, and anyone who murders will be subject to judgment.' [22]But I tell you that anyone who is angry with his brother will be subject to judgment. Again, anyone who says to his brother, 'Raca,' is answerable to the Sanhedrin. But anyone who says, 'You fool!' will be in danger of the fire of hell."

MATTHEW 5:27-30 "You have heard that it was said, 'Do not commit adultery.' [28]But I tell you that anyone who looks at a woman lustfully has already committed adultery with her in his heart. [29]If your right eye causes you to sin, gouge it out and throw it away. It is better for you to lose one part of your body than for your whole body to be thrown into hell.

30And if your right hand causes you to sin, cut it off and throw it away. It is better for you to lose one part of your body than for your whole body to go into hell."

MATTHEW 7:1-3 "Do not judge, or you too will be judged. 2For in the same way you judge others, you will be judged, and with the measure you use, it will be measured to you. 3Why do you look at the speck of sawdust in your brother's eye and pay no attention to the plank in your own eye?"

MATTHEW 7:13-14 "Enter through the narrow gate. For wide is the gate and broad is the road that leads to destruction, and many enter through it. 14But small is the gate and narrow the road that leads to life, and only a few find it."

MATTHEW 7:19 "Every tree that does not bear good fruit is cut down and thrown into the fire."

MATTHEW 7:21-23 "Not everyone who says to Me, 'Lord, Lord,' shall enter the kingdom of heaven, but he who does the will of My Father in heaven. 22Many will say to Me in that day, 'Lord, Lord, have we not prophesied in Your name, cast out demons in Your name, and done many wonders in Your name?' 23And then I will declare to them, 'I never knew you; depart from Me, you who practice lawlessness!'" (NKJV)

MATTHEW 8:10-12 When Jesus heard this [the centurion's testimony], he was astonished and said to those following him, "I tell you the truth, I have not found anyone in Israel with such great faith. 11I say to you that many will come from the east and the west, and will take their places at the feast with Abraham, Isaac and Jacob in the kingdom of heaven. 12But the subjects of the kingdom will be thrown outside, into the darkness, where there will be weeping and gnashing of teeth."

MATTHEW 10:28 "Do not be afraid of those who kill the body but cannot kill the soul. Rather, be afraid of the One who can destroy both soul and body in hell."

MATTHEW 11:20-24 Then Jesus began to denounce the cities in which most of his miracles had been performed, because they did not repent. 21"Woe to you, Korazin! Woe to you, Bethsaida! If the miracles that were performed in you had been performed in Tyre and Sidon, they would have repented long ago in sackcloth and ashes. 22But I tell you, it will be more bearable for Tyre and Sidon on the day of judgment than for you. 23And you, Capernaum, will you be lifted up to the skies? No, you will go down to the depths. If the miracles that were performed in you had been performed in Sodom, it would have remained to this day. 24But I tell you that it will be more bearable for Sodom on the day of judgment than for you." (See also Luke 10:13-15.)

MATTHEW 12:34-37 "You brood of vipers, how can you who are evil say anything good? For out of the overflow of the heart the mouth speaks. 35The good man brings good things out of the good stored up in him, and the evil man brings evil things out of the evil stored up in him. 36But I tell you that men will have to give account on the day of judgment for every careless word they have spoken. 37For by your words you will be acquitted, and by your words you will be condemned."

MATTHEW 12:39-42 He answered, "A wicked and adulterous generation asks for a miraculous sign! But none will be given it except the sign of the prophet Jonah. [40]For as Jonah was three days and three nights in the belly of a huge fish, so the Son of Man will be three days and three nights in the heart of the earth. [41]The men of Nineveh will stand up at the judgment with this generation and condemn it; for they repented at the preaching of Jonah, and now one greater than Jonah is here. [42]The Queen of the South will rise at the judgment with this generation and condemn it; for she came from the ends of the earth to listen to Solomon's wisdom, and now one greater than Solomon is here."

MATTHEW 13:24-30 Jesus told them another parable: "The kingdom of heaven is like a man who sowed good seed in his field. [25]But while everyone was sleeping, his enemy came and sowed weeds among the wheat, and went away. [26]When the wheat sprouted and formed heads, then the weeds also appeared. [27]The owner's servants came to him and said, 'Sir, didn't you sow good seed in your field? Where then did the weeds come from?' [28]'An enemy did this,' he replied. The servants asked him, 'Do you want us to go and pull them up?' [29]'No,' he answered, 'because while you are pulling the weeds, you may root up the wheat with them. [30]Let both grow together until the harvest. At that time I will tell the harvesters: First collect the weeds and tie them in bundles to be burned; then gather the wheat and bring it into my barn.'"

MATTHEW 13:37-43 He answered, "The one who sowed the good seed is the Son of Man. [38]The field is the world, and the good seed stands for the sons of the kingdom. The weeds are the sons of the evil one, [39]and the enemy who sows them is the devil. The harvest is the end of the age, and the harvesters are angels. [40]As the weeds are pulled up and burned in the fire, so it will be at the end of the age. [41]The Son of Man will send out his angels, and they will weed out of his kingdom everything that causes sin and all who do evil. [42]They will throw them into the fiery furnace, where there will be weeping and gnashing of teeth. [43]Then the righteous will shine like the sun in the kingdom of their Father. He who has ears, let him hear."

MATTHEW 13:47-50 "Once again, the kingdom of heaven is like a net that was let down into the lake and caught all kinds of fish. [48]When it was full, the fishermen pulled it up on the shore. Then they sat down and collected the good fish in baskets, but threw the bad away. [49]This is how it will be at the end of the age. The angels will come and separate the wicked from the righteous [50]and throw them into the fiery furnace, where there will be weeping and gnashing of teeth."

MATTHEW 18:8-9 "If your hand or your foot causes you to sin, cut it off and throw it away. It is better for you to enter life maimed or crippled than to have two hands or two feet and be thrown into eternal fire. [9]And if your eye causes you to sin, gouge it out and throw it away. It is better for you to enter life with one eye than to have two eyes and be thrown into the fire of hell."

MATTHEW 21:33-40 "Listen to another parable: There was a landowner who planted a vineyard. He put a wall around it, dug a winepress in it and built a watchtower. Then he rented the vineyard to some farmers and went away on a journey. [34]When the harvest time approached, he sent his servants to the tenants to collect his fruit. [35]The tenants seized his servants; they beat one, killed another, and stoned a third. [36]Then he sent other servants to them, more than the first time, and the tenants treated them the same way. [37]Last of all, he sent his son to them. 'They will respect my son,' he said. [38]But when the tenants saw the son, they said to each other, 'This is the heir. Come, let's kill him and take his inheritance.' [39]So they took him and threw him out of the vineyard and killed him. [40]Therefore, when the owner of the vineyard comes, what will he do to those tenants?"

MATTHEW 21:42-44 Jesus said to them, "Have you never read in the Scriptures: 'The stone the builders rejected has become the capstone; the Lord has done this, and it is marvelous in our eyes'? [43]Therefore I tell you that the kingdom of God will be taken away from you and given to a people who will produce its fruit. [44]He who falls on this stone will be broken to pieces, but he on whom it falls will be crushed."

MATTHEW 22:1-14 Jesus spoke to them again in parables, saying: [2]"The kingdom of heaven is like a king who prepared a wedding banquet for his son. [3]He sent his servants to those who had been invited to the banquet to tell them to come, but they refused to come. [4]Then he sent some more servants and said, 'Tell those who have been invited that I have prepared my dinner: My oxen and fattened cattle have been butchered, and everything is ready. Come to the wedding banquet.' [5]But they paid no attention and went off—one to his field, another to his business. [6]The rest seized his servants, mistreated them and killed them. [7]The king was enraged. He sent his army and destroyed those murderers and burned their city. [8]Then he said to his servants, 'The wedding banquet is ready, but those I invited did not deserve to come. [9]Go to the street corners and invite to the banquet anyone you find.' [10]So the servants went out into the streets and gathered all the people they could find, both good and bad, and the wedding hall was filled with guests. [11]But when the king came in to see the guests, he noticed a man there who was not wearing wedding clothes. [12]'Friend,' he asked, 'how did you get in here without wedding clothes?' The man was speechless. [13]Then the king told the attendants, 'Tie him hand and foot, and throw him outside, into the darkness, where there will be weeping and gnashing of teeth.' [14]For many are invited, but few are chosen."

MATTHEW 23:31-33 "So you testify against yourselves that you are the descendants of those who murdered the prophets. [32]Fill up, then, the measure of the sin of your forefathers! [33]You snakes! You brood of vipers! How will you escape being condemned to hell?"

MATTHEW 24:45-51 "Who then is the faithful and wise servant, whom the master has put in charge of the servants in his household to give them their food at the proper time? [46]It will be good for that servant whose master finds him doing so when he returns. [47]I tell you the truth, he will put him in charge of all his possessions. [48]But suppose that servant is wicked and says to himself, 'My master is staying away a long time,' [49]and he then begins to beat his fellow servants and to eat and drink with drunkards. [50]The master of that servant will come on a day when he does not expect him and at an hour he is not aware of. [51]He will cut him to pieces and assign him a place with the hypocrites, where there will be weeping and gnashing of teeth."

MATTHEW 25:14-30 "Again, it will be like a man going on a journey, who called his servants and entrusted his property to them. [15]To one he gave five talents of money, to another two talents, and to another one talent, each according to his ability. Then he went on his journey. [16]The man who had received the five talents went at once and put his money to work and gained five more. [17]So also, the one with the two talents gained two more. [18]But the man who had received the one talent went off, dug a hole in the ground and hid his master's money. [19]After a long time the master of those servants returned and settled accounts with them. [20]The man who had received the five talents brought the other five. 'Master,' he said, 'you entrusted me with five talents. See, I have gained five more.' [21]His master replied, 'Well done, good and faithful servant! You have been faithful with a few things; I will put you in charge of many things. Come and share your master's happiness!' [22]The man with the two talents also came. 'Master,' he said, 'you entrusted me with two talents; see, I have gained two more.' [23]His master replied, 'Well done, good and faithful servant! You have been faithful with a few things; I will put you in charge of many things. Come and share your master's happiness!' [24]Then the man who had received the one talent came. 'Master,' he said, 'I knew that you are a hard man, harvesting where you have not sown and gathering where you have not scattered seed. [25]So I was afraid and went out and hid your talent in the ground. See, here is what belongs to you.' [26]His master replied, 'You wicked, lazy servant! So you knew that I harvest where I have not sown and gather where I have not scattered seed? [27]Well then, you should have put my money on deposit with the bankers, so that when I returned I would have received it back with interest. [28]Take the talent from him and give it to the one who has the ten talents. [29]For everyone who has will be given more, and he will have an abundance. Whoever does not have, even what he has will be taken from him. [30]And throw that worthless servant outside, into the darkness, where there will be weeping and gnashing of teeth.' "

MATTHEW 25:31-46 "When the Son of Man comes in his glory, and all the angels with him, he will sit on his throne in heavenly glory. [32]All the nations will be gathered before him, and he will separate the people one from another as a shepherd separates the sheep from the goats. [33]He will put the sheep on his right and the goats on his left. ³⁴Then the King will say to those on his right, 'Come, you who are blessed by my Father; take your inheritance, the kingdom prepared for you since the creation of the world. ³⁵For I was hungry and you gave me something to eat, I was thirsty and you gave me something to drink, I was a stranger and you invited me in, ³⁶I needed clothes and you clothed me, I was sick and you looked after me, I was in prison and you came to visit me.' ³⁷Then the righteous will answer him, 'Lord, when did we see you hungry and feed you, or thirsty and give you something to drink? ³⁸When did we see you a stranger and invite you in, or needing clothes and clothe you? ³⁹When did we see you sick or in prison and go to visit you?' ⁴⁰The King will reply, 'I tell you the truth, whatever you did for one of the least of these brothers of mine, you did for me.' ⁴¹Then he will say to those on his left, 'Depart from me, you who are cursed, into the eternal fire prepared for the devil and his angels. ⁴²For I was hungry and you gave me nothing to eat, I was thirsty and you gave me nothing to drink, ⁴³I was a stranger and you did not invite me in, I needed clothes and you did not clothe me, I was sick and in prison and you did not look after me.' ⁴⁴They also will answer, 'Lord, when did we see you hungry or thirsty or a stranger or needing clothes or sick or in prison, and did not help you?' ⁴⁵He will reply, 'I tell you the truth, whatever you did not do for one of the least of these, you did not do for me.' ⁴⁶Then they will go away to eternal punishment, but the righteous to eternal life."

MARK 2:17 On hearing this, Jesus said to them, "It is not the healthy who need a doctor, but the sick. I have not come to call the righteous, but sinners." (See also Luke 5:32.)

MARK 3:28-30 "I tell you the truth, all the sins and blasphemies of men will be forgiven them. ²⁹But whoever blasphemes against the Holy Spirit will never be forgiven; he is guilty of an eternal sin." ³⁰He said this because they were saying, "He has an evil spirit."

MARK 4:21-25 He said to them, "Do you bring in a lamp to put it under a bowl or a bed? Instead, don't you put it on its stand? ²²For whatever is hidden is meant to be disclosed, and whatever is concealed is meant to be brought out into the open. ²³If anyone has ears to hear, let him hear. ²⁴Consider carefully what you hear," he continued. "With the measure you use, it will be measured to you—and even more. ²⁵Whoever has will be given more; whoever does not have, even what he has will be taken from him."

MARK 6:8-11 These were his instructions [to the Twelve]: "Take nothing for the journey except a staff—no bread, no bag, no money in your belts. ⁹Wear sandals but not an extra tunic. ¹⁰Whenever you enter a house, stay there until you leave that town. ¹¹And if any place will not welcome you or listen to you, shake the dust off your feet when you leave, as a testimony against them." (See also Matthew 10:9-15; Luke 9:1-5.)

MARK 9:43, 45, 47-48 "If your hand causes you to sin, cut it off. It is better for you to enter life maimed than with two hands to go into hell, where the fire never goes out. ⁴⁵And if your foot causes you to sin, cut it off. It is better for you to enter life crippled than to have two feet and be thrown into hell. ⁴⁷And if your eye causes you to sin, pluck it out. It is better for you to enter the kingdom of God with one eye than to have two eyes and be thrown into hell, ⁴⁸where 'their worm does not die, and the fire is not quenched.'"

MARK 12:1-11 He then began to speak to them in parables: "A man planted a vineyard. He put a wall around it, dug a pit for the winepress and built a watchtower. Then he rented the vineyard to some farmers and went away on a journey. ²At harvest time he sent a servant to the tenants to collect from them some of the fruit of the vineyard. ³But they seized him, beat him and sent him away empty-handed. ⁴Then he sent another servant to them; they struck this man on the head and treated him shamefully. ⁵He sent still another, and that one they killed. He sent many others; some of them they beat, others they killed. ⁶He had one left to send, a son, whom he loved. He sent him last of all, saying, 'They will respect my son.' ⁷But the tenants said to one another, 'This is the heir. Come, let's kill him, and the inheritance will be ours.' ⁸So they took him and killed him, and threw him out of the vineyard. ⁹What then will the owner of the vineyard do? He will come and kill those tenants and give the vineyard to others. ¹⁰Haven't you read this scripture: 'The stone the builders rejected has become the capstone; ¹¹the Lord has done this, and it is marvelous in our eyes'?"

MARK 16:14-16 Later Jesus appeared to the Eleven as they were eating; he rebuked them for their lack of faith and their stubborn refusal to believe those who had seen him after he had risen. ¹⁵He said to them, "Go into all the world and preach the good news to all creation. ¹⁶Whoever believes and is baptized will be saved, but whoever does not believe will be condemned."ᵛⁱⁱⁱ

LUKE 10:8-12 "When you enter a town and are welcomed, eat what is set before you. ⁹Heal the sick who are there and tell them, 'The kingdom of God is near you.' ¹⁰But when you enter a town and are not welcomed, go into its streets and say, ¹¹'Even the dust of your town that sticks to our feet we wipe off against you. Yet be sure of this: The kingdom of God is near.' ¹²I tell you, it will be more bearable on that day for Sodom than for that town."

LUKE 10:16 "He who listens to you [the seventy-two disciples who were sent out] listens to me; he who rejects you rejects me; but he who rejects me rejects him who sent me."

LUKE 12:1-3 Meanwhile, when a crowd of many thousands had gathered, so that they were trampling on one another, Jesus began to speak first to his disciples, saying: "Be on your guard against the yeast of the Pharisees, which is hypocrisy. ²There is nothing concealed that will not be disclosed, or hidden that will not be made known. ³What you have said in the dark will be heard in the daylight, and what you have whispered in the ear in the inner rooms will be proclaimed from the roofs."

LUKE 12:4-5 "I tell you, my friends, do not be afraid of those who kill the body and after that can do no more. [5]But I will show you whom you should fear: Fear him who, after the killing of the body, has power to throw you into hell. Yes, I tell you, fear him."

LUKE 12:8-10 "I tell you, whoever acknowledges me before men, the Son of Man will also acknowledge him before the angels of God. [9]But he who disowns me before men will be disowned before the angels of God. [10]And everyone who speaks a word against the Son of Man will be forgiven, but anyone who blasphemes against the Holy Spirit will not be forgiven."

LUKE 12:35-40 "Be dressed ready for service and keep your lamps burning, [36]like men waiting for their master to return from a wedding banquet, so that when he comes and knocks they can immediately open the door for him. [37]It will be good for those servants whose master finds them watching when he comes. I tell you the truth, he will dress himself to serve, will have them recline at the table and will come and wait on them. [38]It will be good for those servants whose master finds them ready, even if he comes in the second or third watch of the night. [39]But understand this: If the owner of the house had known at what hour the thief was coming, he would not have let his house be broken into. [40]You also must be ready, because the Son of Man will come at an hour when you do not expect him."

LUKE 12:42-48 The Lord answered, "Who then is the faithful and wise manager, whom the master puts in charge of his servants to give them their food allowance at the proper time? [43]It will be good for that servant whom the master finds doing so when he returns. [44]I tell you the truth, he will put him in charge of all his possessions. [45]But suppose the servant says to himself, 'My master is taking a long time in coming,' and he then begins to beat the menservants and maidservants and to eat and drink and get drunk. [46]The master of that servant will come on a day when he does not expect him and at an hour he is not aware of. He will cut him to pieces and assign him a place with the unbelievers. [47]That servant who knows his master's will and does not get ready or does not do what his master wants will be beaten with many blows. [48]But the one who does not know and does things deserving punishment will be beaten with few blows. From everyone who has been given much, much will be demanded; and from the one who has been entrusted with much, much more will be asked."

LUKE 13:6-9 Then he told this parable: "A man had a fig tree, planted in his vineyard, and he went to look for fruit on it, but did not find any. [7]So he said to the man who took care of the vineyard, 'For three years now I've been coming to look for fruit on this fig tree and haven't found any. Cut it down! Why should it use up the soil?' [8]'Sir,' the man replied, 'leave it alone for one more year, and I'll dig around it and fertilize it. [9]If it bears fruit next year, fine! If not, then cut it down.'"

LUKE 13:23-30 Someone asked him, "Lord, are only a few people going to be saved?" He said to them, [24]"Make every effort to enter through the narrow door, because many, I tell you, will try to enter and will not be able to. ²⁵Once the owner of the house gets up and closes the door, you will stand outside knocking and pleading, 'Sir, open the door for us.' But he will answer, 'I don't know you or where you come from.' ²⁶Then you will say, 'We ate and drank with you, and you taught in our streets.' ²⁷But he will reply, 'I don't know you or where you come from. Away from me, all you evildoers!' ²⁸There will be weeping there, and gnashing of teeth, when you see Abraham, Isaac and Jacob and all the prophets in the kingdom of God, but you yourselves thrown out. ²⁹People will come from east and west and north and south, and will take their places at the feast in the kingdom of God. ³⁰Indeed there are those who are last who will be first, and first who will be last."

LUKE 16:15 He said to them [the Pharisees], "You are the ones who justify yourselves in the eyes of men, but God knows your hearts. What is highly valued among men is detestable in God's sight."

LUKE 16:19-31 "There was a rich man who was dressed in purple and fine linen and lived in luxury every day. ²⁰At his gate was laid a beggar named Lazarus, covered with sores ²¹and longing to eat what fell from the rich man's table. Even the dogs came and licked his sores. ²²The time came when the beggar died and the angels carried him to Abraham's side. The rich man also died and was buried. ²³In hell, where he was in torment, he looked up and saw Abraham far away, with Lazarus by his side. ²⁴So he called to him, 'Father Abraham, have pity on me and send Lazarus to dip the tip of his finger in water and cool my tongue, because I am in agony in this fire.' ²⁵But Abraham replied, 'Son, remember that in your lifetime you received your good things, while Lazarus received bad things, but now he is comforted here and you are in agony. ²⁶And besides all this, between us and you a great chasm has been fixed, so that those who want to go from here to you cannot, nor can anyone cross over from there to us.' ²⁷He answered, 'Then I beg you, father, send Lazarus to my father's house, ²⁸for I have five brothers. Let him warn them, so that they will not also come to this place of torment.' ²⁹Abraham replied, 'They have Moses and the Prophets; let them listen to them.' ³⁰'No, father Abraham,' he said, 'but if someone from the dead goes to them, they will repent.' ³¹He said to him, 'If they do not listen to Moses and the Prophets, they will not be convinced even if someone rises from the dead.'"

LUKE 17:1-2 Jesus said to his disciples: "Things that cause people to sin are bound to come, but woe to that person through whom they come. ²It would be better for him to be thrown into the sea with a millstone tied around his neck than for him to cause one of these little ones to sin."

LUKE 19:12-27 He said: "A man of noble birth went to a distant country to have himself appointed king and then to return. ¹³So he called ten of his servants and gave them ten minas. 'Put this money to work,' he said, 'until I come back.' ¹⁴But his subjects hated him and sent a delegation after him to say, 'We don't want this man to be our king.' [15]He was made king, however, and returned home. Then he sent for the servants to whom he had given the money, in order to find out what they had gained with it. [16]The first one came and said, 'Sir, your mina has earned ten more.' [17]'Well done, my good servant!' his master replied. 'Because you have been trustworthy in a very small matter, take charge of ten cities.' [18]The second came and said, 'Sir, your mina has earned five more.' [19]His master answered, 'You take charge of five cities.' [20]Then another servant came and said, 'Sir, here is your mina; I have kept it laid away in a piece of cloth. [21]I was afraid of you, because you are a hard man. You take out what you did not put in and reap what you did not sow.' [22]His master replied, 'I will judge you by your own words, you wicked servant! You knew, did you, that I am a hard man, taking out what I did not put in, and reaping what I did not sow? [23]Why then didn't you put my money on deposit, so that when I came back, I could have collected it with interest?' [24]Then he said to those standing by, 'Take his mina away from him and give it to the one who has ten minas.' [25]'Sir,' they said, 'he already has ten!' [26]He replied, 'I tell you that to everyone who has, more will be given, but as for the one who has nothing, even what he has will be taken away. [27]But those enemies of mine who did not want me to be king over them—bring them here and kill them in front of me.'"

LUKE 20:45-47 While all the people were listening, Jesus said to his disciples, [46]"Beware of the teachers of the law. They like to walk around in flowing robes and love to be greeted in the marketplaces and have the most important seats in the synagogues and the places of honor at banquets. [47]They devour widows' houses and for a show make lengthy prayers. Such men will be punished most severely."

Justification

JOHN 3:14-19 "Just as Moses lifted up the snake in the desert, so the Son of Man must be lifted up, [15]that everyone who believes in him may have eternal life. [16]For God so loved the world that he gave his one and only Son, that whoever believes in him shall not perish but have eternal life. [17]For God did not send his Son into the world to condemn the world, but to save the world through him. [18]Whoever believes in him is not condemned, but whoever does not believe stands condemned already because he has not believed in the name of God's one and only Son. [19]This is the verdict: Light has come into the world, but men loved darkness instead of light because their deeds were evil."

MATTHEW 12:33-37 "Make a tree good and its fruit will be good, or make a tree bad and its fruit will be bad, for a tree is recognized by its fruit. [34]You brood of vipers, how can you who are evil say anything good? For out of the overflow of the heart the mouth speaks. [35]The good man brings good things out of the good stored up in him, and the evil man brings evil things out of the evil stored up in him. [36]But I tell you that men will have to give account on the day of judgment for every careless word they have spoken. [37]For by your words you will be acquitted, and by your words you will be condemned."

LUKE 18:9-14 To some who were confident of their own righteousness and looked down on everybody else, Jesus told this parable: [10]"Two men went up to the temple to pray, one a Pharisee and the other a tax collector. [11]The Pharisee stood up and prayed about himself: 'God, I thank you that I am not like other men—robbers, evildoers, adulterers—or even like this tax collector. [12]I fast twice a week and give a tenth of all I get.' [13]But the tax collector stood at a distance. He would not even look up to heaven, but beat his breast and said, 'God, have mercy on me, a sinner.' [14]I tell you that this man, rather than the other, went home justified before God. For everyone who exalts himself will be humbled, and he who humbles himself will be exalted."

The Kingdom of God and the Kingdom of Heaven

JOHN 3:3-7 In reply Jesus declared, "I tell you the truth, no one can see the kingdom of God unless he is born again." [4]"How can a man be born when he is old?" Nicodemus asked. "Surely he cannot enter a second time into his mother's womb to be born!" [5]Jesus answered, "I tell you the truth, no one can enter the kingdom of God unless he is born of water and the Spirit. [6]Flesh gives birth to flesh, but the Spirit gives birth to spirit. [7]You should not be surprised at my saying, 'You must be born again.'"

MATTHEW 4:17 From that time on Jesus began to preach, "Repent, for the kingdom of heaven is near."

MATTHEW 5:3 "Blessed are the poor in spirit, for theirs is the kingdom of heaven."

MATTHEW 5:10-11 "Blessed are those who are persecuted because of righteousness, for theirs is the kingdom of heaven. [11]Blessed are you when people insult you, persecute you and falsely say all kinds of evil against you because of me."

MATTHEW 5:19-20 "Anyone who breaks one of the least of these commandments and teaches others to do the same will be called least in the kingdom of heaven, but whoever practices and teaches these commands will be called great in the kingdom of heaven. [20]For I tell you that unless your righteousness surpasses that of the Pharisees and the teachers of the law, you will certainly not enter the kingdom of heaven."

MATTHEW 6:9-13 "This, then, is how you should pray: 'Our Father in heaven, hallowed be your name, [10]your kingdom come, your will be done on earth as it is in heaven. [11]Give us today our daily bread. [12]Forgive us our debts, as we also have forgiven our debtors. [13]And lead us not into temptation, but deliver us from the evil one.'"

MATTHEW 6:31-34 "So do not worry, saying, 'What shall we eat?' or 'What shall we drink?' or 'What shall we wear?' [32]For the pagans run after all these things, and your heavenly Father knows that you need them. [33]But seek first his kingdom and his righteousness, and all these things will be given to you as well.

[34]Therefore do not worry about tomorrow, for tomorrow will worry about itself. Each day has enough trouble of its own."

MATTHEW 7:21-27 "Not everyone who says to Me, 'Lord, Lord,' shall enter the kingdom of heaven, but he who does the will of My Father in heaven. [22]Many will say to Me in that day, 'Lord, Lord, have we not prophesied in Your name, cast out demons in Your name, and done many wonders in Your name?' [23]And then I will declare to them, 'I never knew you; depart from Me, you who practice lawlessness!' [24]Therefore whoever hears these sayings of Mine, and does them, I will liken him to a wise man who built his house on the rock: [25]and the rain descended, the floods came, and the winds blew and beat on that house; and it did not fall, for it was founded on the rock. [26]But everyone who hears these sayings of Mine, and does not do them, will be like a foolish man who built his house on the sand: [27]and the rain descended, the floods came, and the winds blew and beat on that house; and it fell. And great was its fall." (NKJV)

MATTHEW 10:5-7 These twelve Jesus sent out with the following instructions: "Do not go among the Gentiles or enter any town of the Samaritans. [6]Go rather to the lost sheep of Israel. [7]As you go, preach this message: 'The kingdom of heaven is near.'"

MATTHEW 12:25-28 Jesus knew their [the Pharisees'] thoughts and said to them, "Every kingdom divided against itself will be ruined, and every city or household divided against itself will not stand. [26]If Satan drives out Satan, he is divided against himself. How then can his kingdom stand? [27]And if I drive out demons by Beelzebub, by whom do your people drive them out? So then, they will be your judges. [28]But if I drive out demons by the Spirit of God, then the kingdom of God has come upon you."

MATTHEW 13:11-12 He replied, "The knowledge of the secrets of the kingdom of heaven has been given to you, but not to them. [12]Whoever has will be given more, and he will have an abundance. Whoever does not have, even what he has will be taken from him."

MATTHEW 13:31-32 He told them another parable: "The kingdom of heaven is like a mustard seed, which a man took and planted in his field. [32]Though it is the smallest of all your seeds, yet when it grows, it is the largest of garden plants and becomes a tree, so that the birds of the air come and perch in its branches."

MATTHEW 13:33 He told them still another parable: "The kingdom of heaven is like yeast that a woman took and mixed into a large amount of flour until it worked all through the dough."

MATTHEW 13:37-43 He answered, "The one who sowed the good seed is the Son of Man. [38]The field is the world, and the good seed stands for the sons of the kingdom. The weeds are the sons of the evil one, [39]and the enemy who sows them is the devil. The harvest is the end of the age, and the harvesters are angels. [40]As the weeds are pulled up and burned in the fire, so it will be at the end of the age. [41]The Son of Man will send out his angels, and they will weed out of his kingdom everything that causes sin and all who do evil. [42]They will throw them into the fiery furnace, where there will be weeping and gnashing of teeth. [43]Then the righteous will shine like the sun in the kingdom of their Father. He who has ears, let him hear."

MATTHEW 13:44-46 "The kingdom of heaven is like treasure hidden in a field. When a man found it, he hid it again, and then in his joy went and sold all he had and bought that field. [45]Again, the kingdom of heaven is like a merchant looking for fine pearls. [46]When he found one of great value, he went away and sold everything he had and bought it."

MATTHEW 13:47-50 "Once again, the kingdom of heaven is like a net that was let down into the lake and caught all kinds of fish. [48]When it was full, the fishermen pulled it up on the shore. Then they sat down and collected the good fish in baskets, but threw the bad away. [49]This is how it will be at the end of the age. The angels will come and separate the wicked from the righteous [50]and throw them into the fiery furnace, where there will be weeping and gnashing of teeth."

MATTHEW 13:51-52 "Have you understood all these things?" Jesus asked. "Yes," they replied. [52]He said to them, "Therefore every teacher of the law who has been instructed about the kingdom of heaven is like the owner of a house who brings out of his storeroom new treasures as well as old."

MATTHEW 16:16-17 Simon Peter answered, "You are the Christ, the Son of the living God." [17]Jesus replied, "Blessed are you, Simon son of Jonah, for this was not revealed to you by man, but by my Father in heaven."

MATTHEW 16:24-28 Then Jesus said to his disciples, "If anyone would come after me, he must deny himself and take up his cross and follow me. [25]For whoever wants to save his life will lose it, but whoever loses his life for me will find it. [26]What good will it be for a man if he gains the whole world, yet forfeits his soul? Or what can a man give in exchange for his soul? [27]For the Son of Man is going to come in his Father's glory with his angels, and then he will reward each person according to what he has done. [28]I tell you the truth, some who are standing here will not taste death before they see the Son of Man coming in his kingdom."

MATTHEW 18:2-4 He called a little child and had him stand among them. [3]And he said: "I tell you the truth, unless you change and become like little children, you will never enter the kingdom of heaven. [4]Therefore, whoever humbles himself like this child is the greatest in the kingdom of heaven."

MATTHEW 18:21-35 Then Peter came to Jesus and asked, "Lord, how many times shall I forgive my brother when he sins against me? Up to seven times?" [22]Jesus answered, "I tell you, not seven times, but seventy-seven times. [23]Therefore, the kingdom of heaven is like a king who wanted to settle accounts with his servants. [24]As he began the settlement, a man who owed him ten thousand talents was brought to him. [25]Since he was not able to pay, the master ordered that he and his wife and his children and all that he had be sold to repay the debt. [26]The servant fell on his knees before him. 'Be patient with me,' he begged, 'and I will pay back everything.' 27The servant's master took pity on him, canceled the debt and let him go. 28But when that servant went out, he found one of his fellow servants who owed him a hundred denarii. He grabbed him and began to choke him. 'Pay back what you owe me!' he demanded. 29His fellow servant fell to his knees and begged him, 'Be patient with me, and I will pay you back.' 30But he refused. Instead, he went off and had the man thrown into prison until he could pay the debt. 31When the other servants saw what had happened, they were greatly distressed and went and told their master everything that had happened. 32Then the master called the servant in. 'You wicked servant,' he said, 'I canceled all that debt of yours because you begged me to. 33Shouldn't you have had mercy on your fellow servant just as I had on you?' 34In anger his master turned him over to the jailers to be tortured, until he should pay back all he owed. 35This is how my heavenly Father will treat each of you unless you forgive your brother from your heart."

MATTHEW 19:11-12 Jesus replied, "Not everyone can accept this word [on divorce], but only those to whom it has been given. 12For some are eunuchs because they were born that way; others were made that way by men; and others have renounced marriage because of the kingdom of heaven. The one who can accept this should accept it."

MATTHEW 19:14 Jesus said, "Let the little children come to me, and do not hinder them, for the kingdom of heaven belongs to such as these."

MATTHEW 19:23-26 Then Jesus said to his disciples, "I tell you the truth, it is hard for a rich man to enter the kingdom of heaven. 24Again I tell you, it is easier for a camel to go through the eye of a needle than for a rich man to enter the kingdom of God." 25When the disciples heard this, they were greatly astonished and asked, "Who then can be saved?" 26Jesus looked at them and said, "With man this is impossible, but with God all things are possible."

MATTHEW 19:27-30 Peter answered him, "We have left everything to follow you! What then will there be for us?" 28Jesus said to them, "I tell you the truth, at the renewal of all things, when the Son of Man sits on his glorious throne, you who have followed me will also sit on twelve thrones, judging the twelve tribes of Israel. 29And everyone who has left houses or brothers or sisters or father or mother or children or fields for my sake will receive a hundred times as much and will inherit eternal life. 30But many who are first will be last, and many who are last will be first."

MATTHEW 20:1-16 "For the kingdom of heaven is like a landowner who went out early in the morning to hire men to work in his vineyard. 2He agreed to pay them a denarius for the day and sent them into his vineyard. 3About the third hour he went out and saw others standing in the marketplace doing nothing. 4He told them, 'You also go and work in my vineyard, and I will pay you whatever is right.' 5So they went. He went out again about the sixth hour and the ninth hour and did the same thing. 6About the eleventh hour he went out and found still others standing around. He asked them, 'Why have you been standing here all day long doing nothing?' [7]'Because no one has hired us,' they answered. He said to them, 'You also go and work in my vineyard.' [8]When evening came, the owner of the vineyard said to his foreman, 'Call the workers and pay them their wages, beginning with the last ones hired and going on to the first.' [9]The workers who were hired about the eleventh hour came and each received a denarius. [10]So when those came who were hired first, they expected to receive more. But each one of them also received a denarius. [11]When they received it, they began to grumble against the landowner. [12]'These men who were hired last worked only one hour,' they said, 'and you have made them equal to us who have borne the burden of the work and the heat of the day.' [13]But he answered one of them, 'Friend, I am not being unfair to you. Didn't you agree to work for a denarius? [14]Take your pay and go. I want to give the man who was hired last the same as I gave you. [15]Don't I have the right to do what I want with my own money? Or are you envious because I am generous?' [16]So the last will be first, and the first will be last."

MATTHEW 21:28-32 "What do you think? There was a man who had two sons. He went to the first and said, 'Son, go and work today in the vineyard.' [29]'I will not,' he answered, but later he changed his mind and went. [30]Then the father went to the other son and said the same thing. He answered, 'I will, sir,' but he did not go. [31]Which of the two did what his father wanted?" "The first," they

answered. Jesus said to them, "I tell you the truth, the tax collectors and the prostitutes are entering the kingdom of God ahead of you. [32]For John came to you to show you the way of righteousness, and you did not believe him, but the tax collectors and the prostitutes did. And even after you saw this, you did not repent and believe him."

MATTHEW 21:42-44 Jesus said to them, "Have you never read in the Scriptures: 'The stone the builders rejected has become the capstone; the Lord has done this, and it is marvelous in our eyes'? [43]Therefore I tell you that the kingdom of God will be taken away from you and given to a people who will produce its fruit. [44]He who falls on this stone will be broken to pieces, but he on whom it falls will be crushed."

MATTHEW 22:1-14 Jesus spoke to them again in parables, saying: [2]"The kingdom of heaven is like a king who prepared a wedding banquet for his son. [3]He sent his servants to those who had been invited to the banquet to tell them to come, but they refused to come. [4]Then he sent some more servants and said, 'Tell those who have been invited that I have prepared my dinner: My oxen and fattened cattle have been butchered, and everything is ready. Come to the wedding banquet.' [5]But they paid no attention and went off—one to his field, another to his business. [6]The rest seized his servants, mistreated them and killed them. [7]The king was enraged. He sent his army and destroyed those murderers and burned their city. [8]Then he said to his servants, 'The wedding banquet is ready, but those

I invited did not deserve to come. ^{9}Go to the street corners and invite to the banquet anyone you find.' ^{10}So the servants went out into the streets and gathered all the people they could find, both good and bad, and the wedding hall was filled with guests. ^{11}But when the king came in to see the guests, he noticed a man there who was not wearing wedding clothes. ^{12}'Friend,' he asked, 'how did you get in here without wedding clothes?' The man was speechless. ^{13}Then the king told the attendants, 'Tie him hand and foot, and throw him outside, into the darkness, where there will be weeping and gnashing of teeth.' ^{14}For many are invited, but few are chosen."

MATTHEW 25:1-13 "At that time the kingdom of heaven will be like ten virgins who took their lamps and went out to meet the bridegroom. ^{2}Five of them were foolish and five were wise. ^{3}The foolish ones took their lamps but did not take any oil with them. ^{4}The wise, however, took oil in jars along with their lamps. ^{5}The bridegroom was a long time in coming, and they all became drowsy and fell asleep. ^{6}At midnight the cry rang out: 'Here's the bridegroom! Come out to meet him!' ^{7}Then all the virgins woke up and trimmed their lamps. ^{8}The foolish ones said to the wise, 'Give us some of your oil; our lamps are going out.' ^{9}'No,' they replied, 'there may not be enough for both us and you. Instead, go to those who sell oil and buy some for yourselves.' ^{10}But while they were on their way to buy the oil, the bridegroom arrived. The virgins who were ready went in with him to the wedding banquet. And the door was shut.

^{11}Later the others also came. 'Sir! Sir!' they said. 'Open the door for us!' ^{12}But he replied, 'I tell you the truth, I don't know you.' ^{13}Therefore keep watch, because you do not know the day or the hour.

MATTHEW 25:14-30 "Again, it will be like a man going on a journey, who called his servants and entrusted his property to them. ^{15}To one he gave five talents of money, to another two talents, and to another one talent, each according to his ability. Then he went on his journey. ^{16}The man who had received the five talents went at once and put his money to work and gained five more. ^{17}So also, the one with the two talents gained two more. ^{18}But the man who had received the one talent went off, dug a hole in the ground and hid his master's money. ^{19}After a long time the master of those servants returned and settled accounts with them. ^{20}The man who had received the five talents brought the other five. 'Master,' he said, 'you entrusted me with five talents. See, I have gained five more.' ^{21}His master replied, 'Well done, good and faithful servant! You have been faithful with a few things; I will put you in charge of many things. Come and share your master's happiness!' ^{22}The man with the two talents also came. 'Master,' he said, 'you entrusted me with two talents; see, I have gained two more.' ^{23}His master replied, 'Well done, good and faithful servant! You have been faithful with a few things; I will put you in charge of many things. Come and share your master's happiness!' ^{24}Then the man who had received the one talent came. 'Master,' he said, 'I knew that you are a hard man, harvesting where you have not sown and gathering where you have not scattered seed. ^{25}So I was afraid and went out and hid your talent in the ground. See, here is what belongs to you.' ^{26}His master replied, 'You wicked, lazy servant! So you knew that I harvest where I have not sown and gather where I have not scattered seed? ^{27}Well then, you should have put my money on deposit with the bankers, so that when I returned I would have received it back with interest. ^{28}'Take the talent from him and give it to the one who has the ten talents. ^{29}For everyone who has will be given more, and he will have an abundance. Whoever does not have, even what he has will be taken from him. ^{30}And throw that worthless servant outside, into the darkness, where there will be weeping and gnashing of teeth.'"

MATTHEW 25:31-46 "When the Son of Man comes in his glory, and all the angels with him, he will sit on his throne in heavenly glory. ^{32}All the nations will be gathered before him, and he will separate the people one from another as a shepherd separates the sheep from the goats. ^{33}He will put the sheep on his right and the goats on his left. ^{34}Then the King will say to those on his right, 'Come, you who are blessed by my Father; take your inheritance, the kingdom prepared for you since the creation of the world. ^{35}For I was hungry and you gave me something to eat, I was thirsty and you gave me something to drink, I was a stranger and you invited me in, ^{36}I needed clothes and you clothed me, I was sick and you looked after me, I was in prison and you came to visit me.' ^{37}Then the righteous will answer him,

'Lord, when did we see you hungry and feed you, or thirsty and give you something to drink? ^{38}When did we see you a stranger and invite you in, or needing clothes and clothe you? ^{39}When did we see you sick or in prison and go to visit you?' ^{40}The King will reply, 'I tell you the truth, whatever you did for one of the least of these brothers of mine, you did for me.' ^{41}Then he will say to those on his left, 'Depart from me, you who are cursed, into the eternal fire prepared for the devil and his angels. ^{42}For I was hungry and you gave me nothing to eat, I was thirsty and you gave me nothing to drink, ^{43}I was a stranger and you did not invite me in, I needed clothes and you did not clothe me, I was sick and in prison and you did not look after me.' ^{44}They also will answer, 'Lord, when did we see you hungry or thirsty or a stranger or needing clothes or sick or in prison, and did not help you?' ^{45}He will reply, 'I tell you the truth, whatever you did not do for one of the least of these, you did not do for me.' ^{46}Then they will go away to eternal punishment, but the righteous to eternal life."

MATTHEW 26:29 "I tell you, I will not drink of this fruit of the vine from now on until that day when I drink it anew with you in my Father's kingdom."

MARK 1:15 "The time has come," he said. "The kingdom of God is near. Repent and believe the good news!"

MARK 4:26-32 He also said, "This is what the kingdom of God is like. A man scatters seed on the ground. ^{27}Night and day, whether he sleeps or gets up, the seed sprouts and grows, though he does not know how. ^{28}All by itself the soil produc grain—first the stalk, then the head, then the full kernel in the head. [29]As soon as the grain is ripe, he puts the sickle to it, because the harvest has come." [30]Again he said, "What shall we say the kingdom of God is like, or what parable shall we use to describe it? [31]It is like a mustard seed, which is the smallest seed you plant in the ground. [32]Yet when planted, it grows and becomes the largest of all garden plants, with such big branches that the birds of the air can perch in its shade."

MARK 8:34-9:1 Then he called the crowd to him along with his disciples and said: "If anyone would come after me, he must deny himself and take up his cross and follow me. [35]For whoever wants to save his life will lose it, but whoever loses his life for me and for the gospel will save it. [36]What good is it for a man to gain the whole world, yet forfeit his soul? [37]Or what can a man give in exchange for his soul? [38]If anyone is ashamed of me and my words in this adulterous and sinful generation, the Son of Man will be ashamed of him when he comes in his Father's glory with the holy angels." [1]And he said to them, "I tell you the truth, some who are standing here will not taste death before they see the kingdom of God come with power."

MARK 10:13-16 People were bringing little children to Jesus to have him touch them, but the disciples rebuked them. [14]When Jesus saw this, he was indignant. He said to them, "Let the little children come to me, and do not hinder them, for the kingdom of God belongs to these. [15]I tell you the truth, any-

one who will not receive the kingdom of God like a little child will never enter it." [16]And he took the children in his arms, put his hands on them and blessed them.

MARK 10:21 Jesus looked at him [a rich young man] and loved him. "One thing you lack," he said. "Go, sell everything you have and give to the poor, and you will have treasure in heaven. Then come, follow me."

MARK 12:32-34 "Well said, teacher," the man replied. "You are right in saying that God is one and there is no other but him. [33]To love him with all your heart, with all your understanding and with all your strength, and to love your neighbor as yourself is more important than all burnt offerings and sacrifices." [34]When Jesus saw that he had answered wisely, he said to him, "You are not far from the kingdom of God." And from then on no one dared ask him any more questions.

LUKE 4:43 But he said, "I must preach the good news of the kingdom of God to the other towns also, because that is why I was sent."

LUKE 6:20 Looking at his disciples, he said: "Blessed are you who are poor, for yours is the kingdom of God."

LUKE 7:24-28 After John's messengers left, Jesus began to speak to the crowd about John: "What did you go out into the desert to see? A reed swayed by the wind? [25]If not, what did you go out to see? A man dressed in fine clothes? No, those who wear expensive clothes and indulge in luxury are in palaces. [26]But what did you go out to see? A prophet? Yes, I tell you, and more than a prophet. [27]This is the one about whom it is written: 'I will send my messenger ahead of you, who will prepare your way before you. [28]I tell you, among those born of women there is no one greater than John; yet the one who is least in the kingdom of God is greater than he."

LUKE 9:23-27 Then he said to them all: "If anyone would come after me, he must deny himself and take up his cross daily and follow me. [24]For whoever wants to save his life will lose it, but whoever loses his life for me will save it. [25]What good is it for a man to gain the whole world, and yet lose or forfeit his very self? [26]If anyone is ashamed of me and my words, the Son of Man will be ashamed of him when he comes in his glory and in the glory of the Father and of the holy angels. [27]I tell you the truth, some who are standing here will not taste death before they see the kingdom of God."

LUKE 9:59-60 He said to another man, "Follow me." But the man replied, "Lord, first let me go and bury my father." [60]Jesus said to him, "Let the dead bury their own dead, but you go and proclaim the kingdom of God."

LUKE 10:8-12 "When you enter a town and are welcomed, eat what is set before you. [9]Heal the sick who are there and tell them, 'The kingdom of God is near you.' [10]But when you enter a town and are not welcomed, go into its streets and say, [11]'Even the dust of your town that sticks to our feet we wipe off against you. Yet be sure of this: The kingdom of God is near.' [12]I tell you, it will be more

bearable on that day for Sodom than for that town."

LUKE 11:2 He said to them, "When you pray, say: 'Father, hallowed be your name, your kingdom come.'"

LUKE 13:18-19 Then Jesus asked, "What is the kingdom of God like? What shall I compare it to? [19]It is like a mustard seed, which a man took and planted in his garden. It grew and became a tree, and the birds of the air perched in its branches."

LUKE 13:20-21 Again he asked, "What shall I compare the kingdom of God to? [21]It is like yeast that a woman took and mixed into a large amount of flour until it worked all through the dough."

LUKE 16:16 "The Law and the Prophets were proclaimed until John. Since that time, the good news of the kingdom of God is being preached, and everyone is forcing his way into it."

LUKE 17:20-21 Once, having been asked by the Pharisees when the kingdom of God would come, Jesus replied, "The kingdom of God does not come with your careful observation, [21]nor will people say, 'Here it is,' or 'There it is,' because the kingdom of God is within you."

LUKE 18:16-17 But Jesus called the children to him and said, "Let the little children come to me, and do not hinder them, for the kingdom of God belongs to such as these. [17]I tell you the truth, anyone who will not receive the kingdom of God like a little child will never enter it."

LUKE 18:29-30 "I tell you the truth," Jesus said to them, "no one who has left home or wife or brothers or parents or children for the sake of the kingdom of God [30]will fail to receive many times as much in this age and, in the age to come, eternal life."

LUKE 20:34-38 Jesus replied, "The people of this age marry and are given in marriage. [35]But those who are considered worthy of taking part in that age and in the resurrection from the dead will neither marry nor be given in marriage, [36]and they can no longer die; for they are like the angels. They are God's children, since they are children of the resurrection. [37]But in the account of the bush, even Moses showed that the dead rise, for he calls the Lord 'the God of Abraham, and the God of Isaac, and the God of Jacob.' [38]He is not the God of the dead, but of the living, for to him all are alive."

LUKE 22:7-16 Then came the day of Unleavened Bread on which the Passover lamb had to be sacrificed. [8]Jesus sent Peter and John, saying, "Go and make preparations for us to eat the Passover." [9]"Where do you want us to prepare for it?" they asked. [10]He replied, "As you enter the city, a man carrying a jar of water will meet you. Follow him to the house that he enters, [11]and say to the owner of the house, 'The Teacher asks: Where is the guest room, where I may eat the Passover with my disciples?' [12]He will show you a large upper room, all furnished. Make preparations there." [13]They left and found things just as Jesus had told them. So they prepared the Passover. [14]When the hour came, Jesus and his apostles reclined at the table. [15]And he said to them, "I have eagerly desired to eat this Passover with you before I suffer. [16]For I tell you, I will

not eat it again until it finds fulfillment in the kingdom of God."

LUKE 22:25-30 Jesus said to them [the apostles], "The kings of the Gentiles lord it over them; and those who exercise authority over them call themselves Benefactors. [26]But you are not to be like that. Instead, the greatest among you should be like the youngest, and the one who rules like the one who serves. [27]For who is greater, the one who is at the table or the one who serves? Is it not the one who is at the table? But I am among you as one who serves. [28]You are those who have stood by me in my trials. [29]And I confer on you a kingdom, just as my Father conferred one on me, [30]so that you may eat and drink at my table in my kingdom and sit on thrones, judging the twelve tribes of Israel."

The Narrow Way Versus the Broad Way

MATTHEW 7:13-14 "Enter through the narrow gate. For wide is the gate and broad is the road that leads to destruction, and many enter through it. [14]But small is the gate and narrow the road that leads to life, and only a few find it."

LUKE 13:23-30 Someone asked him, "Lord, are only a few people going to be saved?" He said to them, [24]"Make every effort to enter through the narrow door, because many, I tell you, will try to enter and will not be able to. [25]Once the owner of the house gets up and closes the door, you will stand outside knocking and pleading, 'Sir, open the door for us.' But he will answer, 'I don't know you or where you come from.' [26]Then you will say, 'We ate and drank with you, and you taught in our streets.' [27]But he will reply, 'I don't know you or where you come from. Away from me, all you evildoers!' [28]There will be weeping there, and gnashing of teeth, when you see Abraham, Isaac and Jacob and all the prophets in the kingdom of God, but you yourselves thrown out. [29]People will come from east and west and north and south, and will take their places at the feast in the kingdom of God. [30]Indeed there are those who are last who will be first, and first who will be last."

The Resurrection of the Dead

JOHN 5:24-29 "I tell you the truth, whoever hears my word and believes him who sent me has eternal life and will not be condemned; he has crossed over from death to life. [25]I tell you the truth, a time is coming and has now come when the dead will hear the voice of the Son of God and those who hear will live. [26]For as the Father has life in himself, so he has granted the Son to have life in himself. [27]And he has given him authority to judge because he is the Son of Man. [28]Do not be amazed at this, for a time is coming when all who are in their graves will hear his voice [29]and come out—those who have done good will rise to live, and those who have done evil will rise to be condemned."

JOHN 6:37-40 "All that the Father gives me will come to me, and whoever comes to me I will never drive away. [38]For I have come down from heaven not to do my will but to do the will of him who sent me. [39]And this is the will of him who sent me, that I shall lose none of all that he has given me, but raise them up at the last day. [40]For my Father's will is that everyone who looks to the Son and believes in him shall have eternal life, and I will raise him up at the last day."

JOHN 6:43-45 "Stop grumbling among yourselves," Jesus answered. [44]"No one can come to me unless the Father who sent me draws him, and I will raise him up at the last day. [45]It is written in the Prophets: 'They will all be taught by God.' Everyone who listens to the Father and learns from him comes to me."

JOHN 6:54-56 "Whoever eats my flesh and drinks my blood has eternal life, and I will raise him up at the last day. [55]For my flesh is real food and my blood is real drink. [56]Whoever eats my flesh and drinks my blood remains in me, and I in him."

JOHN 11:25-26 Jesus said to her [Martha], "I am the resurrection and the life. He who believes in me will live, even though he dies; [26]and whoever lives and believes in me will never die. Do you believe this?"

MATTHEW 22:29-32 Jesus replied, "You are in error because you do not know the Scriptures or the power of God. [30]At the resurrection people will neither marry nor be given in marriage; they will be like the angels in heaven. [31]But about the resurrection of the dead—have you not read what God said to you, [32]'I am the God of Abraham, the God of Isaac, and the God of Jacob'? He is not the God of the dead but of the living."

MARK 12:24-27 Jesus replied, "Are you not in error because you do not know the Scriptures or the power of God? [25]When the dead rise, they will neither marry nor be given in marriage; they will be like the angels in heaven. [26]Now about the dead rising—have you not read in the book of Moses, in the account of the bush, how God said to him, 'I am the God of Abraham, the God of Isaac, and the God of Jacob'? [27]He is not the God of the dead, but of the living. You are badly mistaken!"

LUKE 16:19-31 "There was a rich man who was dressed in purple and fine linen and lived in luxury every day. [20]At his gate was laid a beggar named Lazarus, covered with sores [21]and longing to eat what fell from the rich man's table. Even the dogs came and licked his sores. [22]The time came when the beggar died and the angels carried him to Abraham's side. The rich man also died and was buried. [23]In hell, where he was in torment, he looked up and saw Abraham far away, with Lazarus by his side. [24]So he called to him, 'Father Abraham, have pity on me and send Lazarus to dip the tip of his finger in water and cool my tongue, because I am in agony in this fire.' [25]But Abraham replied, 'Son, remember that in your lifetime you received your good things, while Lazarus received bad things, but now he is comforted here and you are in agony. [26]And besides all this, between us and you a great chasm has been fixed, so that those who want to go from here to you cannot, nor can anyone cross over from there to us.' [27]He answered, 'Then I beg you, father, send Lazarus to my father's house, [28]for I have five brothers. Let him warn them, so that they will not also come to this place of torment.' [29]Abraham replied, 'They have Moses and the Prophets; let them listen to them.' [30]'No, father Abraham,' he said, 'but if someone from the dead goes to them, they will repent.' [31]He said to him, 'If they do not listen to Moses and the Prophets, they will not be convinced even if someone rises from the dead.'"

LUKE 20:34-38 Jesus replied, "The people of this age marry and are given in marriage. [35]But those who are considered worthy of taking part in that age and in the resurrection from the dead will neither marry nor be given in marriage, [36]and they can no longer die; for they are like the angels. They are God's children, since they are children of the resurrection. [37]But in the account of the bush, even Moses showed that the dead rise, for he calls the Lord 'the God of Abraham, and the God of Isaac, and the God of Jacob.' [38]He is not the God of the dead, but of the living, for to him all are alive."

Rewards

MATTHEW 5:19-20 "Anyone who breaks one of the least of these commandments and teaches others to do the same will be called least in the kingdom of heaven, but whoever practices and teaches these commands will be called great in the kingdom of heaven. [20]For I tell you that unless your righteousness surpasses that of the Pharisees and the teachers of the law, you will certainly not enter the kingdom of heaven."

MATTHEW 5:38-48 "You have heard that it was said, 'Eye for eye, and tooth for tooth.' [39]But I tell you, Do not resist an evil person. If someone strikes you on the right cheek, turn to him the other also. [40]And if someone wants to sue you and take your tunic, let him have your cloak as well. [41]If someone forces you to go one mile, go with him two miles. [42]Give to the one who asks you, and do not turn away from the one who wants to borrow from you. [43]You have heard that it was said, 'Love your neighbor and hate your enemy.' [44]But I tell you: Love your enemies and pray for those who persecute you, [45]that you may be sons of your Father in heaven. He causes his sun to rise on the evil and the good, and sends rain on the righteous and the unrighteous. [46]If you love those who love you, what reward will you get? Are not even the tax collectors doing that? [47]And if you greet only your brothers, what are you doing more than others? Do not even pagans do that? [48]Be perfect, therefore, as your heavenly Father is perfect."

MATTHEW 6:1-4 "Be careful not to do your 'acts of righteousness' before men, to be seen by them. If you do, you will have no reward from your Father in heaven. [2]So when you give to the needy, do not announce it with trumpets, as the hypocrites do in the synagogues and on the streets, to be honored by men. I tell you the truth, they have received their reward in full. [3]But when you give to the needy, do not let your left hand know what your right hand is doing, [4]so that your giving may be in secret. Then your Father, who sees what is done in secret, will reward you."

MATTHEW 6:5-8 "And when you pray, do not be like the hypocrites, for

they love to pray standing in the synagogues and on the street corners to be seen by men. I tell you the truth, they have received their reward in full. [6]But when you pray, go into your room, close the door and pray to your Father, who is unseen. Then your Father, who sees what is done in secret, will reward you. [7]And when you pray, do not keep on babbling like pagans, for they think they will be heard because of their many words. [8]Do not be like them, for your Father knows what you need before you ask him."

MATTHEW 6:16-18 "When you fast, do not look somber as the hypocrites do, for they disfigure their faces to show men they are fasting. I tell you the truth, they have received their reward in full. [17]But when you fast, put oil on your head and wash your face, [18]so that it will not be obvious to men that you are fasting, but only to your Father, who is unseen; and your Father, who sees what is done in secret, will reward you."

MATTHEW 6:19-21 "Do not store up for yourselves treasures on earth, where moth and rust destroy, and where thieves break in and steal. [20]But store up for yourselves treasures in heaven, where moth and rust do not destroy, and where thieves do not break in and steal. [21]For where your treasure is, there your heart will be also."

MATTHEW 10:40-42 "He who receives you receives me, and he who receives me receives the one who sent me. [41]Anyone who receives a prophet because he is a prophet will receive a prophet's reward, and anyone who receives a righteous man because he is a righteous man will receive a righteous man's reward. [42]And if anyone gives even a cup of cold water to one of these little ones because he is my disciple, I tell you the truth, he will certainly not lose his reward."

MATTHEW 16:23-27 Jesus turned and said to Peter, "Get behind me, Satan! You are a stumbling block to me; you do not have in mind the things of God, but the things of men." [24]Then Jesus said to his disciples, "If anyone would come after me, he must deny himself and take up his cross and follow me. [25]For whoever wants to save his life will lose it, but whoever loses his life for me will find it. [26]What good will it be for a man if he gains the whole world, yet forfeits his soul? Or what can a man give in exchange for his soul? [27]For the Son of Man is going to come in his Father's glory with his angels, and then he will reward each person according to what he has done."

MATTHEW 19:17-21 "Why do you ask me about what is good?" Jesus replied. "There is only One who is good. If you want to enter life, obey the commandments." [18]"Which ones?" the man inquired. Jesus replied, " 'Do not murder, do not commit adultery, do not steal, do not give false testimony, [19]honor your father and mother,' and 'love your neighbor as yourself.' " [20]"All these I have kept," the young man said. "What do I still lack?" [21]Jesus answered, "If you want to be perfect, go, sell your possessions and give to the poor, and you will have treasure in heaven. Then come, follow me."

MATTHEW 19:27-30 Peter answered him, "We have left everything to follow you! What then will there be for us?"

[28]Jesus said to them, "I tell you the truth, at the renewal of all things, when the Son of Man sits on his glorious throne, you who have followed me will also sit on twelve thrones, judging the twelve tribes of Israel. [29]And everyone who has left houses or brothers or sisters or father or mother or children or fields for my sake will receive a hundred times as much and will inherit eternal life. [30]But many who are first will be last, and many who are last will be first."

MATTHEW 25:14-29 "Again, it will be like a man going on a journey, who called his servants and entrusted his property to them. [15]To one he gave five talents of money, to another two talents, and to another one talent, each according to his ability. Then he went on his journey. [16]The man who had received the five talents went at once and put his money to work and gained five more. [17]So also, the one with the two talents gained two more. [18]But the man who had received the one talent went off, dug a hole in the ground and hid his master's money. [19]After a long time the master of those servants returned and settled accounts with them. [20]The man who had received the five talents brought the other five. 'Master,' he said, 'you entrusted me with five talents. See, I have gained five more.' [21]His master replied, 'Well done, good and faithful servant! You have been faithful with a few things; I will put you in charge of many things. Come and share your master's happiness!' [22]The man with the two talents also came. 'Master,' he said, 'you entrusted me with two talents; see, I have gained two more.' [23]His master replied, 'Well done, good and faithful servant! You have been faithful with a few things; I will put you in charge of many things. Come and share your master's happiness!' [24]Then the man who had received the one talent came. 'Master,' he said, 'I knew that you are a hard man, harvesting where you have not sown and gathering where you have not scattered seed. [25]So I was afraid and went out and hid your talent in the ground. See, here is what belongs to you.' [26]His master replied, 'You wicked, lazy servant! So you knew that I harvest where I have not sown and gather where I have not scattered seed? [27]Well then, you should have put my money on deposit with the bankers, so that when I returned I would have received it back with interest. [28]'Take the talent from him and give it to the one who has the ten talents. [29]For everyone who has will be given more, and he will have an abundance. Whoever does not have, even what he has will be taken from him."

MARK 10:29-31 "I tell you the truth," Jesus replied, "no one who has left home or brothers or sisters or mother or father or children or fields for me and the gospel [30]will fail to receive a hundred times as much in this present age (homes, brothers, sisters, mothers, children and fields— and with them, persecutions) and in the age to come, eternal life. [31]But many who are first will be last, and the last first."

LUKE 6:22 "Blessed are you when men hate you, when they exclude you and insult you and reject your name as evil, because of the Son of Man."

LUKE 14:12-14 Then Jesus said to his host, "When you give a luncheon or dinner, do not invite your friends, your brothers or relatives, or your rich neighbors; if you do, they may invite you back and so you will be repaid. [13]But when you give a banquet, invite the poor, the crippled, the lame, the blind, [14]and you will be blessed. Although they cannot repay you, you will be repaid at the resurrection of the righteous."

LUKE 18:29-30 "I tell you the truth," Jesus said to them, "no one who has left home or wife or brothers or parents or children for the sake of the kingdom of God [30]will fail to receive many times as much in this age and, in the age to come, eternal life."

Satan and the Nature of the Devil

JOHN 8:42-44 Jesus said to them, "If God were your Father, you would love me, for I came from God and now am here. I have not come on my own; but he sent me. [43]Why is my language not clear to you? Because you are unable to hear what I say. [44]You belong to your father, the devil, and you want to carry out your father's desire. He was a murderer from the beginning, not holding to the truth, for there is no truth in him. When he lies, he speaks his native language, for he is a liar and the father of lies."

JOHN 14:30 "I will not speak with you much longer, for the prince of this world is coming. He has no hold on me."

JOHN 17:15-17 "My prayer is not that you [God] take them out of the world but that you protect them from the evil one. [16]They are not of the world, even as I am not of it. [17]Sanctify them by the truth; your word is truth."

MATTHEW 6:9-13 "This, then, is how you should pray: 'Our Father in heaven, hallowed be your name, [10]your kingdom come, your will be done on earth as it is in heaven. [11]Give us today our daily bread. [12]Forgive us our debts, as we also have forgiven our debtors. [13]And lead us not into temptation, but deliver us from the evil one.'"

MATTHEW 12:25-30 Jesus knew their [the Pharisees'] thoughts and said to them, "Every kingdom divided against itself will be ruined, and every city or household divided against itself will not stand. [26]If Satan drives out Satan, he is divided against himself. How then can his kingdom stand? [27]And if I drive out demons by Beelzebub, by whom do your people drive them out? So then, they will be your judges. [28]But if I drive out demons by the Spirit of God, then the kingdom of God has come upon you. [29]Or again, how can anyone enter a strong man's house and carry off his possessions unless he first ties up the strong man? Then he can rob his house. [30]He who is not with me is against me, and he who does not gather with me scatters."

MATTHEW 13:37-42 He answered, "The one who sowed the good seed is the Son of Man. [38]The field is the world, and the good seed stands for the sons of the kingdom. The weeds are the sons of the evil one, [39]and the enemy who sows them is the devil. The harvest is the end of the age, and the harvesters are angels. [40]As the weeds are pulled up and burned in the fire, so it will be at the end of the age. [41]The Son of Man will send out his angels, and they will weed out of his king-dom everything that causes sin and all who do evil. [42]They will throw them into the fiery furnace, where there will be weeping and gnashing of teeth."

MATTHEW 16:23 Jesus turned and said to Peter, "Get behind me, Satan! You are a stumbling block to me; you do not have in mind the things of God, but the things of men."

MARK 3:23-27 So Jesus called them and spoke to them in parables: "How can Satan drive out Satan? [24]If a kingdom is divided against itself, that kingdom can-not stand. [25]If a house is divided against itself, that house cannot stand. [26]And if Satan opposes himself and is divided, he cannot stand; his end has come. [27]In fact, no one can enter a strong man's house and carry off his possessions unless he first ties up the strong man. Then he can rob his house."

MARK 4:13-15 Then Jesus said to them [the disciples], "Don't you under-stand this parable? How then will you understand any parable? [14]The farmer sows the word. [15]Some people are like seed along the path, where the word is sown. As soon as they hear it, Satan comes and takes away the word that was sown in them."

LUKE 4:1-13 Jesus, full of the Holy Spirit, returned from the Jordan and was led by the Spirit in the desert, [2]where for forty days he was tempted by the devil. He ate nothing during those days, and at the end of them he was hungry. [3]The devil said to him, "If you are the Son of God, tell this stone to become bread." [4]Jesus answered, "It is written: 'Man does not live on bread alone.'" [5]The devil led him up to a high place and showed him in an instant all the kingdoms of the world. [6]And he said to him, "I will give you all their authority and splendor, for it has been given to me, and I can give it to anyone I want to. [7]So if you worship me, it will all be yours." [8]Jesus answered, "It is written: 'Worship the Lord your God and serve him only.'" [9]The devil led him to Jerusalem and had him stand on the highest point of the temple. "If you are the Son of God," he said, "throw yourself down from here. [10]For it is written: 'He will command his angels concerning you to guard you carefully; [11]they will lift you up in their hands, so that you will not strike your foot against a stone.'" [12]Jesus answered, "It says: 'Do not put the Lord your God to the test.'" [13]When the devil had finished all this tempting, he left him until an opportune time. (See also Matthew 4:1-11.)

LUKE 11:2-4 He said to them, "When you pray, say: 'Father, hallowed be your name, your kingdom come. [3]Give us each day our daily bread. [4]Forgive us our sins, for we also forgive everyone who sins against us. And lead us not into temptation.'"

LUKE 11:17-23 Jesus knew their thoughts and said to them: "Any kingdom divided against itself will be ruined, and a house divided against itself will fall. [18]If Satan is divided against himself, how can his kingdom stand? I say this because you claim that I drive out demons by Beelzebub. [19]Now if I drive out demons by Beelzebub, by whom do your followers drive them out? So then, they will be your judges. [20]But if I drive out demons by the finger of God, then the kingdom of God has come to you. [21]When a strong man, fully armed, guards his own house, his possessions are safe. [22]But when someone stronger attacks and overpowers him, he takes away the armor in which the man trusted and divides up the spoils. [23]He who is not with me is against me, and he who does not gather with me, scatters."

LUKE 13:14-16 Indignant because Jesus had healed on the Sabbath, the synagogue ruler said to the people, "There are six days for work. So come and be healed on those days, not on the Sabbath." [15]The Lord answered him, "You hypocrites! Doesn't each of you on the Sabbath untie his ox or donkey from the stall and lead it out to give it water? [16]Then should not this woman, a daughter of Abraham, whom Satan has kept bound for eighteen long years, be set free on the Sabbath day from what bound her?"

LUKE 22:31-32 "Simon, Simon, Satan has asked to sift you as wheat. [32]But I have prayed for you, Simon, that your faith may not fail. And when you have turned back, strengthen your brothers."

ACTS 26:13-18 "About noon, O king, as I [Paul] was on the road, I saw a light from heaven, brighter than the sun, blazing around me and my companions. [14]We all fell to the ground, and I heard a voice saying to me in Aramaic, 'Saul, Saul, why do you persecute me? It is hard for you to kick against the goads.' [15]Then I asked, 'Who are you, Lord?' 'I am Jesus, whom you are persecuting,' the Lord replied. [16]'Now get up and stand on your feet. I have appeared to you to appoint you as a servant and as a witness of what you have seen of me and what I will show you. [17]I will rescue you from your own people and from the Gentiles. I am sending you to them [18]to open their eyes and turn them from darkness to light, and from the power of Satan to God, so that they may receive forgiveness of sins and a place among those who are sanctified by faith in me.'"

The Soul

MATTHEW 10:28 "Do not be afraid of those who kill the body but cannot kill the soul. Rather, be afraid of the One who can destroy both soul and body in hell."

MATTHEW 16:23-27 Jesus turned and said to Peter, "Get behind me, Satan! You are a stumbling block to me; you do not have in mind the things of God, but the things of men." [24]Then Jesus said to his disciples, "If anyone would come after me, he must deny himself and take up his cross and follow me. [25]For whoever wants to save his life will lose it, but whoever loses his life for me will find it. [26]What good will it be for a man if he gains the whole world, yet forfeits his soul? Or what can a man give in exchange for his soul? [27]For the Son of Man is going to come in his Father's glory with his angels, and then he will reward each person according to what he has done." (See also Mark 8:36-37.)

MATTHEW 22:37-38 Jesus replied: "'Love the Lord your God with all your heart and with all your soul and with all your mind.' [38]This is the first and greatest commandment."

MARK 12:30 "Love the Lord your God with all your heart and with all your

soul and with all your mind and with all your strength."

LUKE 12:15-21 Then he said to them, "Watch out! Be on your guard against all kinds of greed; a man's life does not consist in the abundance of his possessions." [16]And he told them this parable: "The ground of a certain rich man produced a good crop. [17]He thought to himself, 'What shall I do? I have no place to store my crops.' [18]Then he said, 'This is what I'll do. I will tear down my barns and build bigger ones, and there I will store all my grain and my goods. [19]And I'll say to myself, "You have plenty of good things laid up for many years. Take life easy; eat, drink and be merry."' [20]But God said to him, 'You fool! This very night your life ["soul" in NKJV] will be demanded from you. Then who will get what you have prepared for yourself?' [21]This is how it will be with anyone who stores up things for himself but is not rich toward God."

Spiritual Birth (Conversion)

JOHN 3:3-8 In reply Jesus declared, "I tell you the truth, no one can see the kingdom of God unless he is born again." [4]"How can a man be born when he is old?" Nicodemus asked. "Surely he cannot enter a second time into his mother's womb to be born!" [5]Jesus answered, "I tell you the truth, no one can enter the kingdom of God unless he is born of water and the Spirit. [6]Flesh gives birth to flesh, but the Spirit gives birth to spirit. [7]You should not be surprised at my saying, 'You must be born again.' [8]The wind blows wherever it pleases. You hear its sound, but you cannot tell where it comes from or where it is going. So it is with everyone born of the Spirit."

MATTHEW 9:16-17 "No one sews a patch of unshrunk cloth on an old garment, for the patch will pull away from the garment, making the tear worse. [17]Neither do men pour new wine into old wineskins. If they do, the skins will burst, the wine will run out and the wineskins will be ruined. No, they pour new wine into new wineskins, and both are preserved." (See also Mark 2:21-22.)

MATTHEW 13:3-9 Then he told them many things in parables, saying: "A farmer went out to sow his seed. [4]As he was scattering the seed, some fell along the path, and the birds came and ate it up. [5]Some fell on rocky places, where it did not have much soil. It sprang up quickly, because the soil was shallow. [6]But when the sun came up, the plants were scorched, and they withered because they had no root. [7]Other seed fell among thorns, which grew up and choked the plants. [8]Still other seed fell on good soil, where it produced a crop—a hundred, sixty or thirty times what was sown. [9]He who has ears, let him hear."

MATTHEW 13:18-23 "Listen then to what the parable of the sower means: [19]When anyone hears the message about the kingdom and does not understand it, the evil one comes and snatches away what was sown in his heart. This is the seed sown along the path. [20]The one who received the seed that fell on rocky places is the man who hears the word and at once receives it with joy. [21]But since he has no root, he lasts only a short time. When

trouble or persecution comes because of the word, he quickly falls away. [22]The one who received the seed that fell among the thorns is the man who hears the word, but the worries of this life and the deceitfulness of wealth choke it, making it unfruitful. [23]But the one who received the seed that fell on good soil is the man who hears the word and understands it. He produces a crop, yielding a hundred, sixty or thirty times what was sown."

MATTHEW 18:2-5 He called a little child and had him stand among them. [3]And he said: "I tell you the truth, unless you change and become like little children, you will never enter the kingdom of heaven. [4]Therefore, whoever humbles himself like this child is the greatest in the kingdom of heaven. [5]And whoever welcomes a little child like this in my name welcomes me."

MARK 4:3-9 "Listen! A farmer went out to sow his seed. [4]As he was scattering the seed, some fell along the path, and the birds came and ate it up. [5]Some fell on rocky places, where it did not have much soil. It sprang up quickly, because the soil was shallow. [6]But when the sun came up, the plants were scorched, and they withered because they had no root. [7]Other seed fell among thorns, which grew up and choked the plants, so that they did not bear grain. [8]Still other seed fell on good soil. It came up, grew and produced a crop, multiplying thirty, sixty, or even a hundred times." [9]Then Jesus said, "He who has ears to hear, let him hear."

MARK 4:13-20 Then Jesus said to them [the disciples], "Don't you understand this parable? How then will you understand any parable? [14]The farmer sows the word. [15]Some people are like seed along the path, where the word is sown. As soon as they hear it, Satan comes and takes away the word that was sown in them. [16]Others, like seed sown on rocky places, hear the word and at once receive it with joy. [17]But since they have no root, they last only a short time. When trouble or persecution comes because of the word, they quickly fall away. [18]Still others, like seed sown among thorns, hear the word; [19]but the worries of this life, the deceitfulness of wealth and the desires for other things come in and choke the word, making it unfruitful. [20]Others, like seed sown on good soil, hear the word, accept it, and produce a crop—thirty, sixty or even a hundred times what was sown."

LUKE 5:36-39 He told them this parable: "No one tears a patch from a new garment and sews it on an old one. If he does, he will have torn the new garment, and the patch from the new will not match the old. [37]And no one pours new wine into old wineskins. If he does, the new wine will burst the skins, the wine will run out and the wineskins will be ruined. [38]No, new wine must be poured into new wineskins. [39]And no one after drinking old wine wants the new, for he says, 'The old is better.'"

LUKE 8:4-8 While a large crowd was gathering and people were coming to Jesus from town after town, he told this parable: [5]"A farmer went out to sow his seed. As he was scattering the seed, some fell along the path; it was trampled on, and the birds of the air ate it up. [6]Some

fell on rock, and when it came up, the plants withered because they had no moisture. [7]Other seed fell among thorns, which grew up with it and choked the plants. [8]Still other seed fell on good soil. It came up and yielded a crop, a hundred times more than was sown." When he said this, he called out, "He who has ears to hear, let him hear."

LUKE 8:11-15 "This is the meaning of the parable: The seed is the word of God. [12]Those along the path are the ones who hear, and then the devil comes and takes away the word from their hearts, so that they may not believe and be saved. [13]Those on the rock are the ones who receive the word with joy when they hear it, but they have no root. They believe for a while, but in the time of testing they fall away. [14]The seed that fell among thorns stands for those who hear, but as they go on their way they are choked by life's worries, riches and pleasures, and they do not mature. [15]But the seed on good soil stands for those with a noble and good heart, who hear the word, retain it, and by persevering produce a crop."

ACTS 9:3-16 As he neared Damascus on his journey, suddenly a light from heaven flashed around him. [4]He fell to the ground and heard a voice say to him, "Saul, Saul, why do you persecute me?" [5]"Who are you, Lord?" Saul asked. "I am Jesus, whom you are persecuting," he replied. [6]"Now get up and go into the city, and you will be told what you must do." [7]The men traveling with Saul stood there speechless; they heard the sound but did not see anyone. [8]Saul got up from the ground, but when he opened his eyes he could see nothing. So they led him by the hand into Damascus. [9]For three days he was blind, and did not eat or drink anything. [10]In Damascus there was a disciple named Ananias. The Lord called to him in a vision, "Ananias!" "Yes, Lord," he answered. [11]The Lord told him, "Go to the house of Judas on Straight Street and ask for a man from Tarsus named Saul, for he is praying. [12]In a vision he has seen a man named Ananias come and place his hands on him to restore his sight."

[13]"Lord," Ananias answered, "I have heard many reports about this man and all the harm he has done to your saints in Jerusalem. [14]And he has come here with authority from the chief priests to arrest all who call on your name." [15]But the Lord said to Ananias, "Go! This man is my chosen instrument to carry my name before the Gentiles and their kings and before the people of Israel. [16]I will show him how much he must suffer for my name." (See also Acts 22:6-10.)

5

THE GREATEST WORDS
EVER SPOKEN
TO JESUS' FOLLOWERS

What Jesus Said to Those Who Believe in Him

Several years ago a string of four letters took the Christian community by storm. It seemed like WWJD, which stands for "What would Jesus do?" was everywhere—and why not? When a choice has to be made, is any other question more important to ask?

The answer is "Yes, one question is more important. One question Christians should ask before choosing any course of action, making any spiritual decision, or adopting any value or belief." That question is "WDJS: What did Jesus say?" This is the question Christians need to ask because in many situations we simply can't know for sure what Jesus would do, so we are left to figure it out for ourselves. And figuring it out may require more wisdom, revelation, insight, and spiritual maturity than we possess at the time.

On the other hand, Jesus made incredible promises to Christians who would learn His words and use those words to guide their decisions, actions, and beliefs. Remember His promise in John 8:31-32: "If you abide in My word, you are My disciples indeed. And you shall know the truth, and the truth shall make you free" (NKJV). Jesus offers three promises that no one else in history could make and deliver on: the promise that you will become one of His intimate followers, the promise that you will discover and know perfect and eternal truth, and the promise that you will be liberated from the most powerful force that enslaves your heart and mind. Jesus promises that if you abide in His word, you will be freed from your self-centered nature and will enjoy the freedom, peace, power, and joy that come from intimacy with Christ.

In Matthew 7:24-25, Jesus uses an analogy of a man building a house. Describing the man who built his house on a rock, Jesus promises a level of wisdom and security that can't be shaken by even the most powerful internal or external forces. This is a level of wisdom and security that is unknown to the world in general and even to most Christians.

Those are just a few of the more than two dozen promises the Lord makes to anyone who begins to "abide" in His words. As noble as it may be to try to figure out what Jesus would do in a certain situation, He made no promises to the man or woman who would commit to such an undertaking. Would you rather base your hopes on your own limited wisdom, insights, and feelings, or on the "rock-solid" foundation of Christ's words?

What Jesus Said to His Followers

In this chapter, hundreds of Jesus' statements are organized into more than seventy topics—topics that deal specifically with those who believe in Him. He made more statements about how His followers should live and what they should believe than about any other group of topics. Our loving Savior spent much more time providing critical lessons, instruction, and encouragement to those who believed than addressing those who did not follow His words. Christ's comments equip us with everything we need to know to follow His guidance in every situation. But the incredible statements you will read in this chapter not only provide guidance; they also give us promises, revelation, and inspiration that enable us to experience God's incomparable grace and power. His words instruct us on how to experience a life full of extraordinary purpose, peace, and joy.

The first three sections of this chapter deal with breathtaking subjects: everything Christ said about abiding in His words, wisdom for dealing with our adversaries, and His revelation and instructions for dealing with anxiety and worry. In the first section alone, you'll find more than a dozen promises to anyone who hears and follows Christ's teachings. These promises don't apply to the followers of any other teacher or system of teaching.

Two of my favorite topics in this chapter are the "The Promises of Christ" and the "Commands of Christ." In the first, we have more than one hundred specific promises that Jesus made to those who truly follow Him. You will find promises regarding routine, day-to-day needs and situations, as well as promises that address your eternal needs. Under the heading "Commands of Christ," there are a handful of commands that apply specifically to Jesus' apostles, but more important you will read more than one hundred and thirty stated or implied commands that are given to all Christians—commands that reveal Jesus' heart and desires for us and for our walk with Him.

Two additional topics that are truly life empowering and life changing are priorities and prayer. If our priorities are not in line with Jesus' priorities, we won't experience all that He wants us to experience nor will we achieve all that He wants us to achieve on earth. As great as a purpose-driven life might be, a purpose-accomplished life is infinitely better. And if you've ever felt like your prayers weren't getting past the ceiling or that your prayer life wasn't all it could be, study what Jesus says about prayer. Jesus gives us everything we need to know, as well as His instructions and promises that we need to be aware of when we pray.

And especially relevant to Christians living in the twenty-first century, the topic of riches and possessions warrants special attention. In comparison to the rest of the world's population, even the poorest American would be regarded as rich. If you are a Christian living in America, you need to be especially aware of Jesus' teachings on riches and possessions. The bad news is, Christ reserved some of His gravest pronouncements and warnings for the rich. The good news is, He gives us wonderful instruction and hope as well. While American culture focuses on the accumulation of "things," in Luke 12:15 Jesus says, "Watch out! Be on your guard against all kinds of greed; a man's life does not consist in the abundance of his possessions." And in Matthew 16:26, Jesus says, "For what profit is it to a man if he gains the whole world, and loses his own soul?" (NKJV).

When Jesus said, "It is easier for a camel to go through the eye of a needle than for a rich man to enter the kingdom of God" (Mark 10:25, NKJV), He meant exactly what He said. In fact, this statement was so shocking that Jesus' disciples were "greatly astonished" and asked, "Who then can be saved?" (10:26, NKJV). By the world's standards at that time, they were considered rich as well. Even though they didn't have an abundance of possessions, they had jobs and were able to put bread on the table without having to beg. Jesus answered His disciples' question: "With men it is impossible, but not with God; for with God all things are possible" (10:27, NKJV).

Every situation you will ever encounter is dealt with by the powerful, illuminating statements of our Lord Jesus. Read His words with a joyful heart. May your faith be strengthened and your path made clear as you build your life on His guidance and admonitions.

Abiding in the Words of Christ

JOHN 5:24 "I tell you the truth, whoever hears my word and believes him who sent me has eternal life and will not be condemned; he has crossed over from death to life."

JOHN 6:63 "The Spirit gives life; the flesh counts for nothing. The words I have spoken to you are spirit and they are life."

JOHN 8:31-32 Then Jesus said to those Jews who believed Him, "If you abide in My word, you are My disciples indeed. 32And you shall know the truth, and the truth shall make you free." (NKJV)

JOHN 8:37-38 "I know you are Abraham's descendants. Yet you are ready to kill me, because you have no room for my word. 38I am telling you what I have seen in the Father's presence, and you do what you have heard from your father."

JOHN 8:51 "I tell you the truth, if anyone keeps my word, he will never see death."

JOHN 11:25-26 Jesus said to her [Martha], "I am the resurrection and the life. He who believes in me will live, even though he dies; 26and whoever lives and believes in me will never die. Do you believe this?"

JOHN 12:47-50 "As for the person who hears my words but does not keep them, I do not judge him. For I did not come to judge the world, but to save it. 48There is a judge for the one who rejects me and does not accept my words; that very word which I spoke will condemn him at the last day. 49For I did not speak of my own accord, but the Father who sent me commanded me what to say and how to say it. 50I know that his command leads to eternal life. So whatever I say is just what the Father has told me to say."

JOHN 14:10 "Don't you believe that I am in the Father, and that the Father is in me? The words I say to you are not just my own. Rather, it is the Father, living in me, who is doing his work."

JOHN 14:23-26 Jesus replied, "If anyone loves me, he will obey my teaching. My Father will love him, and we will come to him and make our home with him. 24He who does not love me will not obey my teaching. These words you hear are not my own; they belong to the Father who sent me. 25All this I have spoken while still with you. 26But the Counselor, the Holy Spirit, whom the Father will send in my name, will teach you all things and will remind you of everything I have said to you."

JOHN 15:3-4 "You are already clean because of the word I have spoken to you. ⁴Remain in me, and I will remain in you. No branch can bear fruit by itself; it must remain in the vine. Neither can you bear fruit unless you remain in me."

JOHN 15:5-8 "I am the vine; you are the branches. If a man remains in me and I in him, he will bear much fruit; apart from me you can do nothing. ⁶If anyone does not remain in me, he is like a branch that is thrown away and withers; such branches are picked up, thrown into the fire and burned. ⁷If you remain in me and my words remain in you, ask whatever you wish, and it will be given you. ⁸This is to my Father's glory, that you bear much fruit, showing yourselves to be my disciples."

JOHN 15:9-11 "As the Father has loved me, so have I loved you. Now remain in my love. ¹⁰If you obey my commands, you will remain in my love, just as I have obeyed my Father's commands and remain in his love. ¹¹I have told you this so that my joy may be in you and that your joy may be complete."

JOHN 17:13-17 "I am coming to you [God the Father] now, but I say these things while I am still in the world, so that they may have the full measure of my joy within them. ¹⁴I have given them your word and the world has hated them, for they are not of the world any more than I am of the world. ¹⁵My prayer is not that you take them out of the world but that you protect them from the evil one. ¹⁶They are not of the world, even as I am

not of it. ¹⁷Sanctify them by the truth; your word is truth."

MATTHEW 4:4 Jesus answered, "It is written: 'Man does not live on bread alone, but on every word that comes from the mouth of God.'" (See also Luke 4:4.)

MATTHEW 7:21-27 "Not everyone who says to Me, 'Lord, Lord,' shall enter the kingdom of heaven, but he who does the will of My Father in heaven. ²²Many will say to Me in that day, 'Lord, Lord, have we not prophesied in Your name, cast out demons in Your name, and done many wonders in Your name?' ²³And then I will declare to them, 'I never knew you; depart from Me, you who practice lawlessness!' ²⁴Therefore whoever hears these sayings of Mine, and does them, I will liken him to a wise man who built his house on the rock: ²⁵and the rain descended, the floods came, and the winds blew and beat on that house; and it did not fall, for it was founded on the rock. ²⁶But everyone who hears these sayings of Mine, and does not do them, will be like a foolish man who built his house on the sand: ²⁷and the rain descended, the floods came, and the winds blew and beat on that house; and it fell. And great was its fall." (NKJV)

MATTHEW 24:34-35 "I tell you the truth, this generation will certainly not pass away until all these things have happened. ³⁵Heaven and earth will pass away, but my words will never pass away." (See also Mark 13:30-31 and Luke 21:32-33.)

MARK 4:13-20 Then Jesus said to them [the disciples], "Don't you understand this parable? How then will you understand any parable? ¹⁴The farmer sows the word. ¹⁵Some people are like seed along the path, where the word is sown. As soon as they hear it, Satan comes and takes away the word that was sown in them. [16]Others, like seed sown on rocky places, hear the word and at once receive it with joy. [17]But since they have no root, they last only a short time. When trouble or persecution comes because of the word, they quickly fall away. [18]Still others, like seed sown among thorns, hear the word; [19]but the worries of this life, the deceitfulness of wealth and the desires for other things come in and choke the word, making it unfruitful. [20]Others, like seed sown on good soil, hear the word, accept it, and produce a crop—thirty, sixty or even a hundred times what was sown."

MARK 7:6-13 He replied, "Isaiah was right when he prophesied about you hypocrites; as it is written: 'These people honor me with their lips, but their hearts are far from me. [7]They worship me in vain; their teachings are but rules taught by men.' [8]You have let go of the commands of God and are holding on to the traditions of men." [9]And he said to them: "You have a fine way of setting aside the commands of God in order to observe your own traditions! [10]For Moses said, 'Honor your father and your mother,' and, 'Anyone who curses his father or mother must be put to death.' [11]But you say that if a man says to his father or mother: 'Whatever help you might otherwise have received from me is Corban' (that is, a gift devoted to God), [12]then you no longer let him do anything for his father or mother. [13]Thus you nullify the word of God by your tradition that you

have handed down. And you do many things like that."

LUKE 6:46-49 "Why do you call me, 'Lord, Lord,' and do not do what I say? [47]I will show you what he is like who comes to me and hears my words and puts them into practice. [48]He is like a man building a house, who dug down deep and laid the foundation on rock. When a flood came, the torrent struck that house but could not shake it, because it was well built. [49]But the one who hears my words and does not put them into practice is like a man who built a house on the ground without a foundation. The moment the torrent struck that house, it collapsed and its destruction was complete."

LUKE 8:21 He replied, "My mother and brothers are those who hear God's word and put it into practice."

LUKE 9:23-26 Then he said to them all: "If anyone would come after me, he must deny himself and take up his cross daily and follow me. [24]For whoever wants to save his life will lose it, but whoever loses his life for me will save it. [25]What good is it for a man to gain the whole world, and yet lose or forfeit his very self? [26]If anyone is ashamed of me and my words, the Son of Man will be ashamed of him when he comes in his glory and in the glory of the Father and of the holy angels."

LUKE 11:28 He replied, "Blessed rather are those who hear the word of God and obey it."

Adversaries and Human Enemies

MATTHEW 5:25-26 "Settle matters quickly with your adversary who is taking you to court. Do it while you are still with him on the way, or he may hand you over to the judge, and the judge may hand you over to the officer, and you may be thrown into prison. [26]I tell you the truth, you will not get out until you have paid the last penny."

MATTHEW 5:38-48 "You have heard that it was said, 'Eye for eye, and tooth for tooth.' [39]But I tell you, Do not resist an evil person. If someone strikes you on the right cheek, turn to him the other also. [40]And if someone wants to sue you and take your tunic, let him have your cloak as well. [41]If someone forces you to go one mile, go with him two miles. [42]Give to the one who asks you, and do not turn away from the one who wants to borrow from you. [43]You have heard that it was said, 'Love your neighbor and hate your enemy.' [44]But I tell you: Love your enemies and pray for those who persecute you, [45]that you may be sons of your Father in heaven. He causes his sun to rise on the evil and the good, and sends rain on the righteous and the unrighteous. [46]If you love those who love you, what reward will you get? Are not even the tax collectors doing that? [47]And if you greet only your brothers, what are you doing more than others? Do not even pagans do that? [48]Be perfect, therefore, as your heavenly Father is perfect."

MATTHEW 10:16-23 "I am sending you out like sheep among wolves. Therefore be as shrewd as snakes and as innocent as doves. [17]Be on your guard against men; they will hand you over to the local councils and flog you in their synagogues. [18]On my account you will be brought before governors and kings as witnesses to them and to the Gentiles. [19]But when they arrest you, do not worry about what to say or how to say it. At that time you will be given what to say, [20]for it will not be you speaking, but the Spirit of your Father speaking through you. [21]Brother will betray brother to death, and a father his child; children will rebel against their parents and have them put to death. [22]All men will hate you because of me, but he who stands firm to the end will be saved. [23]When you are persecuted in one place, flee to another. I tell you the truth, you will not finish going through the cities of Israel before the Son of Man comes."

LUKE 6:27-36 "But I tell you who hear me: Love your enemies, do good to those who hate you, [28]bless those who curse you, pray for those who mistreat you. [29]If someone strikes you on one cheek, turn to him the other also. If someone takes your cloak, do not stop him from taking your tunic. [30]Give to everyone who asks you, and if anyone takes what belongs to you, do not demand it back. [31]Do to others as you would have them do to you. [32]If you love those who love you, what credit is that to you? Even 'sinners' love those who love them. [33]And if you do good to those who are good to you, what credit is that to you? Even 'sinners' do that. [34]And if you lend to those from whom you expect repayment, what credit is that to you? Even 'sinners' lend to 'sinners,' expecting to be repaid in full. [35]But love your enemies, do good to them, and lend to them without expecting to get anything back. Then your reward will be great, and you will be sons of the

Most High, because he is kind to the ungrateful and wicked. ³⁶Be merciful, just as your Father is merciful."

LUKE 12:58-59 "As you are going with your adversary to the magistrate, try hard to be reconciled to him on the way, or he may drag you off to the judge, and the judge turn you over to the officer, and the officer throw you into prison. ⁵⁹I tell you, you will not get out until you have paid the last penny."

Anxiety, Worry, and Fear

JOHN 6:19-20 When they had rowed three or three and a half miles, they saw Jesus approaching the boat, walking on the water; and they were terrified. ²⁰But he said to them, "It is I; don't be afraid."

JOHN 14:1-4 "Do not let your hearts be troubled. Trust in God; trust also in me. ²In my Father's house are many rooms; if it were not so, I would have told you. I am going there to prepare a place for you. ³And if I go and prepare a place for you, I will come back and take you to be with me that you also may be where I am. ⁴You know the way to the place where I am going."

JOHN 14:27-29 "Peace I leave with you; my peace I give you. I do not give to you as the world gives. Do not let your hearts be troubled and do not be afraid. ²⁸You heard me say, 'I am going away and I am coming back to you.' If you loved me, you would be glad that I am going to the Father, for the Father is greater than I. ²⁹I have told you now before it happens, so that when it does happen you will believe."

JOHN 16:31-33 "You believe at last!" Jesus answered. ³²"But a time is coming, and has come, when you will be scattered, each to his own home. You will leave me all alone. Yet I am not alone, for my Father is with me. ³³I have told you these things, so that in me you may have peace. In this world you will have trouble. But take heart! I have overcome the world."

JOHN 20:21-22 Again Jesus said, "Peace be with you! As the Father has sent me, I am sending you." ²²And with that he breathed on them and said, "Receive the Holy Spirit."

JOHN 20:26-27 A week later his disciples were in the house again, and Thomas was with them. Though the doors were locked, Jesus came and stood among them and said, "Peace be with you!" ²⁷Then he said to Thomas, "Put your finger here; see my hands. Reach out your hand and put it into my side. Stop doubting and believe."

MATTHEW 5:4, 9 "Blessed are those who mourn, for they will be comforted. ⁹Blessed are the peacemakers, for they will be called sons of God."

MATTHEW 6:25-34 "Therefore I tell you, do not worry about your life, what you will eat or drink; or about your body, what you will wear. Is not life more important than food, and the body more important than clothes? ²⁶Look at the birds of the air; they do not sow or reap or store away in barns, and yet your heavenly Father feeds them. Are you not much more valuable than they? ²⁷Who of you by worrying can add a single hour to his life? ²⁸And why do you worry about clothes? See how the lilies of the field grow. They do not labor or spin. [29]Yet I tell you that not even Solomon in all his splendor was dressed like one of these. [30]If that is how God clothes the grass of the field, which is here today and tomorrow is thrown into the fire, will he not much more clothe you, O you of little faith? [31]So do not worry, saying, 'What shall we eat?' or 'What shall we drink?' or 'What shall we wear?' [32]For the pagans run after all these things, and your heavenly Father knows that you need them. [33]But seek first his kingdom and his righteousness, and all these things will be given to you as well. [34]Therefore do not worry about tomorrow, for tomorrow will worry about itself. Each day has enough trouble of its own."

MATTHEW 8:25-26 The disciples went and woke him, saying, "Lord, save us! We're going to drown!" [26]He replied, "You of little faith, why are you so afraid?" Then he got up and rebuked the winds and the waves, and it was completely calm.

MATTHEW 10:24-26 "A student is not above his teacher, nor a servant above his master. [25]It is enough for the student to be like his teacher, and the servant like his master. If the head of the house has been called Beelzebub, how much more the members of his household! [26]So do not be afraid of them. There is nothing concealed that will not be disclosed, or hidden that will not be made known."

MATTHEW 10:27-31 "What I tell you in the dark, speak in the daylight; what is whispered in your ear, proclaim from the roofs. [28]Do not be afraid of those who kill the body but cannot kill the soul. Rather, be afraid of the One who can destroy both soul and body in hell. [29]Are not two sparrows sold for a penny? Yet not one of them will fall to the ground apart from the will of your Father. [30]And even the very hairs of your head are all numbered. [31]So don't be afraid; you are worth more than many sparrows."

MATTHEW 10:34-39 "Do not suppose that I have come to bring peace to the earth. I did not come to bring peace, but a sword. [35]For I have come to turn 'a man against his father, a daughter against her mother, a daughter-in-law against her mother-in-law— [36]a man's enemies will be the members of his own household.' [37]Anyone who loves his father or mother more than me is not worthy of me; anyone who loves his son or daughter more than me is not worthy of me; [38]and anyone who does not take his cross and follow me is not worthy of me. [39]Whoever finds his life will lose it, and whoever loses his life for my sake will find it."

MATTHEW 11:28-30 "Come to me, all you who are weary and burdened, and I will give you rest. [29]Take my yoke upon you and learn from me, for I am gentle and humble in heart, and you will find rest for your souls. [30]For my yoke is easy and my burden is light."

MATTHEW 14:26-27 When the disciples saw him walking on the lake, they were terrified. "It's a ghost," they said, and cried out in fear. [27]But Jesus immediately said to them: "Take courage! It is I. Don't be afraid." (See also Mark 6:49-50.)

MATTHEW 17:1-8 After six days Jesus took with him Peter, James and John the brother of James, and led them up a high mountain by themselves. [2]There he was transfigured before them. His face shone like the sun, and his clothes became as white as the light. ³Just then there appeared before them Moses and Elijah, talking with Jesus. ⁴Peter said to Jesus, "Lord, it is good for us to be here. If you wish, I will put up three shelters—one for you, one for Moses and one for Elijah." ⁵While he was still speaking, a bright cloud enveloped them, and a voice from the cloud said, "This is my Son, whom I love; with him I am well pleased. Listen to him!" ⁶When the disciples heard this, they fell facedown to the ground, terrified. ⁷But Jesus came and touched them. "Get up," he said. "Don't be afraid." ⁸When they looked up, they saw no one except Jesus.

MATTHEW 28:9-10 Suddenly Jesus met them. "Greetings," he said. They came to him, clasped his feet and worshiped him. ¹⁰Then Jesus said to them, "Do not be afraid. Go and tell my brothers to go to Galilee; there they will see me."

MARK 4:35-40 That day when evening came, he said to his disciples, "Let us go over to the other side." ³⁶Leaving the crowd behind, they took him along, just as he was, in the boat. There were also other boats with him. ³⁷A furious squall came up, and the waves broke over the boat, so that it was nearly swamped. ³⁸Jesus was in the stern, sleeping on a cushion. The disciples woke him and said to him, "Teacher, don't you care if we drown?" ³⁹He got up, rebuked the wind and said to the waves, "Quiet! Be still!" Then the wind died down and it was completely calm. ⁴⁰He said to his disciples, "Why are you so afraid? Do you still have no faith?"

MARK 5:35-36 While Jesus was still speaking, some men came from the house of Jairus, the synagogue ruler. "Your daughter is dead," they said. "Why bother the teacher any more?" ³⁶Ignoring what they said, Jesus told the synagogue ruler, "Don't be afraid; just believe."

MARK 6:30-32 The apostles gathered around Jesus and reported to him all they had done and taught. ³¹Then, because so many people were coming and going that they did not even have a chance to eat, he said to them, "Come with me by yourselves to a quiet place and get some rest." ³²So they went away by themselves in a boat to a solitary place.

MARK 9:49-50 "Everyone will be salted with fire. ⁵⁰Salt is good, but if it loses its saltiness, how can you make it salty again? Have salt in yourselves, and be at peace with each other."

LUKE 5:10 …Then Jesus said to Simon, "Don't be afraid; from now on you will catch men."

LUKE 12:4-7 "I tell you, my friends, do not be afraid of those who kill the body and after that can do no more. ⁵But I will show you whom you should fear: Fear him who, after the killing of the body, has power to throw you into hell. Yes, I tell you, fear him. ⁶Are not five sparrows sold for two pennies? Yet not one of them is forgotten by God. ⁷Indeed, the very hairs of your head are all numbered. Don't be afraid; you are worth more than many sparrows."

LUKE 12:22-34 Then Jesus said to his disciples: "Therefore I tell you, do not worry about your life, what you will eat; or about your body, what you will wear.

[23]Life is more than food, and the body more than clothes. [24]Consider the ravens: They do not sow or reap, they have no storeroom or barn; yet God feeds them. And how much more valuable you are than birds! [25]Who of you by worrying can add a single hour to his life? [26]Since you cannot do this very little thing, why do you worry about the rest? [27]Consider how the lilies grow. They do not labor or spin. Yet I tell you, not even Solomon in all his splendor was dressed like one of these. [28]If that is how God clothes the grass of the field, which is here today, and tomorrow is thrown into the fire, how much more will he clothe you, O you of little faith! [29]And do not set your heart on what you will eat or drink; do not worry about it. [30]For the pagan world runs after all such things, and your Father knows that you need them. [31]But seek his kingdom, and these things will be given to you as well. [32]Do not be afraid, little flock, for your Father has been pleased to give you the kingdom. [33]Sell your possessions and give to the poor. Provide purses for yourselves that will not wear out, a treasure in heaven that will not be exhausted, where no thief comes near and no moth destroys. [34]For where your treasure is, there your heart will be also."

LUKE 12:51-53 "Do you think I came to bring peace on earth? No, I tell you, but division. [52]From now on there will be five in one family divided against each other, three against two and two against three. [53]They will be divided, father against son and son against father, mother against daughter and daughter against mother, mother-in-law against daughter-in-law and daughter-in-law against mother-in-law."

LUKE 24:36-43 While they [the disciples] were still talking about this, Jesus himself stood among them and said to them, "Peace be with you." [37]They were startled and frightened, thinking they saw a ghost. [38]He said to them, "Why are you troubled, and why do doubts rise in your minds? [39]Look at my hands and my feet. It is I myself! Touch me and see; a ghost does not have flesh and bones, as you see I have." [40]When he had said this, he showed them his hands and feet. [41]And while they still did not believe it because of joy and amazement, he asked them, "Do you have anything here to eat?" [42]They gave him a piece of broiled fish, [43]and he took it and ate it in their presence.

ACTS 18:9-11 One night the Lord spoke to Paul in a vision: "Do not be afraid; keep on speaking, do not be silent. [10]For I am with you, and no one is going to attack and harm you, because I have many people in this city." [11]So Paul stayed for a year and a half, teaching them the word of God.

Apostles

In this section we see instructions and commands that Jesus gave specifically to His apostles. In them, we can see Jesus' will clearly expressed, and in some cases we can apply these same principles to our lives as well. For example in John 20:21-22, Jesus tells the apostles He's sending them out in the same manner that He was sent by His Father. Although this exhortation was specifically for His disciples, we can learn from this admonition that Jesus wants us to go out into the world with the same love, compassion, and truth that He brought to us. *(See also "Following Christ," p. 245.)*

JOHN 15:26-27 "When the Counselor comes, whom I will send to you from the Father, the Spirit of truth who goes out from the Father, he will testify about me. [27]And you also must testify, for you have been with me from the beginning."

JOHN 20:21-23 Again Jesus said, "Peace be with you! As the Father has sent me, I am sending you." [22]And with that he breathed on them and said, "Receive the Holy Spirit. [23]If you forgive anyone his sins, they are forgiven; if you do not forgive them, they are not forgiven."

JOHN 21:15-18 When they had finished eating, Jesus said to Simon Peter, "Simon son of John, do you truly love me more than these?" "Yes, Lord," he said, "you know that I love you." Jesus said, "Feed my lambs." [16]Again Jesus said, "Simon son of John, do you truly love me?" He answered, "Yes, Lord, you know that I love you." Jesus said, "Take care of my sheep." [17]The third time he said to him, "Simon son of John, do you love me?" Peter was hurt because Jesus asked him the third time, "Do you love me?" He said, "Lord, you know all things; you know that I love you." Jesus said, "Feed my sheep. [18]I tell you the truth, when you were younger you dressed yourself and went where you wanted; but when you are old you will stretch out your hands, and someone else will dress you and lead you where you do not want to go."

MATTHEW 10:5-20 These twelve Jesus sent out with the following instructions: "Do not go among the Gentiles or enter any town of the Samaritans. [6]Go rather to the lost sheep of Israel. [7]As you go, preach this message: 'The kingdom of heaven is near.' [8]Heal the sick, raise the dead, cleanse those who have leprosy, drive out demons. Freely you have received, freely give. [9]Do not take along any gold or silver or copper in your belts; [10]take no bag for the journey, or extra tunic, or sandals or a staff; for the worker is worth his keep. [11]Whatever town or village you enter, search for some worthy person there and stay at his house until you leave. [12]As you enter the home, give it your greeting. [13]If the home is deserving, let your peace rest on it; if it is not, let your peace return to you. [14]If anyone will not welcome you or listen to your words, shake the dust off your feet when you leave that home or town. [15]I tell you the truth, it will be more bearable for Sodom and Gomorrah on the day of judgment than for that town. [16]I am sending you out like sheep among wolves. Therefore be as shrewd as snakes and as innocent as doves. [17]Be on your guard against men; they will hand you over to the local councils and flog you in their synagogues. [18]On my account you will be brought before governors and kings as witnesses to them and to the Gentiles. [19]But when they arrest you, do not worry about what to say or how to say it. At that time you will be given what to say, [20]for it will not be you speaking, but the Spirit of your Father speaking through you."

MATTHEW 16:17-20 Jesus replied, "Blessed are you, Simon son of Jonah, for this was not revealed to you by man, but by my Father in heaven. ¹⁸And I tell you that you are Peter, and on this rock I will build my church, and the gates of Hades will not overcome it. ¹⁹I will give you the keys of the kingdom of heaven; whatever you bind on earth will be bound in heaven, and whatever you loose on earth will be loosed in heaven." ²⁰Then he warned his disciples not to tell anyone that he was the Christ.

MATTHEW 19:27-30 Peter answered him, "We have left everything to follow you! What then will there be for us?" ²⁸Jesus said to them, "I tell you the truth, at the renewal of all things, when the Son of Man sits on his glorious throne, you who have followed me will also sit on twelve thrones, judging the twelve tribes of Israel. ²⁹And everyone who has left houses or brothers or sisters or father or mother or children or fields for my sake will receive a hundred times as much and will inherit eternal life. ³⁰But many who are first will be last, and many who are last will be first."

MATTHEW 20:20-23 Then the mother of Zebedee's sons [James and John] came to Jesus with her sons and, kneeling down, asked a favor of him. ²¹"What is it you want?" he asked. She said, "Grant that one of these two sons of mine may sit at your right and the other at your left in your kingdom." ²²"You don't know what you are asking," Jesus said to them. "Can you drink the cup I am going to drink?" "We can," they answered. ²³Jesus said to them, "You will indeed drink from my cup, but to sit at my right or left is not for me to grant. These places

belong to those for whom they have been prepared by my Father."

MATTHEW 28:18-20 Then Jesus came to them [the eleven disciples] and said, "All authority in heaven and on earth has been given to me. ¹⁹Therefore go and make disciples of all nations, baptizing them in the name of the Father and of the Son and of the Holy Spirit, ²⁰and teaching them to obey everything I have commanded you. And surely I am with you always, to the very end of the age."

MARK 6:7 Calling the Twelve to him, he sent them out two by two and gave them authority over evil spirits.

MARK 10:36-40 "What do you want me to do for you?" he asked. ³⁷They [James and John] replied, "Let one of us sit at your right and the other at your left in your glory." ³⁸"You don't know what you are asking," Jesus said. "Can you drink the cup I drink or be baptized with the baptism I am baptized with?" ³⁹"We can," they answered. Jesus said to them, "You will drink the cup I drink and be baptized with the baptism I am baptized with, ⁴⁰but to sit at my right or left is not for me to grant. These places belong to those for whom they have been prepared."

MARK 16:15-18 He said to them [the Eleven], "Go into all the world and preach the good news to all creation. ¹⁶Whoever believes and is baptized will be saved, but whoever does not believe will be condemned. ¹⁷And these signs will accompany those who believe: In my name they will drive out demons; they will speak in new tongues; ¹⁸they will pick up snakes with their hands; and when they drink deadly poison, it will not hurt them at all; they will place their hands on sick people, and they will get well."[ix]

LUKE 9:1 When Jesus had called the Twelve together, he gave them power and authority to drive out all demons and to cure diseases.

LUKE 22:24-32 Also a dispute arose among them as to which of them was considered to be greatest. [25]Jesus said to them, "The kings of the Gentiles lord it over them; and those who exercise authority over them call themselves Benefactors. [26]But you are not to be like that. Instead, the greatest among you should be like the youngest, and the one who rules like the one who serves. [27]For who is greater, the one who is at the table or the one who serves? Is it not the one who is at the table? But I am among you as one who serves. [28]You are those who have stood by me in my trials. [29]And I confer on you a kingdom, just as my Father conferred one on me, [30]so that you may eat and drink at my table in my kingdom and sit on thrones, judging the twelve tribes of Israel. [31]Simon, Simon, Satan has asked to sift you as wheat. [32]But I have prayed for you, Simon, that your faith may not fail. And when you have turned back, strengthen your brothers."

ACTS 1:4-5 On one occasion, while he was eating with them [the apostles], he gave them this command: "Do not leave Jerusalem, but wait for the gift my Father promised, which you have heard me speak about. [5]For John baptized with water, but in a few days you will be baptized with the Holy Spirit." (See also Acts 11:16.)

Attitudes

MATTHEW 5:3-9 "Blessed are the poor in spirit, for theirs is the kingdom of heaven. [4]Blessed are those who mourn, for they will be comforted. [5]Blessed are the meek, for they will inherit the earth. [6]Blessed are those who hunger and thirst for righteousness, for they will be filled. [7]Blessed are the merciful, for they will be shown mercy. [8]Blessed are the pure in heart, for they will see God. [9]Blessed are the peacemakers, for they will be called sons of God."

MATTHEW 5:13 "You are the salt of the earth. But if the salt loses its saltiness, how can it be made salty again? It is no longer good for anything, except to be thrown out and trampled by men."

MATTHEW 5:14-16 "You are the light of the world. A city on a hill cannot be hidden. [15]Neither do people light a lamp and put it under a bowl. Instead they put it on its stand, and it gives light to everyone in the house. [16]In the same way, let your light shine before men, that they may see your good deeds and praise your Father in heaven."

MATTHEW 5:38-48 "You have heard that it was said, 'Eye for eye, and tooth for tooth.' [39]But I tell you, Do not resist an evil person. If someone strikes you on the right cheek, turn to him the other also. [40]And if someone wants to sue you and take your tunic, let him have your cloak as well. [41]If someone forces you to go one mile, go with him two miles. [42]Give to the one who asks you, and do not turn away from the one who wants to borrow from you. ⁴³You have heard that it was said, 'Love your neighbor and hate your enemy.' ⁴⁴But I tell you: Love your enemies and pray for those who persecute you, ⁴⁵that you may be sons of your Father in heaven. He causes his sun to rise on the evil and the good, and sends rain on the righteous and the unrighteous. ⁴⁶If you love those who love you, what reward will you get? Are not even the tax collectors doing that? ⁴⁷And if you greet only your brothers, what are you doing more than others? Do not even pagans do that? ⁴⁸Be perfect, therefore, as your heavenly Father is perfect."

LUKE 12:35-40 "Be dressed ready for service and keep your lamps burning, ³⁶like men waiting for their master to return from a wedding banquet, so that when he comes and knocks they can immediately open the door for him. ³⁷It will be good for those servants whose master finds them watching when he comes. I tell you the truth, he will dress himself to serve, will have them recline at the table and will come and wait on them. ³⁸It will be good for those servants whose master finds them ready, even if he comes in the second or third watch of the night. ³⁹But understand this: If the owner of the house had known at what hour the thief was coming, he would not have let his house be broken into. ⁴⁰You also must be ready, because the Son of Man will come at an hour when you do not expect him."

LUKE 12:42-48 The Lord answered, "Who then is the faithful and wise manager, whom the master puts in charge of his servants to give them their food allowance at the proper time? ⁴³It will be good for that servant whom the master finds doing so when he returns. ⁴⁴I tell you the truth, he will put him in charge of all his possessions. ⁴⁵But suppose the servant says to himself, 'My master is taking a long time in coming,' and he then begins to beat the menservants and maidservants and to eat and drink and get drunk. ⁴⁶The master of that servant will come on a day when he does not expect him and at an hour he is not aware of. He will cut him to pieces and assign him a place with the unbelievers. ⁴⁷That servant who knows his master's will and does not get ready or does not do what his master wants will be beaten with many blows. ⁴⁸But the one who does not know and does things deserving punishment will be beaten with few blows. From everyone who has been given much, much will be demanded; and from the one who has been entrusted with much, much more will be asked."

LUKE 17:7-10 "Suppose one of you had a servant plowing or looking after the sheep. Would he say to the servant when he comes in from the field, 'Come along now and sit down to eat'? ⁸Would he not rather say, 'Prepare my supper, get yourself ready and wait on me while I eat and drink; after that you may eat and drink'? ⁹Would he thank the servant because he did what he was told to do? ¹⁰So you also, when you have done everything you were told to do, should say, 'We are unworthy servants; we have only done our duty.'"

LUKE 18:1-8 Then Jesus told his disciples a parable to show them that they should always pray and not give up. [2]He said: "In a certain town there was a judge who neither feared God nor cared about men. [3]And there was a widow in that town who kept coming to him with the plea, 'Grant me justice against my adversary.' [4]For some time he refused. But finally he said to himself, 'Even though I don't fear God or care about men, [5]yet because this widow keeps bothering me, I will see that she gets justice, so that she won't eventually wear me out with her coming!'" [6]And the Lord said, "Listen to what the unjust judge says. [7]And will not God bring about justice for his chosen ones, who cry out to him day and night? Will he keep putting them off? [8]I tell you, he will see that they get justice, and quickly. However, when the Son of Man comes, will he find faith on the earth?"

Blessings

MATTHEW 5:3-9 "Blessed are the poor in spirit, for theirs is the kingdom of heaven. [4]Blessed are those who mourn, for they will be comforted. [5]Blessed are the meek, for they will inherit the earth. [6]Blessed are those who hunger and thirst for righteousness, for they will be filled. [7]Blessed are the merciful, for they will be shown mercy. [8]Blessed are the pure in heart, for they will see God. [9]Blessed are the peacemakers, for they will be called sons of God."

MATTHEW 5:10-11 "Blessed are those who are persecuted because of righteousness, for theirs is the kingdom of heaven. [11]Blessed are you when people insult you, persecute you and falsely say all kinds of evil against you because of me."

MATTHEW 11:6 "Blessed is the man who does not fall away on account of me." (See also Luke 7:23.)

LUKE 14:12-14 Then Jesus said to his host, "When you give a luncheon or dinner, do not invite your friends, your brothers or relatives, or your rich neighbors; if you do, they may invite you back and so you will be repaid. [13]But when you give a banquet, invite the poor, the crippled, the lame, the blind, [14]and you will be blessed. Although they cannot repay you, you will be repaid at the resurrection of the righteous."

LUKE 14:15-24 When one of those at the table with him heard this, he said to Jesus, "Blessed is the man who will eat at the feast in the kingdom of God." [16]Jesus replied: "A certain man was preparing a great banquet and invited many guests. [17]At the time of the banquet he sent his servant to tell those who had been invited, 'Come, for everything is now ready.' [18]But they all alike began to make excuses. The first said, 'I have just bought a field, and I must go and see it. Please excuse me.' [19]Another said, 'I have just bought five yoke of oxen, and I'm on my way to try them out. Please excuse me.' [20]Still another said, 'I just got married, so I can't come.' [21]The servant came back and reported this to his master. Then the owner of the house became angry and ordered his servant, 'Go out quickly into the streets and alleys of the town and bring in the poor, the crippled, the blind and the lame.' [22]'Sir,' the servant said, 'what you ordered has been done, but there is still room.' [23]Then the master told his servant, 'Go out to the roads and country lanes and make them come in, so that my house will be full. [24]I tell you, not one of those men who were invited will get a taste of my banquet.'"

ACTS 20:35 "In everything I [Paul] did, I showed you that by this kind of hard work we must help the weak, remembering the words the Lord Jesus himself said: 'It is more blessed to give than to receive.'"

REVELATION 22:7 "Behold, I am coming soon! Blessed is he who keeps the words of the prophecy in this book."

REVELATION 22:14 "Blessed are those who wash their robes, that they may have the right to the tree of life and may go through the gates into the city."

Children of God

JOHN 8:42-47 Jesus said to them, "If God were your Father, you would love me, for I came from God and now am here. I have not come on my own; but he sent me. [43]Why is my language not clear to you? Because you are unable to hear what I say. [44]You belong to your father, the devil, and you want to carry out your father's desire. He was a murderer from the beginning, not holding to the truth, for there is no truth in him. When he lies, he speaks his native language, for he is a liar and the father of lies. [45]Yet because I tell the truth, you do not believe me! [46]Can any of you prove me guilty of sin? If I am telling the truth, why don't you believe me? [47]He who belongs to God hears what God says. The reason you do not hear is that you do not belong to God."

JOHN 12:25-26 "The man who loves his life will lose it, while the man who hates his life in this world will keep it for eternal life. [26]Whoever serves me must follow me; and where I am, my servant also will be. My Father will honor the one who serves me."

JOHN 17:9 "I pray for them [the disciples]. I am not praying for the world, but for those you have given me, for they are yours."

MATTHEW 7:11 "If you, then, though you are evil, know how to give good gifts to your children, how much more will your Father in heaven give good gifts to those who ask him!"

MATTHEW 12:49-50 Pointing to his disciples, he said, "Here are my mother and my brothers. [50]For whoever does the will of my Father in heaven is my brother and sister and mother."

MATTHEW 13:37-43 He answered, "The one who sowed the good seed is the Son of Man. [38]The field is the world, and the good seed stands for the sons of the kingdom. The weeds are the sons of the evil one, [39]and the enemy who sows them is the devil. The harvest is the end of the age, and the harvesters are angels. [40]As the weeds are pulled up and burned in the fire, so it will be at the end of the age. [41]The Son of Man will send out his angels, and they will weed out of his kingdom everything that causes sin and all who do evil. [42]They will throw them into the fiery furnace, where there will be weeping and gnashing of teeth. [43]Then the righteous will shine like the sun in the kingdom of their Father. He who has ears, let him hear."

LUKE 6:32-36 "If you love those who love you, what credit is that to you? Even 'sinners' love those who love them. ³³And if you do good to those who are good to you, what credit is that to you? Even 'sinners' do that. ³⁴And if you lend to those from whom you expect repayment, what credit is that to you? Even 'sinners' lend to 'sinners,' expecting to be repaid in full. ³⁵But love your enemies, do good to them, and lend to them without expecting to get anything back. Then your reward will be great, and you will be sons of the Most High, because he is kind to the ungrateful and wicked. ³⁶Be merciful, just as your Father is merciful."

LUKE 20:34-36 Jesus replied, "The people of this age marry and are given in marriage. ³⁵But those who are considered worthy of taking part in that age and in the resurrection from the dead will neither marry nor be given in marriage, ³⁶and they can no longer die; for they are like the angels. They are God's children, since they are children of the resurrection."

Chosen (Those Jesus Chooses)

JOHN 6:36-40 "But as I told you, you have seen me and still you do not believe. ³⁷All that the Father gives me will come to me, and whoever comes to me I will never drive away. ³⁸For I have come down from heaven not to do my will but to do the will of him who sent me. ³⁹And this is the will of him who sent me, that I shall lose none of all that he has given me, but raise them up at the last day. ⁴⁰For my Father's will is that everyone who looks to the Son and believes in him shall have

eternal life, and I will raise him up at the last day."

JOHN 6:64-65 "Yet there are some of you who do not believe." For Jesus had known from the beginning which of them did not believe and who would betray him. ⁶⁵He went on to say, "This is why I told you that no one can come to me unless the Father has enabled him."

JOHN 10:27-30 "My sheep listen to my voice; I know them, and they follow me. ²⁸I give them eternal life, and they shall never perish; no one can snatch them out of my hand. ²⁹My Father, who has given them to me, is greater than all; no one can snatch them out of my Father's hand. ³⁰I and the Father are one."

JOHN 13:18 "I am not referring to all of you; I know those I have chosen. But this is to fulfill the scripture: 'He who shares my bread has lifted up his heel against me.'"

JOHN 15:16-17 "You did not choose me, but I chose you and appointed you to go and bear fruit—fruit that will last. Then the Father will give you whatever you ask in my name. ¹⁷This is my command: Love each other."

JOHN 15:19 "If you belonged to the world, it would love you as its own. As it is, you do not belong to the world, but I have chosen you out of the world. That is why the world hates you."

JOHN 17:2-4 "For you [God] granted him [Christ] authority over all people that he might give eternal life to all those you have given him. ³Now this is eternal life: that they may know you, the only true God, and Jesus Christ, whom you have sent. ⁴I have brought you glory on earth by completing the work you gave me to do."

JOHN 17:6 "I have revealed you [God] to those whom you gave me out of the world. They were yours; you gave them to me and they have obeyed your word."

JOHN 17:9-12 "I pray for them [the disciples]. I am not praying for the world, but for those you have given me, for they are yours. [10]All I have is yours, and all you have is mine. And glory has come to me through them. [11]I will remain in the world no longer, but they are still in the world, and I am coming to you. Holy Father, protect them by the power of your name—the name you gave me—so that they may be one as we are one. [12]While I was with them, I protected them and kept them safe by that name you gave me. None has been lost except the one doomed to destruction so that Scripture would be fulfilled."

MATTHEW 11:27 "All things have been committed to me by my Father. No one knows the Son except the Father, and no one knows the Father except the Son and those to whom the Son chooses to reveal him."

MATTHEW 20:1-16 "For the kingdom of heaven is like a landowner who went out early in the morning to hire men to work in his vineyard. [2]He agreed to pay them a denarius for the day and sent them into his vineyard. [3]About the third hour he went out and saw others standing in the marketplace doing nothing. [4]He told them, 'You also go and work in my vineyard, and I will pay you whatever is right.' [5]So they went. He went out again about

the sixth hour and the ninth hour and did the same thing. [6]About the eleventh hour he went out and found still others standing around. He asked them, 'Why have you been standing here all day long doing nothing?' [7]'Because no one has hired us,' they answered. He said to them, 'You also go and work in my vineyard.' [8]When evening came, the owner of the vineyard said to his foreman, 'Call the workers and pay them their wages, beginning with the last ones hired and going on to the first.' [9]The workers who were hired about the eleventh hour came and each received a denarius. [10]So when those came who were hired first, they expected to receive more. But each one of them also received a denarius. [11]When they received it, they began to grumble against the landowner. [12]'These men who were hired last worked only one hour,' they said, 'and you have made them equal to us who have borne the burden of the work and the heat of the day.' [13]But he answered one of them, 'Friend, I am not being unfair to you. Didn't you agree to work for a denarius? [14]Take your pay and go. I want to give the man who was hired last the same as I gave you. [15]Don't I have the right to do what I want with my own money? Or are you envious because I am generous?' [16]So the last will be first, and the first will be last."

MATTHEW 22:1-14 Jesus spoke to them again in parables, saying: [2]"The kingdom of heaven is like a king who prepared a wedding banquet for his son. [3]He sent his servants to those who had been invited to the banquet to tell them to come, but they refused to come. [4]Then he sent some more servants and said, 'Tell those who have been invited that I have prepared my dinner: My oxen and fattened cattle have been butchered, and everything is ready. Come to the wedding banquet.' [5]But they paid no attention and went off—one to his field, another to his business. [6]The rest seized his servants, mistreated them and killed them. [7]The king was enraged. He sent his army and destroyed those murderers and burned their city. [8]Then he said to his servants, 'The wedding banquet is ready, but those I invited did not deserve to come. [9]Go to the street corners and invite to the banquet anyone you find.' [10]So the servants went out into the streets and gathered all the people they could find, both good and bad, and the wedding hall was filled with guests. [11]But when the king came in to see the guests, he noticed a man there who was not wearing wedding clothes. [12]'Friend,' he asked, 'how did you get in here without wedding clothes?' The man was speechless. [13]Then the king told the attendants, 'Tie him hand and foot, and throw him outside, into the darkness, where there will be weeping and gnashing of teeth.' [14]For many are invited, but few are chosen."

MARK 13:18-20 "Pray that this will not take place in winter, [19]because those will be days of distress unequaled from the beginning, when God created the world, until now—and never to be equaled again. [20]If the Lord had not cut short those days, no one would survive. But for the sake of the elect, whom he has chosen, he has shortened them."

MARK 13:22 "For false Christs and false prophets will appear and perform signs and miracles to deceive the elect—if that were possible."

LUKE 18:6-8 And the Lord said, "Listen to what the unjust judge says. [7]And will not God bring about justice for his chosen ones, who cry out to him day and night? Will he keep putting them off? [8]I tell you, he will see that they get justice, and quickly. However, when the Son of Man comes, will he find faith on the earth?"

Christ Living in the Believer

JOHN 14:20-21 "On that day you will realize that I am in my Father, and you are in me, and I am in you. [21]Whoever has my commands and obeys them, he is the one who loves me. He who loves me will be loved by my Father, and I too will love him and show myself to him."

JOHN 14:23-24 Jesus replied, "If anyone loves me, he will obey my teaching. My Father will love him, and we will come to him and make our home with him. [24]He who does not love me will not obey my teaching. These words you hear are not my own; they belong to the Father who sent me."

JOHN 15:4-5 "Remain in me, and I will remain in you. No branch can bear fruit by itself; it must remain in the vine. Neither can you bear fruit unless you remain in me. [5]I am the vine; you are the branches. If a man remains in me and I in him, he will bear much fruit; apart from me you can do nothing."

JOHN 17:20-23 "My prayer is not for them [the disciples] alone. I pray also for those who will believe in me through their message, [21]that all of them may be one, Father, just as you are in me and I am in you. May they also be in us so that the world may believe that you have sent me. [22]I have given them the glory that you gave me, that they may be one as we are one: [23]I in them and you in me. May they be brought to complete unity to let the world know that you sent me and have loved them even as you have loved me."

REVELATION 3:19-20 "Those whom I love I rebuke and discipline. So be earnest, and repent. [20]Here I am! I stand at the door and knock. If anyone hears my voice and opens the door, I will come in and eat with him, and he with me."

Christ's Family

MATTHEW 12:48-50 He replied to him, "Who is my mother, and who are my brothers?" [49]Pointing to his disciples, he said, "Here are my mother and my brothers. [50]For whoever does the will of my Father in heaven is my brother and sister and mother."

MARK 3:33-35 "Who are my mother and my brothers?" he [Jesus] asked. [34]Then he looked at those seated in a circle around him and said, "Here are my mother and my brothers! [35]Whoever does God's will is my brother and sister and mother."

LUKE 8:21 He replied, "My mother and brothers are those who hear God's word and put it into practice."

The Church

MATTHEW 16:16-19 Simon Peter answered, "You are the Christ, the Son of the living God." [17]Jesus replied, "Blessed are you, Simon son of Jonah, for this was not revealed to you by man, but by my Father in heaven. [18]And I tell you that you are Peter, and on this rock I will build my church, and the gates of Hades will not overcome it. [19]I will give you the keys of the kingdom of heaven; whatever you bind on earth will be bound in heaven, and whatever you loose on earth will be loosed in heaven."

MATTHEW 18:15-17 "If your brother sins against you, go and show him his fault, just between the two of you. If he listens to you, you have won your brother over. [16]But if he will not listen, take one or two others along, so that 'every matter may be established by the testimony of two or three witnesses.' [17]If he refuses to listen to them, tell it to the church; and if he refuses to listen even to the church, treat him as you would a pagan or a tax collector."

REVELATION 2:1-7 "To the angel of the church in Ephesus write: These are the words of him who holds the seven stars in his right hand and walks among the seven golden lampstands: [2]I know your deeds, your hard work and your perseverance. I know that you cannot tolerate wicked men, that you have tested those who claim to be apostles but are not, and have found them false. [3]You have persevered and have endured hardships for my name, and have not grown weary. [4]Yet I hold this against you: You have forsaken your first love. [5]Remember the height from which you have fallen! Repent and do the things you did at first. If you do not repent, I will come to you and remove your lampstand from its place. [6]But you have this in your favor: You hate the practices of the Nicolaitans, which I also hate. [7]He who has an ear, let him hear what the Spirit says to the churches. To him who overcomes, I will give the right to eat from the tree of life, which is in the paradise of God."

REVELATION 2:8-11 "To the angel of the church in Smyrna write: These are the words of him who is the First and the Last, who died and came to life again. [9]I know your afflictions and your poverty— yet you are rich! I know the slander of those who say they are Jews and are not, but are a synagogue of Satan. [10]Do not be afraid of what you are about to suffer. I tell you, the devil will put some of you in prison to test you, and you will suffer persecution for ten days. Be faithful, even to the point of death, and I will give you the crown of life. [11]He who has an ear, let him hear what the Spirit says to the churches. He who overcomes will not be hurt at all by the second death."

REVELATION 2:12-17 "To the angel of the church in Pergamum write: These are the words of him who has the sharp, double-edged sword. [13]I know where you live—where Satan has his throne. Yet you remain true to my name. You did not renounce your faith in me, even in the days of Antipas, my faithful witness, who was put to death in your city—where Satan lives. [14]Nevertheless, I have a few things against you: You have people there who hold to the teaching of Balaam, who taught Balak to entice the Israelites to sin by eating food sacrificed to idols and by committing sexual immorality. [15]Likewise you also have those who hold to the teaching of the Nicolaitans. [16]Repent therefore! Otherwise, I will soon come to you and will fight against them with the sword of my mouth. [17]He who has an ear, let him hear what the Spirit says to the churches. To him who overcomes, I will give some of the hidden manna. I will also give him a white stone with a new name written on it, known only to him who receives it."

REVELATION 2:18-29 "To the angel of the church in Thyatira write: These are the words of the Son of God, whose eyes are like blazing fire and whose feet are like burnished bronze. [19]I know your deeds, your love and faith, your service and perseverance, and that you are now doing more than you did at first. [20]Nevertheless, I have this against you: You tolerate that woman Jezebel, who calls herself a prophetess. By her teaching she misleads my servants into sexual immorality and the eating of food sacrificed to idols. [21]I have given her time to repent of her immorality, but she is unwilling. [22]So I will cast her on a bed of suffering, and I will make those who commit adultery with her suffer intensely, unless they repent of her ways. [23]I will strike her children dead. Then all the churches will know that I am he who searches hearts and minds, and I will repay each of you according to your deeds. [24]Now I say to the rest of you in Thyatira, to you who do not hold to her teaching and have not learned Satan's so-called deep secrets (I will not impose any other burden on you): [25]Only hold on to what you have until I come. [26]To him who overcomes and does my will to the end, I will give authority over the nations— [27]'He will rule them with an iron scepter; he will dash them to pieces like pottery'—just as I have received authority from my Father. [28]I will also give him the morning star. [29]He who has an ear, let him hear what the Spirit says to the churches."

REVELATION 3:1-6 "To the angel of the church in Sardis write: These are the words of him who holds the seven spirits of God and the seven stars. I know your deeds; you have a reputation of being alive, but you are dead. [2]Wake up! Strengthen what remains and is about to die, for I have not found your deeds complete in the sight of my God. [3]Remember, therefore, what you have received and heard; obey it, and repent. But if you do not wake up, I will come like a thief, and you will not know at what time I will come to you. [4]Yet you have a few people in Sardis who have not soiled their clothes. They will walk with me, dressed in white, for they are worthy. [5]He who overcomes will, like them, be dressed in white. I will never blot out his name from the book of life, but will acknowledge his name before my Father and his angels. [6]He who has an ear, let him hear what the Spirit says to the churches."

REVELATION 3:7-13 "To the angel of the church in Philadelphia write: These are the words of him who is holy and true, who holds the key of David. What he opens no one can shut, and what he shuts no one can open. [8]I know your deeds. See, I have placed before you an open door that no one can shut. I know that you have little strength, yet you have kept my word and have not denied my name. [9]I will make those who are of the synagogue of Satan, who claim to be Jews though they are not, but are liars—I will make them come and fall down at your feet and acknowledge that I have loved you. [10]Since you have kept my command to endure patiently, I will also keep you from the hour of trial that is going to come upon the whole world to test those who live on the earth. [11]I am coming soon. Hold on to what you have, so that no one will take your crown. [12]Him who overcomes I will make a pillar in the temple of my God. Never again will he leave it. I will write on him the name of my God and the name of the city of my God, the new Jerusalem, which is coming down out of heaven from my God; and I will also write on him my new name. [13]He who has an ear, let him hear what the Spirit says to the churches."

REVELATION 3:14-22 "To the angel of the church in Laodicea write: These are the words of the Amen, the faithful and true witness, the ruler of God's creation. [15]I know your deeds, that you are neither cold nor hot. I wish you were either one or the other! [16]So, because you are lukewarm—neither hot nor cold—I am about to spit you out of my mouth. [17]You say, 'I am rich; I have acquired wealth and do not need a thing.' But you do not realize that you are wretched, pitiful, poor, blind and naked. [18]I counsel you to buy from me gold refined in the fire, so you can become rich; and white clothes to wear, so you can cover your shameful nakedness; and salve to put on your eyes, so you can see. [19]Those whom I love I rebuke and discipline. So be earnest, and repent. [20]Here I am! I stand at the door and knock. If anyone hears my voice and opens the door, I will come in and eat with him, and he with me. [21]To him who overcomes, I will give the right to sit with me on my throne, just as I overcame and sat down with my Father on his throne. [22]He who has an ear, let him hear what the Spirit says to the churches."

Cleansing Versus False Cleansing

JOHN 15:3-4 "You are already clean because of the word I have spoken to you. [4]Remain in me, and I will remain in you. No branch can bear fruit by itself; it must remain in the vine. Neither can you bear fruit unless you remain in me."

JOHN 17:17-19 "Sanctify them by the truth; your word is truth. [18]As you sent me into the world, I have sent them into the world. [19]For them I sanctify myself, that they too may be truly sanctified."

MATTHEW 10:5-10 These twelve Jesus sent out with the following instructions: "Do not go among the Gentiles or enter any town of the Samaritans. [6]Go rather to the lost sheep of Israel. [7]As you go, preach this message: 'The kingdom of heaven is near.' [8]Heal the sick, raise the dead, cleanse those who have leprosy, drive out demons. Freely you have received, freely give. [9]Do not take along any gold or silver or copper in your belts; [10]take no bag for the journey, or extra tunic, or sandals or a staff; for the worker is worth his keep."

MATTHEW 23:25-28 "Woe to you, teachers of the law and Pharisees, you hypocrites! You clean the outside of the cup and dish, but inside they are full of greed and self-indulgence. [26]Blind Pharisee! First clean the inside of the cup and dish, and then the outside also will be clean. [27]Woe to you, teachers of the law and Pharisees, you hypocrites! You are like whitewashed tombs, which look beautiful on the outside but on the inside are full of dead men's bones and everything unclean. [28]In the same way, on the outside you appear to people as righteous but on the inside you are full of hypocrisy and wickedness."

LUKE 17:17-19 Jesus asked, "Were not all ten cleansed? Where are the other nine? [18]Was no one found to return and give praise to God except this foreigner?" [19]Then he said to him, "Rise and go; your faith has made you well."

Commands of Christ

In Matthew 11:28 Jesus extends one of the most wonderful invitations ever. He tells all of us—who struggle with sin, self-centeredness, worry, guilt, depression, and despair—to "come" to Him. He promises to harness us to His side and says He will gently lead us. He promises that He will carry the burden of our load. And yet, in this section you will find more than 130 stated or implied commands that Jesus gives to His followers. Some were intended solely for His disciples, but they reveal principles that are just as meaningful for us. His commands are not meant to burden us. They are given so we might ascend to the height of joy, fulfillment, and success that lasts for eternity rather than that which ends at death.

The religious leaders of Jesus' day used the commands of God and added the commands of men to manipulate people. The leaders weighed people down with demands they could never meet, loading on guilt they could never escape. That is not what our loving Savior does with His instructions and commands. He provides them as a light that will enable us to find our way through the illusions and darkness of this life and the attractions of this world. Oh what a Savior!

To help you through this wonderful subject, I urge you to underline or highlight Jesus' commands and revelations that you see in each statement.

JOHN 4:35 "Do you not say, 'Four months more and then the harvest'? I tell you, open your eyes and look at the fields! They are ripe for harvest."

JOHN 6:27 "Do not work for food that spoils, but for food that endures to eternal life, which the Son of Man will give you. On him God the Father has placed his seal of approval."

JOHN 13:34-35 "A new command I give you: Love one another. As I have loved you, so you must love one another. [35]By this all men will know that you are my disciples, if you love one another."

JOHN 14:1 "Do not let your hearts be troubled. Trust in God; trust also in me."

JOHN 14:11 "Believe me when I say that I am in the Father and the Father is in me; or at least believe on the evidence of the miracles themselves."

JOHN 14:23 Jesus replied, "If anyone loves me, he will obey my teaching. My Father will love him, and we will come to him and make our home with him."

JOHN 15:4 "Remain in me, and I will remain in you. No branch can bear fruit by itself; it must remain in the vine. Neither can you bear fruit unless you remain in me."

JOHN 15:7-8 "If you remain in me and my words remain in you, ask whatever you wish, and it will be given you. [8]This is to my Father's glory, that you bear much fruit, showing yourselves to be my disciples."

JOHN 15:9-14 "As the Father has loved me, so have I loved you. Now remain in my love. [10]If you obey my commands, you will remain in my love, just as I have obeyed my Father's commands and remain in his love. [11]I have told you this so that my joy may be in you and that your joy may be complete. [12]My command is this: Love each other as I have loved you. [13]Greater love has no one than this, that he lay down his life for his friends. [14]You are my friends if you do what I command."

JOHN 15:17 "This is my command: Love each other."

JOHN 15:27 "And you also must testify, for you have been with me from the beginning."

JOHN 20:22 And with that he breathed on them and said, "Receive the Holy Spirit."

JOHN 20:27 Then he said to Thomas, "Put your finger here; see my hands. Reach out your hand and put it into my side. Stop doubting and believe."

JOHN 21:15-17 When they had finished eating, Jesus said to Simon Peter, "Simon son of John, do you truly love me more than these?" "Yes, Lord," he said, "you know that I love you." Jesus said, "Feed my lambs." [16]Again Jesus said,

"Simon son of John, do you truly love me?" He answered, "Yes, Lord, you know that I love you." Jesus said, "Take care of my sheep." [17]The third time he said to him, "Simon son of John, do you love me?" Peter was hurt because Jesus asked him the third time, "Do you love me?" He said, "Lord, you know all things; you know that I love you." Jesus said, "Feed my sheep."

JOHN 21:19 Jesus said this to indicate the kind of death by which Peter would glorify God. Then he said to him, "Follow me!"

JOHN 21:22-23 Jesus answered, "If I want him to remain alive until I return, what is that to you? You must follow me." [23]Because of this, the rumor spread among the brothers that this disciple would not die. But Jesus did not say that he would not die; he only said, "If I want him to remain alive until I return, what is that to you?"

MATTHEW 4:10 Jesus said to him, "Away from me, Satan! For it is written: 'Worship the Lord your God, and serve him only.'" (See also Luke 4:8.)

MATTHEW 4:17 From that time on Jesus began to preach, "Repent, for the kingdom of heaven is near."

MATTHEW 4:19 "Come, follow me," Jesus said, "and I will make you fishers of men." (See also Mark 1:17.)

MATTHEW 5:11-12 "Blessed are you when people insult you, persecute you and falsely say all kinds of evil against you because of me. [12]Rejoice and be glad, because great is your reward in heaven, for in the same way they persecuted the prophets who were before you."

MATTHEW 5:14-16 "You are the light of the world. A city on a hill cannot be hidden. [15]Neither do people light a lamp and put it under a bowl. Instead they put it on its stand, and it gives light to everyone in the house. [16]In the same way, let your light shine before men, that they may see your good deeds and praise your Father in heaven."

MATTHEW 5:19 "Anyone who breaks one of the least of these commandments and teaches others to do the same will be called least in the kingdom of heaven, but whoever practices and teaches these commands will be called great in the kingdom of heaven."

MATTHEW 5:25 "Settle matters quickly with your adversary who is taking you to court. Do it while you are still with him on the way, or he may hand you over to the judge, and the judge may hand you over to the officer, and you may be thrown into prison."

MATTHEW 5:27-30 "You have heard that it was said, 'Do not commit adultery.' [28]But I tell you that anyone who looks at a woman lustfully has already committed adultery with her in his heart. [29]If your right eye causes you to sin, gouge it out and throw it away. It is better for you to lose one part of your body than for your whole body to be thrown into hell. [30]And if your right hand causes you to sin, cut it off and throw it away. It is better for you to lose one part of your body than for your whole body to go into hell."

MATTHEW 5:31-32 "It has been said, 'Anyone who divorces his wife must give her a certificate of divorce.' [32]But I tell you that anyone who divorces his wife, except for marital unfaithfulness, causes her to become an adulteress, and anyone who marries the divorced woman commits adultery."

MATTHEW 5:33-37 "Again, you have heard that it was said to the people long ago, 'Do not break your oath, but keep the oaths you have made to the Lord.' [34]But I tell you, Do not swear at all: either by heaven, for it is God's throne; [35]or by the earth, for it is his footstool; or by Jerusalem, for it is the city of the Great King. [36]And do not swear by your head, for you cannot make even one hair white or black. [37]Simply let your 'Yes' be 'Yes,' and your 'No,' 'No'; anything beyond this comes from the evil one."

MATTHEW 5:38-48 "You have heard that it was said, 'Eye for eye, and tooth for tooth.' [39]But I tell you, Do not resist an evil person. If someone strikes you on the right cheek, turn to him the other also. [40]And if someone wants to sue you and take your tunic, let him have your cloak as well. [41]If someone forces you to go one mile, go with him two miles. [42]Give to the one who asks you, and do not turn away from the one who wants to borrow from you. [43]You have heard that it was said, 'Love your neighbor and hate your enemy.' [44]But I tell you: Love your enemies and pray for those who persecute you, [45]that you may be sons of your Father in heaven. He causes his sun to rise on the evil and the good, and sends rain on the righteous and the unrighteous. [46]If you love those who love you, what reward will you get? Are not even the tax collectors doing that? [47]And if you greet only your brothers, what are you doing more than others? Do not even pagans do that?

[48]Be perfect, therefore, as your heavenly Father is perfect."

MATTHEW 6:1-4 "Be careful not to do your 'acts of righteousness' before men, to be seen by them. If you do, you will have no reward from your Father in heaven. [2]So when you give to the needy, do not announce it with trumpets, as the hypocrites do in the synagogues and on the streets, to be honored by men. I tell you the truth, they have received their reward in full. [3]But when you give to the needy, do not let your left hand know what your right hand is doing, [4]so that your giving may be in secret. Then your Father, who sees what is done in secret, will reward you."

MATTHEW 6:31-34 "So do not worry, saying, 'What shall we eat?' or 'What shall we drink?' or 'What shall we wear?' [32]For the pagans run after all these things, and your heavenly Father knows that you need them. [33]But seek first his kingdom and his righteousness, and all these things will be given to you as well. [34]Therefore do not worry about tomorrow, for tomorrow will worry about itself. Each day has enough trouble of its own."

MATTHEW 7:13-14 "Enter through the narrow gate. For wide is the gate and broad is the road that leads to destruction, and many enter through it. [14]But small is the gate and narrow the road that leads to life, and only a few find it."

MATTHEW 7:21-27 "Not everyone who says to Me, 'Lord, Lord,' shall enter the kingdom of heaven, but he who does the will of My Father in heaven. [22]Many will say to Me in that day, 'Lord, Lord, have we not prophesied in Your name, cast out demons in Your name, and done many wonders in Your name?' [23]And then I will declare to them, 'I never knew you; depart from Me, you who practice lawlessness!' [24]Therefore whoever hears these sayings of Mine, and does them, I will liken him to a wise man who built his house on the rock: [25]and the rain descended, the floods came, and the winds blew and beat on that house; and it did not fall, for it was founded on the rock. [26]But everyone who hears these sayings of Mine, and does not do them, will be like a foolish man who built his house on the sand: [27]and the rain descended, the floods came, and the winds blew and beat on that house; and it fell. And great was its fall." (NKJV)

MATTHEW 8:21-22 Another disciple said to him, "Lord, first let me go and bury my father." [22]But Jesus told him, "Follow me, and let the dead bury their own dead."

MATTHEW 9:9 As Jesus went on from there, he saw a man named Matthew sitting at the tax collector's booth. "Follow me," he told him, and Matthew got up and followed him.

MATTHEW 9:12-13 On hearing this, Jesus said, "It is not the healthy who need a doctor, but the sick. [13]But go and learn what this means: 'I desire mercy, not sacrifice.' For I have not come to call the righteous, but sinners."

MATTHEW 10:5-10 These twelve Jesus sent out with the following instructions: "Do not go among the Gentiles or enter any town of the Samaritans. [6]Go rather to the lost sheep of Israel. [7]As you go, preach this message: 'The kingdom of heaven is near.' [8]Heal the sick, raise the dead, cleanse those who have leprosy, drive out demons. Freely you have received, freely give. [9]Do not take along any gold or silver or copper in your belts; [10]take no bag for the journey, or extra tunic, or sandals or a staff; for the worker is worth his keep."

MATTHEW 10:16-20 "I am sending you out like sheep among wolves. Therefore be as shrewd as snakes and as innocent as doves. [17]Be on your guard against men; they will hand you over to the local councils and flog you in their synagogues. [18]On my account you will be brought before governors and kings as witnesses to them and to the Gentiles. [19]But when they arrest you, do not worry about what to say or how to say it. At that time you will be given what to say, [20]for it will not be you speaking, but the Spirit of your Father speaking through you."

MATTHEW 10:24-26 "A student is not above his teacher, nor a servant above his master. [25]It is enough for the student to be like his teacher, and the servant like his master. If the head of the house has been called Beelzebub, how much more the members of his household! [26]So do not be afraid of them. There is nothing concealed that will not be disclosed, or hidden that will not be made known."

MATTHEW 10:27 "What I tell you in the dark, speak in the daylight; what is whispered in your ear, proclaim from the roofs."

MATTHEW 10:28-33 "Do not be afraid of those who kill the body but cannot kill the soul. Rather, be afraid of the One who can destroy both soul and body in hell. [29]Are not two sparrows sold for a penny? Yet not one of them will fall to the ground apart from the will of your Father. ³⁰And even the very hairs of your head are all numbered. ³¹So don't be afraid; you are worth more than many sparrows. ³²Whoever acknowledges me before men, I will also acknowledge him before my Father in heaven. ³³But whoever disowns me before men, I will disown him before my Father in heaven."

Matthew 11:28-30 "Come to me, all you who are weary and burdened, and I will give you rest. ²⁹Take my yoke upon you and learn from me, for I am gentle and humble in heart, and you will find rest for your souls. ³⁰For my yoke is easy and my burden is light."

Matthew 12:9-13 Going on from that place, he went into their synagogue, ¹⁰and a man with a shriveled hand was there. Looking for a reason to accuse Jesus, they asked him, "Is it lawful to heal on the Sabbath?" ¹¹He said to them, "If any of you has a sheep and it falls into a pit on the Sabbath, will you not take hold of it and lift it out? ¹²How much more valuable is a man than a sheep! Therefore it is lawful to do good on the Sabbath." ¹³Then he said to the man, "Stretch out your hand." So he stretched it out and it was completely restored, just as sound as the other. (See also Luke 6:6-10.)

Matthew 14:26-27 When the disciples saw him walking on the lake, they were terrified. "It's a ghost," they said, and cried out in fear. ²⁷But Jesus immediately said to them: "Take courage! It is I. Don't be afraid." (See also Mark 6:49-50.)

Matthew 14:29 "Come," he said. Then Peter got down out of the boat, walked on the water and came toward Jesus.

Matthew 15:10-11, 16-20 Jesus called the crowd to him and said, "Listen and understand. ¹¹What goes into a man's mouth does not make him 'unclean,' but what comes out of his mouth, that is what makes him 'unclean.' ¹⁶Are you still so dull?" Jesus asked them. ¹⁷"Don't you see that whatever enters the mouth goes into the stomach and then out of the body? ¹⁸But the things that come out of the mouth come from the heart, and these make a man 'unclean.' ¹⁹For out of the heart come evil thoughts, murder, adultery, sexual immorality, theft, false testimony, slander. ²⁰These are what make a man 'unclean'; but eating with unwashed hands does not make him 'unclean.'"

Matthew 18:8-9 "If your hand or your foot causes you to sin, cut it off and throw it away. It is better for you to enter life maimed or crippled than to have two hands or two feet and be thrown into eternal fire. ⁹And if your eye causes you to sin, gouge it out and throw it away. It is better for you to enter life with one eye than to have two eyes and be thrown into the fire of hell."

Matthew 18:10, 12-14 "See that you do not look down on one of these little ones. For I tell you that their angels in heaven always see the face of my Father in heaven. ¹²What do you think? If a man owns a hundred sheep, and one of them wanders away, will he not leave the ninety-nine on the hills and go to look for the one that wandered off? ¹³And if he finds it, I tell you the truth, he is happier about that one sheep than about the ninety-nine that did not wander off. [14]In the same way your Father in heaven is not willing that any of these little ones should be lost."

MATTHEW 18:15-17 "If your brother sins against you, go and show him his fault, just between the two of you. If he listens to you, you have won your brother over. [16]But if he will not listen, take one or two others along, so that 'every matter may be established by the testimony of two or three witnesses.' [17]If he refuses to listen to them, tell it to the church; and if he refuses to listen even to the church, treat him as you would a pagan or a tax collector."

MATTHEW 18:21-22 Then Peter came to Jesus and asked, "Lord, how many times shall I forgive my brother when he sins against me? Up to seven times?" [22]Jesus answered, "I tell you, not seven times, but seventy-seven times."

MATTHEW 23:23-26 "Woe to you, teachers of the law and Pharisees, you hypocrites! You give a tenth of your spices—mint, dill and cummin. But you have neglected the more important matters of the law—justice, mercy and faithfulness. You should have practiced the latter, without neglecting the former. [24]You blind guides! You strain out a gnat but swallow a camel. [25]Woe to you, teachers of the law and Pharisees, you hypocrites! You clean the outside of the cup and dish, but inside they are full of greed and self-indulgence. [26]Blind Pharisee! First clean the inside of the cup and dish, and then the outside also will be clean."

MATTHEW 24:4-6 Jesus answered: "Watch out that no one deceives you. [5]For many will come in my name, claiming, 'I am the Christ,' and will deceive many. [6]You will hear of wars and rumors of wars, but see to it that you are not alarmed. Such things must happen, but the end is still to come." (See also Mark 13:5-7.)

MATTHEW 24:42-46 "Therefore keep watch, because you do not know on what day your Lord will come. [43]But understand this: If the owner of the house had known at what time of night the thief was coming, he would have kept watch and would not have let his house be broken into. [44]So you also must be ready, because the Son of Man will come at an hour when you do not expect him. [45]Who then is the faithful and wise servant, whom the master has put in charge of the servants in his household to give them their food at the proper time? [46]It will be good for that servant whose master finds him doing so when he returns." (See also Luke 12:39-40.)

MATTHEW 25:13 "Therefore keep watch, because you do not know the day or the hour."

MATTHEW 28:9-10 Suddenly Jesus met them. "Greetings," he said. They came to him, clasped his feet and worshiped him. [10]Then Jesus said to them, "Do not be afraid. Go and tell my brothers to go to Galilee; there they will see me."

MATTHEW 28:19-20 "Therefore go and make disciples of all nations, baptizing them in the name of the Father and of the Son and of the Holy Spirit, [20]and teaching them to obey everything I have commanded you. And surely I am with you always, to the very end of the age."

MARK 1:15 "The time has come," he

said. "The kingdom of God is near. Repent and believe the good news!"

MARK 2:14 As he walked along, he saw Levi son of Alphaeus sitting at the tax collector's booth. "Follow me," Jesus told him, and Levi got up and followed him.

MARK 3:9 Because of the crowd he told his disciples to have a small boat ready for him, to keep the people from crowding him.

MARK 4:24-25 "Consider carefully what you hear," he continued. "With the measure you use, it will be measured to you—and even more. [25]Whoever has will be given more; whoever does not have, even what he has will be taken from him."

MARK 5:19 Jesus did not let him [the man freed of demons go with him], but said, "Go home to your family and tell them how much the Lord has done for you, and how he has had mercy on you." (See also Luke 8:38-39.)

MARK 5:36 Ignoring what they said, Jesus told the synagogue ruler, "Don't be afraid; just believe."

MARK 7:14-15, 17-23 Again Jesus called the crowd to him and said, "Listen to me, everyone, and understand this. [15]Nothing outside a man can make him 'unclean' by going into him. Rather, it is what comes out of a man that makes him 'unclean.'" [17]After he had left the crowd and entered the house, his disciples asked him about this parable. [18]"Are you so dull?" he asked. "Don't you see that nothing that enters a man from the outside can make him 'unclean'? [19]For it doesn't go into his heart but into his stomach, and then out of his body." (In saying this, Jesus declared all foods "clean.") [20]He went on:

"What comes out of a man is what makes him 'unclean.' [21]For from within, out of men's hearts, come evil thoughts, sexual immorality, theft, murder, adultery, [22]greed, malice, deceit, lewdness, envy, slander, arrogance and folly. [23]All these evils come from inside and make a man 'unclean.'"

MARK 11:22-25 "Have faith in God," Jesus answered. [23]"I tell you the truth, if anyone says to this mountain, 'Go, throw yourself into the sea,' and does not doubt in his heart but believes that what he says will happen, it will be done for him. [24]Therefore I tell you, whatever you ask for in prayer, believe that you have received it, and it will be yours. [25]And when you stand praying, if you hold anything against anyone, forgive him, so that your Father in heaven may forgive you your sins."

MARK 12:14-17 They came to him and said, "Teacher, we know you are a man of integrity. You aren't swayed by men, because you pay no attention to who they are; but you teach the way of God in accordance with the truth. Is it right to pay taxes to Caesar or not? [15]Should we pay or shouldn't we?" But Jesus knew their hypocrisy. "Why are you trying to trap me?" he asked. "Bring me a denarius and let me look at it." [16]They brought the coin, and he asked them, "Whose portrait is this? And whose inscription?" "Caesar's," they replied. [17]Then Jesus said to them, "Give to Caesar what is Caesar's and to God what is God's."… (See also Matthew 22:16-21; Luke 20:21-25.)

MARK 13:9-11 "You must be on your guard. You will be handed over to the local councils and flogged in the synagogues. On account of me you will stand before governors and kings as witnesses to them. [10]And the gospel must first be preached to all nations. [11]Whenever you are arrested and brought to trial, do not worry beforehand about what to say. Just say whatever is given you at the time, for it is not you speaking, but the Holy Spirit."

MARK 13:32-33, 35-37 "No one knows about that day or hour, not even the angels in heaven, nor the Son, but only the Father. [33]Be on guard! Be alert! You do not know when that time will come. [35]Therefore keep watch because you do not know when the owner of the house will come back—whether in the evening, or at midnight, or when the rooster crows, or at dawn. [36]If he comes suddenly, do not let him find you sleeping. [37]What I say to you, I say to everyone: 'Watch!'"

MARK 16:15-16 He said to them [the Eleven], "Go into all the world and preach the good news to all creation. [16]Whoever believes and is baptized will be saved, but whoever does not believe will be condemned."[x]

LUKE 4:12 Jesus answered, "It says: 'Do not put the Lord your God to the test.'" (See also Matthew 4:7.)

LUKE 5:10 …Then Jesus said to Simon, "Don't be afraid; from now on you will catch men."

LUKE 5:27-28 After this, Jesus went out and saw a tax collector by the name of Levi sitting at his tax booth. "Follow me," Jesus said to him, [28]and Levi got up, left everything and followed him.

LUKE 6:27-31 "But I tell you who hear me: Love your enemies, do good to those who hate you, [28]bless those who curse you, pray for those who mistreat you. [29]If someone strikes you on one cheek, turn to him the other also. If someone takes your cloak, do not stop him from taking your tunic. [30]Give to everyone who asks you, and if anyone takes what belongs to you, do not demand it back. [31]Do to others as you would have them do to you."

LUKE 6:35-36 "But love your enemies, do good to them, and lend to them without expecting to get anything back. Then your reward will be great, and you will be sons of the Most High, because he is kind to the ungrateful and wicked. [36]Be merciful, just as your Father is merciful."

LUKE 6:37-38 "Do not judge, and you will not be judged. Do not condemn, and you will not be condemned. Forgive, and you will be forgiven. [38]Give, and it will be given to you. A good measure, pressed down, shaken together and running over, will be poured into your lap. For with the measure you use, it will be measured to you."

LUKE 8:18 "Therefore consider carefully how you listen. Whoever has will be given more; whoever does not have, even what he thinks he has will be taken from him."

LUKE 9:62 Jesus replied, "No one who puts his hand to the plow and looks back is fit for service in the kingdom of God."

LUKE 10:2 He told them [the seventy-two who were sent out], "The harvest is plentiful, but the workers are few. Ask the Lord of the harvest, therefore, to send out workers into his harvest field."

LUKE 10:29-37 But he [an expert in the law] wanted to justify himself, so he asked Jesus, "And who is my neighbor?" [30]In reply Jesus said: "A man was going down from Jerusalem to Jericho, when he fell into the hands of robbers. They stripped him of his clothes, beat him and went away, leaving him half dead. [31]A priest happened to be going down the same road, and when he saw the man, he passed by on the other side. [32]So too, a Levite, when he came to the place and saw him, passed by on the other side. [33]But a Samaritan, as he traveled, came where the man was; and when he saw him, he took pity on him. [34]He went to him and bandaged his wounds, pouring on oil and wine. Then he put the man on his own donkey, took him to an inn and took care of him. [35]The next day he took out two silver coins and gave them to the innkeeper. 'Look after him,' he said, 'and when I return, I will reimburse you for any extra expense you may have.' [36]Which of these three do you think was a neighbor to the man who fell into the hands of robbers?" [37]The expert in the law replied, "The one who had mercy on him." Jesus told him, "Go and do likewise."

LUKE 11:9-10 "So I say to you: Ask and it will be given to you; seek and you will find; knock and the door will be opened to you. [10]For everyone who asks receives; he who seeks finds; and to him who knocks, the door will be opened."

LUKE 11:33-36 "No one lights a lamp and puts it in a place where it will be hidden, or under a bowl. Instead he puts it on its stand, so that those who come in may see the light. [34]Your eye is the lamp of your body. When your eyes are good, your whole body also is full of light. But when they are bad, your body also is full of darkness. [35]See to it, then, that the light within you is not darkness. [36]Therefore, if your whole body is full of light, and no part of it dark, it will be completely lighted, as when the light of a lamp shines on you."

LUKE 11:39-41 Then the Lord said to him, "Now then, you Pharisees clean the outside of the cup and dish, but inside you are full of greed and wickedness. [40]You foolish people! Did not the one who made the outside make the inside also? [41]But give what is inside the dish to the poor, and everything will be clean for you."

LUKE 12:1-3 Meanwhile, when a crowd of many thousands had gathered, so that they were trampling on one another, Jesus began to speak first to his disciples, saying: "Be on your guard against the yeast of the Pharisees, which is hypocrisy. [2]There is nothing concealed that will not be disclosed, or hidden that will not be made known. [3]What you have said in the dark will be heard in the daylight, and what you have whispered in the ear in the inner rooms will be proclaimed from the roofs."

LUKE 12:4-5 "I tell you, my friends, do not be afraid of those who kill the body and after that can do no more. [5]But I will show you whom you should fear: Fear him who, after the killing of the body, has power to throw you into hell. Yes, I tell you, fear him."

LUKE 12:6-7 "Are not five sparrows sold for two pennies? Yet not one of them is forgotten by God. [7]Indeed, the very hairs of your head are all numbered. Don't be afraid; you are worth more than many sparrows."

LUKE 12:8-12 "I tell you, whoever acknowledges me before men, the Son of Man will also acknowledge him before the angels of God. [9]But he who disowns me before men will be disowned before the angels of God. [10]And everyone who speaks a word against the Son of Man will be forgiven, but anyone who blasphemes against the Holy Spirit will not be forgiven. [11]When you are brought before synagogues, rulers and authorities, do not worry about how you will defend yourselves or what you will say, [12]for the Holy Spirit will teach you at that time what you should say."

LUKE 12:15 Then he said to them, "Watch out! Be on your guard against all kinds of greed; a man's life does not consist in the abundance of his possessions."

LUKE 12:22-23 Then Jesus said to his disciples: "Therefore I tell you, do not worry about your life, what you will eat; or about your body, what you will wear. [23]Life is more than food, and the body more than clothes."

LUKE 12:29-31 "And do not set your heart on what you will eat or drink; do not worry about it. [30]For the pagan world runs after all such things, and your Father knows that you need them. [31]But seek his kingdom, and these things will be given to you as well."

LUKE 12:32-34 "Do not be afraid, little flock, for your Father has been pleased to give you the kingdom. [33]Sell your possessions and give to the poor. Provide purses for yourselves that will not wear out, a treasure in heaven that will not be exhausted, where no thief comes near and no moth destroys. [34]For where your treasure is, there your heart will be also."

LUKE 12:35-36 "Be dressed ready for service and keep your lamps burning, [36]like men waiting for their master to return from a wedding banquet, so that when he comes and knocks they can immediately open the door for him."

LUKE 12:48 "But the one who does not know and does things deserving punishment will be beaten with few blows. From everyone who has been given much, much will be demanded; and from the one who has been entrusted with much, much more will be asked."

LUKE 17:3-6 "So watch yourselves. If your brother sins, rebuke him, and if he repents, forgive him. [4]If he sins against you seven times in a day, and seven times comes back to you and says, 'I repent,' forgive him." [5]The apostles said to the Lord, "Increase our faith!" [6]He replied, "If you have faith as small as a mustard seed, you can say to this mulberry tree, 'Be uprooted and planted in the sea,' and it will obey you."

LUKE 17:7-10 "Suppose one of you had a servant plowing or looking after the sheep. Would he say to the servant when he comes in from the field, 'Come along now and sit down to eat'? [8]Would he not rather say, 'Prepare my supper, get yourself ready and wait on me while I eat and drink; after that you may eat and drink'? [9]Would he thank the servant because he did what he was told to do? [10]So you also, when you have done everything you were told to do, should say, 'We are unworthy servants; we have only done our duty.' "

LUKE 21:8-9 He replied: "Watch out that you are not deceived. For many will come in my name, claiming, 'I am he,' and, 'The time is near.' Do not follow them. [9]When you hear of wars and revolutions, do not be frightened. These things must happen first, but the end will not come right away."

LUKE 21:12-15 "But before all this, they will lay hands on you and persecute you. They will deliver you to synagogues and prisons, and you will be brought before kings and governors, and all on account of my name. [13]This will result in your being witnesses to them. [14]But make up your mind not to worry beforehand how you will defend yourselves. [15]For I will give you words and wisdom that none of your adversaries will be able to resist or contradict."

LUKE 22:19 And he took bread, gave thanks and broke it, and gave it to them [the apostles], saying, "This is my body given for you; do this in remembrance of me."

LUKE 22:25-27 Jesus said to them [the apostles], "The kings of the Gentiles lord it over them; and those who exercise authority over them call themselves Benefactors. [26]But you are not to be like that. Instead, the greatest among you should be like the youngest, and the one who rules like the one who serves. [27]For who is greater, the one who is at the table or the one who serves? Is it not the one who is at the table? But I am among you as one who serves."

LUKE 22:32 "But I have prayed for you, Simon, that your faith may not fail. And when you have turned back, strengthen your brothers."

LUKE 22:46 "Why are you sleeping?" he asked them. "Get up and pray so that you will not fall into temptation."

LUKE 24:49 "I am going to send you what my Father has promised; but stay in the city until you have been clothed with power from on high."

ACTS 1:4-5 On one occasion, while he was eating with them [the apostles], he gave them this command: "Do not leave Jerusalem, but wait for the gift my Father promised, which you have heard me speak about. [5]For John baptized with water, but in a few days you will be baptized with the Holy Spirit." (See also Acts 11:16.)

ACTS 1:8 "But you will receive power when the Holy Spirit comes on you; and you will be my witnesses in Jerusalem, and in all Judea and Samaria, and to the ends of the earth."

Communion

MATTHEW 26:26-29 While they were eating, Jesus took bread, gave thanks and broke it, and gave it to his disciples, saying, "Take and eat; this is my body." [27]Then he took the cup, gave thanks and offered it to them, saying, "Drink from it, all of you. [28]This is my blood of the covenant, which is poured out for many for the forgiveness of sins. [29]I tell you, I will not drink of this fruit of the vine from now on until that day when I drink it anew with you in my Father's kingdom."

MARK 14:22-25 While they were eating, Jesus took bread, gave thanks and broke it, and gave it to his disciples, saying, "Take it; this is my body." [23]Then he took the cup, gave thanks and offered it to them, and they all drank from it. [24]"This is my blood of the covenant, which is poured out for many," he said to them. [25]"I tell you the truth, I will not drink again of the fruit of the vine until that day when I drink it anew in the kingdom of God."

LUKE 22:17-20 After taking the cup, he gave thanks and said, "Take this and divide it among you. [18]For I tell you I will not drink again of the fruit of the vine until the kingdom of God comes." [19]And he took bread, gave thanks and broke it, and gave it to them, saying, "This is my body given for you; do this in remembrance of me." [20]In the same way, after the supper he took the cup, saying, "This cup is the new covenant in my blood, which is poured out for you."

1 CORINTHIANS 11:23-25 For I received from the Lord what I also passed on to you: The Lord Jesus, on the night he was betrayed, took bread, [24]and when he had given thanks, he broke it and said, "This is my body, which is for you; do this in remembrance of me." [25]In the same way, after supper he took the cup, saying, "This cup is the new covenant in my blood; do this, whenever you drink it, in remembrance of me."

Desires

JOHN 15:7-8 "If you remain in me and my words remain in you, ask whatever you wish, and it will be given you. [8]This is to my Father's glory, that you bear much fruit, showing yourselves to be my disciples."

MATTHEW 5:3-9 "Blessed are the poor in spirit, for theirs is the kingdom of heaven. [4]Blessed are those who mourn, for they will be comforted. [5]Blessed are the meek, for they will inherit the earth. [6]Blessed are those who hunger and thirst for righteousness, for they will be filled. [7]Blessed are the merciful, for they will be shown mercy. [8]Blessed are the pure in heart, for they will see God. [9]Blessed are the peacemakers, for they will be called sons of God."

MATTHEW 6:9-13 "This, then, is how you should pray: 'Our Father in heaven, hallowed be your name, [10]your kingdom come, your will be done on earth as it is in heaven. [11]Give us today our daily bread. [12]Forgive us our debts, as we also have forgiven our debtors. [13]And lead us not into temptation, but deliver us from the evil one.'"

MATTHEW 6:19-21 "Do not store up for yourselves treasures on earth, where moth and rust destroy, and where thieves break in and steal. [20]But store up for yourselves treasures in heaven, where moth and rust do not destroy, and where thieves do not break in and steal. [21]For where your treasure is, there your heart will be also."

MATTHEW 6:24-33 "No one can serve two masters. Either he will hate the one and love the other, or he will be devoted to the one and despise the other. You cannot serve both God and Money. [25]Therefore I tell you, do not worry about your life, what you will eat or drink; or about your body, what you will wear. Is not life more important than food, and the body more important than clothes? [26]Look at the birds of the air; they do not sow or reap or store away in barns, and yet your heavenly Father feeds them. Are you not much more valuable than they? [27]Who of you by worrying can add a single hour to his life? [28]And why do you worry about clothes? See how the lilies of the field grow. They do not labor or spin. [29]Yet I tell you that not even Solomon in all his splendor was dressed like one of these. [30]If that is how God clothes the grass of the field, which is here today and tomorrow is thrown into the fire, will he not much more clothe you, O you of little faith? [31]So do not worry, saying, 'What shall we eat?' or 'What shall we drink?' or 'What shall we wear?' [32]For the pagans run after all these things, and your heavenly Father knows that you need them. [33]But seek first his kingdom and his righteousness, and all these things will be given to you as well."

MATTHEW 7:7-12 "Ask and it will be given to you; seek and you will find; knock and the door will be opened to you. [8]For everyone who asks receives; he who seeks finds; and to him who knocks, the door will be opened. [9]Which of you, if his son asks for bread, will give him a stone? [10]Or if he asks for a fish, will give him a snake? [11]If you, then, though you are evil, know how to give good gifts to your children, how much more will your Father in heaven give good gifts to those who ask him! [12]So in everything, do to others what you would have them do to you, for this sums up the Law and the Prophets."

LUKE 11:9-13 "So I say to you: Ask and it will be given to you; seek and you will find; knock and the door will be opened to you. [10]For everyone who asks receives; he who seeks finds; and to him who knocks, the door will be opened. [11]Which of you fathers, if your son asks for a fish, will give him a snake instead? [12]Or if he asks for an egg, will give him a scorpion? [13]If you then, though you are evil, know how to give good gifts to your children, how much more will your Father in heaven give the Holy Spirit to those who ask him!"

Diligence, Sowing, and Reaping

JOHN 4:31-38 Meanwhile his disciples urged him, "Rabbi, eat something." [32]But he said to them, "I have food to eat that you know nothing about." [33]Then his disciples said to each other, "Could someone have brought him food?" [34]"My food," said Jesus, "is to do the will of him who sent me and to finish his work. [35]Do you not say, 'Four months more and then the harvest'? I tell you, open your eyes and look at the fields! They are ripe for harvest. [36]Even now the reaper draws his wages, even now he harvests the crop for eternal life, so that the sower and the reaper may be glad together. [37]Thus the saying 'One sows and another reaps' is true. [38]I sent you to reap what you have not worked for. Others have done the hard work, and you have reaped the benefits of their labor."

MATTHEW 9:37-38 Then he said to his disciples, "The harvest is plentiful but the workers are few. [38]Ask the Lord of the harvest, therefore, to send out workers into his harvest field."

MATTHEW 25:14-30 "Again, it will be like a man going on a journey, who called his servants and entrusted his property to them. ¹⁵To one he gave five talents of money, to another two talents, and to another one talent, each according to his ability. Then he went on his journey. ¹⁶The man who had received the five talents went at once and put his money to work and gained five more. ¹⁷So also, the one with the two talents gained two more. ¹⁸But the man who had received the one talent went off, dug a hole in the ground and hid his master's money. ¹⁹After a long time the master of those servants returned and settled accounts with them. ²⁰The man who had received the five talents brought the other five. 'Master,' he said, 'you entrusted me with five talents. See, I have gained five more.' ²¹His master replied, 'Well done, good and faithful servant! You have been faithful with a few things; I will put you in charge of many things. Come and share your master's happiness!' ²²The man with the two talents also came. 'Master,' he said, 'you entrusted me with two talents; see, I have gained two more.' ²³His master replied, 'Well done, good and faithful servant! You have been faithful with a few things; I will put you in charge of many things. Come and share your master's happiness!' ²⁴Then the man who had received the one talent came. 'Master,' he said, 'I knew that you are a hard man, harvesting where you have not sown and gathering where you have not scattered seed. ²⁵So I was afraid and went out and hid your talent in the ground. See, here is what belongs to you.' ²⁶His master replied, 'You wicked, lazy servant! So you knew that I harvest where I have not sown and gather where I have not scattered seed? ²⁷Well then, you should have put my money on deposit with the bankers, so that when I returned I would have received it back with interest. ²⁸Take the talent from him and give it to the one who has the ten talents. ²⁹For everyone who has will be given more, and he will have an abundance. Whoever does not have, even what he has will be taken from him. ³⁰And throw that worthless servant outside, into the darkness, where there will be weeping and gnashing of teeth.'"

MARK 4:26-29 He also said, "This is what the kingdom of God is like. A man scatters seed on the ground. ²⁷Night and day, whether he sleeps or gets up, the seed sprouts and grows, though he does not know how. ²⁸All by itself the soil produces grain—first the stalk, then the head, then the full kernel in the head. ²⁹As soon as the grain is ripe, he puts the sickle to it, because the harvest has come."

LUKE 14:25-33 Large crowds were traveling with Jesus, and turning to them he said: ²⁶"If anyone comes to me and does not hate his father and mother, his wife and children, his brothers and sisters—yes, even his own life—he cannot be my disciple. ²⁷And anyone who does not carry his cross and follow me cannot be my disciple. ²⁸Suppose one of you wants to build a tower. Will he not first sit down and estimate the cost to see if he has enough money to complete it? ²⁹For if he lays the foundation and is not able to finish it, everyone who sees it will ridicule him, ³⁰saying, 'This fellow began to build and was not able to finish.' [31]Or suppose a king is about to go to war against another king. Will he not first sit down and consider whether he is able with ten thousand men to oppose the one coming against him with twenty thousand? [32]If he is not able, he will send a delegation while the other is still a long way off and will ask for terms of peace. [33]In the same way, any of you who does not give up everything he has cannot be my disciple."

LUKE 14:34-35 "Salt is good, but if it loses its saltiness, how can it be made salty again? [35]It is fit neither for the soil nor for the manure pile; it is thrown out. He who has ears to hear, let him hear."

The End Times and the Great Tribulation

MATTHEW 24:2-29 "Do you see all these things?" he asked. "I tell you the truth, not one stone here will be left on another; every one will be thrown down." [3]As Jesus was sitting on the Mount of Olives, the disciples came to him privately. "Tell us," they said, "when will this happen, and what will be the sign of your coming and of the end of the age?" [4]Jesus answered: "Watch out that no one deceives you. [5]For many will come in my name, claiming, 'I am the Christ,' and will deceive many. [6]You will hear of wars and rumors of wars, but see to it that you are not alarmed. Such things must happen, but the end is still to come. [7]Nation will rise against nation, and kingdom against kingdom. There will be famines and earthquakes in various places. [8]All these are the beginning of birth pains. [9]Then you will be handed over to be persecuted and put to death, and you will be hated by all nations because of me. [10]At that time many will turn away from the faith and will betray and hate each other, [11]and many false prophets will appear and deceive many people. [12]Because of the increase of wickedness, the love of most will grow cold, [13]but he who stands firm to the end will be saved. [14]And this gospel of the kingdom will be preached in the whole world as a testimony to all nations, and then the end will come. [15]So when you see standing in the holy place 'the abomination that causes desolation,' spoken of through the prophet Daniel—let the reader understand— [16]then let those who are in Judea flee to the mountains. [17]Let no one on the roof of his house go down to take anything out of the house. [18]Let no one in the field go back to get his cloak. [19]How dreadful it will be in those days for pregnant women and nursing mothers! [20]Pray that your flight will not take place in winter or on the Sabbath. [21]For then there will be great distress, unequaled from the beginning of the world until now—and never to be equaled again. [22]If those days had not been cut short, no one would survive, but for the sake of the elect those days will be shortened. [23]At that time if anyone says to you, 'Look, here is the Christ!' or, 'There he is!' do not believe it. [24]For false Christs and false prophets will appear and perform great signs and miracles to deceive even the elect—if that were possible. [25]See, I have told you ahead of time. [26]So if anyone tells you, 'There he is, out in the desert,' do not go out; or, 'Here he is, in the inner rooms,' do not believe it. ²⁷For as lightning that comes from the east is visible even in the west, so will be the coming of the Son of Man. ²⁸Wherever there is a carcass, there the vultures will gather. ²⁹Immediately after the distress of those days 'the sun will be darkened, and the moon will not give its light; the stars will fall from the sky, and the heavenly bodies will be shaken.'"

MATTHEW 24:32-35 "Now learn this lesson from the fig tree: As soon as its twigs get tender and its leaves come out, you know that summer is near. ³³Even so, when you see all these things, you know that it is near, right at the door. ³⁴I tell you the truth, this generation will certainly not pass away until all these things have happened. ³⁵Heaven and earth will pass away, but my words will never pass away."

MARK 13:2-26 "Do you see all these great buildings?" replied Jesus. "Not one stone here will be left on another; every one will be thrown down." ³As Jesus was sitting on the Mount of Olives opposite the temple, Peter, James, John and Andrew asked him privately, ⁴"Tell us, when will these things happen? And what will be the sign that they are all about to be fulfilled?" ⁵Jesus said to them: "Watch out that no one deceives you. ⁶Many will come in my name, claiming, 'I am he,' and will deceive many. ⁷When you hear of wars and rumors of wars, do not be alarmed. Such things must happen, but the end is still to come. ⁸Nation will rise against nation, and kingdom against kingdom. There will be earthquakes in various places, and famines. These are the beginning of birth pains. ⁹You must be on your guard. You will be handed over to the local councils and flogged in the synagogues. On account of me you will stand before governors and kings as witnesses to them. ¹⁰And the gospel must first be preached to all nations. ¹¹Whenever you are arrested and brought to trial, do not worry beforehand about what to say. Just say whatever is given you at the time, for it is not you speaking, but the Holy Spirit. ¹²Brother will betray brother to death, and a father his child. Children will rebel against their parents and have them put to death. ¹³All men will hate you because of me, but he who stands firm to the end will be saved. ¹⁴When you see 'the abomination that causes desolation' standing where it does not belong—let the reader understand—then let those who are in Judea flee to the mountains. ¹⁵Let no one on the roof of his house go down or enter the house to take anything out. ¹⁶Let no one in the field go back to get his cloak. ¹⁷How dreadful it will be in those days for pregnant women and nursing mothers! ¹⁸Pray that this will not take place in winter, ¹⁹because those will be days of distress unequaled from the beginning, when God created the world, until now—and never to be equaled again. ²⁰If the Lord had not cut short those days, no one would survive. But for the sake of the elect, whom he has chosen, he has shortened them. ²¹At that time if anyone says to you, 'Look, here is the Christ!' or, 'Look, there he is!' do not believe it. ²²For false Christs and false prophets will appear and perform signs and miracles to deceive the elect—if that were possible. ²³So be on your guard; I have told you everything ahead of time.

[24]But in those days, following that distress, 'the sun will be darkened, and the moon will not give its light; [25]the stars will fall from the sky, and the heavenly bodies will be shaken.' [26]At that time men will see the Son of Man coming in clouds with great power and glory."

MARK 13:28-33 "Now learn this lesson from the fig tree: As soon as its twigs get tender and its leaves come out, you know that summer is near. [29]Even so, when you see these things happening, you know that it is near, right at the door. [30]I tell you the truth, this generation will certainly not pass away until all these things have happened. [31]Heaven and earth will pass away, but my words will never pass away. [32]No one knows about that day or hour, not even the angels in heaven, nor the Son, but only the Father. [33]Be on guard! Be alert! You do not know when that time will come."

LUKE 21:6-28 "As for what you see here, the time will come when not one stone will be left on another; every one of them will be thrown down." [7]"Teacher," they asked, "when will these things happen? And what will be the sign that they are about to take place?" [8]He replied: "Watch out that you are not deceived. For many will come in my name, claiming, 'I am he,' and, 'The time is near.' Do not follow them. [9]When you hear of wars and revolutions, do not be frightened. These things must happen first, but the end will not come right away." [10]Then he said to them: "Nation will rise against nation, and kingdom against kingdom. [11]There will be great earthquakes, famines and pestilences in various places, and fearful events and great signs from heaven. [12]But before all this, they will lay hands on you and persecute you. They will deliver you to synagogues and prisons, and you will be brought before kings and governors, and all on account of my name. [13]This will result in your being witnesses to them. [14]But make up your mind not to worry beforehand how you will defend yourselves. [15]For I will give you words and wisdom that none of your adversaries will be able to resist or contradict. [16]You will be betrayed even by parents, brothers, relatives and friends, and they will put some of you to death. [17]All men will hate you because of me. [18]But not a hair of your head will perish. [19]By standing firm you will gain life. [20]When you see Jerusalem being surrounded by armies, you will know that its desolation is near. [21]Then let those who are in Judea flee to the mountains, let those in the city get out, and let those in the country not enter the city. [22]For this is the time of punishment in fulfillment of all that has been written. [23]How dreadful it will be in those days for pregnant women and nursing mothers! There will be great distress in the land and wrath against this people. [24]They will fall by the sword and will be taken as prisoners to all the nations. Jerusalem will be trampled on by the Gentiles until the times of the Gentiles are fulfilled. [25]There will be signs in the sun, moon and stars. On the earth, nations will be in anguish and perplexity at the roaring and tossing of the sea. [26]Men will faint from terror, apprehensive of what is coming on the world, for the heavenly bodies will be shaken. [27]At that time they will see the

Son of Man coming in a cloud with power and great glory. [28]When these things begin to take place, stand up and lift up your heads, because your redemption is drawing near."

LUKE 21:29-36 He told them this parable: "Look at the fig tree and all the trees. [30]When they sprout leaves, you can see for yourselves and know that summer is near. [31]Even so, when you see these things happening, you know that the kingdom of God is near. [32]I tell you the truth, this generation will certainly not pass away until all these things have happened. [33]Heaven and earth will pass away, but my words will never pass away. [34]Be careful, or your hearts will be weighed down with dissipation, drunkenness and the anxieties of life, and that day will close on you unexpectedly like a trap. [35]For it will come upon all those who live on the face of the whole earth. [36]Be always on the watch, and pray that you may be able to escape all that is about to happen, and that you may be able to stand before the Son of Man."

Endurance During Persecution in the End Times

MATTHEW 10:16-22 "I am sending you out like sheep among wolves. Therefore be as shrewd as snakes and as innocent as doves. [17]Be on your guard against men; they will hand you over to the local councils and flog you in their synagogues. [18]On my account you will be brought before governors and kings as witnesses to them and to the Gentiles. [19]But when they arrest you, do not worry about what to say or how to say it. At that time you will be given what to say, [20]for it will not be you speaking, but the Spirit of your Father speaking through you. [21]Brother will betray brother to death, and a father his child; children will rebel against their parents and have them put to death. [22]All men will hate you because of me, but he who stands firm to the end will be saved."

MATTHEW 13:3-13, 18-23 Then he told them many things in parables, saying: "A farmer went out to sow his seed. [4]As he was scattering the seed, some fell along the path, and the birds came and ate it up. [5]Some fell on rocky places, where it did not have much soil. It sprang up quickly, because the soil was shallow. [6]But when the sun came up, the plants were scorched, and they withered because they had no root. [7]Other seed fell among thorns, which grew up and choked the plants. [8]Still other seed fell on good soil, where it produced a crop—a hundred, sixty or thirty times what was sown. [9]He who has ears, let him hear." [10]The disciples came to him and asked, "Why do you speak to the people in parables?" [11]He replied, "The knowledge of the secrets of the kingdom of heaven has been given to you, but not to them. [12]Whoever has will be given more, and he will have an abundance. Whoever does not have, even what he has will be taken from him. [13]This is why I speak to them in parables: Though seeing, they do not see; though hearing, they do not hear or understand. [18]Listen then to what the parable of the sower means: [19]When anyone hears the message about the kingdom and does not understand it, the evil one comes and snatches away what was sown in his heart. This is the seed sown along the path. [20]The one who received the seed that fell on rocky places is the man who hears the word and at once receives it with joy. [21]But since he has no root, he lasts only a short time. When trouble or persecution comes because of the word, he quickly falls away. [22]The one who received the seed that fell among the thorns is the man who hears the word, but the worries of this life and the deceitfulness of wealth choke it, making it unfruitful. [23]But the one who received the seed that fell on good soil is the man who hears the word and understands it. He produces a crop, yielding a hundred, sixty or thirty times what was sown."

MATTHEW 24:9-13 "Then you will be handed over to be persecuted and put to death, and you will be hated by all nations because of me. [10]At that time many will turn away from the faith and will betray and hate each other, [11]and many false prophets will appear and deceive many people. [12]Because of the increase of wickedness, the love of most will grow cold, [13]but he who stands firm to the end will be saved."

MARK 4:2-20 He taught them many things by parables, and in his teaching said: [3]"Listen! A farmer went out to sow his seed. [4]As he was scattering the seed, some fell along the path, and the birds came and ate it up. [5]Some fell on rocky places, where it did not have much soil. It sprang up quickly, because the soil was shallow. [6]But when the sun came up, the plants were scorched, and they withered because they had no root. [7]Other seed fell among thorns, which grew up and choked the plants, so that they did not bear grain. [8]Still other seed fell on good soil. It came up, grew and produced a crop, multiplying thirty, sixty, or even a hundred times." [9]Then Jesus said, "He who has ears to hear, let him hear." [10]When he was alone, the Twelve and the others around him asked him about the parables. [11]He told them, "The secret of the kingdom of God has been given to you. But to those on the outside everything is said in parables [12]so that, 'they may be ever seeing but never perceiving, and ever hearing but never understanding; otherwise they might turn and be forgiven!'" [13]Then Jesus said to them, "Don't you understand this parable? How then will you understand any parable? [14]The farmer sows the word. [15]Some people are like seed along the path, where the word is sown. As soon as they hear it, Satan comes and takes away the word that was sown in them. [16]Others, like seed sown on rocky places, hear the word and at once receive it with joy. [17]But since they have no root, they last only a short time. When trouble or persecution comes because of the word, they quickly fall away. [18]Still others, like seed sown among thorns, hear the word; [19]but the worries of this life, the deceitfulness of wealth and the desires for other things come in and choke the word, making it unfruitful. [20]Others, like seed sown on good soil, hear the word, accept it, and produce a crop—thirty, sixty or even a hundred times what was sown."

MARK 13:9-13 "You must be on your guard. You will be handed over to the local councils and flogged in the synagogues. On account of me you will stand before governors and kings as witnesses to them. [10]And the gospel must first be preached to all nations. [11]Whenever you are arrested and brought to trial, do not worry beforehand about what to say. Just say whatever is given you at the time, for it is not you speaking, but the Holy Spirit. [12]Brother will betray brother to death, and a father his child. Children will rebel against their parents and have them put to death. [13]All men will hate you because of me, but he who stands firm to the end will be saved."

LUKE 8:4-15 While a large crowd was gathering and people were coming to Jesus from town after town, he told this parable: [5]"A farmer went out to sow his seed. As he was scattering the seed, some fell along the path; it was trampled on, and the birds of the air ate it up. [6]Some fell on rock, and when it came up, the plants withered because they had no moisture. [7]Other seed fell among thorns, which grew up with it and choked the plants. [8]Still other seed fell on good soil. It came up and yielded a crop, a hundred times more than was sown." When he said this, he called out, "He who has ears to hear, let him hear." [9]His disciples asked him what this parable meant. [10]He said, "The knowledge of the secrets of the kingdom of God has been given to you, but to others I speak in parables, so that, 'though seeing, they may not see; though hearing, they may not understand.' [11]This is the meaning of the parable: The seed is the word of God. [12]Those along the path are the ones who hear, and then the devil comes and takes away the word from their hearts, so that they may not believe and be

saved. [13]Those on the rock are the ones who receive the word with joy when they hear it, but they have no root. They believe for a while, but in the time of testing they fall away. [14]The seed that fell among thorns stands for those who hear, but as they go on their way they are choked by life's worries, riches and pleasures, and they do not mature. [15]But the seed on good soil stands for those with a noble and good heart, who hear the word, retain it, and by persevering produce a crop."

REVELATION 2:7 "He who has an ear, let him hear what the Spirit says to the churches. To him who overcomes, I will give the right to eat from the tree of life, which is in the paradise of God."

REVELATION 2:10 "Do not be afraid of what you are about to suffer. I tell you, the devil will put some of you in prison to test you, and you will suffer persecution for ten days. Be faithful, even to the point of death, and I will give you the crown of life."

REVELATION 2:17 "He who has an ear, let him hear what the Spirit says to the churches. To him who overcomes, I will give some of the hidden manna. I will also give him a white stone with a new name written on it, known only to him who receives it."

REVELATION 2:25-26 "Only hold on to what you have until I come. [26]To him who overcomes and does my will to the end, I will give authority over the nations."

REVELATION 3:4 "Yet you have a few people in Sardis who have not soiled their clothes. They will walk with me, dressed in white, for they are worthy."

REVELATION 3:12 "Him who overcomes I will make a pillar in the temple of my God. Never again will he leave it. I will write on him the name of my God and the name of the city of my God, the new Jerusalem, which is coming down out of heaven from my God; and I will also write on him my new name."

REVELATION 3:21 "To him who overcomes, I will give the right to sit with me on my throne, just as I overcame and sat down with my Father on his throne."

Evangelism

JOHN 15:26-27 "When the Counselor comes, whom I will send to you from the Father, the Spirit of truth who goes out from the Father, he will testify about me. [27]And you also must testify, for you have been with me from the beginning."

MATTHEW 5:14-16 "You are the light of the world. A city on a hill cannot be hidden. [15]Neither do people light a lamp and put it under a bowl. Instead they put it on its stand, and it gives light to everyone in the house. [16]In the same way, let your light shine before men, that they may see your good deeds and praise your Father in heaven."

MATTHEW 7:6 "Do not give dogs what is sacred; do not throw your pearls to pigs. If you do, they may trample them under their feet, and then turn and tear you to pieces."

MATTHEW 9:37-38 Then he said to his disciples, "The harvest is plentiful but the workers are few. [38]Ask the Lord of the harvest, therefore, to send out workers into his harvest field."

MATTHEW 10:5-10 These twelve Jesus sent out with the following instructions: "Do not go among the Gentiles or enter any town of the Samaritans. [6]Go rather to the lost sheep of Israel. [7]As you go, preach this message: 'The kingdom of heaven is near.' [8]Heal the sick, raise the dead, cleanse those who have leprosy, drive out demons. Freely you have received, freely give. [9]Do not take along any gold or silver or copper in your belts; [10]take no bag for the journey, or extra tunic, or sandals or a staff; for the worker is worth his keep."

MATTHEW 10:16-23 "I am sending you out like sheep among wolves. Therefore be as shrewd as snakes and as innocent as doves. [17]Be on your guard against men; they will hand you over to the local councils and flog you in their synagogues. [18]On my account you will be brought before governors and kings as witnesses to them and to the Gentiles. [19]But when they arrest you, do not worry about what to say or how to say it. At that time you will be given what to say, [20]for it will not be you speaking, but the Spirit of your Father speaking through you. [21]Brother will betray brother to death, and a father his child; children will rebel against their parents and have them put to death. [22]All men will hate you because of me, but he who stands firm to the end will be saved. [23]When you are persecuted in one place, flee to another. I tell you the truth, you will not finish going through the cities of Israel before the Son of Man comes."

MATTHEW 10:27-28, 32-33 "What I tell you in the dark, speak in the daylight; what is whispered in your ear, proclaim from the roofs. [28]Do not be afraid of those who kill the body but cannot kill the soul. Rather, be afraid of the One who can destroy both soul and body in hell. [32]Whoever acknowledges me before men, I will also acknowledge him before my Father in heaven. [33]But whoever disowns me before men, I will disown him before my Father in heaven."

MARK 4:21-23 He said to them, "Do you bring in a lamp to put it under a bowl or a bed? Instead, don't you put it on its stand? [22]For whatever is hidden is meant to be disclosed, and whatever is concealed is meant to be brought out into the open. [23]If anyone has ears to hear, let him hear."

MARK 16:15 He said to them [the Eleven], "Go into all the world and preach the good news to all creation."[xi]

LUKE 8:16-17 "No one lights a lamp and hides it in a jar or puts it under a bed. Instead, he puts it on a stand, so that those who come in can see the light. [17]For there is nothing hidden that will not be disclosed, and nothing concealed that will not be known or brought out into the open."

LUKE 8:38-39 The man from whom the demons had gone out begged to go with him, but Jesus sent him away, saying, [39]"Return home and tell how much God has done for you." So the man went away and told all over town how much Jesus had done for him.

LUKE 11:33-36 "No one lights a lamp and puts it in a place where it will be hidden, or under a bowl. Instead he puts it on its stand, so that those who come in may see the light. [34]Your eye is the lamp of your body. When your eyes are good, your whole body also is full of light. But when they are bad, your body also is full of darkness. [35]See to it, then, that the light within you is not darkness. [36]Therefore, if your whole body is full of light, and no part of it dark, it will be completely lighted, as when the light of a lamp shines on you."

LUKE 12:8-12 "I tell you, whoever acknowledges me before men, the Son of Man will also acknowledge him before the angels of God. [9]But he who disowns me before men will be disowned before the angels of God. [10]And everyone who speaks a word against the Son of Man will be forgiven, but anyone who blasphemes against the Holy Spirit will not be forgiven. [11]When you are brought before synagogues, rulers and authorities, do not worry about how you will defend yourselves or what you will say, [12]for the Holy Spirit will teach you at that time what you should say."

LUKE 12:42-48 The Lord answered, "Who then is the faithful and wise manager, whom the master puts in charge of his servants to give them their food allowance at the proper time? [43]It will be good for that servant whom the master finds doing so when he returns. [44]I tell you the truth, he will put him in charge of all his possessions. [45]But suppose the servant says to himself, 'My master is taking a long time in coming,' and he then begins to beat the menservants and maidservants and to eat and drink and get drunk. [46]The master of that servant will come on a day when he does not expect him and at an hour he is not aware of. He will cut him to pieces and assign him a place with the unbelievers. [47]That servant who knows his master's will and does not get ready or does not do what his master wants will be beaten with many blows. [48]But the one who does not know and does things deserving punishment will be beaten with few blows. From everyone who has been given much, much will be demanded; and from the one who has been entrusted with much, much more will be asked."

LUKE 24:46-49 He told them [the disciples], "This is what is written: The Christ will suffer and rise from the dead on the third day, [47]and repentance and forgiveness of sins will be preached in his name to all nations, beginning at Jerusalem. [48]You are witnesses of these things. [49]I am going to send you what my Father has promised; but stay in the city until you have been clothed with power from on high."

ACTS 1:8 "But you will receive power when the Holy Spirit comes on you; and you will be my witnesses in Jerusalem, and in all Judea and Samaria, and to the ends of the earth."

Exaltation and Exalting God, Not Self

MATTHEW 23:8-12 "But you are not to be called 'Rabbi,' for you have only one Master and you are all brothers. [9]And do not call anyone on earth 'father,' for you have one Father, and he is in heaven. [10]Nor are you to be called 'teacher,' for you have one Teacher, the Christ. [11]The greatest among you will be your servant. [12]For whoever exalts himself will be humbled, and whoever humbles himself will be exalted."

LUKE 14:7-11 When he noticed how the guests picked the places of honor at the table, he told them this parable: [8]"When someone invites you to a wedding feast, do not take the place of honor, for a person more distinguished than you may have been invited. [9]If so, the host who invited both of you will come and say to you, 'Give this man your seat.' Then, humiliated, you will have to take the least important place. [10]But when you are invited, take the lowest place, so that when your host comes, he will say to you, 'Friend, move up to a better place.' Then you will be honored in the presence of all your fellow guests. [11]For everyone who exalts himself will be humbled, and he who humbles himself will be exalted."

LUKE 16:15 He said to them [the Pharisees], "You are the ones who justify yourselves in the eyes of men, but God knows your hearts. What is highly valued among men is detestable in God's sight."

LUKE 18:9-14 To some who were confident of their own righteousness and looked down on everybody else, Jesus told this parable: [10]"Two men went up to the temple to pray, one a Pharisee and the other a tax collector. [11]The Pharisee stood up and prayed about himself: 'God, I thank you that I am not like other men—robbers, evildoers, adulterers—or even like this tax collector. [12]I fast twice a week and give a tenth of all I get.' [13]But the tax collector stood at a distance. He would not even look up to heaven, but beat his breast and said, 'God, have mercy on me, a sinner.' [14]I tell you that this man, rather than the other, went home justified before God. For everyone who exalts himself will be humbled, and he who humbles himself will be exalted."

LUKE 20:34-36 Jesus replied, "The people of this age marry and are given in marriage. 35But those who are considered worthy of taking part in that age and in the resurrection from the dead will neither marry nor be given in marriage, 36and they can no longer die; for they are like the angels. They are God's children, since they are children of the resurrection."

The Eye and Seeing with Spiritual Eyes

JOHN 4:31-36 Meanwhile his disciples urged him, "Rabbi, eat something." 32But he said to them, "I have food to eat that you know nothing about." 33Then his disciples said to each other, "Could someone have brought him food?" 34"My food," said Jesus, "is to do the will of him who sent me and to finish his work. 35Do you not say, 'Four months more and then the harvest'? I tell you, open your eyes and look at the fields! They are ripe for harvest. 36Even now the reaper draws his wages, even now he harvests the crop for eternal life, so that the sower and the reaper may be glad together."

MATTHEW 5:27-30 "You have heard that it was said, 'Do not commit adultery.' 28But I tell you that anyone who looks at a woman lustfully has already committed adultery with her in his heart. 29If your right eye causes you to sin, gouge it out and throw it away. It is better for you to lose one part of your body than for

your whole body to be thrown into hell. 30And if your right hand causes you to sin, cut it off and throw it away. It is better for you to lose one part of your body than for your whole body to go into hell."

MATTHEW 6:22-23 "The eye is the lamp of the body. If your eyes are good, your whole body will be full of light. 23But if your eyes are bad, your whole body will be full of darkness. If then the light within you is darkness, how great is that darkness!"

MATTHEW 7:3-5 "Why do you look at the speck of sawdust in your brother's eye and pay no attention to the plank in your own eye? 4How can you say to your brother, 'Let me take the speck out of your eye,' when all the time there is a plank in your own eye? 5You hypocrite, first take the plank out of your own eye, and then you will see clearly to remove the speck from your brother's eye." (See also Luke 6:41-42.)

MATTHEW 13:13-17 "This is why I speak to them in parables: Though seeing, they do not see; though hearing, they do not hear or understand. 14In them is fulfilled the prophecy of Isaiah: 'You will be ever hearing but never understanding; you will be ever seeing but never perceiving. 15For this people's heart has become calloused; they hardly hear with their ears, and they have closed their eyes. Otherwise they might see with their eyes, hear with their ears, understand with their hearts and turn, and I would heal them.' 16But blessed are your eyes because they see, and your ears because they hear. 17For I tell you the truth, many prophets and righteous men longed to see what you see but did not see it, and to hear what you hear but did not hear it."

MATTHEW 18:9 "And if your eye causes you to sin, gouge it out and throw it away. It is better for you to enter life with one eye than to have two eyes and be thrown into the fire of hell."

MARK 7:20-23 He went on: "What comes out of a man is what makes him 'unclean.' [21]For from within, out of men's hearts, come evil thoughts, sexual immorality, theft, murder, adultery, [22]greed, malice, deceit, lewdness, envy, slander, arrogance and folly. [23]All these evils come from inside and make a man 'unclean.' "

MARK 8:17-19 Aware of their [the disciples'] discussion, Jesus asked them: "Why are you talking about having no bread? Do you still not see or understand? Are your hearts hardened? [18]Do you have eyes but fail to see, and ears but fail to hear? And don't you remember? [19]When I broke the five loaves for the five thousand, how many basketfuls of pieces did you pick up?" "Twelve," they replied.

MARK 9:47-48 "And if your eye causes you to sin, pluck it out. It is better for you to enter the kingdom of God with one eye than to have two eyes and be thrown into hell, [48]where 'their worm does not die, and the fire is not quenched.' "

LUKE 11:33-36 "No one lights a lamp and puts it in a place where it will be hidden, or under a bowl. Instead he puts it on its stand, so that those who come in may see the light. [34]Your eye is the lamp of your body. When your eyes are good, your whole body also is full of light. But when they are bad, your body also is full of dark-

ness. [35]See to it, then, that the light within you is not darkness. [36]Therefore, if your whole body is full of light, and no part of it dark, it will be completely lighted, as when the light of a lamp shines on you."

Faith (Examples of)
(See also "Belief and Faith in Christ," p. 445.)

JOHN 2:1-10 On the third day a wedding took place at Cana in Galilee. Jesus' mother was there, [2]and Jesus and his disciples had also been invited to the wedding. [3]When the wine was gone, Jesus' mother said to him, "They have no more wine." [4]"Dear woman, why do you involve me?" Jesus replied. "My time has not yet come." [5]His mother said to the servants, "Do whatever he tells you." [6]Nearby stood six stone water jars, the kind used by the Jews for ceremonial washing, each holding from twenty to thirty gallons. [7]Jesus said to the servants, "Fill the jars with water"; so they filled them to the brim. [8]Then he told them, "Now draw some out and take it to the master of the banquet." They did so, [9]and the master of the banquet tasted the water that had been turned into wine. He did not realize where it had come from, though the servants who had drawn the water knew. Then he called the bridegroom aside [10]and said, "Everyone brings out the choice wine first and then the cheaper wine after the guests have had too much to drink; but you have saved the best till now."

JOHN 4:49-53 The royal official said, "Sir, come down before my child dies." [50]Jesus replied, "You may go. Your son will live." The man took Jesus at his word and departed. [51]While he was still on the way, his servants met him with the news that his boy was living. [52]When he inquired as to the time when his son got better, they said to him, "The fever left him yesterday at the seventh hour." [53]Then the father realized that this was the exact time at which Jesus had said to him, "Your son will live." So he and all his household believed.

JOHN 5:5-14 One who was there had been an invalid for thirty-eight years. [6]When Jesus saw him lying there and learned that he had been in this condition for a long time, he asked him, "Do you want to get well?" [7]"Sir," the invalid replied, "I have no one to help me into the pool when the water is stirred. While I am trying to get in, someone else goes down ahead of me." [8]Then Jesus said to him, "Get up! Pick up your mat and walk." [9]At once the man was cured; he picked up his mat and walked. The day on which this took place was a Sabbath, [10]and so the Jews said to the man who had been healed, "It is the Sabbath; the law forbids you to carry your mat." [11]But he replied, "The man who made me well said to me, 'Pick up your mat and walk.'" [12]So they asked him, "Who is this fellow who told you to pick it up and walk?" [13]The man who was healed had no idea who it was, for Jesus had slipped away into the crowd that was there. [14]Later Jesus found him at the temple and said to him, "See, you are well again. Stop sinning or something worse may happen to you."

JOHN 6:5-13 When Jesus looked up and saw a great crowd coming toward him, he said to Philip, "Where shall we buy bread for these people to eat?" [6]He asked this only to test him, for he already had in mind what he was going to do. [7]Philip answered him, "Eight months' wages would not buy enough bread for each one to have a bite!" [8]Another of his disciples, Andrew, Simon Peter's brother, spoke up, [9]"Here is a boy with five small barley loaves and two small fish, but how far will they go among so many?" [10]Jesus said, "Have the people sit down." There was plenty of grass in that place, and the men sat down, about five thousand of them. [11]Jesus then took the loaves, gave thanks, and distributed to those who were seated as much as they wanted. He did the same with the fish. [12]When they had all had enough to eat, he said to his disciples, "Gather the pieces that are left over. Let nothing be wasted." [13]So they gathered them and filled twelve baskets with the pieces of the five barley loaves left over by those who had eaten.

JOHN 11:11-15 After he had said this, he went on to tell them, "Our friend Lazarus has fallen asleep; but I am going there to wake him up." [12]His disciples replied, "Lord, if he sleeps, he will get better." [13]Jesus had been speaking of his death, but his disciples thought he meant natural sleep. [14]So then he told them plainly, "Lazarus is dead, [15]and for your sake I am glad I was not there, so that you may believe. But let us go to him."

JOHN 20:13-16 They asked her [Mary], "Woman, why are you crying?" "They have taken my Lord away," she said, "and I don't know where they have put him." [14]At this, she turned around and saw Jesus standing there, but she did not realize that it was Jesus. [15]"Woman," he said, "why are you crying? Who is it you are looking for?" Thinking he was the gardener, she said, "Sir, if you have carried him away, tell me where you have put him, and I will get him." [16]Jesus said to her, "Mary." She turned toward him and cried out in Aramaic, "Rabboni!" (which means Teacher).

JOHN 21:4-6, 9-12 Early in the morning, Jesus stood on the shore, but the disciples did not realize that it was Jesus. [5]He called out to them, "Friends, haven't you any fish?" "No," they answered. [6]He said, "Throw your net on the right side of the boat and you will find some." When they did, they were unable to haul the net in because of the large number of fish. [9]When they landed, they saw a fire of burning coals there with fish on it, and some bread. [10]Jesus said to them, "Bring some of the fish you have just caught." [11]Simon Peter climbed aboard and dragged the net ashore. It was full of large fish, 153, but even with so many the net was not torn. [12]Jesus said to them, "Come and have breakfast." None of the disciples dared ask him, "Who are you?" They knew it was the Lord.

MATTHEW 8:2-4 A man with leprosy came and knelt before him and said, "Lord, if you are willing, you can make me clean." [3]Jesus reached out his hand and touched the man. "I am willing," he said. "Be clean!" Immediately he was cured of his leprosy. [4]Then Jesus said to him, "See that you don't tell anyone. But go, show yourself to the priest and offer the gift Moses commanded, as a testi-mony to them." (See also Mark 1:40-44; Luke 5:12-14.)

MATTHEW 9:23-25 When Jesus entered the ruler's house and saw the flute players and the noisy crowd, [24]he said, "Go away. The girl is not dead but asleep." But they laughed at him. [25]After the crowd had been put outside, he went in and took the girl by the hand, and she got up.

MATTHEW 9:27-30 As Jesus went on from there, two blind men followed him, calling out, "Have mercy on us, Son of David!" [28]When he had gone indoors, the blind men came to him, and he asked them, "Do you believe that I am able to do this?" "Yes, Lord," they replied. [29]Then he touched their eyes and said, "According to your faith will it be done to you"; [30]and their sight was restored. Jesus warned them sternly, "See that no one knows about this."

MATTHEW 14:15-20 As evening approached, the disciples came to him and said, "This is a remote place, and it's already getting late. Send the crowds away, so they can go to the villages and buy themselves some food." [16]Jesus replied, "They do not need to go away. You give them something to eat." [17]"We have here only five loaves of bread and two fish," they answered. [18]"Bring them here to me," he said. [19]And he directed the people to sit down on the grass. Taking the five loaves and the two fish and looking up to heaven, he gave thanks and broke the loaves. Then he gave them to the disciples, and the disciples gave them to the people. [20]They all ate and were satisfied, and the disciples picked up twelve basketfuls of broken pieces that were left over.

MATTHEW 15:32-37 Jesus called his disciples to him and said, "I have compassion for these people; they have already been with me three days and have nothing to eat. I do not want to send them away hungry, or they may collapse on the way." [33]His disciples answered, "Where could we get enough bread in this remote place to feed such a crowd?" [34]"How many loaves do you have?" Jesus asked. "Seven," they replied, "and a few small fish." [35]He told the crowd to sit down on the ground. [36]Then he took the seven loaves and the fish, and when he had given thanks, he broke them and gave them to the disciples, and they in turn to the people. [37]They all ate and were satisfied. Afterward the disciples picked up seven basketfuls of broken pieces that were left over.

MATTHEW 16:5-12 When they went across the lake, the disciples forgot to take bread. [6]"Be careful," Jesus said to them. "Be on your guard against the yeast of the Pharisees and Sadducees." [7]They discussed this among themselves and said, "It is because we didn't bring any bread." [8]Aware of their discussion, Jesus asked, "You of little faith, why are you talking among yourselves about having no bread? [9]Do you still not understand? Don't you remember the five loaves for the five thousand, and how many basketfuls you gathered? [10]Or the seven loaves for the four thousand, and how many basketfuls you gathered? [11]How is it you don't understand that I was not talking to you about bread? But be on your guard against the yeast of the Pharisees and Sadducees." [12]Then they understood that he was not telling them to guard against the yeast

used in bread, but against the teaching of the Pharisees and Sadducees. (See also Mark 8:14-15.)

MATTHEW 16:13-16 When Jesus came to the region of Caesarea Philippi, he asked his disciples, "Who do people say the Son of Man is?" [14]They replied, "Some say John the Baptist; others say Elijah; and still others, Jeremiah or one of the prophets." [15]"But what about you?" he asked. "Who do you say I am?" [16]Simon Peter answered, "You are the Christ, the Son of the living God."

MATTHEW 20:30-34 Two blind men were sitting by the roadside, and when they heard that Jesus was going by, they shouted, "Lord, Son of David, have mercy on us!" [31]The crowd rebuked them and told them to be quiet, but they shouted all the louder, "Lord, Son of David, have mercy on us!" [32]Jesus stopped and called them. "What do you want me to do for you?" he asked. [33]"Lord," they answered, "we want our sight." [34]Jesus had compassion on them and touched their eyes. Immediately they received their sight and followed him.

MARK 3:1-5 Another time he went into the synagogue, and a man with a shriveled hand was there. [2]Some of them were looking for a reason to accuse Jesus, so they watched him closely to see if he would heal him on the Sabbath. [3]Jesus said to the man with the shriveled hand, "Stand up in front of everyone." [4]Then Jesus asked them, "Which is lawful on the Sabbath: to do good or to do evil, to save life or to kill?" But they remained silent. [5]He looked around at them in anger and, deeply distressed at their stubborn hearts, said to the man, "Stretch out your hand." He stretched it out, and his hand was completely restored. (See also Luke 6:6-10.)

MARK 5:38-42 When they came to the home of the synagogue ruler, Jesus saw a commotion, with people crying and wailing loudly. [39]He went in and said to them, "Why all this commotion and wailing? The child is not dead but asleep." [40]But they laughed at him. After he put them all out, he took the child's father and mother and the disciples who were with him, and went in where the child was. [41]He took her by the hand and said to her, *"Talitha koum!"* (which means, "Little girl, I say to you, get up!"). [42]Immediately the girl stood up and walked around (she was twelve years old). At this they were completely astonished.

MARK 6:35-43 By this time it was late in the day, so his disciples came to him. "This is a remote place," they said, "and it's already very late. [36]Send the people away so they can go to the surrounding countryside and villages and buy themselves something to eat." [37]But he answered, "You give them something to eat." They said to him, "That would take eight months of a man's wages! Are we to go and spend that much on bread and give it to them to eat?" [38]"How many loaves do you have?" he asked. "Go and see." When they found out, they said, "Five—and two fish." [39]Then Jesus directed them to have all the people sit down in groups on the green grass. [40]So they sat down in groups of hundreds and fifties. [41]Taking the five loaves and the two fish and looking up to heaven, he gave thanks and broke the loaves. Then he gave

them to his disciples to set before the people. He also divided the two fish among them all. [42]They all ate and were satisfied, [43]and the disciples picked up twelve basketfuls of broken pieces of bread and fish.

MARK 7:32-35 There some people brought to him a man who was deaf and could hardly talk, and they begged him to place his hand on the man. [33]After he took him aside, away from the crowd, Jesus put his fingers into the man's ears. Then he spit and touched the man's tongue. [34]He looked up to heaven and with a deep sigh said to him, *"Ephphatha!"* (which means, "Be opened!"). [35]At this, the man's ears were opened, his tongue was loosened and he began to speak plainly.

MARK 8:22-26 They came to Bethsaida, and some people brought a blind man and begged Jesus to touch him. [23]He took the blind man by the hand and led him outside the village. When he had spit on the man's eyes and put his hands on him, Jesus asked, "Do you see anything?" [24]He looked up and said, "I see people; they look like trees walking around." [25]Once more Jesus put his hands on the man's eyes. Then his eyes were opened, his sight was restored, and he saw everything clearly. [26]Jesus sent him home, saying, "Don't go into the village."

MARK 10:46-52 Then they came to Jericho. As Jesus and his disciples, together with a large crowd, were leaving the city, a blind man, Bartimaeus (that is, the Son of Timaeus), was sitting by the roadside begging. [47]When he heard that it was Jesus of Nazareth, he began to shout, "Jesus, Son of David, have mercy on me!" [48]Many rebuked him and told him to be quiet, but he shouted all the more, "Son of David, have mercy on me!" ⁴⁹Jesus stopped and said, "Call him." So they called to the blind man, "Cheer up! On your feet! He's calling you." ⁵⁰Throwing his cloak aside, he jumped to his feet and came to Jesus. ⁵¹"What do you want me to do for you?" Jesus asked him. The blind man said, "Rabbi, I want to see." ⁵²"Go," said Jesus, "your faith has healed you." Immediately he received his sight and followed Jesus along the road.

LUKE 5:4-6 When he had finished speaking, he said to Simon, "Put out into deep water, and let down the nets for a catch." ⁵Simon answered, "Master, we've worked hard all night and haven't caught anything. But because you say so, I will let down the nets." ⁶When they had done so, they caught such a large number of fish that their nets began to break.

LUKE 8:22-25 One day Jesus said to his disciples, "Let's go over to the other side of the lake." So they got into a boat and set out. ²³As they sailed, he fell asleep. A squall came down on the lake, so that the boat was being swamped, and they were in great danger. ²⁴The disciples went and woke him, saying, "Master, Master, we're going to drown!" He got up and rebuked the wind and the raging waters; the storm subsided, and all was calm. ²⁵"Where is your faith?" he asked his disciples. In fear and amazement they asked one another, "Who is this? He commands even the winds and the water, and they obey him." (See also Matthew 8:23-27; Mark 4:35-41.)

LUKE 9:12-17 Late in the afternoon the Twelve came to him and said, "Send the crowd away so they can go to the surrounding villages and countryside and find food and lodging, because we are in a remote place here." ¹³He replied, "You give them something to eat." They answered, "We have only five loaves of bread and two fish—unless we go and buy food for all this crowd." ¹⁴(About five thousand men were there.) But he said to his disciples, "Have them sit down in groups of about fifty each." ¹⁵The disciples did so, and everybody sat down. ¹⁶Taking the five loaves and the two fish and looking up to heaven, he gave thanks and broke them. Then he gave them to the disciples to set before the people. ¹⁷They all ate and were satisfied, and the disciples picked up twelve basketfuls of broken pieces that were left over.

LUKE 17:12-14 As he was going into a village, ten men who had leprosy met him. They stood at a distance ¹³and called out in a loud voice, "Jesus, Master, have pity on us!" ¹⁴When he saw them, he said, "Go, show yourselves to the priests." And as they went, they were cleansed.

LUKE 18:35, 38, 40-42 As Jesus approached Jericho, a blind man was sitting by the roadside begging. ³⁸He called out, "Jesus, Son of David, have mercy on me!" ⁴⁰Jesus stopped and ordered the man to be brought to him. When he came near, Jesus asked him, ⁴¹"What do you want me to do for you?" "Lord, I want to see," he replied. ⁴²Jesus said to him, "Receive your sight; your faith has healed you."

LUKE 22:7-16 Then came the day of Unleavened Bread on which the Passover lamb had to be sacrificed. [8]Jesus sent Peter and John, saying, "Go and make preparations for us to eat the Passover." [9]"Where do you want us to prepare for it?" they asked. [10]He replied, "As you enter the city, a man carrying a jar of water will meet you. Follow him to the house that he enters, [11]and say to the owner of the house, 'The Teacher asks: Where is the guest room, where I may eat the Passover with my disciples?' [12]He will show you a large upper room, all furnished. Make preparations there." [13]They left and found things just as Jesus had told them. So they prepared the Passover. [14]When the hour came, Jesus and his apostles reclined at the table. [15]And he said to them, "I have eagerly desired to eat this Passover with you before I suffer. [16]For I tell you, I will not eat it again until it finds fulfillment in the kingdom of God."

ACTS 26:13-18 "About noon, O king, as I [Paul] was on the road, I saw a light from heaven, brighter than the sun, blazing around me and my companions. [14]We all fell to the ground, and I heard a voice saying to me in Aramaic, 'Saul, Saul, why do you persecute me? It is hard for you to kick against the goads.' [15]Then I asked, 'Who are you, Lord?' 'I am Jesus, whom you are persecuting,' the Lord replied. [16]'Now get up and stand on your feet. I have appeared to you to appoint you as a servant and as a witness of what you have seen of me and what I will show you. [17]I will rescue you from your own people and from the Gentiles. I am sending you to them [18]to open their eyes and turn them from darkness to light, and from the power of Satan to God, so that they may receive forgiveness of sins and a place among those who are sanctified by faith in me.'"

Faithfulness

MATTHEW 10:21-22 "Brother will betray brother to death, and a father his child; children will rebel against their parents and have them put to death. [22]All men will hate you because of me, but he who stands firm to the end will be saved."

MATTHEW 11:6 "Blessed is the man who does not fall away on account of me." (See also Luke 7:23.)

MATTHEW 23:23 "Woe to you, teachers of the law and Pharisees, you hypocrites! You give a tenth of your spices—mint, dill and cummin. But you have neglected the more important matters of the law—justice, mercy and faithfulness. You should have practiced the latter, without neglecting the former."

MATTHEW 24:42-51 "Therefore keep watch, because you do not know on what day your Lord will come. [43]But understand this: If the owner of the house had known at what time of night the thief was coming, he would have kept watch and would not have let his house be broken into. [44]So you also must be ready, because the Son of Man will come at an hour when you do not expect him. [45]Who then is the faithful and wise servant, whom the master has put in charge of the servants in his household to give them their food at the proper time? [46]It will be good for that servant whose master finds him doing so when he returns. [47]I tell you the truth, he will put him in charge of all his possessions. [48]But suppose that servant is wicked and says to himself, 'My master is staying away a long time,' [49]and he then begins to beat his fellow servants and to eat and drink with drunkards. [50]The master of that servant will come on a day when he does not expect him and at an hour he is not aware of. [51]He will cut him to pieces and assign him a place with the hypocrites, where there will be weeping and gnashing of teeth."

MATTHEW 25:1-13 "At that time the kingdom of heaven will be like ten virgins who took their lamps and went out to meet the bridegroom. [2]Five of them were foolish and five were wise. [3]The foolish ones took their lamps but did not take any oil with them. [4]The wise, however, took oil in jars along with their lamps. [5]The bridegroom was a long time in coming, and they all became drowsy and fell asleep. [6]At midnight the cry rang out: 'Here's the bridegroom! Come out to meet him!' [7]Then all the virgins woke up and trimmed their lamps. [8]The foolish ones said to the wise, 'Give us some of your oil; our lamps are going out.' [9]'No,' they replied, 'there may not be enough for both us and you. Instead, go to those who sell oil and buy some for yourselves.' [10]But while they were on their way to buy the oil, the bridegroom arrived. The virgins who were ready went in with him to the wedding banquet. And the door was shut. [11]Later the others also came. 'Sir! Sir!' they said. 'Open the door for us!' [12]But he

replied, 'I tell you the truth, I don't know you.' [13]Therefore keep watch, because you do not know the day or the hour."

MATTHEW 25:14-30 "Again, it will be like a man going on a journey, who called his servants and entrusted his property to them. [15]To one he gave five talents of money, to another two talents, and to another one talent, each according to his ability. Then he went on his journey. [16]The man who had received the five talents went at once and put his money to work and gained five more. [17]So also, the one with the two talents gained two more. [18]But the man who had received the one talent went off, dug a hole in the ground and hid his master's money. [19]After a long time the master of those servants returned and settled accounts with them. [20]The man who had received the five talents brought the other five. 'Master,' he said, 'you entrusted me with five talents. See, I have gained five more.' [21]His master replied, 'Well done, good and faithful servant! You have been faithful with a few things; I will put you in charge of many things. Come and share your master's happiness!' [22]The man with the two talents also came. 'Master,' he said, 'you entrusted me with two talents; see, I have gained two more.' [23]His master replied, 'Well done, good and faithful servant! You have been faithful with a few things; I will put you in charge of many things. Come and share your master's happiness!' [24]Then the man who had received the one talent came. 'Master,' he said, 'I knew that you are a hard man, harvesting where you have not sown and gathering where you have not scattered seed. [25]So I was afraid and went out and hid your talent in the ground. See, here is what belongs to you.' ²⁶His master replied, 'You wicked, lazy servant! So you knew that I harvest where I have not sown and gather where I have not scattered seed? ²⁷Well then, you should have put my money on deposit with the bankers, so that when I returned I would have received it back with interest. ²⁸Take the talent from him and give it to the one who has the ten talents. ²⁹For everyone who has will be given more, and he will have an abundance. Whoever does not have, even what he has will be taken from him. ³⁰And throw that worthless servant outside, into the darkness, where there will be weeping and gnashing of teeth.' "

LUKE 12:42-48 The Lord answered, "Who then is the faithful and wise manager, whom the master puts in charge of his servants to give them their food allowance at the proper time? ⁴³It will be good for that servant whom the master finds doing so when he returns. ⁴⁴I tell you the truth, he will put him in charge of all his possessions. ⁴⁵But suppose the servant says to himself, 'My master is taking a long time in coming,' and he then begins to beat the menservants and maidservants and to eat and drink and get drunk. ⁴⁶The master of that servant will come on a day when he does not expect him and at an hour he is not aware of. He will cut him to pieces and assign him a place with the unbelievers. ⁴⁷That servant who knows his master's will and does not get ready or does not do what his master wants will be beaten with many blows. ⁴⁸But the one who does not know and

does things deserving punishment will be beaten with few blows. From everyone who has been given much, much will be demanded; and from the one who has been entrusted with much, much more will be asked."

LUKE 15:4-7 "Suppose one of you has a hundred sheep and loses one of them. Does he not leave the ninety-nine in the open country and go after the lost sheep until he finds it? ⁵And when he finds it, he joyfully puts it on his shoulders ⁶and goes home. Then he calls his friends and neighbors together and says, 'Rejoice with me; I have found my lost sheep.' ⁷I tell you that in the same way there will be more rejoicing in heaven over one sinner who repents than over ninety-nine righteous persons who do not need to repent."

LUKE 16:9-13 "I tell you, use worldly wealth to gain friends for yourselves, so that when it is gone, you will be welcomed into eternal dwellings. ¹⁰Whoever can be trusted with very little can also be trusted with much, and whoever is dishonest with very little will also be dishonest with much. ¹¹So if you have not been trustworthy in handling worldly wealth, who will trust you with true riches? ¹²And if you have not been trustworthy with someone else's property, who will give you property of your own? ¹³No servant can serve two masters. Either he will hate the one and love the other, or he will be devoted to the one and despise the other. You cannot serve both God and Money."

LUKE 19:12-26 He said: "A man of noble birth went to a distant country to have himself appointed king and then to return. ¹³So he called ten of his servants and gave them ten minas. 'Put this money to work,' he said, 'until I come back.' ¹⁴But his subjects hated him and sent a delegation after him to say, 'We don't want this man to be our king.' ¹⁵He was made king, however, and returned home. Then he sent for the servants to whom he had given the money, in order to find out what they had gained with it. ¹⁶The first one came and said, 'Sir, your mina has earned ten more.' ¹⁷'Well done, my good servant!' his master replied. 'Because you have been trustworthy in a very small matter, take charge of ten cities.' ¹⁸The second came and said, 'Sir, your mina has earned five more.' ¹⁹His master answered, 'You take charge of five cities.' ²⁰Then another servant came and said, 'Sir, here is your mina; I have kept it laid away in a piece of cloth. ²¹I was afraid of you, because you are a hard man. You take out what you did not put in and reap what you did not sow.' ²²His master replied, 'I will judge you by your own words, you wicked servant! You knew, did you, that I am a hard man, taking out what I did not put in, and reaping what I did not sow? ²³Why then didn't you put my money on deposit, so that when I came back, I could have collected it with interest?' ²⁴Then he said to those standing by, 'Take his mina away from him and give it to the one who has ten minas.' ²⁵'Sir,' they said, 'he already has ten!' ²⁶He replied, 'I tell you that to everyone who has, more will be given, but as for the one who has nothing, even what he has will be taken away.'"

LUKE 21:19 "By standing firm you will gain life."

REVELATION 2:10 "Do not be afraid of what you are about to suffer. I tell you, the devil will put some of you in prison to test you, and you will suffer persecution for ten days. Be faithful, even to the point of death, and I will give you the crown of life."

Family

JOHN 8:35 "Now a slave has no permanent place in the family, but a son belongs to it forever."

JOHN 19:26-27 When Jesus saw his mother there, and the disciple whom he loved standing nearby, he said to his mother, "Dear woman, here is your son," ²⁷and to the disciple, "Here is your mother." From that time on, this disciple took her into his home.

MATTHEW 5:31-32 "It has been said, 'Anyone who divorces his wife must give her a certificate of divorce.' ³²But I tell you that anyone who divorces his wife, except for marital unfaithfulness, causes her to become an adulteress, and anyone who marries the divorced woman commits adultery."

MATTHEW 7:9-11 "Which of you, if his son asks for bread, will give him a stone? ¹⁰Or if he asks for a fish, will give him a snake? ¹¹If you, then, though you are evil, know how to give good gifts to your children, how much more will your Father in heaven give good gifts to those who ask him!" (See also Luke 11:11-13.)

MATTHEW 10:34-39 "Do not suppose that I have come to bring peace to the earth. I did not come to bring peace, but a sword. ³⁵For I have come to turn 'a man against his father, a daughter against her mother, a daughter-in-law against her mother-in-law— [36]a man's enemies will be the members of his own household.' [37]Anyone who loves his father or mother more than me is not worthy of me; anyone who loves his son or daughter more than me is not worthy of me; [38]and anyone who does not take his cross and follow me is not worthy of me. [39]Whoever finds his life will lose it, and whoever loses his life for my sake will find it." (See also Luke 12:51-53.)

MATTHEW 12:48-50 He replied to him, "Who is my mother, and who are my brothers?" [49]Pointing to his disciples, he said, "Here are my mother and my brothers. [50]For whoever does the will of my Father in heaven is my brother and sister and mother." (See also Luke 8:21.)

MATTHEW 15:3-6 Jesus replied, "And why do you break the command of God for the sake of your tradition? [4]For God said, 'Honor your father and mother' and 'Anyone who curses his father or mother must be put to death.' [5]But you say that if a man says to his father or mother, 'Whatever help you might otherwise have received from me is a gift devoted to God,' [6]he is not to 'honor his father' with it. Thus you nullify the word of God for the sake of your tradition."

MATTHEW 19:4-9 "Haven't you read," he replied, "that at the beginning the Creator 'made them male and female,' [5]and said, 'For this reason a man will leave his father and mother and be united to his wife, and the two will become one flesh'? [6]So they are no longer two, but one. Therefore what God has joined together, let man not separate." [7]"Why then," they

asked, "did Moses command that a man give his wife a certificate of divorce and send her away?" [8]Jesus replied, "Moses permitted you to divorce your wives because your hearts were hard. But it was not this way from the beginning. [9]I tell you that anyone who divorces his wife, except for marital unfaithfulness, and marries another woman commits adultery."

MATTHEW 19:29 "And everyone who has left houses or brothers or sisters or father or mother or children or fields for my sake will receive a hundred times as much and will inherit eternal life."

MATTHEW 22:29-30 Jesus replied, "You are in error because you do not know the Scriptures or the power of God. [30]At the resurrection people will neither marry nor be given in marriage; they will be like the angels in heaven."

MARK 10:3-12 "What did Moses command you?" he replied. [4]They said, "Moses permitted a man to write a certificate of divorce and send her away." [5]"It was because your hearts were hard that Moses wrote you this law," Jesus replied. [6]"But at the beginning of creation God 'made them male and female.' [7]'For this reason a man will leave his father and mother and be united to his wife, [8]and the two will become one flesh.' So they are no longer two, but one. [9]Therefore what God has joined together, let man not separate." [10]When they were in the house again, the disciples asked Jesus about this. [11]He answered, "Anyone who divorces his wife and marries another woman commits adultery against her. [12]And if she divorces her husband and marries another man, she commits adultery."

LUKE 14:25-33 Large crowds were traveling with Jesus, and turning to them he said: [26]"If anyone comes to me and does not hate his father and mother, his wife and children, his brothers and sisters—yes, even his own life—he cannot be my disciple. [27]And anyone who does not carry his cross and follow me cannot be my disciple. [28]Suppose one of you wants to build a tower. Will he not first sit down and estimate the cost to see if he has enough money to complete it? [29]For if he lays the foundation and is not able to finish it, everyone who sees it will ridicule him, [30]saying, 'This fellow began to build and was not able to finish.' [31]Or suppose a king is about to go to war against another king. Will he not first sit down and consider whether he is able with ten thousand men to oppose the one coming against him with twenty thousand? [32]If he is not able, he will send a delegation while the other is still a long way off and will ask for terms of peace. [33]In the same way, any of you who does not give up everything he has cannot be my disciple."

LUKE 15:11-32 Jesus continued: "There was a man who had two sons. [12]The younger one said to his father, 'Father, give me my share of the estate.' So he divided his property between them. [13]Not long after that, the younger son got together all he had, set off for a distant country and there squandered his wealth in wild living. [14]After he had spent everything, there was a severe famine in that whole country, and he began to be in need. [15]So he went and hired himself out to a citizen of that country, who sent him to his fields to feed pigs. [16]He longed to fill his stomach with the pods that the pigs were eating, but no one gave him anything. [17]When he came to his senses, he said, 'How many of my father's hired men have food to spare, and here I am starving to death! [18]I will set out and go back to my father and say to him: Father, I have sinned against heaven and against you. [19]I am no longer worthy to be called your son; make me like one of your hired men.' [20]So he got up and went to his father. But while he was still a long way off, his father saw him and was filled with compassion for him; he ran to his son, threw his arms around him and kissed him. [21]The son said to him, 'Father, I have sinned against heaven and against you. I am no longer worthy to be called your son.' [22]But the father said to his servants, 'Quick! Bring the best robe and put it on him. Put a ring on his finger and sandals on his feet. [23]Bring the fattened calf and kill it. Let's have a feast and celebrate. [24]For this son of mine was dead and is alive again; he was lost and is found.' So they began to celebrate. [25]Meanwhile, the older son was in the field. When he came near the house, he heard music and dancing. [26]So he called one of the servants and asked him what was going on. [27]'Your brother has come,' he replied, 'and your father has killed the fattened calf because he has him back safe and sound.' [28]The older brother became angry and refused to go in. So his father went out and pleaded with him. [29]But he answered his father, 'Look! All these years I've been slaving for you and never disobeyed your orders. Yet you never gave me even a young goat so I could celebrate with my friends. [30]But when this son of yours who has squandered your property with prostitutes comes home, you kill the fattened calf for him!' [31]'My son,' the father said, 'you are always with me, and everything I have is yours. [32]But we had to celebrate and be glad, because this brother of yours was dead and is alive again; he was lost and is found.'"

LUKE 16:18 "Anyone who divorces his wife and marries another woman commits adultery, and the man who marries a divorced woman commits adultery."

LUKE 20:34-36 Jesus replied, "The people of this age marry and are given in marriage. [35]But those who are considered worthy of taking part in that age and in the resurrection from the dead will neither marry nor be given in marriage, [36]and they can no longer die; for they are like the angels. They are God's children, since they are children of the resurrection."

Fasting

MATTHEW 6:16-18 "When you fast, do not look somber as the hypocrites do, for they disfigure their faces to show men they are fasting. I tell you the truth, they have received their reward in full. [17]But when you fast, put oil on your head and wash your face, [18]so that it will not be obvious to men that you are fasting, but only to your Father, who is unseen; and your Father, who sees what is done in secret, will reward you."

MATTHEW 9:15 Jesus answered, "How can the guests of the bridegroom mourn while he is with them? The time will come when the bridegroom will be taken from them; then they will fast." (See also Luke 5:34-35.)

MATTHEW 17:19-21 Then the disciples came to Jesus privately and said, "Why could we not cast it [the demon] out?" [20]So Jesus said to them, "Because of your unbelief; for assuredly, I say to you, if you have faith as a mustard seed, you will say to this mountain, 'Move from here to there,' and it will move; and nothing will be impossible for you. [21]However, this kind does not go out except by prayer and fasting." (NKJV)

MARK 2:19-20 Jesus answered, "How can the guests of the bridegroom fast while he is with them? They cannot, so long as they have him with them. [20]But the time will come when the bridegroom will be taken from them, and on that day they will fast."

MARK 9:28-29 And when He had come into the house, His disciples asked Him privately, "Why could we not cast it out?" [29]So He said to them, "This kind can come out by nothing but prayer and fasting." (NKJV)

The Fear of God

MATTHEW 10:27-31 "What I tell you in the dark, speak in the daylight; what is whispered in your ear, proclaim from the roofs. [28]Do not be afraid of those who kill the body but cannot kill the soul. Rather, be afraid of the One who can destroy both soul and body in hell. [29]Are not two sparrows sold for a penny? Yet not one of them will fall to the ground apart from the will of your Father. [30]And even the very hairs of your head are all numbered. [31]So don't be afraid; you are worth more than many sparrows."

LUKE 12:4-7 "I tell you, my friends, do not be afraid of those who kill the body and after that can do no more. [5]But I will show you whom you should fear: Fear him who, after the killing of the body, has power to throw you into hell. Yes, I tell you, fear him. [6]Are not five sparrows sold for two pennies? Yet not one of them is forgotten by God. [7]Indeed, the very hairs of your head are all numbered. Don't be afraid; you are worth more than many sparrows."

Focus

MATTHEW 6:24-34 "No one can serve two masters. Either he will hate the one and love the other, or he will be devoted to the one and despise the other. You cannot serve both God and Money. [25]Therefore I tell you, do not worry about your life, what you will eat or drink; or about your body, what you will wear. Is not life more important than food, and the body more important than clothes? [26]Look at the birds of the air; they do not sow or reap or store away in barns, and yet your heavenly Father feeds them. Are you not much more valuable than they? [27]Who of you by worrying can add a single hour to his life? [28]And why do you worry about clothes? See how the lilies of the field grow. They do not labor or spin. [29]Yet I tell you that not even Solomon in all his splendor was dressed like one of these. [30]If that is how God clothes the grass of the field, which is here today and

tomorrow is thrown into the fire, will he not much more clothe you, O you of little faith? [31]So do not worry, saying, 'What shall we eat?' or 'What shall we drink?' or 'What shall we wear?' [32]For the pagans run after all these things, and your heavenly Father knows that you need them. [33]But seek first his kingdom and his righteousness, and all these things will be given to you as well. [34]Therefore do not worry about tomorrow, for tomorrow will worry about itself. Each day has enough trouble of its own."

MATTHEW 10:34-39 "Do not suppose that I have come to bring peace to the earth. I did not come to bring peace, but a sword. [35]For I have come to turn 'a man against his father, a daughter against her mother, a daughter-in-law against her mother-in-law— [36]a man's enemies will be the members of his own household.' [37]Anyone who loves his father or mother more than me is not worthy of me; anyone who loves his son or daughter more than me is not worthy of me; [38]and anyone who does not take his cross and follow me is not worthy of me. [39]Whoever finds his life will lose it, and whoever loses his life for my sake will find it."

MATTHEW 16:23-28 Jesus turned and said to Peter, "Get behind me, Satan! You are a stumbling block to me; you do not have in mind the things of God, but the things of men." [24]Then Jesus said to his disciples, "If anyone would come after me, he must deny himself and take up his cross and follow me. [25]For whoever wants to save his life will lose it, but whoever loses his life for me will find it. [26]What good will it be for a man if he gains the whole world, yet forfeits his soul? Or what can a man give in exchange for his soul? 27For the Son of Man is going to come in his Father's glory with his angels, and then he will reward each person according to what he has done. 28I tell you the truth, some who are standing here will not taste death before they see the Son of Man coming in his kingdom."

LUKE 10:41-42 "Martha, Martha," the Lord answered, "you are worried and upset about many things, 42but only one thing is needed. Mary has chosen what is better, and it will not be taken away from her."

LUKE 12:22-34 Then Jesus said to his disciples: "Therefore I tell you, do not worry about your life, what you will eat; or about your body, what you will wear. 23Life is more than food, and the body more than clothes. 24Consider the ravens: They do not sow or reap, they have no storeroom or barn; yet God feeds them. And how much more valuable you are than birds! 25Who of you by worrying can add a single hour to his life? 26Since you cannot do this very little thing, why do you worry about the rest? 27Consider how the lilies grow. They do not labor or spin. Yet I tell you, not even Solomon in all his splendor was dressed like one of these. 28If that is how God clothes the grass of the field, which is here today, and tomorrow is thrown into the fire, how much more will he clothe you, O you of little faith! 29And do not set your heart on what you will eat or drink; do not worry about it. 30For the pagan world runs after all such things, and your Father knows that you need them. 31But seek his king-

dom, and these things will be given to you as well. 32Do not be afraid, little flock, for your Father has been pleased to give you the kingdom. 33Sell your possessions and give to the poor. Provide purses for yourselves that will not wear out, a treasure in heaven that will not be exhausted, where no thief comes near and no moth destroys. 34For where your treasure is, there your heart will be also."

Following Christ (Discipleship)

JOHN 1:35-43 The next day John was there again with two of his disciples. 36When he saw Jesus passing by, he said, "Look, the Lamb of God!" 37When the two disciples heard him say this, they followed Jesus. 38Turning around, Jesus saw them following and asked, "What do you want?" They said, "Rabbi" (which means Teacher), "where are you staying?" 39"Come," he replied, "and you will see." So they went and saw where he was staying, and spent that day with him. It was about the tenth hour. 40Andrew, Simon Peter's brother, was one of the two who heard what John had said and who had followed Jesus. 41The first thing Andrew did was to find his brother Simon and tell him, "We have found the Messiah" (that is, the Christ). 42And he brought him to Jesus. Jesus looked at him and said, "You are Simon son of John. You will be called Cephas" (which, when translated, is Peter). 43The next day Jesus decided to leave for Galilee. Finding Philip, he said to him, "Follow me."

JOHN 3:19-21 "This is the verdict: Light has come into the world, but men loved darkness instead of light because their deeds were evil. [20]Everyone who does evil hates the light, and will not come into the light for fear that his deeds will be exposed. [21]But whoever lives by the truth comes into the light, so that it may be seen plainly that what he has done has been done through God."

JOHN 5:21-24 "For just as the Father raises the dead and gives them life, even so the Son gives life to whom he is pleased to give it. [22]Moreover, the Father judges no one, but has entrusted all judgment to the Son, [23]that all may honor the Son just as they honor the Father. He who does not honor the Son does not honor the Father, who sent him. [24]I tell you the truth, whoever hears my word and believes him who sent me has eternal life and will not be condemned; he has crossed over from death to life."

JOHN 6:26-27 Jesus answered, "I tell you the truth, you are looking for me, not because you saw miraculous signs but because you ate the loaves and had your fill. [27]Do not work for food that spoils, but for food that endures to eternal life, which the Son of Man will give you. On him God the Father has placed his seal of approval."

JOHN 6:35-37 Then Jesus declared, "I am the bread of life. He who comes to me will never go hungry, and he who believes in me will never be thirsty. [36]But as I told you, you have seen me and still you do not believe. [37]All that the Father gives me will come to me, and whoever comes to me I will never drive away."

JOHN 6:43-44 "Stop grumbling among yourselves," Jesus answered. [44]"No one can come to me unless the Father who sent me draws him, and I will raise him up at the last day."

JOHN 6:63-65 "The Spirit gives life; the flesh counts for nothing. The words I have spoken to you are spirit and they are life. [64]Yet there are some of you who do not believe." For Jesus had known from the beginning which of them did not believe and who would betray him. [65]He went on to say, "This is why I told you that no one can come to me unless the Father has enabled him."

JOHN 7:37-38 On the last and greatest day of the Feast, Jesus stood and said in a loud voice, "If anyone is thirsty, let him come to me and drink. [38]Whoever believes in me, as the Scripture has said, streams of living water will flow from within him."

JOHN 8:31-32 Then Jesus said to those Jews who believed Him, "If you abide in My word, you are My disciples indeed. [32]And you shall know the truth, and the truth shall make you free." (NKJV)

JOHN 10:9-10 "I am the gate; whoever enters through me will be saved. He will come in and go out, and find pasture. [10]The thief comes only to steal and kill and destroy; I have come that they may have life, and have it to the full."

JOHN 10:14-16 "I am the good shepherd; I know my sheep and my sheep know me— [15]just as the Father knows me and I know the Father—and I lay down my life for the sheep. [16]I have other sheep that are not of this sheep pen. I must bring them also. They too will listen to my voice, and there shall be one flock and one shepherd."

JOHN 10:27-30 "My sheep listen to my voice; I know them, and they follow me. ²⁸I give them eternal life, and they shall never perish; no one can snatch them out of my hand. ²⁹My Father, who has given them to me, is greater than all; no one can snatch them out of my Father's hand. ³⁰I and the Father are one."

JOHN 12:25-26 "The man who loves his life will lose it, while the man who hates his life in this world will keep it for eternal life. ²⁶Whoever serves me must follow me; and where I am, my servant also will be. My Father will honor the one who serves me."

JOHN 12:44-46 Then Jesus cried out, "When a man believes in me, he does not believe in me only, but in the one who sent me. ⁴⁵When he looks at me, he sees the one who sent me. ⁴⁶I have come into the world as a light, so that no one who believes in me should stay in darkness."

JOHN 13:8-17 "No," said Peter, "you shall never wash my feet." Jesus answered, "Unless I wash you, you have no part with me." ⁹"Then, Lord," Simon Peter replied, "not just my feet but my hands and my head as well!" ¹⁰Jesus answered, "A person who has had a bath needs only to wash his feet; his whole body is clean. And you are clean, though not every one of you." ¹¹For he knew who was going to betray him, and that was why he said not every one was clean. ¹²When he had finished washing their feet, he put on his clothes and returned to his place. "Do you understand what I have done for you?" he asked them. ¹³"You call me 'Teacher' and 'Lord,' and rightly so, for that is what I am. ¹⁴Now

that I, your Lord and Teacher, have washed your feet, you also should wash one another's feet. ¹⁵I have set you an example that you should do as I have done for you. ¹⁶I tell you the truth, no servant is greater than his master, nor is a messenger greater than the one who sent him. ¹⁷Now that you know these things, you will be blessed if you do them."

JOHN 13:20 "I tell you the truth, whoever accepts anyone I send accepts me; and whoever accepts me accepts the one who sent me."

JOHN 13:34-35 "A new command I give you: Love one another. As I have loved you, so you must love one another. ³⁵By this all men will know that you are my disciples, if you love one another."

JOHN 14:1-4 "Do not let your hearts be troubled. Trust in God; trust also in me. ²In my Father's house are many rooms; if it were not so, I would have told you. I am going there to prepare a place for you. ³And if I go and prepare a place for you, I will come back and take you to be with me that you also may be where I am. ⁴You know the way to the place where I am going."

JOHN 14:12-16 "I tell you the truth, anyone who has faith in me will do what I have been doing. He will do even greater things than these, because I am going to the Father. ¹³And I will do whatever you ask in my name, so that the Son may bring glory to the Father. ¹⁴You may ask me for anything in my name, and I will do it. ¹⁵If you love me, you will obey what I command. ¹⁶And I will ask the Father, and he will give you another Counselor to be with you forever."

JOHN 14:20-21 "On that day you will realize that I am in my Father, and you are in me, and I am in you. [21]Whoever has my commands and obeys them, he is the one who loves me. He who loves me will be loved by my Father, and I too will love him and show myself to him."

JOHN 14:23-24 Jesus replied, "If anyone loves me, he will obey my teaching. My Father will love him, and we will come to him and make our home with him. [24]He who does not love me will not obey my teaching. These words you hear are not my own; they belong to the Father who sent me."

JOHN 15:1-21 "I am the true vine, and my Father is the gardener. [2]He cuts off every branch in me that bears no fruit, while every branch that does bear fruit he prunes so that it will be even more fruitful. [3]You are already clean because of the word I have spoken to you. [4]Remain in me, and I will remain in you. No branch can bear fruit by itself; it must remain in the vine. Neither can you bear fruit unless you remain in me. [5]I am the vine; you are the branches. If a man remains in me and I in him, he will bear much fruit; apart from me you can do nothing. [6]If anyone does not remain in me, he is like a branch that is thrown away and withers; such branches are picked up, thrown into the fire and burned. [7]If you remain in me and my words remain in you, ask whatever you wish, and it will be given you. [8]This is to my Father's glory, that you bear much fruit, showing yourselves to be my disciples. [9]As the Father has loved me, so have I loved you. Now remain in my love. [10]If you obey my commands, you will remain in my love, just as I have obeyed my Father's commands and remain in his love. [11]I have told you this so that my joy may be in you and that your joy may be complete. [12]My command is this: Love each other as I have loved you. [13]Greater love has no one than this, that he lay down his life for his friends. [14]You are my friends if you do what I command. [15]I no longer call you servants, because a servant does not know his master's business. Instead, I have called you friends, for everything that I learned from my Father I have made known to you. [16]You did not choose me, but I chose you and appointed you to go and bear fruit—fruit that will last. Then the Father will give you whatever you ask in my name. [17]This is my command: Love each other. [18]If the world hates you, keep in mind that it hated me first. [19]If you belonged to the world, it would love you as its own. As it is, you do not belong to the world, but I have chosen you out of the world. That is why the world hates you. [20]Remember the words I spoke to you: 'No servant is greater than his master.' If they persecuted me, they will persecute you also. If they obeyed my teaching, they will obey yours also. [21]They will treat you this way because of my name, for they do not know the One who sent me."

JOHN 15:27 "And you also must testify, for you have been with me from the beginning."

JOHN 17:6-8 "I have revealed you [God] to those whom you gave me out of the world. They were yours; you gave them to me and they have obeyed your word. [7]Now they know that everything you have given me comes from you. [8]For I gave them the words you gave me and they accepted them. They knew with certainty that I came from you, and they believed that you sent me."

MATTHEW 4:4 Jesus answered, "It is written: 'Man does not live on bread alone, but on every word that comes from the mouth of God.'" (See also Luke 4:4.)

MATTHEW 4:19 "Come, follow me," Jesus said, "and I will make you fishers of men."

MATTHEW 7:20-25 "Therefore by their fruits you will know them. [21]Not everyone who says to Me, 'Lord, Lord,' shall enter the kingdom of heaven, but he who does the will of My Father in heaven. [22]Many will say to Me in that day, 'Lord, Lord, have we not prophesied in Your name, cast out demons in Your name, and done many wonders in Your name?' [23]And then I will declare to them, 'I never knew you; depart from Me, you who practice lawlessness!' [24]Therefore whoever hears these sayings of Mine, and does them, I will liken him to a wise man who built his house on the rock: [25]and the rain descended, the floods came, and the winds blew and beat on that house; and it did not fall, for it was founded on the rock." (NKJV)

MATTHEW 8:19-22 Then a teacher of the law came to him and said, "Teacher, I will follow you wherever you go." [20]Jesus replied, "Foxes have holes and birds of the air have nests, but the Son of Man has no place to lay his head." [21]Another disciple said to him, "Lord, first let me go and bury my father." [22]But Jesus told him, "Follow me, and let the dead bury their own dead."

MATTHEW 10:24-26 "A student is not above his teacher, nor a servant above his master. [25]It is enough for the student to be like his teacher, and the servant like his master. If the head of the house has been called Beelzebub, how much more the members of his household! [26]So do not be afraid of them. There is nothing concealed that will not be disclosed, or hidden that will not be made known."

MATTHEW 10:32-33 "Whoever acknowledges me before men, I will also acknowledge him before my Father in heaven. [33]But whoever disowns me before men, I will disown him before my Father in heaven."

MATTHEW 10:34-39 "Do not suppose that I have come to bring peace to the earth. I did not come to bring peace, but a sword. [35]For I have come to turn 'a man against his father, a daughter against her mother, a daughter-in-law against her mother-in-law— [36]a man's enemies will be the members of his own household.' [37]Anyone who loves his father or mother more than me is not worthy of me; anyone who loves his son or daughter more than me is not worthy of me; [38]and anyone who does not take his cross and follow me is not worthy of me. [39]Whoever finds his life will lose it, and whoever loses his life for my sake will find it."

MATTHEW 11:28-30 "Come to me, all you who are weary and burdened, and I will give you rest. [29]Take my yoke upon you and learn from me, for I am gentle and humble in heart, and you will find rest for your souls. [30]For my yoke is easy and my burden is light."

MATTHEW 16:23-27 Jesus turned and said to Peter, "Get behind me, Satan! You are a stumbling block to me; you do not have in mind the things of God, but the things of men." [24]Then Jesus said to his disciples, "If anyone would come after me, he must deny himself and take up his cross and follow me. [25]For whoever wants to save his life will lose it, but whoever loses his life for me will find it. [26]What good will it be for a man if he gains the whole world, yet forfeits his soul? Or what can a man give in exchange for his soul? [27]For the Son of Man is going to come in his Father's glory with his angels, and then he will reward each person according to what he has done."

MATTHEW 18:18-20 "I tell you the truth, whatever you bind on earth will be bound in heaven, and whatever you loose on earth will be loosed in heaven. [19]Again, I tell you that if two of you on earth agree about anything you ask for, it will be done for you by my Father in heaven. [20]For where two or three come together in my name, there am I with them."

MATTHEW 19:21 Jesus answered, "If you want to be perfect, go, sell your possessions and give to the poor, and you will have treasure in heaven. Then come, follow me."

MATTHEW 19:27-30 Peter answered him, "We have left everything to follow you! What then will there be for us?" [28]Jesus said to them, "I tell you the truth, at the renewal of all things, when the Son of Man sits on his glorious throne, you

who have followed me will also sit on twelve thrones, judging the twelve tribes of Israel. [29]And everyone who has left houses or brothers or sisters or father or mother or children or fields for my sake will receive a hundred times as much and will inherit eternal life. [30]But many who are first will be last, and many who are last will be first."

MATTHEW 28:18-20 Then Jesus came to them [the eleven disciples] and said, "All authority in heaven and on earth has been given to me. [19]Therefore go and make disciples of all nations, baptizing them in the name of the Father and of the Son and of the Holy Spirit, [20]and teaching them to obey everything I have commanded you. And surely I am with you always, to the very end of the age."

MARK 3:33-35 "Who are my mother and my brothers?" he [Jesus] asked. [34]Then he looked at those seated in a circle around him and said, "Here are my mother and my brothers! [35]Whoever does God's will is my brother and sister and mother."

MARK 8:34 Then he called the crowd to him along with his disciples and said: "If anyone would come after me, he must deny himself and take up his cross and follow me."

MARK 9:38-42 "Teacher," said John, "we saw a man driving out demons in your name and we told him to stop, because he was not one of us." [39]"Do not stop him," Jesus said. "No one who does a miracle in my name can in the next moment say anything bad about me, [40]for whoever is not against us is for us. [41]I tell you the truth, anyone who gives you a cup of water in my name because you belong to Christ will certainly not lose his reward. [42]And if anyone causes one of these little ones who believe in me to sin, it would be better for him to be thrown into the sea with a large millstone tied around his neck."

MARK 10:18-21 "Why do you call me good?" Jesus answered. "No one is good—except God alone. [19]You know the commandments: 'Do not murder, do not commit adultery, do not steal, do not give false testimony, do not defraud, honor your father and mother.'" [20]"Teacher," he declared, "all these I have kept since I was a boy." [21]Jesus looked at him and loved him. "One thing you lack," he said. "Go, sell everything you have and give to the poor, and you will have treasure in heaven. Then come, follow me."

LUKE 5:9-10 For he [Simon Peter] and all his companions were astonished at the catch of fish they had taken, [10]and so were James and John, the sons of Zebedee, Simon's partners. Then Jesus said to Simon, "Don't be afraid; from now on you will catch men."

LUKE 5:27-28 After this, Jesus went out and saw a tax collector by the name of Levi sitting at his tax booth. "Follow me," Jesus said to him, [28]and Levi got up, left everything and followed him.

LUKE 6:39-40 He also told them this parable: "Can a blind man lead a blind man? Will they not both fall into a pit? [40]A student is not above his teacher, but everyone who is fully trained will be like his teacher."

LUKE 6:46-49 "Why do you call me, 'Lord, Lord,' and do not do what I say? [47]I will show you what he is like who comes to me and hears my words and puts them into practice. [48]He is like a man building a house, who dug down deep and laid the foundation on rock. When a flood came, the torrent struck that house but could not shake it, because it was well built. [49]But the one who hears my words and does not put them into practice is like a man who built a house on the ground without a foundation. The moment the torrent struck that house, it collapsed and its destruction was complete."

LUKE 8:16-17 "No one lights a lamp and hides it in a jar or puts it under a bed. Instead, he puts it on a stand, so that those who come in can see the light. [17]For there is nothing hidden that will not be disclosed, and nothing concealed that will not be known or brought out into the open."

LUKE 9:23-26 Then he said to them all: "If anyone would come after me, he must deny himself and take up his cross daily and follow me. [24]For whoever wants to save his life will lose it, but whoever loses his life for me will save it. [25]What good is it for a man to gain the whole world, and yet lose or forfeit his very self? [26]If anyone is ashamed of me and my words, the Son of Man will be ashamed of him when he comes in his glory and in the glory of the Father and of the holy angels."

LUKE 9:57-58 As they were walking along the road, a man said to him, "I will follow you wherever you go." [58]Jesus replied, "Foxes have holes and birds of the air have nests, but the Son of Man has no place to lay his head."

LUKE 9:59-60 He said to another man, "Follow me." But the man replied, "Lord, first let me go and bury my father." [60]Jesus said to him, "Let the dead bury their own dead, but you go and proclaim the kingdom of God."

LUKE 10:2-12 He told them [the seventy-two who were sent out], "The harvest is plentiful, but the workers are few. Ask the Lord of the harvest, therefore, to send out workers into his harvest field. [3]Go! I am sending you out like lambs among wolves. [4]Do not take a purse or bag or sandals; and do not greet anyone on the road. [5]When you enter a house, first say, 'Peace to this house.' [6]If a man of peace is there, your peace will rest on him; if not, it will return to you. [7]Stay in that house, eating and drinking whatever they give you, for the worker deserves his wages. Do not move around from house to house. [8]When you enter a town and are welcomed, eat what is set before you. [9]Heal the sick who are there and tell them, 'The kingdom of God is near you.' [10]But when you enter a town and are not welcomed, go into its streets and say, [11]'Even the dust of your town that sticks to our feet we wipe off against you. Yet be sure of this: The kingdom of God is near.' [12]I tell you, it will be more bearable on that day for Sodom than for that town." (See also Matthew 9:37-38.)

LUKE 12:8-9 "I tell you, whoever acknowledges me before men, the Son of Man will also acknowledge him before the angels of God. [9]But he who disowns me before men will be disowned before the angels of God."

LUKE 14:25-35 Large crowds were traveling with Jesus, and turning to them he said: [26]"If anyone comes to me and does not hate his father and mother, his wife and children, his brothers and sisters—yes, even his own life—he cannot be my disciple. [27]And anyone who does not carry his cross and follow me cannot be my disciple. [28]Suppose one of you wants to build a tower. Will he not first sit down and estimate the cost to see if he has enough money to complete it? [29]For if he lays the foundation and is not able to finish it, everyone who sees it will ridicule him, [30]saying, 'This fellow began to build and was not able to finish.' [31]Or suppose a king is about to go to war against another king. Will he not first sit down and consider whether he is able with ten thousand men to oppose the one coming against him with twenty thousand? [32]If he is not able, he will send a delegation while the other is still a long way off and will ask for terms of peace. [33]In the same way, any of you who does not give up everything he has cannot be my disciple. [34]Salt is good, but if it loses its saltiness, how can it be made salty again? [35]It is fit neither for the soil nor for the manure pile; it is thrown out. He who has ears to hear, let him hear."

ACTS 1:4-5 On one occasion, while he was eating with them [the apostles], he gave them this command: "Do not leave Jerusalem, but wait for the gift my Father promised, which you have heard me speak about. [5]For John baptized with water, but in a few days you will be baptized with the Holy Spirit." (See also Acts 11:16.)

REVELATION 2:10 "Do not be afraid of what you are about to suffer. I tell you, the devil will put some of you in prison to test you, and you will suffer persecution for ten days. Be faithful, even to the point of death, and I will give you the crown of life."

REVELATION 2:19 "I know your deeds, your love and faith, your service and perseverance, and that you are now doing more than you did at first."

REVELATION 3:4-5 "Yet you have a few people in Sardis who have not soiled their clothes. They will walk with me, dressed in white, for they are worthy. [5]He who overcomes will, like them, be dressed in white. I will never blot out his name from the book of life, but will acknowledge his name before my Father and his angels."

REVELATION 3:8-12 "I know your deeds. See, I have placed before you an open door that no one can shut. I know that you have little strength, yet you have kept my word and have not denied my name. [9]I will make those who are of the synagogue of Satan, who claim to be Jews though they are not, but are liars—I will make them come and fall down at your feet and acknowledge that I have loved you. [10]Since you have kept my command to endure patiently, I will also keep you from the hour of trial that is going to come upon the whole world to test those who live on the earth. [11]I am coming soon. Hold on to what you have, so that no one will take your crown. [12]Him who overcomes I will make a pillar in the temple of my God. Never again will he leave it. I will write on him the name of my

God and the name of the city of my God, the new Jerusalem, which is coming down out of heaven from my God; and I will also write on him my new name."

REVELATION 3:15-22 "I know your deeds, that you are neither cold nor hot. I wish you were either one or the other! [16]So, because you are lukewarm—neither hot nor cold—I am about to spit you out of my mouth. [17]You say, 'I am rich; I have acquired wealth and do not need a thing.' But you do not realize that you are wretched, pitiful, poor, blind and naked. [18]I counsel you to buy from me gold refined in the fire, so you can become rich; and white clothes to wear, so you can cover your shameful nakedness; and salve to put on your eyes, so you can see. [19]Those whom I love I rebuke and discipline. So be earnest, and repent. [20]Here I am! I stand at the door and knock. If anyone hears my voice and opens the door, I will come in and eat with him, and he with me. [21]To him who overcomes, I will give the right to sit with me on my throne, just as I overcame and sat down with my Father on his throne. [22]He who has an ear, let him hear what the Spirit says to the churches."

Forgiveness

(See also pages 142 and 481.)

JOHN 3:14-21 "Just as Moses lifted up the snake in the desert, so the Son of Man must be lifted up, [15]that everyone who believes in him may have eternal life. [16]For God so loved the world that he gave his one and only Son, that whoever believes in him shall not perish but have eternal life. [17]For God did not send his Son into the world to condemn the world, but to save the world through him. [18]Whoever believes in him is not condemned, but whoever does not believe stands condemned already because he has not believed in the name of God's one and only Son. [19]This is the verdict: Light has come into the world, but men loved darkness instead of light because their deeds were evil. [20]Everyone who does evil hates the light, and will not come into the light for fear that his deeds will be exposed. [21]But whoever lives by the truth comes into the light, so that it may be seen plainly that what he has done has been done through God."

JOHN 8:7-12 When they kept on questioning him, he straightened up and said to them, "If any one of you is without sin, let him be the first to throw a stone at her." [8]Again he stooped down and wrote on the ground. [9]At this, those who heard began to go away one at a time, the older ones first, until only Jesus was left, with the woman still standing there. [10]Jesus straightened up and asked her, "Woman, where are they? Has no one condemned you?" [11]"No one, sir," she said. "Then neither do I condemn you," Jesus declared. "Go now and leave your life of sin." [12]When Jesus spoke again to the people, he said, "I am the light of the world. Whoever follows me will never walk in darkness, but will have the light of life."

JOHN 8:21, 23-24 Once more Jesus said to them, "I am going away, and you will look for me, and you will die in your sin. Where I go, you cannot come." [23]But

he continued, "You are from below; I am from above. You are of this world; I am not of this world. [24]I told you that you would die in your sins; if you do not believe that I am the one I claim to be, you will indeed die in your sins."

JOHN 20:22-23 And with that he breathed on them and said, "Receive the Holy Spirit. [23]If you forgive anyone his sins, they are forgiven; if you do not forgive them, they are not forgiven."

MATTHEW 6:9-13 "This, then, is how you should pray: 'Our Father in heaven, hallowed be your name, [10]your kingdom come, your will be done on earth as it is in heaven. [11]Give us today our daily bread. [12]Forgive us our debts, as we also have forgiven our debtors. [13]And lead us not into temptation, but deliver us from the evil one.'"

MATTHEW 6:14-15 "For if you forgive men when they sin against you, your heavenly Father will also forgive you. [15]But if you do not forgive men their sins, your Father will not forgive your sins."

MATTHEW 9:2-6 Some men brought to him a paralytic, lying on a mat. When Jesus saw their faith, he said to the paralytic, "Take heart, son; your sins are forgiven." [3]At this, some of the teachers of the law said to themselves, "This fellow is blaspheming!" [4]Knowing their thoughts, Jesus said, "Why do you entertain evil thoughts in your hearts? [5]Which is easier: to say, 'Your sins are forgiven,' or to say, 'Get up and walk'? [6]But so that you may know that the Son of Man has authority on earth to forgive sins...." Then he said to the paralytic, "Get up, take your mat and go home."

MATTHEW 12:31-32 "And so I tell you, every sin and blasphemy will be forgiven men, but the blasphemy against the Spirit will not be forgiven. [32]Anyone who speaks a word against the Son of Man will be forgiven, but anyone who speaks against the Holy Spirit will not be forgiven, either in this age or in the age to come."

MATTHEW 18:15-17 "If your brother sins against you, go and show him his fault, just between the two of you. If he listens to you, you have won your brother over. [16]But if he will not listen, take one or two others along, so that 'every matter may be established by the testimony of two or three witnesses.' [17]If he refuses to listen to them, tell it to the church; and if he refuses to listen even to the church, treat him as you would a pagan or a tax collector."

MATTHEW 18:21-35 Then Peter came to Jesus and asked, "Lord, how many times shall I forgive my brother when he sins against me? Up to seven times?" [22]Jesus answered, "I tell you, not seven times, but seventy-seven times. [23]Therefore, the kingdom of heaven is like a king who wanted to settle accounts with his servants. [24]As he began the settlement, a man who owed him ten thousand talents was brought to him. [25]Since he was not able to pay, the master ordered that he and his wife and his children and all that he had be sold to repay the debt. [26]The servant fell on his knees before him. 'Be patient with me,' he begged, 'and I will pay back everything.' [27]The servant's master took pity on him, canceled the debt and let him go. [28]But when that servant went out, he found one of his fellow servants who owed him a hundred denarii. He grabbed him and began to choke him. 'Pay back what you owe me!' he demanded. [29]His fellow servant fell to his knees and begged him, 'Be patient with me, and I will pay you back.' [30]"But he refused. Instead, he went off and had the man thrown into prison until he could pay the debt. [31]When the other servants saw what had happened, they were greatly distressed and went and told their master everything that had happened. [32]Then the master called the servant in. 'You wicked servant,' he said, 'I canceled all that debt of yours because you begged me to. [33]Shouldn't you have had mercy on your fellow servant just as I had on you?' [34]In anger his master turned him over to the jailers to be tortured, until he should pay back all he owed. [35]This is how my heavenly Father will treat each of you unless you forgive your brother from your heart."

MARK 2:3-11 Some men came, bringing to him a paralytic, carried by four of them. [4]Since they could not get him to Jesus because of the crowd, they made an opening in the roof above Jesus and, after digging through it, lowered the mat the paralyzed man was lying on. [5]When Jesus saw their faith, he said to the paralytic, "Son, your sins are forgiven." [6]Now some teachers of the law were sitting there, thinking to themselves, [7]"Why does this fellow talk like that? He's blaspheming! Who can forgive sins but God alone?" [8]Immediately Jesus knew in his spirit that this was what they were thinking in their hearts, and he said to them, "Why are you thinking these things?

[9]Which is easier: to say to the paralytic, 'Your sins are forgiven,' or to say, 'Get up, take your mat and walk'? [10]But that you may know that the Son of Man has authority on earth to forgive sins...." He said to the paralytic, [11]"I tell you, get up, take your mat and go home."

MARK 2:17 On hearing this, Jesus said to them, "It is not the healthy who need a doctor, but the sick. I have not come to call the righteous, but sinners."

MARK 3:28-30 "I tell you the truth, all the sins and blasphemies of men will be forgiven them. [29]But whoever blasphemes against the Holy Spirit will never be forgiven; he is guilty of an eternal sin." [30]He said this because they were saying, "He has an evil spirit."

MARK 11:24-25 "Therefore I tell you, whatever you ask for in prayer, believe that you have received it, and it will be yours. [25]And when you stand praying, if you hold anything against anyone, forgive him, so that your Father in heaven may forgive you your sins."

LUKE 5:18-24 Some men came carrying a paralytic on a mat and tried to take him into the house to lay him before Jesus. [19]When they could not find a way to do this because of the crowd, they went up on the roof and lowered him on his mat through the tiles into the middle of the crowd, right in front of Jesus. [20]When Jesus saw their faith, he said, "Friend, your sins are forgiven." [21]The Pharisees and the teachers of the law began thinking to themselves, "Who is this fellow who speaks blasphemy? Who can forgive sins but God alone?" [22]Jesus knew what they were thinking and asked, "Why are you thinking these things in your hearts? [23]Which is easier: to say, 'Your sins are forgiven,' or to say, 'Get up and walk'? [24]But that you may know that the Son of Man has authority on earth to forgive sins...." He said to the paralyzed man, "I tell you, get up, take your mat and go home."

LUKE 6:37-38 "Do not judge, and you will not be judged. Do not condemn, and you will not be condemned. Forgive, and you will be forgiven. [38]Give, and it will be given to you. A good measure, pressed down, shaken together and running over, will be poured into your lap. For with the measure you use, it will be measured to you."

LUKE 7:41-50 "Two men owed money to a certain moneylender. One owed him five hundred denarii, and the other fifty. [42]Neither of them had the money to pay him back, so he canceled the debts of both. Now which of them will love him more?" [43]Simon replied, "I suppose the one who had the bigger debt canceled." "You have judged correctly," Jesus said. [44]Then he turned toward the woman and said to Simon, "Do you see this woman? I came into your house. You did not give me any water for my feet, but she wet my feet with her tears and wiped them with her hair. [45]You did not give me a kiss, but this woman, from the time I entered, has not stopped kissing my feet. [46]You did not put oil on my head, but she has poured perfume on my feet. [47]Therefore, I tell you, her many sins have been forgiven—for she loved much. But he who has been forgiven little loves little." [48]Then Jesus said to her, "Your sins are forgiven." [49]The other guests began to say among themselves, "Who is this who even forgives sins?" [50]Jesus said to the woman, "Your faith has saved you; go in peace."

LUKE 12:10 "And everyone who speaks a word against the Son of Man will be forgiven, but anyone who blasphemes against the Holy Spirit will not be forgiven."

LUKE 17:3-6 "So watch yourselves. If your brother sins, rebuke him, and if he repents, forgive him. [4]If he sins against you seven times in a day, and seven times comes back to you and says, 'I repent,' forgive him." [5]The apostles said to the Lord, "Increase our faith!" [6]He replied, "If you have faith as small as a mustard seed, you can say to this mulberry tree, 'Be uprooted and planted in the sea,' and it will obey you."

LUKE 23:34 Jesus said, "Father, forgive them, for they do not know what they are doing."…

LUKE 23:42-43 Then he [a criminal crucified with Jesus] said, "Jesus, remember me when you come into your kingdom." [43]Jesus answered him, "I tell you the truth, today you will be with me in paradise."

ACTS 26:13-18 "About noon, O king, as I [Paul] was on the road, I saw a light from heaven, brighter than the sun, blazing around me and my companions. [14]We all fell to the ground, and I heard a voice saying to me in Aramaic, 'Saul, Saul, why do you persecute me? It is hard for you to kick against the goads.' [15]Then I asked, 'Who are you, Lord?' 'I am Jesus, whom you are persecuting,' the Lord replied. [16]'Now get up and stand on your feet. I have appeared to you to appoint you as a servant and as a witness of what you have seen of me and what I will show you. [17]I will rescue you from your own people and from the Gentiles. I am sending you to them [18]to open their eyes and turn them from darkness to light, and from the power of Satan to God, so that they may receive forgiveness of sins and a place among those who are sanctified by faith in me.'"

Fruitbearing

JOHN 4:36-38 "Even now the reaper draws his wages, even now he harvests the crop for eternal life, so that the sower and the reaper may be glad together. [37]Thus the saying 'One sows and another reaps' is true. [38]I sent you to reap what you have not worked for. Others have done the hard work, and you have reaped the benefits of their labor."

JOHN 15:1-4 "I am the true vine, and my Father is the gardener. [2]He cuts off every branch in me that bears no fruit, while every branch that does bear fruit he prunes so that it will be even more fruitful. [3]You are already clean because of the word I have spoken to you. [4]Remain in me, and I will remain in you. No branch can bear fruit by itself; it must remain in the vine. Neither can you bear fruit unless you remain in me."

JOHN 15:5-6 "I am the vine; you are the branches. If a man remains in me and I in him, he will bear much fruit; apart from me you can do nothing. [6]If anyone does not remain in me, he is like a branch that is thrown away and withers; such branches are picked up, thrown into the fire and burned."

JOHN 15:7-8 "If you remain in me and my words remain in you, ask whatever you wish, and it will be given you. [8]This is to my Father's glory, that you bear much fruit, showing yourselves to be my disciples."

JOHN 15:16 "You did not choose me, but I chose you and appointed you to go and bear fruit—fruit that will last. Then the Father will give you whatever you ask in my name."

MATTHEW 7:15-20 "Watch out for false prophets. They come to you in sheep's clothing, but inwardly they are ferocious wolves. [16]By their fruit you will recognize them. Do people pick grapes from thornbushes, or figs from thistles? [17]Likewise every good tree bears good fruit, but a bad tree bears bad fruit. [18]A good tree cannot bear bad fruit, and a bad tree cannot bear good fruit. [19]Every tree that does not bear good fruit is cut down and thrown into the fire. [20]Thus, by their fruit you will recognize them."

MATTHEW 13:3-13, 18-23 Then he told them many things in parables, saying: "A farmer went out to sow his seed. [4]As he was scattering the seed, some fell along the path, and the birds came and ate it up. [5]Some fell on rocky places, where it did not have much soil. It sprang up quickly, because the soil was shallow. [6]But when the sun came up, the plants were scorched, and they withered because they had no root. [7]Other seed fell among thorns, which grew up and choked the plants. [8]Still other seed fell on good soil, where it produced a crop—a hundred, sixty or thirty times what was sown. [9]He who has ears, let him hear." [10]The disciples came to him and asked, "Why do you speak to the people in parables?" [11]He replied, "The knowledge of the secrets of the kingdom of heaven has been given to you, but not to them. [12]Whoever has will be given more, and he will have an abundance. Whoever does not have, even what he has will be taken from him. [13]This is why I speak to them in parables: Though seeing, they do not see; though hearing, they do not hear or understand. [18]Listen then to what the parable of the sower means: [19]When anyone hears the message about the kingdom and does not understand it, the evil one comes and snatches away what was sown in his heart. This is the seed sown along the path. [20]The one who received the seed that fell on rocky places is the man who hears the word and at once receives it with joy. [21]But since he has no root, he lasts only a short time. When trouble or persecution comes because of the word, he quickly falls away. [22]The one who received the seed that fell among the thorns is the man who hears the word, but the worries of this life and the deceitfulness of wealth choke it, making it unfruitful. [23]But the one who received the seed that fell on good soil is the man who hears the word and understands it. He produces a crop, yielding a hundred, sixty or thirty times what was sown."

MARK 4:2-20 He taught them many things by parables, and in his teaching said: [3]"Listen! A farmer went out to sow his seed. [4]As he was scattering the seed, some fell along the path, and the birds came and ate it up. [5]Some fell on rocky places, where it did not have much soil. It sprang up quickly, because the soil was shallow. [6]But when the sun came up, the plants were scorched, and they withered because they had no root. [7]Other seed fell among thorns, which grew up and choked the plants, so that they did not bear grain. [8]Still other seed fell on good soil. It came up, grew and produced a crop, multiplying thirty, sixty, or even a hundred times." [9]Then Jesus said, "He who has ears to hear, let him hear." [10]When he was alone, the Twelve and the others around him asked him about the parables. [11]He told them, "The secret of the kingdom of God has been given to you. But to those on the outside everything is said in parables [12]so that, 'they may be ever seeing but never perceiving, and ever hearing but never understanding; otherwise they might turn and be forgiven!'" [13]Then Jesus said to them, "Don't you understand this parable? How then will you understand any parable? [14]The farmer sows the word. [15]Some people are like seed along the path, where the word is sown. As soon as they hear it, Satan comes and takes away the word that was sown in them. [16]Others, like seed sown on rocky places, hear the word and at once receive it with joy. [17]But since they have no root, they last only a short time. When trouble or persecution comes because of the word, they quickly fall away. [18]Still others, like seed sown among thorns, hear the word; [19]but the worries of this life, the deceitfulness of wealth and the desires for other things come in and choke the word, making it unfruitful. [20]Others, like seed sown on good soil, hear the word, accept it, and produce a crop—thirty, sixty or even a hundred times what was sown."

MARK 4:24-25 "Consider carefully what you hear," he continued. "With the measure you use, it will be measured to you—and even more. [25]Whoever has will be given more; whoever does not have, even what he has will be taken from him."

LUKE 6:43-45 "No good tree bears bad fruit, nor does a bad tree bear good fruit. [44]Each tree is recognized by its own fruit. People do not pick figs from thornbushes, or grapes from briers. [45]The good man brings good things out of the good stored up in his heart, and the evil man brings evil things out of the evil stored up in his heart. For out of the overflow of his heart his mouth speaks."

LUKE 8:4-15 While a large crowd was gathering and people were coming to Jesus from town after town, he told this parable: [5]"A farmer went out to sow his seed. As he was scattering the seed, some fell along the path; it was trampled on, and the birds of the air ate it up. [6]Some fell on rock, and when it came up, the plants withered because they had no moisture. [7]Other seed fell among thorns, which grew up with it and choked the plants. [8]Still other seed fell on good soil. It came up and yielded a crop, a hundred times more than was sown." When he said this, he called out, "He who has ears to hear, let him hear." [9]His disciples asked him what this parable meant. [10]He said, "The knowledge of the secrets of the kingdom of God has been given to you, but to others I speak in parables, so that, 'though seeing, they may not see; though hearing, they may not understand.' [11]This is the meaning of the parable: The seed is the word of God. [12]Those along the path are the ones who hear, and then the devil comes and takes away the word from their hearts, so that they may not believe and be saved. [13]Those on the rock are the ones who receive the word with joy when they hear it, but they have no root. They believe for a while, but in the time of testing they fall away. [14]The seed that fell among thorns stands for those who hear, but as they go on their way they are choked by life's worries, riches and pleasures, and they do not mature. [15]But the seed on good soil stands for those with a noble and good heart, who hear the word, retain it, and by persevering produce a crop."

LUKE 13:6-9 Then he told this parable: "A man had a fig tree, planted in his vineyard, and he went to look for fruit on it, but did not find any. [7]So he said to the man who took care of the vineyard, 'For three years now I've been coming to look for fruit on this fig tree and haven't found any. Cut it down! Why should it use up the soil?' [8]'Sir,' the man replied, 'leave it alone for one more year, and I'll dig around it and fertilize it. [9]If it bears fruit next year, fine! If not, then cut it down.'"

Fulfillment

MATTHEW 5:3-9 "Blessed are the poor in spirit, for theirs is the kingdom of heaven. [4]Blessed are those who mourn, for they will be comforted. [5]Blessed are the meek, for they will inherit the earth. [6]Blessed are those who hunger and thirst for righteousness, for they will be filled. [7]Blessed are the merciful, for they will be shown mercy. [8]Blessed are the pure in heart, for they will see God. [9]Blessed are the peacemakers, for they will be called sons of God."

MATTHEW 6:25-33 "Therefore I tell you, do not worry about your life, what you will eat or drink; or about your body, what you will wear. Is not life more important than food, and the body more important than clothes? [26]Look at the birds of the air; they do not sow or reap or store away in barns, and yet your heavenly Father feeds them. Are you not much more valuable than they? [27]Who of you by worrying can add a single hour to his life? [28]And why do you worry about clothes? See how the lilies of the field grow. They do not labor or spin. [29]Yet I tell you that not even Solomon in all his splendor was dressed like one of these. [30]If that is how God clothes the grass of the field, which is here today and tomorrow is thrown into the fire, will he not much more clothe you, O you of little faith? [31]So do not worry, saying, 'What shall we eat?' or 'What shall we drink?' or 'What shall we wear?' [32]For the pagans run after all these things, and your heavenly Father knows that you need them. [33]But seek first his kingdom and his righteousness, and all these things will be given to you as well."

MATTHEW 7:8 "For everyone who asks receives; he who seeks finds; and to him who knocks, the door will be opened."

LUKE 12:16-21 And he told them this parable: "The ground of a certain rich man produced a good crop. [17]He thought to himself, 'What shall I do? I have no place to store my crops.' [18]Then he said, 'This is what I'll do. I will tear down my barns and build bigger ones, and there I will store all my grain and my goods. [19]And I'll say to myself, "You have plenty of good things laid up for many years. Take life easy; eat, drink and be merry."' [20]But God said to him, 'You fool! This very night your life will be demanded from you. Then who will get what you have prepared for yourself?' [21]This is how it will be with anyone who stores up things for himself but is not rich toward God."

Gentleness

MATTHEW 5:3, 5 "Blessed are the poor in spirit, for theirs is the kingdom of heaven. [5]Blessed are the meek, for they will inherit the earth."

MATTHEW 5:38-42 "You have heard that it was said, 'Eye for eye, and tooth for tooth.' [39]But I tell you, Do not resist an evil person. If someone strikes you on the right cheek, turn to him the other also. [40]And if someone wants to sue you and take your tunic, let him have your cloak as well. [41]If someone forces you to go one mile, go with him two miles. [42]Give to the one who asks you, and do not turn away from the one who wants to borrow from you."

MATTHEW 10:16 "I am sending you out like sheep among wolves. Therefore be as shrewd as snakes and as innocent as doves."

MATTHEW 11:28-29 "Come to me, all you who are weary and burdened, and I will give you rest. [29]Take my yoke upon you and learn from me, for I am gentle and humble in heart, and you will find rest for your souls."

The Gospel

MATTHEW 4:17 From that time on Jesus began to preach, "Repent, for the kingdom of heaven is near."

MATTHEW 11:4-6 Jesus replied, "Go back and report to John what you hear and see: [5]The blind receive sight, the lame walk, those who have leprosy are cured, the deaf hear, the dead are raised, and the good news is preached to the poor. [6]Blessed is the man who does not fall away on account of me." (See also Luke 7:22-23.)

MATTHEW 24:14 "And this gospel of the kingdom will be preached in the whole world as a testimony to all nations, and then the end will come."

MATTHEW 26:13 "I tell you the truth, wherever this gospel is preached throughout the world, what she has done will also be told, in memory of her."

MARK 1:15 "The time has come," he said. "The kingdom of God is near. Repent and believe the good news!"

MARK 13:9-10 "You must be on your guard. You will be handed over to the local councils and flogged in the synagogues. On account of me you will stand before governors and kings as witnesses to them. [10]And the gospel must first be preached to all nations."

MARK 16:15-16 He said to them [the Eleven], "Go into all the world and preach the good news to all creation.

[16]Whoever believes and is baptized will be saved, but whoever does not believe will be condemned."[xii]

LUKE 4:18-21 "The Spirit of the Lord is on me, because he has anointed me to preach good news to the poor. He has sent me to proclaim freedom for the prisoners and recovery of sight for the blind, to release the oppressed, [19]to proclaim the year of the Lord's favor." [20]Then he rolled up the scroll, gave it back to the attendant and sat down. The eyes of everyone in the synagogue were fastened on him, [21]and he began by saying to them, "Today this scripture is fulfilled in your hearing."

LUKE 4:43 But he said, "I must preach the good news of the kingdom of God to the other towns also, because that is why I was sent."

LUKE 16:16 "The Law and the Prophets were proclaimed until John. Since that time, the good news of the kingdom of God is being preached, and everyone is forcing his way into it."

ACTS 22:17-21 "When I [Paul] returned to Jerusalem and was praying at the temple, I fell into a trance [18]and saw the Lord speaking. 'Quick!' he said to me. 'Leave Jerusalem immediately, because they will not accept your testimony about me.' [19]'Lord,' I replied, 'these men know that I went from one synagogue to another to imprison and beat those who believe in you. [20]And when the blood of your martyr Stephen was shed, I stood there giving my approval and guarding the clothes of those who were killing him.' [21]Then the Lord said to me, 'Go; I will send you far away to the Gentiles.'"

ACTS 23:11 The following night the Lord stood near Paul and said, "Take courage! As you have testified about me in Jerusalem, so you must also testify in Rome."

Gratitude

MARK 5:19 Jesus did not let him [the man freed of demons go with him], but said, "Go home to your family and tell them how much the Lord has done for you, and how he has had mercy on you." (See also Luke 8:38-39.)

LUKE 7:40-48 Jesus answered him, "Simon, I have something to tell you." "Tell me, teacher," he said. [41]"Two men owed money to a certain moneylender. One owed him five hundred denarii, and the other fifty. [42]Neither of them had the money to pay him back, so he canceled the debts of both. Now which of them will love him more?" [43]Simon replied, "I suppose the one who had the bigger debt canceled." "You have judged correctly," Jesus said. [44]Then he turned toward the woman and said to Simon, "Do you see this woman? I came into your house. You did not give me any water for my feet, but she wet my feet with her tears and wiped them with her hair. [45]You did not give me a kiss, but this woman, from the time I entered, has not stopped kissing my feet. [46]You did not put oil on my head, but she has poured perfume on my feet. [47]Therefore, I tell you, her many sins have been forgiven—for she loved much. But he who has been forgiven little loves little." [48]Then Jesus said to her, "Your sins are forgiven."

LUKE 10:19-20 "I have given you authority to trample on snakes and scorpions and to overcome all the power of the enemy; nothing will harm you. [20]However, do not rejoice that the spirits submit to you, but rejoice that your names are written in heaven."

LUKE 17:17-19 Jesus asked, "Were not all ten cleansed? Where are the other nine? [18]Was no one found to return and give praise to God except this foreigner?" [19]Then he said to him, "Rise and go; your faith has made you well."

The Great Commission

MATTHEW 28:18-20 Then Jesus came to them [the eleven disciples] and said, "All authority in heaven and on earth has been given to me. [19]Therefore go and make disciples of all nations, baptizing them in the name of the Father and of the Son and of the Holy Spirit, [20]and teaching them to obey everything I have commanded you. And surely I am with you always, to the very end of the age."

MARK 16:15-16 He said to them [the Eleven], "Go into all the world and preach the good news to all creation. [16]Whoever believes and is baptized will be saved, but whoever does not believe will be condemned."[xiii]

ACTS 1:7-8 He said to them: "It is not for you to know the times or dates the Father has set by his own authority. [8]But you will receive power when the Holy Spirit comes on you; and you will be my witnesses in Jerusalem, and in all Judea and Samaria, and to the ends of the earth."

Healing

JOHN 4:49-53 The royal official said, "Sir, come down before my child dies." [50]Jesus replied, "You may go. Your son will live." The man took Jesus at his word and departed. [51]While he was still on the way, his servants met him with the news that his boy was living. [52]When he inquired as to the time when his son got better, they said to him, "The fever left him yesterday at the seventh hour." [53]Then the father realized that this was the exact time at which Jesus had said to him, "Your son will live." So he and all his household believed.

JOHN 5:5-14 One who was there had been an invalid for thirty-eight years. [6]When Jesus saw him lying there and learned that he had been in this condition for a long time, he asked him, "Do you want to get well?" [7]"Sir," the invalid replied, "I have no one to help me into the pool when the water is stirred. While I am trying to get in, someone else goes down ahead of me." [8]Then Jesus said to him, "Get up! Pick up your mat and walk." [9]At once the man was cured; he picked up his mat and walked. The day on which this took place was a Sabbath, [10]and so the Jews said to the man who had been healed, "It is the Sabbath; the law forbids you to carry your mat." [11]But he replied, "The man who made me well said to me, 'Pick up your mat and walk.'" [12]So they asked him, "Who is this fellow who told you to pick it up and walk?" [13]The man who was healed had no idea who it was, for Jesus had slipped away into the crowd that was there. [14]Later Jesus found him at the temple and said to him, "See, you are well again. Stop sinning or something worse may happen to you."

JOHN 9:1-7 As he went along, he saw a man blind from birth. [2]His disciples asked him, "Rabbi, who sinned, this man or his parents, that he was born blind?" [3]"Neither this man nor his parents sinned," said Jesus, "but this happened so that the work of God might be displayed in his life. [4]As long as it is day, we must do the work of him who sent me. Night is coming, when no one can work. [5]While I am in the world, I am the light of the world." [6]Having said this, he spit on the ground, made some mud with the saliva, and put it on the man's eyes. [7]"Go," he told him, "wash in the Pool of Siloam" (this word means Sent). So the man went and washed, and came home seeing.

MATTHEW 8:2-4 A man with leprosy came and knelt before him and said, "Lord, if you are willing, you can make me clean." [3]Jesus reached out his hand and touched the man. "I am willing," he said. "Be clean!" Immediately he was cured of his leprosy. [4]Then Jesus said to him, "See that you don't tell anyone. But go, show yourself to the priest and offer the gift Moses commanded, as a testimony to them." (See also Mark 1:40-44; Luke 5:12-14.)

MATTHEW 9:22 Jesus turned and saw her. "Take heart, daughter," he said, "your faith has healed you." And the woman was healed from that moment.

MATTHEW 9:23-25 When Jesus entered the ruler's house and saw the flute players and the noisy crowd, [24]he said, "Go away. The girl is not dead but asleep."

But they laughed at him. [25]After the crowd had been put outside, he went in and took the girl by the hand, and she got up.

MATTHEW 9:27-30 As Jesus went on from there, two blind men followed him, calling out, "Have mercy on us, Son of David!" [28]When he had gone indoors, the blind men came to him, and he asked them, "Do you believe that I am able to do this?" "Yes, Lord," they replied. [29]Then he touched their eyes and said, "According to your faith will it be done to you"; [30]and their sight was restored. Jesus warned them sternly, "See that no one knows about this."

MATTHEW 10:5-8 These twelve Jesus sent out with the following instructions: "Do not go among the Gentiles or enter any town of the Samaritans. [6]Go rather to the lost sheep of Israel. [7]As you go, preach this message: 'The kingdom of heaven is near.' [8]Heal the sick, raise the dead, cleanse those who have leprosy, drive out demons. Freely you have received, freely give."

MATTHEW 20:30-34 Two blind men were sitting by the roadside, and when they heard that Jesus was going by, they shouted, "Lord, Son of David, have mercy on us!" [31]The crowd rebuked them and told them to be quiet, but they shouted all the louder, "Lord, Son of David, have mercy on us!" [32]Jesus stopped and called them. "What do you want me to do for you?" he asked. [33]"Lord," they answered, "we want our sight." [34]Jesus had compassion on them and touched their eyes. Immediately they received their sight and followed him.

MARK 2:8-9 Immediately Jesus

knew in his spirit that this was what they were thinking in their hearts, and he said to them, "Why are you thinking these things? ⁹Which is easier: to say to the paralytic, 'Your sins are forgiven,' or to say, 'Get up, take your mat and walk'?"

MARK 3:1-5 Another time he went into the synagogue, and a man with a shriveled hand was there. ²Some of them were looking for a reason to accuse Jesus, so they watched him closely to see if he would heal him on the Sabbath. ³Jesus said to the man with the shriveled hand, "Stand up in front of everyone." ⁴Then Jesus asked them, "Which is lawful on the Sabbath: to do good or to do evil, to save life or to kill?" But they remained silent. ⁵He looked around at them in anger and, deeply distressed at their stubborn hearts, said to the man, "Stretch out your hand." He stretched it out, and his hand was completely restored. (See also Luke 6:6-10.)

MARK 5:38-42 When they came to the home of the synagogue ruler, Jesus saw a commotion, with people crying and wailing loudly. ³⁹He went in and said to them, "Why all this commotion and wailing? The child is not dead but asleep." ⁴⁰But they laughed at him. After he put them all out, he took the child's father and mother and the disciples who were with him, and went in where the child was. ⁴¹He took her by the hand and said to her, "Talitha koum!" (which means, "Little girl, I say to you, get up!"). ⁴²Immediately the girl stood up and walked around (she was twelve years old). At this they were completely astonished.

MARK 7:32-35 There some people brought to him a man who was deaf and could hardly talk, and they begged him to place his hand on the man. ³³After he took him aside, away from the crowd, Jesus put his fingers into the man's ears. Then he spit and touched the man's tongue. ³⁴He looked up to heaven and with a deep sigh said to him, "Ephphatha!" (which means, "Be opened!"). ³⁵At this, the man's ears were opened, his tongue was loosened and he began to speak plainly.

MARK 8:22-26 They came to Bethsaida, and some people brought a blind man and begged Jesus to touch him. ²³He took the blind man by the hand and led him outside the village. When he had spit on the man's eyes and put his hands on him, Jesus asked, "Do you see anything?" ²⁴He looked up and said, "I see people; they look like trees walking around." ²⁵Once more Jesus put his hands on the man's eyes. Then his eyes were opened, his sight was restored, and he saw everything clearly. ²⁶Jesus sent him home, saying, "Don't go into the village."

MARK 10:46-52 Then they came to Jericho. As Jesus and his disciples, together with a large crowd, were leaving the city, a blind man, Bartimaeus (that is, the Son of Timaeus), was sitting by the roadside begging. ⁴⁷When he heard that it was Jesus of Nazareth, he began to shout, "Jesus, Son of David, have mercy on me!" ⁴⁸Many rebuked him and told him to be quiet, but he shouted all the more, "Son of David, have mercy on me!" ⁴⁹Jesus stopped and said, "Call him." So they called to the blind man, "Cheer up! On your feet! He's calling you." ⁵⁰Throwing his cloak aside, he jumped to his feet and came to Jesus.

51"What do you want me to do for you?" Jesus asked him. The blind man said, "Rabbi, I want to see." 52"Go," said Jesus, "your faith has healed you." Immediately he received his sight and followed Jesus along the road.

MARK 16:15-18 He said to them [the Eleven], "Go into all the world and preach the good news to all creation. 16Whoever believes and is baptized will be saved, but whoever does not believe will be condemned. 17And these signs will accompany those who believe: In my name they will drive out demons; they will speak in new tongues; 18they will pick up snakes with their hands; and when they drink deadly poison, it will not hurt them at all; they will place their hands on sick people, and they will get well."xiv

LUKE 4:18-21 "The Spirit of the Lord is on me, because he has anointed me to preach good news to the poor. He has sent me to proclaim freedom for the prisoners and recovery of sight for the blind, to release the oppressed, 19to proclaim the year of the Lord's favor." 20Then he rolled up the scroll, gave it back to the attendant and sat down. The eyes of everyone in the synagogue were fastened on him, 21and he began by saying to them, "Today this scripture is fulfilled in your hearing."

LUKE 4:24-27 "I tell you the truth," he continued, "no prophet is accepted in his hometown. 25I assure you that there were many widows in Israel in Elijah's time, when the sky was shut for three and a half years and there was a severe famine throughout the land. 26Yet Elijah was not sent to any of them, but to a widow in Zarephath in the region of Sidon. 27And there were many in Israel with leprosy in the time of Elisha the prophet, yet not one of them was cleansed—only Naaman the Syrian."

LUKE 7:12-15 As he approached the town gate, a dead person was being carried out—the only son of his mother, and she was a widow. And a large crowd from the town was with her. 13When the Lord saw her, his heart went out to her and he said, "Don't cry." 14Then he went up and touched the coffin, and those carrying it stood still. He said, "Young man, I say to you, get up!" 15The dead man sat up and began to talk, and Jesus gave him back to his mother.

LUKE 10:2-9 He told them [the seventy-two who were sent out], "The harvest is plentiful, but the workers are few. Ask the Lord of the harvest, therefore, to send out workers into his harvest field. 3Go! I am sending you out like lambs among wolves. 4Do not take a purse or bag or sandals; and do not greet anyone on the road. 5When you enter a house, first say, 'Peace to this house.' 6If a man of peace is there, your peace will rest on him; if not, it will return to you. 7Stay in that house, eating and drinking whatever they give you, for the worker deserves his wages. Do not move around from house to house. 8When you enter a town and are welcomed, eat what is set before you. 9Heal the sick who are there and tell them, 'The kingdom of God is near you.'"

LUKE 13:10-13 On a Sabbath Jesus was teaching in one of the synagogues, 11and a woman was there who had been crippled by a spirit for eighteen years. She was bent over and could not straighten up at all. ¹²When Jesus saw her, he called her forward and said to her, "Woman, you are set free from your infirmity." ¹³Then he put his hands on her, and immediately she straightened up and praised God.

LUKE 13:14-16 Indignant because Jesus had healed on the Sabbath, the synagogue ruler said to the people, "There are six days for work. So come and be healed on those days, not on the Sabbath." ¹⁵The Lord answered him, "You hypocrites! Doesn't each of you on the Sabbath untie his ox or donkey from the stall and lead it out to give it water? ¹⁶Then should not this woman, a daughter of Abraham, whom Satan has kept bound for eighteen long years, be set free on the Sabbath day from what bound her?"

LUKE 17:12-14 As he was going into a village, ten men who had leprosy met him. They stood at a distance ¹³and called out in a loud voice, "Jesus, Master, have pity on us!" ¹⁴When he saw them, he said, "Go, show yourselves to the priests." And as they went, they were cleansed.

LUKE 17:17-19 Jesus asked, "Were not all ten cleansed? Where are the other nine? ¹⁸Was no one found to return and give praise to God except this foreigner?" ¹⁹Then he said to him, "Rise and go; your faith has made you well."

LUKE 18:35, 38, 40-42 As Jesus approached Jericho, a blind man was sitting by the roadside begging. ³⁸He called out, "Jesus, Son of David, have mercy on me!" ⁴⁰Jesus stopped and ordered the man to be brought to him. When he came near, Jesus asked, ⁴¹"What do you want me to do for you?" "Lord, I want to see," he

replied. ⁴²Jesus said to him, "Receive your sight; your faith has healed you."

ACTS 9:10-16 In Damascus there was a disciple named Ananias. The Lord called to him in a vision, "Ananias!" "Yes, Lord," he answered. ¹¹The Lord told him, "Go to the house of Judas on Straight Street and ask for a man from Tarsus named Saul, for he is praying. ¹²In a vision he has seen a man named Ananias come and place his hands on him to restore his sight." ¹³"Lord," Ananias answered, "I have heard many reports about this man and all the harm he has done to your saints in Jerusalem. ¹⁴And he has come here with authority from the chief priests to arrest all who call on your name." ¹⁵But the Lord said to Ananias, "Go! This man is my chosen instrument to carry my name before the Gentiles and their kings and before the people of Israel. ¹⁶I will show him how much he must suffer for my name." (See also Acts 22:6-10.)

Honoring and Glorifying Christ; the Glory of Christ

JOHN 5:21-23 "For just as the Father raises the dead and gives them life, even so the Son gives life to whom he is pleased to give it. ²²Moreover, the Father judges no one, but has entrusted all judgment to the Son, ²³that all may honor the Son just as they honor the Father. He who does not honor the Son does not honor the Father, who sent him."

JOHN 5:41-43 "I do not accept praise from men, ⁴²but I know you. I know that you do not have the love of God in your hearts. ⁴³I have come in my

Father's name, and you do not accept me; but if someone else comes in his own name, you will accept him."

JOHN 8:31 Then Jesus said to those Jews who believed Him, "If you abide in My word, you are My disciples indeed." (NKJV)

JOHN 8:54-56 Jesus replied, "If I glorify myself, my glory means nothing. My Father, whom you claim as your God, is the one who glorifies me. [55]Though you do not know him, I know him. If I said I did not, I would be a liar like you, but I do know him and keep his word. [56]Your father Abraham rejoiced at the thought of seeing my day; he saw it and was glad."

JOHN 11:4 When he heard this [Lazarus was sick], Jesus said, "This sickness will not end in death. No, it is for God's glory so that God's Son may be glorified through it."

JOHN 12:23-24 Jesus replied, "The hour has come for the Son of Man to be glorified. [24]I tell you the truth, unless a kernel of wheat falls to the ground and dies, it remains only a single seed. But if it dies, it produces many seeds."

JOHN 12:26 "Whoever serves me must follow me; and where I am, my servant also will be. My Father will honor the one who serves me."

JOHN 13:31-33 When he [Judas] was gone, Jesus said, "Now is the Son of Man glorified and God is glorified in him. [32]If God is glorified in him, God will glorify the Son in himself, and will glorify him at once. [33]My children, I will be with you only a little longer. You will look for me, and just as I told the Jews, so I tell you

now: Where I am going, you cannot come."

JOHN 14:15 "If you love me, you will obey what I command."

JOHN 14:23-24 Jesus replied, "If anyone loves me, he will obey my teaching. My Father will love him, and we will come to him and make our home with him. [24]He who does not love me will not obey my teaching. These words you hear are not my own; they belong to the Father who sent me."

JOHN 17:1-5 After Jesus said this, he looked toward heaven and prayed: "Father, the time has come. Glorify your Son, that your Son may glorify you. [2]For you granted him authority over all people that he might give eternal life to all those you have given him. [3]Now this is eternal life: that they may know you, the only true God, and Jesus Christ, whom you have sent. [4]I have brought you glory on earth by completing the work you gave me to do. [5]And now, Father, glorify me in your presence with the glory I had with you before the world began."

JOHN 17:9-10 "I pray for them [the disciples]. I am not praying for the world, but for those you have given me, for they are yours. [10]All I have is yours, and all you have is mine. And glory has come to me through them."

JOHN 17:22-23 "I have given them the glory that you [God] gave me, that they may be one as we are one: [23]I in them and you in me. May they be brought to complete unity to let the world know that you sent me and have loved them even as you have loved me."

JOHN 17:24 "Father, I want those you have given me to be with me where I am, and to see my glory, the glory you have given me because you loved me before the creation of the world."

MATTHEW 7:21-25 "Not everyone who says to Me, 'Lord, Lord,' shall enter the kingdom of heaven, but he who does the will of My Father in heaven. 22Many will say to Me in that day, 'Lord, Lord, have we not prophesied in Your name, cast out demons in Your name, and done many wonders in Your name?' 23And then I will declare to them, 'I never knew you; depart from Me, you who practice lawlessness!' 24Therefore whoever hears these sayings of Mine, and does them, I will liken him to a wise man who built his house on the rock: 25and the rain descended, the floods came, and the winds blew and beat on that house; and it did not fall, for it was founded on the rock." (NKJV)

MATTHEW 15:8-9 "These people honor me with their lips, but their hearts are far from me. 9They worship me in vain; their teachings are but rules taught by men."

MATTHEW 16:27 "For the Son of Man is going to come in his Father's glory with his angels, and then he will reward each person according to what he has done."

MATTHEW 19:28 Jesus said to them [the disciples], "I tell you the truth, at the renewal of all things, when the Son of Man sits on his glorious throne, you who have followed me will also sit on twelve thrones, judging the twelve tribes of Israel."

MATTHEW 23:6-12 "[T]hey love the place of honor at banquets and the most important seats in the synagogues; 7they love to be greeted in the marketplaces and to have men call them 'Rabbi.' 8But you are not to be called 'Rabbi,' for you have only one Master and you are all brothers. 9And do not call anyone on earth 'father,' for you have one Father, and he is in heaven. 10Nor are you to be called 'teacher,' for you have one Teacher, the Christ. 11The greatest among you will be your servant. 12For whoever exalts himself will be humbled, and whoever humbles himself will be exalted."

MATTHEW 23:39 "For I tell you, you will not see me again until you say, 'Blessed is he who comes in the name of the Lord.'"

MATTHEW 24:30 "At that time the sign of the Son of Man will appear in the sky, and all the nations of the earth will mourn. They will see the Son of Man coming on the clouds of the sky, with power and great glory."

MATTHEW 25:31-32 "When the Son of Man comes in his glory, and all the angels with him, he will sit on his throne in heavenly glory. 32All the nations will be gathered before him, and he will separate the people one from another as a shepherd separates the sheep from the goats."

MARK 13:26-27 "At that time men will see the Son of Man coming in clouds with great power and glory. 27And he will send his angels and gather his elect from the four winds, from the ends of the earth to the ends of the heavens."

LUKE 21:25-27 "There will be signs in the sun, moon and stars. On the earth, nations will be in anguish and perplexity at the roaring and tossing of the sea. 26Men will faint from terror, apprehensive of what is coming on the world, for the heavenly bodies will be shaken. 27At that time they will see the Son of Man coming in a cloud with power and great glory."

LUKE 24:25-26 He said to them [two people on the road to Emmaus], "How foolish you are, and how slow of heart to believe all that the prophets have spoken! 26Did not the Christ have to suffer these things and then enter his glory?"

Honoring and Glorifying God; the Glory of God

JOHN 4:23-24 "Yet a time is coming and has now come when the true worshipers will worship the Father in spirit and truth, for they are the kind of worshipers the Father seeks. 24God is spirit, and his worshipers must worship in spirit and in truth."

JOHN 5:21-23 "For just as the Father raises the dead and gives them life, even so the Son gives life to whom he is pleased to give it. 22Moreover, the Father judges no one, but has entrusted all judgment to the Son, 23that all may honor the Son just as they honor the Father. He who does not honor the Son does not honor the Father, who sent him."

JOHN 7:17-19 "If anyone chooses to do God's will, he will find out whether my teaching comes from God or whether I speak on my own. 18He who speaks on his own does so to gain honor for himself, but he who works for the honor of the one who sent him is a man of truth; there is nothing false about him. 19Has not Moses given you the law? Yet not one of you keeps the law. Why are you trying to kill me?"

JOHN 11:4 When he heard this [Lazarus was sick], Jesus said, "This sickness will not end in death. No, it is for God's glory so that God's Son may be glorified through it."

JOHN 11:40 Then Jesus said, "Did I not tell you that if you believed, you would see the glory of God?"

JOHN 13:31-33 When he [Judas] was gone, Jesus said, "Now is the Son of Man glorified and God is glorified in him. 32If God is glorified in him, God will glorify the Son in himself, and will glorify him at once. 33My children, I will be with you only a little longer. You will look for me, and just as I told the Jews, so I tell you now: Where I am going, you cannot come."

JOHN 14:12-13 "I tell you the truth, anyone who has faith in me will do what I have been doing. He will do even greater things than these, because I am going to the Father. 13And I will do whatever you ask in my name, so that the Son may bring glory to the Father."

JOHN 15:5-8 "I am the vine; you are the branches. If a man remains in me and I in him, he will bear much fruit; apart from me you can do nothing. 6If anyone does not remain in me, he is like a branch that is thrown away and withers; such branches are picked up, thrown into the fire and burned. 7If you remain in me and my words remain in you, ask whatever you wish, and it will be given you. [8]This is to my Father's glory, that you bear much fruit, showing yourselves to be my disciples."

JOHN 17:1-5 After Jesus said this, he looked toward heaven and prayed: "Father, the time has come. Glorify your Son, that your Son may glorify you. [2]For you granted him authority over all people that he might give eternal life to all those you have given him. [3]Now this is eternal life: that they may know you, the only true God, and Jesus Christ, whom you have sent. [4]I have brought you glory on earth by completing the work you gave me to do. [5]And now, Father, glorify me in your presence with the glory I had with you before the world began."

MATTHEW 5:14-16 "You are the light of the world. A city on a hill cannot be hidden. [15]Neither do people light a lamp and put it under a bowl. Instead they put it on its stand, and it gives light to everyone in the house. [16]In the same way, let your light shine before men, that they may see your good deeds and praise your Father in heaven."

MATTHEW 6:13 "And lead us not into temptation, but deliver us from the evil one."

MATTHEW 23:6-12 "[T]hey love the place of honor at banquets and the most important seats in the synagogues; [7]they love to be greeted in the market-places and to have men call them 'Rabbi.' [8]But you are not to be called 'Rabbi,' for you have only one Master and you are all brothers. [9]And do not call anyone on earth 'father,' for you have one Father, and he is in heaven. [10]Nor are you to be called

'teacher,' for you have one Teacher, the Christ. [11]The greatest among you will be your servant. [12]For whoever exalts himself will be humbled, and whoever humbles himself will be exalted."

MARK 7:6-8 He replied, "Isaiah was right when he prophesied about you hypocrites; as it is written: 'These people honor me with their lips, but their hearts are far from me. [7]They worship me in vain; their teachings are but rules taught by men.' [8]You have let go of the commands of God and are holding on to the traditions of men."

LUKE 17:17-18 Jesus asked, "Were not all ten cleansed? Where are the other nine? [18]Was no one found to return and give praise to God except this foreigner?"

Humility

JOHN 13:12-17 When he [Jesus] had finished washing their [the disciples'] feet, he put on his clothes and returned to his place. "Do you understand what I have done for you?" he asked them. [13]"You call me 'Teacher' and 'Lord,' and rightly so, for that is what I am. [14]Now that I, your Lord and Teacher, have washed your feet, you also should wash one another's feet. [15]I have set you an example that you should do as I have done for you. [16]I tell you the truth, no servant is greater than his master, nor is a messenger greater than the one who sent him. [17]Now that you know these things, you will be blessed if you do them."

MATTHEW 5:3-9 "Blessed are the poor in spirit, for theirs is the kingdom of heaven. [4]Blessed are those who mourn, for they will be comforted. [5]Blessed are the meek, for they will inherit the earth. [6]Blessed are those who hunger and thirst for righteousness, for they will be filled. [7]Blessed are the merciful, for they will be shown mercy. [8]Blessed are the pure in heart, for they will see God. [9]Blessed are the peacemakers, for they will be called sons of God."

MATTHEW 11:29 "Take my yoke upon you and learn from me, for I am gentle and humble in heart, and you will find rest for your souls."

MATTHEW 18:2-4 He called a little child and had him stand among them. [3]And he said: "I tell you the truth, unless you change and become like little children, you will never enter the kingdom of heaven. [4]Therefore, whoever humbles himself like this child is the greatest in the kingdom of heaven."

MATTHEW 20:25-28 Jesus called them [the disciples] together and said, "You know that the rulers of the Gentiles lord it over them, and their high officials exercise authority over them. [26]Not so with you. Instead, whoever wants to become great among you must be your servant, [27]and whoever wants to be first must be your slave— [28]just as the Son of Man did not come to be served, but to serve, and to give his life as a ransom for many."

MATTHEW 23:1-8 Then Jesus said to the crowds and to his disciples: [2]"The teachers of the law and the Pharisees sit in Moses' seat. [3]So you must obey them and do everything they tell you. But do not do what they do, for they do not practice what they preach. [4]They tie up heavy loads and put them on men's shoulders, but they themselves are not willing to lift a finger to move them. [5]Everything they do is done for men to see: They make their phylacteries wide and the tassels on their garments long; [6]they love the place of honor at banquets and the most important seats in the synagogues; [7]they love to be greeted in the marketplaces and to have men call them 'Rabbi.' [8]But you are not to be called 'Rabbi,' for you have only one Master and you are all brothers."

LUKE 14:8-11 "When someone invites you to a wedding feast, do not take the place of honor, for a person more distinguished than you may have been invited. [9]If so, the host who invited both of you will come and say to you, 'Give this man your seat.' Then, humiliated, you will have to take the least important place. [10]But when you are invited, take the lowest place, so that when your host comes, he will say to you, 'Friend, move up to a better place.' Then you will be honored in the presence of all your fellow guests. [11]For everyone who exalts himself will be humbled, and he who humbles himself will be exalted."

LUKE 17:7-10 "Suppose one of you had a servant plowing or looking after the sheep. Would he say to the servant when he comes in from the field, 'Come along now and sit down to eat'? [8]Would he not rather say, 'Prepare my supper, get yourself ready and wait on me while I eat and drink; after that you may eat and drink'? [9]Would he thank the servant because he did what he was told to do? [10]So you also, when you have done everything you were told to do, should say, 'We are unworthy servants; we have only done our duty.'"

LUKE 18:9-14 To some who were confident of their own righteousness and looked down on everybody else, Jesus told this parable: [10]"Two men went up to the temple to pray, one a Pharisee and the other a tax collector. [11]The Pharisee stood up and prayed about himself: 'God, I thank you that I am not like other men—robbers, evildoers, adulterers—or even like this tax collector. [12]I fast twice a week and give a tenth of all I get.' [13]But the tax collector stood at a distance. He would not even look up to heaven, but beat his breast and said, 'God, have mercy on me, a sinner.' [14]I tell you that this man, rather than the other, went home justified before God. For everyone who exalts himself will be humbled, and he who humbles himself will be exalted."

Jesus' Body

JOHN 6:47-51 "I tell you the truth, he who believes has everlasting life. [48]I am the bread of life. [49]Your forefathers ate the manna in the desert, yet they died. [50]But here is the bread that comes down from heaven, which a man may eat and not die. [51]I am the living bread that came down from heaven. If anyone eats of this bread, he will live forever. This bread is my flesh, which I will give for the life of the world."

JOHN 6:61-64 Aware that his disciples were grumbling about this, Jesus said to them, "Does this offend you? [62]What if you see the Son of Man ascend to where he was before! [63]The Spirit gives life; the flesh counts for nothing. The words I have spoken to you are spirit and they are life. [64]Yet there are some of you who do not

believe." For Jesus had known from the beginning which of them did not believe and who would betray him.

MATTHEW 26:26-29 While they were eating, Jesus took bread, gave thanks and broke it, and gave it to his disciples, saying, "Take and eat; this is my body." [27]Then he took the cup, gave thanks and offered it to them, saying, "Drink from it, all of you. [28]This is my blood of the covenant, which is poured out for many for the forgiveness of sins. [29]I tell you, I will not drink of this fruit of the vine from now on until that day when I drink it anew with you in my Father's kingdom." (See also Mark 14:22-25.)

LUKE 22:19 And he took bread, gave thanks and broke it, and gave it to them [the apostles], saying, "This is my body given for you; do this in remembrance of me."

1 CORINTHIANS 11:23-26 For I received from the Lord what I also passed on to you: The Lord Jesus, on the night he was betrayed, took bread, [24]and when he had given thanks, he broke it and said, "This is my body, which is for you; do this in remembrance of me." [25]In the same way, after supper he took the cup, saying, "This cup is the new covenant in my blood; do this, whenever you drink it, in remembrance of me." [26]For whenever you eat this bread and drink this cup, you proclaim the Lord's death until he comes.

Joy

JOHN 10:10 "The thief does not come except to steal, and to kill, and to destroy. I have come that they may have life, and that they may have it more abundantly." (NKJV)

JOHN 15:9-14 "As the Father has loved me, so have I loved you. Now remain in my love. [10]If you obey my commands, you will remain in my love, just as I have obeyed my Father's commands and remain in his love. [11]I have told you this so that my joy may be in you and that your joy may be complete. [12]My command is this: Love each other as I have loved you. [13]Greater love has no one than this, that he lay down his life for his friends. [14]You are my friends if you do what I command."

JOHN 16:20-24 "I tell you the truth, you will weep and mourn while the world rejoices. You will grieve, but your grief will turn to joy. [21]A woman giving birth to a child has pain because her time has come; but when her baby is born she forgets the anguish because of her joy that a child is born into the world. [22]So with you: Now is your time of grief, but I will see you again and you will rejoice, and no one will take away your joy. [23]In that day you will no longer ask me anything. I tell you the truth, my Father will give you whatever you ask in my name. [24]Until now you have not asked for anything in my name. Ask and you will receive, and your joy will be complete."

JOHN 16:31-33 "You believe at last!" Jesus answered. [32]"But a time is coming, and has come, when you will be scattered, each to his own home. You will leave me all alone. Yet I am not alone, for my Father is with me. [33]I have told you these things, so that in me you may have peace. In this world you will have trouble. But take heart! I have overcome the world."

JOHN 17:13-14 "I am coming to you [God the Father] now, but I say these things while I am still in the world, so that they may have the full measure of my joy within them. [14]I have given them your word and the world has hated them, for they are not of the world any more than I am of the world."

MATTHEW 9:2 Some men brought to him a paralytic, lying on a mat. When Jesus saw their faith, he said to the paralytic, "Take heart, son; your sins are forgiven."

MATTHEW 9:22 Jesus turned and saw her. "Take heart, daughter," he said, "your faith has healed you."...

MATTHEW 14:27 But Jesus immediately said to them: "Take courage! It is I. Don't be afraid."

MARK 6:50 ... they all saw him and were terrified. Immediately he spoke to them and said, "Take courage! It is I. Don't be afraid."

LUKE 6:20-21 Looking at his disciples, he said: "Blessed are you who are poor, for yours is the kingdom of God. [21]Blessed are you who hunger now, for you will be satisfied. Blessed are you who weep now, for you will laugh."

LUKE 6:22-23 "Blessed are you when men hate you, when they exclude you and insult you and reject your name as evil, because of the Son of Man. [23]Rejoice in that day and leap for joy, because great is your reward in heaven. For that is how their fathers treated the prophets."

LUKE 10:17-20 The seventy-two returned with joy and said, "Lord, even the demons submit to us in your name."

[18]He replied, "I saw Satan fall like lightning from heaven. [19]I have given you authority to trample on snakes and scorpions and to overcome all the power of the enemy; nothing will harm you. [20]However, do not rejoice that the spirits submit to you, but rejoice that your names are written in heaven."

Justification

JOHN 3:14-19 "Just as Moses lifted up the snake in the desert, so the Son of Man must be lifted up, [15]that everyone who believes in him may have eternal life. [16]For God so loved the world that he gave his one and only Son, that whoever believes in him shall not perish but have eternal life. [17]For God did not send his Son into the world to condemn the world, but to save the world through him. [18]Whoever believes in him is not condemned, but whoever does not believe stands condemned already because he has not believed in the name of God's one and only Son. [19]This is the verdict: Light has come into the world, but men loved darkness instead of light because their deeds were evil."

MATTHEW 12:33-37 "Make a tree good and its fruit will be good, or make a tree bad and its fruit will be bad, for a tree is recognized by its fruit. [34]You brood of vipers, how can you who are evil say anything good? For out of the overflow of the heart the mouth speaks. [35]The good man brings good things out of the good stored up in him, and the evil man brings evil things out of the evil stored up in him. [36]But I tell you that men will have to give account on the day of judgment for every careless word they have spoken. [37]For by your words you will be acquitted, and by your words you will be condemned."

LUKE 16:14-15 The Pharisees, who loved money, heard all this and were sneering at Jesus. [15]He said to them, "You are the ones who justify yourselves in the eyes of men, but God knows your hearts. What is highly valued among men is detestable in God's sight."

LUKE 18:9-14 To some who were confident of their own righteousness and looked down on everybody else, Jesus told this parable: [10]"Two men went up to the temple to pray, one a Pharisee and the other a tax collector. [11]The Pharisee stood up and prayed about himself: 'God, I thank you that I am not like other men—robbers, evildoers, adulterers—or even like this tax collector. [12]I fast twice a week and give a tenth of all I get.' [13]But the tax collector stood at a distance. He would not even look up to heaven, but beat his breast and said, 'God, have mercy on me, a sinner.' [14]I tell you that this man, rather than the other, went home justified before God. For everyone who exalts himself will be humbled, and he who humbles himself will be exalted."

Knowing God and Knowing Christ

JOHN 10:14-16 "I am the good shepherd; I know my sheep and my sheep know me— [15]just as the Father knows me and I know the Father—and I lay down my life for the sheep. [16]I have other sheep that are not of this sheep pen. I must bring them also. They too will listen to my voice, and there shall be one flock and one shepherd."

JOHN 10:27-30 "My sheep listen to my voice; I know them, and they follow me. [28]I give them eternal life, and they shall never perish; no one can snatch them out of my hand. [29]My Father, who has given them to me, is greater than all; no one can snatch them out of my Father's hand. [30]I and the Father are one."

JOHN 14:6-7 Jesus answered, "I am the way and the truth and the life. No one comes to the Father except through me. [7]If you really knew me, you would know my Father as well. From now on, you do know him and have seen him."

JOHN 14:9-11 Jesus answered: "Don't you know me, Philip, even after I have been among you such a long time? Anyone who has seen me has seen the Father. How can you say, 'Show us the Father'? [10]Don't you believe that I am in the Father, and that the Father is in me? The words I say to you are not just my own. Rather, it is the Father, living in me, who is doing his work. [11]Believe me when I say that I am in the Father and the Father is in me; or at least believe on the evidence of the miracles themselves."

JOHN 14:15 "If you love me, you will obey what I command."

JOHN 14:23-24 Jesus replied, "If anyone loves me, he will obey my teaching. My Father will love him, and we will come to him and make our home with him. [24]He who does not love me will not obey my teaching. These words you hear are not my own; they belong to the Father who sent me."

JOHN 15:5-7 "I am the vine; you are the branches. If a man remains in me and I in him, he will bear much fruit; apart from me you can do nothing. [6]If anyone does not remain in me, he is like a branch that is thrown away and withers; such branches are picked up, thrown into the fire and burned. [7]If you remain in me and my words remain in you, ask whatever you wish, and it will be given you."

JOHN 15:9-17 "As the Father has loved me, so have I loved you. Now remain in my love. [10]If you obey my commands, you will remain in my love, just as I have obeyed my Father's commands and remain in his love. [11]I have told you this so that my joy may be in you and that your joy may be complete. [12]My command is this: Love each other as I have loved you. [13]Greater love has no one than this, that he lay down his life for his friends. [14]You are my friends if you do what I command. [15]I no longer call you servants, because a servant does not know his master's business. Instead, I have called you friends, for everything that I learned from my Father I have made known to you. [16]You did not choose me, but I chose you and appointed you to go and bear fruit—fruit that will last. Then the Father will give you whatever you ask in my name. [17]This is my command: Love each other."

JOHN 15:20-21 "Remember the words I spoke to you: 'No servant is greater than his master.' If they persecuted me, they will persecute you also. If they obeyed my teaching, they will obey yours also. [21]They will treat you this way because of my name, for they do not know the One who sent me."

JOHN 16:1-3 "All this I have told you so that you will not go astray. ²They will put you out of the synagogue; in fact, a time is coming when anyone who kills you will think he is offering a service to God. ³They will do such things because they have not known the Father or me."

JOHN 17:3-4 "Now this is eternal life: that they may know you, the only true God, and Jesus Christ, whom you have sent. ⁴I have brought you glory on earth by completing the work you gave me to do."

MATTHEW 7:21-23 "Not everyone who says to Me, 'Lord, Lord,' shall enter the kingdom of heaven, but he who does the will of My Father in heaven. ²²Many will say to Me in that day, 'Lord, Lord, have we not prophesied in Your name, cast out demons in Your name, and done many wonders in Your name?' ²³And then I will declare to them, 'I never knew you; depart from Me, you who practice lawlessness!'" (NKJV)

LUKE 13:23-30 Someone asked him, "Lord, are only a few people going to be saved?" He said to them, ²⁴"Make every effort to enter through the narrow door, because many, I tell you, will try to enter and will not be able to. ²⁵Once the owner of the house gets up and closes the door, you will stand outside knocking and pleading, 'Sir, open the door for us.' But he will answer, 'I don't know you or where you come from.' ²⁶Then you will say, 'We ate and drank with you, and you taught in our streets.' ²⁷But he will reply, 'I don't know you or where you come from. Away from me, all you evildoers!' ²⁸There will be weeping there, and gnashing of teeth, when you see Abraham, Isaac and Jacob and all the prophets in the kingdom of God, but you yourselves thrown out. ²⁹People will come from east and west and north and south, and will take their places at the feast in the kingdom of God. ³⁰Indeed there are those who are last who will be first, and first who will be last."

Living in the Present

JOHN 4:35-38 "Do you not say, 'Four months more and then the harvest'? I tell you, open your eyes and look at the fields! They are ripe for harvest. ³⁶Even now the reaper draws his wages, even now he harvests the crop for eternal life, so that the sower and the reaper may be glad together. ³⁷Thus the saying 'One sows and another reaps' is true. ³⁸I sent you to reap what you have not worked for. Others have done the hard work, and you have reaped the benefits of their labor."

MATTHEW 6:11 "Give us today our daily bread."

MATTHEW 6:31-34 "So do not worry, saying, 'What shall we eat?' or 'What shall we drink?' or 'What shall we wear?' ³²For the pagans run after all these things, and your heavenly Father knows that you need them. ³³But seek first his kingdom and his righteousness, and all these things will be given to you as well. ³⁴Therefore do not worry about tomorrow, for tomorrow will worry about itself. Each day has enough trouble of its own."

LUKE 9:62 Jesus replied, "No one who puts his hand to the plow and looks back is fit for service in the kingdom of God."

LUKE 10:2-12 He told them [the seventy-two who were sent out], "The harvest is plentiful, but the workers are few. Ask the Lord of the harvest, therefore, to send out workers into his harvest field. [3]Go! I am sending you out like lambs among wolves. [4]Do not take a purse or bag or sandals; and do not greet anyone on the road. [5]When you enter a house, first say, 'Peace to this house.' [6]If a man of peace is there, your peace will rest on him; if not, it will return to you. [7]Stay in that house, eating and drinking whatever they give you, for the worker deserves his wages. Do not move around from house to house. [8]When you enter a town and are welcomed, eat what is set before you. [9]Heal the sick who are there and tell them, 'The kingdom of God is near you.' [10]But when you enter a town and are not welcomed, go into its streets and say, [11]'Even the dust of your town that sticks to our feet we wipe off against you. Yet be sure of this: The kingdom of God is near.' [12]I tell you, it will be more bearable on that day for Sodom than for that town."

LUKE 12:16-21 And he told them this parable: "The ground of a certain rich man produced a good crop. [17]He thought to himself, 'What shall I do? I have no place to store my crops.' [18]Then he said, 'This is what I'll do. I will tear down my barns and build bigger ones, and there I will store all my grain and my goods. [19]And I'll say to myself, "You have plenty of good things laid up for many years. Take life easy; eat, drink and be merry."' [20]But God said to him, 'You fool! This very night your life will be demanded from you. Then who will get what you have prepared for yourself?' [21]This is how it will be with anyone who stores up things for himself but is not rich toward God."

Living Water

JOHN 4:7-11, 13-14 When a Samaritan woman came to draw water, Jesus said to her, "Will you give me a drink?" [8](His disciples had gone into the town to buy food.) [9]The Samaritan woman said to him, "You are a Jew and I am a Samaritan woman. How can you ask me for a drink?" (For Jews do not associate with Samaritans.) [10]Jesus answered her, "If you knew the gift of God and who it is that asks you for a drink, you would have asked him and he would have given you living water." [11]"Sir," the woman said, "you have nothing to draw with and the well is deep. Where can you get this living water?" [13]Jesus answered, "Everyone who drinks this water will be thirsty again, [14]but whoever drinks the water I give him will never thirst. Indeed, the water I give him will become in him a spring of water welling up to eternal life."

JOHN 7:37-38 On the last and greatest day of the Feast, Jesus stood and said in a loud voice, "If anyone is thirsty, let him come to me and drink. [38]Whoever believes in me, as the Scripture has said, streams of living water will flow from within him."

Love

JOHN 13:34-35 "A new command I give you: Love one another. As I have loved you, so you must love one another. [35]By this all men will know that you are my disciples, if you love one another."

JOHN 15:11-13 "I have told you this so that my joy may be in you and that your joy may be complete. [12]My command is this: Love each other as I have loved you. [13]Greater love has no one than this, that he lay down his life for his friends."

JOHN 15:16-17 "You did not choose me, but I chose you and appointed you to go and bear fruit—fruit that will last. Then the Father will give you whatever you ask in my name. [17]This is my command: Love each other."

MATTHEW 5:43-46 "You have heard that it was said, 'Love your neighbor and hate your enemy.' [44]But I tell you: Love your enemies and pray for those who persecute you, [45]that you may be sons of your Father in heaven. He causes his sun to rise on the evil and the good, and sends rain on the righteous and the unrighteous. [46]If you love those who love you, what reward will you get? Are not even the tax collectors doing that?"

MATTHEW 19:19 " '[H]onor your father and mother,' and 'love your neighbor as yourself.' "

MARK 12:30-31 " 'Love the Lord your God with all your heart and with all your soul and with all your mind and with all your strength.' [31]The second is this: 'Love your neighbor as yourself.' There is no commandment greater than these."

LUKE 6:27-36 "But I tell you who hear me: Love your enemies, do good to those who hate you, [28]bless those who curse you, pray for those who mistreat you. [29]If someone strikes you on one cheek, turn to him the other also. If someone takes your cloak, do not stop him from taking your tunic. [30]Give to everyone who asks you, and if anyone takes what belongs to you, do not demand it back. [31]Do to others as you would have them do to you. [32]If you love those who love you, what credit is that to you? Even 'sinners' love those who love them. [33]And if you do good to those who are good to you, what credit is that to you? Even 'sinners' do that. [34]And if you lend to those from whom you expect repayment, what credit is that to you? Even 'sinners' lend to 'sinners,' expecting to be repaid in full. [35]But love your enemies, do good to them, and lend to them without expecting to get anything back. Then your reward will be great, and you will be sons of the Most High, because he is kind to the ungrateful and wicked. [36]Be merciful, just as your Father is merciful."

LUKE 10:29-37 But he [an expert in the law] wanted to justify himself, so he asked Jesus, "And who is my neighbor?" [30]In reply Jesus said: "A man was going down from Jerusalem to Jericho, when he fell into the hands of robbers. They stripped him of his clothes, beat him and went away, leaving him half dead. [31]A priest happened to be going down the same road, and when he saw the man, he passed by on the other side. [32]So too, a Levite, when he came to the place and saw him, passed by on the other side. [33]But a Samaritan, as he traveled, came where the man was; and when he saw him, he took pity on him. [34]He went to him and bandaged his wounds, pouring on oil and wine. Then he put the man on his own donkey, took him to an inn and took care of him. 35The next day he took out two silver coins and gave them to the innkeeper. 'Look after him,' he said, 'and when I return, I will reimburse you for any extra expense you may have.' 36Which of these three do you think was a neighbor to the man who fell into the hands of robbers?" 37The expert in the law replied, "The one who had mercy on him." Jesus told him, "Go and do likewise."

Loving Christ

JOHN 10:27 "My sheep listen to my voice; I know them, and they follow me."

JOHN 14:15-16 "If you love me, you will obey what I command. 16And I will ask the Father, and he will give you another Counselor to be with you forever."

JOHN 14:21 "Whoever has my commands and obeys them, he is the one who loves me. He who loves me will be loved by my Father, and I too will love him and show myself to him."

JOHN 14:23-24 Jesus replied, "If anyone loves me, he will obey my teaching. My Father will love him, and we will come to him and make our home with him. 24He who does not love me will not obey my teaching. These words you hear are not my own; they belong to the Father who sent me."

JOHN 21:15-17 When they had finished eating, Jesus said to Simon Peter, "Simon son of John, do you truly love me more than these?" "Yes, Lord," he said, "you know that I love you." Jesus said,

"Feed my lambs." 16Again Jesus said, "Simon son of John, do you truly love me?" He answered, "Yes, Lord, you know that I love you." Jesus said, "Take care of my sheep." 17The third time he said to him, "Simon son of John, do you love me?" Peter was hurt because Jesus asked him the third time, "Do you love me?" He said, "Lord, you know all things; you know that I love you." Jesus said, "Feed my sheep."

LUKE 7:41-48 "Two men owed money to a certain moneylender. One owed him five hundred denarii, and the other fifty. 42Neither of them had the money to pay him back, so he canceled the debts of both. Now which of them will love him more?" 43Simon replied, "I suppose the one who had the bigger debt canceled." "You have judged correctly," Jesus said. 44Then he turned toward the woman and said to Simon, "Do you see this woman? I came into your house. You did not give me any water for my feet, but she wet my feet with her tears and wiped them with her hair. 45You did not give me a kiss, but this woman, from the time I entered, has not stopped kissing my feet. 46You did not put oil on my head, but she has poured perfume on my feet. 47Therefore, I tell you, her many sins have been forgiven—for she loved much. But he who has been forgiven little loves little." 48Then Jesus said to her, "Your sins are forgiven."

LUKE 10:41-42 "Martha, Martha," the Lord answered, "you are worried and upset about many things, 42but only one thing is needed. Mary has chosen what is better, and it will not be taken away from her."

Masters and Those in Authority

JOHN 8:32-34 "And you shall know the truth, and the truth shall make you free." [33]They answered Him, "We are Abraham's descendants, and have never been in bondage to anyone. How can you say, 'You will be made free'?" [34]Jesus answered them, "Most assuredly, I say to you, whoever commits sin is a slave of sin." (NKJV)

JOHN 13:12-17 When he [Jesus] had finished washing their [the disciples'] feet, he put on his clothes and returned to his place. "Do you understand what I have done for you?" he asked them. [13]"You call me 'Teacher' and 'Lord,' and rightly so, for that is what I am. [14]Now that I, your Lord and Teacher, have washed your feet, you also should wash one another's feet. [15]I have set you an example that you should do as I have done for you. [16]I tell you the truth, no servant is greater than his master, nor is a messenger greater than the one who sent him. [17]Now that you know these things, you will be blessed if you do them."

JOHN 15:15-17 "I no longer call you servants, because a servant does not know his master's business. Instead, I have called you friends, for everything that I learned from my Father I have made known to you. [16]You did not choose me, but I chose you and appointed you to go and bear fruit—fruit that will last. Then the Father will give you whatever you ask in my name. [17]This is my command: Love each other."

MATTHEW 6:24 "No one can serve two masters. Either he will hate the one and love the other, or he will be devoted to the one and despise the other. You cannot serve both God and Money."

MATTHEW 10:24 "A student is not above his teacher, nor a servant above his master."

MATTHEW 23:8 "But you are not to be called 'Rabbi,' for you have only one Master and you are all brothers."

MATTHEW 24:45-46 "Who then is the faithful and wise servant, whom the master has put in charge of the servants in his household to give them their food at the proper time? [46]It will be good for that servant whose master finds him doing so when he returns."

MATTHEW 28:18 Then Jesus came to them [the eleven disciples] and said, "All authority in heaven and on earth has been given to me."

LUKE 16:13 "No servant can serve two masters. Either he will hate the one and love the other, or he will be devoted to the one and despise the other. You cannot serve both God and Money."

The Mission of a Christian

In chapter 1 of this book, Jesus revealed more than twenty missions that He came to earth to fulfill. In His short life He fulfilled every one of them, and most were fulfilled in less than four years during His public ministry. In this section we look at the various missions Jesus calls us to fulfill. Some are stated in general terms; others are more specific. Some are implied from statements that Jesus made to His apostles, such as telling Peter to "feed my lambs" and "take care of my sheep."

Others—like "store up…treasures in heaven" rather than treasures on earth—are given directly to all who desire to follow Christ. We're told to bear fruit, to sow seeds and reap the harvest. There are many extraordinary insights and revelations in this section; don't try to take in all that Jesus said in a single sitting. Underline the statements and missions that you feel relate to your specific callings and opportunities right now. As you'll see, it's not enough to be "purpose driven." Jesus wants us to be "purpose accomplished"—Christians who are driven by their missions and accomplish the missions they are called to fulfill. Entire sermons could be preached on any one of these passages, so prayerfully approach each one.

JOHN 4:35-38 "Do you not say, 'Four months more and then the harvest'? I tell you, open your eyes and look at the fields! They are ripe for harvest. ³⁶Even now the reaper draws his wages, even now he harvests the crop for eternal life, so that the sower and the reaper may be glad together. ³⁷Thus the saying 'One sows and another reaps' is true. ³⁸I sent you to reap what you have not worked for. Others have done the hard work, and you have reaped the benefits of their labor."

JOHN 15:1-8 "I am the true vine, and my Father is the gardener. ²He cuts off every branch in me that bears no fruit, while every branch that does bear fruit he prunes so that it will be even more fruitful. ³You are already clean because of the word I have spoken to you. ⁴Remain in me, and I will remain in you. No branch can bear fruit by itself; it must remain in the vine.

Neither can you bear fruit unless you remain in me. ⁵I am the vine; you are the branches. If a man remains in me and I in him, he will bear much fruit; apart from me you can do nothing. ⁶If anyone does not remain in me, he is like a branch that is thrown away and withers; such branches are picked up, thrown into the fire and burned. ⁷If you remain in me and my words remain in you, ask whatever you wish, and it will be given you. ⁸This is to my Father's glory, that you bear much fruit, showing yourselves to be my disciples."

JOHN 15:11-15 "I have told you this so that my joy may be in you and that your joy may be complete. ¹²My command is this: Love each other as I have loved you. ¹³Greater love has no one than this, that he lay down his life for his friends. ¹⁴You are my friends if you do what I command. ¹⁵I no longer call you servants, because a servant does not know his master's business. Instead, I have called you friends, for everything that I learned from my Father I have made known to you."

JOHN 17:13-26 "I am coming to you [God the Father] now, but I say these things while I am still in the world, so that they may have the full measure of my joy within them. ¹⁴I have given them your word and the world has hated them, for they are not of the world any more than I am of the world. ¹⁵My prayer is not that you take them out of the world but that you protect them from the evil one. ¹⁶They are not of the world, even as I am not of it. ¹⁷Sanctify them by the truth; your word is truth. ¹⁸As you sent me into the world, I have sent them into the world. [19]For them I sanctify myself, that they too may be truly sanctified. [20]My prayer is not for them alone. I pray also for those who will believe in me through their message, [21]that all of them may be one, Father, just as you are in me and I am in you. May they also be in us so that the world may believe that you have sent me. [22]I have given them the glory that you gave me, that they may be one as we are one: [23]I in them and you in me. May they be brought to complete unity to let the world know that you sent me and have loved them even as you have loved me. [24]Father, I want those you have given me to be with me where I am, and to see my glory, the glory you have given me because you loved me before the creation of the world. [25]Righteous Father, though the world does not know you, I know you, and they know that you have sent me. [26]I have made you known to them, and will continue to make you known in order that the love you have for me may be in them and that I myself may be in them."

JOHN 21:15-17 When they had finished eating, Jesus said to Simon Peter, "Simon son of John, do you truly love me more than these?" "Yes, Lord," he said, "you know that I love you." Jesus said, "Feed my lambs." [16]Again Jesus said, "Simon son of John, do you truly love me?" He answered, "Yes, Lord, you know that I love you." Jesus said, "Take care of my sheep." [17]The third time he said to him, "Simon son of John, do you love me?" Peter was hurt because Jesus asked him the third time, "Do you love me?" He said, "Lord, you know all things; you know that I love you." Jesus said, "Feed my sheep."

MATTHEW 4:19 "Come, follow me," Jesus said, "and I will make you fishers of men."

MATTHEW 5:10-11 "Blessed are those who are persecuted because of righteousness, for theirs is the kingdom of heaven. [11]Blessed are you when people insult you, persecute you and falsely say all kinds of evil against you because of me."

MATTHEW 5:13 "You are the salt of the earth. But if the salt loses its saltiness, how can it be made salty again? It is no longer good for anything, except to be thrown out and trampled by men."

MATTHEW 5:14-16 "You are the light of the world. A city on a hill cannot be hidden. [15]Neither do people light a lamp and put it under a bowl. Instead they put it on its stand, and it gives light to everyone in the house. [16]In the same way, let your light shine before men, that they may see your good deeds and praise your Father in heaven."

MATTHEW 5:19-20 "Anyone who breaks one of the least of these commandments and teaches others to do the same will be called least in the kingdom of heaven, but whoever practices and teaches these commands will be called great in the kingdom of heaven. [20]For I tell you that unless your righteousness surpasses that of the Pharisees and the teachers of the law, you will certainly not enter the kingdom of heaven."

MATTHEW 5:38-46 "You have heard that it was said, 'Eye for eye, and tooth for tooth.' [39]But I tell you, Do not resist an evil person. If someone strikes you on the right cheek, turn to him the other also. [40]And if someone wants to sue you and take your tunic, let him have your cloak as well. ⁴¹If someone forces you to go one mile, go with him two miles. ⁴²Give to the one who asks you, and do not turn away from the one who wants to borrow from you. ⁴³You have heard that it was said, 'Love your neighbor and hate your enemy.' ⁴⁴But I tell you: Love your enemies and pray for those who persecute you, ⁴⁵that you may be sons of your Father in heaven. He causes his sun to rise on the evil and the good, and sends rain on the righteous and the unrighteous. ⁴⁶If you love those who love you, what reward will you get? Are not even the tax collectors doing that?"

MATTHEW 5:48 "Be perfect, therefore, as your heavenly Father is perfect."

MATTHEW 6:19-21 "Do not store up for yourselves treasures on earth, where moth and rust destroy, and where thieves break in and steal. ²⁰But store up for yourselves treasures in heaven, where moth and rust do not destroy, and where thieves do not break in and steal. ²¹For where your treasure is, there your heart will be also."

MATTHEW 6:24-34 "No one can serve two masters. Either he will hate the one and love the other, or he will be devoted to the one and despise the other. You cannot serve both God and Money. ²⁵Therefore I tell you, do not worry about your life, what you will eat or drink; or about your body, what you will wear. Is not life more important than food, and the body more important than clothes? ²⁶Look at the birds of the air; they do not sow or reap or store away in barns, and yet your heavenly Father feeds them. Are you not much more valuable than they? ²⁷Who of

you by worrying can add a single hour to his life? ²⁸And why do you worry about clothes? See how the lilies of the field grow. They do not labor or spin. ²⁹Yet I tell you that not even Solomon in all his splendor was dressed like one of these. ³⁰If that is how God clothes the grass of the field, which is here today and tomorrow is thrown into the fire, will he not much more clothe you, O you of little faith? ³¹So do not worry, saying, 'What shall we eat?' or 'What shall we drink?' or 'What shall we wear?' ³²For the pagans run after all these things, and your heavenly Father knows that you need them. ³³But seek first his kingdom and his righteousness, and all these things will be given to you as well. ³⁴Therefore do not worry about tomorrow, for tomorrow will worry about itself. Each day has enough trouble of its own."

MATTHEW 10:27 "What I tell you in the dark, speak in the daylight; what is whispered in your ear, proclaim from the roofs."

MATTHEW 10:28-31 "Do not be afraid of those who kill the body but cannot kill the soul. Rather, be afraid of the One who can destroy both soul and body in hell. ²⁹Are not two sparrows sold for a penny? Yet not one of them will fall to the ground apart from the will of your Father. ³⁰And even the very hairs of your head are all numbered. ³¹So don't be afraid; you are worth more than many sparrows."

MATTHEW 10:32-33 "Whoever acknowledges me before men, I will also acknowledge him before my Father in heaven. ³³But whoever disowns me before men, I will disown him before my Father in heaven."

MATTHEW 10:34-39 "Do not suppose that I have come to bring peace to the earth. I did not come to bring peace, but a sword. [35]For I have come to turn 'a man against his father, a daughter against her mother, a daughter-in-law against her mother-in-law— [36]a man's enemies will be the members of his own household.' [37]Anyone who loves his father or mother more than me is not worthy of me; anyone who loves his son or daughter more than me is not worthy of me; [38]and anyone who does not take his cross and follow me is not worthy of me. [39]Whoever finds his life will lose it, and whoever loses his life for my sake will find it."

MATTHEW 11:28-30 "Come to me, all you who are weary and burdened, and I will give you rest. [29]Take my yoke upon you and learn from me, for I am gentle and humble in heart, and you will find rest for your souls. [30]For my yoke is easy and my burden is light."

MATTHEW 12:50 "For whoever does the will of my Father in heaven is my brother and sister and mother."

MATTHEW 13:16-17 "But blessed are your eyes because they see, and your ears because they hear. [17]For I tell you the truth, many prophets and righteous men longed to see what you see but did not see it, and to hear what you hear but did not hear it."

MATTHEW 20:25-28 Jesus called them [the disciples] together and said, "You know that the rulers of the Gentiles lord it over them, and their high officials exercise authority over them. [26]Not so with you. Instead, whoever wants to become great among you must be your serv-ant, [27]and whoever wants to be first must be your slave— [28]just as the Son of Man did not come to be served, but to serve, and to give his life as a ransom for many."

MATTHEW 28:18-20 Then Jesus came to them [the eleven disciples] and said, "All authority in heaven and on earth has been given to me. [19]Therefore go and make disciples of all nations, baptizing them in the name of the Father and of the Son and of the Holy Spirit, [20]and teaching them to obey everything I have commanded you. And surely I am with you always, to the very end of the age."

MARK 9:41 "I tell you the truth, anyone who gives you a cup of water in my name because you belong to Christ will certainly not lose his reward."

MARK 16:15-18 He said to them [the Eleven], "Go into all the world and preach the good news to all creation. [16]Whoever believes and is baptized will be saved, but whoever does not believe will be condemned. [17]And these signs will accompany those who believe: In my name they will drive out demons; they will speak in new tongues; [18]they will pick up snakes with their hands; and when they drink deadly poison, it will not hurt them at all; they will place their hands on sick people, and they will get well."[xv]

LUKE 4:8 Jesus answered, "It is written: 'Worship the Lord your God and serve him only.'" (See also Matthew 4:10.)

LUKE 4:12 Jesus answered, "It says: 'Do not put the Lord your God to the test.'" (See also Matthew 4:7.)

LUKE 5:9-10 For he [Simon Peter] and all his companions were astonished at the catch of fish they had taken, [10]and so were James and John, the sons of Zebedee, Simon's partners. Then Jesus said to Simon, "Don't be afraid; from now on you will catch men."

LUKE 5:27 After this, Jesus went out and saw a tax collector by the name of Levi sitting at his tax booth. "Follow me," Jesus said to him, 28and Levi got up, left everything and followed him.

LUKE 6:46-49 "Why do you call me, 'Lord, Lord,' and do not do what I say? 47I will show you what he is like who comes to me and hears my words and puts them into practice. 48He is like a man building a house, who dug down deep and laid the foundation on rock. When a flood came, the torrent struck that house but could not shake it, because it was well built. 49But the one who hears my words and does not put them into practice is like a man who built a house on the ground without a foundation. The moment the torrent struck that house, it collapsed and its destruction was complete."

LUKE 9:62 Jesus replied, "No one who puts his hand to the plow and looks back is fit for service in the kingdom of God."

LUKE 10:2-3 He told them [the seventy-two who were sent out], "The harvest is plentiful, but the workers are few. Ask the Lord of the harvest, therefore, to send out workers into his harvest field. 3Go! I am sending you out like lambs among wolves."

LUKE 12:1 Meanwhile, when a crowd of many thousands had gathered, so that they were trampling on one another, Jesus began to speak first to his disciples, saying: "Be on your guard against the yeast of the Pharisees, which is hypocrisy."

LUKE 12:22-23 Then Jesus said to his disciples: "Therefore I tell you, do not worry about your life, what you will eat; or about your body, what you will wear. 23Life is more than food, and the body more than clothes."

LUKE 12:29-34 "And do not set your heart on what you will eat or drink; do not worry about it. 30For the pagan world runs after all such things, and your Father knows that you need them. 31But seek his kingdom, and these things will be given to you as well. 32Do not be afraid, little flock, for your Father has been pleased to give you the kingdom. 33Sell your possessions and give to the poor. Provide purses for yourselves that will not wear out, a treasure in heaven that will not be exhausted, where no thief comes near and no moth destroys. 34For where your treasure is, there your heart will be also."

LUKE 12:35-37 "Be dressed ready for service and keep your lamps burning, 36like men waiting for their master to return from a wedding banquet, so that when he comes and knocks they can immediately open the door for him. 37It will be good for those servants whose master finds them watching when he comes. I tell you the truth, he will dress himself to serve, will have them recline at the table and will come and wait on them."

LUKE 12:42-48 The Lord answered, "Who then is the faithful and wise manager, whom the master puts in charge of his servants to give them their food allowance at the proper time? 43It will be good for that servant whom the master finds doing so when he returns. ⁴⁴I tell you the truth, he will put him in charge of all his possessions. ⁴⁵But suppose the servant says to himself, 'My master is taking a long time in coming,' and he then begins to beat the menservants and maidservants and to eat and drink and get drunk. ⁴⁶The master of that servant will come on a day when he does not expect him and at an hour he is not aware of. He will cut him to pieces and assign him a place with the unbelievers. ⁴⁷That servant who knows his master's will and does not get ready or does not do what his master wants will be beaten with many blows. ⁴⁸But the one who does not know and does things deserving punishment will be beaten with few blows. From everyone who has been given much, much will be demanded; and from the one who has been entrusted with much, much more will be asked."

LUKE 13:6-9 Then he told this parable: "A man had a fig tree, planted in his vineyard, and he went to look for fruit on it, but did not find any. ⁷So he said to the man who took care of the vineyard, 'For three years now I've been coming to look for fruit on this fig tree and haven't found any. Cut it down! Why should it use up the soil?' ⁸'Sir,' the man replied, 'leave it alone for one more year, and I'll dig around it and fertilize it. ⁹If it bears fruit next year, fine! If not, then cut it down.' "

LUKE 17:7-10 "Suppose one of you had a servant plowing or looking after the sheep. Would he say to the servant when he comes in from the field, 'Come along now and sit down to eat'? ⁸Would he not rather say, 'Prepare my supper, get yourself

ready and wait on me while I eat and drink; after that you may eat and drink'? ⁹Would he thank the servant because he did what he was told to do? ¹⁰So you also, when you have done everything you were told to do, should say, 'We are unworthy servants; we have only done our duty.' "

LUKE 20:22-25 "Is it right for us to pay taxes to Caesar or not?" ²³He [Jesus] saw through their duplicity and said to them, ²⁴"Show me a denarius. Whose portrait and inscription are on it?" ²⁵"Caesar's," they replied. He said to them, "Then give to Caesar what is Caesar's, and to God what is God's." (See also Matthew 22:17-21; Mark 12:14-17.)

LUKE 22:31-32 "Simon, Simon, Satan has asked to sift you as wheat. ³²But I have prayed for you, Simon, that your faith may not fail. And when you have turned back, strengthen your brothers."

LUKE 24:46-49 He told them [the disciples], "This is what is written: The Christ will suffer and rise from the dead on the third day, ⁴⁷and repentance and forgiveness of sins will be preached in his name to all nations, beginning at Jerusalem. ⁴⁸You are witnesses of these things. ⁴⁹I am going to send you what my Father has promised; but stay in the city until you have been clothed with power from on high."

ACTS 1:8 "But you will receive power when the Holy Spirit comes on you; and you will be my witnesses in Jerusalem, and in all Judea and Samaria, and to the ends of the earth."

REVELATION 2:2-5 "I know your deeds, your hard work and your perseverance. I know that you cannot tolerate wicked men, that you have tested those who claim to be apostles but are not, and have found them false. [3]You have persevered and have endured hardships for my name, and have not grown weary. [4]Yet I hold this against you: You have forsaken your first love. [5]Remember the height from which you have fallen! Repent and do the things you did at first. If you do not repent, I will come to you and remove your lampstand from its place."

REVELATION 2:7 "He who has an ear, let him hear what the Spirit says to the churches. To him who overcomes, I will give the right to eat from the tree of life, which is in the paradise of God."

REVELATION 2:9-11 "I know your afflictions and your poverty—yet you are rich! I know the slander of those who say they are Jews and are not, but are a synagogue of Satan. [10]Do not be afraid of what you are about to suffer. I tell you, the devil will put some of you in prison to test you, and you will suffer persecution for ten days. Be faithful, even to the point of death, and I will give you the crown of life. [11]He who has an ear, let him hear what the Spirit says to the churches. He who overcomes will not be hurt at all by the second death."

REVELATION 2:13 "I know where you live—where Satan has his throne. Yet you remain true to my name. You did not renounce your faith in me, even in the days of Antipas, my faithful witness, who was put to death in your city—where Satan lives."

REVELATION 2:17 "He who has an ear, let him hear what the Spirit says to the churches. To him who overcomes, I will

give some of the hidden manna. I will also give him a white stone with a new name written on it, known only to him who receives it."

REVELATION 2:19 "I know your deeds, your love and faith, your service and perseverance, and that you are now doing more than you did at first."

REVELATION 2:25-26 "Only hold on to what you have until I come. [26]To him who overcomes and does my will to the end, I will give authority over the nations."

REVELATION 3:2-4 "Wake up! Strengthen what remains and is about to die, for I have not found your deeds complete in the sight of my God. [3]Remember, therefore, what you have received and heard; obey it, and repent. But if you do not wake up, I will come like a thief, and you will not know at what time I will come to you. [4]Yet you have a few people in Sardis who have not soiled their clothes. They will walk with me, dressed in white, for they are worthy."

REVELATION 3:8 "I know your deeds. See, I have placed before you an open door that no one can shut. I know that you have little strength, yet you have kept my word and have not denied my name."

REVELATION 3:10-12 "Since you have kept my command to endure patiently, I will also keep you from the hour of trial that is going to come upon the whole world to test those who live on the earth. [11]I am coming soon. Hold on to what you have, so that no one will take your crown. [12]Him who overcomes I will make a pillar in the temple of my God.

Never again will he leave it. I will write on him the name of my God and the name of the city of my God, the new Jerusalem, which is coming down out of heaven from my God; and I will also write on him my new name."

REVELATION 3:15-18 "I know your deeds, that you are neither cold nor hot. I wish you were either one or the other! [16]So, because you are lukewarm—neither hot nor cold—I am about to spit you out of my mouth. [17]You say, 'I am rich; I have acquired wealth and do not need a thing.' But you do not realize that you are wretched, pitiful, poor, blind and naked. [18]I counsel you to buy from me gold refined in the fire, so you can become rich; and white clothes to wear, so you can cover your shameful nakedness; and salve to put on your eyes, so you can see."

Obedience and Good Works

JOHN 4:49-53 The royal official said, "Sir, come down before my child dies." [50]Jesus replied, "You may go. Your son will live." The man took Jesus at his word and departed. [51]While he was still on the way, his servants met him with the news that his boy was living. [52]When he inquired as to the time when his son got better, they said to him, "The fever left him yesterday at the seventh hour." [53]Then the father realized that this was the exact time at which Jesus had said to him, "Your son will live." So he and all his household believed.

JOHN 5:5-14 One who was there had been an invalid for thirty-eight years.

[6]When Jesus saw him lying there and learned that he had been in this condition for a long time, he asked him, "Do you want to get well?" [7]"Sir," the invalid replied, "I have no one to help me into the pool when the water is stirred. While I am trying to get in, someone else goes down ahead of me." [8]Then Jesus said to him, "Get up! Pick up your mat and walk." [9]At once the man was cured; he picked up his mat and walked. The day on which this took place was a Sabbath, [10]and so the Jews said to the man who had been healed, "It is the Sabbath; the law forbids you to carry your mat." [11]But he replied, "The man who made me well said to me, 'Pick up your mat and walk.'" [12]So they asked him, "Who is this fellow who told you to pick it up and walk?" [13]The man who was healed had no idea who it was, for Jesus had slipped away into the crowd that was there. [14]Later Jesus found him at the temple and said to him, "See, you are well again. Stop sinning or something worse may happen to you."

JOHN 6:5-13 When Jesus looked up and saw a great crowd coming toward him, he said to Philip, "Where shall we buy bread for these people to eat?" [6]He asked this only to test him, for he already had in mind what he was going to do. [7]Philip answered him, "Eight months' wages would not buy enough bread for each one to have a bite!" [8]Another of his disciples, Andrew, Simon Peter's brother, spoke up, [9]"Here is a boy with five small barley loaves and two small fish, but how far will they go among so many?" [10]Jesus said, "Have the people sit down." There was plenty of grass in that place, and the men sat down, about five thousand of them. [11]Jesus then took the loaves, gave thanks, and distributed to those who were seated as much as they wanted. He did the same with the fish. [12]When they had all had enough to eat, he said to his disciples, "Gather the pieces that are left over. Let nothing be wasted." [13]So they gathered them and filled twelve baskets with the pieces of the five barley loaves left over by those who had eaten.

John 8:51 "I tell you the truth, if anyone keeps my word, he will never see death."

John 10:27 "My sheep listen to my voice; I know them, and they follow me."

John 14:12 "I tell you the truth, anyone who has faith in me will do what I have been doing. He will do even greater things than these, because I am going to the Father."

John 14:15 "If you love me, you will obey what I command."

John 14:21 "Whoever has my commands and obeys them, he is the one who loves me. He who loves me will be loved by my Father, and I too will love him and show myself to him."

John 14:23-24 Jesus replied, "If anyone loves me, he will obey my teaching. My Father will love him, and we will come to him and make our home with him. [24]He who does not love me will not obey my teaching. These words you hear are not my own; they belong to the Father who sent me."

John 15:10 "If you obey my commands, you will remain in my love, just as I have obeyed my Father's commands and remain in his love."

John 15:14 "You are my friends if you do what I command."

John 15:16-17 "You did not choose me, but I chose you and appointed you to go and bear fruit—fruit that will last. Then the Father will give you whatever you ask in my name. [17]This is my command: Love each other."

Matthew 5:14-20 "You are the light of the world. A city on a hill cannot be hidden. [15]Neither do people light a lamp and put it under a bowl. Instead they put it on its stand, and it gives light to everyone in the house. [16]In the same way, let your light shine before men, that they may see your good deeds and praise your Father in heaven. [17]Do not think that I have come to abolish the Law or the Prophets; I have not come to abolish them but to fulfill them. [18]I tell you the truth, until heaven and earth disappear, not the smallest letter, not the least stroke of a pen, will by any means disappear from the Law until everything is accomplished. [19]Anyone who breaks one of the least of these commandments and teaches others to do the same will be called least in the kingdom of heaven, but whoever practices and teaches these commands will be called great in the kingdom of heaven. [20]For I tell you that unless your righteousness surpasses that of the Pharisees and the teachers of the law, you will certainly not enter the kingdom of heaven."

Matthew 7:21-27 "Not everyone who says to Me, 'Lord, Lord,' shall enter the kingdom of heaven, but he who does the will of My Father in heaven. [22]Many will say to Me in that day, 'Lord, Lord, have we not prophesied in Your name, cast out demons in Your name, and done many wonders in Your name?' ²³And then I will declare to them, 'I never knew you; depart from Me, you who practice lawlessness!' ²⁴Therefore whoever hears these sayings of Mine, and does them, I will liken him to a wise man who built his house on the rock: ²⁵and the rain descended, the floods came, and the winds blew and beat on that house; and it did not fall, for it was founded on the rock. ²⁶But everyone who hears these sayings of Mine, and does not do them, will be like a foolish man who built his house on the sand: ²⁷and the rain descended, the floods came, and the winds blew and beat on that house; and it fell. And great was its fall." (NKJV)

MATTHEW 12:49-50 Pointing to his disciples, he said, "Here are my mother and my brothers. ⁵⁰For whoever does the will of my Father in heaven is my brother and sister and mother." (See also Mark 3:34-35.)

MATTHEW 14:15-20 As evening approached, the disciples came to him and said, "This is a remote place, and it's already getting late. Send the crowds away, so they can go to the villages and buy themselves some food." ¹⁶Jesus replied, "They do not need to go away. You give them something to eat." ¹⁷"We have here only five loaves of bread and two fish," they answered. ¹⁸"Bring them here to me," he said. ¹⁹And he directed the people to sit down on the grass. Taking the five loaves and the two fish and looking up to heaven, he gave thanks and broke the loaves. Then he gave them to the disciples, and the disciples gave them to the people. ²⁰They all ate and were satisfied, and the

disciples picked up twelve basketfuls of broken pieces that were left over.

MATTHEW 15:32-37 Jesus called his disciples to him and said, "I have compassion for these people; they have already been with me three days and have nothing to eat. I do not want to send them away hungry, or they may collapse on the way." ³³His disciples answered, "Where could we get enough bread in this remote place to feed such a crowd?" ³⁴"How many loaves do you have?" Jesus asked. "Seven," they replied, "and a few small fish." ³⁵He told the crowd to sit down on the ground. ³⁶Then he took the seven loaves and the fish, and when he had given thanks, he broke them and gave them to the disciples, and they in turn to the people. ³⁷They all ate and were satisfied. Afterward the disciples picked up seven basketfuls of broken pieces that were left over.

MATTHEW 26:42-46 He went away a second time and prayed, "My Father, if it is not possible for this cup to be taken away unless I drink it, may your will be done." ⁴³When he came back, he again found them sleeping, because their eyes were heavy. ⁴⁴So he left them and went away once more and prayed the third time, saying the same thing. ⁴⁵Then he returned to the disciples and said to them, "Are you still sleeping and resting? Look, the hour is near, and the Son of Man is betrayed into the hands of sinners. ⁴⁶Rise, let us go! Here comes my betrayer!" (See also Mark 14:39-42.)

MARK 6:35-43 By this time it was late in the day, so his disciples came to him. "This is a remote place," they said, "and it's already very late. ³⁶Send the people away so they can go to the surrounding countryside and villages and buy themselves something to eat." [37]But he answered, "You give them something to eat." They said to him, "That would take eight months of a man's wages! Are we to go and spend that much on bread and give it to them to eat?" [38]"How many loaves do you have?" he asked. "Go and see." When they found out, they said, "Five—and two fish." [39]Then Jesus directed them to have all the people sit down in groups on the green grass. [40]So they sat down in groups of hundreds and fifties. [41]Taking the five loaves and the two fish and looking up to heaven, he gave thanks and broke the loaves. Then he gave them to his disciples to set before the people. He also divided the two fish among them all. [42]They all ate and were satisfied, [43]and the disciples picked up twelve basketfuls of broken pieces of bread and fish.

MARK 11:1-3 As they approached Jerusalem and came to Bethphage and Bethany at the Mount of Olives, Jesus sent two of his disciples, [2]saying to them, "Go to the village ahead of you, and just as you enter it, you will find a colt tied there, which no one has ever ridden. Untie it and bring it here. [3]If anyone asks you, 'Why are you doing this?' tell him, 'The Lord needs it and will send it back here shortly.'" (See also Matthew 21:1-3; Luke 19:29-31.)

MARK 14:12-16 On the first day of the Feast of Unleavened Bread, when it was customary to sacrifice the Passover lamb, Jesus' disciples asked him, "Where do you want us to go and make prepara-

tions for you to eat the Passover?" [13]So he sent two of his disciples, telling them, "Go into the city, and a man carrying a jar of water will meet you. Follow him. [14]Say to the owner of the house he enters, 'The Teacher asks: Where is my guest room, where I may eat the Passover with my disciples?' [15]He will show you a large upper room, furnished and ready. Make preparations for us there." [16]The disciples left, went into the city and found things just as Jesus had told them. So they prepared the Passover.

LUKE 5:4-6 When he had finished speaking, he said to Simon, "Put out into deep water, and let down the nets for a catch." [5]Simon answered, "Master, we've worked hard all night and haven't caught anything. But because you say so, I will let down the nets." [6]When they had done so, they caught such a large number of fish that their nets began to break.

LUKE 6:46-49 "Why do you call me, 'Lord, Lord,' and do not do what I say? [47]I will show you what he is like who comes to me and hears my words and puts them into practice. [48]He is like a man building a house, who dug down deep and laid the foundation on rock. When a flood came, the torrent struck that house but could not shake it, because it was well built. [49]But the one who hears my words and does not put them into practice is like a man who built a house on the ground without a foundation. The moment the torrent struck that house, it collapsed and its destruction was complete."

LUKE 8:11-15 "This is the meaning of the parable: The seed is the word of God. [12]Those along the path are the ones who hear, and then the devil comes and takes away the word from their hearts, so that they may not believe and be saved. [13]Those on the rock are the ones who receive the word with joy when they hear it, but they have no root. They believe for a while, but in the time of testing they fall away. [14]The seed that fell among thorns stands for those who hear, but as they go on their way they are choked by life's worries, riches and pleasures, and they do not mature. [15]But the seed on good soil stands for those with a noble and good heart, who hear the word, retain it, and by persevering produce a crop."

LUKE 8:21 He replied, "My mother and brothers are those who hear God's word and put it into practice."

LUKE 9:12-17 Late in the afternoon the Twelve came to him and said, "Send the crowd away so they can go to the surrounding villages and countryside and find food and lodging, because we are in a remote place here." [13]He replied, "You give them something to eat." They answered, "We have only five loaves of bread and two fish—unless we go and buy food for all this crowd." [14](About five thousand men were there.) But he said to his disciples, "Have them sit down in groups of about fifty each." [15]The disciples did so, and everybody sat down. [16]Taking the five loaves and the two fish and looking up to heaven, he gave thanks and broke them. Then he gave them to the disciples to set before the people. [17]They all ate and were satisfied, and the disciples picked up twelve basketfuls of broken pieces that were left over.

LUKE 11:28 He replied, "Blessed rather are those who hear the word of God and obey it."

LUKE 22:7-16 Then came the day of Unleavened Bread on which the Passover lamb had to be sacrificed. [8]Jesus sent Peter and John, saying, "Go and make preparations for us to eat the Passover." [9]"Where do you want us to prepare for it?" they asked. [10]He replied, "As you enter the city, a man carrying a jar of water will meet you. Follow him to the house that he enters, [11]and say to the owner of the house, 'The Teacher asks: Where is the guest room, where I may eat the Passover with my disciples?' [12]He will show you a large upper room, all furnished. Make preparations there." [13]They left and found things just as Jesus had told them. So they prepared the Passover. [14]When the hour came, Jesus and his apostles reclined at the table. [15]And he said to them, "I have eagerly desired to eat this Passover with you before I suffer. [16]For I tell you, I will not eat it again until it finds fulfillment in the kingdom of God."

ACTS 9:3-16 As he neared Damascus on his journey, suddenly a light from heaven flashed around him. [4]He fell to the ground and heard a voice say to him, "Saul, Saul, why do you persecute me?" [5]"Who are you, Lord?" Saul asked. "I am Jesus, whom you are persecuting," he replied. [6]"Now get up and go into the city, and you will be told what you must do." [7]The men traveling with Saul stood there speechless; they heard the sound but did not see anyone. [8]Saul got up from the ground, but when he opened his eyes he could see nothing. So they led him by the hand into Damascus. [9]For three days he was blind, and did not eat or drink anything. ¹⁰In Damascus there was a disciple named Ananias. The Lord called to him in a vision, "Ananias!" "Yes, Lord," he answered. ¹¹The Lord told him, "Go to the house of Judas on Straight Street and ask for a man from Tarsus named Saul, for he is praying. ¹²In a vision he has seen a man named Ananias come and place his hands on him to restore his sight." ¹³"Lord," Ananias answered, "I have heard many reports about this man and all the harm he has done to your saints in Jerusalem. ¹⁴And he has come here with authority from the chief priests to arrest all who call on your name." ¹⁵But the Lord said to Ananias, "Go! This man is my chosen instrument to carry my name before the Gentiles and their kings and before the people of Israel. ¹⁶I will show him how much he must suffer for my name." (See also Acts 22:6-10.)

Patience

LUKE 21:8-19 He replied: "Watch out that you are not deceived. For many will come in my name, claiming, 'I am he,' and, 'The time is near.' Do not follow them. ⁹When you hear of wars and revolutions, do not be frightened. These things must happen first, but the end will not come right away." ¹⁰Then he said to them: "Nation will rise against nation, and kingdom against kingdom. ¹¹There will be great earthquakes, famines and pestilences in various places, and fearful events and great signs from heaven. ¹²But before all this, they will lay hands on you and persecute you. They will deliver you

to synagogues and prisons, and you will be brought before kings and governors, and all on account of my name. ¹³This will result in your being witnesses to them. ¹⁴But make up your mind not to worry beforehand how you will defend yourselves. ¹⁵For I will give you words and wisdom that none of your adversaries will be able to resist or contradict. ¹⁶You will be betrayed even by parents, brothers, relatives and friends, and they will put some of you to death. ¹⁷All men will hate you because of me. ¹⁸But not a hair of your head will perish. ¹⁹By standing firm you will gain life."

REVELATION 3:10-11 "Since you have kept my command to endure patiently, I will also keep you from the hour of trial that is going to come upon the whole world to test those who live on the earth. ¹¹I am coming soon. Hold on to what you have, so that no one will take your crown."

Praise

JOHN 5:41-44 "I do not accept praise from men, ⁴²but I know you. I know that you do not have the love of God in your hearts. ⁴³I have come in my Father's name, and you do not accept me; but if someone else comes in his own name, you will accept him. ⁴⁴How can you believe if you accept praise from one another, yet make no effort to obtain the praise that comes from the only God?"

MATTHEW 5:16 "In the same way, let your light shine before men, that they may see your good deeds and praise your Father in heaven."

MATTHEW 11:25-26 At that time Jesus said, "I praise you, Father, Lord of heaven and earth, because you have hidden these things from the wise and learned, and revealed them to little children. ²⁶Yes, Father, for this was your good pleasure."

MATTHEW 21:16 "Do you hear what these children are saying?" they asked him. "Yes," replied Jesus, "have you never read, 'From the lips of children and infants you have ordained praise'?"

LUKE 11:2-4 He said to them, "When you pray, say: 'Father, hallowed be your name, your kingdom come. ³Give us each day our daily bread. ⁴Forgive us our sins, for we also forgive everyone who sins against us. And lead us not into temptation.'"

LUKE 17:17-18 Jesus asked, "Were not all ten cleansed? Where are the other nine? ¹⁸Was no one found to return and give praise to God except this foreigner?"

LUKE 19:37-40 When he came near the place where the road goes down the Mount of Olives, the whole crowd of disciples began joyfully to praise God in loud voices for all the miracles they had seen: ³⁸"Blessed is the king who comes in the name of the Lord!" "Peace in heaven and glory in the highest!" ³⁹Some of the Pharisees in the crowd said to Jesus, "Teacher, rebuke your disciples!" ⁴⁰"I tell you," he replied, "if they keep quiet, the stones will cry out."

Prayer

JOHN 14:12-14 "I tell you the truth, anyone who has faith in me will do what I have been doing. He will do even greater things than these, because I am going to the Father. ¹³And I will do whatever you ask in my name, so that the Son may bring glory to the Father. ¹⁴You may ask me for anything in my name, and I will do it."

JOHN 15:7-8 "If you remain in me and my words remain in you, ask whatever you wish, and it will be given you. ⁸This is to my Father's glory, that you bear much fruit, showing yourselves to be my disciples."

JOHN 16:23-24 "In that day you will no longer ask me anything. I tell you the truth, my Father will give you whatever you ask in my name. ²⁴Until now you have not asked for anything in my name. Ask and you will receive, and your joy will be complete."

JOHN 16:26-28 "In that day you will ask in my name. I am not saying that I will ask the Father on your behalf. ²⁷No, the Father himself loves you because you have loved me and have believed that I came from God. ²⁸I came from the Father and entered the world; now I am leaving the world and going back to the Father."

MATTHEW 6:5-8 "And when you pray, do not be like the hypocrites, for they love to pray standing in the synagogues and on the street corners to be seen by men. I tell you the truth, they have received their reward in full. ⁶But when you pray, go into your room, close the door and pray to your Father, who is unseen. Then your Father, who sees what is done in secret, will reward you. ⁷And when you pray, do not keep on babbling like pagans, for they think they will be heard because of their many words. ⁸Do not be like them, for your Father knows what you need before you ask him."

MATTHEW 6:9-13 "This, then, is how you should pray: 'Our Father in heaven, hallowed be your name, [10]your kingdom come, your will be done on earth as it is in heaven. [11]Give us today our daily bread. [12]Forgive us our debts, as we also have forgiven our debtors. [13]And lead us not into temptation, but deliver us from the evil one.'" (See also Luke 11:2-4.)

MATTHEW 7:7-11 "Ask and it will be given to you; seek and you will find; knock and the door will be opened to you. [8]For everyone who asks receives; he who seeks finds; and to him who knocks, the door will be opened. [9]Which of you, if his son asks for bread, will give him a stone? [10]Or if he asks for a fish, will give him a snake? [11]If you, then, though you are evil, know how to give good gifts to your children, how much more will your Father in heaven give good gifts to those who ask him!"

MATTHEW 9:37-38 Then he said to his disciples, "The harvest is plentiful but the workers are few. [38]Ask the Lord of the harvest, therefore, to send out workers into his harvest field."

MATTHEW 17:19-21 Then the disciples came to Jesus privately and said, "Why could we not cast it [the demon] out?" [20]So Jesus said to them, "Because of your unbelief; for assuredly, I say to you, if you have faith as a mustard seed, you will say to this mountain, 'Move from here to there,' and it will move; and nothing will be impossible for you. [21]However, this kind does not go out except by prayer and fasting." (NKJV)

MATTHEW 18:18-20 "I tell you the truth, whatever you bind on earth will be bound in heaven, and whatever you loose on earth will be loosed in heaven. [19]Again, I tell you that if two of you on earth agree about anything you ask for, it will be done for you by my Father in heaven. [20]For where two or three come together in my name, there am I with them."

MATTHEW 21:12-13 Jesus entered the temple area and drove out all who were buying and selling there. He overturned the tables of the money changers and the benches of those selling doves. [13]"It is written," he said to them, "'My house will be called a house of prayer,' but you are making it a 'den of robbers.'"

MATTHEW 21:18-22 Early in the morning, as he was on his way back to the city, he was hungry. [19]Seeing a fig tree by the road, he went up to it but found nothing on it except leaves. Then he said to it, "May you never bear fruit again!" Immediately the tree withered. [20]When the disciples saw this, they were amazed. "How did the fig tree wither so quickly?" they asked. [21]Jesus replied, "I tell you the truth, if you have faith and do not doubt, not only can you do what was done to the fig tree, but also you can say to this mountain, 'Go, throw yourself into the sea,' and it will be done. [22]If you believe, you will receive whatever you ask for in prayer." (See also Mark 11:12-14.)

MATTHEW 26:36-38 Then Jesus went with his disciples to a place called Gethsemane, and he said to them, "Sit here while I go over there and pray." [37]He took Peter and the two sons of Zebedee along with him, and he began to be sorrowful and troubled. [38]Then he said to them, "My soul is overwhelmed with sorrow to the point of death. Stay here and keep watch with me." (See also Mark 14:32-34.)

MATTHEW 26:42-46 He went away a second time and prayed, "My Father, if it is not possible for this cup to be taken away unless I drink it, may your will be done." [43]When he came back, he again found them sleeping, because their eyes were heavy. [44]So he left them and went away once more and prayed the third time, saying the same thing. [45]Then he returned to the disciples and said to them, "Are you still sleeping and resting? Look, the hour is near, and the Son of Man is betrayed into the hands of sinners. [46]Rise, let us go! Here comes my betrayer!" (See also Mark 14:39-42.)

MARK 9:25-29 When Jesus saw that the people came running together, He rebuked the unclean spirit, saying to it, "Deaf and dumb spirit, I command you, come out of him and enter him no more!" [26]Then the spirit cried out, convulsed him greatly, and came out of him. And he became as one dead, so that many said, "He is dead." [27]But Jesus took him by the hand and lifted him up, and he arose. [28]And when He had come into the house, His disciples asked Him privately, "Why could we not cast it out?" [29]So He said to them, "This kind can come out by nothing but prayer and fasting." (NKJV)

MARK 11:15-17 On reaching Jerusalem, Jesus entered the temple area and began driving out those who were buying and selling there. He overturned the tables of the money changers and the benches of those selling doves, [16]and would not allow anyone to carry merchandise through the temple courts. [17]And as he taught them, he said, "Is it not written: 'My house will be called a house of prayer for all nations'? But you have made it 'a den of robbers.'"

MARK 11:22-24 "Have faith in God," Jesus answered. [23]"I tell you the truth, if anyone says to this mountain, 'Go, throw yourself into the sea,' and does not doubt in his heart but believes that what he says will happen, it will be done for him. [24]Therefore I tell you, whatever you ask for in prayer, believe that you have received it, and it will be yours."

LUKE 11:5-10 Then he said to them, "Suppose one of you has a friend, and he goes to him at midnight and says, 'Friend, lend me three loaves of bread, [6]because a friend of mine on a journey has come to me, and I have nothing to set before him.' [7]Then the one inside answers, 'Don't bother me. The door is already locked, and my children are with me in bed. I can't get up and give you anything.' [8]I tell you, though he will not get up and give him the bread because he is his friend, yet because of the man's boldness he will get up and give him as much as he needs. [9]So I say to you: Ask and it will be given to you; seek and you will find; knock and the door will be opened to you. [10]For everyone who asks receives; he who seeks finds; and to him who knocks, the door will be opened."

LUKE 11:11-13 "Which of you fathers, if your son asks for a fish, will give him a snake instead? [12]Or if he asks for an egg, will give him a scorpion? [13]If you then, though you are evil, know how to give good gifts to your children, how much more will your Father in heaven give the Holy Spirit to those who ask him!"

LUKE 18:1-8 Then Jesus told his disciples a parable to show them that they should always pray and not give up. ²He said: "In a certain town there was a judge who neither feared God nor cared about men. ³And there was a widow in that town who kept coming to him with the plea, 'Grant me justice against my adversary.' ⁴For some time he refused. But finally he said to himself, 'Even though I don't fear God or care about men, ⁵yet because this widow keeps bothering me, I will see that she gets justice, so that she won't eventually wear me out with her coming!'" ⁶And the Lord said, "Listen to what the unjust judge says. ⁷And will not God bring about justice for his chosen ones, who cry out to him day and night? Will he keep putting them off? ⁸I tell you, he will see that they get justice, and quickly. However, when the Son of Man comes, will he find faith on the earth?"

LUKE 18:9-14 To some who were confident of their own righteousness and looked down on everybody else, Jesus told this parable: ¹⁰"Two men went up to the temple to pray, one a Pharisee and the other a tax collector. ¹¹The Pharisee stood up and prayed about himself: 'God, I thank you that I am not like other men—robbers, evildoers, adulterers—or even like this tax collector. ¹²I fast twice a week and give a tenth of all I get.' ¹³But the tax collector stood at a distance. He would not even look up to heaven, but beat his breast and said, 'God, have mercy on me, a sinner.' ¹⁴I tell you that this man, rather than the other, went home justified before God. For everyone who exalts himself will be humbled, and he who humbles himself will be exalted."

LUKE 19:45-46 Then he entered the temple area and began driving out those who were selling. ⁴⁶"It is written," he said to them, "'My house will be a house of prayer'; but you have made it 'a den of robbers.'"

LUKE 22:31-32 "Simon, Simon, Satan has asked to sift you as wheat. ³²But I have prayed for you, Simon, that your faith may not fail. And when you have turned back, strengthen your brothers."

LUKE 22:40 On reaching the place, he said to them, "Pray that you will not fall into temptation."

LUKE 22:46 "Why are you sleeping?" he asked them. "Get up and pray so that you will not fall into temptation."

The Promises of Christ

In this section you will find more than one hundred promises that our Savior makes to those who follow Him and do what He says. You'll discover His promises about eternal life, answers to prayer, contentment, forgiveness, rewards, peace, miracles, and eternal blessings—just to name a few. Most of His promises are conditional: they call on you to fulfill a condition, and when it is met, Jesus promises that a benefit or blessing will follow. In my personal study of this subject, I found it helpful to underline the condition that

Jesus asks me to fulfill and the benefit He promises to deliver.

You should note that when a promise is made to an individual or a group, it may be so specific as to apply only to that person or group. Such a promise may reflect a principle that applies to others, but it may not. Also, a number of promises at first glance seem to contradict reality. But with additional study of the context or the meaning of the words in the original language, the apparent contradictions are quickly eliminated. For example, in John 8:51 Jesus promises that anyone who "keeps my word...will never see death." All of us die physically, so at first glance it appears to contradict reality. It could mean that if you truly keep His word, you will avoid spiritual death. Or it could mean that when you die, you will simply fall asleep and wake up in eternity without seeing a terrible death experience. Either way, it's a great promise.

If you prayerfully study this section and begin to walk in Jesus' promises, your life will experience supernatural changes that the world can't explain.

JOHN 3:14-18 "Just as Moses lifted up the snake in the desert, so the Son of Man must be lifted up, [15]that everyone who believes in him may have eternal life. [16]For God so loved the world that he gave his one and only Son, that whoever believes in him shall not perish but have eternal life. [17]For God did not send his Son into the world to condemn the world, but to save the world through him. [18]Whoever believes in him is not con-demned, but whoever does not believe stands condemned already because he has not believed in the name of God's one and only Son."

JOHN 4:13-14 Jesus answered, "Everyone who drinks this water will be thirsty again, [14]but whoever drinks the water I give him will never thirst. Indeed, the water I give him will become in him a spring of water welling up to eternal life."

JOHN 5:24-25 "I tell you the truth, whoever hears my word and believes him who sent me has eternal life and will not be condemned; he has crossed over from death to life. [25]I tell you the truth, a time is coming and has now come when the dead will hear the voice of the Son of God and those who hear will live."

JOHN 5:28-29 "Do not be amazed at this, for a time is coming when all who are in their graves will hear his voice [29]and come out—those who have done good will rise to live, and those who have done evil will rise to be condemned."

JOHN 6:35 Then Jesus declared, "I am the bread of life. He who comes to me will never go hungry, and he who believes in me will never be thirsty."

JOHN 6:37 "All that the Father gives me will come to me, and whoever comes to me I will never drive away."

JOHN 6:40 "For my Father's will is that everyone who looks to the Son and believes in him shall have eternal life, and I will raise him up at the last day."

JOHN 6:44 "No one can come to me unless the Father who sent me draws him, and I will raise him up at the last day."

JOHN 6:54-57 "Whoever eats my flesh and drinks my blood has eternal life, and I will raise him up at the last day. [55]For my flesh is real food and my blood is real drink. [56]Whoever eats my flesh and drinks my blood remains in me, and I in him. [57]Just as the living Father sent me and I live because of the Father, so the one who feeds on me will live because of me."

JOHN 7:37-38 On the last and greatest day of the Feast, Jesus stood and said in a loud voice, "If anyone is thirsty, let him come to me and drink. [38]Whoever believes in me, as the Scripture has said, streams of living water will flow from within him."

JOHN 8:12 When Jesus spoke again to the people, he said, "I am the light of the world. Whoever follows me will never walk in darkness, but will have the light of life."

JOHN 8:31-32 Then Jesus said to those Jews who believed Him, "If you abide in My word, you are My disciples indeed. [32]And you shall know the truth, and the truth shall make you free." (NKJV)

JOHN 8:51 "I tell you the truth, if anyone keeps my word, he will never see death."

JOHN 10:9-10 "I am the gate; whoever enters through me will be saved. He will come in and go out, and find pasture. [10]The thief comes only to steal and kill and destroy; I have come that they may have life, and have it to the full."

JOHN 10:14-16 "I am the good shepherd; I know my sheep and my sheep know me— [15]just as the Father knows me and I know the Father—and I lay down my life for the sheep. [16]I have other sheep that are not of this sheep pen. I must bring them also. They too will listen to my voice, and there shall be one flock and one shepherd."

JOHN 10:27-29 "My sheep listen to my voice; I know them, and they follow me. [28]I give them eternal life, and they shall never perish; no one can snatch them out of my hand. [29]My Father, who has given them to me, is greater than all; no one can snatch them out of my Father's hand."

JOHN 11:25-26 Jesus said to her [Martha], "I am the resurrection and the life. He who believes in me will live, even though he dies; [26]and whoever lives and believes in me will never die. Do you believe this?"

JOHN 12:25-26 "The man who loves his life will lose it, while the man who hates his life in this world will keep it for eternal life. [26]Whoever serves me must follow me; and where I am, my servant also will be. My Father will honor the one who serves me."

JOHN 12:46 "I have come into the world as a light, so that no one who believes in me should stay in darkness."

JOHN 14:2-4 "In my Father's house are many rooms; if it were not so, I would have told you. I am going there to prepare a place for you. [3]And if I go and prepare a place for you, I will come back and take you to be with me that you also may be where I am. [4]You know the way to the place where I am going."

JOHN 14:12-14 "I tell you the truth, anyone who has faith in me will do what I have been doing. He will do even greater things than these, because I am going to the Father. [13]And I will do whatever you ask in my name, so that the Son may bring glory to the Father. [14]You may ask me for anything in my name, and I will do it."

JOHN 14:18 "I will not leave you as orphans; I will come to you."

JOHN 14:19 "Before long, the world will not see me anymore, but you will see me. Because I live, you also will live."

JOHN 14:20 "On that day you will realize that I am in my Father, and you are in me, and I am in you."

JOHN 14:21 "Whoever has my commands and obeys them, he is the one who loves me. He who loves me will be loved by my Father, and I too will love him and show myself to him."

JOHN 14:23 Jesus replied, "If anyone loves me, he will obey my teaching. My Father will love him, and we will come to him and make our home with him."

JOHN 14:26 "But the Counselor, the Holy Spirit, whom the Father will send in my name, will teach you all things and will remind you of everything I have said to you."

JOHN 14:27 "Peace I leave with you; my peace I give you. I do not give to you as the world gives. Do not let your hearts be troubled and do not be afraid."

JOHN 15:5 "I am the vine; you are the branches. If a man remains in me and I in him, he will bear much fruit; apart from me you can do nothing."

JOHN 15:7 "If you remain in me and my words remain in you, ask whatever you wish, and it will be given you."

JOHN 15:10 "If you obey my commands, you will remain in my love, just as I have obeyed my Father's commands and remain in his love."

JOHN 15:11 "I have told you this so that my joy may be in you and that your joy may be complete."

JOHN 15:16 "You did not choose me, but I chose you and appointed you to go and bear fruit—fruit that will last. Then the Father will give you whatever you ask in my name."

JOHN 15:26 "When the Counselor comes, whom I will send to you from the Father, the Spirit of truth who goes out from the Father, he will testify about me."

JOHN 16:12-15 "I have much more to say to you, more than you can now bear. [13]But when he, the Spirit of truth, comes, he will guide you into all truth. He will not speak on his own; he will speak only what he hears, and he will tell you what is yet to come. [14]He will bring glory to me by taking from what is mine and making it known to you. [15]All that belongs to the Father is mine. That is why I said the Spirit will take from what is mine and make it known to you."

JOHN 16:23-24 "In that day you will no longer ask me anything. I tell you the truth, my Father will give you whatever you ask in my name. [24]Until now you have not asked for anything in my name. Ask and you will receive, and your joy will be complete."

JOHN 16:33 "I have told you these things, so that in me you may have peace. In this world you will have trouble. But take heart! I have overcome the world."

MATTHEW 5:3-11 "Blessed are the poor in spirit, for theirs is the kingdom of heaven. [4]Blessed are those who mourn, for they will be comforted. [5]Blessed are the meek, for they will inherit the earth. [6]Blessed are those who hunger and thirst for righteousness, for they will be filled. [7]Blessed are the merciful, for they will be shown mercy. [8]Blessed are the pure in heart, for they will see God. [9]Blessed are the peacemakers, for they will be called sons of God. [10]Blessed are those who are persecuted because of righteousness, for theirs is the kingdom of heaven. [11]Blessed are you when people insult you, persecute you and falsely say all kinds of evil against you because of me."

MATTHEW 5:19 "Anyone who breaks one of the least of these commandments and teaches others to do the same will be called least in the kingdom of heaven, but whoever practices and teaches these commands will be called great in the kingdom of heaven."

MATTHEW 6:3-4 "But when you give to the needy, do not let your left hand know what your right hand is doing, [4]so that your giving may be in secret. Then your Father, who sees what is done in secret, will reward you."

MATTHEW 6:6 "But when you pray, go into your room, close the door and pray to your Father, who is unseen. Then your Father, who sees what is done in secret, will reward you."

MATTHEW 6:14 "For if you forgive men when they sin against you, your heavenly Father will also forgive you."

MATTHEW 6:33 "But seek first his kingdom and his righteousness, and all these things will be given to you as well."

MATTHEW 7:7-8 "Ask and it will be given to you; seek and you will find; knock and the door will be opened to you. [8]For everyone who asks receives; he who seeks finds; and to him who knocks, the door will be opened." (See also Luke 11:9-10.)

MATTHEW 7:11 "If you, then, though you are evil, know how to give good gifts to your children, how much more will your Father in heaven give good gifts to those who ask him!"

MATTHEW 7:21, 24-25 "Not everyone who says to Me, 'Lord, Lord,' shall enter the kingdom of heaven, but he who does the will of My Father in heaven. [24]Therefore whoever hears these sayings of Mine, and does them, I will liken him to a wise man who built his house on the rock: [25]and the rain descended, the floods came, and the winds blew and beat on that house; and it did not fall, for it was founded on the rock." (NKJV)

MATTHEW 10:32 "Whoever acknowledges me before men, I will also acknowledge him before my Father in heaven."

MATTHEW 10:42 "And if anyone gives even a cup of cold water to one of these little ones because he is my disciple, I tell you the truth, he will certainly not lose his reward."

MATTHEW 11:6 "Blessed is the man who does not fall away on account of me."

MATTHEW 11:28-30 "Come to me, all you who are weary and burdened, and I will give you rest. [29]Take my yoke upon you and learn from me, for I am gentle and humble in heart, and you will find rest for your souls. [30]For my yoke is easy and my burden is light."

MATTHEW 12:49-50 Pointing to his disciples, he said, "Here are my mother and my brothers. [50]For whoever does the will of my Father in heaven is my brother and sister and mother."

MATTHEW 18:18-20 "I tell you the truth, whatever you bind on earth will be bound in heaven, and whatever you loose on earth will be loosed in heaven. [19]Again, I tell you that if two of you on earth agree about anything you ask for, it will be done for you by my Father in heaven. [20]For where two or three come together in my name, there am I with them."

MATTHEW 19:29-30 "And everyone who has left houses or brothers or sisters or father or mother or children or fields for my sake will receive a hundred times as much and will inherit eternal life. [30]But many who are first will be last, and many who are last will be first."

MATTHEW 21:18-22 Early in the morning, as he was on his way back to the city, he was hungry. [19]Seeing a fig tree by the road, he went up to it but found nothing on it except leaves. Then he said to it, "May you never bear fruit again!" Immediately the tree withered. [20]When the disciples saw this, they were amazed. "How did the fig tree wither so quickly?" they asked. [21]Jesus replied, "I tell you the truth, if you have faith and do not doubt, not only can you do what was done to the fig tree, but also you can say to this mountain, 'Go, throw yourself into the sea,' and it will be done. [22]If you believe, you will receive whatever you ask for in prayer." (See also Mark 11:12-14.)

MATTHEW 25:34-36 "Then the King will say to those on his right, 'Come, you who are blessed by my Father; take your inheritance, the kingdom prepared for you since the creation of the world. [35]For I was hungry and you gave me something to eat, I was thirsty and you gave me something to drink, I was a stranger and you invited me in, [36]I needed clothes and you clothed me, I was sick and you looked after me, I was in prison and you came to visit me.'"

MATTHEW 28:18-20 Then Jesus came to them [the eleven disciples] and said, "All authority in heaven and on earth has been given to me. [19]Therefore go and make disciples of all nations, baptizing them in the name of the Father and of the Son and of the Holy Spirit, [20]and teaching them to obey everything I have commanded you. And surely I am with you always, to the very end of the age."

LUKE 6:35 "But love your enemies, do good to them, and lend to them without expecting to get anything back. Then your reward will be great, and you will be sons of the Most High, because he is kind to the ungrateful and wicked."

LUKE 6:37-38 "Do not judge, and you will not be judged. Do not condemn, and you will not be condemned. Forgive, and you will be forgiven. [38]Give, and it will be given to you. A good measure, pressed down, shaken together and running over, will be poured into your lap. For with the measure you use, it will be measured to you."

LUKE 9:48 Then he said to them, "Whoever welcomes this little child in my name welcomes me; and whoever welcomes me welcomes the one who sent me. For he who is least among you all—he is the greatest."

LUKE 11:11-13 "Which of you fathers, if your son asks for a fish, will give him a snake instead? [12]Or if he asks for an egg, will give him a scorpion? [13]If you then, though you are evil, know how to give good gifts to your children, how much more will your Father in heaven give the Holy Spirit to those who ask him!"

LUKE 11:28 He replied, "Blessed rather are those who hear the word of God and obey it."

LUKE 21:33 "Heaven and earth will pass away, but my words will never pass away."

Prophets

MATTHEW 11:11-15 "I tell you the truth: Among those born of women there has not risen anyone greater than John the Baptist; yet he who is least in the kingdom of heaven is greater than he. [12]From the days of John the Baptist until now, the kingdom of heaven has been forcefully advancing, and forceful men lay hold of it. [13]For all the Prophets and the Law prophesied until John. [14]And if you are willing to accept it, he is the Elijah who was to come. [15]He who has ears, let him hear."

MATTHEW 11:16-19 "To what can I compare this generation? They are like children sitting in the marketplaces and calling out to others: [17]'We played the flute for you, and you did not dance; we sang a dirge, and you did not mourn.' [18]For John came neither eating nor drinking, and they say, 'He has a demon.' [19]The Son of Man came eating and drinking, and they say, 'Here is a glutton and a drunkard, a friend of tax collectors and "sinners." ' But wisdom is proved right by her actions."

MATTHEW 13:54-57 Coming to his hometown, he began teaching the people in their synagogue, and they were amazed. "Where did this man get this wisdom and these miraculous powers?" they asked. [55]"Isn't this the carpenter's son? Isn't his mother's name Mary, and aren't his brothers James, Joseph, Simon and Judas? [56]Aren't all his sisters with us? Where then did this man get all these things?" [57]And they took offense at him. But Jesus said to them, "Only in his hometown and in his own house is a prophet without honor."

MATTHEW 21:23-27 Jesus entered the temple courts, and, while he was teaching, the chief priests and the elders of the people came to him. "By what authority are you doing these things?" they asked. "And who gave you this authority?" [24]Jesus replied, "I will also ask you one question. If you answer me, I will tell you by what authority I am doing these things. [25]John's baptism—where did it come from? Was it from heaven, or from men?" They discussed it among themselves and said, "If we say, 'From heaven,' he will ask, 'Then why didn't you believe him?' [26]But if we say, 'From men'—we are afraid of the people, for they all hold that John was a prophet." [27]So they answered Jesus, "We don't know." Then he said, "Neither will I tell you by what authority I am doing these things." (See also Mark 11:27-33; Luke 20:1-8.)

MATTHEW 26:55-56 At that time Jesus said to the crowd, "Am I leading a rebellion, that you have come out with swords and clubs to capture me? Every day I sat in the temple courts teaching, and you did not arrest me. [56]But this has all taken place that the writings of the prophets might be fulfilled." Then all the disciples deserted him and fled.

LUKE 4:24-27 "I tell you the truth," he continued, "no prophet is accepted in his hometown. [25]I assure you that there were many widows in Israel in Elijah's time, when the sky was shut for three and a half years and there was a severe famine throughout the land. [26]Yet Elijah was not sent to any of them, but to a widow in Zarephath in the region of Sidon. [27]And there were many in Israel with leprosy in the time of Elisha the prophet, yet not one of them was cleansed—only Naaman the Syrian."

LUKE 7:24-27 After John's messengers left, Jesus began to speak to the crowd about John: "What did you go out into the desert to see? A reed swayed by the wind? [25]If not, what did you go out to see? A man dressed in fine clothes? No, those who wear expensive clothes and indulge in luxury are in palaces. [26]But what did you go out to see? A prophet? Yes, I tell you, and more than a prophet. [27]This is the one about whom it is written: 'I will send my messenger ahead of you, who will prepare your way before you.'" (See also Matthew 11:7-10.)

LUKE 24:15-27 As they talked and discussed these things with each other, Jesus himself came up and walked along with them; [16]but they were kept from recognizing him. [17]He asked them, "What are you discussing together as you walk along?" They stood still, their faces downcast. [18]One of them, named Cleopas, asked him, "Are you only a visitor to Jerusalem and do not know the things that have happened there in these days?" [19]"What things?" he asked. "About Jesus of Nazareth," they replied. "He was a prophet, powerful in word and deed before God and all the people. [20]The chief priests and our rulers handed him over to be sentenced to death, and they crucified him; [21]but we had hoped that he was the one who was going to redeem Israel. And what is more, it is the third day since all this took place. [22]In addition, some of our women amazed us. They went to the tomb early this morning [23]but didn't find his body. They came and told us that they had seen a vision of angels, who said he was alive. [24]Then some of our companions went to the tomb and found it just as the women had said, but him they did not see." [25]He said to them, "How foolish you are, and how slow of heart to believe all that the prophets have spoken! [26]Did not the Christ have to suffer these things and then enter his glory?" [27]And beginning with Moses and all the Prophets, he explained to them what was said in all the Scriptures concerning himself.

Purity

MATTHEW 5:8 "Blessed are the pure in heart, for they will see God."

The Pursuit of Righteousness

JOHN 14:15-16 "If you love me, you will obey what I command. [16]And I will ask the Father, and he will give you another Counselor to be with you forever."

JOHN 14:26-27 "But the Counselor, the Holy Spirit, whom the Father will send in my name, will teach you all things and will remind you of everything I have said to you. ²⁷Peace I leave with you; my peace I give you. I do not give to you as the world gives. Do not let your hearts be troubled and do not be afraid."

JOHN 17:15-19 "My prayer is not that you [God] take them out of the world but that you protect them from the evil one. ¹⁶They are not of the world, even as I am not of it. ¹⁷Sanctify them by the truth; your word is truth. ¹⁸As you sent me into the world, I have sent them into the world. ¹⁹For them I sanctify myself, that they too may be truly sanctified."

MATTHEW 5:6 "Blessed are those who hunger and thirst for righteousness, for they will be filled."

MATTHEW 5:10-11 "Blessed are those who are persecuted because of righteousness, for theirs is the kingdom of heaven. ¹¹Blessed are you when people insult you, persecute you and falsely say all kinds of evil against you because of me."

MATTHEW 5:19-20 "Anyone who breaks one of the least of these commandments and teaches others to do the same will be called least in the kingdom of heaven, but whoever practices and teaches these commands will be called great in the kingdom of heaven. ²⁰For I tell you that unless your righteousness surpasses that of the Pharisees and the teachers of the law, you will certainly not enter the kingdom of heaven."

MATTHEW 5:29-30 "If your right eye causes you to sin, gouge it out and throw it away. It is better for you to lose one part of your body than for your whole body to be thrown into hell. ³⁰And if your right hand causes you to sin, cut it off and throw it away. It is better for you to lose one part of your body than for your whole body to go into hell."

MATTHEW 5:48 "Be perfect, therefore, as your heavenly Father is perfect."

MATTHEW 6:31-34 "So do not worry, saying, 'What shall we eat?' or 'What shall we drink?' or 'What shall we wear?' ³²For the pagans run after all these things, and your heavenly Father knows that you need them. ³³But seek first his kingdom and his righteousness, and all these things will be given to you as well. ³⁴Therefore do not worry about tomorrow, for tomorrow will worry about itself. Each day has enough trouble of its own."

MATTHEW 13:37-43 He answered, "The one who sowed the good seed is the Son of Man. ³⁸The field is the world, and the good seed stands for the sons of the kingdom. The weeds are the sons of the evil one, ³⁹and the enemy who sows them is the devil. The harvest is the end of the age, and the harvesters are angels. ⁴⁰As the weeds are pulled up and burned in the fire, so it will be at the end of the age. ⁴¹The Son of Man will send out his angels, and they will weed out of his kingdom everything that causes sin and all who do evil. ⁴²They will throw them into the fiery furnace, where there will be weeping and gnashing of teeth. ⁴³Then the righteous will shine like the sun in the kingdom of their Father. He who has ears, let him hear."

MATTHEW 19:17-21 "Why do you ask me about what is good?" Jesus replied.

"There is only One who is good. If you want to enter life, obey the commandments." [18]"Which ones?" the man inquired. Jesus replied, " 'Do not murder, do not commit adultery, do not steal, do not give false testimony, [19]honor your father and mother,' and 'love your neighbor as yourself.' " [20]"All these I have kept," the young man said. "What do I still lack?" [21]Jesus answered, "If you want to be perfect, go, sell your possessions and give to the poor, and you will have treasure in heaven. Then come, follow me."

Reconciliation Between People

MATTHEW 5:21-24 "You have heard that it was said to the people long ago, 'Do not murder, and anyone who murders will be subject to judgment.' [22]But I tell you that anyone who is angry with his brother will be subject to judgment. Again, anyone who says to his brother, 'Raca,' is answerable to the Sanhedrin. But anyone who says, 'You fool!' will be in danger of the fire of hell. [23]Therefore, if you are offering your gift at the altar and there remember that your brother has something against you, [24]leave your gift there in front of the altar. First go and be reconciled to your brother; then come and offer your gift."

MATTHEW 18:15-17 "If your brother sins against you, go and show him his fault, just between the two of you. If he listens to you, you have won your brother over. [16]But if he will not listen, take one or two others along, so that 'every matter may be established by the testimony of two or three witnesses.' [17]If he refuses to listen to them, tell it to the church; and if he refuses to listen even to the church, treat him as you would a pagan or a tax collector."

MATTHEW 18:21-35 Then Peter came to Jesus and asked, "Lord, how many times shall I forgive my brother when he sins against me? Up to seven times?" [22]Jesus answered, "I tell you, not seven times, but seventy-seven times. [23]Therefore, the kingdom of heaven is like a king who wanted to settle accounts with his servants. [24]As he began the settlement, a man who owed him ten thousand talents was brought to him. [25]Since he was not able to pay, the master ordered that he and his wife and his children and all that he had be sold to repay the debt. [26]The servant fell on his knees before him. 'Be patient with me,' he begged, 'and I will pay back everything.' [27]The servant's master took pity on him, canceled the debt and let him go. [28]But when that servant went out, he found one of his fellow servants who owed him a hundred denarii. He grabbed him and began to choke him. 'Pay back what you owe me!' he demanded. [29]His fellow servant fell to his knees and begged him, 'Be patient with me, and I will pay you back.' [30]But he refused. Instead, he went off and had the man thrown into prison until he could pay the debt. [31]When the other servants saw what had happened, they were greatly distressed and went and told their master everything that had happened. [32]Then the master called the servant in. 'You wicked servant,' he said, 'I canceled all that debt of yours because you begged me to. [33]Shouldn't you have had mercy on your fellow servant just as I had on you?' [34]In anger his master turned him over to the jailers to be tortured, until he should pay back all he owed. [35]This is how my heavenly Father will treat each of you unless you forgive your brother from your heart."

Luke 12:58 "As you are going with your adversary to the magistrate, try hard to be reconciled to him on the way, or he may drag you off to the judge, and the judge turn you over to the officer, and the officer throw you into prison."

Luke 17:3-4 "So watch yourselves. If your brother sins, rebuke him, and if he repents, forgive him. [4]If he sins against you seven times in a day, and seven times comes back to you and says, 'I repent,' forgive him."

Rejection and Persecution of Christians

John 15:18-23 "If the world hates you, keep in mind that it hated me first. [19]If you belonged to the world, it would love you as its own. As it is, you do not belong to the world, but I have chosen you out of the world. That is why the world hates you. [20]Remember the words I spoke to you: 'No servant is greater than his master.' If they persecuted me, they will persecute you also. If they obeyed my teaching, they will obey yours also. [21]They will treat you this way because of my name, for they do not know the One who sent me. [22]If I had not come and spoken to them, they would not be guilty of sin. Now, however, they have no excuse for

their sin. [23]He who hates me hates my Father as well."

John 16:1-4 "All this I have told you so that you will not go astray. [2]They will put you out of the synagogue; in fact, a time is coming when anyone who kills you will think he is offering a service to God. [3]They will do such things because they have not known the Father or me. [4]I have told you this, so that when the time comes you will remember that I warned you. I did not tell you this at first because I was with you."

John 16:32-33 "But a time is coming, and has come, when you will be scattered, each to his own home. You will leave me all alone. Yet I am not alone, for my Father is with me. [33]I have told you these things, so that in me you may have peace. In this world you will have trouble. But take heart! I have overcome the world."

John 17:14 "I have given them your [God's] word and the world has hated them, for they are not of the world any more than I am of the world."

John 18:19-24 Meanwhile, the high priest questioned Jesus about his disciples and his teaching. [20]"I have spoken openly to the world," Jesus replied. "I always taught in synagogues or at the temple, where all the Jews come together. I said nothing in secret. [21]Why question me? Ask those who heard me. Surely they know what I said." [22]When Jesus said this, one of the officials nearby struck him in the face. "Is this the way you answer the high priest?" he demanded. [23]"If I said something wrong," Jesus replied, "testify as to what is wrong. But if I spoke the truth, why did you strike me?" ²⁴Then Annas sent him, still bound, to Caiaphas the high priest.

MATTHEW 5:10-11 "Blessed are those who are persecuted because of righteousness, for theirs is the kingdom of heaven. ¹¹Blessed are you when people insult you, persecute you and falsely say all kinds of evil against you because of me."

MATTHEW 5:44-46 "But I tell you: Love your enemies and pray for those who persecute you, ⁴⁵that you may be sons of your Father in heaven. He causes his sun to rise on the evil and the good, and sends rain on the righteous and the unrighteous. ⁴⁶If you love those who love you, what reward will you get? Are not even the tax collectors doing that?"

MATTHEW 10:16-23 "I am sending you out like sheep among wolves. Therefore be as shrewd as snakes and as innocent as doves. ¹⁷Be on your guard against men; they will hand you over to the local councils and flog you in their synagogues. ¹⁸On my account you will be brought before governors and kings as witnesses to them and to the Gentiles. ¹⁹But when they arrest you, do not worry about what to say or how to say it. At that time you will be given what to say, ²⁰for it will not be you speaking, but the Spirit of your Father speaking through you. ²¹Brother will betray brother to death, and a father his child; children will rebel against their parents and have them put to death. ²²All men will hate you because of me, but he who stands firm to the end will be saved. ²³When you are persecuted in one place,

flee to another. I tell you the truth, you will not finish going through the cities of Israel before the Son of Man comes."

MATTHEW 24:4-29 Jesus answered: "Watch out that no one deceives you. ⁵For many will come in my name, claiming, 'I am the Christ,' and will deceive many. ⁶You will hear of wars and rumors of wars, but see to it that you are not alarmed. Such things must happen, but the end is still to come. ⁷Nation will rise against nation, and kingdom against kingdom. There will be famines and earthquakes in various places. ⁸All these are the beginning of birth pains. ⁹Then you will be handed over to be persecuted and put to death, and you will be hated by all nations because of me. ¹⁰At that time many will turn away from the faith and will betray and hate each other, ¹¹and many false prophets will appear and deceive many people. ¹²Because of the increase of wickedness, the love of most will grow cold, ¹³but he who stands firm to the end will be saved. ¹⁴And this gospel of the kingdom will be preached in the whole world as a testimony to all nations, and then the end will come. ¹⁵So when you see standing in the holy place 'the abomination that causes desolation,' spoken of through the prophet Daniel—let the reader understand— ¹⁶then let those who are in Judea flee to the mountains. ¹⁷Let no one on the roof of his house go down to take anything out of the house. ¹⁸Let no one in the field go back to get his cloak. ¹⁹How dreadful it will be in those days for pregnant women and nursing mothers! ²⁰Pray that your flight will not take place in winter or on the Sabbath. [21]For then there will be great distress, unequaled from the beginning of the world until now—and never to be equaled again. [22]If those days had not been cut short, no one would survive, but for the sake of the elect those days will be shortened. [23]At that time if anyone says to you, 'Look, here is the Christ!' or, 'There he is!' do not believe it. [24]For false Christs and false prophets will appear and perform great signs and miracles to deceive even the elect—if that were possible. [25]See, I have told you ahead of time. [26]So if anyone tells you, 'There he is, out in the desert,' do not go out; or, 'Here he is, in the inner rooms,' do not believe it. [27]For as lightning that comes from the east is visible even in the west, so will be the coming of the Son of Man. [28]Wherever there is a carcass, there the vultures will gather. [29]Immediately after the distress of those days 'the sun will be darkened, and the moon will not give its light; the stars will fall from the sky, and the heavenly bodies will be shaken.' "

MARK 6:8-11 These were his instructions: "Take nothing for the journey except a staff—no bread, no bag, no money in your belts. [9]Wear sandals but not an extra tunic. [10]Whenever you enter a house, stay there until you leave that town. [11]And if any place will not welcome you or listen to you, shake the dust off your feet when you leave, as a testimony against them." (See also Matthew 10:9-15; Luke 9:1-5.)

MARK 13:9-20 "You must be on your guard. You will be handed over to the local councils and flogged in the synagogues. On account of me you will stand before governors and kings as witnesses to them. [10]And the gospel must first be preached to all nations. [11]Whenever you are arrested and brought to trial, do not worry beforehand about what to say. Just say whatever is given you at the time, for it is not you speaking, but the Holy Spirit. [12]Brother will betray brother to death, and a father his child. Children will rebel against their parents and have them put to death. [13]All men will hate you because of me, but he who stands firm to the end will be saved. [14]When you see 'the abomination that causes desolation' standing where it does not belong— let the reader understand—then let those who are in Judea flee to the mountains. [15]Let no one on the roof of his house go down or enter the house to take anything out. [16]Let no one in the field go back to get his cloak. [17]How dreadful it will be in those days for pregnant women and nursing mothers! [18]Pray that this will not take place in winter, [19]because those will be days of distress unequaled from the beginning, when God created the world, until now—and never to be equaled again. [20]If the Lord had not cut short those days, no one would survive. But for the sake of the elect, whom he has chosen, he has shortened them."

LUKE 6:22 "Blessed are you when men hate you, when they exclude you and insult you and reject your name as evil, because of the Son of Man."

LUKE 21:8-28 He replied: "Watch out that you are not deceived. For many will come in my name, claiming, 'I am he,' and, 'The time is near.' Do not follow them. [9]When you hear of wars and revolutions, do not be frightened. These things must happen first, but the end will not come right away." [10]Then he said to them: "Nation will rise against nation, and kingdom against kingdom. [11]There will be great earthquakes, famines and pestilences in various places, and fearful events and great signs from heaven. [12]But before all this, they will lay hands on you and persecute you. They will deliver you to synagogues and prisons, and you will be brought before kings and governors, and all on account of my name. [13]This will result in your being witnesses to them. [14]But make up your mind not to worry beforehand how you will defend yourselves. [15]For I will give you words and wisdom that none of your adversaries will be able to resist or contradict. [16]You will be betrayed even by parents, brothers, relatives and friends, and they will put some of you to death. [17]All men will hate you because of me. [18]But not a hair of your head will perish. [19]By standing firm you will gain life. [20]When you see Jerusalem being surrounded by armies, you will know that its desolation is near. [21]Then let those who are in Judea flee to the mountains, let those in the city get out, and let those in the country not enter the city. [22]For this is the time of punishment in fulfillment of all that has been written. [23]How dreadful it will be in those days for pregnant women and nursing mothers! There will be great distress in the land and wrath against this people. [24]They will fall by the sword and will be taken as prisoners to all the nations. Jerusalem will be trampled on by the Gentiles until the times of the Gentiles are fulfilled. [25]There will be signs in the sun, moon and stars. On the earth, nations will be in anguish and perplexity at the roaring and tossing of the sea. [26]Men will faint from terror, apprehensive of what is coming on the world, for the heavenly bodies will be shaken. [27]At that time they will see the Son of Man coming in a cloud with power and great glory. [28]When these things begin to take place, stand up and lift up your heads, because your redemption is drawing near."

ACTS 9:3-16 As he neared Damascus on his journey, suddenly a light from heaven flashed around him. [4]He fell to the ground and heard a voice say to him, "Saul, Saul, why do you persecute me?" [5]"Who are you, Lord?" Saul asked. "I am Jesus, whom you are persecuting," he replied. [6]"Now get up and go into the city, and you will be told what you must do." [7]The men traveling with Saul stood there speechless; they heard the sound but did not see anyone. [8]Saul got up from the ground, but when he opened his eyes he could see nothing. So they led him by the hand into Damascus. [9]For three days he was blind, and did not eat or drink anything. [10]In Damascus there was a disciple named Ananias. The Lord called to him in a vision, "Ananias!" "Yes, Lord," he answered. [11]The Lord told him, "Go to the house of Judas on Straight Street and ask for a man from Tarsus named Saul, for he is praying. [12]In a vision he has seen a man named Ananias come and place his hands on him to restore his sight." [13]"Lord," Ananias answered, "I have heard many reports about this man and all the harm he has done to your saints in Jerusalem. [14]And he has come here with authority from the chief priests to arrest all who call on your name." [15]But the Lord said to Ananias, "Go! This man is my chosen instrument to carry my name before the Gentiles and their kings and before the people of Israel. [16]I will show him how much he must suffer for my name." (See also Acts 22:6-10.)

ACTS 26:13-18 "About noon, O king, as I [Paul] was on the road, I saw a light from heaven, brighter than the sun, blazing around me and my companions. [14]We all fell to the ground, and I heard a voice saying to me in Aramaic, 'Saul, Saul, why do you persecute me? It is hard for you to kick against the goads.' [15]Then I asked, 'Who are you, Lord?' 'I am Jesus, whom you are persecuting,' the Lord replied. [16]'Now get up and stand on your feet. I have appeared to you to appoint you as a servant and as a witness of what you have seen of me and what I will show you. [17]I will rescue you from your own people and from the Gentiles. I am sending you to them [18]to open their eyes and turn them from darkness to light, and from the power of Satan to God, so that they may receive forgiveness of sins and a place among those who are sanctified by faith in me.' "

REVELATION 2:10 "Do not be afraid of what you are about to suffer. I tell you, the devil will put some of you in prison to test you, and you will suffer persecution for ten days. Be faithful, even to the point of death, and I will give you the crown of life."

Revelation of God's Truth

JOHN 14:6-7 Jesus answered, "I am the way and the truth and the life. No one comes to the Father except through me. [7]If you really knew me, you would know my Father as well. From now on, you do know him and have seen him."

JOHN 16:13 "But when he, the Spirit of truth, comes, he will guide you into all truth. He will not speak on his own; he will speak only what he hears, and he will tell you what is yet to come."

JOHN 18:37 "You are a king, then!" said Pilate. Jesus answered, "You are right in saying I am a king. In fact, for this reason I was born, and for this I came into the world, to testify to the truth. Everyone on the side of truth listens to me."

MATTHEW 10:24-26 "A student is not above his teacher, nor a servant above his master. [25]It is enough for the student to be like his teacher, and the servant like his master. If the head of the house has been called Beelzebub, how much more the members of his household! [26]So do not be afraid of them. There is nothing concealed that will not be disclosed, or hidden that will not be made known."

MATTHEW 11:25-26 At that time Jesus said, "I praise you, Father, Lord of heaven and earth, because you have hidden these things from the wise and learned, and revealed them to little children. [26]Yes, Father, for this was your good pleasure."

MATTHEW 11:27 "All things have been committed to me by my Father. No one knows the Son except the Father, and no one knows the Father except the Son and those to whom the Son chooses to reveal him."

MATTHEW 13:11-15 He replied, "The knowledge of the secrets of the kingdom of heaven has been given to you, but not to them. [12]Whoever has will be given more, and he will have an abundance. Whoever does not have, even what he has will be taken from him. [13]This is why I speak to them in parables: Though seeing, they do not see; though hearing, they do not hear or understand. [14]In them is fulfilled the prophecy of Isaiah: 'You will be ever hearing but never understanding; you will be ever seeing but never perceiving. [15]For this people's heart has become calloused; they hardly hear with their ears, and they have closed their eyes. Otherwise they might see with their eyes, hear with their ears, understand with their hearts and turn, and I would heal them.'"

MATTHEW 16:17 Jesus replied, "Blessed are you, Simon son of Jonah, for this was not revealed to you by man, but by my Father in heaven."

Sacrifice and Self-Denial

MATTHEW 10:34-39 "Do not suppose that I have come to bring peace to the earth. I did not come to bring peace, but a sword. [35]For I have come to turn 'a man against his father, a daughter against her mother, a daughter-in-law against her mother-in-law— [36]a man's enemies will be the members of his own household.' [37]Anyone who loves his father or mother more than me is not worthy of me; any-

one who loves his son or daughter more than me is not worthy of me; [38]and anyone who does not take his cross and follow me is not worthy of me. [39]Whoever finds his life will lose it, and whoever loses his life for my sake will find it."

MATTHEW 16:24-26 Then Jesus said to his disciples, "If anyone would come after me, he must deny himself and take up his cross and follow me. [25]For whoever wants to save his life will lose it, but whoever loses his life for me will find it. [26]What good will it be for a man if he gains the whole world, yet forfeits his soul? Or what can a man give in exchange for his soul?"

MATTHEW 19:27-30 Peter answered him, "We have left everything to follow you! What then will there be for us?" [28]Jesus said to them, "I tell you the truth, at the renewal of all things, when the Son of Man sits on his glorious throne, you who have followed me will also sit on twelve thrones, judging the twelve tribes of Israel. [29]And everyone who has left houses or brothers or sisters or father or mother or children or fields for my sake will receive a hundred times as much and will inherit eternal life. [30]But many who are first will be last, and many who are last will be first."

MARK 8:34-38 Then he called the crowd to him along with his disciples and said: "If anyone would come after me, he must deny himself and take up his cross and follow me. [35]For whoever wants to save his life will lose it, but whoever loses his life for me and for the gospel will save it. [36]What good is it for a man to gain the whole world, yet forfeit his soul? [37]Or what can a man give in exchange for his soul? [38]If anyone is ashamed of me and my words in this adulterous and sinful generation, the Son of Man will be ashamed of him when he comes in his Father's glory with the holy angels."

MARK 10:29-31 "I tell you the truth," Jesus replied, "no one who has left home or brothers or sisters or mother or father or children or fields for me and the gospel [30]will fail to receive a hundred times as much in this present age (homes, brothers, sisters, mothers, children and fields—and with them, persecutions) and in the age to come, eternal life. [31]But many who are first will be last, and the last first."

MARK 12:38-40 As he taught, Jesus said, "Watch out for the teachers of the law. They like to walk around in flowing robes and be greeted in the marketplaces, [39]and have the most important seats in the synagogues and the places of honor at banquets. [40]They devour widows' houses and for a show make lengthy prayers. Such men will be punished most severely."

MARK 12:42-44 But a poor widow came and put in two very small copper coins, worth only a fraction of a penny. [43]Calling his disciples to him, Jesus said, "I tell you the truth, this poor widow has put more into the treasury than all the others. [44]They all gave out of their wealth; but she, out of her poverty, put in everything—all she had to live on." (See also Luke 21:2-4.)

LUKE 9:23 Then he said to them all: "If anyone would come after me, he must deny himself and take up his cross daily and follow me."

LUKE 14:25-33 Large crowds were traveling with Jesus, and turning to them he said: [26]"If anyone comes to me and does not hate his father and mother, his wife and children, his brothers and sisters—yes, even his own life—he cannot be my disciple. [27]And anyone who does not carry his cross and follow me cannot be my disciple. [28]Suppose one of you wants to build a tower. Will he not first sit down and estimate the cost to see if he has enough money to complete it? [29]For if he lays the foundation and is not able to finish it, everyone who sees it will ridicule him, [30]saying, 'This fellow began to build and was not able to finish.' [31]Or suppose a king is about to go to war against another king. Will he not first sit down and consider whether he is able with ten thousand men to oppose the one coming against him with twenty thousand? [32]If he is not able, he will send a delegation while the other is still a long way off and will ask for terms of peace. [33]In the same way, any of you who does not give up everything he has cannot be my disciple."

LUKE 18:29-30 "I tell you the truth," Jesus said to them, "no one who has left home or wife or brothers or parents or children for the sake of the kingdom of God [30]will fail to receive many times as much in this age and, in the age to come, eternal life."

Salt

MATTHEW 5:13 "You are the salt of the earth. But if the salt loses its saltiness, how can it be made salty again? It is no longer good for anything, except to be thrown out and trampled by men."

MARK 9:50 "Salt is good, but if it loses its saltiness, how can you make it salty again? Have salt in yourselves, and be at peace with each other."

LUKE 14:34-35 "Salt is good, but if it loses its saltiness, how can it be made salty again? 35It is fit neither for the soil nor for the manure pile; it is thrown out. He who has ears to hear, let him hear."

Sanctification

JOHN 17:15-19 "My prayer is not that you [God] take them out of the world but that you protect them from the evil one. 16They are not of the world, even as I am not of it. 17Sanctify them by the truth; your word is truth. 18As you sent me into the world, I have sent them into the world. 19For them I sanctify myself, that they too may be truly sanctified."

MATTHEW 5:29-30 "If your right eye causes you to sin, gouge it out and throw it away. It is better for you to lose one part of your body than for your whole body to be thrown into hell. 30And if your right hand causes you to sin, cut it off and throw it away. It is better for you to lose one part of your body than for your whole body to go into hell."

MATTHEW 5:48 "Be perfect, therefore, as your heavenly Father is perfect."

Security

JOHN 3:14-18 "Just as Moses lifted up the snake in the desert, so the Son of Man must be lifted up, 15that everyone who believes in him may have eternal life. 16For God so loved the world that he gave his one and only Son, that whoever believes in him shall not perish but have eternal life. 17For God did not send his Son into the world to condemn the world, but to save the world through him. 18Whoever believes in him is not condemned, but whoever does not believe stands condemned already because he has not believed in the name of God's one and only Son."

JOHN 10:27-30 "My sheep listen to my voice; I know them, and they follow me. 28I give them eternal life, and they shall never perish; no one can snatch them out of my hand. 29My Father, who has given them to me, is greater than all; no one can snatch them out of my Father's hand. 30I and the Father are one."

JOHN 14:2-4 "In my Father's house are many rooms; if it were not so, I would have told you. I am going there to prepare a place for you. 3And if I go and prepare a place for you, I will come back and take you to be with me that you also may be where I am. 4You know the way to the place where I am going."

JOHN 17:1-4 After Jesus said this, he looked toward heaven and prayed: "Father, the time has come. Glorify your Son, that your Son may glorify you. 2For you granted him authority over all people that he might give eternal life to all those you have given him. 3Now this is eternal life: that they may know you, the only true God, and Jesus Christ, whom you have sent. 4I have brought you glory on earth by completing the work you gave me to do."

Servants

JOHN 12:26 "Whoever serves me must follow me; and where I am, my servant also will be. My Father will honor the one who serves me."

JOHN 13:12-17 When he [Jesus] had finished washing their [the disciples'] feet, he put on his clothes and returned to his place. "Do you understand what I have done for you?" he asked them. [13]"You call me 'Teacher' and 'Lord,' and rightly so, for that is what I am. [14]Now that I, your Lord and Teacher, have washed your feet, you also should wash one another's feet. [15]I have set you an example that you should do as I have done for you. [16]I tell you the truth, no servant is greater than his master, nor is a messenger greater than the one who sent him. [17]Now that you know these things, you will be blessed if you do them."

JOHN 15:20-21 "Remember the words I spoke to you: 'No servant is greater than his master.' If they persecuted me, they will persecute you also. If they obeyed my teaching, they will obey yours also. [21]They will treat you this way because of my name, for they do not know the One who sent me."

MATTHEW 6:24 "No one can serve two masters. Either he will hate the one and love the other, or he will be devoted to the one and despise the other. You cannot serve both God and Money." (See also Luke 16:13.)

MATTHEW 10:24-25 "A student is not above his teacher, nor a servant above his master. [25]It is enough for the student to be like his teacher, and the servant like his master. If the head of the house has been called Beelzebub, how much more the members of his household!"

MATTHEW 10:42 "And if anyone gives even a cup of cold water to one of these little ones because he is my disciple, I tell you the truth, he will certainly not lose his reward."

MATTHEW 18:23-35 "Therefore, the kingdom of heaven is like a king who wanted to settle accounts with his servants. [24]As he began the settlement, a man who owed him ten thousand talents was brought to him. [25]Since he was not able to pay, the master ordered that he and his wife and his children and all that he had be sold to repay the debt. [26]The servant fell on his knees before him. 'Be patient with me,' he begged, 'and I will pay back everything.' [27]The servant's master took pity on him, canceled the debt and let him go. [28]But when that servant went out, he found one of his fellow servants who owed him a hundred denarii. He grabbed him and began to choke him. 'Pay back what you owe me!' he demanded. [29]His fellow servant fell to his knees and begged him, 'Be patient with me, and I will pay you back.' [30]But he refused. Instead, he went off and had the man thrown into prison until he could pay the debt. [31]When the other servants saw what had happened, they were greatly distressed and went and told their master everything that had happened. [32]Then the master called the servant in. 'You wicked servant,' he said, 'I canceled all that debt of yours because you begged me to. [33]Shouldn't you have had mercy on your fellow servant just as I had on you?' [34]In anger his master turned him over to the jailers to be tortured, until he should pay back all he owed. [35]This is how my heavenly Father will treat each of you unless you forgive your brother from your heart."

MATTHEW 20:25-28 Jesus called them [the disciples] together and said, "You know that the rulers of the Gentiles lord it over them, and their high officials exercise authority over them. [26]Not so with you. Instead, whoever wants to become great among you must be your servant, [27]and whoever wants to be first must be your slave— [28]just as the Son of Man did not come to be served, but to serve, and to give his life as a ransom for many."

MATTHEW 23:9-12 "And do not call anyone on earth 'father,' for you have one Father, and he is in heaven. [10]Nor are you to be called 'teacher,' for you have one Teacher, the Christ. [11]The greatest among you will be your servant. [12]For whoever exalts himself will be humbled, and whoever humbles himself will be exalted."

MATTHEW 24:43-51 "But understand this: If the owner of the house had known at what time of night the thief was coming, he would have kept watch and would not have let his house be broken into. [44]So you also must be ready, because the Son of Man will come at an hour when you do not expect him. [45]Who then is the faithful and wise servant, whom the master has put in charge of the servants in his household to give them their food at the proper time? [46]It will be good for that servant whose master finds him doing so when he returns. [47]I tell you the truth, he will put him in charge of all his posses-

sions. [48]But suppose that servant is wicked and says to himself, 'My master is staying away a long time,' [49]and he then begins to beat his fellow servants and to eat and drink with drunkards. [50]The master of that servant will come on a day when he does not expect him and at an hour he is not aware of. [51]He will cut him to pieces and assign him a place with the hypocrites, where there will be weeping and gnashing of teeth."

MATTHEW 25:14-30 "Again, it will be like a man going on a journey, who called his servants and entrusted his property to them. [15]To one he gave five talents of money, to another two talents, and to another one talent, each according to his ability. Then he went on his journey. [16]The man who had received the five talents went at once and put his money to work and gained five more. [17]So also, the one with the two talents gained two more. [18]But the man who had received the one talent went off, dug a hole in the ground and hid his master's money. [19]After a long time the master of those servants returned and settled accounts with them. [20]The man who had received the five talents brought the other five. 'Master,' he said, 'you entrusted me with five talents. See, I have gained five more.' [21]His master replied, 'Well done, good and faithful servant! You have been faithful with a few things; I will put you in charge of many things. Come and share your master's happiness!' [22]The man with the two talents also came. 'Master,' he said, 'you entrusted me with two talents; see, I have gained two more.' [23]His master replied, 'Well done, good and faithful servant! You have been faithful with a few things; I will put you in charge of many things. Come and share your master's happiness!' ²⁴Then the man who had received the one talent came. 'Master,' he said, 'I knew that you are a hard man, harvesting where you have not sown and gathering where you have not scattered seed. ²⁵So I was afraid and went out and hid your talent in the ground. See, here is what belongs to you.' ²⁶His master replied, 'You wicked, lazy servant! So you knew that I harvest where I have not sown and gather where I have not scattered seed? ²⁷Well then, you should have put my money on deposit with the bankers, so that when I returned I would have received it back with interest. ²⁸Take the talent from him and give it to the one who has the ten talents. ²⁹For everyone who has will be given more, and he will have an abundance. Whoever does not have, even what he has will be taken from him. ³⁰And throw that worthless servant outside, into the darkness, where there will be weeping and gnashing of teeth.' "

MARK 9:33-35 They came to Capernaum. When he was in the house, he asked them, "What were you arguing about on the road?" ³⁴But they kept quiet because on the way they had argued about who was the greatest. ³⁵Sitting down, Jesus called the Twelve and said, "If anyone wants to be first, he must be the very last, and the servant of all."

LUKE 12:35-40 "Be dressed ready for service and keep your lamps burning, ³⁶like men waiting for their master to return from a wedding banquet, so that when he comes and knocks they can

immediately open the door for him. ³⁷It will be good for those servants whose master finds them watching when he comes. I tell you the truth, he will dress himself to serve, will have them recline at the table and will come and wait on them. ³⁸It will be good for those servants whose master finds them ready, even if he comes in the second or third watch of the night. ³⁹But understand this: If the owner of the house had known at what hour the thief was coming, he would not have let his house be broken into. ⁴⁰You also must be ready, because the Son of Man will come at an hour when you do not expect him."

LUKE 12:42-48 The Lord answered, "Who then is the faithful and wise manager, whom the master puts in charge of his servants to give them their food allowance at the proper time? ⁴³It will be good for that servant whom the master finds doing so when he returns. ⁴⁴I tell you the truth, he will put him in charge of all his possessions. ⁴⁵But suppose the servant says to himself, 'My master is taking a long time in coming,' and he then begins to beat the menservants and maidservants and to eat and drink and get drunk. ⁴⁶The master of that servant will come on a day when he does not expect him and at an hour he is not aware of. He will cut him to pieces and assign him a place with the unbelievers. ⁴⁷That servant who knows his master's will and does not get ready or does not do what his master wants will be beaten with many blows. ⁴⁸But the one who does not know and does things deserving punishment will be beaten with few blows. From everyone who has been given much, much will be demanded; and from the one who has been entrusted with much, much more will be asked."

LUKE 17:7-10 "Suppose one of you had a servant plowing or looking after the sheep. Would he say to the servant when he comes in from the field, 'Come along now and sit down to eat'? [8]Would he not rather say, 'Prepare my supper, get yourself ready and wait on me while I eat and drink; after that you may eat and drink'? [9]Would he thank the servant because he did what he was told to do? [10]So you also, when you have done everything you were told to do, should say, 'We are unworthy servants; we have only done our duty.'"

LUKE 22:25-30 Jesus said to them [the apostles], "The kings of the Gentiles lord it over them; and those who exercise authority over them call themselves Benefactors. [26]But you are not to be like that. Instead, the greatest among you should be like the youngest, and the one who rules like the one who serves. [27]For who is greater, the one who is at the table or the one who serves? Is it not the one who is at the table? But I am among you as one who serves. [28]You are those who have stood by me in my trials. [29]And I confer on you a kingdom, just as my Father conferred one on me, [30]so that you may eat and drink at my table in my kingdom and sit on thrones, judging the twelve tribes of Israel."

Serving Others and Serving God

JOHN 13:12-17 When he [Jesus] had finished washing their [the disciples'] feet, he put on his clothes and returned to his place. "Do you understand what I have done for you?" he asked them. [13]"You call me 'Teacher' and 'Lord,' and rightly so, for that is what I am. [14]Now that I, your Lord and Teacher, have washed your feet, you also should wash one another's feet. [15]I have set you an example that you should do as I have done for you. [16]I tell you the truth, no servant is greater than his master, nor is a messenger greater than the one who sent him. [17]Now that you know these things, you will be blessed if you do them."

MATTHEW 20:25-28 Jesus called them [the disciples] together and said, "You know that the rulers of the Gentiles lord it over them, and their high officials exercise authority over them. [26]Not so with you. Instead, whoever wants to become great among you must be your servant, [27]and whoever wants to be first must be your slave— [28]just as the Son of Man did not come to be served, but to serve, and to give his life as a ransom for many." (See also Mark 10:42-45.)

MATTHEW 23:11-12 "The greatest among you will be your servant. [12]For whoever exalts himself will be humbled, and whoever humbles himself will be exalted."

LUKE 16:13 "No servant can serve two masters. Either he will hate the one and love the other, or he will be devoted to the one and despise the other. You cannot serve both God and Money."

LUKE 17:7-10 "Suppose one of you had a servant plowing or looking after the sheep. Would he say to the servant when he comes in from the field, 'Come along now and sit down to eat'? [8]Would he not rather say, 'Prepare my supper, get yourself ready and wait on me while I eat and drink; after that you may eat and drink'? [9]Would he thank the servant because he did what he was told to do? [10]So you also, when you have done everything you were told to do, should say, 'We are unworthy servants; we have only done our duty.'"

LUKE 19:12-27 He said: "A man of noble birth went to a distant country to have himself appointed king and then to return. [13]So he called ten of his servants and gave them ten minas. 'Put this money to work,' he said, 'until I come back.' [14]But his subjects hated him and sent a delegation after him to say, 'We don't want this man to be our king.' [15]He was made king, however, and returned home. Then he sent for the servants to whom he had given the money, in order to find out what they had gained with it. [16]The first one came and said, 'Sir, your mina has earned ten more.' [17]'Well done, my good servant!' his master replied. 'Because you have been trustworthy in a very small matter, take charge of ten cities.' [18]The second came and said, 'Sir, your mina has earned five more.' [19]His master answered, 'You take charge of five cities.' [20]Then another servant came and said, 'Sir, here is your mina; I have kept it laid away in a piece of cloth. [21]I was afraid of you, because you are a hard man. You take out what you did not put in and reap what you did not sow.' [22]His master replied, 'I will judge you by your own words, you wicked servant! You knew, did you, that I am a hard man, taking out what I did not put in, and reaping what I did not sow? [23]Why then didn't you put my money on deposit, so that when I came back, I could have collected it with interest?' [24]Then he said to those standing by, 'Take his mina away from him and give it to the one who has ten minas.' [25]'Sir,' they said, 'he already has ten!' [26]He replied, 'I tell you that to everyone who has, more will be given, but as for the one who has nothing, even what he has will be taken away. [27]But those enemies of mine who did not want me to be king over them—bring them here and kill them in front of me.'"

LUKE 22:25-30 Jesus said to them [the apostles], "The kings of the Gentiles lord it over them; and those who exercise authority over them call themselves Benefactors. [26]But you are not to be like that. Instead, the greatest among you should be like the youngest, and the one who rules like the one who serves. [27]For who is greater, the one who is at the table or the one who serves? Is it not the one who is at the table? But I am among you as one who serves. [28]You are those who have stood by me in my trials. [29]And I confer on you a kingdom, just as my Father conferred one on me, [30]so that you may eat and drink at my table in my kingdom and sit on thrones, judging the twelve tribes of Israel."

The Shepherd and His Sheep (Jesus Leading and Providing for His Followers)

JOHN 3:14-18 "Just as Moses lifted up the snake in the desert, so the Son of Man must be lifted up, [15]that everyone who believes in him may have eternal life. [16]For God so loved the world that he gave his one and only Son, that whoever believes in him shall not perish but have eternal life. [17]For God did not send his Son into the world to condemn the world, but to save the world through him. [18]Whoever believes in him is not condemned, but whoever does not believe stands condemned already because he has not believed in the name of God's one and only Son."

JOHN 10:1-5 "I tell you the truth, the man who does not enter the sheep pen by the gate, but climbs in by some other way, is a thief and a robber. [2]The man who enters by the gate is the shepherd of his sheep. [3]The watchman opens the gate for him, and the sheep listen to his voice. He calls his own sheep by name and leads them out. [4]When he has brought out all his own, he goes on ahead of them, and his sheep follow him because they know his voice. [5]But they will never follow a stranger; in fact, they will run away from him because they do not recognize a stranger's voice."

JOHN 10:11-16 "I am the good shepherd. The good shepherd lays down his life for the sheep. [12]The hired hand is not the shepherd who owns the sheep. So when he sees the wolf coming, he abandons the sheep and runs away. Then the wolf attacks the flock and scatters it. [13]The man runs away because he is a hired hand and cares nothing for the sheep. [14]I am the good shepherd; I know my sheep and my sheep know me— [15]just as the Father knows me and I know the Father—and I lay down my life for the sheep. [16]I have other sheep that are not of this sheep pen. I must bring them also.

They too will listen to my voice, and there shall be one flock and one shepherd."

JOHN 10:27-29 "My sheep listen to my voice; I know them, and they follow me. [28]I give them eternal life, and they shall never perish; no one can snatch them out of my hand. [29]My Father, who has given them to me, is greater than all; no one can snatch them out of my Father's hand."

JOHN 12:25-26 "The man who loves his life will lose it, while the man who hates his life in this world will keep it for eternal life. [26]Whoever serves me must follow me; and where I am, my servant also will be. My Father will honor the one who serves me."

JOHN 12:44-46 Then Jesus cried out, "When a man believes in me, he does not believe in me only, but in the one who sent me. [45]When he looks at me, he sees the one who sent me. [46]I have come into the world as a light, so that no one who believes in me should stay in darkness."

JOHN 13:7-10 Jesus replied, "You do not realize now what I am doing, but later you will understand." [8]"No," said Peter, "you shall never wash my feet." Jesus answered, "Unless I wash you, you have no part with me." [9]"Then, Lord," Simon Peter replied, "not just my feet but my hands and my head as well!" [10]Jesus answered, "A person who has had a bath needs only to wash his feet; his whole body is clean. And you are clean, though not every one of you."

JOHN 13:12-17 When he [Jesus] had finished washing their [the disciples'] feet, he put on his clothes and returned to his place. "Do you understand what I have done for you?" he asked them. ¹³"You call me 'Teacher' and 'Lord,' and rightly so, for that is what I am. ¹⁴Now that I, your Lord and Teacher, have washed your feet, you also should wash one another's feet. ¹⁵I have set you an example that you should do as I have done for you. ¹⁶I tell you the truth, no servant is greater than his master, nor is a messenger greater than the one who sent him. ¹⁷Now that you know these things, you will be blessed if you do them."

John 13:20 "I tell you the truth, whoever accepts anyone I send accepts me; and whoever accepts me accepts the one who sent me."

John 15:2-5 "He [the Father] cuts off every branch in me that bears no fruit, while every branch that does bear fruit he prunes so that it will be even more fruitful. ³You are already clean because of the word I have spoken to you. ⁴Remain in me, and I will remain in you. No branch can bear fruit by itself; it must remain in the vine. Neither can you bear fruit unless you remain in me. ⁵I am the vine; you are the branches. If a man remains in me and I in him, he will bear much fruit; apart from me you can do nothing."

John 17:6-11 "I have revealed you to those whom you gave me out of the world. They were yours; you gave them to me and they have obeyed your word. ⁷Now they know that everything you have given me comes from you. ⁸For I gave them the words you gave me and they accepted them. They knew with certainty that I came from you, and they believed that you sent me. ⁹I pray for them. I am not praying for the world, but for those

you have given me, for they are yours. ¹⁰All I have is yours, and all you have is mine. And glory has come to me through them. ¹¹I will remain in the world no longer, but they are still in the world, and I am coming to you. Holy Father, protect them by the power of your name—the name you gave me—so that they may be one as we are one."

John 17:20-26 "My prayer is not for them [the disciples] alone. I pray also for those who will believe in me through their message, ²¹that all of them may be one, Father, just as you are in me and I am in you. May they also be in us so that the world may believe that you have sent me. ²²I have given them the glory that you gave me, that they may be one as we are one: ²³I in them and you in me. May they be brought to complete unity to let the world know that you sent me and have loved them even as you have loved me. ²⁴Father, I want those you have given me to be with me where I am, and to see my glory, the glory you have given me because you loved me before the creation of the world. ²⁵Righteous Father, though the world does not know you, I know you, and they know that you have sent me. ²⁶I have made you known to them, and will continue to make you known in order that the love you have for me may be in them and that I myself may be in them."

Matthew 18:10, 12-14 "See that you do not look down on one of these little ones. For I tell you that their angels in heaven always see the face of my Father in heaven. ¹²What do you think? If a man owns a hundred sheep, and one of them wanders away, will he not leave the ninety-nine on the hills and go to look for the one that wandered off? [13]And if he finds it, I tell you the truth, he is happier about that one sheep than about the ninety-nine that did not wander off. [14]In the same way your Father in heaven is not willing that any of these little ones should be lost."

MATTHEW 18:18-20 "I tell you the truth, whatever you bind on earth will be bound in heaven, and whatever you loose on earth will be loosed in heaven. [19]Again, I tell you that if two of you on earth agree about anything you ask for, it will be done for you by my Father in heaven. [20]For where two or three come together in my name, there am I with them."

MATTHEW 26:31-32 Then Jesus told them [the disciples], "This very night you will all fall away on account of me, for it is written: 'I will strike the shepherd, and the sheep of the flock will be scattered.' [32]But after I have risen, I will go ahead of you into Galilee." (See also Mark 14:27-28.)

MARK 3:33-35 "Who are my mother and my brothers?" he [Jesus] asked. [34]Then he looked at those seated in a circle around him and said, "Here are my mother and my brothers! [35]Whoever does God's will is my brother and sister and mother."

MARK 4:9, 11 Then Jesus said, "He who has ears to hear, let him hear." [11]He told them, "The secret of the kingdom of God has been given to you. But to those on the outside everything is said in parables."

MARK 6:30-32 The apostles gathered around Jesus and reported to him all they had done and taught. [31]Then, because so many people were coming and going that they did not even have a chance to eat, he said to them, "Come with me by yourselves to a quiet place and get some rest." [32]So they went away by themselves in a boat to a solitary place.

LUKE 8:16 "No one lights a lamp and hides it in a jar or puts it under a bed. Instead, he puts it on a stand, so that those who come in can see the light."

LUKE 8:21 He replied, "My mother and brothers are those who hear God's word and put it into practice."

LUKE 15:4-7 "Suppose one of you has a hundred sheep and loses one of them. Does he not leave the ninety-nine in the open country and go after the lost sheep until he finds it? [5]And when he finds it, he joyfully puts it on his shoulders [6]and goes home. Then he calls his friends and neighbors together and says, 'Rejoice with me; I have found my lost sheep.' [7]I tell you that in the same way there will be more rejoicing in heaven over one sinner who repents than over ninety-nine righteous persons who do not need to repent."

Signs and Miracles

JOHN 2:1-10 On the third day a wedding took place at Cana in Galilee. Jesus' mother was there, [2]and Jesus and his disciples had also been invited to the wedding. [3]When the wine was gone, Jesus' mother said to him, "They have no more wine." [4]"Dear woman, why do you involve me?" Jesus replied. "My time has not yet come." [5]His mother said to the servants, "Do whatever he tells you." [6]Nearby stood six stone water jars, the kind used by the Jews for ceremonial washing, each holding from twenty to thirty gallons. [7]Jesus said to the servants, "Fill the jars with water"; so they filled them to the brim. [8]Then he told them, "Now draw some out and take it to the master of the banquet." They did so, [9]and the master of the banquet tasted the water that had been turned into wine. He did not realize where it had come from, though the servants who had drawn the water knew. Then he called the bridegroom aside [10]and said, "Everyone brings out the choice wine first and then the cheaper wine after the guests have had too much to drink; but you have saved the best till now."

JOHN 4:49-53 The royal official said, "Sir, come down before my child dies." [50]Jesus replied, "You may go. Your son will live." The man took Jesus at his word and departed. [51]While he was still on the way, his servants met him with the news that his boy was living. [52]When he inquired as to the time when his son got better, they said to him, "The fever left him yesterday at the seventh hour." [53]Then the father realized that this was the exact time at which Jesus had said to him, "Your son will live." So he and all his household believed.

JOHN 5:5-14 One who was there had been an invalid for thirty-eight years. [6]When Jesus saw him lying there and learned that he had been in this condition for a long time, he asked him, "Do you want to get well?" [7]"Sir," the invalid replied, "I have no one to help me into the pool when the water is stirred. While I am trying to get in, someone else goes down ahead of me." [8]Then Jesus said to him,

"Get up! Pick up your mat and walk." [9]At once the man was cured; he picked up his mat and walked. The day on which this took place was a Sabbath, [10]and so the Jews said to the man who had been healed, "It is the Sabbath; the law forbids you to carry your mat." [11]But he replied, "The man who made me well said to me, 'Pick up your mat and walk.'" [12]So they asked him, "Who is this fellow who told you to pick it up and walk?" [13]The man who was healed had no idea who it was, for Jesus had slipped away into the crowd that was there. [14]Later Jesus found him at the temple and said to him, "See, you are well again. Stop sinning or something worse may happen to you."

JOHN 6:5-13 When Jesus looked up and saw a great crowd coming toward him, he said to Philip, "Where shall we buy bread for these people to eat?" [6]He asked this only to test him, for he already had in mind what he was going to do. [7]Philip answered him, "Eight months' wages would not buy enough bread for each one to have a bite!" [8]Another of his disciples, Andrew, Simon Peter's brother, spoke up, [9]"Here is a boy with five small barley loaves and two small fish, but how far will they go among so many?" [10]Jesus said, "Have the people sit down." There was plenty of grass in that place, and the men sat down, about five thousand of them. [11]Jesus then took the loaves, gave thanks, and distributed to those who were seated as much as they wanted. He did the same with the fish. [12]When they had all had enough to eat, he said to his disciples, "Gather the pieces that are left over. Let nothing be wasted." [13]So they gathered them and filled twelve baskets with the pieces of the five barley loaves left over by those who had eaten.

JOHN 11:11-15 After he had said this, he went on to tell them, "Our friend Lazarus has fallen asleep; but I am going there to wake him up." [12]His disciples replied, "Lord, if he sleeps, he will get better." [13]Jesus had been speaking of his death, but his disciples thought he meant natural sleep. [14]So then he told them plainly, "Lazarus is dead, [15]and for your sake I am glad I was not there, so that you may believe. But let us go to him."

JOHN 11:21-23 "Lord," Martha said to Jesus, "if you had been here, my brother would not have died. [22]But I know that even now God will give you whatever you ask." [23]Jesus said to her, "Your brother will rise again."

JOHN 14:12-14 "I tell you the truth, anyone who has faith in me will do what I have been doing. He will do even greater things than these, because I am going to the Father. [13]And I will do whatever you ask in my name, so that the Son may bring glory to the Father. [14]You may ask me for anything in my name, and I will do it."

JOHN 21:4-6, 9-12 Early in the morning, Jesus stood on the shore, but the disciples did not realize that it was Jesus. [5]He called out to them, "Friends, haven't you any fish?" "No," they answered. [6]He said, "Throw your net on the right side of the boat and you will find some." When they did, they were unable to haul the net in because of the large number of fish. [9]When they landed, they saw a fire of burning coals there with fish on it, and some bread. [10]Jesus said to them, "Bring some of the fish you have just caught." [11]Simon Peter climbed aboard and dragged the net ashore. It was full of large fish, 153, but even with so many the net was not torn. [12]Jesus said to them, "Come and have breakfast." None of the disciples dared ask him, "Who are you?" They knew it was the Lord.

MATTHEW 7:21-23 "Not everyone who says to Me, 'Lord, Lord,' shall enter the kingdom of heaven, but he who does the will of My Father in heaven. [22]Many will say to Me in that day, 'Lord, Lord, have we not prophesied in Your name, cast out demons in Your name, and done many wonders in Your name?' [23]And then I will declare to them, 'I never knew you; depart from Me, you who practice lawlessness!' " (NKJV)

MATTHEW 14:15-20 As evening approached, the disciples came to him and said, "This is a remote place, and it's already getting late. Send the crowds away, so they can go to the villages and buy themselves some food." [16]Jesus replied, "They do not need to go away. You give them something to eat." [17]"We have here only five loaves of bread and two fish," they answered. [18]"Bring them here to me," he said. [19]And he directed the people to sit down on the grass. Taking the five loaves and the two fish and looking up to heaven, he gave thanks and broke the loaves. Then he gave them to the disciples, and the disciples gave them to the people. [20]They all ate and were satisfied, and the disciples picked up twelve basketfuls of broken pieces that were left over.

MARK 6:35-43 By this time it was late in the day, so his disciples came to him. "This is a remote place," they said, "and it's already very late. ³⁶Send the people away so they can go to the surrounding countryside and villages and buy themselves something to eat." ³⁷But he answered, "You give them something to eat." They said to him, "That would take eight months of a man's wages! Are we to go and spend that much on bread and give it to them to eat?" ³⁸"How many loaves do you have?" he asked. "Go and see." When they found out, they said, "Five—and two fish." ³⁹Then Jesus directed them to have all the people sit down in groups on the green grass. ⁴⁰So they sat down in groups of hundreds and fifties. ⁴¹Taking the five loaves and the two fish and looking up to heaven, he gave thanks and broke the loaves. Then he gave them to his disciples to set before the people. He also divided the two fish among them all. ⁴²They all ate and were satisfied, ⁴³and the disciples picked up twelve basketfuls of broken pieces of bread and fish.

MARK 9:38-40 "Teacher," said John, "we saw a man driving out demons in your name and we told him to stop, because he was not one of us." ³⁹"Do not stop him," Jesus said. "No one who does a miracle in my name can in the next moment say anything bad about me, ⁴⁰for whoever is not against us is for us."

MARK 16:14-18 Later Jesus appeared to the Eleven as they were eating; he rebuked them for their lack of faith and their stubborn refusal to believe those who had seen him after he had risen. ¹⁵He said to them, "Go into all the world and preach the good news to all creation.

¹⁶Whoever believes and is baptized will be saved, but whoever does not believe will be condemned. ¹⁷And these signs will accompany those who believe: In my name they will drive out demons; they will speak in new tongues; ¹⁸they will pick up snakes with their hands; and when they drink deadly poison, it will not hurt them at all; they will place their hands on sick people, and they will get well."ˣᵛⁱ

LUKE 8:22-25 One day Jesus said to his disciples, "Let's go over to the other side of the lake." So they got into a boat and set out. ²³As they sailed, he fell asleep. A squall came down on the lake, so that the boat was being swamped, and they were in great danger. ²⁴The disciples went and woke him, saying, "Master, Master, we're going to drown!" He got up and rebuked the wind and the raging waters; the storm subsided, and all was calm. ²⁵"Where is your faith?" he asked his disciples. In fear and amazement they asked one another, "Who is this? He commands even the winds and the water, and they obey him." (See also Matthew 8:23-27; Mark 4:35-41.)

LUKE 9:12-17 Late in the afternoon the Twelve came to him and said, "Send the crowd away so they can go to the surrounding villages and countryside and find food and lodging, because we are in a remote place here." ¹³He replied, "You give them something to eat." They answered, "We have only five loaves of bread and two fish—unless we go and buy food for all this crowd." ¹⁴(About five thousand men were there.) But he said to his disciples, "Have them sit down in groups of about fifty each." ¹⁵The disciples did so, and everybody sat down. [16]Taking the five loaves and the two fish and looking up to heaven, he gave thanks and broke them. Then he gave them to the disciples to set before the people. [17]They all ate and were satisfied, and the disciples picked up twelve basketfuls of broken pieces that were left over.

LUKE 10:17-20 The seventy-two returned with joy and said, "Lord, even the demons submit to us in your name." [18]He replied, "I saw Satan fall like lightning from heaven. [19]I have given you authority to trample on snakes and scorpions and to overcome all the power of the enemy; nothing will harm you. [20]However, do not rejoice that the spirits submit to you, but rejoice that your names are written in heaven."

Small Beginnings, Big Outcomes

MATTHEW 10:42 "And if anyone gives even a cup of cold water to one of these little ones because he is my disciple, I tell you the truth, he will certainly not lose his reward."

MATTHEW 13:33 He told them still another parable: "The kingdom of heaven is like yeast that a woman took and mixed into a large amount of flour until it worked all through the dough."

MARK 4:26-29 He also said, "This is what the kingdom of God is like. A man scatters seed on the ground. [27]Night and day, whether he sleeps or gets up, the seed sprouts and grows, though he does not know how. [28]All by itself the soil produces grain—first the stalk, then the head, then the full kernel in the head. [29]As soon as

the grain is ripe, he puts the sickle to it, because the harvest has come."

MARK 4:30-32 Again he said, "What shall we say the kingdom of God is like, or what parable shall we use to describe it? [31]It is like a mustard seed, which is the smallest seed you plant in the ground. [32]Yet when planted, it grows and becomes the largest of all garden plants, with such big branches that the birds of the air can perch in its shade."

Sons of God

JOHN 12:36 "Put your trust in the light while you have it, so that you may become sons of light." When he had finished speaking, Jesus left and hid himself from them.

MATTHEW 5:9 "Blessed are the peacemakers, for they will be called sons of God."

MATTHEW 5:43-48 "You have heard that it was said, 'Love your neighbor and hate your enemy.' [44]But I tell you: Love your enemies and pray for those who persecute you, [45]that you may be sons of your Father in heaven. He causes his sun to rise on the evil and the good, and sends rain on the righteous and the unrighteous. [46]If you love those who love you, what reward will you get? Are not even the tax collectors doing that? [47]And if you greet only your brothers, what are you doing more than others? Do not even pagans do that? [48]Be perfect, therefore, as your heavenly Father is perfect."

LUKE 6:32-36 "If you love those who love you, what credit is that to you? Even 'sinners' love those who love them.

[33]And if you do good to those who are good to you, what credit is that to you? Even 'sinners' do that. [34]And if you lend to those from whom you expect repayment, what credit is that to you? Even 'sinners' lend to 'sinners,' expecting to be repaid in full. [35]But love your enemies, do good to them, and lend to them without expecting to get anything back. Then your reward will be great, and you will be sons of the Most High, because he is kind to the ungrateful and wicked. [36]Be merciful, just as your Father is merciful."

LUKE 20:34-36 Jesus replied, "The people of this age marry and are given in marriage. [35]But those who are considered worthy of taking part in that age and in the resurrection from the dead will neither marry nor be given in marriage, [36]and they can no longer die; for they are like the angels. They are God's children, since they are children of the resurrection."

Spiritual Maturity

MATTHEW 5:6 "Blessed are those who hunger and thirst for righteousness, for they will be filled."

MATTHEW 5:38-48 "You have heard that it was said, 'Eye for eye, and tooth for tooth.' [39]But I tell you, Do not resist an evil person. If someone strikes you on the right cheek, turn to him the other also. [40]And if someone wants to sue you and take your tunic, let him have your cloak as well. [41]If someone forces you to go one mile, go with him two miles. [42]Give to the one who asks you, and do not turn away from the one who wants to borrow from you. [43]You have heard that it

was said, 'Love your neighbor and hate your enemy.' [44]But I tell you: Love your enemies and pray for those who persecute you, [45]that you may be sons of your Father in heaven. He causes his sun to rise on the evil and the good, and sends rain on the righteous and the unrighteous. [46]If you love those who love you, what reward will you get? Are not even the tax collectors doing that? [47]And if you greet only your brothers, what are you doing more than others? Do not even pagans do that? [48]Be perfect, therefore, as your heavenly Father is perfect."

MATTHEW 7:24-25 "Therefore whoever hears these sayings of Mine, and does them, I will liken him to a wise man who built his house on the rock: [25]and the rain descended, the floods came, and the winds blew and beat on that house; and it did not fall, for it was founded on the rock." (NKJV)

REVELATION 2:19 "I know your deeds, your love and faith, your service and perseverance, and that you are now doing more than you did at first."

Spiritual Priorities

At the end of a day, a week, or even a year, have you ever felt as if you didn't accomplish all that much? Have you been discouraged that even though you took care of a lot of less-important matters, you didn't progress in the most important matter—the spiritual side of your life? The good news is, no matter how discouraged you have been, it can all change in a matter of minutes. If anyone knows what really matters and what doesn't, it's Jesus.

And fortunately for us, He doesn't keep us in the dark. In the passages you'll read in this section, you will find that Jesus clearly reveals the things that matter most to God and what should matter most to you. As you begin to see the priorities He lays before you, write down how they relate to your daily life and what you can do to embrace His priorities as your own. As Jesus' priorities begin to influence your attitudes and activities, your sense of joy and fulfillment will rise to a level that can't be reached any other way.

JOHN 6:27 "Do not work for food that spoils, but for food that endures to eternal life, which the Son of Man will give you. On him God the Father has placed his seal of approval."

JOHN 6:63 "The Spirit gives life; the flesh counts for nothing. The words I have spoken to you are spirit and they are life."

JOHN 12:25-26 "The man who loves his life will lose it, while the man who hates his life in this world will keep it for eternal life. 26Whoever serves me must follow me; and where I am, my servant also will be. My Father will honor the one who serves me."

JOHN 21:15-17 When they had finished eating, Jesus said to Simon Peter, "Simon son of John, do you truly love me more than these?" "Yes, Lord," he said, "you know that I love you." Jesus said, "Feed my lambs." 16Again Jesus said, "Simon son of John, do you truly love me?" He answered, "Yes, Lord, you know that I love you." Jesus said, "Take care of my sheep." 17The third time he said to him, "Simon son of John, do you love

me?" Peter was hurt because Jesus asked him the third time, "Do you love me?" He said, "Lord, you know all things; you know that I love you." Jesus said, "Feed my sheep."

MATTHEW 4:4 Jesus answered, "It is written: 'Man does not live on bread alone, but on every word that comes from the mouth of God.'" (See also Luke 4:4.)

MATTHEW 4:10 Jesus said to him, "Away from me, Satan! For it is written: 'Worship the Lord your God, and serve him only.'" (See also Luke 4:8.)

MATTHEW 5:3-9 "Blessed are the poor in spirit, for theirs is the kingdom of heaven. 4Blessed are those who mourn, for they will be comforted. 5Blessed are the meek, for they will inherit the earth. 6Blessed are those who hunger and thirst for righteousness, for they will be filled. 7Blessed are the merciful, for they will be shown mercy. 8Blessed are the pure in heart, for they will see God. 9Blessed are the peacemakers, for they will be called sons of God."

MATTHEW 5:27-30 "You have heard that it was said, 'Do not commit adultery.' 28But I tell you that anyone who looks at a woman lustfully has already committed adultery with her in his heart. 29If your right eye causes you to sin, gouge it out and throw it away. It is better for you to lose one part of your body than for your whole body to be thrown into hell. 30And if your right hand causes you to sin, cut it off and throw it away. It is better for you to lose one part of your body than for your whole body to go into hell."

MATTHEW 6:1-4 "Be careful not to do your 'acts of righteousness' before men, to be seen by them. If you do, you will have no reward from your Father in heaven. [2]So when you give to the needy, do not announce it with trumpets, as the hypocrites do in the synagogues and on the streets, to be honored by men. I tell you the truth, they have received their reward in full. [3]But when you give to the needy, do not let your left hand know what your right hand is doing, [4]so that your giving may be in secret. Then your Father, who sees what is done in secret, will reward you."

MATTHEW 6:19-21 "Do not store up for yourselves treasures on earth, where moth and rust destroy, and where thieves break in and steal. [20]But store up for yourselves treasures in heaven, where moth and rust do not destroy, and where thieves do not break in and steal. [21]For where your treasure is, there your heart will be also."

MATTHEW 6:22-23 "The eye is the lamp of the body. If your eyes are good, your whole body will be full of light. [23]But if your eyes are bad, your whole body will be full of darkness. If then the light within you is darkness, how great is that darkness!"

MATTHEW 6:24-34 "No one can serve two masters. Either he will hate the one and love the other, or he will be devoted to the one and despise the other. You cannot serve both God and Money. [25]Therefore I tell you, do not worry about your life, what you will eat or drink; or about your body, what you will wear. Is not life more important than food, and the body more important than clothes? [26]Look at the birds of the air; they do not sow or reap or store away in barns, and yet your heavenly Father feeds them. Are you not much more valuable than they? [27]Who of you by worrying can add a single hour to his life? [28]And why do you worry about clothes? See how the lilies of the field grow. They do not labor or spin. [29]Yet I tell you that not even Solomon in all his splendor was dressed like one of these. [30]If that is how God clothes the grass of the field, which is here today and tomorrow is thrown into the fire, will he not much more clothe you, O you of little faith? [31]So do not worry, saying, 'What shall we eat?' or 'What shall we drink?' or 'What shall we wear?' [32]For the pagans run after all these things, and your heavenly Father knows that you need them. [33]But seek first his kingdom and his righteousness, and all these things will be given to you as well. [34]Therefore do not worry about tomorrow, for tomorrow will worry about itself. Each day has enough trouble of its own."

MATTHEW 7:21-27 "Not everyone who says to Me, 'Lord, Lord,' shall enter the kingdom of heaven, but he who does the will of My Father in heaven. [22]Many will say to Me in that day, 'Lord, Lord, have we not prophesied in Your name, cast out demons in Your name, and done many wonders in Your name?' [23]And then I will declare to them, 'I never knew you; depart from Me, you who practice lawlessness!' [24]Therefore whoever hears these sayings of Mine, and does them, I will liken him to a wise man who built his house on the rock: [25]and the rain descended, the floods came, and the winds blew and beat on that house; and it did not fall, for it was founded on the rock. [26]But everyone who hears these sayings of Mine, and does not do them, will be like a foolish man who built his house on the sand: [27]and the rain descended, the floods came, and the winds blew and beat on that house; and it fell. And great was its fall." (NKJV)

Matthew 8:19-22 Then a teacher of the law came to him and said, "Teacher, I will follow you wherever you go." [20]Jesus replied, "Foxes have holes and birds of the air have nests, but the Son of Man has no place to lay his head." [21]Another disciple said to him, "Lord, first let me go and bury my father." [22]But Jesus told him, "Follow me, and let the dead bury their own dead."

Matthew 9:12-13 On hearing this, Jesus said, "It is not the healthy who need a doctor, but the sick. [13]But go and learn what this means: 'I desire mercy, not sacrifice.' For I have not come to call the righteous, but sinners."

Matthew 9:15-17 Jesus answered, "How can the guests of the bridegroom mourn while he is with them? The time will come when the bridegroom will be taken from them; then they will fast. [16]No one sews a patch of unshrunk cloth on an old garment, for the patch will pull away from the garment, making the tear worse. [17]Neither do men pour new wine into old wineskins. If they do, the skins will burst, the wine will run out and the wineskins will be ruined. No, they pour new wine into new wineskins, and both are preserved."

Matthew 10:24-26 "A student is not above his teacher, nor a servant above his master. [25]It is enough for the student to be like his teacher, and the servant like his master. If the head of the house has been called Beelzebub, how much more the members of his household! [26]So do not be afraid of them. There is nothing concealed that will not be disclosed, or hidden that will not be made known."

Matthew 13:44-46 "The kingdom of heaven is like treasure hidden in a field. When a man found it, he hid it again, and then in his joy went and sold all he had and bought that field. [45]Again, the kingdom of heaven is like a merchant looking for fine pearls. [46]When he found one of great value, he went away and sold everything he had and bought it."

Matthew 18:8-9 "If your hand or your foot causes you to sin, cut it off and throw it away. It is better for you to enter life maimed or crippled than to have two hands or two feet and be thrown into eternal fire. [9]And if your eye causes you to sin, gouge it out and throw it away. It is better for you to enter life with one eye than to have two eyes and be thrown into the fire of hell."

Matthew 19:27-30 Peter answered him, "We have left everything to follow you! What then will there be for us?" [28]Jesus said to them, "I tell you the truth, at the renewal of all things, when the Son of Man sits on his glorious throne, you who have followed me will also sit on twelve thrones, judging the twelve tribes of Israel. [29]And everyone who has left houses or brothers or sisters or father or mother or children or fields for my sake will receive a hundred times as much and will inherit eternal life. [30]But many who are first will be last, and many who are last will be first."

MATTHEW 20:1-16 "For the kingdom of heaven is like a landowner who went out early in the morning to hire men to work in his vineyard. [2]He agreed to pay them a denarius for the day and sent them into his vineyard. [3]About the third hour he went out and saw others standing in the marketplace doing nothing. [4]He told them, 'You also go and work in my vineyard, and I will pay you whatever is right.' [5]So they went. He went out again about the sixth hour and the ninth hour and did the same thing. [6]About the eleventh hour he went out and found still others standing around. He asked them, 'Why have you been standing here all day long doing nothing?' [7]'Because no one has hired us,' they answered. He said to them, 'You also go and work in my vineyard.' [8]"When evening came, the owner of the vineyard said to his foreman, 'Call the workers and pay them their wages, beginning with the last ones hired and going on to the first.' [9]The workers who were hired about the eleventh hour came and each received a denarius. [10]So when those came who were hired first, they expected to receive more. But each one of them also received a denarius. [11]When they received it, they began to grumble against the landowner. [12]'These men who were hired last worked only one hour,' they said, 'and you have made them equal to us who have borne the burden of the work and the heat of the day.' [13]But he answered one of them, 'Friend, I am not being unfair to you. Didn't you agree to work for a denarius? [14]Take your pay and go. I want to give the man who was hired last the same as I gave you. [15]Don't I have the right to do what I want with my own money? Or are you envious because I am generous?' [16]So the last will be first, and the first will be last."

MATTHEW 20:25-28 Jesus called them [the disciples] together and said, "You know that the rulers of the Gentiles lord it over them, and their high officials exercise authority over them. [26]Not so with you. Instead, whoever wants to become great among you must be your servant, [27]and whoever wants to be first must be your slave— [28]just as the Son of Man did not come to be served, but to serve, and to give his life as a ransom for many."

MATTHEW 26:10-13 Aware of this, Jesus said to them, "Why are you bothering this woman? She has done a beautiful thing to me. [11]The poor you will always have with you, but you will not always have me. [12]When she poured this perfume on my body, she did it to prepare me for burial. [13]I tell you the truth, wherever this gospel is preached throughout the world, what she has done will also be told, in memory of her."

MARK 4:9 Then Jesus said, "He who has ears to hear, let him hear."

MARK 8:33-37 But when Jesus turned and looked at his disciples, he rebuked Peter. "Get behind me, Satan!" he said. "You do not have in mind the things of God, but the things of men." [34]Then he called the crowd to him along with his disciples and said: "If anyone would come after me, he must deny himself and take up his cross and follow me. [35]For whoever wants to save his life will lose it, but whoever loses his life for me and for the gospel will save it. [36]What good is it for a man to gain the whole world, yet forfeit his soul? [37]Or what can a man give in exchange for his soul?"

MARK 9:35-37 Sitting down, Jesus called the Twelve and said, "If anyone wants to be first, he must be the very last, and the servant of all." [36]He took a little child and had him stand among them. Taking him in his arms, he said to them, [37]"Whoever welcomes one of these little children in my name welcomes me; and whoever welcomes me does not welcome me but the one who sent me."

MARK 9:43, 45, 47-48 "If your hand causes you to sin, cut it off. It is better for you to enter life maimed than with two hands to go into hell, where the fire never goes out. [45]And if your foot causes you to sin, cut it off. It is better for you to enter life crippled than to have two feet and be thrown into hell. [47]And if your eye causes you to sin, pluck it out. It is better for you to enter the kingdom of God with one eye than to have two eyes and be thrown into hell, [48]where 'their worm does not die, and the fire is not quenched.'"

MARK 9:50 "Salt is good, but if it loses its saltiness, how can you make it salty again? Have salt in yourselves, and be at peace with each other."

MARK 10:29-31 "I tell you the truth," Jesus replied, "no one who has left home or brothers or sisters or mother or father or children or fields for me and the gospel [30]will fail to receive a hundred times as much in this present age (homes, brothers, sisters, mothers, children and fields—and with them, persecutions) and in the age to come, eternal life. [31]But

many who are first will be last, and the last first."

MARK 12:14-17 They came to him and said, "Teacher, we know you are a man of integrity. You aren't swayed by men, because you pay no attention to who they are; but you teach the way of God in accordance with the truth. Is it right to pay taxes to Caesar or not? [15]Should we pay or shouldn't we?" But Jesus knew their hypocrisy. "Why are you trying to trap me?" he asked. "Bring me a denarius and let me look at it." [16]They brought the coin, and he asked them, "Whose portrait is this? And whose inscription?" "Caesar's," they replied. [17]Then Jesus said to them, "Give to Caesar what is Caesar's and to God what is God's.".... (See also Matthew 22:16-21; Luke 20:21-25.)

LUKE 6:46-49 "Why do you call me, 'Lord, Lord,' and do not do what I say? [47]I will show you what he is like who comes to me and hears my words and puts them into practice. [48]He is like a man building a house, who dug down deep and laid the foundation on rock. When a flood came, the torrent struck that house but could not shake it, because it was well built. [49]But the one who hears my words and does not put them into practice is like a man who built a house on the ground without a foundation. The moment the torrent struck that house, it collapsed and its destruction was complete."

LUKE 7:40-47 Jesus answered him, "Simon, I have something to tell you." "Tell me, teacher," he said. [41]"Two men owed money to a certain moneylender. One owed him five hundred denarii, and the other fifty. [42]Neither of them had the money to pay him back, so he canceled the debts of both. Now which of them will love him more?" ⁴³Simon replied, "I suppose the one who had the bigger debt canceled." "You have judged correctly," Jesus said. ⁴⁴Then he turned toward the woman and said to Simon, "Do you see this woman? I came into your house. You did not give me any water for my feet, but she wet my feet with her tears and wiped them with her hair. ⁴⁵You did not give me a kiss, but this woman, from the time I entered, has not stopped kissing my feet. ⁴⁶You did not put oil on my head, but she has poured perfume on my feet. ⁴⁷Therefore, I tell you, her many sins have been forgiven—for she loved much. But he who has been forgiven little loves little."

LUKE 9:23-26 Then he said to them all: "If anyone would come after me, he must deny himself and take up his cross daily and follow me. ²⁴For whoever wants to save his life will lose it, but whoever loses his life for me will save it. ²⁵What good is it for a man to gain the whole world, and yet lose or forfeit his very self? ²⁶If anyone is ashamed of me and my words, the Son of Man will be ashamed of him when he comes in his glory and in the glory of the Father and of the holy angels."

LUKE 9:57 As they were walking along the road, a man said to him, "I will follow you wherever you go."

LUKE 10:38-42 As Jesus and his disciples were on their way, he came to a village where a woman named Martha opened her home to him. ³⁹She had a sister called Mary, who sat at the Lord's feet listening to what he said. ⁴⁰But Martha was distracted by all the preparations that

had to be made. She came to him and asked, "Lord, don't you care that my sister has left me to do the work by myself? Tell her to help me!" ⁴¹"Martha, Martha," the Lord answered, "you are worried and upset about many things, ⁴²but only one thing is needed. Mary has chosen what is better, and it will not be taken away from her."

LUKE 12:4-7 "I tell you, my friends, do not be afraid of those who kill the body and after that can do no more. ⁵But I will show you whom you should fear: Fear him who, after the killing of the body, has power to throw you into hell. Yes, I tell you, fear him. ⁶Are not five sparrows sold for two pennies? Yet not one of them is forgotten by God. ⁷Indeed, the very hairs of your head are all numbered. Don't be afraid; you are worth more than many sparrows."

LUKE 12:13-21 Someone in the crowd said to him, "Teacher, tell my brother to divide the inheritance with me." ¹⁴Jesus replied, "Man, who appointed me a judge or an arbiter between you?" ¹⁵Then he said to them, "Watch out! Be on your guard against all kinds of greed; a man's life does not consist in the abundance of his possessions." ¹⁶And he told them this parable: "The ground of a certain rich man produced a good crop. ¹⁷He thought to himself, 'What shall I do? I have no place to store my crops.' ¹⁸Then he said, 'This is what I'll do. I will tear down my barns and build bigger ones, and there I will store all my grain and my goods. ¹⁹And I'll say to myself, "You have plenty of good things laid up for many years. Take life easy; eat, drink and be merry." ' ²⁰But God said to him, 'You fool!

This very night your life will be demanded from you. Then who will get what you have prepared for yourself?' [21]This is how it will be with anyone who stores up things for himself but is not rich toward God."

LUKE 12:22-34 Then Jesus said to his disciples: "Therefore I tell you, do not worry about your life, what you will eat; or about your body, what you will wear. [23]Life is more than food, and the body more than clothes. [24]Consider the ravens: They do not sow or reap, they have no storeroom or barn; yet God feeds them. And how much more valuable you are than birds! [25]Who of you by worrying can add a single hour to his life? [26]Since you cannot do this very little thing, why do you worry about the rest? [27]Consider how the lilies grow. They do not labor or spin. Yet I tell you, not even Solomon in all his splendor was dressed like one of these. [28]If that is how God clothes the grass of the field, which is here today, and tomorrow is thrown into the fire, how much more will he clothe you, O you of little faith! [29]And do not set your heart on what you will eat or drink; do not worry about it. [30]For the pagan world runs after all such things, and your Father knows that you need them. [31]But seek his kingdom, and these things will be given to you as well. [32]Do not be afraid, little flock, for your Father has been pleased to give you the kingdom. [33]Sell your possessions and give to the poor. Provide purses for yourselves that will not wear out, a treasure in heaven that will not be exhausted, where no thief comes near and no moth destroys. [34]For where your treasure is, there your heart will be also."

LUKE 12:35-40 "Be dressed ready for service and keep your lamps burning, [36]like men waiting for their master to return from a wedding banquet, so that when he comes and knocks they can immediately open the door for him. [37]It will be good for those servants whose master finds them watching when he comes. I tell you the truth, he will dress himself to serve, will have them recline at the table and will come and wait on them. [38]It will be good for those servants whose master finds them ready, even if he comes in the second or third watch of the night. [39]But understand this: If the owner of the house had known at what hour the thief was coming, he would not have let his house be broken into. [40]You also must be ready, because the Son of Man will come at an hour when you do not expect him."

LUKE 12:42-53 The Lord answered, "Who then is the faithful and wise manager, whom the master puts in charge of his servants to give them their food allowance at the proper time? [43]It will be good for that servant whom the master finds doing so when he returns. [44]I tell you the truth, he will put him in charge of all his possessions. [45]But suppose the servant says to himself, 'My master is taking a long time in coming,' and he then begins to beat the menservants and maidservants and to eat and drink and get drunk. [46]The master of that servant will come on a day when he does not expect him and at an hour he is not aware of. He will cut him to pieces and assign him a place with the unbelievers. [47]That servant who knows his master's will and does not get ready or does not do what his master wants will be beaten with many blows. [48]But the one who does not know and does things deserving punishment will be beaten with few blows. From everyone who has been given much, much will be demanded; and from the one who has been entrusted with much, much more will be asked. [49]I have come to bring fire on the earth, and how I wish it were already kindled! [50]But I have a baptism to undergo, and how distressed I am until it is completed! [51]Do you think I came to bring peace on earth? No, I tell you, but division. [52]From now on there will be five in one family divided against each other, three against two and two against three. [53]They will be divided, father against son and son against father, mother against daughter and daughter against mother, mother-in-law against daughter-in-law and daughter-in-law against mother-in-law."

LUKE 13:23-30 Someone asked him, "Lord, are only a few people going to be saved?" He said to them, [24]"Make every effort to enter through the narrow door, because many, I tell you, will try to enter and will not be able to. [25]Once the owner of the house gets up and closes the door, you will stand outside knocking and pleading, 'Sir, open the door for us.' But he will answer, 'I don't know you or where you come from.' [26]Then you will say, 'We ate and drank with you, and you taught in our streets.' [27]But he will reply, 'I don't know you or where you come from. Away from me, all you evildoers!' [28]There will be weeping there, and gnashing of teeth, when you see Abraham, Isaac and Jacob and all the prophets in the kingdom of God, but you yourselves thrown out. [29]People will come from east and west and north and south, and will take their places at the feast in the kingdom of God. [30]Indeed there are those who are last who will be first, and first who will be last."

LUKE 14:12-14 Then Jesus said to his host, "When you give a luncheon or dinner, do not invite your friends, your brothers or relatives, or your rich neighbors; if you do, they may invite you back and so you will be repaid. [13]But when you give a banquet, invite the poor, the crippled, the lame, the blind, [14]and you will be blessed. Although they cannot repay you, you will be repaid at the resurrection of the righteous."

LUKE 14:25-35 Large crowds were traveling with Jesus, and turning to them he said: [26]"If anyone comes to me and does not hate his father and mother, his wife and children, his brothers and sisters—yes, even his own life—he cannot be my disciple. [27]And anyone who does not carry his cross and follow me cannot be my disciple. [28]Suppose one of you wants to build a tower. Will he not first sit down and estimate the cost to see if he has enough money to complete it? [29]For if he lays the foundation and is not able to finish it, everyone who sees it will ridicule him, [30]saying, 'This fellow began to build and was not able to finish.' [31]Or suppose a king is about to go to war against another king. Will he not first sit down and consider whether he is able with ten thousand men to oppose the one coming against him with twenty thousand? [32]If he is not able, he will send a delegation while the other is still a long way off and will ask for terms of peace. [33]In the same way, any of you who does not give up everything he has cannot be my disciple. [34]Salt is good, but if it loses its saltiness, how can it be made salty again? [35]It is fit neither for the soil nor for the manure pile; it is thrown out. He who has ears to hear, let him hear."

LUKE 16:9-12 "I tell you, use worldly wealth to gain friends for yourselves, so that when it is gone, you will be welcomed into eternal dwellings. [10]Whoever can be trusted with very little can also be trusted with much, and whoever is dishonest with very little will also be dishonest with much. [11]So if you have not been trustworthy in handling worldly wealth, who will trust you with true riches? [12]And if you have not been trustworthy with someone else's property, who will give you property of your own?"

LUKE 16:13 "No servant can serve two masters. Either he will hate the one and love the other, or he will be devoted to the one and despise the other. You cannot serve both God and Money."

LUKE 16:15 He said to them [the Pharisees], "You are the ones who justify yourselves in the eyes of men, but God knows your hearts. What is highly valued among men is detestable in God's sight."

LUKE 22:25-30 Jesus said to them [the apostles], "The kings of the Gentiles lord it over them; and those who exercise authority over them call themselves Benefactors. [26]But you are not to be like that. Instead, the greatest among you should be like the youngest, and the one who rules like the one who serves. [27]For who is greater, the one who is at the table or the one who serves? Is it not the one who is at the table? But I am among you as one who serves. [28]You are those who have stood by me in my trials. [29]And I confer on you a kingdom, just as my Father conferred one on me, [30]so that you may eat and drink at my table in my kingdom and sit on thrones, judging the twelve tribes of Israel."

The Spirit Versus the Flesh

JOHN 3:5-8 Jesus answered, "I tell you the truth, no one can enter the kingdom of God unless he is born of water and the Spirit. [6]Flesh gives birth to flesh, but the Spirit gives birth to spirit. [7]You should not be surprised at my saying, 'You must be born again.' [8]The wind blows wherever it pleases. You hear its sound, but you cannot tell where it comes from or where it is going. So it is with everyone born of the Spirit."

JOHN 4:23-24 "Yet a time is coming and has now come when the true worshipers will worship the Father in spirit and truth, for they are the kind of worshipers the Father seeks. [24]God is spirit, and his worshipers must worship in spirit and in truth."

MATTHEW 26:40-41 Then he returned to his disciples and found them sleeping. "Could you men not keep watch with me for one hour?" he asked Peter. [41]"Watch and pray so that you will not fall into temptation. The spirit is willing, but the body is weak."

MARK 14:37-38 Then he returned to his disciples and found them sleeping. "Simon," he said to Peter, "are you asleep?

Could you not keep watch for one hour? [38]Watch and pray so that you will not fall into temptation. The spirit is willing, but the body is weak."

Stewardship, Generosity, and Giving

MATTHEW 5:38-48 "You have heard that it was said, 'Eye for eye, and tooth for tooth.' [39]But I tell you, Do not resist an evil person. If someone strikes you on the right cheek, turn to him the other also. [40]And if someone wants to sue you and take your tunic, let him have your cloak as well. [41]If someone forces you to go one mile, go with him two miles. [42]Give to the one who asks you, and do not turn away from the one who wants to borrow from you. [43]You have heard that it was said, 'Love your neighbor and hate your enemy.' [44]But I tell you: Love your enemies and pray for those who persecute you, [45]that you may be sons of your Father in heaven. He causes his sun to rise on the evil and the good, and sends rain on the righteous and the unrighteous. [46]If you love those who love you, what reward will you get? Are not even the tax collectors doing that? [47]And if you greet only your brothers, what are you doing more than others? Do not even pagans do that? [48]Be perfect, therefore, as your heavenly Father is perfect."

MATTHEW 10:5-10 These twelve Jesus sent out with the following instructions: "Do not go among the Gentiles or enter any town of the Samaritans. [6]Go rather to the lost sheep of Israel. [7]As you go, preach this message: 'The kingdom of heaven is near.' [8]Heal the sick, raise the dead, cleanse those who have leprosy, drive out demons. Freely you have received, freely give. [9]Do not take along any gold or silver or copper in your belts; [10]take no bag for the journey, or extra tunic, or sandals or a staff; for the worker is worth his keep."

MATTHEW 10:40-42 "He who receives you receives me, and he who receives me receives the one who sent me. [41]Anyone who receives a prophet because he is a prophet will receive a prophet's reward, and anyone who receives a righteous man because he is a righteous man will receive a righteous man's reward. [42]And if anyone gives even a cup of cold water to one of these little ones because he is my disciple, I tell you the truth, he will certainly not lose his reward."

MATTHEW 19:21 Jesus answered, "If you want to be perfect, go, sell your possessions and give to the poor, and you will have treasure in heaven. Then come, follow me."

MATTHEW 25:14-30 "Again, it will be like a man going on a journey, who called his servants and entrusted his property to them. [15]To one he gave five talents of money, to another two talents, and to another one talent, each according to his ability. Then he went on his journey. [16]The man who had received the five talents went at once and put his money to work and gained five more. [17]So also, the one with the two talents gained two more. [18]But the man who had received the one talent went off, dug a hole in the ground and hid his master's money. [19]After a long time the master of those servants returned and settled accounts with them. [20]The man who had received the five talents brought the other five. 'Master,' he said, 'you entrusted me with five talents. See, I have gained five more.' [21]His master replied, 'Well done, good and faithful servant! You have been faithful with a few things; I will put you in charge of many things. Come and share your master's happiness!' [22]The man with the two talents also came. 'Master,' he said, 'you entrusted me with two talents; see, I have gained two more.' [23]His master replied, 'Well done, good and faithful servant! You have been faithful with a few things; I will put you in charge of many things. Come and share your master's happiness!' [24]Then the man who had received the one talent came. 'Master,' he said, 'I knew that you are a hard man, harvesting where you have not sown and gathering where you have not scattered seed. [25]So I was afraid and went out and hid your talent in the ground. See, here is what belongs to you.' [26]His master replied, 'You wicked, lazy servant! So you knew that I harvest where I have not sown and gather where I have not scattered seed? [27]Well then, you should have put my money on deposit with the bankers, so that when I returned I would have received it back with interest. [28]Take the talent from him and give it to the one who has the ten talents. [29]For everyone who has will be given more, and he will have an abundance. Whoever does not have, even what he has will be taken from him. [30]And throw that worthless servant outside, into the darkness, where there will be weeping and gnashing of teeth.'"

MARK 4:24-25 "Consider carefully what you hear," he continued. "With the measure you use, it will be measured to you—and even more. [25]Whoever has will be given more; whoever does not have, even what he has will be taken from him."

MARK 10:21 Jesus looked at him [a rich young man] and loved him. "One thing you lack," he said. "Go, sell everything you have and give to the poor, and you will have treasure in heaven. Then come, follow me."

MARK 12:38-40 As he taught, Jesus said, "Watch out for the teachers of the law. They like to walk around in flowing robes and be greeted in the marketplaces, [39]and have the most important seats in the synagogues and the places of honor at banquets. [40]They devour widows' houses and for a show make lengthy prayers. Such men will be punished most severely."

MARK 12:42-44 But a poor widow came and put in two very small copper coins, worth only a fraction of a penny. [43]Calling his disciples to him, Jesus said, "I tell you the truth, this poor widow has put more into the treasury than all the others. [44]They all gave out of their wealth; but she, out of her poverty, put in everything—all she had to live on."

LUKE 6:27-36 "But I tell you who hear me: Love your enemies, do good to those who hate you, [28]bless those who curse you, pray for those who mistreat you. [29]If someone strikes you on one cheek, turn to him the other also. If someone takes your cloak, do not stop him from taking your tunic. [30]Give to everyone who asks you, and if anyone takes what belongs to you, do not demand it back. [31]Do to others as you would have them do to you. [32]If you love those who love you, what credit is that to you? Even 'sinners' love those who love them. ³³And if you do good to those who are good to you, what credit is that to you? Even 'sinners' do that. ³⁴And if you lend to those from whom you expect repayment, what credit is that to you? Even 'sinners' lend to 'sinners,' expecting to be repaid in full. ³⁵But love your enemies, do good to them, and lend to them without expecting to get anything back. Then your reward will be great, and you will be sons of the Most High, because he is kind to the ungrateful and wicked. ³⁶Be merciful, just as your Father is merciful."

LUKE 6:38 "Give, and it will be given to you. A good measure, pressed down, shaken together and running over, will be poured into your lap. For with the measure you use, it will be measured to you."

LUKE 12:35-40 "Be dressed ready for service and keep your lamps burning, ³⁶like men waiting for their master to return from a wedding banquet, so that when he comes and knocks they can immediately open the door for him. ³⁷It will be good for those servants whose master finds them watching when he comes. I tell you the truth, he will dress himself to serve, will have them recline at the table and will come and wait on them. ³⁸It will be good for those servants whose master finds them ready, even if he comes in the second or third watch of the night. ³⁹But understand this: If the owner of the house had known at what hour the thief was coming, he would not have let his house be broken into. ⁴⁰You also must be ready, because the Son of Man will

come at an hour when you do not expect him."

LUKE 12:42-48 The Lord answered, "Who then is the faithful and wise manager, whom the master puts in charge of his servants to give them their food allowance at the proper time? ⁴³It will be good for that servant whom the master finds doing so when he returns. ⁴⁴I tell you the truth, he will put him in charge of all his possessions. ⁴⁵But suppose the servant says to himself, 'My master is taking a long time in coming,' and he then begins to beat the menservants and maidservants and to eat and drink and get drunk. ⁴⁶The master of that servant will come on a day when he does not expect him and at an hour he is not aware of. He will cut him to pieces and assign him a place with the unbelievers. ⁴⁷That servant who knows his master's will and does not get ready or does not do what his master wants will be beaten with many blows. ⁴⁸But the one who does not know and does things deserving punishment will be beaten with few blows. From everyone who has been given much, much will be demanded; and from the one who has been entrusted with much, much more will be asked."

LUKE 16:9-12 "I tell you, use worldly wealth to gain friends for yourselves, so that when it is gone, you will be welcomed into eternal dwellings. ¹⁰Whoever can be trusted with very little can also be trusted with much, and whoever is dishonest with very little will also be dishonest with much. ¹¹So if you have not been trustworthy in handling worldly wealth, who will trust you with true riches? ¹²And if you have not been trustworthy with someone else's property, who will give you property of your own?'"

LUKE 19:12-27 He said: "A man of noble birth went to a distant country to have himself appointed king and then to return. [13]So he called ten of his servants and gave them ten minas. 'Put this money to work,' he said, 'until I come back.' [14]But his subjects hated him and sent a delegation after him to say, 'We don't want this man to be our king.' [15]He was made king, however, and returned home. Then he sent for the servants to whom he had given the money, in order to find out what they had gained with it. [16]The first one came and said, 'Sir, your mina has earned ten more.' [17]'Well done, my good servant!' his master replied. 'Because you have been trustworthy in a very small matter, take charge of ten cities.' [18]The second came and said, 'Sir, your mina has earned five more.' [19]His master answered, 'You take charge of five cities.' [20]Then another servant came and said, 'Sir, here is your mina; I have kept it laid away in a piece of cloth. [21]I was afraid of you, because you are a hard man. You take out what you did not put in and reap what you did not sow.' [22]His master replied, 'I will judge you by your own words, you wicked servant! You knew, did you, that I am a hard man, taking out what I did not put in, and reaping what I did not sow? [23]Why then didn't you put my money on deposit, so that when I came back, I could have collected it with interest?' [24]Then he said to those standing by, 'Take his mina away from him and give it to the one who has ten minas.' [25]'Sir,' they said, 'he already has ten!' [26]He replied, 'I tell you

that to everyone who has, more will be given, but as for the one who has nothing, even what he has will be taken away. [27]But those enemies of mine who did not want me to be king over them—bring them here and kill them in front of me.'"

LUKE 21:3-4 "I tell you the truth," he said, "this poor widow has put in more than all the others. [4]All these people gave their gifts out of their wealth; but she out of her poverty put in all she had to live on."

ACTS 20:35 "In everything I [Paul] did, I showed you that by this kind of hard work we must help the weak, remembering the words the Lord Jesus himself said: 'It is more blessed to give than to receive.'"

Temptation

MATTHEW 18:6-9 "But if anyone causes one of these little ones who believe in me to sin, it would be better for him to have a large millstone hung around his neck and to be drowned in the depths of the sea. [7]Woe to the world because of the things that cause people to sin! Such things must come, but woe to the man through whom they come! [8]If your hand or your foot causes you to sin, cut it off and throw it away. It is better for you to enter life maimed or crippled than to have two hands or two feet and be thrown into eternal fire. [9]And if your eye causes you to sin, gouge it out and throw it away. It is better for you to enter life with one eye than to have two eyes and be thrown into the fire of hell."

MATTHEW 26:41 "Watch and pray so that you will not fall into temptation.

The spirit is willing, but the body is weak." (See also Mark 14:38.)

LUKE 11:2-4 He said to them, "When you pray, say: 'Father, hallowed be your name, your kingdom come. ³Give us each day our daily bread. ⁴Forgive us our sins, for we also forgive everyone who sins against us. And lead us not into temptation.'"

Unity Versus Division

JOHN 10:16 "I have other sheep that are not of this sheep pen. I must bring them also. They too will listen to my voice, and there shall be one flock and one shepherd."

JOHN 13:13-15 "You call me 'Teacher' and 'Lord,' and rightly so, for that is what I am. ¹⁴Now that I, your Lord and Teacher, have washed your feet, you also should wash one another's feet. ¹⁵I have set you an example that you should do as I have done for you."

JOHN 13:34-35 "A new command I give you: Love one another. As I have loved you, so you must love one another. ³⁵By this all men will know that you are my disciples, if you love one another."

JOHN 17:20-23 "My prayer is not for them [the disciples] alone. I pray also for those who will believe in me through their message, ²¹that all of them may be one, Father, just as you are in me and I am in you. May they also be in us so that the world may believe that you have sent me. ²²I have given them the glory that you gave me, that they may be one as we are one: ²³I in them and you in me. May they

be brought to complete unity to let the world know that you sent me and have loved them even as you have loved me."

MATTHEW 23:8 "But you are not to be called 'Rabbi,' for you have only one Master and you are all brothers."

LUKE 11:17-23 Jesus knew their thoughts and said to them: "Any kingdom divided against itself will be ruined, and a house divided against itself will fall. ¹⁸If Satan is divided against himself, how can his kingdom stand? I say this because you claim that I drive out demons by Beelzebub. ¹⁹Now if I drive out demons by Beelzebub, by whom do your followers drive them out? So then, they will be your judges. ²⁰But if I drive out demons by the finger of God, then the kingdom of God has come to you. ²¹When a strong man, fully armed, guards his own house, his possessions are safe. ²²But when someone stronger attacks and overpowers him, he takes away the armor in which the man trusted and divides up the spoils. ²³He who is not with me is against me, and he who does not gather with me, scatters."

Vigilance

MATTHEW 24:4-29 Jesus answered: "Watch out that no one deceives you. ⁵For many will come in my name, claiming, 'I am the Christ,' and will deceive many. ⁶You will hear of wars and rumors of wars, but see to it that you are not alarmed. Such things must happen, but the end is still to come. ⁷Nation will rise against nation, and kingdom against kingdom. There will be famines and earthquakes in various places. [8]All these are the beginning of birth pains. [9]Then you will be handed over to be persecuted and put to death, and you will be hated by all nations because of me. [10]At that time many will turn away from the faith and will betray and hate each other, [11]and many false prophets will appear and deceive many people. [12]Because of the increase of wickedness, the love of most will grow cold, [13]but he who stands firm to the end will be saved. [14]And this gospel of the kingdom will be preached in the whole world as a testimony to all nations, and then the end will come. [15]So when you see standing in the holy place 'the abomination that causes desolation,' spoken of through the prophet Daniel—let the reader understand— [16]then let those who are in Judea flee to the mountains. [17]Let no one on the roof of his house go down to take anything out of the house. [18]Let no one in the field go back to get his cloak. [19]How dreadful it will be in those days for pregnant women and nursing mothers! [20]Pray that your flight will not take place in winter or on the Sabbath. [21]For then there will be great distress, unequaled from the beginning of the world until now—and never to be equaled again. [22]If those days had not been cut short, no one would survive, but for the sake of the elect those days will be shortened. [23]At that time if anyone says to you, 'Look, here is the Christ!' or, 'There he is!' do not believe it. [24]For false Christs and false prophets will appear and perform great signs and miracles to deceive even the elect—if that were possible.

[25]See, I have told you ahead of time. [26]So if anyone tells you, 'There he is, out in the desert,' do not go out; or, 'Here he is, in the inner rooms,' do not believe it. [27]For as lightning that comes from the east is visible even in the west, so will be the coming of the Son of Man. [28]Wherever there is a carcass, there the vultures will gather. [29]Immediately after the distress of those days 'the sun will be darkened, and the moon will not give its light; the stars will fall from the sky, and the heavenly bodies will be shaken.'"

MATTHEW 25:1-13 "At that time the kingdom of heaven will be like ten virgins who took their lamps and went out to meet the bridegroom. [2]Five of them were foolish and five were wise. [3]The foolish ones took their lamps but did not take any oil with them. [4]The wise, however, took oil in jars along with their lamps. [5]The bridegroom was a long time in coming, and they all became drowsy and fell asleep. [6]At midnight the cry rang out: 'Here's the bridegroom! Come out to meet him!' [7]Then all the virgins woke up and trimmed their lamps. [8]The foolish ones said to the wise, 'Give us some of your oil; our lamps are going out.' [9]'No,' they replied, 'there may not be enough for both us and you. Instead, go to those who sell oil and buy some for yourselves.' [10]But while they were on their way to buy the oil, the bridegroom arrived. The virgins who were ready went in with him to the wedding banquet. And the door was shut. [11]Later the others also came. 'Sir! Sir!' they said. 'Open the door for us!' [12]But he replied, 'I tell you the truth, I don't know you.' [13]Therefore keep watch, because you do not know the day or the hour."

MARK 13:5 Jesus said to them [Peter, James, John, Andrew]: "Watch out that no one deceives you."

MARK 13:28-37 "Now learn this lesson from the fig tree: As soon as its twigs get tender and its leaves come out, you know that summer is near. [29]Even so, when you see these things happening, you know that it is near, right at the door. [30]I tell you the truth, this generation will certainly not pass away until all these things have happened. [31]Heaven and earth will pass away, but my words will never pass away. [32]No one knows about that day or hour, not even the angels in heaven, nor the Son, but only the Father. [33]Be on guard! Be alert! You do not know when that time will come. [34]It's like a man going away: He leaves his house and puts his servants in charge, each with his assigned task, and tells the one at the door to keep watch. [35]Therefore keep watch because you do not know when the owner of the house will come back—whether in the evening, or at midnight, or when the rooster crows, or at dawn. [36]If he comes suddenly, do not let him find you sleeping. [37]What I say to you, I say to everyone: 'Watch!'"

Wealth and Possessions

MATTHEW 6:19-21 "Do not store up for yourselves treasures on earth, where moth and rust destroy, and where thieves break in and steal. [20]But store up for yourselves treasures in heaven, where moth and rust do not destroy, and where thieves do not break in and steal. [21]For where your treasure is, there your heart will be also."

MATTHEW 6:24 "No one can serve two masters. Either he will hate the one and love the other, or he will be devoted to the one and despise the other. You cannot serve both God and Money."

MATTHEW 6:30-34 "If that is how God clothes the grass of the field, which is here today and tomorrow is thrown into the fire, will he not much more clothe you, O you of little faith? [31]So do not worry, saying, 'What shall we eat?' or 'What shall we drink?' or 'What shall we wear?' [32]For the pagans run after all these things, and your heavenly Father knows that you need them. [33]But seek first his kingdom and his righteousness, and all these things will be given to you as well. [34]Therefore do not worry about tomorrow, for tomorrow will worry about itself. Each day has enough trouble of its own."

MATTHEW 16:24-27 Then Jesus said to his disciples, "If anyone would come after me, he must deny himself and take up his cross and follow me. [25]For whoever wants to save his life will lose it, but whoever loses his life for me will find it. [26]What good will it be for a man if he gains the whole world, yet forfeits his soul? Or what can a man give in exchange for his soul? [27]For the Son of Man is going to come in his Father's glory with his angels, and then he will reward each person according to what he has done."

MATTHEW 19:17-21 "Why do you ask me about what is good?" Jesus replied. "There is only One who is good. If you want to enter life, obey the commandments." [18]"Which ones?" the man inquired. Jesus replied, " 'Do not murder, do not commit adultery, do not steal, do not give false testimony, [19]honor your father and mother,' and 'love your neighbor as yourself.' " [20]"All these I have kept," the young man said. "What do I still lack?" [21]Jesus answered, "If you want to be perfect, go, sell your possessions and give to the poor, and you will have treasure in heaven. Then come, follow me."

MATTHEW 19:23-26 Then Jesus said to his disciples, "I tell you the truth, it is hard for a rich man to enter the kingdom of heaven. [24]Again I tell you, it is easier for a camel to go through the eye of a needle than for a rich man to enter the kingdom of God." [25]When the disciples heard this, they were greatly astonished and asked, "Who then can be saved?" [26]Jesus looked at them and said, "With man this is impossible, but with God all things are possible."

MARK 4:18-19 "Still others, like seed sown among thorns, hear the word; [19]but the worries of this life, the deceitfulness of wealth and the desires for other things come in and choke the word, making it unfruitful."

MARK 10:18-21 "Why do you call me good?" Jesus answered. "No one is good—except God alone. [19]You know the commandments: 'Do not murder, do not commit adultery, do not steal, do not give false testimony, do not defraud, honor your father and mother.' " [20]"Teacher," he declared, "all these I have kept since I was a boy." [21]Jesus looked at him and loved him. "One thing you lack," he said. "Go, sell everything you have and give to the

poor, and you will have treasure in heaven. Then come, follow me."

MARK 10:23-27 Jesus looked around and said to his disciples, "How hard it is for the rich to enter the kingdom of God!" [24]The disciples were amazed at his words. But Jesus said again, "Children, how hard it is to enter the kingdom of God! [25]It is easier for a camel to go through the eye of a needle than for a rich man to enter the kingdom of God." [26]The disciples were even more amazed, and said to each other, "Who then can be saved?" [27]Jesus looked at them and said, "With man this is impossible, but not with God; all things are possible with God."

MARK 12:16-17 They brought the coin, and he asked them, "Whose portrait is this? And whose inscription?" "Caesar's," they replied. [17]Then Jesus said to them, "Give to Caesar what is Caesar's and to God what is God's." And they were amazed at him.

LUKE 6:24-25 "But woe to you who are rich, for you have already received your comfort. [25]Woe to you who are well fed now, for you will go hungry. Woe to you who laugh now, for you will mourn and weep."

LUKE 9:23-26 Then he said to them all: "If anyone would come after me, he must deny himself and take up his cross daily and follow me. [24]For whoever wants to save his life will lose it, but whoever loses his life for me will save it. [25]What good is it for a man to gain the whole world, and yet lose or forfeit his very self? [26]If anyone is ashamed of me and my words, the Son of Man will be ashamed of him when he comes in his glory and in the glory of the Father and of the holy angels."

Luke 12:13-21 Someone in the crowd said to him, "Teacher, tell my brother to divide the inheritance with me." [14]Jesus replied, "Man, who appointed me a judge or an arbiter between you?" [15]Then he said to them, "Watch out! Be on your guard against all kinds of greed; a man's life does not consist in the abundance of his possessions." [16]And he told them this parable: "The ground of a certain rich man produced a good crop. [17]He thought to himself, 'What shall I do? I have no place to store my crops.' [18]Then he said, 'This is what I'll do. I will tear down my barns and build bigger ones, and there I will store all my grain and my goods. [19]And I'll say to myself, "You have plenty of good things laid up for many years. Take life easy; eat, drink and be merry." ' [20]But God said to him, 'You fool! This very night your life will be demanded from you. Then who will get what you have prepared for yourself?' [21]This is how it will be with anyone who stores up things for himself but is not rich toward God."

Luke 16:9-12 "I tell you, use worldly wealth to gain friends for yourselves, so that when it is gone, you will be welcomed into eternal dwellings. [10]Whoever can be trusted with very little can also be trusted with much, and whoever is dishonest with very little will also be dishonest with much. [11]So if you have not been trustworthy in handling worldly wealth, who will trust you with true riches? [12]And if you have not been trustworthy with someone else's property, who will give you property of your own?"

Luke 16:13 "No servant can serve two masters. Either he will hate the one and love the other, or he will be devoted to the one and despise the other. You cannot serve both God and Money."

Luke 16:15 He said to them [the Pharisees], "You are the ones who justify yourselves in the eyes of men, but God knows your hearts. What is highly valued among men is detestable in God's sight."

Luke 16:19-31 "There was a rich man who was dressed in purple and fine linen and lived in luxury every day. [20]At his gate was laid a beggar named Lazarus, covered with sores [21]and longing to eat what fell from the rich man's table. Even the dogs came and licked his sores. [22]The time came when the beggar died and the angels carried him to Abraham's side. The rich man also died and was buried. [23]In hell, where he was in torment, he looked up and saw Abraham far away, with Lazarus by his side. [24]So he called to him, 'Father Abraham, have pity on me and send Lazarus to dip the tip of his finger in water and cool my tongue, because I am in agony in this fire.' [25]But Abraham replied, 'Son, remember that in your lifetime you received your good things, while Lazarus received bad things, but now he is comforted here and you are in agony. [26]And besides all this, between us and you a great chasm has been fixed, so that those who want to go from here to you cannot, nor can anyone cross over from there to us.' [27]He answered, 'Then I beg you, father, send Lazarus to my father's house, [28]for I have five brothers. Let him warn them, so that they will not also come to this place of torment.' ²⁹Abraham replied, 'They have Moses and the Prophets; let them listen to them.' ³⁰'No, father Abraham,' he said, 'but if someone from the dead goes to them, they will repent.' ³¹He said to him, 'If they do not listen to Moses and the Prophets, they will not be convinced even if someone rises from the dead.'"

LUKE 18:19-27 "Why do you call me good?" Jesus answered. "No one is good—except God alone. ²⁰You know the commandments: 'Do not commit adultery, do not murder, do not steal, do not give false testimony, honor your father and mother.'" ²¹"All these I have kept since I was a boy," he said. ²²When Jesus heard this, he said to him, "You still lack one thing. Sell everything you have and give to the poor, and you will have treasure in heaven. Then come, follow me." ²³When he heard this, he became very sad, because he was a man of great wealth. ²⁴Jesus looked at him and said, "How hard it is for the rich to enter the kingdom of God! ²⁵Indeed, it is easier for a camel to go through the eye of a needle than for a rich man to enter the kingdom of God." ²⁶Those who heard this asked, "Who then can be saved?" ²⁷Jesus replied, "What is impossible with men is possible with God."

REVELATION 3:15-18 "I know your deeds, that you are neither cold nor hot. I wish you were either one or the other! ¹⁶So, because you are lukewarm—neither hot nor cold—I am about to spit you out of my mouth. ¹⁷You say, 'I am rich; I have acquired wealth and do not need a thing.' But you do not realize that you are wretched, pitiful, poor, blind and naked. ¹⁸I counsel you to buy from me gold refined in the fire, so you can become rich; and white clothes to wear, so you can cover your shameful nakedness; and salve to put on your eyes, so you can see."

Wisdom and Understanding

JOHN 6:45 "It is written in the Prophets: 'They will all be taught by God.' Everyone who listens to the Father and learns from him comes to me."

JOHN 7:16-19 Jesus answered, "My teaching is not my own. It comes from him who sent me. ¹⁷If anyone chooses to do God's will, he will find out whether my teaching comes from God or whether I speak on my own. ¹⁸He who speaks on his own does so to gain honor for himself, but he who works for the honor of the one who sent him is a man of truth; there is nothing false about him. ¹⁹Has not Moses given you the law? Yet not one of you keeps the law. Why are you trying to kill me?"

JOHN 8:12 When Jesus spoke again to the people, he said, "I am the light of the world. Whoever follows me will never walk in darkness, but will have the light of life."

JOHN 8:31-32 Then Jesus said to those Jews who believed Him, "If you abide in My word, you are My disciples indeed. ³²And you shall know the truth, and the truth shall make you free." (NKJV)

JOHN 9:39 Jesus said, "For judgment I have come into this world, so that the blind will see and those who see will become blind."

JOHN 12:46 "I have come into the world as a light, so that no one who believes in me should stay in darkness."

JOHN 14:6 Jesus answered, "I am the way and the truth and the life. No one comes to the Father except through me."

JOHN 14:16 "And I will ask the Father, and he will give you another Counselor to be with you forever."

JOHN 16:12-14 "I have much more to say to you, more than you can now bear. [13]But when he, the Spirit of truth, comes, he will guide you into all truth. He will not speak on his own; he will speak only what he hears, and he will tell you what is yet to come. [14]He will bring glory to me by taking from what is mine and making it known to you."

JOHN 17:3 "Now this is eternal life: that they may know you, the only true God, and Jesus Christ, whom you have sent."

JOHN 17:7-8 "Now they know that everything you have given me comes from you. [8]For I gave them the words you gave me and they accepted them. They knew with certainty that I came from you, and they believed that you sent me."

JOHN 17:17 "Sanctify them by the truth; your word is truth."

JOHN 17:19 "For them I sanctify myself, that they too may be truly sanctified."

JOHN 18:37 "You are a king, then!" said Pilate. Jesus answered, "You are right in saying I am a king. In fact, for this reason I was born, and for this I came into the world, to testify to the truth. Everyone on the side of truth listens to me."

MATTHEW 6:22-23 "The eye is the lamp of the body. If your eyes are good, your whole body will be full of light. [23]But if your eyes are bad, your whole body will be full of darkness. If then the light within you is darkness, how great is that darkness!" (See also Luke 11:34-36.)

MATTHEW 7:21-27 "Not everyone who says to Me, 'Lord, Lord,' shall enter the kingdom of heaven, but he who does the will of My Father in heaven. [22]Many will say to Me in that day, 'Lord, Lord, have we not prophesied in Your name, cast out demons in Your name, and done many wonders in Your name?' [23]And then I will declare to them, 'I never knew you; depart from Me, you who practice lawlessness!' [24]Therefore whoever hears these sayings of Mine, and does them, I will liken him to a wise man who built his house on the rock: [25]and the rain descended, the floods came, and the winds blew and beat on that house; and it did not fall, for it was founded on the rock. [26]But everyone who hears these sayings of Mine, and does not do them, will be like a foolish man who built his house on the sand: [27]and the rain descended, the floods came, and the winds blew and beat on that house; and it fell. And great was its fall." (NKJV)

MATTHEW 10:16-20 "I am sending you out like sheep among wolves. Therefore be as shrewd as snakes and as innocent as doves. [17]Be on your guard against men; they will hand you over to the local councils and flog you in their synagogues. [18]On my account you will be brought before governors and kings as witnesses to them and to the Gentiles. [19]But when they arrest you, do not worry about what to say or how to say it. At that time you will be given what to say, [20]for it will not be you speaking, but the Spirit of your Father speaking through you."

MATTHEW 11:16-19 "To what can I compare this generation? They are like children sitting in the marketplaces and calling out to others: [17]'We played the flute for you, and you did not dance; we sang a dirge, and you did not mourn.' [18]For John came neither eating nor drinking, and they say, 'He has a demon.' [19]The Son of Man came eating and drinking, and they say, 'Here is a glutton and a drunkard, a friend of tax collectors and "sinners."' But wisdom is proved right by her actions."

MATTHEW 11:25-26 At that time Jesus said, "I praise you, Father, Lord of heaven and earth, because you have hidden these things from the wise and learned, and revealed them to little children. [26]Yes, Father, for this was your good pleasure."

MATTHEW 13:10-17 The disciples came to him and asked, "Why do you speak to the people in parables?" [11]He replied, "The knowledge of the secrets of the kingdom of heaven has been given to you, but not to them. [12]Whoever has will be given more, and he will have an abundance. Whoever does not have, even what he has will be taken from him. [13]This is why I speak to them in parables: Though seeing, they do not see; though hearing, they do not hear or understand. [14]In them is fulfilled the prophecy of Isaiah: 'You will be ever hearing but never understanding; you will be ever seeing but never perceiving. [15]For this people's heart has become calloused; they hardly hear with their ears, and they have closed their eyes. Otherwise they might see with their eyes, hear with their ears, understand with their hearts and turn, and I would heal them.' [16]But blessed are your eyes because they see, and your ears because they hear. [17]For I tell you the truth, many prophets and righteous men longed to see what you see but did not see it, and to hear what you hear but did not hear it."

MATTHEW 16:17 Jesus replied, "Blessed are you, Simon son of Jonah, for this was not revealed to you by man, but by my Father in heaven."

LUKE 11:52 "Woe to you experts in the law, because you have taken away the key to knowledge. You yourselves have not entered, and you have hindered those who were entering."

LUKE 12:11-12 "When you are brought before synagogues, rulers and authorities, do not worry about how you will defend yourselves or what you will say, [12]for the Holy Spirit will teach you at that time what you should say."

LUKE 12:16-21 And he told them this parable: "The ground of a certain rich man produced a good crop. [17]He thought to himself, 'What shall I do? I have no place to store my crops.' [18]Then he said, 'This is what I'll do. I will tear down my barns and build bigger ones, and there I will store all my grain and my goods. [19]And I'll say to myself, "You have plenty of good things laid up for many years. Take life easy; eat, drink and be merry."' [20]But God said to him, 'You fool! This very night your life will be demanded from you. Then who will get what you have prepared for yourself?' ²¹This is how it will be with anyone who stores up things for himself but is not rich toward God."

LUKE 14:27-33 "And anyone who does not carry his cross and follow me cannot be my disciple. ²⁸Suppose one of you wants to build a tower. Will he not first sit down and estimate the cost to see if he has enough money to complete it? ²⁹For if he lays the foundation and is not able to finish it, everyone who sees it will ridicule him, ³⁰saying, 'This fellow began to build and was not able to finish.' ³¹Or suppose a king is about to go to war against another king. Will he not first sit down and consider whether he is able with ten thousand men to oppose the one coming against him with twenty thousand? ³²If he is not able, he will send a delegation while the other is still a long way off and will ask for terms of peace. ³³In the same way, any of you who does not give up everything he has cannot be my disciple."

LUKE 16:8 "The master commended the dishonest manager because he had acted shrewdly. For the people of this world are more shrewd in dealing with their own kind than are the people of the light."

LUKE 21:14-15 "But make up your mind not to worry beforehand how you will defend yourselves. ¹⁵For I will give you words and wisdom that none of your adversaries will be able to resist or contradict."

Worthiness

MATTHEW 10:34-39 "Do not suppose that I have come to bring peace to the earth. I did not come to bring peace, but a sword. ³⁵For I have come to turn 'a man against his father, a daughter against her mother, a daughter-in-law against her mother-in-law— ³⁶a man's enemies will be the members of his own household.' ³⁷Anyone who loves his father or mother more than me is not worthy of me; anyone who loves his son or daughter more than me is not worthy of me; ³⁸and anyone who does not take his cross and follow me is not worthy of me. ³⁹Whoever finds his life will lose it, and whoever loses his life for my sake will find it."

LUKE 20:34-36 Jesus replied, "The people of this age marry and are given in marriage. ³⁵But those who are considered worthy of taking part in that age and in the resurrection from the dead will neither marry nor be given in marriage, ³⁶and they can no longer die; for they are like the angels. They are God's children, since they are children of the resurrection."

LUKE 21:34-36 "Be careful, or your hearts will be weighed down with dissipation, drunkenness and the anxieties of life, and that day will close on you unexpectedly like a trap. ³⁵For it will come upon all those who live on the face of the whole earth. ³⁶Be always on the watch, and pray that you may be able to escape all that is about to happen, and that you may be able to stand before the Son of Man."

THE GREATEST WORDS
EVER SPOKEN
ABOUT HUMANITY

What Jesus Said About Our Nature,
Our Struggles, and Our Future

"How could something that felt so right turn out so bad?" It's a question we all have asked at one time or another. Our feelings tend to be the most powerful driving force in our lives. Unfortunately, feelings can lead us to make choices that range from less than the best to catastrophic. They can cause us to be lazy when we should be diligent, panicked when we should be calm, or overconfident when we should be careful. Equally destructive, our feelings can motivate us to follow a foolish course of action completely at odds with the guidance Christ offers.

We make many of our worst mistakes because we don't know the *ultimate* truth about a situation, nor do we understand the grave consequences of choosing the wrong course of action. There is a bias built into our nature. Our selfcenteredness not only blurs our vision; it affects our behavior in the same way a magnet affects a nearby piece of iron. Selfcenteredness creates an almost irresistible pull, causing us to do what we want to do rather than what we *should* do, regardless of how damaging that behavior may be.

Making Titanic Mistakes

When the *Titanic* struck an iceberg shortly before midnight on April 14, 1912, the passengers didn't believe their lives were at risk. On the contrary, for the first hour they continued their activities as if nothing had happened. When they were told to begin boarding lifeboats, most refused. Who in their right mind would want to leave the safety and comfort of the world's largest and most luxurious ocean liner to crowd into a tiny boat and venture onto the open seas on a cold North Atlantic night? When the crew's requests became demands, some passengers were so angered that they ridiculed the very crew members who were trying to save their lives.

Why would people resist the efforts of a person who was trying to save them? First, the passengers trusted their feelings of safety more than the word of the crew members. Second, they made decisions without having an accurate understanding of the harsh realities of their situation. They weren't aware of the severity of the damage to the ship's hull, nor did they know there were only enough lifeboats to hold half of the passengers. Consequently, the first boats were lowered half-empty. By the time most of the passengers realized the terrible truth of their circumstances, it was too late to seek refuge.

Far more tragic than the life-and-death plight of the *Titanic*'s passengers is the ultimate, *eternal* life-and-death plight that each of us faces. We overlook the power and the bias inherent in human nature, and we fail to understand the eternal consequences of our decisions. The result is that we make the same critical mistakes that were made by most of the *Titanic*'s passengers. Placing our confidence in our feelings, we make choices based on our limited (and often inaccurate) assessment of the situation we're in. We choose to remain in the middle of our comfort zone, or we choose to move in the wrong direction rather than the best one.

Here again, the incomparable words of Christ are a beacon, shedding divine light on our path. His assessments of humanity, human nature, our faults, and our future are based on His perfect knowledge and infinite understanding of the realities of everything about us and our future. Most important, Christ understands these things from an *eternal* perspective, and He knows the issues that matter most to God. In Luke 9:25 He asks: "What profit is it to a man if he gains the whole world, and is himself destroyed or lost?" (NKJV). By nature, we evaluate nearly every situation according to its immediate impact on our desires, and we make our choices accordingly. Consequently, we often sacrifice that which would bring infinite eternal benefit in exchange for temporary gratification.

Christ's statements in this chapter will give you God's perspective on humanity and the issues that often divert our path from the positive to the negative. Many of Christ's pronouncements are hard to accept, similar to the urgent—but unwelcome—instructions given to the doomed passengers on the *Titanic*. But when we realize His pronouncements are based on eternal realities and are given to provide us with a true source of love, joy, and security, then we see them for what they really are—powerful revelations of God's unfathomable love.

How Could a Loving God Allow This?

Perhaps the most frequent question asked by those who struggle with the difficulty of life is "If God is all-powerful and loving, how could He allow so many terrible things to happen?" The answer might exhaust the wisdom of Solomon, but it doesn't overwhelm the wisdom found in the words of Christ. In Mark 12:30-31, Jesus tells us that the greatest of God's commandments are to "love the LORD your God with all your heart, with all your soul, with all your mind, and with all your strength" and to *"love your neighbor as yourself"* (NKJV). Too often we choose to love ourselves above God, and in doing so we love ourselves more than others. As our selfcenteredness grows, the terrible consequences it can produce also grow. In John 3:19, Jesus revealed a tragic side to our basic nature. He said people "loved darkness rather than light, because their deeds were evil" (NKJV). In other words, if left unchecked, our selfcenteredness can evolve into an existence without a conscience, making it possible for even the worst people to justify their terrible behavior.

Even though we recognize the tragedies that result from the exercise of unrestrained human nature, we fail to see that God often intervenes to prevent even greater evils from taking place. His perfect nature of infinite love, ultimate righteousness, and unequivocal justice protects us from the full earthly consequences of our foolish choices. God can do anything except violate His perfect character. His ultimate plan for humanity reflects these three aspects of His nature—love, righteousness, and justice—without diminishing any of them.

But even this doesn't explain why God allows bad things to happen. God is infinitely intelligent, and His dealings with humanity are based on His *eternal* perspective rather than a finite, nearsighted perspective. Our short life on earth is like a drop of water in the oceans of eternity. While we look at disasters, tragedies, and death as if they are the final pages in the book of life, in truth they are only the first pages of the introduction.

Christ's statements in this chapter shed light on our hearts, our minds, and our natural tendencies. You'll see why worldly happiness ultimately fails to provide lasting contentment and consistent joy. You'll see why women get it right more often than men and why it's so easy to deceive ourselves. And in the last section of this chapter, you'll gain an understanding of your unimaginable worth to God. As you read Jesus' words, you will gain a clearer understanding of your true nature and your need before God, and you will see His love and understand His amazing grace more fully than ever before.

Accountability Before God

MATTHEW 12:36-37 "But I tell you that men will have to give account on the day of judgment for every careless word they have spoken. [37]For by your words you will be acquitted, and by your words you will be condemned."

MATTHEW 25:14-30 "Again, it will be like a man going on a journey, who called his servants and entrusted his property to them. [15]To one he gave five talents of money, to another two talents, and to another one talent, each according to his ability. Then he went on his journey. [16]The man who had received the five talents went at once and put his money to work and gained five more. [17]So also, the one with the two talents gained two more. [18]But the man who had received the one talent went off, dug a hole in the ground and hid his master's money. [19]After a long time the master of those servants returned and settled accounts with them. [20]The man who had received the five talents brought the other five. 'Master,' he said, 'you entrusted me with five talents. See, I have gained five more.' [21]His master replied, 'Well done, good and faithful servant! You have been faithful with a few things; I will put you in charge of many things. Come and share your master's happiness!' [22]The man with the two talents also came. 'Master,' he said, 'you entrusted me with two talents; see, I have gained two more.' [23]His master replied, 'Well done, good and faithful servant! You have been faithful with a few things; I will put you in charge of many things. Come and share your master's happiness!' [24]Then the man who had received the one talent came. 'Master,' he said, 'I knew that you are a hard man, harvesting where you have not sown and gathering where you have not scattered seed. [25]So I was afraid and went out and hid your talent in the ground. See, here is what belongs to you.' [26]His master replied, 'You wicked, lazy servant! So you knew that I harvest where I have not sown and gather where I have not scattered seed? [27]Well then, you should have put my money on deposit with the bankers, so that when I returned I would have received it back with interest. [28]Take the talent from him and give it to the one who has the ten talents. [29]For everyone who has will be given more, and he will have an abundance. Whoever does not have, even what he has will be taken from him. [30]And throw that worthless servant outside, into the darkness, where there will be weeping and gnashing of teeth.'"

LUKE 8:17 "For there is nothing hidden that will not be disclosed, and nothing concealed that will not be known or brought out into the open."

LUKE 17:1-2 Jesus said to his disciples: "Things that cause people to sin are bound to come, but woe to that person through whom they come. [2]It would be better for him to be thrown into the sea with a millstone tied around his neck than for him to cause one of these little ones to sin."

Betrayal

JOHN 6:66-71 From this time many of his disciples turned back and no longer followed him. [67]"You do not want to leave too, do you?" Jesus asked the Twelve. [68]Simon Peter answered him, "Lord, to whom shall we go? You have the words of eternal life. [69]We believe and know that you are the Holy One of God." [70]Then Jesus replied, "Have I not chosen you, the Twelve? Yet one of you is a devil!" [71](He meant Judas, the son of Simon Iscariot, who, though one of the Twelve, was later to betray him.)

JOHN 13:21-28 After he had said this, Jesus was troubled in spirit and testified, "I tell you the truth, one of you is going to betray me." [22]His disciples stared at one another, at a loss to know which of them he meant. [23]One of them, the disciple whom Jesus loved, was reclining next to him. [24]Simon Peter motioned to this disciple and said, "Ask him which one he means." [25]Leaning back against Jesus, he asked him, "Lord, who is it?" [26]Jesus answered, "It is the one to whom I will give this piece of bread when I have dipped it in the dish." Then, dipping the piece of bread, he gave it to Judas Iscariot, son of Simon. [27]As soon as Judas took the bread, Satan entered into him. "What you are about to do, do quickly," Jesus told him, [28]but no one at the meal understood why Jesus said this to him.

JOHN 18:3-9 So Judas came to the grove, guiding a detachment of soldiers and some officials from the chief priests and Pharisees. They were carrying torches, lanterns and weapons. [4]Jesus, knowing all that was going to happen to him, went out and asked them, "Who is it you want?" [5]"Jesus of Nazareth," they replied. "I am he," Jesus said. (And Judas the traitor was standing there with them.) [6]When Jesus said, "I am he," they drew back and fell to the ground. [7]Again he asked them, "Who is it you want?" And they said,

"Jesus of Nazareth." [8]"I told you that I am he," Jesus answered. "If you are looking for me, then let these men go." [9]This happened so that the words he had spoken would be fulfilled: "I have not lost one of those you gave me."

MATTHEW 26:17-25 On the first day of the Feast of Unleavened Bread, the disciples came to Jesus and asked, "Where do you want us to make preparations for you to eat the Passover?" [18]He replied, "Go into the city to a certain man and tell him, 'The Teacher says: My appointed time is near. I am going to celebrate the Passover with my disciples at your house.'" [19]So the disciples did as Jesus had directed them and prepared the Passover. [20]When evening came, Jesus was reclining at the table with the Twelve. [21]And while they were eating, he said, "I tell you the truth, one of you will betray me." [22]They were very sad and began to say to him one after the other, "Surely not I, Lord?" [23]Jesus replied, "The one who has dipped his hand into the bowl with me will betray me. [24]The Son of Man will go just as it is written about him. But woe to that man who betrays the Son of Man! It would be better for him if he had not been born." [25]Then Judas, the one who would betray him, said, "Surely not I, Rabbi?" Jesus answered, "Yes, it is you."

MATTHEW 26:42-46 He went away a second time and prayed, "My Father, if it is not possible for this cup to be taken away unless I drink it, may your will be done." [43]When he came back, he again found them sleeping, because their eyes were heavy. [44]So he left them and went away once more and prayed the third time, saying the same thing. [45]Then he returned to the disciples and said to them, "Are you still sleeping and resting? Look, the hour is near, and the Son of Man is betrayed into the hands of sinners. [46]Rise, let us go! Here comes my betrayer!" (See also Mark 14:39-42.)

MATTHEW 26:55-56 At that time Jesus said to the crowd, "Am I leading a rebellion, that you have come out with swords and clubs to capture me? Every day I sat in the temple courts teaching, and you did not arrest me. [56]But this has all taken place that the writings of the prophets might be fulfilled." Then all the disciples deserted him and fled.

MATTHEW 26:69-70, 74-75 Now Peter was sitting out in the courtyard, and a servant girl came to him. "You also were with Jesus of Galilee," she said. [70]But he denied it before them all. "I don't know what you're talking about," he said. [74]Then he began to call down curses on himself and he swore to them, "I don't know the man!" Immediately a rooster crowed. [75]Then Peter remembered the word Jesus had spoken: "Before the rooster crows, you will disown me three times." And he went outside and wept bitterly. (See also Mark 14:66-72; Luke 22:55-62.)

MARK 14:17-21 When evening came, Jesus arrived with the Twelve. [18]While they were reclining at the table eating, he said, "I tell you the truth, one of you will betray me—one who is eating with me." [19]They were saddened, and one by one they said to him, "Surely not I?" [20]"It is one of the Twelve," he replied, "one who dips bread into the bowl with me.

[21]The Son of Man will go just as it is written about him. But woe to that man who betrays the Son of Man! It would be better for him if he had not been born."

LUKE 22:20-22 In the same way, after the supper he took the cup, saying, "This cup is the new covenant in my blood, which is poured out for you. [21]But the hand of him who is going to betray me is with mine on the table. [22]The Son of Man will go as it has been decreed, but woe to that man who betrays him."

LUKE 22:47-51 While he was still speaking a crowd came up, and the man who was called Judas, one of the Twelve, was leading them. He approached Jesus to kiss him, [48]but Jesus asked him, "Judas, are you betraying the Son of Man with a kiss?" [49]When Jesus' followers saw what was going to happen, they said, "Lord, should we strike with our swords?" [50]And one of them struck the servant of the high priest, cutting off his right ear. [51]But Jesus answered, "No more of this!" And he touched the man's ear and healed him.

A Broken Heart

MATTHEW 5:4 "Blessed are those who mourn, for they will be comforted."

LUKE 4:18-21 "The Spirit of the Lord is on me, because he has anointed me to preach good news to the poor. He has sent me to proclaim freedom for the prisoners and recovery of sight for the blind, to release the oppressed, [19]to proclaim the year of the Lord's favor." [20]Then he rolled up the scroll, gave it back to the attendant and sat down. The eyes of everyone in the synagogue were fastened on him, [21]and he began by saying to them, "Today this scripture is fulfilled in your hearing."

Children

MATTHEW 7:9-11 "Which of you, if his son asks for bread, will give him a stone? [10]Or if he asks for a fish, will give him a snake? [11]If you, then, though you are evil, know how to give good gifts to your children, how much more will your Father in heaven give good gifts to those who ask him!"

MATTHEW 10:34-39 "Do not suppose that I have come to bring peace to the earth. I did not come to bring peace, but a sword. [35]For I have come to turn 'a man against his father, a daughter against her mother, a daughter-in-law against her mother-in-law— [36]a man's enemies will be the members of his own household.' [37]Anyone who loves his father or mother more than me is not worthy of me; anyone who loves his son or daughter more than me is not worthy of me; [38]and anyone who does not take his cross and follow me is not worthy of me. [39]Whoever finds his life will lose it, and whoever loses his life for my sake will find it."

MATTHEW 10:42 "And if anyone gives even a cup of cold water to one of these little ones because he is my disciple, I tell you the truth, he will certainly not lose his reward."

MATTHEW 18:2-7 He called a little child and had him stand among them. [3]And he said: "I tell you the truth, unless you change and become like little children, you will never enter the kingdom of heaven. ⁴Therefore, whoever humbles himself like this child is the greatest in the kingdom of heaven. ⁵And whoever welcomes a little child like this in my name welcomes me. ⁶But if anyone causes one of these little ones who believe in me to sin, it would be better for him to have a large millstone hung around his neck and to be drowned in the depths of the sea. ⁷Woe to the world because of the things that cause people to sin! Such things must come, but woe to the man through whom they come!"

MATTHEW 18:10, 12-14 "See that you do not look down on one of these little ones. For I tell you that their angels in heaven always see the face of my Father in heaven. ¹²What do you think? If a man owns a hundred sheep, and one of them wanders away, will he not leave the ninety-nine on the hills and go to look for the one that wandered off? ¹³And if he finds it, I tell you the truth, he is happier about that one sheep than about the ninety-nine that did not wander off. ¹⁴In the same way your Father in heaven is not willing that any of these little ones should be lost."

MATTHEW 19:14 Jesus said, "Let the little children come to me, and do not hinder them, for the kingdom of heaven belongs to such as these."

MARK 9:35-37 Sitting down, Jesus called the Twelve and said, "If anyone wants to be first, he must be the very last, and the servant of all." ³⁶He took a little child and had him stand among them. Taking him in his arms, he said to them, ³⁷"Whoever welcomes one of these little children in my name welcomes me; and

whoever welcomes me does not welcome me but the one who sent me."

MARK 9:39-42 …"No one who does a miracle in my name can in the next moment say anything bad about me, ⁴⁰for whoever is not against us is for us. ⁴¹I tell you the truth, anyone who gives you a cup of water in my name because you belong to Christ will certainly not lose his reward. ⁴²And if anyone causes one of these little ones who believe in me to sin, it would be better for him to be thrown into the sea with a large millstone tied around his neck."

MARK 10:14-16 When Jesus saw this, he was indignant. He said to them, "Let the little children come to me, and do not hinder them, for the kingdom of God belongs to such as these. ¹⁵I tell you the truth, anyone who will not receive the kingdom of God like a little child will never enter it." ¹⁶And he took the children in his arms, put his hands on them and blessed them.

LUKE 14:26 "If anyone comes to me and does not hate his father and mother, his wife and children, his brothers and sisters—yes, even his own life—he cannot be my disciple."

LUKE 17:1-2 Jesus said to his disciples: "Things that cause people to sin are bound to come, but woe to that person through whom they come. ²It would be better for him to be thrown into the sea with a millstone tied around his neck than for him to cause one of these little ones to sin."

LUKE 18:16-17 But Jesus called the children to him and said, "Let the little children come to me, and do not hinder them, for the kingdom of God belongs to such as these. [17]I tell you the truth, anyone who will not receive the kingdom of God like a little child will never enter it."

LUKE 18:29-30 "I tell you the truth," Jesus said to them, "no one who has left home or wife or brothers or parents or children for the sake of the kingdom of God [30]will fail to receive many times as much in this age and, in the age to come, eternal life."

Children of the Devil

JOHN 8:39-47 "Abraham is our father," they answered. "If you were Abraham's children," said Jesus, "then you would do the things Abraham did. [40]As it is, you are determined to kill me, a man who has told you the truth that I heard from God. Abraham did not do such things. [41]You are doing the things your own father does." "We are not illegitimate children," they protested. "The only Father we have is God himself." [42]Jesus said to them, "If God were your Father, you would love me, for I came from God and now am here. I have not come on my own; but he sent me. [43]Why is my language not clear to you? Because you are unable to hear what I say. [44]You belong to your father, the devil, and you want to carry out your father's desire. He was a murderer from the beginning, not holding to the truth, for there is no truth in him. When he lies, he speaks his native language, for he is a liar and the father of lies. [45]Yet because I tell the truth, you do not believe me! [46]Can any of you prove me guilty of sin? If I am telling the truth,

why don't you believe me? [47]He who belongs to God hears what God says. The reason you do not hear is that you do not belong to God."

MATTHEW 13:37-43 He answered, "The one who sowed the good seed is the Son of Man. [38]The field is the world, and the good seed stands for the sons of the kingdom. The weeds are the sons of the evil one, [39]and the enemy who sows them is the devil. The harvest is the end of the age, and the harvesters are angels. [40]As the weeds are pulled up and burned in the fire, so it will be at the end of the age. [41]The Son of Man will send out his angels, and they will weed out of his kingdom everything that causes sin and all who do evil. [42]They will throw them into the fiery furnace, where there will be weeping and gnashing of teeth. [43]Then the righteous will shine like the sun in the kingdom of their Father. He who has ears, let him hear."

Defilement of the Heart

MATTHEW 12:33-35 "Make a tree good and its fruit will be good, or make a tree bad and its fruit will be bad, for a tree is recognized by its fruit. [34]You brood of vipers, how can you who are evil say anything good? For out of the overflow of the heart the mouth speaks. [35]The good man brings good things out of the good stored up in him, and the evil man brings evil things out of the evil stored up in him." (See also Luke 6:43-45.)

MATTHEW 15:7-9 "You hypocrites! Isaiah was right when he prophesied about you: [8]'These people honor me with their lips, but their hearts are far from me. [9]They worship me in vain; their teachings are but rules taught by men.'"

MATTHEW 15:10-11 Jesus called the crowd to him and said, "Listen and understand. [11]What goes into a man's mouth does not make him 'unclean,' but what comes out of his mouth, that is what makes him 'unclean.'"

MATTHEW 15:16-20 "Are you still so dull?" Jesus asked them. [17]"Don't you see that whatever enters the mouth goes into the stomach and then out of the body? [18]But the things that come out of the mouth come from the heart, and these make a man 'unclean.' [19]For out of the heart come evil thoughts, murder, adultery, sexual immorality, theft, false testimony, slander. [20]These are what make a man 'unclean'; but eating with unwashed hands does not make him 'unclean.'"

MATTHEW 23:27-28 "Woe to you, teachers of the law and Pharisees, you hypocrites! You are like whitewashed tombs, which look beautiful on the outside but on the inside are full of dead men's bones and everything unclean. [28]In the same way, on the outside you appear to people as righteous but on the inside you are full of hypocrisy and wickedness."

MARK 7:14-15, 17-23 Again Jesus called the crowd to him and said, "Listen to me, everyone, and understand this. [15]Nothing outside a man can make him 'unclean' by going into him. Rather, it is what comes out of a man that makes him 'unclean.'" [17]After he had left the crowd and entered the house, his disciples asked him about this parable. [18]"Are you so

dull?" he asked. "Don't you see that nothing that enters a man from the outside can make him 'unclean'? [19]For it doesn't go into his heart but into his stomach, and then out of his body." (In saying this, Jesus declared all foods "clean.") [20]He went on: "What comes out of a man is what makes him 'unclean.' [21]For from within, out of men's hearts, come evil thoughts, sexual immorality, theft, murder, adultery, [22]greed, malice, deceit, lewdness, envy, slander, arrogance and folly. [23]All these evils come from inside and make a man 'unclean.'"

LUKE 11:39-44 Then the Lord said to him, "Now then, you Pharisees clean the outside of the cup and dish, but inside you are full of greed and wickedness. [40]You foolish people! Did not the one who made the outside make the inside also? [41]But give what is inside the dish to the poor, and everything will be clean for you. [42]Woe to you Pharisees, because you give God a tenth of your mint, rue and all other kinds of garden herbs, but you neglect justice and the love of God. You should have practiced the latter without leaving the former undone. [43]Woe to you Pharisees, because you love the most important seats in the synagogues and greetings in the marketplaces. [44]Woe to you, because you are like unmarked graves, which men walk over without knowing it."

LUKE 16:15 He said to them [the Pharisees], "You are the ones who justify yourselves in the eyes of men, but God knows your hearts. What is highly valued among men is detestable in God's sight."

Eating

MATTHEW 15:10-11 Jesus called the crowd to him and said, "Listen and understand. [11]What goes into a man's mouth does not make him 'unclean,' but what comes out of his mouth, that is what makes him 'unclean.'"

MATTHEW 15:16-20 "Are you still so dull?" Jesus asked them. [17]"Don't you see that whatever enters the mouth goes into the stomach and then out of the body? [18]But the things that come out of the mouth come from the heart, and these make a man 'unclean.' [19]For out of the heart come evil thoughts, murder, adultery, sexual immorality, theft, false testimony, slander. [20]These are what make a man 'unclean'; but eating with unwashed hands does not make him 'unclean.'"

MARK 7:15, 17-20 "Nothing outside a man can make him 'unclean' by going into him. Rather, it is what comes out of a man that makes him 'unclean.'" [17]After he had left the crowd and entered the house, his disciples asked him about this parable. [18]"Are you so dull?" he asked. "Don't you see that nothing that enters a man from the outside can make him 'unclean'? [19]For it doesn't go into his heart but into his stomach, and then out of his body." (In saying this, Jesus declared all foods "clean.") [20]He went on: "What comes out of a man is what makes him 'unclean.'"

Enemies of Christ

JOHN 8:37-49 "I know you are Abraham's descendants. Yet you are ready to kill me, because you have no room for my word. [38]I am telling you what I have seen in the Father's presence, and you do what you have heard from your father." [39]"Abraham is our father," they answered. "If you were Abraham's children," said Jesus, "then you would do the things Abraham did. [40]As it is, you are determined to kill me, a man who has told you the truth that I heard from God. Abraham did not do such things. [41]You are doing the things your own father does." "We are not illegitimate children," they protested. "The only Father we have is God himself." [42]Jesus said to them, "If God were your Father, you would love me, for I came from God and now am here. I have not come on my own; but he sent me. [43]Why is my language not clear to you? Because you are unable to hear what I say. [44]You belong to your father, the devil, and you want to carry out your father's desire. He was a murderer from the beginning, not holding to the truth, for there is no truth in him. When he lies, he speaks his native language, for he is a liar and the father of lies. [45]Yet because I tell the truth, you do not believe me! [46]Can any of you prove me guilty of sin? If I am telling the truth, why don't you believe me? [47]He who belongs to God hears what God says. The reason you do not hear is that you do not belong to God." [48]The Jews answered him, "Aren't we right in saying that you are a Samaritan and demon-possessed?" [49]"I am not possessed by a demon," said Jesus, "but I honor my Father and you dishonor me."

MATTHEW 5:10-11 "Blessed are those who are persecuted because of righteousness, for theirs is the kingdom of heaven. [11]Blessed are you when people insult you, persecute you and falsely say all kinds of evil against you because of me."

MATTHEW 5:38-48 "You have heard that it was said, 'Eye for eye, and tooth for tooth.' [39]But I tell you, Do not resist an evil person. If someone strikes you on the right cheek, turn to him the other also. [40]And if someone wants to sue you and take your tunic, let him have your cloak as well. [41]If someone forces you to go one mile, go with him two miles. [42]Give to the one who asks you, and do not turn away from the one who wants to borrow from you. [43]You have heard that it was said, 'Love your neighbor and hate your enemy.' [44]But I tell you: Love your enemies and pray for those who persecute you, [45]that you may be sons of your Father in heaven. He causes his sun to rise on the evil and the good, and sends rain on the righteous and the unrighteous. [46]If you love those who love you, what reward will you get? Are not even the tax collectors doing that? [47]And if you greet only your brothers, what are you doing more than others? Do not even pagans do that? [48]Be perfect, therefore, as your heavenly Father is perfect."

MATTHEW 10:21-26 "Brother will betray brother to death, and a father his child; children will rebel against their parents and have them put to death. [22]All men will hate you because of me, but he who stands firm to the end will be saved. [23]When you are persecuted in one place, flee to another. I tell you the truth, you will not finish going through the cities of Israel before the Son of Man comes. [24]A student is not above his teacher, nor a servant above his master. [25]It is enough for the student to be like his teacher, and the servant like his master. If the head of the house has been called Beelzebub, how much more the members of his household! [26]So do not be afraid of them. There is nothing concealed that will not be disclosed, or hidden that will not be made known."

MATTHEW 24:9-10 "Then you will be handed over to be persecuted and put to death, and you will be hated by all nations because of me. [10]At that time many will turn away from the faith and will betray and hate each other."

MARK 9:38-42 "Teacher," said John, "we saw a man driving out demons in your name and we told him to stop, because he was not one of us." [39]"Do not stop him," Jesus said. "No one who does a miracle in my name can in the next moment say anything bad about me, [40]for whoever is not against us is for us. [41]I tell you the truth, anyone who gives you a cup of water in my name because you belong to Christ will certainly not lose his reward. [42]And if anyone causes one of these little ones who believe in me to sin, it would be better for him to be thrown into the sea with a large millstone tied around his neck."

MARK 13:9-13 "You must be on your guard. You will be handed over to the local councils and flogged in the synagogues. On account of me you will stand before governors and kings as witnesses to them. [10]And the gospel must first be preached to all nations. [11]Whenever you are arrested and brought to trial, do not worry beforehand about what to say. Just say whatever is given you at the time, for it is not you speaking, but the Holy Spirit. [12]Brother will betray brother to death, and a father his child. Children will rebel against their parents and have them put to death. [13]All men will hate you because of me, but he who stands firm to the end will be saved."

LUKE 11:17-26 Jesus knew their thoughts and said to them: "Any kingdom divided against itself will be ruined, and a house divided against itself will fall. [18]If Satan is divided against himself, how can his kingdom stand? I say this because you claim that I drive out demons by Beelzebub. [19]Now if I drive out demons by Beelzebub, by whom do your followers drive them out? So then, they will be your judges. [20]But if I drive out demons by the finger of God, then the kingdom of God has come to you. [21]When a strong man, fully armed, guards his own house, his possessions are safe. [22]But when someone stronger attacks and overpowers him, he takes away the armor in which the man trusted and divides up the spoils. [23]He who is not with me is against me, and he who does not gather with me, scatters. [24]When an evil spirit comes out of a man, it goes through arid places seeking rest and does not find it. Then it says, 'I will return to the house I left.' [25]When it arrives, it finds the house swept clean and put in order. [26]Then it goes and takes seven other spirits more wicked than itself, and they go in and live there. And the final condition of that man is worse than the first."

LUKE 21:12-19 "But before all this, they will lay hands on you and persecute you. They will deliver you to synagogues and prisons, and you will be brought before kings and governors, and all on account of my name. [13]This will result in your being witnesses to them. [14]But make up your mind not to worry beforehand how you will defend yourselves. [15]For I will give you words and wisdom that none of your adversaries will be able to resist or contradict. [16]You will be betrayed even by parents, brothers, relatives and friends, and they will put some of you to death. [17]All men will hate you because of me. [18]But not a hair of your head will perish. [19]By standing firm you will gain life."

LUKE 23:34 Jesus said, "Father, forgive them, for they do not know what they are doing." And they divided up his clothes by casting lots.

Evil

JOHN 3:19-20 "This is the verdict: Light has come into the world, but men loved darkness instead of light because their deeds were evil. [20]Everyone who does evil hates the light, and will not come into the light for fear that his deeds will be exposed."

JOHN 5:28-29 "Do not be amazed at this, for a time is coming when all who are in their graves will hear his voice [29]and come out—those who have done good will rise to live, and those who have done evil will rise to be condemned."

JOHN 7:7-8 "The world cannot hate you, but it hates me because I testify that what it does is evil. [8]You go to the Feast. I am not yet going up to this Feast, because for me the right time has not yet come."

Matthew 5:44-46 "But I tell you: Love your enemies and pray for those who persecute you, [45]that you may be sons of your Father in heaven. He causes his sun to rise on the evil and the good, and sends rain on the righteous and the unrighteous. [46]If you love those who love you, what reward will you get? Are not even the tax collectors doing that?"

Matthew 6:9-13 "This, then, is how you should pray: 'Our Father in heaven, hallowed be your name, [10]your kingdom come, your will be done on earth as it is in heaven. [11]Give us today our daily bread. [12]Forgive us our debts, as we also have forgiven our debtors. [13]And lead us not into temptation, but deliver us from the evil one.'" (See also Luke 11:2-4.)

Matthew 9:2, 4-5 Some men brought to him a paralytic, lying on a mat. When Jesus saw their faith, he said to the paralytic, "Take heart, son; your sins are forgiven." [4]Knowing their thoughts, Jesus said, "Why do you entertain evil thoughts in your hearts? [5]Which is easier: to say, 'Your sins are forgiven,' or to say, 'Get up and walk'?"

Matthew 12:34-35 "You brood of vipers, how can you who are evil say anything good? For out of the overflow of the heart the mouth speaks. [35]The good man brings good things out of the good stored up in him, and the evil man brings evil things out of the evil stored up in him."

Matthew 12:39 He answered, "A wicked and adulterous generation asks for a miraculous sign! But none will be given it except the sign of the prophet Jonah."

Matthew 15:10-11, 18-20 Jesus called the crowd to him and said, "Listen and understand. [11]What goes into a man's mouth does not make him 'unclean,' but what comes out of his mouth, that is what makes him 'unclean.' [18]But the things that come out of the mouth come from the heart, and these make a man 'unclean.' [19]For out of the heart come evil thoughts, murder, adultery, sexual immorality, theft, false testimony, slander. [20]These are what make a man 'unclean'; but eating with unwashed hands does not make him 'unclean.'"

Matthew 24:48-51 "But suppose that servant is wicked and says to himself, 'My master is staying away a long time,' [49]and he then begins to beat his fellow servants and to eat and drink with drunkards. [50]The master of that servant will come on a day when he does not expect him and at an hour he is not aware of. [51]He will cut him to pieces and assign him a place with the hypocrites, where there will be weeping and gnashing of teeth."

Mark 7:18-23 "Are you so dull?" he asked. "Don't you see that nothing that enters a man from the outside can make him 'unclean'? [19]For it doesn't go into his heart but into his stomach, and then out of his body." (In saying this, Jesus declared all foods "clean.") [20]He went on: "What comes out of a man is what makes him 'unclean.' [21]For from within, out of men's hearts, come evil thoughts, sexual immorality, theft, murder, adultery, [22]greed, malice, deceit, lewdness, envy, slander, arrogance and folly. [23]All these evils come from inside and make a man 'unclean.'"

Luke 6:35-36 "But love your enemies, do good to them, and lend to them without expecting to get anything back. Then your reward will be great, and you will be sons of the Most High, because he is kind to the ungrateful and wicked. [36]Be merciful, just as your Father is merciful."

LUKE 11:5-13 Then he said to them, "Suppose one of you has a friend, and he goes to him at midnight and says, 'Friend, lend me three loaves of bread, [6]because a friend of mine on a journey has come to me, and I have nothing to set before him.' [7]Then the one inside answers, 'Don't bother me. The door is already locked, and my children are with me in bed. I can't get up and give you anything.' [8]I tell you, though he will not get up and give him the bread because he is his friend, yet because of the man's boldness he will get up and give him as much as he needs. [9]So I say to you: Ask and it will be given to you; seek and you will find; knock and the door will be opened to you. [10]For everyone who asks receives; he who seeks finds; and to him who knocks, the door will be opened. [11]Which of you fathers, if your son asks for a fish, will give him a snake instead? [12]Or if he asks for an egg, will give him a scorpion? [13]If you then, though you are evil, know how to give good gifts to your children, how much more will your Father in heaven give the Holy Spirit to those who ask him!"

LUKE 11:29 As the crowds increased, Jesus said, "This is a wicked generation. It asks for a miraculous sign, but none will be given it except the sign of Jonah."

LUKE 11:39-44 Then the Lord said to him, "Now then, you Pharisees clean the outside of the cup and dish, but inside you are full of greed and wickedness.

[40]You foolish people! Did not the one who made the outside make the inside also? [41]But give what is inside the dish to the poor, and everything will be clean for you. [42]Woe to you Pharisees, because you give God a tenth of your mint, rue and all other kinds of garden herbs, but you neglect justice and the love of God. You should have practiced the latter without leaving the former undone. [43]Woe to you Pharisees, because you love the most important seats in the synagogues and greetings in the marketplaces. [44]Woe to you, because you are like unmarked graves, which men walk over without knowing it."

REVELATION 2:2-3 "I know your deeds, your hard work and your perseverance. I know that you cannot tolerate wicked men, that you have tested those who claim to be apostles but are not, and have found them false. [3]You have persevered and have endured hardships for my name, and have not grown weary."

Evildoers

MATTHEW 7:21-27 "Not everyone who says to Me, 'Lord, Lord,' shall enter the kingdom of heaven, but he who does the will of My Father in heaven. [22]Many will say to Me in that day, 'Lord, Lord, have we not prophesied in Your name, cast out demons in Your name, and done many wonders in Your name?' [23]And then I will declare to them, 'I never knew you; depart from Me, you who practice lawlessness!' [24]Therefore whoever hears these sayings of Mine, and does them, I will liken him to a wise man who built his house on the rock: [25]and the rain descended, the floods came, and the winds blew and beat on that house; and it did not fall, for it was founded on the rock. [26]But everyone who hears these sayings of Mine, and does not do them, will be like a foolish man who built his house on the sand: [27]and the rain descended, the floods came, and the winds blew and beat on that house; and it fell. And great was its fall." (NKJV)

LUKE 13:23-30 Someone asked him, "Lord, are only a few people going to be saved?" He said to them, [24]"Make every effort to enter through the narrow door, because many, I tell you, will try to enter and will not be able to. [25]Once the owner of the house gets up and closes the door, you will stand outside knocking and pleading, 'Sir, open the door for us.' But he will answer, 'I don't know you or where you come from.' [26]Then you will say, 'We ate and drank with you, and you taught in our streets.' [27]But he will reply, 'I don't know you or where you come from. Away from me, all you evildoers!' [28]There will be weeping there, and gnashing of teeth, when you see Abraham, Isaac and Jacob and all the prophets in the kingdom of God, but you yourselves thrown out. [29]People will come from east and west and north and south, and will take their places at the feast in the kingdom of God. [30]Indeed there are those who are last who will be first, and first who will be last."

The Eyes and Spiritual Eyesight

JOHN 4:31-36 Meanwhile his disciples urged him, "Rabbi, eat something." [32]But he said to them, "I have food to eat that you know nothing about." [33]Then his disciples said to each other, "Could someone have brought him food?" [34]"My food," said Jesus, "is to do the will of him who sent me and to finish his work. [35]Do you not say, 'Four months more and then the harvest'? I tell you, open your eyes and look at the fields! They are ripe for harvest. [36]Even now the reaper draws his wages, even now he harvests the crop for eternal life, so that the sower and the reaper may be glad together."

MATTHEW 5:27-30 "You have heard that it was said, 'Do not commit adultery.' [28]But I tell you that anyone who looks at a woman lustfully has already committed adultery with her in his heart. [29]If your right eye causes you to sin, gouge it out and throw it away. It is better for you to lose one part of your body than for your whole body to be thrown into hell. [30]And if your right hand causes you to sin, cut it off and throw it away. It is better for you to lose one part of your body than for your whole body to go into hell."

MATTHEW 6:22-23 "The eye is the lamp of the body. If your eyes are good, your whole body will be full of light. [23]But if your eyes are bad, your whole body will be full of darkness. If then the light within you is darkness, how great is that darkness!"

MATTHEW 7:3-5 "Why do you look at the speck of sawdust in your brother's eye and pay no attention to the plank in your own eye? [4]How can you say to your brother, 'Let me take the speck out of your eye,' when all the time there is a plank in your own eye? [5]You hypocrite, first take the plank out of your own eye, and then you will see clearly to remove the speck from your brother's eye."

MATTHEW 13:13-17 "This is why I speak to them in parables: Though seeing, they do not see; though hearing, they do not hear or understand. [14]In them is fulfilled the prophecy of Isaiah: 'You will be ever hearing but never understanding; you will be ever seeing but never perceiving. [15]For this people's heart has become calloused; they hardly hear with their ears, and they have closed their eyes. Otherwise they might see with their eyes, hear with their ears, understand with their hearts and turn, and I would heal them.' [16]But blessed are your eyes because they see, and your ears because they hear. [17]For I tell you the truth, many prophets and righteous men longed to see what you see but did not see it, and to hear what you hear but did not hear it."

MATTHEW 18:9 "And if your eye causes you to sin, gouge it out and throw it away. It is better for you to enter life with one eye than to have two eyes and be thrown into the fire of hell."

MARK 7:20-23 He went on: "What comes out of a man is what makes him 'unclean.' [21]For from within, out of men's hearts, come evil thoughts, sexual immorality, theft, murder, adultery, [22]greed, malice, deceit, lewdness, envy, slander, arrogance and folly. [23]All these evils come from inside and make a man 'unclean.'"

MARK 8:17-19 Aware of their [the disciples'] discussion, Jesus asked them: "Why are you talking about having no bread? Do you still not see or understand? Are your hearts hardened? [18]Do you have eyes but fail to see, and ears but fail to hear? And don't you remember? [19]When I broke the five loaves for the five thousand, how many basketfuls of pieces did you pick up?" "Twelve," they replied.

MARK 9:47-48 "And if your eye causes you to sin, pluck it out. It is better for you to enter the kingdom of God with one eye than to have two eyes and be thrown into hell, [48]where 'their worm does not die, and the fire is not quenched.'"

LUKE 6:41-42 "Why do you look at the speck of sawdust in your brother's eye and pay no attention to the plank in your own eye? [42]How can you say to your brother, 'Brother, let me take the speck out of your eye,' when you yourself fail to see the plank in your own eye? You hypocrite, first take the plank out of your eye, and then you will see clearly to remove the speck from your brother's eye."

LUKE 11:33-36 "No one lights a lamp and puts it in a place where it will be hidden, or under a bowl. Instead he puts it on its stand, so that those who come in may see the light. [34]Your eye is the lamp of your body. When your eyes are good, your whole body also is full of light. But when they are bad, your body also is full of darkness. [35]See to it, then, that the light within you is not darkness. [36]Therefore, if your whole body is full of light, and no part of it dark, it will be completely lighted, as when the light of a lamp shines on you."

False Doctrine

MARK 7:6-13 He replied, "Isaiah was right when he prophesied about you hypocrites; as it is written: 'These people honor me with their lips, but their hearts are far from me. [7]They worship me in vain; their teachings are but rules taught by men.' [8]You have let go of the commands of God and are holding on to the traditions of men." [9]And he said to them: "You have a fine way of setting aside the commands of God in order to observe your own traditions! [10]For Moses said, 'Honor your father and your mother,' and, 'Anyone who curses his father or mother must be put to death.' [11]But you say that if a man says to his father or mother: 'Whatever help you might otherwise have received from me is Corban' (that is, a gift devoted to God), [12]then you no longer let him do anything for his father or mother. [13]Thus you nullify the word of God by your tradition that you have handed down. And you do many things like that."

False Prophets

JOHN 10:1-5 "I tell you the truth, the man who does not enter the sheep pen by the gate, but climbs in by some other way, is a thief and a robber. [2]The man who enters by the gate is the shepherd of his sheep. [3]The watchman opens the gate for him, and the sheep listen to his voice. He calls his own sheep by name and leads them out. [4]When he has brought out all his own, he goes on ahead of them, and his sheep follow him because they know his voice. [5]But they will never follow a stranger; in fact, they will run away from him because they do not recognize a stranger's voice."

JOHN 10:7-16 Therefore Jesus said again, "I tell you the truth, I am the gate for the sheep. [8]All who ever came before me were thieves and robbers, but the sheep did not listen to them. [9]I am the gate; whoever enters through me will be saved. He will come in and go out, and find pasture. [10]The thief comes only to steal and kill and destroy; I have come that they may have life, and have it to the full. [11]I am the good shepherd. The good shepherd lays down his life for the sheep. [12]The hired hand is not the shepherd who owns the sheep. So when he sees the wolf coming, he abandons the sheep and runs away. Then the wolf attacks the flock and scatters it. [13]The man runs away because he is a hired hand and cares nothing for the sheep. [14]I am the good shepherd; I know my sheep and my sheep know me— [15]just as the Father knows me and I know the Father—and I lay down my life for the sheep. [16]I have other sheep that are not of this sheep pen. I must bring them also. They too will listen to my voice, and there shall be one flock and one shepherd."

MATTHEW 7:15-20 "Watch out for false prophets. They come to you in sheep's clothing, but inwardly they are ferocious wolves. [16]By their fruit you will recognize them. Do people pick grapes from thornbushes, or figs from thistles? [17]Likewise every good tree bears good fruit, but a bad tree bears bad fruit. [18]A good tree cannot bear bad fruit, and a bad tree cannot bear good fruit. [19]Every tree that does not bear good fruit is cut down and thrown into the fire. [20]Thus, by their fruit you will recognize them."

MATTHEW 24:4-5 Jesus answered: "Watch out that no one deceives you. [5]For many will come in my name, claiming, 'I am the Christ,' and will deceive many."

MATTHEW 24:15-16 "So when you see standing in the holy place 'the abomination that causes desolation,' spoken of through the prophet Daniel—let the reader understand— [16]then let those who are in Judea flee to the mountains."

MATTHEW 24:23-27 "At that time if anyone says to you, 'Look, here is the Christ!' or, 'There he is!' do not believe it. [24]For false Christs and false prophets will appear and perform great signs and miracles to deceive even the elect—if that were possible. [25]See, I have told you ahead of time. [26]So if anyone tells you, 'There he is, out in the desert,' do not go out; or, 'Here he is, in the inner rooms,' do not believe it. [27]For as lightning that comes from the east is visible even in the west, so will be the coming of the Son of Man."

MARK 13:5-6 Jesus said to them [Peter, James, John, Andrew]: "Watch out that no one deceives you. [6]Many will come in my name, claiming, 'I am he,' and will deceive many."

MARK 13:14 "When you see 'the abomination that causes desolation' standing where it does not belong—let the reader understand—then let those who are in Judea flee to the mountains."

LUKE 17:22-24 Then he said to his disciples, "The time is coming when you will long to see one of the days of the Son of Man, but you will not see it. [23]Men will tell you, 'There he is!' or 'Here he is!' Do not go running off after them. [24]For the Son of Man in his day will be like the lightning, which flashes and lights up the sky from one end to the other."

LUKE 21:8 He replied: "Watch out that you are not deceived. For many will come in my name, claiming, 'I am he,' and, 'The time is near.' Do not follow them."

Flattery

LUKE 6:26 "Woe to you when all men speak well of you, for that is how their fathers treated the false prophets."

Foolishness

MATTHEW 7:21-27 "Not everyone who says to Me, 'Lord, Lord,' shall enter the kingdom of heaven, but he who does the will of My Father in heaven. [22]Many will say to Me in that day, 'Lord, Lord, have we not prophesied in Your name, cast out demons in Your name, and done many wonders in Your name?' [23]And then I will declare to them, 'I never knew you; depart from Me, you who practice lawlessness!' [24]Therefore whoever hears these sayings of Mine, and does them, I will liken him to a wise man who built his house on the rock: [25]and the rain descended, the floods came, and the winds blew and beat on that house; and it did not fall, for it was founded on the rock. [26]But everyone who hears these sayings of Mine, and does not do them, will be like a foolish man who built his house on the sand: [27]and the rain descended, the floods came, and the winds blew and beat on that house; and it fell. And great was its fall." (NKJV)

LUKE 11:39-44 Then the Lord said to him, "Now then, you Pharisees clean the outside of the cup and dish, but inside you are full of greed and wickedness. [40]You foolish people! Did not the one who made the outside make the inside also? [41]But give what is inside the dish to the poor, and everything will be clean for you. [42]Woe to you Pharisees, because you give God a tenth of your mint, rue and all other kinds of garden herbs, but you neglect justice and the love of God. You should have practiced the latter without leaving the former undone. [43]Woe to you Pharisees, because you love the most important seats in the synagogues and greetings in the marketplaces. [44]Woe to you, because you are like unmarked graves, which men walk over without knowing it."

LUKE 12:13-21 Someone in the crowd said to him, "Teacher, tell my brother to divide the inheritance with me." [14]Jesus replied, "Man, who appointed me a judge or an arbiter between you?" [15]Then he said to them, "Watch out! Be on your guard against all kinds of greed; a man's life does not consist in the abundance of his possessions." [16]And he told them this parable: "The ground of a certain rich man produced a good crop. [17]He thought to himself, 'What shall I do? I have no place to store my crops.' [18]Then he said, 'This is what I'll do. I will tear down my barns and build bigger ones, and there I will store all my grain and my goods. [19]And I'll say to myself, "You have plenty of good things laid up for many years. Take life easy; eat, drink and be merry." ' [20]But God said to him, 'You fool! This very night your life will be demanded from you. Then who will get what you have prepared for yourself?' [21]This is how it will be with anyone who stores up things for himself but is not rich toward God."

LUKE 12:42-49 The Lord answered, "Who then is the faithful and wise manager, whom the master puts in charge of his servants to give them their food allowance at the proper time? [43]It will be good for that servant whom the master finds doing so when he returns. [44]I tell you the truth, he will put him in charge of all his possessions. [45]But suppose the servant says to himself, 'My master is taking a long time in coming,' and he then begins to beat the menservants and maidservants and to eat and drink and get drunk. [46]The master of that servant will come on a day when he does not expect him and at an hour he is not aware of. He will cut him to pieces and assign him a place with the unbelievers. [47]That servant who knows his master's will and does not get ready or does not do what his master wants will be beaten with many blows. [48]But the one who does not know and does things deserving punishment will be beaten with few blows. From everyone who has been given much, much will be demanded; and from the one who has been entrusted with much, much more will be asked. [49]I have come to bring fire on the earth, and how I wish it were already kindled!"

LUKE 14:27-33 "And anyone who does not carry his cross and follow me cannot be my disciple. [28]Suppose one of you wants to build a tower. Will he not first sit down and estimate the cost to see if he has enough money to complete it? [29]For if he lays the foundation and is not able to finish it, everyone who sees it will ridicule him, [30]saying, 'This fellow began to build and was not able to finish.' [31]Or suppose a king is about to go to war against another king. Will he not first sit down and consider whether he is able with ten thousand men to oppose the one coming against him with twenty thousand? [32]If he is not able, he will send a delegation while the other is still a long way off and will ask for terms of peace. [33]In the same way, any of you who does not give up everything he has cannot be my disciple."

Good People Versus Evil People

JOHN 3:19-21 "This is the verdict: Light has come into the world, but men loved darkness instead of light because their deeds were evil. [20]Everyone who does evil hates the light, and will not come into the light for fear that his deeds will be exposed. [21]But whoever lives by the truth comes into the light, so that it may be seen plainly that what he has done has been done through God."

MATTHEW 12:33-37 "Make a tree good and its fruit will be good, or make a tree bad and its fruit will be bad, for a tree is recognized by its fruit. [34]You brood of vipers, how can you who are evil say anything good? For out of the overflow of the heart the mouth speaks. [35]The good man brings good things out of the good stored up in him, and the evil man brings evil things out of the evil stored up in him.

[36]But I tell you that men will have to give account on the day of judgment for every careless word they have spoken. [37]For by your words you will be acquitted, and by your words you will be condemned."

MATTHEW 15:10-20 Jesus called the crowd to him and said, "Listen and understand. [11]What goes into a man's mouth does not make him 'unclean,' but what comes out of his mouth, that is what makes him 'unclean.' " [12]Then the disciples came to him and asked, "Do you know that the Pharisees were offended when they heard this?" [13]He replied, "Every plant that my heavenly Father has not planted will be pulled up by the roots. [14]Leave them; they are blind guides. If a blind man leads a blind man, both will fall into a pit." [15]Peter said, "Explain the parable to us." [16]"Are you still so dull?" Jesus asked them. [17]"Don't you see that whatever enters the mouth goes into the stomach and then out of the body? [18]But the things that come out of the mouth come from the heart, and these make a man 'unclean.' [19]For out of the heart come evil thoughts, murder, adultery, sexual immorality, theft, false testimony, slander. [20]These are what make a man 'unclean'; but eating with unwashed hands does not make him 'unclean.' "

MATTHEW 23:25-28 "Woe to you, teachers of the law and Pharisees, you hypocrites! You clean the outside of the cup and dish, but inside they are full of greed and self-indulgence. [26]Blind Pharisee! First clean the inside of the cup and dish, and then the outside also will be clean. [27]Woe to you, teachers of the law and Pharisees, you hypocrites! You are like whitewashed tombs, which look beautiful on the outside but on the inside are full of dead men's bones and everything unclean. [28]In the same way, on the outside you appear to people as righteous but on the inside you are full of hypocrisy and wickedness."

LUKE 6:43-45 "No good tree bears bad fruit, nor does a bad tree bear good fruit. [44]Each tree is recognized by its own fruit. People do not pick figs from thornbushes, or grapes from briers. [45]The good man brings good things out of the good stored up in his heart, and the evil man brings evil things out of the evil stored up in his heart. For out of the overflow of his heart his mouth speaks."

LUKE 11:39-40 Then the Lord said to him, "Now then, you Pharisees clean the outside of the cup and dish, but inside you are full of greed and wickedness. [40]You foolish people! Did not the one who made the outside make the inside also?"

LUKE 12:1-3 Meanwhile, when a crowd of many thousands had gathered, so that they were trampling on one another, Jesus began to speak first to his disciples, saying: "Be on your guard against the yeast of the Pharisees, which is hypocrisy. [2]There is nothing concealed that will not be disclosed, or hidden that will not be made known. [3]What you have said in the dark will be heard in the daylight, and what you have whispered in the ear in the inner rooms will be proclaimed from the roofs."

LUKE 18:9-14 To some who were confident of their own righteousness and looked down on everybody else, Jesus told this parable: [10]"Two men went up to the temple to pray, one a Pharisee and the other a tax collector. [11]The Pharisee stood up and prayed about himself: 'God, I thank you that I am not like other men—robbers, evildoers, adulterers—or even like this tax collector. [12]I fast twice a week and give a tenth of all I get.' [13]But the tax collector stood at a distance. He would not even look up to heaven, but beat his breast and said, 'God, have mercy on me, a sinner.' [14]I tell you that this man, rather than the other, went home justified before God. For everyone who exalts himself will be humbled, and he who humbles himself will be exalted."

Greed and Covetousness

JOHN 6:26 Jesus answered, "I tell you the truth, you are looking for me, not because you saw miraculous signs but because you ate the loaves and had your fill."

MATTHEW 6:19-21 "Do not store up for yourselves treasures on earth, where moth and rust destroy, and where thieves break in and steal. [20]But store up for yourselves treasures in heaven, where moth and rust do not destroy, and where thieves do not break in and steal. [21]For where your treasure is, there your heart will be also."

MATTHEW 6:24-34 "No one can serve two masters. Either he will hate the one and love the other, or he will be devoted to the one and despise the other. You cannot serve both God and Money.

²⁵Therefore I tell you, do not worry about your life, what you will eat or drink; or about your body, what you will wear. Is not life more important than food, and the body more important than clothes? ²⁶Look at the birds of the air; they do not sow or reap or store away in barns, and yet your heavenly Father feeds them. Are you not much more valuable than they? ²⁷Who of you by worrying can add a single hour to his life? ²⁸And why do you worry about clothes? See how the lilies of the field grow. They do not labor or spin. ²⁹Yet I tell you that not even Solomon in all his splendor was dressed like one of these. ³⁰If that is how God clothes the grass of the field, which is here today and tomorrow is thrown into the fire, will he not much more clothe you, O you of little faith? ³¹So do not worry, saying, 'What shall we eat?' or 'What shall we drink?' or 'What shall we wear?' ³²For the pagans run after all these things, and your heavenly Father knows that you need them. ³³But seek first his kingdom and his righteousness, and all these things will be given to you as well. ³⁴Therefore do not worry about tomorrow, for tomorrow will worry about itself. Each day has enough trouble of its own."

MATTHEW 13:22 "The one who received the seed that fell among the thorns is the man who hears the word, but the worries of this life and the deceitfulness of wealth choke it, making it unfruitful."

MATTHEW 16:24-26 Then Jesus said to his disciples, "If anyone would come after me, he must deny himself and take up his cross and follow me. ²⁵For whoever wants to save his life will lose it, but whoever loses his life for me will find it. ²⁶What good will it be for a man if he gains the whole world, yet forfeits his soul? Or what can a man give in exchange for his soul?"

MATTHEW 19:21-24 Jesus answered, "If you want to be perfect, go, sell your possessions and give to the poor, and you will have treasure in heaven. Then come, follow me." ²²When the young man heard this, he went away sad, because he had great wealth. ²³Then Jesus said to his disciples, "I tell you the truth, it is hard for a rich man to enter the kingdom of heaven. ²⁴Again I tell you, it is easier for a camel to go through the eye of a needle than for a rich man to enter the kingdom of God." (See also Luke 18:24-25.)

MATTHEW 23:25-26 "Woe to you, teachers of the law and Pharisees, you hypocrites! You clean the outside of the cup and dish, but inside they are full of greed and self-indulgence. ²⁶Blind Pharisee! First clean the inside of the cup and dish, and then the outside also will be clean."

MARK 4:18-19 "Still others, like seed sown among thorns, hear the word; ¹⁹but the worries of this life, the deceitfulness of wealth and the desires for other things come in and choke the word, making it unfruitful."

MARK 7:20-23 He went on: "What comes out of a man is what makes him 'unclean.' ²¹For from within, out of men's hearts, come evil thoughts, sexual immorality, theft, murder, adultery, ²²greed, malice, deceit, lewdness, envy, slander, arrogance and folly. [23]All these evils come from inside and make a man 'unclean.'"

LUKE 11:39 Then the Lord said to him, "Now then, you Pharisees clean the outside of the cup and dish, but inside you are full of greed and wickedness."

LUKE 12:13-21 Someone in the crowd said to him, "Teacher, tell my brother to divide the inheritance with me." [14]Jesus replied, "Man, who appointed me a judge or an arbiter between you?" [15]Then he said to them, "Watch out! Be on your guard against all kinds of greed; a man's life does not consist in the abundance of his possessions." [16]And he told them this parable: "The ground of a certain rich man produced a good crop. [17]He thought to himself, 'What shall I do? I have no place to store my crops.' [18]Then he said, 'This is what I'll do. I will tear down my barns and build bigger ones, and there I will store all my grain and my goods. [19]And I'll say to myself, "You have plenty of good things laid up for many years. Take life easy; eat, drink and be merry."' [20]But God said to him, 'You fool! This very night your life will be demanded from you. Then who will get what you have prepared for yourself?' [21]This is how it will be with anyone who stores up things for himself but is not rich toward God."

LUKE 12:33-34 "Sell your possessions and give to the poor. Provide purses for yourselves that will not wear out, a treasure in heaven that will not be exhausted, where no thief comes near and no moth destroys. [34]For where your treasure is, there your heart will be also."

The Heart

JOHN 7:37-39 On the last and greatest day of the Feast, Jesus stood and said in a loud voice, "If anyone is thirsty, let him come to me and drink. [38]Whoever believes in me, as the Scripture has said, streams of living water will flow from within him." [39]By this he meant the Spirit, whom those who believed in him were later to receive. Up to that time the Spirit had not been given, since Jesus had not yet been glorified.

JOHN 14:1 "Do not let your hearts be troubled. Trust in God; trust also in me."

JOHN 14:27 "Peace I leave with you; my peace I give you. I do not give to you as the world gives. Do not let your hearts be troubled and do not be afraid."

JOHN 16:22 "So with you: Now is your time of grief, but I will see you again and you will rejoice, and no one will take away your joy."

MATTHEW 5:8 "Blessed are the pure in heart, for they will see God."

MATTHEW 5:28 "But I tell you that anyone who looks at a woman lustfully has already committed adultery with her in his heart."

MATTHEW 6:19-21 "Do not store up for yourselves treasures on earth, where moth and rust destroy, and where thieves break in and steal. [20]But store up for yourselves treasures in heaven, where moth and rust do not destroy, and where thieves do not break in and steal. [21]For where your treasure is, there your heart will be also."

MATTHEW 11:29-30 "Take my yoke upon you and learn from me, for I am gentle and humble in heart, and you will find rest for your souls. ³⁰For my yoke is easy and my burden is light."

MATTHEW 12:34-35 "You brood of vipers, how can you who are evil say anything good? For out of the overflow of the heart the mouth speaks. ³⁵The good man brings good things out of the good stored up in him, and the evil man brings evil things out of the evil stored up in him."

MATTHEW 13:11-15 He replied, "The knowledge of the secrets of the kingdom of heaven has been given to you, but not to them. ¹²Whoever has will be given more, and he will have an abundance. Whoever does not have, even what he has will be taken from him. ¹³This is why I speak to them in parables: Though seeing, they do not see; though hearing, they do not hear or understand. ¹⁴In them is fulfilled the prophecy of Isaiah: 'You will be ever hearing but never understanding; you will be ever seeing but never perceiving. ¹⁵For this people's heart has become calloused; they hardly hear with their ears, and they have closed their eyes. Otherwise they might see with their eyes, hear with their ears, understand with their hearts and turn, and I would heal them.'"

MATTHEW 15:3-9 Jesus replied, "And why do you break the command of God for the sake of your tradition? ⁴For God said, 'Honor your father and mother' and 'Anyone who curses his father or mother must be put to death.' ⁵But you say that if a man says to his father or mother, 'Whatever help you might otherwise have received from me is a gift devoted to God,' ⁶he is not to 'honor his father' with it. Thus you nullify the word

of God for the sake of your tradition. ⁷You hypocrites! Isaiah was right when he prophesied about you: ⁸'These people honor me with their lips, but their hearts are far from me. ⁹They worship me in vain; their teachings are but rules taught by men.'"

MATTHEW 15:10-11, 13-20 Jesus called the crowd to him and said, "Listen and understand. ¹¹What goes into a man's mouth does not make him 'unclean,' but what comes out of his mouth, that is what makes him 'unclean.'" ¹³He replied, "Every plant that my heavenly Father has not planted will be pulled up by the roots. ¹⁴Leave them; they are blind guides. If a blind man leads a blind man, both will fall into a pit." ¹⁵Peter said, "Explain the parable to us." ¹⁶"Are you still so dull?" Jesus asked them. ¹⁷"Don't you see that whatever enters the mouth goes into the stomach and then out of the body? ¹⁸But the things that come out of the mouth come from the heart, and these make a man 'unclean.' ¹⁹For out of the heart come evil thoughts, murder, adultery, sexual immorality, theft, false testimony, slander. ²⁰These are what make a man 'unclean'; but eating with unwashed hands does not make him 'unclean.'"

MATTHEW 22:37-40 Jesus replied: "'Love the Lord your God with all your heart and with all your soul and with all your mind.' ³⁸This is the first and greatest commandment. ³⁹And the second is like it: 'Love your neighbor as yourself.' ⁴⁰All the Law and the Prophets hang on these two commandments."

MATTHEW 24:48-51 "But suppose that servant is wicked and says to himself,

'My master is staying away a long time,' [49]and he then begins to beat his fellow servants and to eat and drink with drunkards. [50]The master of that servant will come on a day when he does not expect him and at an hour he is not aware of. [51]He will cut him to pieces and assign him a place with the hypocrites, where there will be weeping and gnashing of teeth."

MARK 7:6 He replied, "Isaiah was right when he prophesied about you hypocrites; as it is written: 'These people honor me with their lips, but their hearts are far from me.'"

MARK 7:14-15, 17-23 Again Jesus called the crowd to him and said, "Listen to me, everyone, and understand this. [15]Nothing outside a man can make him 'unclean' by going into him. Rather, it is what comes out of a man that makes him 'unclean.'" [17]After he had left the crowd and entered the house, his disciples asked him about this parable. [18]"Are you so dull?" he asked. "Don't you see that nothing that enters a man from the outside can make him 'unclean'? [19]For it doesn't go into his heart but into his stomach, and then out of his body." (In saying this, Jesus declared all foods "clean.") [20]He went on: "What comes out of a man is what makes him 'unclean.' [21]For from within, out of men's hearts, come evil thoughts, sexual immorality, theft, murder, adultery, [22]greed, malice, deceit, lewdness, envy, slander, arrogance and folly. [23]All these evils come from inside and make a man 'unclean.'"

MARK 8:17-18 Aware of their [the disciples'] discussion, Jesus asked them:

"Why are you talking about having no bread? Do you still not see or understand? Are your hearts hardened? [18]Do you have eyes but fail to see, and ears but fail to hear? And don't you remember?"

MARK 10:2-9 Some Pharisees came and tested him by asking, "Is it lawful for a man to divorce his wife?" [3]"What did Moses command you?" he replied. [4]They said, "Moses permitted a man to write a certificate of divorce and send her away." [5]"It was because your hearts were hard that Moses wrote you this law," Jesus replied. [6]"But at the beginning of creation God 'made them male and female.' [7]For this reason a man will leave his father and mother and be united to his wife, [8]and the two will become one flesh.' So they are no longer two, but one. [9]Therefore what God has joined together, let man not separate."

MARK 11:22-24 "Have faith in God," Jesus answered. [23]"I tell you the truth, if anyone says to this mountain, 'Go, throw yourself into the sea,' and does not doubt in his heart but believes that what he says will happen, it will be done for him. [24]Therefore I tell you, whatever you ask for in prayer, believe that you have received it, and it will be yours."

MARK 12:29-30 "The most important one [commandment]," answered Jesus, "is this: 'Hear, O Israel, the Lord our God, the Lord is one. [30]Love the Lord your God with all your heart and with all your soul and with all your mind and with all your strength.'"

LUKE 6:43-45 "No good tree bears bad fruit, nor does a bad tree bear good fruit. [44]Each tree is recognized by its own fruit. People do not pick figs from thornbushes, or grapes from briers. [45]The good man brings good things out of the good stored up in his heart, and the evil man brings evil things out of the evil stored up in his heart. For out of the overflow of his heart his mouth speaks."

LUKE 8:15 "But the seed on good soil stands for those with a noble and good heart, who hear the word, retain it, and by persevering produce a crop."

LUKE 10:27 He answered: " 'Love the Lord your God with all your heart and with all your soul and with all your strength and with all your mind'; and, 'Love your neighbor as yourself.' "

LUKE 12:22-34 Then Jesus said to his disciples: "Therefore I tell you, do not worry about your life, what you will eat; or about your body, what you will wear. [23]Life is more than food, and the body more than clothes. [24]Consider the ravens: They do not sow or reap, they have no storeroom or barn; yet God feeds them. And how much more valuable you are than birds! [25]Who of you by worrying can add a single hour to his life? [26]Since you cannot do this very little thing, why do you worry about the rest? [27]Consider how the lilies grow. They do not labor or spin. Yet I tell you, not even Solomon in all his splendor was dressed like one of these. [28]If that is how God clothes the grass of the field, which is here today, and tomorrow is thrown into the fire, how much more will he clothe you, O you of little faith! [29]And do not set your heart on what you will eat or drink; do not worry about it. [30]For the pagan world runs after all such things, and your Father knows that you need them. [31]But seek his kingdom, and these things will be given to you as well. [32]Do not be afraid, little flock, for your Father has been pleased to give you the kingdom. [33]Sell your possessions and give to the poor. Provide purses for yourselves that will not wear out, a treasure in heaven that will not be exhausted, where no thief comes near and no moth destroys. [34]For where your treasure is, there your heart will be also."

LUKE 12:42-46 The Lord answered, "Who then is the faithful and wise manager, whom the master puts in charge of his servants to give them their food allowance at the proper time? [43]It will be good for that servant whom the master finds doing so when he returns. [44]I tell you the truth, he will put him in charge of all his possessions. [45]But suppose the servant says to himself, 'My master is taking a long time in coming,' and he then begins to beat the menservants and maidservants and to eat and drink and get drunk. [46]The master of that servant will come on a day when he does not expect him and at an hour he is not aware of. He will cut him to pieces and assign him a place with the unbelievers."

LUKE 16:15 He said to them [the Pharisees], "You are the ones who justify yourselves in the eyes of men, but God knows your hearts. What is highly valued among men is detestable in God's sight."

LUKE 24:25-26 He said to them [two people on the road to Emmaus], "How foolish you are, and how slow of heart to believe all that the prophets have spoken! ²⁶Did not the Christ have to suffer these things and then enter his glory?"

Honesty

MATTHEW 5:33-37 "Again, you have heard that it was said to the people long ago, 'Do not break your oath, but keep the oaths you have made to the Lord.' ³⁴But I tell you, Do not swear at all: either by heaven, for it is God's throne; ³⁵or by the earth, for it is his footstool; or by Jerusalem, for it is the city of the Great King. ³⁶And do not swear by your head, for you cannot make even one hair white or black. ³⁷Simply let your 'Yes' be 'Yes,' and your 'No,' 'No'; anything beyond this comes from the evil one."

Humans and Human Nature

JOHN 3:19-21 "This is the verdict: Light has come into the world, but men loved darkness instead of light because their deeds were evil. ²⁰Everyone who does evil hates the light, and will not come into the light for fear that his deeds will be exposed. ²¹But whoever lives by the truth comes into the light, so that it may be seen plainly that what he has done has been done through God."

JOHN 8:21, 23-24 Once more Jesus said to them, "I am going away, and you will look for me, and you will die in your sin. Where I go, you cannot come." ²³But he continued, "You are from below; I am from above. You are of this world; I am not of this world. ²⁴I told you that you would die in your sins; if you do not believe that I am the one I claim to be, you will indeed die in your sins."

MARK 12:14-17 They came to him and said, "Teacher, we know you are a man of integrity. You aren't swayed by men, because you pay no attention to who they are; but you teach the way of God in accordance with the truth. Is it right to pay taxes to Caesar or not? ¹⁵Should we pay or shouldn't we?" But Jesus knew their hypocrisy. "Why are you trying to trap me?" he asked. "Bring me a denarius and let me look at it." ¹⁶They brought the coin, and he asked them, "Whose portrait is this? And whose inscription?" "Caesar's," they replied. ¹⁷Then Jesus said to them, "Give to Caesar what is Caesar's and to God what is God's."... (See also Matthew 22:16-21; Luke 20:21-25.)

LUKE 16:15 He said to them [the Pharisees], "You are the ones who justify yourselves in the eyes of men, but God knows your hearts. What is highly valued among men is detestable in God's sight."

Hypocrites, Hypocrisy, and Self-Righteousness

MATTHEW 6:1-4 "Be careful not to do your 'acts of righteousness' before men, to be seen by them. If you do, you will have no reward from your Father in heaven. ²So when you give to the needy, do not announce it with trumpets, as the hypocrites do in the synagogues and on the streets, to be honored by men. I tell you the truth, they have received their reward in full. ³But when you give to the needy, do not let your left hand know what your right hand is doing, [4]so that your giving may be in secret. Then your Father, who sees what is done in secret, will reward you."

MATTHEW 6:5-8 "And when you pray, do not be like the hypocrites, for they love to pray standing in the synagogues and on the street corners to be seen by men. I tell you the truth, they have received their reward in full. [6]But when you pray, go into your room, close the door and pray to your Father, who is unseen. Then your Father, who sees what is done in secret, will reward you. [7]And when you pray, do not keep on babbling like pagans, for they think they will be heard because of their many words. [8]Do not be like them, for your Father knows what you need before you ask him."

MATTHEW 6:16-18 "When you fast, do not look somber as the hypocrites do, for they disfigure their faces to show men they are fasting. I tell you the truth, they have received their reward in full. [17]But when you fast, put oil on your head and wash your face, [18]so that it will not be obvious to men that you are fasting, but only to your Father, who is unseen; and your Father, who sees what is done in secret, will reward you."

MATTHEW 7:1-5 "Do not judge, or you too will be judged. [2]For in the same way you judge others, you will be judged, and with the measure you use, it will be measured to you. [3]Why do you look at the speck of sawdust in your brother's eye and pay no attention to the plank in your own eye? [4]How can you say to your brother, 'Let me take the speck out of your eye,' when all the time there is a plank in your own eye? [5]You hypocrite, first take the plank out of your own eye, and then you will see clearly to remove the speck from your brother's eye."

MATTHEW 15:3-9 Jesus replied, "And why do you break the command of God for the sake of your tradition? [4]For God said, 'Honor your father and mother' and 'Anyone who curses his father or mother must be put to death.' [5]But you say that if a man says to his father or mother, 'Whatever help you might otherwise have received from me is a gift devoted to God,' [6]he is not to 'honor his father' with it. Thus you nullify the word of God for the sake of your tradition. [7]You hypocrites! Isaiah was right when he prophesied about you: [8]'These people honor me with their lips, but their hearts are far from me. [9]They worship me in vain; their teachings are but rules taught by men.' "

MATTHEW 16:2-3 He replied, "When evening comes, you say, 'It will be fair weather, for the sky is red,' [3]and in the morning, 'Today it will be stormy, for the sky is red and overcast.' You know how to interpret the appearance of the sky, but you cannot interpret the signs of the times."

MATTHEW 16:5-12 When they went across the lake, the disciples forgot to take bread. [6]"Be careful," Jesus said to them. "Be on your guard against the yeast of the Pharisees and Sadducees." [7]They discussed this among themselves and said, "It is because we didn't bring any bread." [8]Aware of their discussion, Jesus asked, "You of little faith, why are you talking among yourselves about having no bread?

[9]Do you still not understand? Don't you remember the five loaves for the five thousand, and how many basketfuls you gathered? [10]Or the seven loaves for the four thousand, and how many basketfuls you gathered? [11]How is it you don't understand that I was not talking to you about bread? But be on your guard against the yeast of the Pharisees and Sadducees." [12]Then they understood that he was not telling them to guard against the yeast used in bread, but against the teaching of the Pharisees and Sadducees. (See also Mark 8:14-18.)

MATTHEW 22:16-21 They sent their disciples to him along with the Herodians. "Teacher," they said, "we know you are a man of integrity and that you teach the way of God in accordance with the truth. You aren't swayed by men, because you pay no attention to who they are. [17]Tell us then, what is your opinion? Is it right to pay taxes to Caesar or not?" [18]But Jesus, knowing their evil intent, said, "You hypocrites, why are you trying to trap me? [19]Show me the coin used for paying the tax." They brought him a denarius, [20]and he asked them, "Whose portrait is this? And whose inscription?" [21]"Caesar's," they replied. Then he said to them, "Give to Caesar what is Caesar's, and to God what is God's." (See also Mark 12:13-17; Luke 20:20-25.)

MATTHEW 23:1-13, 15 Then Jesus said to the crowds and to his disciples: [2]"The teachers of the law and the Pharisees sit in Moses' seat. [3]So you must obey them and do everything they tell you. But do not do what they do, for they do not practice what they preach. [4]They tie up heavy loads and put them on men's shoulders, but they themselves are not willing to lift a finger to move them. [5]Everything they do is done for men to see: They make their phylacteries wide and the tassels on their garments long; [6]they love the place of honor at banquets and the most important seats in the synagogues; [7]they love to be greeted in the marketplaces and to have men call them 'Rabbi.' [8]But you are not to be called 'Rabbi,' for you have only one Master and you are all brothers. [9]And do not call anyone on earth 'father,' for you have one Father, and he is in heaven. [10]Nor are you to be called 'teacher,' for you have one Teacher, the Christ. [11]The greatest among you will be your servant. [12]For whoever exalts himself will be humbled, and whoever humbles himself will be exalted. [13]Woe to you, teachers of the law and Pharisees, you hypocrites! You shut the kingdom of heaven in men's faces. You yourselves do not enter, nor will you let those enter who are trying to. [15]Woe to you, teachers of the law and Pharisees, you hypocrites! You travel over land and sea to win a single convert, and when he becomes one, you make him twice as much a son of hell as you are."

MATTHEW 23:23-39 "Woe to you, teachers of the law and Pharisees, you hypocrites! You give a tenth of your spices—mint, dill and cummin. But you have neglected the more important matters of the law—justice, mercy and faithfulness. You should have practiced the latter, without neglecting the former. [24]You blind guides! You strain out a gnat but swallow a camel. [25]Woe to you, teachers of the law and Pharisees, you hypocrites! You clean the outside of the cup and dish, but inside they are full of greed and self-indulgence. 26Blind Pharisee! First clean the inside of the cup and dish, and then the outside also will be clean. 27Woe to you, teachers of the law and Pharisees, you hypocrites! You are like whitewashed tombs, which look beautiful on the outside but on the inside are full of dead men's bones and everything unclean. 28In the same way, on the outside you appear to people as righteous but on the inside you are full of hypocrisy and wickedness. 29Woe to you, teachers of the law and Pharisees, you hypocrites! You build tombs for the prophets and decorate the graves of the righteous. 30And you say, 'If we had lived in the days of our forefathers, we would not have taken part with them in shedding the blood of the prophets.' 31So you testify against yourselves that you are the descendants of those who murdered the prophets. 32Fill up, then, the measure of the sin of your forefathers! 33You snakes! You brood of vipers! How will you escape being condemned to hell? 34Therefore I am sending you prophets and wise men and teachers. Some of them you will kill and crucify; others you will flog in your synagogues and pursue from town to town. 35And so upon you will come all the righteous blood that has been shed on earth, from the blood of righteous Abel to the blood of Zechariah son of Berekiah, whom you murdered between the temple and the altar. 36I tell you the truth, all this will come upon this generation. 37O Jerusalem, Jerusalem, you who kill the prophets and stone those sent to you, how often I have longed to gather your children together, as a hen gathers her chicks under her wings, but you were not willing. 38Look, your house is left to you desolate. 39For I tell you, you will not see me again until you say, 'Blessed is he who comes in the name of the Lord.'"

MARK 7:6-13 He replied, "Isaiah was right when he prophesied about you hypocrites; as it is written: 'These people honor me with their lips, but their hearts are far from me. 7They worship me in vain; their teachings are but rules taught by men.' 8You have let go of the commands of God and are holding on to the traditions of men." 9And he said to them: "You have a fine way of setting aside the commands of God in order to observe your own traditions! 10For Moses said, 'Honor your father and your mother,' and, 'Anyone who curses his father or mother must be put to death.' 11But you say that if a man says to his father or mother: 'Whatever help you might otherwise have received from me is Corban' (that is, a gift devoted to God), 12then you no longer let him do anything for his father or mother. 13Thus you nullify the word of God by your tradition that you have handed down. And you do many things like that."

MARK 12:38-40 As he taught, Jesus said, "Watch out for the teachers of the law. They like to walk around in flowing robes and be greeted in the marketplaces, 39and have the most important seats in the synagogues and the places of honor at banquets. 40They devour widows' houses and for a show make lengthy prayers.

Such men will be punished most severely." (See also Luke 20:45-47.)

LUKE 6:24-26 "But woe to you who are rich, for you have already received your comfort. 25Woe to you who are well fed now, for you will go hungry. Woe to you who laugh now, for you will mourn and weep. 26Woe to you when all men speak well of you, for that is how their fathers treated the false prophets."

LUKE 6:41 "Why do you look at the speck of sawdust in your brother's eye and pay no attention to the plank in your own eye?"

LUKE 11:39-44 Then the Lord said to him, "Now then, you Pharisees clean the outside of the cup and dish, but inside you are full of greed and wickedness. 40You foolish people! Did not the one who made the outside make the inside also? 41But give what is inside the dish to the poor, and everything will be clean for you. 42Woe to you Pharisees, because you give God a tenth of your mint, rue and all other kinds of garden herbs, but you neglect justice and the love of God. You should have practiced the latter without leaving the former undone. 43Woe to you Pharisees, because you love the most important seats in the synagogues and greetings in the marketplaces. 44Woe to you, because you are like unmarked graves, which men walk over without knowing it."

LUKE 11:46-51 Jesus replied, "And you experts in the law, woe to you, because you load people down with burdens they can hardly carry, and you yourselves will not lift one finger to help them. 47Woe to you, because you build tombs for the prophets, and it was your forefathers who killed them. 48So you testify that you approve of what your forefathers did; they killed the prophets, and you build their tombs. 49Because of this, God in his wisdom said, 'I will send them prophets and apostles, some of whom they will kill and others they will persecute.' 50Therefore this generation will be held responsible for the blood of all the prophets that has been shed since the beginning of the world, 51from the blood of Abel to the blood of Zechariah, who was killed between the altar and the sanctuary. Yes, I tell you, this generation will be held responsible for it all."

LUKE 12:1-3 Meanwhile, when a crowd of many thousands had gathered, so that they were trampling on one another, Jesus began to speak first to his disciples, saying: "Be on your guard against the yeast of the Pharisees, which is hypocrisy. 2There is nothing concealed that will not be disclosed, or hidden that will not be made known. 3What you have said in the dark will be heard in the daylight, and what you have whispered in the ear in the inner rooms will be proclaimed from the roofs."

LUKE 13:14-16 Indignant because Jesus had healed on the Sabbath, the synagogue ruler said to the people, "There are six days for work. So come and be healed on those days, not on the Sabbath." 15The Lord answered him, "You hypocrites! Doesn't each of you on the Sabbath untie his ox or donkey from the stall and lead it out to give it water? 16Then should not this woman, a daughter of Abraham, whom Satan has kept bound for eighteen long years, be set free on the Sabbath day from what bound her?"

LUKE 16:15 He said to them [the Pharisees], "You are the ones who justify yourselves in the eyes of men, but God knows your hearts. What is highly valued among men is detestable in God's sight."

LUKE 18:9-14 To some who were confident of their own righteousness and looked down on everybody else, Jesus told this parable: [10]"Two men went up to the temple to pray, one a Pharisee and the other a tax collector. [11]The Pharisee stood up and prayed about himself: 'God, I thank you that I am not like other men—robbers, evildoers, adulterers—or even like this tax collector. [12]I fast twice a week and give a tenth of all I get.' [13]But the tax collector stood at a distance. He would not even look up to heaven, but beat his breast and said, 'God, have mercy on me, a sinner.' [14]I tell you that this man, rather than the other, went home justified before God. For everyone who exalts himself will be humbled, and he who humbles himself will be exalted."

Jealousy

LUKE 15:11-32 Jesus continued: "There was a man who had two sons. [12]The younger one said to his father, 'Father, give me my share of the estate.' So he divided his property between them. [13]Not long after that, the younger son got together all he had, set off for a distant country and there squandered his wealth in wild living. [14]After he had spent everything, there was a severe famine in that whole country, and he began to be in need. [15]So he went and hired himself out to a citizen of that country, who sent him to his fields to feed pigs. [16]He longed to fill his stomach with the pods that the pigs were eating, but no one gave him anything. [17]When he came to his senses, he said, 'How many of my father's hired men have food to spare, and here I am starving to death! [18]I will set out and go back to my father and say to him: Father, I have sinned against heaven and against you. [19]I am no longer worthy to be called your son; make me like one of your hired men.' [20]So he got up and went to his father. But while he was still a long way off, his father saw him and was filled with compassion for him; he ran to his son, threw his arms around him and kissed him. [21]The son said to him, 'Father, I have sinned against heaven and against you. I am no longer worthy to be called your son.' [22]But the father said to his servants, 'Quick! Bring the best robe and put it on him. Put a ring on his finger and sandals on his feet. [23]Bring the fattened calf and kill it. Let's have a feast and celebrate. [24]For this son of mine was dead and is alive again; he was lost and is found.' So they began to celebrate. [25]Meanwhile, the older son was in the field. When he came near the house, he heard music and dancing. [26]So he called one of the servants and asked him what was going on. [27]'Your brother has come,' he replied, 'and your father has killed the fattened calf because he has him back safe and sound.' [28]The older brother became angry and refused to go in. So his father went out and pleaded with him. [29]But he answered his father, 'Look! All these years I've been slaving for you and never disobeyed your orders. Yet you never gave me even a young goat so I could celebrate with my friends. [30]But when this son of yours who has squandered your property with prostitutes comes home, you kill the fattened calf for him!' [31]'My son,' the father said, 'you are always with me, and everything I have is yours. [32]But we had to celebrate and be glad, because this brother of yours was dead and is alive again; he was lost and is found.'"

Light Versus Darkness

JOHN 3:18-21 "Whoever believes in him [Christ] is not condemned, but whoever does not believe stands condemned already because he has not believed in the name of God's one and only Son. [19]This is the verdict: Light has come into the world, but men loved darkness instead of light because their deeds were evil. [20]Everyone who does evil hates the light, and will not come into the light for fear that his deeds will be exposed. [21]But whoever lives by the truth comes into the light, so that it may be seen plainly that what he has done has been done through God."

JOHN 8:12 When Jesus spoke again to the people, he said, "I am the light of the world. Whoever follows me will never walk in darkness, but will have the light of life."

JOHN 9:4-5 "As long as it is day, we must do the work of him who sent me. Night is coming, when no one can work. [5]While I am in the world, I am the light of the world."

JOHN 11:9-10 Jesus answered, "Are there not twelve hours of daylight? A man who walks by day will not stumble, for he sees by this world's light. [10]It is when he walks by night that he stumbles, for he has no light."

JOHN 12:35 Then Jesus told them, "You are going to have the light just a little while longer. Walk while you have the light, before darkness overtakes you. The man who walks in the dark does not know where he is going."

JOHN 12:46 "I have come into the world as a light, so that no one who believes in me should stay in darkness."

MATTHEW 5:14-16 "You are the light of the world. A city on a hill cannot be hidden. [15]Neither do people light a lamp and put it under a bowl. Instead they put it on its stand, and it gives light to everyone in the house. [16]In the same way, let your light shine before men, that they may see your good deeds and praise your Father in heaven."

MATTHEW 6:22-23 "The eye is the lamp of the body. If your eyes are good, your whole body will be full of light. [23]But if your eyes are bad, your whole body will be full of darkness. If then the light within you is darkness, how great is that darkness!"

LUKE 8:16-17 "No one lights a lamp and hides it in a jar or puts it under a bed. Instead, he puts it on a stand, so that those who come in can see the light. [17]For there is nothing hidden that will not be disclosed, and nothing concealed that will not be known or brought out into the open."

LUKE 11:33-36 "No one lights a lamp and puts it in a place where it will be hidden, or under a bowl. Instead he puts it on its stand, so that those who come in may see the light. [34]Your eye is the lamp of your body. When your eyes are good, your whole body also is full of light. But when they are bad, your body also is full of darkness. [35]See to it, then, that the light within you is not darkness. [36]Therefore, if your whole body is full of light, and no part of it dark, it will be completely lighted, as when the light of a lamp shines on you."

Lust

MATTHEW 5:27-30 "You have heard that it was said, 'Do not commit adultery.' [28]But I tell you that anyone who looks at a woman lustfully has already committed adultery with her in his heart. [29]If your right eye causes you to sin, gouge it out and throw it away. It is better for you to lose one part of your body than for your whole body to be thrown into hell. [30]And if your right hand causes you to sin, cut it off and throw it away. It is better for you to lose one part of your body than for your whole body to go into hell."

MATTHEW 15:19-20 "For out of the heart come evil thoughts, murder, adultery, sexual immorality, theft, false testimony, slander. [20]These are what make a man 'unclean'; but eating with unwashed hands does not make him 'unclean.'"

The Mind

MATTHEW 6:22-23 "The eye is the lamp of the body. If your eyes are good, your whole body will be full of light. [23]But if your eyes are bad, your whole body will be full of darkness. If then the light within you is darkness, how great is that darkness!"

MATTHEW 15:18-20 "But the things that come out of the mouth come from the heart, and these make a man 'unclean.' [19]For out of the heart come evil thoughts, murder, adultery, sexual immorality, theft, false testimony, slander. [20]These are what make a man 'unclean'; but eating with unwashed hands does not make him 'unclean.'"

MATTHEW 22:37-38 Jesus replied: "'Love the Lord your God with all your heart and with all your soul and with all your mind.' [38]This is the first and greatest commandment."

MARK 7:20-23 He went on: "What comes out of a man is what makes him 'unclean.' [21]For from within, out of men's hearts, come evil thoughts, sexual immorality, theft, murder, adultery, [22]greed, malice, deceit, lewdness, envy, slander, arrogance and folly. [23]All these evils come from inside and make a man 'unclean.'"

MARK 12:29-30 "The most important one [commandment]," answered Jesus, "is this: 'Hear, O Israel, the Lord our God, the Lord is one. [30]Love the Lord your God with all your heart and with all your soul and with all your mind and with all your strength.'"

LUKE 10:27 He answered: "'Love the Lord your God with all your heart and with all your soul and with all your strength and with all your mind'; and, 'Love your neighbor as yourself.'"

LUKE 12:29-31 "And do not set your heart on what you will eat or drink; do not worry about it. [30]For the pagan world runs after all such things, and your Father knows that you need them. ³¹But seek his kingdom, and these things will be given to you as well."

Motives

MATTHEW 5:16-18 "In the same way, let your light shine before men, that they may see your good deeds and praise your Father in heaven. ¹⁷Do not think that I have come to abolish the Law or the Prophets; I have not come to abolish them but to fulfill them. ¹⁸I tell you the truth, until heaven and earth disappear, not the smallest letter, not the least stroke of a pen, will by any means disappear from the Law until everything is accomplished."

MATTHEW 6:1-4 "Be careful not to do your 'acts of righteousness' before men, to be seen by them. If you do, you will have no reward from your Father in heaven. ²So when you give to the needy, do not announce it with trumpets, as the hypocrites do in the synagogues and on the streets, to be honored by men. I tell you the truth, they have received their reward in full. ³But when you give to the needy, do not let your left hand know what your right hand is doing, ⁴so that your giving may be in secret. Then your Father, who sees what is done in secret, will reward you."

MATTHEW 6:5-8 "And when you pray, do not be like the hypocrites, for they love to pray standing in the synagogues and on the street corners to be seen by men. I tell you the truth, they have received their reward in full. ⁶But when you pray, go into your room, close the door and pray to your Father, who is unseen. Then your Father, who sees what is done in secret, will reward you. ⁷And when you pray, do not keep on babbling like pagans, for they think they will be heard because of their many words. ⁸Do not be like them, for your Father knows what you need before you ask him."

LUKE 16:15 He said to them [the Pharisees], "You are the ones who justify yourselves in the eyes of men, but God knows your hearts. What is highly valued among men is detestable in God's sight."

Oaths

MATTHEW 5:33-37 "Again, you have heard that it was said to the people long ago, 'Do not break your oath, but keep the oaths you have made to the Lord.' ³⁴But I tell you, Do not swear at all: either by heaven, for it is God's throne; ³⁵or by the earth, for it is his footstool; or by Jerusalem, for it is the city of the Great King. ³⁶And do not swear by your head, for you cannot make even one hair white or black. ³⁷Simply let your 'Yes' be 'Yes,' and your 'No,' 'No'; anything beyond this comes from the evil one."

Parents

MATTHEW 10:34-37 "Do not suppose that I have come to bring peace to the earth. I did not come to bring peace, but a sword. ³⁵For I have come to turn 'a man against his father, a daughter against her mother, a daughter-in-law against her mother-in-law— ³⁶a man's enemies will be the members of his own household.'

[37]Anyone who loves his father or mother more than me is not worthy of me; anyone who loves his son or daughter more than me is not worthy of me."

MATTHEW 15:3-9 Jesus replied, "And why do you break the command of God for the sake of your tradition? [4]For God said, 'Honor your father and mother' and 'Anyone who curses his father or mother must be put to death.' [5]But you say that if a man says to his father or mother, 'Whatever help you might otherwise have received from me is a gift devoted to God,' [6]he is not to 'honor his father' with it. Thus you nullify the word of God for the sake of your tradition. [7]You hypocrites! Isaiah was right when he prophesied about you: [8]'These people honor me with their lips, but their hearts are far from me. [9]They worship me in vain; their teachings are but rules taught by men.'"

MATTHEW 19:29 "And everyone who has left houses or brothers or sisters or father or mother or children or fields for my sake will receive a hundred times as much and will inherit eternal life."

MARK 10:29-30 "I tell you the truth," Jesus replied, "no one who has left home or brothers or sisters or mother or father or children or fields for me and the gospel [30]will fail to receive a hundred times as much in this present age (homes, brothers, sisters, mothers, children and fields—and with them, persecutions) and in the age to come, eternal life."

Pharisees

MATTHEW 5:20 "For I tell you that unless your righteousness surpasses that of the Pharisees and the teachers of the law, you will certainly not enter the kingdom of heaven."

MATTHEW 16:5-6 When they went across the lake, the disciples forgot to take bread. [6]"Be careful," Jesus said to them. "Be on your guard against the yeast of the Pharisees and Sadducees."

MATTHEW 19:3-6 Some Pharisees came to him to test him. They asked, "Is it lawful for a man to divorce his wife for any and every reason?" [4]"Haven't you read," he replied, "that at the beginning the Creator 'made them male and female,' [5]and said, 'For this reason a man will leave his father and mother and be united to his wife, and the two will become one flesh'? [6]So they are no longer two, but one. Therefore what God has joined together, let man not separate."

MATTHEW 23:1-13, 15-36 Then Jesus said to the crowds and to his disciples: [2]"The teachers of the law and the Pharisees sit in Moses' seat. [3]So you must obey them and do everything they tell you. But do not do what they do, for they do not practice what they preach. [4]They tie up heavy loads and put them on men's shoulders, but they themselves are not willing to lift a finger to move them. [5]Everything they do is done for men to see: They make their phylacteries wide and the tassels on their garments long; [6]they love the place of honor at banquets and the most important seats in the synagogues; [7]they love to be greeted in the marketplaces and to have men call them 'Rabbi.' [8]But you are not to be called 'Rabbi,' for you have only one Master and you are all brothers. [9]And do not call anyone on earth 'father,' for you have one Father, and he is in heaven. [10]Nor are you to be called 'teacher,' for you have one Teacher, the Christ. [11]The greatest among you will be your servant. [12]For whoever exalts himself will be humbled, and whoever humbles himself will be exalted. [13]Woe to you, teachers of the law and Pharisees, you hypocrites! You shut the kingdom of heaven in men's faces. You yourselves do not enter, nor will you let those enter who are trying to. [15]Woe to you, teachers of the law and Pharisees, you hypocrites! You travel over land and sea to win a single convert, and when he becomes one, you make him twice as much a son of hell as you are. [16]Woe to you, blind guides! You say, 'If anyone swears by the temple, it means nothing; but if anyone swears by the gold of the temple, he is bound by his oath.' [17]You blind fools! Which is greater: the gold, or the temple that makes the gold sacred? [18]You also say, 'If anyone swears by the altar, it means nothing; but if anyone swears by the gift on it, he is bound by his oath.' [19]You blind men! Which is greater: the gift, or the altar that makes the gift sacred? [20]Therefore, he who swears by the altar swears by it and by everything on it. [21]And he who swears by the temple swears by it and by the one who dwells in it. [22]And he who swears by heaven swears by God's throne and by the one who sits on it. [23]Woe to you, teachers of the law and Pharisees, you hypocrites! You give a tenth of your spices—mint, dill and cummin. But you have neglected the more important matters of the law—justice, mercy and faithfulness. You should have prac-

ticed the latter, without neglecting the former. [24]You blind guides! You strain out a gnat but swallow a camel. [25]Woe to you, teachers of the law and Pharisees, you hypocrites! You clean the outside of the cup and dish, but inside they are full of greed and self-indulgence. [26]Blind Pharisee! First clean the inside of the cup and dish, and then the outside also will be clean. [27]Woe to you, teachers of the law and Pharisees, you hypocrites! You are like whitewashed tombs, which look beautiful on the outside but on the inside are full of dead men's bones and everything unclean. [28]In the same way, on the outside you appear to people as righteous but on the inside you are full of hypocrisy and wickedness. [29]Woe to you, teachers of the law and Pharisees, you hypocrites! You build tombs for the prophets and decorate the graves of the righteous. [30]And you say, 'If we had lived in the days of our forefathers, we would not have taken part with them in shedding the blood of the prophets.' [31]So you testify against yourselves that you are the descendants of those who murdered the prophets. [32]Fill up, then, the measure of the sin of your forefathers! [33]You snakes! You brood of vipers! How will you escape being condemned to hell? [34]Therefore I am sending you prophets and wise men and teachers. Some of them you will kill and crucify; others you will flog in your synagogues and pursue from town to town. [35]And so upon you will come all the righteous blood that has been shed on earth, from the blood of righteous Abel to the blood of Zechariah son of Berekiah, whom you murdered between the temple and the altar. [36]I tell you the truth, all this will come upon this generation."

LUKE 11:39-44 Then the Lord said to him, "Now then, you Pharisees clean the outside of the cup and dish, but inside you are full of greed and wickedness. [40]You foolish people! Did not the one who made the outside make the inside also? [41]But give what is inside the dish to the poor, and everything will be clean for you. [42]Woe to you Pharisees, because you give God a tenth of your mint, rue and all other kinds of garden herbs, but you neglect justice and the love of God. You should have practiced the latter without leaving the former undone. [43]Woe to you Pharisees, because you love the most important seats in the synagogues and greetings in the marketplaces. [44]Woe to you, because you are like unmarked graves, which men walk over without knowing it."

LUKE 12:1-3 Meanwhile, when a crowd of many thousands had gathered, so that they were trampling on one another, Jesus began to speak first to his disciples, saying: "Be on your guard against the yeast of the Pharisees, which is hypocrisy. [2]There is nothing concealed that will not be disclosed, or hidden that will not be made known. [3]What you have said in the dark will be heard in the daylight, and what you have whispered in the ear in the inner rooms will be proclaimed from the roofs."

LUKE 16:15 He said to them [the Pharisees], "You are the ones who justify yourselves in the eyes of men, but God knows your hearts. What is highly valued among men is detestable in God's sight."

LUKE 18:9-14 To some who were confident of their own righteousness and looked down on everybody else, Jesus told this parable: [10]"Two men went up to the temple to pray, one a Pharisee and the other a tax collector. [11]The Pharisee stood up and prayed about himself: 'God, I thank you that I am not like other men— robbers, evildoers, adulterers—or even like this tax collector. [12]I fast twice a week and give a tenth of all I get.' [13]But the tax collector stood at a distance. He would not even look up to heaven, but beat his breast and said, 'God, have mercy on me, a sinner.' [14]I tell you that this man, rather than the other, went home justified before God. For everyone who exalts himself will be humbled, and he who humbles himself will be exalted."

The Poor

MATTHEW 5:42 "Give to the one who asks you, and do not turn away from the one who wants to borrow from you."

MATTHEW 11:4-5 Jesus replied, "Go back and report to John what you hear and see: [5]The blind receive sight, the lame walk, those who have leprosy are cured, the deaf hear, the dead are raised, and the good news is preached to the poor." (See also Luke 7:22.)

MATTHEW 25:33-46 "He will put the sheep on his right and the goats on his left. [34]Then the King will say to those on his right, 'Come, you who are blessed by my Father; take your inheritance, the kingdom prepared for you since the creation of the world. [35]For I was hungry and you gave me something to eat, I was thirsty and you gave me something to drink, I was a stranger and you invited me in, ³⁶I needed clothes and you clothed me, I was sick and you looked after me, I was in prison and you came to visit me.' ³⁷Then the righteous will answer him, 'Lord, when did we see you hungry and feed you, or thirsty and give you something to drink? ³⁸When did we see you a stranger and invite you in, or needing clothes and clothe you? ³⁹When did we see you sick or in prison and go to visit you?' ⁴⁰The King will reply, 'I tell you the truth, whatever you did for one of the least of these brothers of mine, you did for me.' ⁴¹Then he will say to those on his left, 'Depart from me, you who are cursed, into the eternal fire prepared for the devil and his angels. ⁴²For I was hungry and you gave me nothing to eat, I was thirsty and you gave me nothing to drink, ⁴³I was a stranger and you did not invite me in, I needed clothes and you did not clothe me, I was sick and in prison and you did not look after me.' ⁴⁴They also will answer, 'Lord, when did we see you hungry or thirsty or a stranger or needing clothes or sick or in prison, and did not help you?' ⁴⁵He will reply, 'I tell you the truth, whatever you did not do for one of the least of these, you did not do for me.' ⁴⁶Then they will go away to eternal punishment, but the righteous to eternal life."

MATTHEW 26:10-11 Aware of this, Jesus said to them, "Why are you bothering this woman? She has done a beautiful thing to me. ¹¹The poor you will always have with you, but you will not always have me."

MARK 12:42-44 But a poor widow came and put in two very small copper coins, worth only a fraction of a penny. ⁴³Calling his disciples to him, Jesus said, "I tell you the truth, this poor widow has put more into the treasury than all the others. ⁴⁴They all gave out of their wealth; but she, out of her poverty, put in everything—all she had to live on."

MARK 14:7 "The poor you will always have with you, and you can help them any time you want. But you will not always have me."

LUKE 4:18-21 "The Spirit of the Lord is on me, because he has anointed me to preach good news to the poor. He has sent me to proclaim freedom for the prisoners and recovery of sight for the blind, to release the oppressed, ¹⁹to proclaim the year of the Lord's favor." ²⁰Then he rolled up the scroll, gave it back to the attendant and sat down. The eyes of everyone in the synagogue were fastened on him, ²¹and he began by saying to them, "Today this scripture is fulfilled in your hearing."

LUKE 6:20-21 Looking at his disciples, he said: "Blessed are you who are poor, for yours is the kingdom of God. ²¹Blessed are you who hunger now, for you will be satisfied. Blessed are you who weep now, for you will laugh."

LUKE 6:30-36 "Give to everyone who asks you, and if anyone takes what belongs to you, do not demand it back. ³¹Do to others as you would have them do to you. ³²If you love those who love you, what credit is that to you? Even 'sinners' love those who love them. ³³And if you do good to those who are good to you, what credit is that to you? Even 'sinners' do that. ³⁴And if you lend to those from whom you expect repayment, what credit is that to you? Even 'sinners' lend to 'sinners,' expecting to be repaid in full. ³⁵But love your enemies, do good to them, and lend to them without expecting to get anything back. Then your reward will be great, and you will be sons of the Most High, because he is kind to the ungrateful and wicked. ³⁶Be merciful, just as your Father is merciful."

LUKE 16:19-25 "There was a rich man who was dressed in purple and fine linen and lived in luxury every day. ²⁰At his gate was laid a beggar named Lazarus, covered with sores ²¹and longing to eat what fell from the rich man's table. Even the dogs came and licked his sores. ²²The time came when the beggar died and the angels carried him to Abraham's side. The rich man also died and was buried. ²³In hell, where he was in torment, he looked up and saw Abraham far away, with Lazarus by his side. ²⁴So he called to him, 'Father Abraham, have pity on me and send Lazarus to dip the tip of his finger in water and cool my tongue, because I am in agony in this fire.' ²⁵But Abraham replied, 'Son, remember that in your lifetime you received your good things, while Lazarus received bad things, but now he is comforted here and you are in agony.' "

Presumption

MATTHEW 7:21-23 "Not everyone who says to Me, 'Lord, Lord,' shall enter the kingdom of heaven, but he who does the will of My Father in heaven. ²²Many will say to Me in that day, 'Lord, Lord, have we not prophesied in Your name, cast out demons in Your name, and done many wonders in Your name?' ²³And then I will declare to them, 'I never knew you; depart from Me, you who practice lawlessness!' " (NKJV)

LUKE 12:13-21 Someone in the crowd said to him, "Teacher, tell my brother to divide the inheritance with me." ¹⁴Jesus replied, "Man, who appointed me a judge or an arbiter between you?" ¹⁵Then he said to them, "Watch out! Be on your guard against all kinds of greed; a man's life does not consist in the abundance of his possessions." ¹⁶And he told them this parable: "The ground of a certain rich man produced a good crop. ¹⁷He thought to himself, 'What shall I do? I have no place to store my crops.' ¹⁸Then he said, 'This is what I'll do. I will tear down my barns and build bigger ones, and there I will store all my grain and my goods. ¹⁹And I'll say to myself, "You have plenty of good things laid up for many years. Take life easy; eat, drink and be merry." ' ²⁰But God said to him, 'You fool! This very night your life will be demanded from you. Then who will get what you have prepared for yourself?' ²¹This is how it will be with anyone who stores up things for himself but is not rich toward God."

Pride

MATTHEW 7:1-5 "Do not judge, or you too will be judged. ²For in the same way you judge others, you will be judged, and with the measure you use, it will be measured to you. [3]Why do you look at the speck of sawdust in your brother's eye and pay no attention to the plank in your own eye? [4]How can you say to your brother, 'Let me take the speck out of your eye,' when all the time there is a plank in your own eye? [5]You hypocrite, first take the plank out of your own eye, and then you will see clearly to remove the speck from your brother's eye."

MATTHEW 20:25-28 Jesus called them [the disciples] together and said, "You know that the rulers of the Gentiles lord it over them, and their high officials exercise authority over them. [26]Not so with you. Instead, whoever wants to become great among you must be your servant, [27]and whoever wants to be first must be your slave— [28]just as the Son of Man did not come to be served, but to serve, and to give his life as a ransom for many." (See also Mark 10:42-45.)

MATTHEW 23:2-12 "The teachers of the law and the Pharisees sit in Moses' seat. [3]So you must obey them and do everything they tell you. But do not do what they do, for they do not practice what they preach. [4]They tie up heavy loads and put them on men's shoulders, but they themselves are not willing to lift a finger to move them. [5]Everything they do is done for men to see: They make their phylacteries wide and the tassels on their garments long; [6]they love the place of honor at banquets and the most important seats in the synagogues; [7]they love to be greeted in the marketplaces and to have men call them 'Rabbi.' [8]But you are not to be called 'Rabbi,' for you have only one Master and you are all brothers. [9]And do not call anyone on earth 'father,' for you have one Father, and he is in heaven. [10]Nor are you to be called 'teacher,' for you have one Teacher, the Christ. [11]The greatest among you will be your servant. [12]For whoever exalts himself will be humbled, and whoever humbles himself will be exalted."

MATTHEW 23:25-28 "Woe to you, teachers of the law and Pharisees, you hypocrites! You clean the outside of the cup and dish, but inside they are full of greed and self-indulgence. [26]Blind Pharisee! First clean the inside of the cup and dish, and then the outside also will be clean. [27]Woe to you, teachers of the law and Pharisees, you hypocrites! You are like whitewashed tombs, which look beautiful on the outside but on the inside are full of dead men's bones and everything unclean. [28]In the same way, on the outside you appear to people as righteous but on the inside you are full of hypocrisy and wickedness."

MARK 12:38-40 As he taught, Jesus said, "Watch out for the teachers of the law. They like to walk around in flowing robes and be greeted in the marketplaces, [39]and have the most important seats in the synagogues and the places of honor at banquets. [40]They devour widows' houses and for a show make lengthy prayers. Such men will be punished most severely."

LUKE 11:43 "Woe to you Pharisees, because you love the most important seats in the synagogues and greetings in the marketplaces."

LUKE 12:16-21 And he told them this parable: "The ground of a certain rich man produced a good crop. [17]He thought to himself, 'What shall I do? I have no place to store my crops.' [18]Then he said, 'This is what I'll do. I will tear down my barns and build bigger ones, and there I will store all my grain and my goods. [19]And I'll say to myself, "You have plenty of good things laid up for many years. Take life easy; eat, drink and be merry."' [20]But God said to him, 'You fool! This very night your life will be demanded from you. Then who will get what you have prepared for yourself?' [21]This is how it will be with anyone who stores up things for himself but is not rich toward God."

LUKE 14:8-11 "When someone invites you to a wedding feast, do not take the place of honor, for a person more distinguished than you may have been invited. [9]If so, the host who invited both of you will come and say to you, 'Give this man your seat.' Then, humiliated, you will have to take the least important place. [10]But when you are invited, take the lowest place, so that when your host comes, he will say to you, 'Friend, move up to a better place.' Then you will be honored in the presence of all your fellow guests. [11]For everyone who exalts himself will be humbled, and he who humbles himself will be exalted."

LUKE 16:15 He said to them [the Pharisees], "You are the ones who justify yourselves in the eyes of men, but God knows your hearts. What is highly valued among men is detestable in God's sight."

LUKE 18:9-14 To some who were confident of their own righteousness and looked down on everybody else, Jesus told this parable: [10]"Two men went up to the temple to pray, one a Pharisee and the other a tax collector. [11]The Pharisee stood up and prayed about himself: 'God, I thank you that I am not like other men—robbers, evildoers, adulterers—or even like this tax collector. [12]I fast twice a week and give a tenth of all I get.' [13]But the tax collector stood at a distance. He would not even look up to heaven, but beat his breast and said, 'God, have mercy on me, a sinner.' [14]I tell you that this man, rather than the other, went home justified before God. For everyone who exalts himself will be humbled, and he who humbles himself will be exalted."

LUKE 20:46-47 "Beware of the teachers of the law. They like to walk around in flowing robes and love to be greeted in the marketplaces and have the most important seats in the synagogues and the places of honor at banquets. [47]They devour widows' houses and for a show make lengthy prayers. Such men will be punished most severely."

Pursuits of Life

MATTHEW 6:19-33 "Do not store up for yourselves treasures on earth, where moth and rust destroy, and where thieves break in and steal. [20]But store up for yourselves treasures in heaven, where moth and rust do not destroy, and where thieves do not break in and steal. [21]For where your treasure is, there your heart will be also. [22]The eye is the lamp of the body. If your eyes are good, your whole body will be full of light. [23]But if your eyes are bad, your whole body will be full of darkness. If then the light within you is darkness, how great is that darkness! [24]No one can serve two masters. Either he will hate the one and love the other, or he will be devoted to the one and despise the other. You cannot serve both God and Money. [25]Therefore I tell you, do not worry about your life, what you will eat or drink; or about your body, what you will wear. Is not life more important than food, and the body more important than clothes? [26]Look at the birds of the air; they do not sow or reap or store away in barns, and yet your heavenly Father feeds them. Are you not much more valuable than they? [27]Who of you by worrying can add a single hour to his life? [28]And why do you worry about clothes? See how the lilies of the field grow. They do not labor or spin. [29]Yet I tell you that not even Solomon in all his splendor was dressed like one of these. [30]If that is how God clothes the grass of the field, which is here today and tomorrow is thrown into the fire, will he not much more clothe you, O you of little faith? [31]So do not worry, saying, 'What shall we eat?' or 'What shall we drink?' or 'What shall we wear?' [32]For the pagans run after all these things, and your heavenly Father knows that you need them. [33]But seek first his kingdom and his righteousness, and all these things will be given to you as well."

MATTHEW 7:7-11 "Ask and it will be given to you; seek and you will find; knock and the door will be opened to you. [8]For everyone who asks receives; he who seeks finds; and to him who knocks, the door will be opened. [9]Which of you, if his son asks for bread, will give him a stone? [10]Or if he asks for a fish, will give him a

snake? [11]If you, then, though you are evil, know how to give good gifts to your children, how much more will your Father in heaven give good gifts to those who ask him!"

MATTHEW 10:38-39 "...anyone who does not take his cross and follow me is not worthy of me. [39]Whoever finds his life will lose it, and whoever loses his life for my sake will find it."

LUKE 12:5-9 "But I will show you whom you should fear: Fear him who, after the killing of the body, has power to throw you into hell. Yes, I tell you, fear him. [6]Are not five sparrows sold for two pennies? Yet not one of them is forgotten by God. [7]Indeed, the very hairs of your head are all numbered. Don't be afraid; you are worth more than many sparrows. [8]I tell you, whoever acknowledges me before men, the Son of Man will also acknowledge him before the angels of God. [9]But he who disowns me before men will be disowned before the angels of God."

Self-Deception and Self-Justification

MATTHEW 10:39 "Whoever finds his life will lose it, and whoever loses his life for my sake will find it."

MARK 8:35-38 "For whoever wants to save his life will lose it, but whoever loses his life for me and for the gospel will save it. [36]What good is it for a man to gain the whole world, yet forfeit his soul? [37]Or what can a man give in exchange for his soul? [38]If anyone is ashamed of me and my words in this adulterous and sinful generation, the Son of Man will be ashamed of him when he comes in his Father's glory with the holy angels."

Mark 10:18-23 "Why do you call me good?" Jesus answered. "No one is good—except God alone. [19]You know the commandments: 'Do not murder, do not commit adultery, do not steal, do not give false testimony, do not defraud, honor your father and mother.'" [20]"Teacher," he declared, "all these I have kept since I was a boy." [21]Jesus looked at him and loved him. "One thing you lack," he said. "Go, sell everything you have and give to the poor, and you will have treasure in heaven. Then come, follow me." [22]At this the man's face fell. He went away sad, because he had great wealth. [23]Jesus looked around and said to his disciples, "How hard it is for the rich to enter the kingdom of God!"

Luke 16:15 He said to them [the Pharisees], "You are the ones who justify yourselves in the eyes of men, but God knows your hearts. What is highly valued among men is detestable in God's sight."

Luke 18:9-14 To some who were confident of their own righteousness and looked down on everybody else, Jesus told this parable: [10]"Two men went up to the temple to pray, one a Pharisee and the other a tax collector. [11]The Pharisee stood up and prayed about himself: 'God, I thank you that I am not like other men— robbers, evildoers, adulterers—or even like this tax collector. [12]I fast twice a week and give a tenth of all I get.' [13]But the tax collector stood at a distance. He would not even look up to heaven, but beat his breast and said, 'God, have mercy on me, a sinner.' [14]I tell you that this man, rather than the other, went home justified before

God. For everyone who exalts himself will be humbled, and he who humbles himself will be exalted."

Sickness

John 9:3 "Neither this man nor his parents sinned," said Jesus, "but this happened so that the work of God might be displayed in his life."

John 11:4 When he heard this [that Lazarus was sick], Jesus said, "This sickness will not end in death. No, it is for God's glory so that God's Son may be glorified through it."

Matthew 10:5-8 These twelve Jesus sent out with the following instructions: "Do not go among the Gentiles or enter any town of the Samaritans. [6]Go rather to the lost sheep of Israel. [7]As you go, preach this message: 'The kingdom of heaven is near.' [8]Heal the sick, raise the dead, cleanse those who have leprosy, drive out demons. Freely you have received, freely give."

Matthew 25:33-40 "He will put the sheep on his right and the goats on his left. [34]Then the King will say to those on his right, 'Come, you who are blessed by my Father; take your inheritance, the kingdom prepared for you since the creation of the world. [35]For I was hungry and you gave me something to eat, I was thirsty and you gave me something to drink, I was a stranger and you invited me in, [36]I needed clothes and you clothed me, I was sick and you looked after me, I was in prison and you came to visit me.' [37]Then the righteous will answer him, 'Lord, when did we see you hungry and feed you, or thirsty and give you something to drink? ³⁸When did we see you a stranger and invite you in, or needing clothes and clothe you? ³⁹When did we see you sick or in prison and go to visit you?' ⁴⁰The King will reply, 'I tell you the truth, whatever you did for one of the least of these brothers of mine, you did for me.'"

LUKE 10:8-9 "When you enter a town and are welcomed, eat what is set before you. ⁹Heal the sick who are there and tell them, 'The kingdom of God is near you.'"

Signs and Seeking a Sign

MATTHEW 12:39-45 He answered, "A wicked and adulterous generation asks for a miraculous sign! But none will be given it except the sign of the prophet Jonah. ⁴⁰For as Jonah was three days and three nights in the belly of a huge fish, so the Son of Man will be three days and three nights in the heart of the earth. ⁴¹The men of Nineveh will stand up at the judgment with this generation and condemn it; for they repented at the preaching of Jonah, and now one greater than Jonah is here. ⁴²The Queen of the South will rise at the judgment with this generation and condemn it; for she came from the ends of the earth to listen to Solomon's wisdom, and now one greater than Solomon is here. ⁴³When an evil spirit comes out of a man, it goes through arid places seeking rest and does not find it. ⁴⁴Then it says, 'I will return to the house I left.' When it arrives, it finds the house unoccupied, swept clean and put in order. ⁴⁵Then it goes and takes with it seven other spirits more wicked

than itself, and they go in and live there. And the final condition of that man is worse than the first. That is how it will be with this wicked generation."

MATTHEW 16:2-4 He replied, "When evening comes, you say, 'It will be fair weather, for the sky is red,' ³and in the morning, 'Today it will be stormy, for the sky is red and overcast.' You know how to interpret the appearance of the sky, but you cannot interpret the signs of the times. ⁴A wicked and adulterous generation looks for a miraculous sign, but none will be given it except the sign of Jonah." Jesus then left them and went away.

MARK 8:12 He sighed deeply and said, "Why does this generation ask for a miraculous sign? I tell you the truth, no sign will be given to it."

LUKE 11:29 As the crowds increased, Jesus said, "This is a wicked generation. It asks for a miraculous sign, but none will be given it except the sign of Jonah."

Sin

JOHN 8:3-11 The teachers of the law and the Pharisees brought in a woman caught in adultery. They made her stand before the group ⁴and said to Jesus, "Teacher, this woman was caught in the act of adultery. ⁵In the Law Moses commanded us to stone such women. Now what do you say?" ⁶They were using this question as a trap, in order to have a basis for accusing him. But Jesus bent down and started to write on the ground with his finger. ⁷When they kept on questioning him, he straightened up and said to them, "If any one of you is without sin, let him be the first to throw a stone at her." [8]Again he stooped down and wrote on the ground. [9]At this, those who heard began to go away one at a time, the older ones first, until only Jesus was left, with the woman still standing there. [10]Jesus straightened up and asked her, "Woman, where are they? Has no one condemned you?" [11]"No one, sir," she said. "Then neither do I condemn you," Jesus declared. "Go now and leave your life of sin."

JOHN 8:21, 23-24 Once more Jesus said to them, "I am going away, and you will look for me, and you will die in your sin. Where I go, you cannot come." [23]But he continued, "You are from below; I am from above. You are of this world; I am not of this world. [24]I told you that you would die in your sins; if you do not believe that I am the one I claim to be, you will indeed die in your sins."

JOHN 8:34-36 Jesus replied, "I tell you the truth, everyone who sins is a slave to sin. [35]Now a slave has no permanent place in the family, but a son belongs to it forever. [36]So if the Son sets you free, you will be free indeed."

JOHN 9:41 Jesus said, "If you were blind, you would not be guilty of sin; but now that you claim you can see, your guilt remains."

JOHN 16:8-11 "When he [the Holy Spirit] comes, he will convict the world of guilt in regard to sin and righteousness and judgment: [9]in regard to sin, because men do not believe in me; [10]in regard to righteousness, because I am going to the Father, where you can see me no longer; [11]and in regard to judgment, because the prince of this world now stands condemned."

MATTHEW 5:27-30 "You have heard that it was said, 'Do not commit adultery.' [28]But I tell you that anyone who looks at a woman lustfully has already committed adultery with her in his heart. [29]If your right eye causes you to sin, gouge it out and throw it away. It is better for you to lose one part of your body than for your whole body to be thrown into hell. [30]And if your right hand causes you to sin, cut it off and throw it away. It is better for you to lose one part of your body than for your whole body to go into hell."

MATTHEW 15:10-20 Jesus called the crowd to him and said, "Listen and understand. [11]What goes into a man's mouth does not make him 'unclean,' but what comes out of his mouth, that is what makes him 'unclean.'" [12]Then the disciples came to him and asked, "Do you know that the Pharisees were offended when they heard this?" [13]He replied, "Every plant that my heavenly Father has not planted will be pulled up by the roots. [14]Leave them; they are blind guides. If a blind man leads a blind man, both will fall into a pit." [15]Peter said, "Explain the parable to us." [16]"Are you still so dull?" Jesus asked them. [17]"Don't you see that whatever enters the mouth goes into the stomach and then out of the body? [18]But the things that come out of the mouth come from the heart, and these make a man 'unclean.' [19]For out of the heart come evil thoughts, murder, adultery, sexual immorality, theft, false testimony, slander. [20]These are what make a man 'unclean'; but eating with unwashed hands does not make him 'unclean.'"

MATTHEW 18:8 "If your hand or your foot causes you to sin, cut it off and throw it away. It is better for you to enter life maimed or crippled than to have two hands or two feet and be thrown into eternal fire."

MARK 2:10-11 "But that you may know that the Son of Man has authority on earth to forgive sins...." He said to the paralytic, [11]"I tell you, get up, take your mat and go home."

MARK 2:17 On hearing this, Jesus said to them, "It is not the healthy who need a doctor, but the sick. I have not come to call the righteous, but sinners."

MARK 3:28-30 "I tell you the truth, all the sins and blasphemies of men will be forgiven them. [29]But whoever blasphemes against the Holy Spirit will never be forgiven; he is guilty of an eternal sin." [30]He said this because they were saying, "He has an evil spirit."

MARK 4:21-23 He said to them, "Do you bring in a lamp to put it under a bowl or a bed? Instead, don't you put it on its stand? [22]For whatever is hidden is meant to be disclosed, and whatever is concealed is meant to be brought out into the open. [23]If anyone has ears to hear, let him hear."

MARK 7:14-15, 17-23 Again Jesus called the crowd to him and said, "Listen to me, everyone, and understand this. [15]Nothing outside a man can make him 'unclean' by going into him. Rather, it is what comes out of a man that makes him 'unclean.'" [17]After he had left the crowd and entered the house, his disciples asked him about this parable. [18]"Are you so dull?" he asked. "Don't you see that nothing that enters a man from the outside can make him 'unclean'? [19]For it doesn't go into his heart but into his stomach, and then out of his body." (In saying this, Jesus declared all foods "clean.") [20]He went on: "What comes out of a man is what makes him 'unclean.' [21]For from within, out of men's hearts, come evil thoughts, sexual immorality, theft, murder, adultery, [22]greed, malice, deceit, lewdness, envy, slander, arrogance and folly. [23]All these evils come from inside and make a man 'unclean.'"

MARK 9:43, 45, 47 "If your hand causes you to sin, cut it off. It is better for you to enter life maimed than with two hands to go into hell, where the fire never goes out. [45]And if your foot causes you to sin, cut it off. It is better for you to enter life crippled than to have two feet and be thrown into hell. [47]And if your eye causes you to sin, pluck it out. It is better for you to enter the kingdom of God with one eye than to have two eyes and be thrown into hell."

LUKE 4:18-21 "The Spirit of the Lord is on me, because he has anointed me to preach good news to the poor. He has sent me to proclaim freedom for the prisoners and recovery of sight for the blind, to release the oppressed, [19]to proclaim the year of the Lord's favor." [20]Then he rolled up the scroll, gave it back to the attendant and sat down. The eyes of everyone in the synagogue were fastened on him, [21]and he began by saying to them, "Today this scripture is fulfilled in your hearing."

LUKE 5:22-23 Jesus knew what they were thinking and asked, "Why are you thinking these things in your hearts? [23]Which is easier: to say, 'Your sins are forgiven,' or to say, 'Get up and walk'?"

LUKE 5:31-32 Jesus answered them, "It is not the healthy who need a doctor, but the sick. [32]I have not come to call the righteous, but sinners to repentance."

LUKE 7:40-48 Jesus answered him, "Simon, I have something to tell you." "Tell me, teacher," he said. [41]"Two men owed money to a certain moneylender. One owed him five hundred denarii, and the other fifty. [42]Neither of them had the money to pay him back, so he canceled the debts of both. Now which of them will love him more?" [43]Simon replied, "I suppose the one who had the bigger debt canceled." "You have judged correctly," Jesus said. [44]Then he turned toward the woman and said to Simon, "Do you see this woman? I came into your house. You did not give me any water for my feet, but she wet my feet with her tears and wiped them with her hair. [45]You did not give me a kiss, but this woman, from the time I entered, has not stopped kissing my feet. [46]You did not put oil on my head, but she has poured perfume on my feet. [47]Therefore, I tell you, her many sins have been forgiven—for she loved much. But he who has been forgiven little loves little." [48]Then Jesus said to her, "Your sins are forgiven."

LUKE 13:2-5 Jesus answered, "Do you think that these Galileans were worse sinners than all the other Galileans because they suffered this way? [3]I tell you, no! But unless you repent, you too will all perish. [4]Or those eighteen who died when the tower in Siloam fell on them— do you think they were more guilty than all the others living in Jerusalem? [5]I tell you, no! But unless you repent, you too will all perish."

LUKE 17:3-6 "So watch yourselves. If your brother sins, rebuke him, and if he repents, forgive him. [4]If he sins against you seven times in a day, and seven times comes back to you and says, 'I repent,' forgive him." [5]The apostles said to the Lord, "Increase our faith!" [6]He replied, "If you have faith as small as a mustard seed, you can say to this mulberry tree, 'Be uprooted and planted in the sea,' and it will obey you."

LUKE 24:46-47 He told them [the disciples], "This is what is written: The Christ will suffer and rise from the dead on the third day, [47]and repentance and forgiveness of sins will be preached in his name to all nations, beginning at Jerusalem."

REVELATION 22:15-16 "Outside are the dogs, those who practice magic arts, the sexually immoral, the murderers, the idolaters and everyone who loves and practices falsehood. [16]I, Jesus, have sent my angel to give you this testimony for the churches. I am the Root and the Offspring of David, and the bright Morning Star."

Sinful Generation

MATTHEW 12:39-45 He answered, "A wicked and adulterous generation asks for a miraculous sign! But none will be given it except the sign of the prophet Jonah. [40]For as Jonah was three days and three nights in the belly of a huge fish, so the Son of Man will be three days and three nights in the heart of the earth. [41]The men of Nineveh will stand up at the judgment with this generation and condemn it; for they repented at the preaching of Jonah, and now one greater than Jonah is here. [42]The Queen of the South will rise at the judgment with this generation and condemn it; for she came from the ends of the earth to listen to Solomon's wisdom, and now one greater than Solomon is here. [43]When an evil spirit comes out of a man, it goes through arid places seeking rest and does not find it. [44]Then it says, 'I will return to the house I left.' When it arrives, it finds the house unoccupied, swept clean and put in order. [45]Then it goes and takes with it seven other spirits more wicked than itself, and they go in and live there. And the final condition of that man is worse than the first. That is how it will be with this wicked generation."

MATTHEW 16:2-4 He replied, "When evening comes, you say, 'It will be fair weather, for the sky is red,' [3]and in the morning, 'Today it will be stormy, for the sky is red and overcast.' You know how to interpret the appearance of the sky, but you cannot interpret the signs of the times. [4]A wicked and adulterous generation looks for a miraculous sign, but none will be given it except the sign of Jonah." Jesus then left them and went away.

MATTHEW 17:17 "O unbelieving and perverse generation," Jesus replied,

"how long shall I stay with you? How long shall I put up with you? Bring the boy here to me."

MARK 8:38 "If anyone is ashamed of me and my words in this adulterous and sinful generation, the Son of Man will be ashamed of him when he comes in his Father's glory with the holy angels."

LUKE 7:31-35 "To what, then, can I compare the people of this generation? What are they like? [32]They are like children sitting in the marketplace and calling out to each other: 'We played the flute for you, and you did not dance; we sang a dirge, and you did not cry.' [33]For John the Baptist came neither eating bread nor drinking wine, and you say, 'He has a demon.' [34]The Son of Man came eating and drinking, and you say, 'Here is a glutton and a drunkard, a friend of tax collectors and "sinners."' [35]But wisdom is proved right by all her children."

LUKE 9:41 "O unbelieving and perverse generation," Jesus replied, "how long shall I stay with you and put up with you? Bring your son here."

LUKE 11:29-32 As the crowds increased, Jesus said, "This is a wicked generation. It asks for a miraculous sign, but none will be given it except the sign of Jonah. [30]For as Jonah was a sign to the Ninevites, so also will the Son of Man be to this generation. [31]The Queen of the South will rise at the judgment with the men of this generation and condemn them; for she came from the ends of the earth to listen to Solomon's wisdom, and now one greater than Solomon is here. [32]The men of Nineveh will stand up at the judgment with this generation and condemn it; for they repented at the preaching of Jonah, and now one greater than Jonah is here."

Sinners

LUKE 13:2-5 Jesus answered, "Do you think that these Galileans were worse sinners than all the other Galileans because they suffered this way? [3]I tell you, no! But unless you repent, you too will all perish. [4]Or those eighteen who died when the tower in Siloam fell on them—do you think they were more guilty than all the others living in Jerusalem? [5]I tell you, no! But unless you repent, you too will all perish."

LUKE 13:23-30 Someone asked him, "Lord, are only a few people going to be saved?" He said to them, [24]"Make every effort to enter through the narrow door, because many, I tell you, will try to enter and will not be able to. [25]Once the owner of the house gets up and closes the door, you will stand outside knocking and pleading, 'Sir, open the door for us.' But he will answer, 'I don't know you or where you come from.' [26]Then you will say, 'We ate and drank with you, and you taught in our streets.' [27]But he will reply, 'I don't know you or where you come from. Away from me, all you evildoers!' [28]There will be weeping there, and gnashing of teeth, when you see Abraham, Isaac and Jacob and all the prophets in the kingdom of God, but you yourselves thrown out. [29]People will come from east and west and north and south, and will take their places

at the feast in the kingdom of God. [30]Indeed there are those who are last who will be first, and first who will be last."

LUKE 14:12-24 Then Jesus said to his host, "When you give a luncheon or dinner, do not invite your friends, your brothers or relatives, or your rich neighbors; if you do, they may invite you back and so you will be repaid. [13]But when you give a banquet, invite the poor, the crippled, the lame, the blind, [14]and you will be blessed. Although they cannot repay you, you will be repaid at the resurrection of the righteous." [15]When one of those at the table with him heard this, he said to Jesus, "Blessed is the man who will eat at the feast in the kingdom of God." [16]Jesus replied: "A certain man was preparing a great banquet and invited many guests. [17]At the time of the banquet he sent his servant to tell those who had been invited, 'Come, for everything is now ready.' [18]But they all alike began to make excuses. The first said, 'I have just bought a field, and I must go and see it. Please excuse me.' [19]Another said, 'I have just bought five yoke of oxen, and I'm on my way to try them out. Please excuse me.' [20]Still another said, 'I just got married, so I can't come.' [21]The servant came back and reported this to his master. Then the owner of the house became angry and ordered his servant, 'Go out quickly into the streets and alleys of the town and bring in the poor, the crippled, the blind and the lame.' [22]'Sir,' the servant said, 'what you ordered has been done, but there is still room.' [23]Then the master told his servant, 'Go out to the roads and country lanes and make them come in, so that my house will be full. ²⁴I tell you, not one of those men who were invited will get a taste of my banquet.'"

LUKE 15:4-10 "Suppose one of you has a hundred sheep and loses one of them. Does he not leave the ninety-nine in the open country and go after the lost sheep until he finds it? ⁵And when he finds it, he joyfully puts it on his shoulders ⁶and goes home. Then he calls his friends and neighbors together and says, 'Rejoice with me; I have found my lost sheep.' ⁷I tell you that in the same way there will be more rejoicing in heaven over one sinner who repents than over ninety-nine right-eous persons who do not need to repent. ⁸Or suppose a woman has ten silver coins and loses one. Does she not light a lamp, sweep the house and search carefully until she finds it? ⁹And when she finds it, she calls her friends and neighbors together and says, 'Rejoice with me; I have found my lost coin.' ¹⁰In the same way, I tell you, there is rejoicing in the presence of the angels of God over one sinner who repents."

LUKE 18:9-14 To some who were confident of their own righteousness and looked down on everybody else, Jesus told this parable: ¹⁰"Two men went up to the temple to pray, one a Pharisee and the other a tax collector. ¹¹The Pharisee stood up and prayed about himself: 'God, I thank you that I am not like other men—robbers, evildoers, adulterers—or even like this tax collector. ¹²I fast twice a week and give a tenth of all I get.' ¹³But the tax collector stood at a distance. He would

not even look up to heaven, but beat his breast and said, 'God, have mercy on me, a sinner.' ¹⁴I tell you that this man, rather than the other, went home justified before God. For everyone who exalts himself will be humbled, and he who humbles himself will be exalted."

The Soul

MATTHEW 10:28 "Do not be afraid of those who kill the body but cannot kill the soul. Rather, be afraid of the One who can destroy both soul and body in hell."

MATTHEW 16:23-27 Jesus turned and said to Peter, "Get behind me, Satan! You are a stumbling block to me; you do not have in mind the things of God, but the things of men." ²⁴Then Jesus said to his disciples, "If anyone would come after me, he must deny himself and take up his cross and follow me. ²⁵For whoever wants to save his life will lose it, but whoever loses his life for me will find it. ²⁶What good will it be for a man if he gains the whole world, yet forfeits his soul? Or what can a man give in exchange for his soul? ²⁷For the Son of Man is going to come in his Father's glory with his angels, and then he will reward each person according to what he has done."

MATTHEW 22:37-38 Jesus replied: "'Love the Lord your God with all your heart and with all your soul and with all your mind.' ³⁸This is the first and greatest commandment."

MATTHEW 26:40-41 Then he re-turned to his disciples and found them sleeping. "Could you men not keep watch with me for one hour?" he asked Peter. [41]"Watch and pray so that you will not fall into temptation. The spirit is willing, but the body is weak."

MARK 8:36-37 "What good is it for a man to gain the whole world, yet forfeit his soul? [37]Or what can a man give in exchange for his soul?"

MARK 12:30 "Love the Lord your God with all your heart and with all your soul and with all your mind and with all your strength."

LUKE 10:27 He answered: " 'Love the Lord your God with all your heart and with all your soul and with all your strength and with all your mind'; and, 'Love your neighbor as yourself.' "

LUKE 12:13-21 Someone in the crowd said to him, "Teacher, tell my brother to divide the inheritance with me." [14]Jesus replied, "Man, who appointed me a judge or an arbiter between you?" [15]Then he said to them, "Watch out! Be on your guard against all kinds of greed; a man's life does not consist in the abundance of his possessions." [16]And he told them this parable: "The ground of a certain rich man produced a good crop. [17]He thought to himself, 'What shall I do? I have no place to store my crops.' [18]Then he said, 'This is what I'll do. I will tear down my barns and build bigger ones, and there I will store all my grain and my goods. [19]And I'll say to myself, "You have plenty of good things laid up for many years. Take life easy; eat, drink and be merry." ' [20]But God said to him, 'You fool! This very night your life ["soul" in NKJV] will be demanded from you. Then who

will get what you have prepared for yourself?' [21]This is how it will be with anyone who stores up things for himself but is not rich toward God."

The Spirit and the Flesh

JOHN 3:5-8 Jesus answered, "I tell you the truth, no one can enter the kingdom of God unless he is born of water and the Spirit. [6]Flesh gives birth to flesh, but the Spirit gives birth to spirit. [7]You should not be surprised at my saying, 'You must be born again.' [8]The wind blows wherever it pleases. You hear its sound, but you cannot tell where it comes from or where it is going. So it is with everyone born of the Spirit."

MATTHEW 26:40-41 Then he returned to his disciples and found them sleeping. "Could you men not keep watch with me for one hour?" he asked Peter. [41]"Watch and pray so that you will not fall into temptation. The spirit is willing, but the body is weak."

MARK 14:37-38 Then he returned to his disciples and found them sleeping. "Simon," he said to Peter, "are you asleep? Could you not keep watch for one hour? [38]Watch and pray so that you will not fall into temptation. The spirit is willing, but the body is weak."

Taxes and Government

LUKE 20:23-25 He saw through their duplicity and said to them, [24]"Show me a denarius. Whose portrait and inscription are on it?" [25]"Caesar's," they replied. He said to them, "Then give to Caesar what is Caesar's, and to God what is God's." (See also Matthew 22:18-21; Mark 12:15-17.)

The Traditions of Men

MARK 7:6-13 He replied, "Isaiah was right when he prophesied about you hypocrites; as it is written: 'These people honor me with their lips, but their hearts are far from me. [7]They worship me in vain; their teachings are but rules taught by men.' [8]You have let go of the commands of God and are holding on to the traditions of men." [9]And he said to them: "You have a fine way of setting aside the commands of God in order to observe your own traditions! [10]For Moses said, 'Honor your father and your mother,' and, 'Anyone who curses his father or mother must be put to death.' [11]But you say that if a man says to his father or mother: 'Whatever help you might otherwise have received from me is Corban' (that is, a gift devoted to God), [12]then you no longer let him do anything for his father or mother. [13]Thus you nullify the word of God by your tradition that you have handed down. And you do many things like that."

Unrighteous Leaders

LUKE 11:46-52 Jesus replied, "And you experts in the law, woe to you, because you load people down with burdens they can hardly carry, and you yourselves will not lift one finger to help them. [47]Woe to you, because you build tombs for the prophets, and it was your forefathers who killed them. [48]So you testify that you approve of what your forefathers did; they killed the prophets, and you build their tombs. [49]Because of this, God in his wisdom said, 'I will send them prophets and apostles, some of whom they will kill and others they will persecute.' [50]Therefore this generation will be held responsible for the blood of all the prophets that has been shed since the beginning of the world, [51]from the blood of Abel to the blood of Zechariah, who was killed between the altar and the sanctuary. Yes, I tell you, this generation will be held responsible for it all. [52]Woe to you experts in the law, because you have taken away the key to knowledge. You yourselves have not entered, and you have hindered those who were entering."

The Wicked

JOHN 3:18-20 "Whoever believes in him [Christ] is not condemned, but whoever does not believe stands condemned already because he has not believed in the name of God's one and only Son. [19]This is the verdict: Light has come into the world, but men loved darkness instead of light because their deeds were evil. [20]Everyone who does evil hates the light, and will not come into the light for fear that his deeds will be exposed."

JOHN 8:34 Jesus replied, "I tell you the truth, everyone who sins is a slave to sin."

JOHN 8:44 "You belong to your father, the devil, and you want to carry out your father's desire. He was a murderer from the beginning, not holding to the truth, for there is no truth in him. When he lies, he speaks his native language, for he is a liar and the father of lies."

MATTHEW 13:47-50 "Once again, the kingdom of heaven is like a net that was let down into the lake and caught all kinds of fish. [48]When it was full, the fishermen pulled it up on the shore. Then they sat down and collected the good fish in baskets, but threw the bad away. [49]This is how it will be at the end of the age. The angels will come and separate the wicked from the righteous [50]and throw them into the fiery furnace, where there will be weeping and gnashing of teeth."

MATTHEW 16:4 "A wicked and adulterous generation looks for a miraculous sign, but none will be given it except the sign of Jonah." Jesus then left them and went away.

MATTHEW 18:23-35 "Therefore, the kingdom of heaven is like a king who wanted to settle accounts with his servants. [24]As he began the settlement, a man who owed him ten thousand talents was brought to him. [25]Since he was not able to pay, the master ordered that he and his wife and his children and all that he had be sold to repay the debt. [26]The servant fell on his knees before him. 'Be patient with me,' he begged, 'and I will pay back everything.' [27]The servant's master took pity on him, canceled the debt and let him go. [28]But when that servant went out, he found one of his fellow servants who owed him a hundred denarii. He grabbed him and began to choke him. 'Pay back what you owe me!' he demanded. [29]His fellow servant fell to his knees and begged him, 'Be patient with me, and I will pay you back.' [30]But he refused. Instead, he went off and had the man thrown into prison until he could pay the debt. [31]When the other servants saw what had happened, they were greatly distressed and went and told their master everything that had happened. [32]Then the master called the servant in. 'You wicked servant,' he said, 'I canceled all that debt of yours because you begged me to. [33]Shouldn't you have had mercy on your fellow servant just as I had on you?' [34]In anger his master turned him over to the jailers to be tortured, until he should pay back all he owed. [35]This is how my heavenly Father will treat each of you unless you forgive your brother from your heart."

MATTHEW 22:18 But Jesus, knowing their evil intent, said, "You hypocrites, why are you trying to trap me?" (See also Mark 12:15.)

MATTHEW 25:24-30 "Then the man who had received the one talent came. 'Master,' he said, 'I knew that you are a hard man, harvesting where you have not sown and gathering where you have not scattered seed. [25]So I was afraid and went out and hid your talent in the ground. See, here is what belongs to you.' [26]His master replied, 'You wicked, lazy servant! So you knew that I harvest where I have not sown and gather where I have not scattered seed? [27]Well then, you should have put my money on deposit with the bankers, so that when I returned I would have received it back with interest. [28]Take the talent from him and give it to the one who has the ten talents. [29]For everyone who has will be given more, and he will have an abundance. Whoever does not have, even what he has will be taken from him. ³⁰And throw that worthless servant outside, into the darkness, where there will be weeping and gnashing of teeth.'"

LUKE 11:39-41 Then the Lord said to him, "Now then, you Pharisees clean the outside of the cup and dish, but inside you are full of greed and wickedness. ⁴⁰You foolish people! Did not the one who made the outside make the inside also? ⁴¹But give what is inside the dish to the poor, and everything will be clean for you."

LUKE 19:9-10 Jesus said to him [Zacchaeus], "Today salvation has come to this house, because this man, too, is a son of Abraham. ¹⁰For the Son of Man came to seek and to save what was lost."

REVELATION 3:15-18 "I know your deeds, that you are neither cold nor hot. I wish you were either one or the other! ¹⁶So, because you are lukewarm—neither hot nor cold—I am about to spit you out of my mouth. ¹⁷You say, 'I am rich; I have acquired wealth and do not need a thing.' But you do not realize that you are wretched, pitiful, poor, blind and naked. ¹⁸I counsel you to buy from me gold refined in the fire, so you can become rich; and white clothes to wear, so you can cover your shameful nakedness; and salve to put on your eyes, so you can see."

Women Honored by Jesus

MATTHEW 15:24-28 He answered, "I was sent only to the lost sheep of Israel." ²⁵The woman came and knelt before him. "Lord, help me!" she said. ²⁶He replied, "It is not right to take the children's bread and toss it to their dogs." ²⁷"Yes, Lord," she said, "but even the dogs eat the crumbs that fall from their masters' table." ²⁸Then Jesus answered, "Woman, you have great faith! Your request is granted." And her daughter was healed from that very hour.

MATTHEW 26:10-13 Aware of this, Jesus said to them, "Why are you bothering this woman? She has done a beautiful thing to me. ¹¹The poor you will always have with you, but you will not always have me. ¹²When she poured this perfume on my body, she did it to prepare me for burial. ¹³I tell you the truth, wherever this gospel is preached throughout the world, what she has done will also be told, in memory of her."

MARK 12:42-44 But a poor widow came and put in two very small copper coins, worth only a fraction of a penny. ⁴³Calling his disciples to him, Jesus said, "I tell you the truth, this poor widow has put more into the treasury than all the others. ⁴⁴They all gave out of their wealth; but she, out of her poverty, put in everything—all she had to live on."

LUKE 7:44-48 Then he turned toward the woman and said to Simon, "Do you see this woman? I came into your house. You did not give me any water for my feet, but she wet my feet with her tears and wiped them with her hair. ⁴⁵You did not give me a kiss, but this woman, from the time I entered, has not stopped kissing my feet. ⁴⁶You did not put oil on my head, but she has poured perfume on my feet. ⁴⁷Therefore, I tell you, her many sins have been forgiven—for she loved much. But he who has been forgiven little loves little." [48]Then Jesus said to her, "Your sins are forgiven."

LUKE 10:38-42 As Jesus and his disciples were on their way, he came to a village where a woman named Martha opened her home to him. [39]She had a sister called Mary, who sat at the Lord's feet listening to what he said. [40]But Martha was distracted by all the preparations that had to be made. She came to him and asked, "Lord, don't you care that my sister has left me to do the work by myself? Tell her to help me!" [41]"Martha, Martha," the Lord answered, "you are worried and upset about many things, [42]but only one thing is needed. Mary has chosen what is better, and it will not be taken away from her."

The Words We Speak

MATTHEW 12:33-37 "Make a tree good and its fruit will be good, or make a tree bad and its fruit will be bad, for a tree is recognized by its fruit. [34]You brood of vipers, how can you who are evil say anything good? For out of the overflow of the heart the mouth speaks. [35]The good man brings good things out of the good stored up in him, and the evil man brings evil things out of the evil stored up in him. [36]But I tell you that men will have to give account on the day of judgment for every careless word they have spoken. [37]For by your words you will be acquitted, and by your words you will be condemned."

MATTHEW 15:10-11 Jesus called the crowd to him and said, "Listen and understand. [11]What goes into a man's mouth does not make him 'unclean,' but what comes out of his mouth, that is what makes him 'unclean.'"

MATTHEW 15:13-20 He replied, "Every plant that my heavenly Father has not planted will be pulled up by the roots. [14]Leave them; they are blind guides. If a blind man leads a blind man, both will fall into a pit." [15]Peter said, "Explain the parable to us." [16]"Are you still so dull?" Jesus asked them. [17]"Don't you see that whatever enters the mouth goes into the stomach and then out of the body? [18]But the things that come out of the mouth come from the heart, and these make a man 'unclean.' [19]For out of the heart come evil thoughts, murder, adultery, sexual immorality, theft, false testimony, slander. [20]These are what make a man 'unclean'; but eating with unwashed hands does not make him 'unclean.'"

MARK 7:14-15, 17-23 Again Jesus called the crowd to him and said, "Listen to me, everyone, and understand this. [15]Nothing outside a man can make him 'unclean' by going into him. Rather, it is what comes out of a man that makes him 'unclean.'" [17]After he had left the crowd and entered the house, his disciples asked him about this parable. [18]"Are you so dull?" he asked. "Don't you see that nothing that enters a man from the outside can make him 'unclean'? [19]For it doesn't go into his heart but into his stomach, and then out of his body." (In saying this, Jesus declared all foods "clean.") [20]He went on: "What comes out of a man is what makes him 'unclean.' [21]For from within, out of men's hearts, come evil thoughts, sexual immorality, theft, murder, adultery,

[22]greed, malice, deceit, lewdness, envy, slander, arrogance and folly. [23]All these evils come from inside and make a man 'unclean.'"

The World

JOHN 7:7-8 "The world cannot hate you, but it hates me because I testify that what it does is evil. [8]You go to the Feast. I am not yet going up to this Feast, because for me the right time has not yet come."

JOHN 12:31 "Now is the time for judgment on this world; now the prince of this world will be driven out."

JOHN 12:46 "I have come into the world as a light, so that no one who believes in me should stay in darkness."

JOHN 14:16-17 "And I will ask the Father, and he will give you another Counselor to be with you forever— [17]the Spirit of truth. The world cannot accept him, because it neither sees him nor knows him. But you know him, for he lives with you and will be in you."

JOHN 14:27 "Peace I leave with you; my peace I give you. I do not give to you as the world gives. Do not let your hearts be troubled and do not be afraid."

JOHN 15:18-19 "If the world hates you, keep in mind that it hated me first. [19]If you belonged to the world, it would love you as its own. As it is, you do not belong to the world, but I have chosen you out of the world. That is why the world hates you."

JOHN 16:8-11 "When he [the Holy Spirit] comes, he will convict the world of guilt in regard to sin and righteousness and judgment: [9]in regard to sin, because men do not believe in me; [10]in regard to righteousness, because I am going to the Father, where you can see me no longer; [11]and in regard to judgment, because the prince of this world now stands condemned."

JOHN 16:19-20 Jesus saw that they wanted to ask him about this, so he said to them, "Are you asking one another what I meant when I said, 'In a little while you will see me no more, and then after a little while you will see me'? [20]I tell you the truth, you will weep and mourn while the world rejoices. You will grieve, but your grief will turn to joy."

JOHN 16:33 "I have told you these things, so that in me you may have peace. In this world you will have trouble. But take heart! I have overcome the world."

JOHN 17:13-19 "I am coming to you [God the Father] now, but I say these things while I am still in the world, so that they may have the full measure of my joy within them. [14]I have given them your word and the world has hated them, for they are not of the world any more than I am of the world. [15]My prayer is not that you take them out of the world but that you protect them from the evil one. [16]They are not of the world, even as I am not of it. [17]Sanctify them by the truth; your word is truth. [18]As you sent me into the world, I have sent them into the world. [19]For them I sanctify myself, that they too may be truly sanctified."

JOHN 17:20-23 "My prayer is not for them [the disciples] alone. I pray also for those who will believe in me through their message, ²¹that all of them may be one, Father, just as you are in me and I am in you. May they also be in us so that the world may believe that you have sent me. ²²I have given them the glory that you gave me, that they may be one as we are one: ²³I in them and you in me. May they be brought to complete unity to let the world know that you sent me and have loved them even as you have loved me."

JOHN 17:25-26 "Righteous Father, though the world does not know you, I know you, and they know that you have sent me. ²⁶I have made you known to them, and will continue to make you known in order that the love you have for me may be in them and that I myself may be in them."

JOHN 18:36 Jesus said, "My kingdom is not of this world. If it were, my servants would fight to prevent my arrest by the Jews. But now my kingdom is from another place."

MATTHEW 13:22 "The one who received the seed that fell among the thorns is the man who hears the word, but the worries of this life and the deceitfulness of wealth choke it, making it unfruitful."

MATTHEW 18:7 "Woe to the world because of the things that cause people to sin! Such things must come, but woe to the man through whom they come!"

MARK 8:36-37 "What good is it for a man to gain the whole world, yet forfeit his soul? ³⁷Or what can a man give in exchange for his soul?"

LUKE 9:25 "What good is it for a man to gain the whole world, and yet lose or forfeit his very self?"

Worldly Happiness

MATTHEW 6:19-21 "Do not store up for yourselves treasures on earth, where moth and rust destroy, and where thieves break in and steal. ²⁰But store up for yourselves treasures in heaven, where moth and rust do not destroy, and where thieves do not break in and steal. ²¹For where your treasure is, there your heart will be also."

MATTHEW 16:24-26 Then Jesus said to his disciples, "If anyone would come after me, he must deny himself and take up his cross and follow me. ²⁵For whoever wants to save his life will lose it, but whoever loses his life for me will find it. ²⁶What good will it be for a man if he gains the whole world, yet forfeits his soul? Or what can a man give in exchange for his soul?"

MATTHEW 19:21-24 Jesus answered, "If you want to be perfect, go, sell your possessions and give to the poor, and you will have treasure in heaven. Then come, follow me." ²²When the young man heard this, he went away sad, because he had great wealth. ²³Then Jesus said to his disciples, "I tell you the truth, it is hard for a rich man to enter the kingdom of heaven. ²⁴Again I tell you, it is easier for a camel to go through the eye of a needle than for a rich man to enter the kingdom of God."

LUKE 6:24-26 "But woe to you who are rich, for you have already received your comfort. ²⁵Woe to you who are well fed now, for you will go hungry. Woe to you who laugh now, for you will mourn and weep. ²⁶Woe to you when all men speak well of you, for that is how their fathers treated the false prophets."

LUKE 16:19-26 "There was a rich man who was dressed in purple and fine linen and lived in luxury every day. [20]At his gate was laid a beggar named Lazarus, covered with sores [21]and longing to eat what fell from the rich man's table. Even the dogs came and licked his sores. [22]The time came when the beggar died and the angels carried him to Abraham's side. The rich man also died and was buried. [23]In hell, where he was in torment, he looked up and saw Abraham far away, with Lazarus by his side. [24]So he called to him, 'Father Abraham, have pity on me and send Lazarus to dip the tip of his finger in water and cool my tongue, because I am in agony in this fire.' [25]But Abraham replied, 'Son, remember that in your lifetime you received your good things, while Lazarus received bad things, but now he is comforted here and you are in agony. [26]And besides all this, between us and you a great chasm has been fixed, so that those who want to go from here to you cannot, nor can anyone cross over from there to us.'"

The Worth of an Individual

JOHN 3:16-17 "For God so loved the world that he gave his one and only Son, that whoever believes in him shall not perish but have eternal life. [17]For God did not send his Son into the world to condemn the world, but to save the world through him."

JOHN 6:32-33 Jesus said to them, "I tell you the truth, it is not Moses who has given you the bread from heaven, but it is my Father who gives you the true bread from heaven. [33]For the bread of God is he who comes down from heaven and gives life to the world."

JOHN 6:37-40 "All that the Father gives me will come to me, and whoever comes to me I will never drive away. [38]For I have come down from heaven not to do my will but to do the will of him who sent me. [39]And this is the will of him who sent me, that I shall lose none of all that he has given me, but raise them up at the last day. [40]For my Father's will is that everyone who looks to the Son and believes in him shall have eternal life, and I will raise him up at the last day."

JOHN 6:50-51 "But here is the bread that comes down from heaven, which a man may eat and not die. [51]I am the living bread that came down from heaven. If anyone eats of this bread, he will live forever. This bread is my flesh, which I will give for the life of the world."

JOHN 8:12 When Jesus spoke again to the people, he said, "I am the light of the world. Whoever follows me will never walk in darkness, but will have the light of life."

JOHN 8:31-32 Then Jesus said to those Jews who believed Him, "If you abide in My word, you are My disciples indeed. [32]And you shall know the truth, and the truth shall make you free." (NKJV)

JOHN 10:9-16 "I am the gate; whoever enters through me will be saved. He will come in and go out, and find pasture. [10]The thief comes only to steal and kill and destroy; I have come that they may have life, and have it to the full. [11]I am the good shepherd. The good shepherd lays down his life for the sheep. [12]The hired hand is not the shepherd who owns the sheep. So when he sees the wolf coming, he abandons the sheep and runs away. Then the wolf attacks the flock and scatters it. [13]The man runs away because he is a hired hand and cares nothing for the sheep. [14]I am the good shepherd; I know my sheep and my sheep know me— [15]just as the Father knows me and I know the Father—and I lay down my life for the sheep. [16]I have other sheep that are not of this sheep pen. I must bring them also. They too will listen to my voice, and there shall be one flock and one shepherd."

JOHN 10:27-30 "My sheep listen to my voice; I know them, and they follow me. [28]I give them eternal life, and they shall never perish; no one can snatch them out of my hand. [29]My Father, who has given them to me, is greater than all; no one can snatch them out of my Father's hand. [30]I and the Father are one."

JOHN 12:46 "I have come into the world as a light, so that no one who believes in me should stay in darkness."

JOHN 14:1-4 "Do not let your hearts be troubled. Trust in God; trust also in me. [2]In my Father's house are many rooms; if it were not so, I would have told you. I am going there to prepare a place for you. [3]And if I go and prepare a place for you, I will come back and take you to be with me that you also may be where I am. [4]You know the way to the place where I am going."

JOHN 14:15-16 "If you love me, you will obey what I command. [16]And I will ask the Father, and he will give you another Counselor to be with you forever."

JOHN 14:23 Jesus replied, "If anyone loves me, he will obey my teaching. My Father will love him, and we will come to him and make our home with him."

JOHN 15:7-17 "If you remain in me and my words remain in you, ask whatever you wish, and it will be given you. [8]This is to my Father's glory, that you bear much fruit, showing yourselves to be my disciples. [9]As the Father has loved me, so have I loved you. Now remain in my love. [10]If you obey my commands, you will remain in my love, just as I have obeyed my Father's commands and remain in his love. [11]I have told you this so that my joy may be in you and that your joy may be complete. [12]My command is this: Love each other as I have loved you. [13]Greater love has no one than this, that he lay down his life for his friends. [14]You are my friends if you do what I command. [15]I no longer call you servants, because a servant does not know his master's business. Instead, I have called you friends, for everything that I learned from my Father I have made known to you. [16]You did not choose me, but I chose you and appointed you to go and bear fruit—fruit that will last. Then the Father will give you whatever you ask in my name. [17]This is my command: Love each other."

JOHN 16:23-27 "In that day you will no longer ask me anything. I tell you the truth, my Father will give you whatever you ask in my name. [24]Until now you have not asked for anything in my name. Ask and you will receive, and your joy will be complete. [25]Though I have been speaking figuratively, a time is coming when I will no longer use this kind of language but will tell you plainly about my Father. [26]In that day you will ask in my name. I am not saying that I will ask the Father on your behalf. [27]No, the Father himself loves you because you have loved me and have believed that I came from God."

JOHN 17:9-11 "I pray for them [the disciples]. I am not praying for the world, but for those you have given me, for they are yours. [10]All I have is yours, and all you have is mine. And glory has come to me through them. [11]I will remain in the world no longer, but they are still in the world, and I am coming to you. Holy Father, protect them by the power of your name—the name you gave me—so that they may be one as we are one."

JOHN 17:13 "I am coming to you [God the Father] now, but I say these things while I am still in the world, so that they may have the full measure of my joy within them."

JOHN 17:20-24 "My prayer is not for them [the disciples] alone. I pray also for those who will believe in me through their message, [21]that all of them may be one, Father, just as you are in me and I am in you. May they also be in us so that the world may believe that you have sent me. [22]I have given them the glory that you gave me, that they may be one as we are one: [23]I in them and you in me. May they be brought to complete unity to let the world know that you sent me and have loved them even as you have loved me. [24]Father, I want those you have given me to be with me where I am, and to see my glory, the glory you have given me because

you loved me before the creation of the world."

JOHN 20:29 Then Jesus told him [Thomas], "Because you have seen me, you have believed; blessed are those who have not seen and yet have believed."

MATTHEW 6:25-34 "Therefore I tell you, do not worry about your life, what you will eat or drink; or about your body, what you will wear. Is not life more important than food, and the body more important than clothes? [26]Look at the birds of the air; they do not sow or reap or store away in barns, and yet your heavenly Father feeds them. Are you not much more valuable than they? [27]Who of you by worrying can add a single hour to his life? [28]And why do you worry about clothes? See how the lilies of the field grow. They do not labor or spin. [29]Yet I tell you that not even Solomon in all his splendor was dressed like one of these. [30]If that is how God clothes the grass of the field, which is here today and tomorrow is thrown into the fire, will he not much more clothe you, O you of little faith? [31]So do not worry, saying, 'What shall we eat?' or 'What shall we drink?' or 'What shall we wear?' [32]For the pagans run after all these things, and your heavenly Father knows that you need them. [33]But seek first his kingdom and his righteousness, and all these things will be given to you as well. [34]Therefore do not worry about tomorrow, for tomorrow will worry about itself. Each day has enough trouble of its own."

MATTHEW 10:27-33 "What I tell you in the dark, speak in the daylight; what is whispered in your ear, proclaim from the roofs. [28]Do not be afraid of those who kill the body but cannot kill the soul. Rather, be afraid of the One who can destroy both soul and body in hell. [29]Are not two sparrows sold for a penny? Yet not one of them will fall to the ground apart from the will of your Father. [30]And even the very hairs of your head are all numbered. [31]So don't be afraid; you are worth more than many sparrows. [32]Whoever acknowledges me before men, I will also acknowledge him before my Father in heaven. [33]But whoever disowns me before men, I will disown him before my Father in heaven."

MATTHEW 12:9-13 Going on from that place, he went into their synagogue, [10]and a man with a shriveled hand was there. Looking for a reason to accuse Jesus, they asked him, "Is it lawful to heal on the Sabbath?" [11]He said to them, "If any of you has a sheep and it falls into a pit on the Sabbath, will you not take hold of it and lift it out? [12]How much more valuable is a man than a sheep! Therefore it is lawful to do good on the Sabbath." [13]Then he said to the man, "Stretch out your hand." So he stretched it out and it was completely restored, just as sound as the other. (See also Luke 6:6-10.)

MATTHEW 16:24-27 Then Jesus said to his disciples, "If anyone would come after me, he must deny himself and take up his cross and follow me. [25]For whoever wants to save his life will lose it, but whoever loses his life for me will find it. [26]What good will it be for a man if he gains the whole world, yet forfeits his soul? Or what can a man give in exchange for his soul? [27]For the Son of Man is going to come in his Father's glory with his angels, and then he will reward each person according to what he has done."

LUKE 12:4-7 "I tell you, my friends, do not be afraid of those who kill the body and after that can do no more. [5]But I will show you whom you should fear: Fear him who, after the killing of the body, has power to throw you into hell. Yes, I tell you, fear him. [6]Are not five sparrows sold for two pennies? Yet not one of them is forgotten by God. [7]Indeed, the very hairs of your head are all numbered. Don't be afraid; you are worth more than many sparrows."

LUKE 15:4-6 "Suppose one of you has a hundred sheep and loses one of them. Does he not leave the ninety-nine in the open country and go after the lost sheep until he finds it? [5]And when he finds it, he joyfully puts it on his shoulders [6]and goes home. Then he calls his friends and neighbors together and says, 'Rejoice with me; I have found my lost sheep.'"

LUKE 15:11-32 Jesus continued: "There was a man who had two sons. [12]The younger one said to his father, 'Father, give me my share of the estate.' So he divided his property between them. [13]Not long after that, the younger son got together all he had, set off for a distant country and there squandered his wealth in wild living. [14]After he had spent everything, there was a severe famine in that whole country, and he began to be in need. [15]So he went and hired himself out to a citizen of that country, who sent him to his fields to feed pigs. [16]He longed to fill his stomach with the pods that the pigs were eating, but no one gave him anything. [17]When he came to his senses, he said, 'How many of my father's hired men have food to spare, and here I am starving to death! [18]I will set out and go back to my father and say to him: Father, I have sinned against heaven and against you. [19]I am no longer worthy to be called your son; make me like one of your hired men.' [20]So he got up and went to his father. But while he was still a long way off, his father saw him and was filled with compassion for him; he ran to his son, threw his arms around him and kissed him. [21]The son said to him, 'Father, I have sinned against heaven and against you. I am no longer worthy to be called your son.' [22]But the father said to his servants, 'Quick! Bring the best robe and put it on him. Put a ring on his finger and sandals on his feet. [23]Bring the fattened calf and kill it. Let's have a feast and celebrate. [24]For this son of mine was dead and is alive again; he was lost and is found.' So they began to celebrate. [25]Meanwhile, the older son was in the field. When he came near the house, he heard music and dancing. [26]So he called one of the servants and asked him what was going on. [27]'Your brother has come,' he replied, 'and your father has killed the fattened calf because he has him back safe and sound.' [28]The older brother became angry and refused to go in. So his father went out and pleaded with him.

[29]But he answered his father, 'Look! All these years I've been slaving for you and never disobeyed your orders. Yet you never gave me even a young goat so I could celebrate with my friends. [30]But when this son of yours who has squandered your property with prostitutes comes home, you kill the fattened calf for him!' [31]'My son,' the father said, 'you are always with me, and everything I have is yours. [32]But we had to celebrate and be glad, because this brother of yours was dead and is alive again; he was lost and is found.' "

Luke 23:32-34, 39-43 Two other men, both criminals, were also led out with him to be executed. [33]When they came to the place called the Skull, there they crucified him, along with the criminals—one on his right, the other on his left. [34]Jesus said, "Father, forgive them, for they do not know what they are doing." And they divided up his clothes by casting lots. [39]One of the criminals who hung there hurled insults at him: "Aren't you the Christ? Save yourself and us!" [40]But the other criminal rebuked him. "Don't you fear God," he said, "since you are under the same sentence? [41]We are punished justly, for we are getting what our deeds deserve. But this man has done nothing wrong." [42]Then he said, "Jesus, remember me when you come into your kingdom." [43]Jesus answered him, "I tell you the truth, today you will be with me in paradise."

7

THE GREATEST WORDS
EVER SPOKEN ABOUT GOD
REACHING OUT TO US

What Jesus Said About God's Tireless Efforts to Save Humanity

It was five o'clock when Sharon told her seven-year-old daughter, Julie, to come in for dinner. Julie said she wanted to find their cat, so she set out on her bicycle. When she didn't return, Sharon went looking for her. Not far from their home, she found Julie's bike lying on the ground next to the body of their cat. Julie was nowhere to be seen.

Two days later Julie's body was found in the desert. The man who had abducted and murdered this precious little girl was later arrested, tried, and convicted. As I learned the details of the horrific crime, my heart was consumed with hatred. For a very long time, I could not forgive the man who committed this act of senseless violence.

If that had happened to *your* daughter, how much rage would you have felt? What vengeance would you have wanted to mete out? Be honest. Would you have considered reaching out to the murderer and offering forgiveness? Even more, would you have considered sacrificing the life of your child to save the life of such a murderer? As inconceivable as that sounds, it provides but a tiny glimpse of what God did for us.

God allowed those who hated Him to torture and kill His only Son so God could rescue the killers from the eternal punishment that they deserved—and that His righteousness and justice demanded. When you think about those who tortured and killed Jesus, don't picture Pontius Pilate, who ordered the execution, or the Roman guards who administered it. And don't concentrate on the religious leaders who demanded the execution or the angry mob that begged for Jesus' death. None of these people was truly responsible for Jesus' crucifixion.

When Pilate scolded Jesus for not answering his questions, he stated, "Do You not know that I have power to crucify You, and power to release You?" Jesus answered, "You could have no power at all against Me unless it had been given you from above" (John 19:10-11, NKJV). In other words, it was God the Father who was offering His perfect Son as a sacrifice for the sins of every person who disobeys God's will. And that includes all of us. God's holiness does not allow Him to embrace for eternity anyone whose soul is stained with sin. His uncompromising justice demands that all who have sinned must be kept separate from Him in eternal death. But God's love, mercy, and grace chose to provide the *only* perfect sacrifice, the one sacrifice that was sufficient to save men and women from their sins. He sacrificed His only begotten Son, Jesus, the Christ.

We can't comprehend the miracle of this act, because none of us views our sin for what it really is. None of us sees it the way God sees it. We violate God's commandments many times every day. We've created a debt of sin so great that, according to the Torah and the New Testament, no one could ever pay off his or her own debt. And without full payment being made, the rightful penalty comes into play, which is eternal separation from God.

That is why God sacrificed His only begotten Son: so our incalculable debt of sin could be paid in full. Because of Jesus' perfect sacrifice, we can be cleansed from our sin and receive eternal life. This is not only an expression of God's love for us; it's also an expression of Jesus' matchless love. He chose to obey His Father's will and lay down His life for us. In Mark 10:45 Jesus stated, "For even the Son of Man did not come to be served, but to serve, and to give His life a ransom for many" (NKJV).

In the topics covered in this chapter, we will examine Jesus' statements that reveal the depths of God's grace and mercy, as well as the kind of mercy God wants us to offer to others. But God's reaching out to us doesn't stop with the sacrifice of His Son. He not only sent His Son to save us from the consequences of our sin; He sent Jesus to *call* us to repentance and into a personal, intimate, and eternal relationship with Him. As you read His statements under the heading "The Call of Christ," you'll be amazed by the depth of Christ's love and the patience and tenderness with which He calls each of us to come to Him. Christianity isn't just about eternal issues; it's also about the issues that face us in everyday life. Under the heading "Blessings and Happiness," you'll see the incredible blessings that God promises to every person who embraces His values and receives the gift of His Son.

Acts Performed in Secret

MATTHEW 6:3-6 "But when you give to the needy, do not let your left hand know what your right hand is doing, ⁴so that your giving may be in secret. Then your Father, who sees what is done in secret, will reward you. ⁵And when you pray, do not be like the hypocrites, for they love to pray standing in the synagogues and on the street corners to be seen by men. I tell you the truth, they have received their reward in full. ⁶But when you pray, go into your room, close the door and pray to your Father, who is unseen. Then your Father, who sees what is done in secret, will reward you."

MATTHEW 6:17-18 "But when you fast, put oil on your head and wash your face, ¹⁸so that it will not be obvious to men that you are fasting, but only to your Father, who is unseen; and your Father, who sees what is done in secret, will reward you."

MARK 4:21-23 He said to them, "Do you bring in a lamp to put it under a bowl or a bed? Instead, don't you put it on its stand? ²²For whatever is hidden is meant to be disclosed, and whatever is concealed is meant to be brought out into the open. ²³If anyone has ears to hear, let him hear."

LUKE 8:17 "For there is nothing hidden that will not be disclosed, and nothing concealed that will not be known or brought out into the open."

LUKE 11:33 "No one lights a lamp and puts it in a place where it will be hidden, or under a bowl. Instead he puts it on its stand, so that those who come in may see the light."

Blessings and Happiness

MATTHEW 5:3-11 "Blessed are the poor in spirit, for theirs is the kingdom of heaven. ⁴Blessed are those who mourn, for they will be comforted. ⁵Blessed are the meek, for they will inherit the earth. ⁶Blessed are those who hunger and thirst for righteousness, for they will be filled. ⁷Blessed are the merciful, for they will be shown mercy. ⁸Blessed are the pure in heart, for they will see God. ⁹Blessed are the peacemakers, for they will be called sons of God. ¹⁰Blessed are those who are persecuted because of righteousness, for theirs is the kingdom of heaven. ¹¹Blessed are you when people insult you, persecute you and falsely say all kinds of evil against you because of me."

MATTHEW 11:6 "Blessed is the man who does not fall away on account of me."

LUKE 10:23-24 Then he turned to his disciples and said privately, "Blessed are the eyes that see what you see. [24]For I tell you that many prophets and kings wanted to see what you see but did not see it, and to hear what you hear but did not hear it."

LUKE 14:12-14 Then Jesus said to his host, "When you give a luncheon or dinner, do not invite your friends, your brothers or relatives, or your rich neighbors; if you do, they may invite you back and so you will be repaid. [13]But when you give a banquet, invite the poor, the crippled, the lame, the blind, [14]and you will be blessed. Although they cannot repay you, you will be repaid at the resurrection of the righteous."

LUKE 14:15-24 When one of those at the table with him heard this, he said to Jesus, "Blessed is the man who will eat at the feast in the kingdom of God." [16]Jesus replied: "A certain man was preparing a great banquet and invited many guests. [17]At the time of the banquet he sent his servant to tell those who had been invited, 'Come, for everything is now ready.' [18]But they all alike began to make excuses. The first said, 'I have just bought a field, and I must go and see it. Please excuse me.' [19]Another said, 'I have just bought five yoke of oxen, and I'm on my way to try them out. Please excuse me.' [20]Still another said, 'I just got married, so I can't come.' [21]The servant came back and reported this to his master. Then the owner of the house became angry and ordered his servant, 'Go out quickly into the streets and alleys of the town and bring in the poor, the crippled, the blind and the lame.' [22]'Sir,' the servant said, 'what you ordered has been done, but there is still room.' [23]Then the master told his servant, 'Go out to the roads and country lanes and make them come in, so that my house will be full. [24]I tell you, not one of those men who were invited will get a taste of my banquet.'"

The Call of Christ

JOHN 6:37-40 "All that the Father gives me will come to me, and whoever comes to me I will never drive away. [38]For I have come down from heaven not to do my will but to do the will of him who sent me. [39]And this is the will of him who sent me, that I shall lose none of all that he has given me, but raise them up at the last day. [40]For my Father's will is that everyone who looks to the Son and believes in him shall have eternal life, and I will raise him up at the last day."

JOHN 6:45-47 "It is written in the Prophets: 'They will all be taught by God.' Everyone who listens to the Father and learns from him comes to me. [46]No one has seen the Father except the one who is from God; only he has seen the Father. [47]I tell you the truth, he who believes has everlasting life."

JOHN 6:65 He went on to say, "This is why I told you that no one can come to me unless the Father has enabled him."

JOHN 7:37-40 On the last and greatest day of the Feast, Jesus stood and said in a loud voice, "If anyone is thirsty, let him come to me and drink. [38]Whoever believes in me, as the Scripture has said, streams of living water will flow from within him." [39]By this he meant the Spirit, whom those who believed in him were later to receive. Up to that time the Spirit had not been given, since Jesus had not yet been glorified. [40]On hearing his words, some of the people said, "Surely this man is the Prophet."

JOHN 8:31-32 Then Jesus said to those Jews who believed Him, "If you abide in My word, you are My disciples indeed. [32]And you shall know the truth, and the truth shall make you free." (NKJV)

JOHN 10:1-5 "I tell you the truth, the man who does not enter the sheep pen by the gate, but climbs in by some other way, is a thief and a robber. [2]The man who enters by the gate is the shepherd of his sheep. [3]The watchman opens the gate for him, and the sheep listen to his voice. He calls his own sheep by name and leads them out. [4]When he has brought out all his own, he goes on ahead of them, and his sheep follow him because they know his voice. [5]But they will never follow a stranger; in fact, they will run away from him because they do not recognize a stranger's voice."

JOHN 14:6 Jesus answered, "I am the way and the truth and the life. No one comes to the Father except through me."

JOHN 17:14-19 "I have given them your [God's] word and the world has hated them, for they are not of the world any more than I am of the world. [15]My prayer is not that you take them out of the world but that you protect them from the evil one. [16]They are not of the world, even as I am not of it. [17]Sanctify them by the truth; your word is truth. [18]As you sent me into the world, I have sent them into the world. [19]For them I sanctify myself, that they too may be truly sanctified."

JOHN 18:37 "You are a king, then!" said Pilate. Jesus answered, "You are right in saying I am a king. In fact, for this reason I was born, and for this I came into the world, to testify to the truth. Everyone on the side of truth listens to me."

MATTHEW 11:28-30 "Come to me, all you who are weary and burdened, and I will give you rest. [29]Take my yoke upon you and learn from me, for I am gentle and humble in heart, and you will find rest for your souls. [30]For my yoke is easy and my burden is light."

MATTHEW 16:23-27 Jesus turned and said to Peter, "Get behind me, Satan! You are a stumbling block to me; you do not have in mind the things of God, but the things of men." [24]Then Jesus said to his disciples, "If anyone would come after me, he must deny himself and take up his cross and follow me. [25]For whoever wants to save his life will lose it, but whoever loses his life for me will find it. [26]What good will it be for a man if he gains the whole world, yet forfeits his soul? Or what can a man give in exchange for his soul? [27]For the Son of Man is going to come in his Father's glory with his angels, and then he will reward each person according to what he has done."

MATTHEW 22:1-14 Jesus spoke to them again in parables, saying: [2]"The kingdom of heaven is like a king who prepared a wedding banquet for his son. [3]He sent his servants to those who had been invited to the banquet to tell them to come, but they refused to come. ⁴Then he sent some more servants and said, 'Tell those who have been invited that I have prepared my dinner: My oxen and fattened cattle have been butchered, and everything is ready. Come to the wedding banquet.' ⁵But they paid no attention and went off—one to his field, another to his business. ⁶The rest seized his servants, mistreated them and killed them. ⁷The king was enraged. He sent his army and destroyed those murderers and burned their city. ⁸Then he said to his servants, 'The wedding banquet is ready, but those I invited did not deserve to come. ⁹Go to the street corners and invite to the banquet anyone you find.' ¹⁰So the servants went out into the streets and gathered all the people they could find, both good and bad, and the wedding hall was filled with guests. ¹¹But when the king came in to see the guests, he noticed a man there who was not wearing wedding clothes. ¹²'Friend,' he asked, 'how did you get in here without wedding clothes?' The man was speechless. ¹³Then the king told the attendants, 'Tie him hand and foot, and throw him outside, into the darkness, where there will be weeping and gnashing of teeth.' ¹⁴For many are invited, but few are chosen."

MARK 8:34-38 Then he called the crowd to him along with his disciples and said: "If anyone would come after me, he must deny himself and take up his cross and follow me. ³⁵For whoever wants to save his life will lose it, but whoever loses his life for me and for the gospel will save it. ³⁶What good is it for a man to gain the whole world, yet forfeit his soul? ³⁷Or

what can a man give in exchange for his soul? ³⁸If anyone is ashamed of me and my words in this adulterous and sinful generation, the Son of Man will be ashamed of him when he comes in his Father's glory with the holy angels."

LUKE 6:46-49 "Why do you call me, 'Lord, Lord,' and do not do what I say? ⁴⁷I will show you what he is like who comes to me and hears my words and puts them into practice. ⁴⁸He is like a man building a house, who dug down deep and laid the foundation on rock. When a flood came, the torrent struck that house but could not shake it, because it was well built. ⁴⁹But the one who hears my words and does not put them into practice is like a man who built a house on the ground without a foundation. The moment the torrent struck that house, it collapsed and its destruction was complete."

LUKE 10:17-20 The seventy-two returned with joy and said, "Lord, even the demons submit to us in your name." ¹⁸He replied, "I saw Satan fall like lightning from heaven. ¹⁹I have given you authority to trample on snakes and scorpions and to overcome all the power of the enemy; nothing will harm you. ²⁰However, do not rejoice that the spirits submit to you, but rejoice that your names are written in heaven."

ACTS 10:11-15 He [Peter] saw heaven opened and something like a large sheet being let down to earth by its four corners. ¹²It contained all kinds of four-footed animals, as well as reptiles of the earth and birds of the air. ¹³Then a voice told him, "Get up, Peter. Kill and eat." ¹⁴"Surely not, Lord!" Peter replied. "I have never eaten anything impure or unclean." [15]The voice spoke to him a second time, "Do not call anything impure that God has made clean."

Eternal Laws

In this section, you will read Jesus' statements about God's eternal principles of life and the benefits of following those principles—as well as the consequences of ignoring them. As you discover these unchangeable principles, you will begin to identify the invisible chains that have held you captive to the problems that plague you. At the same time, Jesus' revelations in this section provide you with the means and power to cut the chains and become the joy-filled, victorious person that God created you to be.

MATTHEW 5:3-11 "Blessed are the poor in spirit, for theirs is the kingdom of heaven. [4]Blessed are those who mourn, for they will be comforted. [5]Blessed are the meek, for they will inherit the earth. [6]Blessed are those who hunger and thirst for righteousness, for they will be filled. [7]Blessed are the merciful, for they will be shown mercy. [8]Blessed are the pure in heart, for they will see God. [9]Blessed are the peacemakers, for they will be called sons of God. [10]Blessed are those who are persecuted because of righteousness, for theirs is the kingdom of heaven. [11]Blessed are you when people insult you, persecute you and falsely say all kinds of evil against you because of me."

MATTHEW 5:18-20 "I tell you the truth, until heaven and earth disappear, not the smallest letter, not the least stroke of a pen, will by any means disappear from the Law until everything is accomplished. [19]Anyone who breaks one of the least of these commandments and teaches others to do the same will be called least in the kingdom of heaven, but whoever practices and teaches these commands will be called great in the kingdom of heaven. [20]For I tell you that unless your righteousness surpasses that of the Pharisees and the teachers of the law, you will certainly not enter the kingdom of heaven."

MATTHEW 5:29-30 "If your right eye causes you to sin, gouge it out and throw it away. It is better for you to lose one part of your body than for your whole body to be thrown into hell. [30]And if your right hand causes you to sin, cut it off and throw it away. It is better for you to lose one part of your body than for your whole body to go into hell."

MATTHEW 6:6 "But when you pray, go into your room, close the door and pray to your Father, who is unseen. Then your Father, who sees what is done in secret, will reward you."

MATTHEW 6:14-15 "For if you forgive men when they sin against you, your heavenly Father will also forgive you. [15]But if you do not forgive men their sins, your Father will not forgive your sins."

MATTHEW 6:24 "No one can serve two masters. Either he will hate the one and love the other, or he will be devoted to the one and despise the other. You cannot serve both God and Money."

MATTHEW 6:31-34 "So do not worry, saying, 'What shall we eat?' or 'What shall we drink?' or 'What shall we wear?' ³²For the pagans run after all these things, and your heavenly Father knows that you need them. ³³But seek first his kingdom and his righteousness, and all these things will be given to you as well. ³⁴Therefore do not worry about tomorrow, for tomorrow will worry about itself. Each day has enough trouble of its own."

MATTHEW 7:1-2 "Do not judge, or you too will be judged. ²For in the same way you judge others, you will be judged, and with the measure you use, it will be measured to you."

MATTHEW 7:7-12 "Ask and it will be given to you; seek and you will find; knock and the door will be opened to you. ⁸For everyone who asks receives; he who seeks finds; and to him who knocks, the door will be opened. ⁹Which of you, if his son asks for bread, will give him a stone? ¹⁰Or if he asks for a fish, will give him a snake? ¹¹If you, then, though you are evil, know how to give good gifts to your children, how much more will your Father in heaven give good gifts to those who ask him! ¹²So in everything, do to others what you would have them do to you, for this sums up the Law and the Prophets."

MATTHEW 7:13-14 "Enter through the narrow gate. For wide is the gate and broad is the road that leads to destruction, and many enter through it. ¹⁴But small is the gate and narrow the road that leads to life, and only a few find it."

MATTHEW 7:17-20 "Likewise every good tree bears good fruit, but a bad tree bears bad fruit. ¹⁸A good tree cannot bear bad fruit, and a bad tree cannot bear good fruit. ¹⁹Every tree that does not bear good fruit is cut down and thrown into the fire. ²⁰Thus, by their fruit you will recognize them."

MATTHEW 7:21-27 "Not everyone who says to Me, 'Lord, Lord,' shall enter the kingdom of heaven, but he who does the will of My Father in heaven. ²²Many will say to Me in that day, 'Lord, Lord, have we not prophesied in Your name, cast out demons in Your name, and done many wonders in Your name?' ²³And then I will declare to them, 'I never knew you; depart from Me, you who practice lawlessness!' ²⁴Therefore whoever hears these sayings of Mine, and does them, I will liken him to a wise man who built his house on the rock: ²⁵and the rain descended, the floods came, and the winds blew and beat on that house; and it did not fall, for it was founded on the rock. ²⁶But everyone who hears these sayings of Mine, and does not do them, will be like a foolish man who built his house on the sand: ²⁷and the rain descended, the floods came, and the winds blew and beat on that house; and it fell. And great was its fall." (NKJV)

MARK 9:36-37 He took a little child and had him stand among them. Taking him in his arms, he said to them, ³⁷"Whoever welcomes one of these little children in my name welcomes me; and whoever welcomes me does not welcome me but the one who sent me."

MARK 9:43, 45, 47-48 "If your hand causes you to sin, cut it off. It is better for you to enter life maimed than with two hands to go into hell, where the fire never goes out. ⁴⁵And if your foot causes you to sin, cut it off. It is better for you to enter life crippled than to have two feet and be thrown into hell. ⁴⁷And if your eye causes you to sin, pluck it out. It is better for you to enter the kingdom of God with one eye than to have two eyes and be thrown into hell, [48]where 'their worm does not die, and the fire is not quenched.'"

MARK 10:29-31 "I tell you the truth," Jesus replied, "no one who has left home or brothers or sisters or mother or father or children or fields for me and the gospel [30]will fail to receive a hundred times as much in this present age (homes, brothers, sisters, mothers, children and fields—and with them, persecutions) and in the age to come, eternal life. [31]But many who are first will be last, and the last first."

MARK 10:42-45 Jesus called them together and said, "You know that those who are regarded as rulers of the Gentiles lord it over them, and their high officials exercise authority over them. [43]Not so with you. Instead, whoever wants to become great among you must be your servant, [44]and whoever wants to be first must be slave of all. [45]For even the Son of Man did not come to be served, but to serve, and to give his life as a ransom for many."

MARK 11:22-25 "Have faith in God," Jesus answered. [23]"I tell you the truth, if anyone says to this mountain, 'Go, throw yourself into the sea,' and does not doubt in his heart but believes that what he says will happen, it will be done for him. [24]Therefore I tell you, whatever you ask for in prayer, believe that you have received it, and it will be yours. [25]And when you stand praying, if you hold anything against anyone, forgive him, so that

your Father in heaven may forgive you your sins."

MARK 12:38-40 As he taught, Jesus said, "Watch out for the teachers of the law. They like to walk around in flowing robes and be greeted in the marketplaces, [39]and have the most important seats in the synagogues and the places of honor at banquets. [40]They devour widows' houses and for a show make lengthy prayers. Such men will be punished most severely."

MARK 12:42-44 But a poor widow came and put in two very small copper coins, worth only a fraction of a penny. [43]Calling his disciples to him, Jesus said, "I tell you the truth, this poor widow has put more into the treasury than all the others. [44]They all gave out of their wealth; but she, out of her poverty, put in everything—all she had to live on."

LUKE 20:46-47 "Beware of the teachers of the law. They like to walk around in flowing robes and love to be greeted in the marketplaces and have the most important seats in the synagogues and the places of honor at banquets. [47]They devour widows' houses and for a show make lengthy prayers. Such men will be punished most severely."

Freedom

JOHN 8:31-32 Then Jesus said to those Jews who believed Him, "If you abide in My word, you are My disciples indeed. [32]And you shall know the truth, and the truth shall make you free." (NKJV)

JOHN 8:34-36 Jesus replied, "I tell you the truth, everyone who sins is a slave to sin. [35]Now a slave has no permanent place in the family, but a son belongs to it forever. ³⁶So if the Son sets you free, you will be free indeed."

Grace and Mercy

JOHN 3:14-17 "Just as Moses lifted up the snake in the desert, so the Son of Man must be lifted up, ¹⁵that everyone who believes in him may have eternal life. ¹⁶For God so loved the world that he gave his one and only Son, that whoever believes in him shall not perish but have eternal life. ¹⁷For God did not send his Son into the world to condemn the world, but to save the world through him."

MATTHEW 5:3-9 "Blessed are the poor in spirit, for theirs is the kingdom of heaven. ⁴Blessed are those who mourn, for they will be comforted. ⁵Blessed are the meek, for they will inherit the earth. ⁶Blessed are those who hunger and thirst for righteousness, for they will be filled. ⁷Blessed are the merciful, for they will be shown mercy. ⁸Blessed are the pure in heart, for they will see God. ⁹Blessed are the peacemakers, for they will be called sons of God."

MATTHEW 7:7-12 "Ask and it will be given to you; seek and you will find; knock and the door will be opened to you. ⁸For everyone who asks receives; he who seeks finds; and to him who knocks, the door will be opened. ⁹Which of you, if his son asks for bread, will give him a stone? ¹⁰Or if he asks for a fish, will give him a snake? ¹¹If you, then, though you are evil, know how to give good gifts to your children, how much more will your Father in heaven give good gifts to those who ask

him! ¹²So in everything, do to others what you would have them do to you, for this sums up the Law and the Prophets."

MATTHEW 9:12-13 On hearing this, Jesus said, "It is not the healthy who need a doctor, but the sick. ¹³But go and learn what this means: 'I desire mercy, not sacrifice.' For I have not come to call the righteous, but sinners."

MATTHEW 12:3-8 He answered, "Haven't you read what David did when he and his companions were hungry? ⁴He entered the house of God, and he and his companions ate the consecrated bread— which was not lawful for them to do, but only for the priests. ⁵Or haven't you read in the Law that on the Sabbath the priests in the temple desecrate the day and yet are innocent? ⁶I tell you that one greater than the temple is here. ⁷If you had known what these words mean, 'I desire mercy, not sacrifice,' you would not have condemned the innocent. ⁸For the Son of Man is Lord of the Sabbath."

MATTHEW 18:12-14 "What do you think? If a man owns a hundred sheep, and one of them wanders away, will he not leave the ninety-nine on the hills and go to look for the one that wandered off? ¹³And if he finds it, I tell you the truth, he is happier about that one sheep than about the ninety-nine that did not wander off. ¹⁴In the same way your Father in heaven is not willing that any of these little ones should be lost."

MATTHEW 20:30-34 Two blind men were sitting by the roadside, and when they heard that Jesus was going by, they shouted, "Lord, Son of David, have mercy on us!" ³¹The crowd rebuked them and told them to be quiet, but they shouted all the louder, "Lord, Son of David, have mercy on us!" [32]Jesus stopped and called them. "What do you want me to do for you?" he asked. [33]"Lord," they answered, "we want our sight." [34]Jesus had compassion on them and touched their eyes. Immediately they received their sight and followed him.

MATTHEW 23:23-24 "Woe to you, teachers of the law and Pharisees, you hypocrites! You give a tenth of your spices—mint, dill and cummin. But you have neglected the more important matters of the law—justice, mercy and faithfulness. You should have practiced the latter, without neglecting the former. [24]You blind guides! You strain out a gnat but swallow a camel."

MARK 10:46-52 Then they came to Jericho. As Jesus and his disciples, together with a large crowd, were leaving the city, a blind man, Bartimaeus (that is, the Son of Timaeus), was sitting by the roadside begging. [47]When he heard that it was Jesus of Nazareth, he began to shout, "Jesus, Son of David, have mercy on me!" [48]Many rebuked him and told him to be quiet, but he shouted all the more, "Son of David, have mercy on me!" [49]Jesus stopped and said, "Call him." So they called to the blind man, "Cheer up! On your feet! He's calling you." [50]Throwing his cloak aside, he jumped to his feet and came to Jesus. [51]"What do you want me to do for you?" Jesus asked him. The blind man said, "Rabbi, I want to see." [52]"Go," said Jesus, "your faith has healed you." Immediately he received his sight and followed Jesus along the road.

LUKE 6:27-36 "But I tell you who hear me: Love your enemies, do good to those who hate you, [28]bless those who curse you, pray for those who mistreat you. [29]If someone strikes you on one cheek, turn to him the other also. If someone takes your cloak, do not stop him from taking your tunic. [30]Give to everyone who asks you, and if anyone takes what belongs to you, do not demand it back. [31]Do to others as you would have them do to you. [32]If you love those who love you, what credit is that to you? Even 'sinners' love those who love them. [33]And if you do good to those who are good to you, what credit is that to you? Even 'sinners' do that. [34]And if you lend to those from whom you expect repayment, what credit is that to you? Even 'sinners' lend to 'sinners,' expecting to be repaid in full. [35]But love your enemies, do good to them, and lend to them without expecting to get anything back. Then your reward will be great, and you will be sons of the Most High, because he is kind to the ungrateful and wicked. [36]Be merciful, just as your Father is merciful."

LUKE 15:4-7 "Suppose one of you has a hundred sheep and loses one of them. Does he not leave the ninety-nine in the open country and go after the lost sheep until he finds it? [5]And when he finds it, he joyfully puts it on his shoulders [6]and goes home. Then he calls his friends and neighbors together and says, 'Rejoice with me; I have found my lost sheep.' [7]I tell you that in the same way there will be more rejoicing in heaven over one sinner who repents than over ninety-nine righteous persons who do not need to repent."

LUKE 15:8-10 "Or suppose a woman has ten silver coins and loses one. Does she not light a lamp, sweep the house and search carefully until she finds it? [9]And when she finds it, she calls her friends and neighbors together and says, 'Rejoice with me; I have found my lost coin.' [10]In the same way, I tell you, there is rejoicing in the presence of the angels of God over one sinner who repents."

LUKE 15:11-32 Jesus continued: "There was a man who had two sons. [12]The younger one said to his father, 'Father, give me my share of the estate.' So he divided his property between them. [13]Not long after that, the younger son got together all he had, set off for a distant country and there squandered his wealth in wild living. [14]After he had spent everything, there was a severe famine in that whole country, and he began to be in need. [15]So he went and hired himself out to a citizen of that country, who sent him to his fields to feed pigs. [16]He longed to fill his stomach with the pods that the pigs were eating, but no one gave him anything. [17]When he came to his senses, he said, 'How many of my father's hired men have food to spare, and here I am starving to death! [18]I will set out and go back to my father and say to him: Father, I have sinned against heaven and against you. [19]I am no longer worthy to be called your son; make me like one of your hired men.' [20]So he got up and went to his father. But while he was still a long way off, his father saw him and was filled with compassion for him; he ran to his son, threw his arms around him and kissed him. [21]The son said to him, 'Father, I have sinned against heaven and against you. I am no longer worthy to be called your son.' [22]But the father said to his servants, 'Quick! Bring the best robe and put it on him. Put a ring on his finger and sandals on his feet. [23]Bring the fattened calf and kill it. Let's have a feast and celebrate. [24]For this son of mine was dead and is alive again; he was lost and is found.' So they began to celebrate. [25]Meanwhile, the older son was in the field. When he came near the house, he heard music and dancing. [26]So he called one of the servants and asked him what was going on. [27]'Your brother has come,' he replied, 'and your father has killed the fattened calf because he has him back safe and sound.' [28]The older brother became angry and refused to go in. So his father went out and pleaded with him. [29]But he answered his father, 'Look! All these years I've been slaving for you and never disobeyed your orders. Yet you never gave me even a young goat so I could celebrate with my friends. [30]But when this son of yours who has squandered your property with prostitutes comes home, you kill the fattened calf for him!' [31]'My son,' the father said, 'you are always with me, and everything I have is yours. [32]But we had to celebrate and be glad, because this brother of yours was dead and is alive again; he was lost and is found.'"

ACTS 10:11-15 He [Peter] saw heaven opened and something like a large sheet being let down to earth by its four corners. [12]It contained all kinds of four-footed animals, as well as reptiles of the earth and birds of the air. [13]Then a voice told him, "Get up, Peter. Kill and eat."

[14]"Surely not, Lord!" Peter replied. "I have never eaten anything impure or unclean." [15]The voice spoke to him a second time, "Do not call anything impure that God has made clean."

2 CORINTHIANS 12:7-9 To keep me [Paul] from becoming conceited because of these surpassingly great revelations, there was given me a thorn in my flesh, a messenger of Satan, to torment me. [8]Three times I pleaded with the Lord to take it away from me. [9]But he said to me, "My grace is sufficient for you, for my power is made perfect in weakness." Therefore I will boast all the more gladly about my weaknesses, so that Christ's power may rest on me.

Justification

JOHN 3:14-19 "Just as Moses lifted up the snake in the desert, so the Son of Man must be lifted up, [15]that everyone who believes in him may have eternal life. [16]For God so loved the world that he gave his one and only Son, that whoever believes in him shall not perish but have eternal life. [17]For God did not send his Son into the world to condemn the world, but to save the world through him. [18]Whoever believes in him is not condemned, but whoever does not believe stands condemned already because he has not believed in the name of God's one and only Son. [19]This is the verdict: Light has come into the world, but men loved darkness instead of light because their deeds were evil."

MATTHEW 12:33-37 "Make a tree good and its fruit will be good, or make a tree bad and its fruit will be bad, for a tree is recognized by its fruit. [34]You brood of vipers, how can you who are evil say anything good? For out of the overflow of the heart the mouth speaks. [35]The good man brings good things out of the good stored up in him, and the evil man brings evil things out of the evil stored up in him. [36]But I tell you that men will have to give account on the day of judgment for every careless word they have spoken. [37]For by your words you will be acquitted, and by your words you will be condemned."

LUKE 18:9-14 To some who were confident of their own righteousness and looked down on everybody else, Jesus told this parable: [10]"Two men went up to the temple to pray, one a Pharisee and the other a tax collector. [11]The Pharisee stood up and prayed about himself: 'God, I thank you that I am not like other men—robbers, evildoers, adulterers—or even like this tax collector. [12]I fast twice a week and give a tenth of all I get.' [13]But the tax collector stood at a distance. He would not even look up to heaven, but beat his breast and said, 'God, have mercy on me, a sinner.' [14]I tell you that this man, rather than the other, went home justified before God. For everyone who exalts himself will be humbled, and he who humbles himself will be exalted."

ACTS 10:11-15 He [Peter] saw heaven opened and something like a large sheet being let down to earth by its four corners. [12]It contained all kinds of four-footed animals, as well as reptiles of the earth and birds of the air. [13]Then a voice told him, "Get up, Peter. Kill and eat." [14]"Surely not, Lord!" Peter replied. "I have never eaten anything impure or unclean." [15]The voice spoke to him a second time, "Do not call anything impure that God has made clean."

The Laws of God

MATTHEW 5:17 "Do not think that I have come to abolish the Law or the Prophets; I have not come to abolish them but to fulfill them."

MATTHEW 5:19-20 "Anyone who breaks one of the least of these commandments and teaches others to do the same will be called least in the kingdom of heaven, but whoever practices and teaches these commands will be called great in the kingdom of heaven. [20]For I tell you that unless your righteousness surpasses that of the Pharisees and the teachers of the law, you will certainly not enter the kingdom of heaven."

MATTHEW 5:21-24 "You have heard that it was said to the people long ago, 'Do not murder, and anyone who murders will be subject to judgment.' [22]But I tell you that anyone who is angry with his brother will be subject to judgment. Again, anyone who says to his brother, 'Raca,' is answerable to the Sanhedrin. But anyone who says, 'You fool!' will be in danger of the fire of hell. [23]Therefore, if you are offering your gift at the altar and there remember that your brother has something against you, [24]leave your gift there in front of the altar. First go and be reconciled to your brother; then come and offer your gift."

MATTHEW 5:27-30 "You have heard that it was said, 'Do not commit adultery.' [28]But I tell you that anyone who looks at a woman lustfully has already committed adultery with her in his heart. [29]If your right eye causes you to sin, gouge it out and throw it away. It is better for you to lose one part of your body than for your whole body to be thrown into hell. [30]And if your right hand causes you to sin, cut it off and throw it away. It is better for you to lose one part of your body than for your whole body to go into hell."

MATTHEW 5:31-32 "It has been said, 'Anyone who divorces his wife must give her a certificate of divorce.' [32]But I tell you that anyone who divorces his wife, except for marital unfaithfulness, causes her to become an adulteress, and anyone who marries the divorced woman commits adultery."

MATTHEW 5:38-48 "You have heard that it was said, 'Eye for eye, and tooth for tooth.' [39]But I tell you, Do not resist an evil person. If someone strikes you on the right cheek, turn to him the other also. [40]And if someone wants to sue you and take your tunic, let him have your cloak as well. [41]If someone forces you to go one mile, go with him two miles. [42]Give to the one who asks you, and do not turn away from the one who wants to borrow from you. [43]You have heard that it was said, 'Love your neighbor and hate your enemy.' [44]But I tell you: Love your enemies and pray for those who persecute you, [45]that you may be sons of your Father in heaven. He causes his sun to rise on the evil and the good, and sends rain on the righteous and the unrighteous. [46]If you love those who love you, what reward will you get? Are not even the tax collectors doing that? ⁴⁷And if you greet only your brothers, what are you doing more than others? Do not even pagans do that? ⁴⁸Be perfect, therefore, as your heavenly Father is perfect."

MATTHEW 15:3-9 Jesus replied, "And why do you break the command of God for the sake of your tradition? ⁴For God said, 'Honor your father and mother' and 'Anyone who curses his father or mother must be put to death.' ⁵But you say that if a man says to his father or mother, 'Whatever help you might otherwise have received from me is a gift devoted to God,' ⁶he is not to 'honor his father' with it. Thus you nullify the word of God for the sake of your tradition. ⁷You hypocrites! Isaiah was right when he prophesied about you: ⁸'These people honor me with their lips, but their hearts are far from me. ⁹They worship me in vain; their teachings are but rules taught by men.'"

MATTHEW 19:17-21 "Why do you ask me about what is good?" Jesus replied. "There is only One who is good. If you want to enter life, obey the commandments." ¹⁸"Which ones?" the man inquired. Jesus replied, "'Do not murder, do not commit adultery, do not steal, do not give false testimony, ¹⁹honor your father and mother,' and 'love your neighbor as yourself.'" ²⁰"All these I have kept," the young man said. "What do I still lack?" ²¹Jesus answered, "If you want to be perfect, go, sell your possessions and give to the poor, and you will have treasure in heaven. Then come, follow me." (See also Luke 18:19-22.)

MATTHEW 22:37-40 Jesus replied:

"'Love the Lord your God with all your heart and with all your soul and with all your mind.' ³⁸This is the first and greatest commandment. ³⁹And the second is like it: 'Love your neighbor as yourself.' ⁴⁰All the Law and the Prophets hang on these two commandments."

MARK 2:24-28 The Pharisees said to him, "Look, why are they doing what is unlawful on the Sabbath?" ²⁵He answered, "Have you never read what David did when he and his companions were hungry and in need? ²⁶In the days of Abiathar the high priest, he entered the house of God and ate the consecrated bread, which is lawful only for priests to eat. And he also gave some to his companions." ²⁷Then he said to them, "The Sabbath was made for man, not man for the Sabbath. ²⁸So the Son of Man is Lord even of the Sabbath."

MARK 3:4 Then Jesus asked them, "Which is lawful on the Sabbath: to do good or to do evil, to save life or to kill?" But they remained silent.

MARK 7:6-7 He replied, "Isaiah was right when he prophesied about you hypocrites; as it is written: 'These people honor me with their lips, but their hearts are far from me. ⁷They worship me in vain; their teachings are but rules taught by men.'"

MARK 7:8-13 "You have let go of the commands of God and are holding on to the traditions of men." ⁹And he said to them: "You have a fine way of setting aside the commands of God in order to observe your own traditions! ¹⁰For Moses said, 'Honor your father and your mother,' and, 'Anyone who curses his father or mother must be put to death.' ¹¹But you say that if a man says to his father or mother: 'Whatever help you might otherwise have received from me is Corban' (that is, a gift devoted to God), ¹²then you no longer let him do anything for his father or mother. ¹³Thus you nullify the word of God by your tradition that you have handed down. And you do many things like that."

MARK 8:34-38 Then he called the crowd to him along with his disciples and said: "If anyone would come after me, he must deny himself and take up his cross and follow me. ³⁵For whoever wants to save his life will lose it, but whoever loses his life for me and for the gospel will save it. ³⁶What good is it for a man to gain the whole world, yet forfeit his soul? ³⁷Or what can a man give in exchange for his soul? ³⁸If anyone is ashamed of me and my words in this adulterous and sinful generation, the Son of Man will be ashamed of him when he comes in his Father's glory with the holy angels."

MARK 10:18-21 "Why do you call me good?" Jesus answered. "No one is good—except God alone. ¹⁹You know the commandments: 'Do not murder, do not commit adultery, do not steal, do not give false testimony, do not defraud, honor your father and mother.'" ²⁰"Teacher," he declared, "all these I have kept since I was a boy." ²¹Jesus looked at him and loved him. "One thing you lack," he said. "Go, sell everything you have and give to the poor, and you will have treasure in heaven. Then come, follow me."

MARK 12:28-31 One of the teachers of the law came and heard them [Jesus and the Sadducees] debating. Noticing that Jesus had given them a good answer, he asked him, "Of all the commandments, which is the most important?" ²⁹"The most important one," answered Jesus, "is this: 'Hear, O Israel, the Lord our God, the Lord is one. ³⁰Love the Lord your God with all your heart and with all your soul and with all your mind and with all your strength.' ³¹The second is this: 'Love your neighbor as yourself.' There is no commandment greater than these."

LUKE 4:8, 12 Jesus answered, "It is written: 'Worship the Lord your God and serve him only.'" ¹²Jesus answered, "It says: 'Do not put the Lord your God to the test.'" (See also Matthew 4:7, 10.)

LUKE 10:25-37 On one occasion an expert in the law stood up to test Jesus. "Teacher," he asked, "what must I do to inherit eternal life?" ²⁶"What is written in the Law?" he replied. "How do you read it?" ²⁷He answered: "'Love the Lord your God with all your heart and with all your soul and with all your strength and with all your mind'; and, 'Love your neighbor as yourself.'" ²⁸"You have answered correctly," Jesus replied. "Do this and you will live." ²⁹But he wanted to justify himself, so he asked Jesus, "And who is my neighbor?" ³⁰In reply Jesus said: "A man was going down from Jerusalem to Jericho, when he fell into the hands of robbers. They stripped him of his clothes, beat him and went away, leaving him half dead. ³¹A priest happened to be going down the same road, and when he saw the man, he passed by on the other side. ³²So too, a Levite, when he came to the place and saw him, passed by on the other side.

[33]But a Samaritan, as he traveled, came where the man was; and when he saw him, he took pity on him. [34]He went to him and bandaged his wounds, pouring on oil and wine. Then he put the man on his own donkey, took him to an inn and took care of him. [35]The next day he took out two silver coins and gave them to the innkeeper. 'Look after him,' he said, 'and when I return, I will reimburse you for any extra expense you may have.' [36]Which of these three do you think was a neighbor to the man who fell into the hands of robbers?" [37]The expert in the law replied, "The one who had mercy on him." Jesus told him, "Go and do likewise."

LUKE 16:16 "The Law and the Prophets were proclaimed until John. Since that time, the good news of the kingdom of God is being preached, and everyone is forcing his way into it."

LUKE 16:17 "It is easier for heaven and earth to disappear than for the least stroke of a pen to drop out of the Law."

LUKE 24:44 He said to them, "This is what I told you while I was still with you: Everything must be fulfilled that is written about me in the Law of Moses, the Prophets and the Psalms."

Prophesied Events and Fulfilled Prophecy

JOHN 1:47-51 When Jesus saw Nathanael approaching, he said of him, "Here is a true Israelite, in whom there is nothing false." [48]"How do you know me?" Nathanael asked. Jesus answered, "I saw you while you were still under the fig tree before Philip called you." [49]Then Nathanael declared, "Rabbi, you are the Son of God; you are the King of Israel." [50]Jesus said, "You believe because I told you I saw you under the fig tree. You shall see greater things than that." [51]He then added, "I tell you the truth, you shall see heaven open, and the angels of God ascending and descending on the Son of Man."

JOHN 2:14-19 In the temple courts he found men selling cattle, sheep and doves, and others sitting at tables exchanging money. [15]So he made a whip out of cords, and drove all from the temple area, both sheep and cattle; he scattered the coins of the money changers and overturned their tables. [16]To those who sold doves he said, "Get these out of here! How dare you turn my Father's house into a market!" [17]His disciples remembered that it is written: "Zeal for your house will consume me." [18]Then the Jews demanded of him, "What miraculous sign can you show us to prove your authority to do all this?" [19]Jesus answered them, "Destroy this temple, and I will raise it again in three days."

JOHN 4:15-19 The woman [at the well] said to him, "Sir, give me this water so that I won't get thirsty and have to keep coming here to draw water." [16]He told her, "Go, call your husband and come back." [17]"I have no husband," she replied. Jesus said to her, "You are right when you say you have no husband. [18]The fact is, you have had five husbands, and the man you now have is not your husband. What you have just said is quite true." [19]"Sir," the woman said, "I can see that you are a prophet."

JOHN 13:21-28 After he had said this, Jesus was troubled in spirit and testified, "I tell you the truth, one of you is going to betray me." [22]His disciples stared at one another, at a loss to know which of them he meant. [23]One of them, the disciple whom Jesus loved, was reclining next to him. [24]Simon Peter motioned to this disciple and said, "Ask him which one he means." [25]Leaning back against Jesus, he asked him, "Lord, who is it?" [26]Jesus answered, "It is the one to whom I will give this piece of bread when I have dipped it in the dish." Then, dipping the piece of bread, he gave it to Judas Iscariot, son of Simon. [27]As soon as Judas took the bread, Satan entered into him. "What you are about to do, do quickly," Jesus told him, [28]but no one at the meal understood why Jesus said this to him.

JOHN 16:17-18 Some of his disciples said to one another, "What does he mean by saying, 'In a little while you will see me no more, and then after a little while you will see me,' and 'Because I am going to the Father'?" [18]They kept asking, "What does he mean by 'a little while'? We don't understand what he is saying."

JOHN 18:3-9 So Judas came to the grove, guiding a detachment of soldiers and some officials from the chief priests and Pharisees. They were carrying torches, lanterns and weapons. [4]Jesus, knowing all that was going to happen to him, went out and asked them, "Who is it you want?" [5]"Jesus of Nazareth," they replied. "I am he," Jesus said. (And Judas the traitor was standing there with them.) [6]When Jesus said, "I am he," they drew back and fell to the ground. [7]Again he asked them, "Who is it you want?" And they said, "Jesus of Nazareth." [8]"I told you that I am he," Jesus answered. "If you are looking for me, then let these men go." [9]This happened so that the words he had spoken would be fulfilled: "I have not lost one of those you gave me."

MATTHEW 3:13-16 Then Jesus came from Galilee to the Jordan to be baptized by John. [14]But John tried to deter him, saying, "I need to be baptized by you, and do you come to me?" [15]Jesus replied, "Let it be so now; it is proper for us to do this to fulfill all righteousness." Then John consented. [16]As soon as Jesus was baptized, he went up out of the water. At that moment heaven was opened, and he saw the Spirit of God descending like a dove and lighting on him.

MATTHEW 11:11-15 "I tell you the truth: Among those born of women there has not risen anyone greater than John the Baptist; yet he who is least in the kingdom of heaven is greater than he. [12]From the days of John the Baptist until now, the kingdom of heaven has been forcefully advancing, and forceful men lay hold of it. [13]For all the Prophets and the Law prophesied until John. [14]And if you are willing to accept it, he is the Elijah who was to come. [15]He who has ears, let him hear."

MATTHEW 24:2-29 "Do you see all these things?" he asked. "I tell you the truth, not one stone here will be left on another; every one will be thrown down." [3]As Jesus was sitting on the Mount of Olives, the disciples came to him privately. "Tell us," they said, "when will this happen, and what will be the sign of your coming and of the end of the age?" [4]Jesus answered: "Watch out that no one deceives you. [5]For many will come in my name, claiming, 'I am the Christ,' and will deceive many. [6]You will hear of wars and rumors of wars, but see to it that you are not alarmed. Such things must happen, but the end is still to come. [7]Nation will rise against nation, and kingdom against kingdom. There will be famines and earthquakes in various places. [8]All these are the beginning of birth pains. [9]Then you will be handed over to be persecuted and put to death, and you will be hated by all nations because of me. [10]At that time many will turn away from the faith and will betray and hate each other, [11]and many false prophets will appear and deceive many people. [12]Because of the increase of wickedness, the love of most will grow cold, [13]but he who stands firm to the end will be saved. [14]And this gospel of the kingdom will be preached in the whole world as a testimony to all nations, and then the end will come. [15]So when you see standing in the holy place 'the abomination that causes desolation,' spoken of through the prophet Daniel—let the reader understand— [16]then let those who are in Judea flee to the mountains. [17]Let no one on the roof of his house go down to take anything out of the house. [18]Let no one in the field go back to get his cloak. [19]How dreadful it will be in those days for pregnant women and nursing mothers! [20]Pray that your flight will not take place in winter or on the Sabbath. [21]For then there will be great distress, unequaled from the beginning of the world until now—and never to be equaled again. [22]If those days had not been cut short, no one would survive, but for the sake of the elect those days will be shortened. [23]At that time if anyone says to you, 'Look, here is the Christ!' or, 'There he is!' do not believe it. [24]For false Christs and false prophets will appear and perform great signs and miracles to deceive even the elect—if that were possible. [25]See, I have told you ahead of time. [26]So if anyone tells you, 'There he is, out in the desert,' do not go out; or, 'Here he is, in the inner rooms,' do not believe it. [27]For as lightning that comes from the east is visible even in the west, so will be the coming of the Son of Man. [28]Wherever there is a carcass, there the vultures will gather. [29]Immediately after the distress of those days 'the sun will be darkened, and the moon will not give its light; the stars will fall from the sky, and the heavenly bodies will be shaken.' "

MATTHEW 26:1-4 When Jesus had finished saying all these things, he said to his disciples, [2]"As you know, the Passover is two days away—and the Son of Man will be handed over to be crucified." [3]Then the chief priests and the elders of the people assembled in the palace of the high priest, whose name was Caiaphas, [4]and they plotted to arrest Jesus in some sly way and kill him.

MATTHEW 26:17-25 On the first day of the Feast of Unleavened Bread, the disciples came to Jesus and asked, "Where do you want us to make preparations for you to eat the Passover?" [18]He replied, "Go into the city to a certain man and tell him, 'The Teacher says: My appointed time is near. I am going to celebrate the

Passover with my disciples at your house.'" [19]So the disciples did as Jesus had directed them and prepared the Passover. [20]When evening came, Jesus was reclining at the table with the Twelve. [21]And while they were eating, he said, "I tell you the truth, one of you will betray me." [22]They were very sad and began to say to him one after the other, "Surely not I, Lord?" [23]Jesus replied, "The one who has dipped his hand into the bowl with me will betray me. [24]The Son of Man will go just as it is written about him. But woe to that man who betrays the Son of Man! It would be better for him if he had not been born." [25]Then Judas, the one who would betray him, said, "Surely not I, Rabbi?" Jesus answered, "Yes, it is you."

MATTHEW 26:50-54 Jesus replied, "Friend [Judas], do what you came for." Then the men stepped forward, seized Jesus and arrested him. [51]With that, one of Jesus' companions reached for his sword, drew it out and struck the servant of the high priest, cutting off his ear. [52]"Put your sword back in its place," Jesus said to him, "for all who draw the sword will die by the sword. [53]Do you think I cannot call on my Father, and he will at once put at my disposal more than twelve legions of angels? [54]But how then would the Scriptures be fulfilled that say it must happen in this way?"

MATTHEW 26:55-56 At that time Jesus said to the crowd, "Am I leading a rebellion, that you have come out with swords and clubs to capture me? Every day I sat in the temple courts teaching, and you did not arrest me. [56]But this has all taken place that the writings of the

prophets might be fulfilled." Then all the disciples deserted him and fled.

MATTHEW 26:69-70, 74-75 Now Peter was sitting out in the courtyard, and a servant girl came to him. "You also were with Jesus of Galilee," she said. [70]But he denied it before them all. "I don't know what you're talking about," he said. [74]Then he began to call down curses on himself and he swore to them, "I don't know the man!" Immediately a rooster crowed. [75]Then Peter remembered the word Jesus had spoken: "Before the rooster crows, you will disown me three times." And he went outside and wept bitterly. (See also Mark 14:66-72; Luke 22:55-62.)

MARK 11:1-3 As they approached Jerusalem and came to Bethphage and Bethany at the Mount of Olives, Jesus sent two of his disciples, [2]saying to them, "Go to the village ahead of you, and just as you enter it, you will find a colt tied there, which no one has ever ridden. Untie it and bring it here. [3]If anyone asks you, 'Why are you doing this?' tell him, 'The Lord needs it and will send it back here shortly.'" (See also Matthew 21:1-3; Luke 19:29-31.)

MARK 13:2-27 "Do you see all these great buildings?" replied Jesus. "Not one stone here will be left on another; every one will be thrown down." [3]As Jesus was sitting on the Mount of Olives opposite the temple, Peter, James, John and Andrew asked him privately, [4]"Tell us, when will these things happen? And what will be the sign that they are all about to be fulfilled?" [5]Jesus said to them: "Watch out that no one deceives you. [6]Many will come in my name, claiming, 'I am he,' and will deceive many. [7]When you hear of wars and rumors of wars, do not be alarmed. Such things must happen, but the end is still to come. [8]Nation will rise against nation, and kingdom against kingdom. There will be earthquakes in various places, and famines. These are the beginning of birth pains. [9]You must be on your guard. You will be handed over to the local councils and flogged in the synagogues. On account of me you will stand before governors and kings as witnesses to them. [10]And the gospel must first be preached to all nations. [11]Whenever you are arrested and brought to trial, do not worry beforehand about what to say. Just say whatever is given you at the time, for it is not you speaking, but the Holy Spirit. [12]Brother will betray brother to death, and a father his child. Children will rebel against their parents and have them put to death. [13]All men will hate you because of me, but he who stands firm to the end will be saved. [14]When you see 'the abomination that causes desolation' standing where it does not belong—let the reader understand—then let those who are in Judea flee to the mountains. [15]Let no one on the roof of his house go down or enter the house to take anything out. [16]Let no one in the field go back to get his cloak. [17]How dreadful it will be in those days for pregnant women and nursing mothers! [18]Pray that this will not take place in winter, [19]because those will be days of distress unequaled from the beginning, when God created the world, until now—and never to be equaled again. [20]If the Lord had not cut short those days, no one would survive. But for

the sake of the elect, whom he has chosen, he has shortened them. [21]At that time if anyone says to you, 'Look, here is the Christ!' or, 'Look, there he is!' do not believe it. [22]For false Christs and false prophets will appear and perform signs and miracles to deceive the elect—if that were possible. [23]So be on your guard; I have told you everything ahead of time. [24]But in those days, following that distress, 'the sun will be darkened, and the moon will not give its light; [25]the stars will fall from the sky, and the heavenly bodies will be shaken.' [26]At that time men will see the Son of Man coming in clouds with great power and glory. [27]And he will send his angels and gather his elect from the four winds, from the ends of the earth to the ends of the heavens."

MARK 14:12-16 On the first day of the Feast of Unleavened Bread, when it was customary to sacrifice the Passover lamb, Jesus' disciples asked him, "Where do you want us to go and make preparations for you to eat the Passover?" [13]So he sent two of his disciples, telling them, "Go into the city, and a man carrying a jar of water will meet you. Follow him. [14]Say to the owner of the house he enters, 'The Teacher asks: Where is my guest room, where I may eat the Passover with my disciples?' [15]He will show you a large upper room, furnished and ready. Make preparations for us there." [16]The disciples left, went into the city and found things just as Jesus had told them. So they prepared the Passover.

MARK 14:17-21 When evening came, Jesus arrived with the Twelve. [18]While they were reclining at the table eating, he said, "I tell you the truth, one of you will betray me—one who is eating with me." [19]They were saddened, and one by one they said to him, "Surely not I?" [20]"It is one of the Twelve," he replied, "one who dips bread into the bowl with me. [21]The Son of Man will go just as it is written about him. But woe to that man who betrays the Son of Man! It would be better for him if he had not been born."

MARK 14:27-30 "You will all fall away," Jesus told them, "for it is written: 'I will strike the shepherd, and the sheep will be scattered.' [28]But after I have risen, I will go ahead of you into Galilee." [29]Peter declared, "Even if all fall away, I will not." [30]"I tell you the truth," Jesus answered, "today—yes, tonight—before the rooster crows twice you yourself will disown me three times." (See also Matthew 26:31-34; John 13:37-38.)

LUKE 12:54-56 He said to the crowd: "When you see a cloud rising in the west, immediately you say, 'It's going to rain,' and it does. [55]And when the south wind blows, you say, 'It's going to be hot,' and it is. [56]Hypocrites! You know how to interpret the appearance of the earth and the sky. How is it that you don't know how to interpret this present time?"

LUKE 17:30-35, 37 "It will be just like this on the day the Son of Man is revealed. [31]On that day no one who is on the roof of his house, with his goods inside, should go down to get them. Likewise, no one in the field should go back for anything. [32]Remember Lot's wife! [33]Whoever tries to keep his life will lose it, and whoever loses his life will preserve it. [34]I tell you, on that night two people will be in one bed; one will be taken and the other left. [35]Two women will be grinding grain together; one will be taken and the other left." [37]"Where, Lord?" they asked. He replied, "Where there is a dead body, there the vultures will gather."

LUKE 21:6-28 "As for what you see here, the time will come when not one stone will be left on another; every one of them will be thrown down." [7]"Teacher," they asked, "when will these things happen? And what will be the sign that they are about to take place?" [8]He replied: "Watch out that you are not deceived. For many will come in my name, claiming, 'I am he,' and, 'The time is near.' Do not follow them. [9]When you hear of wars and revolutions, do not be frightened. These things must happen first, but the end will not come right away." [10]Then he said to them: "Nation will rise against nation, and kingdom against kingdom. [11]There will be great earthquakes, famines and pestilences in various places, and fearful events and great signs from heaven. [12]But before all this, they will lay hands on you and persecute you. They will deliver you to synagogues and prisons, and you will be brought before kings and governors, and all on account of my name. [13]This will result in your being witnesses to them. [14]But make up your mind not to worry beforehand how you will defend yourselves. [15]For I will give you words and wisdom that none of your adversaries will be able to resist or contradict. [16]You will be betrayed even by parents, brothers, relatives and friends, and they will put some of you to death. [17]All men will hate you because of me. [18]But not a hair of your head will perish. [19]By standing firm you will gain life. [20]When you see Jerusalem being surrounded by armies, you will know that its desolation is near. [21]Then let those who are in Judea flee to the mountains, let those in the city get out, and let those in the country not enter the city. [22]For this is the time of punishment in fulfillment of all that has been written. [23]How dreadful it will be in those days for pregnant women and nursing mothers! There will be great distress in the land and wrath against this people. [24]They will fall by the sword and will be taken as prisoners to all the nations. Jerusalem will be trampled on by the Gentiles until the times of the Gentiles are fulfilled. [25]There will be signs in the sun, moon and stars. On the earth, nations will be in anguish and perplexity at the roaring and tossing of the sea. [26]Men will faint from terror, apprehensive of what is coming on the world, for the heavenly bodies will be shaken. [27]At that time they will see the Son of Man coming in a cloud with power and great glory. [28]When these things begin to take place, stand up and lift up your heads, because your redemption is drawing near."

LUKE 22:7-16 Then came the day of Unleavened Bread on which the Passover lamb had to be sacrificed. [8]Jesus sent Peter and John, saying, "Go and make preparations for us to eat the Passover." [9]"Where do you want us to prepare for it?" they asked. [10]He replied, "As you enter the city, a man carrying a jar of water will meet you. Follow him to the house that he enters, [11]and say to the owner of the house, 'The Teacher asks: Where is the guest room, where I may eat the Passover with my disciples?' [12]He will show you a large upper room, all furnished. Make preparations there." [13]They left and found things just as Jesus had told them. So they prepared the Passover. [14]When the hour came, Jesus and his apostles reclined at the table. [15]And he said to them, "I have eagerly desired to eat this Passover with you before I suffer. [16]For I tell you, I will not eat it again until it finds fulfillment in the kingdom of God."

LUKE 22:20-22 In the same way, after the supper he took the cup, saying, "This cup is the new covenant in my blood, which is poured out for you. [21]But the hand of him who is going to betray me is with mine on the table. [22]The Son of Man will go as it has been decreed, but woe to that man who betrays him."

LUKE 22:31-34 "Simon, Simon, Satan has asked to sift you as wheat. [32]But I have prayed for you, Simon, that your faith may not fail. And when you have turned back, strengthen your brothers." [33]But he replied, "Lord, I am ready to go with you to prison and to death." [34]Jesus answered, "I tell you, Peter, before the rooster crows today, you will deny three times that you know me."

LUKE 22:35-38 Then Jesus asked them, "When I sent you without purse, bag or sandals, did you lack anything?" "Nothing," they answered. [36]He said to them, "But now if you have a purse, take it, and also a bag; and if you don't have a sword, sell your cloak and buy one. [37]It is written: 'And he was numbered with the transgressors'; and I tell you that this must be fulfilled in me. Yes, what is written about me is reaching its fulfillment." [38]The disciples said, "See, Lord, here are two swords." "That is enough," he replied.

LUKE 22:52-53 Then Jesus said to the chief priests, the officers of the temple guard, and the elders, who had come for him, "Am I leading a rebellion, that you have come with swords and clubs? [53]Every day I was with you in the temple courts, and you did not lay a hand on me. But this is your hour—when darkness reigns."

LUKE 23:26-31 As they led him away, they seized Simon from Cyrene, who was on his way in from the country, and put the cross on him and made him carry it behind Jesus. [27]A large number of people followed him, including women who mourned and wailed for him. [28]Jesus turned and said to them, "Daughters of Jerusalem, do not weep for me; weep for yourselves and for your children. [29]For the time will come when you will say, 'Blessed are the barren women, the wombs that never bore and the breasts that never nursed!' [30]Then 'they will say to the mountains, "Fall on us!" and to the hills, "Cover us!"' [31]For if men do these things when the tree is green, what will happen when it is dry?"

LUKE 24:15-27 As they talked and discussed these things with each other, Jesus himself came up and walked along with them; [16]but they were kept from recognizing him. [17]He asked them, "What are you discussing together as you walk along?" They stood still, their faces downcast. [18]One of them, named Cleopas, asked him, "Are you only a visitor to Jerusalem and do not know the things that have happened there in these days?"

[19]"What things?" he asked. "About Jesus of Nazareth," they replied. "He was a prophet, powerful in word and deed before God and all the people. [20]The chief priests and our rulers handed him over to be sentenced to death, and they crucified him; [21]but we had hoped that he was the one who was going to redeem Israel. And what is more, it is the third day since all this took place. [22]In addition, some of our women amazed us. They went to the tomb early this morning [23]but didn't find his body. They came and told us that they had seen a vision of angels, who said he was alive. [24]Then some of our companions went to the tomb and found it just as the women had said, but him they did not see." [25]He said to them, "How foolish you are, and how slow of heart to believe all that the prophets have spoken! [26]Did not the Christ have to suffer these things and then enter his glory?" [27]And beginning with Moses and all the Prophets, he explained to them what was said in all the Scriptures concerning himself.

ACTS 22:17-21 "When I [Paul] returned to Jerusalem and was praying at the temple, I fell into a trance [18]and saw the Lord speaking. 'Quick!' he said to me. 'Leave Jerusalem immediately, because they will not accept your testimony about me.' [19]'Lord,' I replied, 'these men know that I went from one synagogue to another to imprison and beat those who believe in you. [20]And when the blood of your martyr Stephen was shed, I stood there giving my approval and guarding the clothes of those who were killing him.' [21]Then the Lord said to me, 'Go; I will send you far away to the Gentiles.'"

REVELATION 1:10-11, 17-20 On the Lord's Day I [John] was in the Spirit, and I heard behind me a loud voice like a trumpet, [11]which said: "Write on a scroll what you see and send it to the seven churches: to Ephesus, Smyrna, Pergamum, Thyatira, Sardis, Philadelphia and Laodicea." [17]When I saw him, I fell at his feet as though dead. Then he placed his right hand on me and said: "Do not be afraid. I am the First and the Last. [18]I am the Living One; I was dead, and behold I am alive for ever and ever! And I hold the keys of death and Hades. [19]Write, therefore, what you have seen, what is now and what will take place later. [20]The mystery of the seven stars that you saw in my right hand and of the seven golden lampstands is this: The seven stars are the angels of the seven churches, and the seven lampstands are the seven churches."

REVELATION 22:15-16 "Outside are the dogs, those who practice magic arts, the sexually immoral, the murderers, the idolaters and everyone who loves and practices falsehood. [16]I, Jesus, have sent my angel to give you this testimony for the churches. I am the Root and the Offspring of David, and the bright Morning Star."

The Sabbath

JOHN 5:16-17 So, because Jesus was doing these things on the Sabbath, the Jews persecuted him. [17]Jesus said to them, "My Father is always at his work to this very day, and I, too, am working."

JOHN 7:21-24 Jesus said to them, "I did one miracle, and you are all astonished. [22]Yet, because Moses gave you circumcision (though actually it did not come from Moses, but from the patriarchs), you circumcise a child on the Sabbath. [23]Now if a child can be circumcised on the Sabbath so that the law of Moses may not be broken, why are you angry with me for healing the whole man on the Sabbath? [24]Stop judging by mere appearances, and make a right judgment."

MATTHEW 12:3-8 He answered, "Haven't you read what David did when he and his companions were hungry? [4]He entered the house of God, and he and his companions ate the consecrated bread—which was not lawful for them to do, but only for the priests. [5]Or haven't you read in the Law that on the Sabbath the priests in the temple desecrate the day and yet are innocent? [6]I tell you that one greater than the temple is here. [7]If you had known what these words mean, 'I desire mercy, not sacrifice,' you would not have condemned the innocent. [8]For the Son of Man is Lord of the Sabbath."

MATTHEW 12:9-13 Going on from that place, he went into their synagogue, [10]and a man with a shriveled hand was there. Looking for a reason to accuse Jesus, they asked him, "Is it lawful to heal on the Sabbath?" [11]He said to them, "If any of you has a sheep and it falls into a pit on the Sabbath, will you not take hold of it and lift it out? [12]How much more valuable is a man than a sheep! Therefore it is lawful to do good on the Sabbath." [13]Then he said to the man, "Stretch out your hand." So he stretched it out and it was completely restored, just as sound as the other. (See also Luke 6:6-10.)

MARK 2:25-28 He answered, "Have you never read what David did when he and his companions were hungry and in need? [26]In the days of Abiathar the high priest, he entered the house of God and ate the consecrated bread, which is lawful only for priests to eat. And he also gave some to his companions." [27]Then he said to them, "The Sabbath was made for man, not man for the Sabbath. [28]So the Son of Man is Lord even of the Sabbath."

MARK 3:1-5 Another time he went into the synagogue, and a man with a shriveled hand was there. [2]Some of them were looking for a reason to accuse Jesus, so they watched him closely to see if he would heal him on the Sabbath. [3]Jesus said to the man with the shriveled hand, "Stand up in front of everyone." [4]Then Jesus asked them, "Which is lawful on the Sabbath: to do good or to do evil, to save life or to kill?" But they remained silent. [5]He looked around at them in anger and, deeply distressed at their stubborn hearts, said to the man, "Stretch out your hand." He stretched it out, and his hand was completely restored. (See also Luke 6:6-10.)

LUKE 6:3-5 Jesus answered them, "Have you never read what David did when he and his companions were hungry? [4]He entered the house of God, and taking the consecrated bread, he ate what is lawful only for priests to eat. And he also gave some to his companions." [5]Then Jesus said to them, "The Son of Man is Lord of the Sabbath."

LUKE 13:10-13 On a Sabbath Jesus was teaching in one of the synagogues, [11]and a woman was there who had been crippled by a spirit for eighteen years. She was bent over and could not straighten up at all. [12]When Jesus saw her, he called her forward and said to her, "Woman, you are set free from your infirmity." [13]Then he put his hands on her, and immediately she straightened up and praised God.

LUKE 13:14-16 Indignant because Jesus had healed on the Sabbath, the synagogue ruler said to the people, "There are six days for work. So come and be healed on those days, not on the Sabbath." [15]The Lord answered him, "You hypocrites! Doesn't each of you on the Sabbath untie his ox or donkey from the stall and lead it out to give it water? [16]Then should not this woman, a daughter of Abraham, whom Satan has kept bound for eighteen long years, be set free on the Sabbath day from what bound her?"

LUKE 14:3-5 Jesus asked the Pharisees and experts in the law, "Is it lawful to heal on the Sabbath or not?" [4]But they remained silent. So taking hold of the man [suffering from dropsy], he healed him and sent him away. [5]Then he asked them, "If one of you has a son or an ox that falls into a well on the Sabbath day, will you not immediately pull him out?"

The Scriptures

JOHN 5:39 "You diligently study the Scriptures because you think that by them you possess eternal life. These are the Scriptures that testify about me."

MATTHEW 5:17-18 "Do not think that I have come to abolish the Law or the Prophets; I have not come to abolish them but to fulfill them. [18]I tell you the truth, until heaven and earth disappear, not the smallest letter, not the least stroke of a pen, will by any means disappear from the Law until everything is accomplished."

MARK 14:48-49 "Am I leading a rebellion," said Jesus, "that you have come out with swords and clubs to capture me? [49]Every day I was with you, teaching in the temple courts, and you did not arrest me. But the Scriptures must be fulfilled."

Truth

JOHN 8:31-32 Then Jesus said to those Jews who believed Him, "If you abide in My word, you are My disciples indeed. [32]And you shall know the truth, and the truth shall make you free." (NKJV)

JOHN 8:40-41 "As it is, you are determined to kill me, a man who has told you the truth that I heard from God. Abraham did not do such things. [41]You are doing the things your own father does." "We are not illegitimate children," they protested. "The only Father we have is God himself."

JOHN 14:6 Jesus answered, "I am the way and the truth and the life. No one comes to the Father except through me."

JOHN 17:14-19 "I have given them your [God's] word and the world has hated them, for they are not of the world any more than I am of the world. [15]My prayer is not that you take them out of the world but that you protect them from the evil one. [16]They are not of the world, even as I am not of it. [17]Sanctify them by the truth; your word is truth. [18]As you sent me into the world, I have sent them into the world. [19]For them I sanctify myself, that they too may be truly sanctified."

JOHN 18:19-24 Meanwhile, the high priest questioned Jesus about his disciples and his teaching. [20]"I have spoken openly to the world," Jesus replied. "I always taught in synagogues or at the temple, where all the Jews come together. I said nothing in secret. [21]Why question me? Ask those who heard me. Surely they know what I said." [22]When Jesus said this, one of the officials nearby struck him in the face. "Is this the way you answer the high priest?" he demanded. [23]"If I said something wrong," Jesus replied, "testify as to what is wrong. But if I spoke the truth, why did you strike me?" [24]Then Annas sent him, still bound, to Caiaphas the high priest.

JOHN 18:37 "You are a king, then!" said Pilate. Jesus answered, "You are right in saying I am a king. In fact, for this reason I was born, and for this I came into the world, to testify to the truth. Everyone on the side of truth listens to me."

8

THE GREATEST WORDS
EVER SPOKEN ABOUT
HOW TO KNOW GOD

*What Jesus Told Us About Starting
and Deepening a Relationship with God*

I've never known a married man who isn't frustrated when it comes to figuring out what his wife wants and needs. My friend and mentor, marriage expert Gary Smalley, taught me that there is only one way to know what my wife wants or needs at any given moment. I can't figure it out by reading a book or a magazine article or even by asking an expert. The only way I can know what my wife wants or needs is to ask her.

Similarly, Gary points out, the only way for a man to *truly* love his wife is to love her in the ways she wants to be loved.

Both of these truths parallel our relationship with God. If I want to have an intimate relationship with God, I must know what He requires in that kind of relationship. It's not important that I offer what comes most naturally to me or even what I *think* God wants most. The only thing that matters is what He actually wants.

Fortunately, Christ has not left us guessing. In His statements about seeking and knowing God, Jesus reveals exactly what God desires from us. Unlike your relationship with your spouse, with God there is no need for guesswork. Jesus gave us all the information and direction we need. It takes a humble and repentant heart to love God the way He wants to be loved—and such a heart comes only as we embrace what God has offered us through His grace and the gift of His Son. As we come into a saving relationship with Christ, we can enter into the intimate relationship with God that He desires for each of us.

In chapter 5, we focused on Christ's statements that show how believers follow Him, love Him, and grow in daily intimacy with Him. In this chapter we will look at Jesus' statements that reveal how people who do *not* have a saving relationship with God can have one. The topics include repentance, faith, fearing God, and worshiping God. But this chapter focuses not only on how men and women can move toward a relationship with God. It also reveals how people often move away from Him and shows the terrible consequences they face when doing so.

You'll see how most of humanity lives in darkness by *choice*. You'll also discover the incredible blessings that come to those who choose to live in Christ's light. You'll see that hatred for God doesn't mean shaking a fist in His face but rather rejecting Him and what He values. You'll discover the dire, eternal consequences of rejecting Jesus Christ and His gospel. In this chapter, Christ shines the floodlight of His words on the pathway that leads to God's kingdom as well as the pathway that leads people *away* from that kingdom. The contrast is stark, and no matter which path you choose, the outcome is eternal and irreversible.

The word *gospel* means "good news." Part of the good news is that as you read the words of Jesus grouped under the headings "Accepting and Receiving Christ," "Belief and Faith in Christ," and "Coming to Christ," you will understand how God has provided for your sin and how you can gain a saving faith in Christ. Under the topics "Honoring and Exalting Christ" and "Knowing God," you'll discover that your love for God is not measured by your feelings but rather by how you respond to the words and commands of Christ and to God's will, which is revealed by Christ's words. This is great news because it takes the guesswork out of loving God. My love for Him is not dependent on my generating loving feelings. According to Christ's statements in Matthew 7 and John 14, I show my love for God by what I do, not by what I feel.

As you study the words of Christ on the matter of faith, you'll discover that faith always includes an act that demonstrates that faith. Such an act may be as subtle as a change in attitude or as visible as a physical action. You'll also discover that true faith is founded on the words of God. When your faith is based on anything other than God's Word, it is neither well founded nor secure.

If you are a believer reading Christ's words in this chapter, you will begin to understand the nature and state of your unbelieving friends. And more important, you will discover how to clarify the essentials of the gospel as you talk to them. May God add His grace and blessing to your study of His words.

Accepting and Receiving Christ

JOHN 12:48-49 "There is a judge for the one who rejects me and does not accept my words; that very word which I spoke will condemn him at the last day. [49]For I did not speak of my own accord, but the Father who sent me commanded me what to say and how to say it."

JOHN 13:20 "I tell you the truth, whoever accepts anyone I send accepts me; and whoever accepts me accepts the one who sent me."

MATTHEW 10:40-41 "He who receives you receives me, and he who receives me receives the one who sent me. [41]Anyone who receives a prophet because he is a prophet will receive a prophet's reward, and anyone who receives a righteous man because he is a righteous man will receive a righteous man's reward."

MATTHEW 18:5-6 "And whoever welcomes a little child like this in my name welcomes me. [6]But if anyone causes one of these little ones who believe in me to sin, it would be better for him to have a large millstone hung around his neck and to be drowned in the depths of the sea."

MARK 9:37 "Whoever welcomes one of these little children in my name

welcomes me; and whoever welcomes me does not welcome me but the one who sent me."

LUKE 9:48 Then he said to them, "Whoever welcomes this little child in my name welcomes me; and whoever welcomes me welcomes the one who sent me. For he who is least among you all—he is the greatest."

REVELATION 3:20 "Here I am! I stand at the door and knock. If anyone hears my voice and opens the door, I will come in and eat with him, and he with me."

Belief and Faith in Christ

JOHN 3:14-16 "Just as Moses lifted up the snake in the desert, so the Son of Man must be lifted up, [15]that everyone who believes in him may have eternal life. [16]For God so loved the world that he gave his one and only Son, that whoever believes in him shall not perish but have eternal life."

JOHN 3:18 "Whoever believes in him [Christ] is not condemned, but whoever does not believe stands condemned already because he has not believed in the name of God's one and only Son."

JOHN 5:24 "I tell you the truth, whoever hears my word and believes him who sent me has eternal life and will not be condemned; he has crossed over from death to life."

JOHN 6:29 Jesus answered, "The work of God is this: to believe in the one he has sent."

JOHN 6:37-40 "All that the Father gives me will come to me, and whoever comes to me I will never drive away. [38]For I have come down from heaven not to do my will but to do the will of him who sent me. [39]And this is the will of him who sent me, that I shall lose none of all that he has given me, but raise them up at the last day. [40]For my Father's will is that everyone who looks to the Son and believes in him shall have eternal life, and I will raise him up at the last day."

JOHN 6:44-47 "No one can come to me unless the Father who sent me draws him, and I will raise him up at the last day. [45]It is written in the Prophets: 'They will all be taught by God.' Everyone who listens to the Father and learns from him comes to me. [46]No one has seen the Father except the one who is from God; only he has seen the Father. [47]I tell you the truth, he who believes has everlasting life."

JOHN 7:37-38 On the last and greatest day of the Feast, Jesus stood and said in a loud voice, "If anyone is thirsty, let him come to me and drink. [38]Whoever believes in me, as the Scripture has said, streams of living water will flow from within him."

JOHN 10:1-5 "I tell you the truth, the man who does not enter the sheep pen by the gate, but climbs in by some other way, is a thief and a robber. [2]The man who enters by the gate is the shepherd of his sheep. [3]The watchman opens the gate for him, and the sheep listen to his voice. He calls his own sheep by name and leads them out. [4]When he has brought out all his own, he goes on ahead of them, and his sheep follow him because they know his voice. [5]But they will never follow a stranger; in fact, they will run away from him because they do not recognize a stranger's voice."

JOHN 10:37-38 "Do not believe me unless I do what my Father does. [38]But if I do it, even though you do not believe me, believe the miracles, that you may know and understand that the Father is in me, and I in the Father."

JOHN 11:25-26 Jesus said to her [Martha], "I am the resurrection and the life. He who believes in me will live, even though he dies; [26]and whoever lives and believes in me will never die. Do you believe this?"

JOHN 11:40-43 Then Jesus said, "Did I not tell you that if you believed, you would see the glory of God?" [41]So they took away the stone. Then Jesus looked up and said, "Father, I thank you that you have heard me. [42]I knew that you always hear me, but I said this for the benefit of the people standing here, that they may believe that you sent me." [43]When he had said this, Jesus called in a loud voice, "Lazarus, come out!"

JOHN 12:44-46 Then Jesus cried out, "When a man believes in me, he does not believe in me only, but in the one who sent me. [45]When he looks at me, he sees the one who sent me. [46]I have come into the world as a light, so that no one who believes in me should stay in darkness."

JOHN 13:19-20 "I am telling you now before it happens, so that when it does happen you will believe that I am He. [20]I tell you the truth, whoever accepts anyone I send accepts me; and whoever accepts me accepts the one who sent me."

JOHN 14:1-4 "Do not let your hearts be troubled. Trust in God; trust also in me. [2]In my Father's house are many rooms; if it were not so, I would have told you. I am going there to prepare a place for you. [3]And if I go and prepare a place for you, I will come back and take you to be with me that you also may be where I am. [4]You know the way to the place where I am going."

JOHN 14:11 "Believe me when I say that I am in the Father and the Father is in me; or at least believe on the evidence of the miracles themselves."

JOHN 14:12-14 "I tell you the truth, anyone who has faith in me will do what I have been doing. He will do even greater things than these, because I am going to the Father. [13]And I will do whatever you ask in my name, so that the Son may bring glory to the Father. [14]You may ask me for anything in my name, and I will do it."

JOHN 20:29 Then Jesus told him [Thomas], "Because you have seen me, you have believed; blessed are those who have not seen and yet have believed."

MATTHEW 8:5-13 When Jesus had entered Capernaum, a centurion came to him, asking for help. [6]"Lord," he said, "my servant lies at home paralyzed and in terrible suffering." [7]Jesus said to him, "I will go and heal him." [8]The centurion replied, "Lord, I do not deserve to have you come under my roof. But just say the word, and my servant will be healed. [9]For I myself am a man under authority, with soldiers under me. I tell this one, 'Go,' and he goes; and that one, 'Come,' and he comes. I say to my servant, 'Do this,' and he does it." [10]When Jesus heard this, he was astonished and said to those following him, "I tell you the truth, I have not found anyone in Israel with such great faith. [11]I say to you that many will come from the east and the west, and will take their places at the feast with Abraham, Isaac and Jacob in the kingdom of heaven. [12]But the subjects of the kingdom will be thrown outside, into the darkness, where there will be weeping and gnashing of teeth." [13]Then Jesus said to the centurion, "Go! It will be done just as you believed it would." And his servant was healed at that very hour.

MATTHEW 8:25-26 The disciples went and woke him, saying, "Lord, save us! We're going to drown!" [26]He replied, "You of little faith, why are you so afraid?" Then he got up and rebuked the winds and the waves, and it was completely calm.

MATTHEW 9:2-5 Some men brought to him a paralytic, lying on a mat. When Jesus saw their faith, he said to the paralytic, "Take heart, son; your sins are forgiven." [3]At this, some of the teachers of the law said to themselves, "This fellow is blaspheming!" [4]Knowing their thoughts, Jesus said, "Why do you entertain evil thoughts in your hearts? [5]Which is easier: to say, 'Your sins are forgiven,' or to say, 'Get up and walk'?"

MATTHEW 9:22 Jesus turned and saw her. "Take heart, daughter," he said, "your faith has healed you." And the woman was healed from that moment.

MATTHEW 9:27-30 As Jesus went on from there, two blind men followed him, calling out, "Have mercy on us, Son of David!" [28]When he had gone indoors, the blind men came to him, and he asked them, "Do you believe that I am able to do this?" "Yes, Lord," they replied. [29]Then he touched their eyes and said, "According to your faith will it be done to you"; [30]and their sight was restored. Jesus warned them sternly, "See that no one knows about this."

MATTHEW 14:29 "Come," he said. Then Peter got down out of the boat, walked on the water and came toward Jesus.

MATTHEW 15:24-28 He answered, "I was sent only to the lost sheep of Israel." [25]The woman came and knelt before him. "Lord, help me!" she said. [26]He replied, "It is not right to take the children's bread and toss it to their dogs." [27]"Yes, Lord," she said, "but even the dogs eat the crumbs that fall from their masters' table." [28]Then Jesus answered, "Woman, you have great faith! Your request is granted." And her daughter was healed from that very hour.

MATTHEW 17:20 So Jesus said to them, "Because of your unbelief; for assuredly, I say to you, if you have faith as a mustard seed, you will say to this mountain, 'Move from here to there,' and it will move; and nothing will be impossible for you." (NKJV)

MATTHEW 21:18-22 Early in the morning, as he was on his way back to the city, he was hungry. [19]Seeing a fig tree by the road, he went up to it but found nothing on it except leaves. Then he said to it, "May you never bear fruit again!" Immediately the tree withered. [20]When the disciples saw this, they were amazed. "How did the fig tree wither so quickly?" they asked. [21]Jesus replied, "I tell you the truth, if you have faith and do not doubt, not only can you do what was done to the fig tree, but also you can say to this mountain, 'Go, throw yourself into the sea,' and it will be done. [22]If you believe, you will receive whatever you ask for in prayer." (See also Mark 11:12-14.)

MARK 1:15 "The time has come," he said. "The kingdom of God is near. Repent and believe the good news!"

MARK 4:35-40 That day when evening came, he said to his disciples, "Let us go over to the other side." [36]Leaving the crowd behind, they took him along, just as he was, in the boat. There were also other boats with him. [37]A furious squall came up, and the waves broke over the boat, so that it was nearly swamped. [38]Jesus was in the stern, sleeping on a cushion. The disciples woke him and said to him, "Teacher, don't you care if we drown?" [39]He got up, rebuked the wind and said to the waves, "Quiet! Be still!" Then the wind died down and it was completely calm. [40]He said to his disciples, "Why are you so afraid? Do you still have no faith?"

MARK 5:30-34 At once Jesus realized that power had gone out from him. He turned around in the crowd and asked, "Who touched my clothes?"

[31]"You see the people crowding against you," his disciples answered, "and yet you can ask, 'Who touched me?'" [32]But Jesus kept looking around to see who had done it. [33]Then the woman, knowing what had happened to her, came and fell at his feet and, trembling with fear, told him the whole truth. [34]He said to her, "Daughter, your faith has healed you. Go in peace and be freed from your suffering."

MARK 7:27-29 "First let the children eat all they want," he told her, "for it is not right to take the children's bread and toss it to their dogs." [28]"Yes, Lord," she replied, "but even the dogs under the table eat the children's crumbs." [29]Then he told her, "For such a reply, you may go; the demon has left your daughter."

MARK 9:1 And he said to them, "I tell you the truth, some who are standing here will not taste death before they see the kingdom of God come with power."

MARK 10:51-52 "What do you want me to do for you?" Jesus asked him. The blind man said, "Rabbi, I want to see." [52]"Go," said Jesus, "your faith has healed you." Immediately he received his sight and followed Jesus along the road.

MARK 11:22-24 "Have faith in God," Jesus answered. [23]"I tell you the truth, if anyone says to this mountain, 'Go, throw yourself into the sea,' and does not doubt in his heart but believes that what he says will happen, it will be done for him. [24]Therefore I tell you, whatever you ask for in prayer, believe that you have received it, and it will be yours."

LUKE 7:6-9 So Jesus went with them. He was not far from the house when the centurion sent friends to say to him: "Lord, don't trouble yourself, for I do not deserve to have you come under my roof. [7]That is why I did not even consider myself worthy to come to you. But say the word, and my servant will be healed. [8]For I myself am a man under authority, with soldiers under me. I tell this one, 'Go,' and he goes; and that one, 'Come,' and he comes. I say to my servant, 'Do this,' and he does it." [9]When Jesus heard this, he was amazed at him, and turning to the crowd following him, he said, "I tell you, I have not found such great faith even in Israel."

LUKE 7:40-50 Jesus answered him, "Simon, I have something to tell you." "Tell me, teacher," he said. [41]"Two men owed money to a certain moneylender. One owed him five hundred denarii, and the other fifty. [42]Neither of them had the money to pay him back, so he canceled the debts of both. Now which of them will love him more?" [43]Simon replied, "I suppose the one who had the bigger debt canceled." "You have judged correctly," Jesus said. [44]Then he turned toward the woman and said to Simon, "Do you see this woman? I came into your house. You did not give me any water for my feet, but she wet my feet with her tears and wiped them with her hair. [45]You did not give me a kiss, but this woman, from the time I entered, has not stopped kissing my feet. [46]You did not put oil on my head, but she has poured perfume on my feet. [47]Therefore, I tell you, her many sins have been forgiven—for she loved much. But he who has been forgiven little loves little." [48]Then Jesus said to her, "Your sins are forgiven." [49]The other guests began to say among themselves, "Who is this who even forgives sins?" [50]Jesus said to the woman, "Your faith has saved you; go in peace."

LUKE 8:24-25 The disciples went and woke him, saying, "Master, Master, we're going to drown!" He got up and rebuked the wind and the raging waters; the storm subsided, and all was calm. [25]"Where is your faith?" he asked his disciples. In fear and amazement they asked one another, "Who is this? He commands even the winds and the water, and they obey him."

LUKE 8:43-48 And a woman was there who had been subject to bleeding for twelve years, but no one could heal her. [44]She came up behind him and touched the edge of his cloak, and immediately her bleeding stopped. [45]"Who touched me?" Jesus asked. When they all denied it, Peter said, "Master, the people are crowding and pressing against you." [46]But Jesus said, "Someone touched me; I know that power has gone out from me." [47]Then the woman, seeing that she could not go unnoticed, came trembling and fell at his feet. In the presence of all the people, she told why she had touched him and how she had been instantly healed. [48]Then he said to her, "Daughter, your faith has healed you. Go in peace."

LUKE 8:50-55 Hearing this, Jesus said to Jairus, "Don't be afraid; just believe, and she will be healed." [51]When he arrived at the house of Jairus, he did not let anyone go in with him except Peter, John and James, and the child's father and mother. [52]Meanwhile, all the people were wailing and mourning for her. "Stop wailing," Jesus said. "She is not dead but asleep." [53]They laughed at him, knowing that she was dead. [54]But he took her by the hand and said, "My child, get up!" [55]Her spirit returned, and at once she stood up. Then Jesus told them to give her something to eat.

LUKE 12:22-34 Then Jesus said to his disciples: "Therefore I tell you, do not worry about your life, what you will eat; or about your body, what you will wear. [23]Life is more than food, and the body more than clothes. [24]Consider the ravens: They do not sow or reap, they have no storeroom or barn; yet God feeds them. And how much more valuable you are than birds! [25]Who of you by worrying can add a single hour to his life? [26]Since you cannot do this very little thing, why do you worry about the rest? [27]Consider how the lilies grow. They do not labor or spin. Yet I tell you, not even Solomon in all his splendor was dressed like one of these. [28]If that is how God clothes the grass of the field, which is here today, and tomorrow is thrown into the fire, how much more will he clothe you, O you of little faith! [29]And do not set your heart on what you will eat or drink; do not worry about it. [30]For the pagan world runs after all such things, and your Father knows that you need them. [31]But seek his kingdom, and these things will be given to you as well. [32]Do not be afraid, little flock, for your Father has been pleased to give you the kingdom. [33]Sell your possessions and give to the poor. Provide purses for yourselves that will not wear out, a treasure in heaven that will not be exhausted, where no thief comes near and no moth destroys. [34]For where your treasure is, there your heart will be also."

LUKE 17:3-6 "So watch yourselves. If your brother sins, rebuke him, and if he repents, forgive him. ⁴If he sins against you seven times in a day, and seven times comes back to you and says, 'I repent,' forgive him." ⁵The apostles said to the Lord, "Increase our faith!" ⁶He replied, "If you have faith as small as a mustard seed, you can say to this mulberry tree, 'Be uprooted and planted in the sea,' and it will obey you."

LUKE 17:17-19 Jesus asked, "Were not all ten cleansed? Where are the other nine? ¹⁸Was no one found to return and give praise to God except this foreigner?" ¹⁹Then he said to him, "Rise and go; your faith has made you well."

LUKE 18:1-8 Then Jesus told his disciples a parable to show them that they should always pray and not give up. ²He said: "In a certain town there was a judge who neither feared God nor cared about men. ³And there was a widow in that town who kept coming to him with the plea, 'Grant me justice against my adversary.' ⁴For some time he refused. But finally he said to himself, 'Even though I don't fear God or care about men, ⁵yet because this widow keeps bothering me, I will see that she gets justice, so that she won't eventually wear me out with her coming!'" ⁶And the Lord said, "Listen to what the unjust judge says. ⁷And will not God bring about justice for his chosen ones, who cry out to him day and night? Will he keep putting them off? ⁸I tell you, he will see that they get justice, and quickly. However, when the Son of Man comes, will he find faith on the earth?"

LUKE 18:35, 38, 40-42 As Jesus approached Jericho, a blind man was sitting by the roadside begging. ³⁸He called out, "Jesus, Son of David, have mercy on me!" ⁴⁰Jesus stopped and ordered the man to be brought to him. When he came near, Jesus asked him, ⁴¹"What do you want me to do for you?" "Lord, I want to see," he replied. ⁴²Jesus said to him, "Receive your sight; your faith has healed you."

LUKE 22:31-32 "Simon, Simon, Satan has asked to sift you as wheat. ³²But I have prayed for you, Simon, that your faith may not fail. And when you have turned back, strengthen your brothers."

LUKE 23:42-43 Then he [a criminal crucified with Jesus] said, "Jesus, remember me when you come into your kingdom." ⁴³Jesus answered him, "I tell you the truth, today you will be with me in paradise."

Blasphemy of the Holy Spirit

MATTHEW 12:25-32 Jesus knew their [the Pharisees'] thoughts and said to them, "Every kingdom divided against itself will be ruined, and every city or household divided against itself will not stand. ²⁶If Satan drives out Satan, he is divided against himself. How then can his kingdom stand? ²⁷And if I drive out demons by Beelzebub, by whom do your people drive them out? So then, they will be your judges. ²⁸But if I drive out demons by the Spirit of God, then the kingdom of God has come upon you. ²⁹Or again, how can anyone enter a strong man's house and carry off his possessions unless he first ties up the strong man? Then he can rob his house. [30]He who is not with me is against me, and he who does not gather with me scatters. [31]And so I tell you, every sin and blasphemy will be forgiven men, but the blasphemy against the Spirit will not be forgiven. [32]Anyone who speaks a word against the Son of Man will be forgiven, but anyone who speaks against the Holy Spirit will not be forgiven, either in this age or in the age to come."

MARK 3:28-30 "I tell you the truth, all the sins and blasphemies of men will be forgiven them. [29]But whoever blasphemes against the Holy Spirit will never be forgiven; he is guilty of an eternal sin." [30]He said this because they were saying, "He has an evil spirit."

Coming to Christ

JOHN 5:39-43 "You diligently study the Scriptures because you think that by them you possess eternal life. These are the Scriptures that testify about me, [40]yet you refuse to come to me to have life. [41]I do not accept praise from men, [42]but I know you. I know that you do not have the love of God in your hearts. [43]I have come in my Father's name, and you do not accept me; but if someone else comes in his own name, you will accept him."

JOHN 6:35-36 Then Jesus declared, "I am the bread of life. He who comes to me will never go hungry, and he who believes in me will never be thirsty. [36]But as I told you, you have seen me and still you do not believe."

JOHN 6:65 He went on to say, "This is why I told you that no one can come to me unless the Father has enabled him."

JOHN 7:37-38 On the last and greatest day of the Feast, Jesus stood and said in a loud voice, "If anyone is thirsty, let him come to me and drink. [38]Whoever believes in me, as the Scripture has said, streams of living water will flow from within him."

JOHN 10:1-5 "I tell you the truth, the man who does not enter the sheep pen by the gate, but climbs in by some other way, is a thief and a robber. [2]The man who enters by the gate is the shepherd of his sheep. [3]The watchman opens the gate for him, and the sheep listen to his voice. He calls his own sheep by name and leads them out. [4]When he has brought out all his own, he goes on ahead of them, and his sheep follow him because they know his voice. [5]But they will never follow a stranger; in fact, they will run away from him because they do not recognize a stranger's voice."

JOHN 10:27-29 "My sheep listen to my voice; I know them, and they follow me. [28]I give them eternal life, and they shall never perish; no one can snatch them out of my hand. [29]My Father, who has given them to me, is greater than all; no one can snatch them out of my Father's hand."

MATTHEW 11:28-30 "Come to me, all you who are weary and burdened, and I will give you rest. [29]Take my yoke upon you and learn from me, for I am gentle and humble in heart, and you will find rest for your souls. [30]For my yoke is easy and my burden is light."

MARK 8:34-38 Then he called the crowd to him along with his disciples and said: "If anyone would come after me, he must deny himself and take up his cross and follow me. [35]For whoever wants to save his life will lose it, but whoever loses his life for me and for the gospel will save it. [36]What good is it for a man to gain the whole world, yet forfeit his soul? [37]Or what can a man give in exchange for his soul? [38]If anyone is ashamed of me and my words in this adulterous and sinful generation, the Son of Man will be ashamed of him when he comes in his Father's glory with the holy angels."

Denying Christ

MATTHEW 10:32-33 "Whoever acknowledges me before men, I will also acknowledge him before my Father in heaven. [33]But whoever disowns me before men, I will disown him before my Father in heaven."

MATTHEW 26:34 "I tell you [Peter] the truth," Jesus answered, "this very night, before the rooster crows, you will disown me three times." (See also Mark 14:30; Luke 22:34; John 13:38.)

LUKE 12:8-10 "I tell you, whoever acknowledges me before men, the Son of Man will also acknowledge him before the angels of God. [9]But he who disowns me before men will be disowned before the angels of God. [10]And everyone who speaks a word against the Son of Man will be forgiven, but anyone who blasphemes against the Holy Spirit will not be forgiven."

Fearing God

MATTHEW 10:27-31 "What I tell you in the dark, speak in the daylight; what is whispered in your ear, proclaim from the roofs. [28]Do not be afraid of those who kill the body but cannot kill the soul. Rather, be afraid of the One who can destroy both soul and body in hell. [29]Are not two sparrows sold for a penny? Yet not one of them will fall to the ground apart from the will of your Father. [30]And even the very hairs of your head are all numbered. [31]So don't be afraid; you are worth more than many sparrows."

MATTHEW 17:1-8 After six days Jesus took with him Peter, James and John the brother of James, and led them up a high mountain by themselves. [2]There he was transfigured before them. His face shone like the sun, and his clothes became as white as the light. [3]Just then there appeared before them Moses and Elijah, talking with Jesus. [4]Peter said to Jesus, "Lord, it is good for us to be here. If you wish, I will put up three shelters—one for you, one for Moses and one for Elijah." [5]While he was still speaking, a bright cloud enveloped them, and a voice from the cloud said, "This is my Son, whom I love; with him I am well pleased. Listen to him!" [6]When the disciples heard this, they fell facedown to the ground, terrified. [7]But Jesus came and touched them. "Get up," he said. "Don't be afraid." [8]When they looked up, they saw no one except Jesus.

LUKE 12:4-7 "I tell you, my friends, do not be afraid of those who kill the body and after that can do no more. [5]But I will show you whom you should fear: Fear him who, after the killing of the body, has power to throw you into hell. Yes, I tell you, fear him. [6]Are not five sparrows sold for two pennies? Yet not one of them is forgotten by God. [7]Indeed, the very hairs of your head are all numbered. Don't be afraid; you are worth more than many sparrows."

Fruit, Both Good and Bad

JOHN 4:31-38 Meanwhile his disciples urged him, "Rabbi, eat something." [32]But he said to them, "I have food to eat that you know nothing about." [33]Then his disciples said to each other, "Could someone have brought him food?" [34]"My food," said Jesus, "is to do the will of him who sent me and to finish his work. [35]Do you not say, 'Four months more and then the harvest'? I tell you, open your eyes and look at the fields! They are ripe for harvest. [36]Even now the reaper draws his wages, even now he harvests the crop for eternal life, so that the sower and the reaper may be glad together. [37]Thus the saying 'One sows and another reaps' is true. [38]I sent you to reap what you have not worked for. Others have done the hard work, and you have reaped the benefits of their labor."

JOHN 15:1-8 "I am the true vine, and my Father is the gardener. [2]He cuts off every branch in me that bears no fruit, while every branch that does bear fruit he prunes so that it will be even more fruitful. [3]You are already clean because of the word I have spoken to you. [4]Remain in me, and I will remain in you. No branch can bear fruit by itself; it must remain in the vine. Neither can you bear fruit unless you remain in me. [5]I am the vine; you are the branches. If a man remains in me and I in him, he will bear much fruit; apart from me you can do nothing. [6]If anyone does not remain in me, he is like a branch that is thrown away and withers; such branches are picked up, thrown into the fire and burned. [7]If you remain in me and my words remain in you, ask whatever you wish, and it will be given you. [8]This is to my Father's glory, that you bear much fruit, showing yourselves to be my disciples."

JOHN 15:16-17 "You did not choose me, but I chose you and appointed you to go and bear fruit—fruit that will last. Then the Father will give you whatever you ask in my name. [17]This is my command: Love each other."

MATTHEW 7:15-20 "Watch out for false prophets. They come to you in sheep's clothing, but inwardly they are ferocious wolves. [16]By their fruit you will recognize them. Do people pick grapes from thornbushes, or figs from thistles? [17]Likewise every good tree bears good fruit, but a bad tree bears bad fruit. [18]A good tree cannot bear bad fruit, and a bad tree cannot bear good fruit. [19]Every tree that does not bear good fruit is cut down and thrown into the fire. [20]Thus, by their fruit you will recognize them."

MATTHEW 12:33-37 "Make a tree good and its fruit will be good, or make a tree bad and its fruit will be bad, for a tree is recognized by its fruit. [34]You brood of vipers, how can you who are evil say anything good? For out of the overflow of the heart the mouth speaks. [35]The good man brings good things out of the good stored up in him, and the evil man brings evil things out of the evil stored up in him. [36]But I tell you that men will have to give account on the day of judgment for every careless word they have spoken. [37]For by your words you will be acquitted, and by your words you will be condemned."

MATTHEW 13:23 "But the one who received the seed that fell on good soil is the man who hears the word and understands it. He produces a crop, yielding a hundred, sixty or thirty times what was sown."

MARK 4:20 "Others, like seed sown on good soil, hear the word, accept it, and produce a crop—thirty, sixty or even a hundred times what was sown."

LUKE 6:43-45 "No good tree bears bad fruit, nor does a bad tree bear good fruit. [44]Each tree is recognized by its own fruit. People do not pick figs from thornbushes, or grapes from briers. [45]The good man brings good things out of the good stored up in his heart, and the evil man brings evil things out of the evil stored up in his heart. For out of the overflow of his heart his mouth speaks."

LUKE 8:15 "But the seed on good soil stands for those with a noble and good heart, who hear the word, retain it, and by persevering produce a crop."

Hatred for God

JOHN 3:19-20 "This is the verdict: Light has come into the world, but men loved darkness instead of light because their deeds were evil. [20]Everyone who does evil hates the light, and will not come into the light for fear that his deeds will be exposed."

JOHN 5:22-23 "Moreover, the Father judges no one, but has entrusted all judgment to the Son, [23]that all may honor the

Son just as they honor the Father. He who does not honor the Son does not honor the Father, who sent him."

JOHN 7:6-8 Therefore Jesus told them, "The right time for me has not yet come; for you any time is right. [7]The world cannot hate you, but it hates me because I testify that what it does is evil. [8]You go to the Feast. I am not yet going up to this Feast, because for me the right time has not yet come."

JOHN 15:18 "If the world hates you, keep in mind that it hated me first."

JOHN 15:23-25 "He who hates me hates my Father as well. [24]If I had not done among them what no one else did, they would not be guilty of sin. But now they have seen these miracles, and yet they have hated both me and my Father. [25]But this is to fulfill what is written in their Law: 'They hated me without reason.'"

Honoring and Exalting Christ

JOHN 5:22-23 "Moreover, the Father judges no one, but has entrusted all judgment to the Son, [23]that all may honor the Son just as they honor the Father. He who does not honor the Son does not honor the Father, who sent him."

JOHN 5:41-43 "I do not accept praise from men, [42]but I know you. I know that you do not have the love of God in your hearts. [43]I have come in my Father's name, and you do not accept me; but if someone else comes in his own name, you will accept him."

JOHN 8:28-29 So Jesus said, "When you have lifted up the Son of Man, then you will know that I am the one I claim to be and that I do nothing on my own but speak just what the Father has taught me. [29]The one who sent me is with me; he has not left me alone, for I always do what pleases him."

John 8:31 Then Jesus said to those Jews who believed Him, "If you abide in My word, you are My disciples indeed." (NKJV)

John 8:54-56 Jesus replied, "If I glorify myself, my glory means nothing. My Father, whom you claim as your God, is the one who glorifies me. [55]Though you do not know him, I know him. If I said I did not, I would be a liar like you, but I do know him and keep his word. [56]Your father Abraham rejoiced at the thought of seeing my day; he saw it and was glad."

John 12:26 "Whoever serves me must follow me; and where I am, my servant also will be. My Father will honor the one who serves me."

John 14:15 "If you love me, you will obey what I command."

John 14:23-24 Jesus replied, "If anyone loves me, he will obey my teaching. My Father will love him, and we will come to him and make our home with him. [24]He who does not love me will not obey my teaching. These words you hear are not my own; they belong to the Father who sent me."

Matthew 7:21-25 "Not everyone who says to Me, 'Lord, Lord,' shall enter the kingdom of heaven, but he who does the will of My Father in heaven. [22]Many will say to Me in that day, 'Lord, Lord, have we not prophesied in Your name, cast out demons in Your name, and done many wonders in Your name?' [23]And then

I will declare to them, 'I never knew you; depart from Me, you who practice lawlessness!' [24]Therefore whoever hears these sayings of Mine, and does them, I will liken him to a wise man who built his house on the rock: [25]and the rain descended, the floods came, and the winds blew and beat on that house; and it did not fall, for it was founded on the rock." (NKJV)

Matthew 15:8-9 "These people honor me with their lips, but their hearts are far from me. [9]They worship me in vain; their teachings are but rules taught by men."

Knowing God

John 8:19 Then they asked him, "Where is your father?" "You do not know me or my Father," Jesus replied. "If you knew me, you would know my Father also."

John 8:54-55 Jesus replied, "If I glorify myself, my glory means nothing. My Father, whom you claim as your God, is the one who glorifies me. [55]Though you do not know him, I know him. If I said I did not, I would be a liar like you, but I do know him and keep his word."

John 14:6-11 Jesus answered, "I am the way and the truth and the life. No one comes to the Father except through me. [7]If you really knew me, you would know my Father as well. From now on, you do know him and have seen him." [8]Philip said, "Lord, show us the Father and that will be enough for us." [9]Jesus answered: "Don't you know me, Philip, even after I have been among you such a long time? Anyone who has seen me has seen the

Father. How can you say, 'Show us the Father'? [10]Don't you believe that I am in the Father, and that the Father is in me? The words I say to you are not just my own. Rather, it is the Father, living in me, who is doing his work. [11]Believe me when I say that I am in the Father and the Father is in me; or at least believe on the evidence of the miracles themselves."

JOHN 14:23-24 Jesus replied, "If anyone loves me, he will obey my teaching. My Father will love him, and we will come to him and make our home with him. [24]He who does not love me will not obey my teaching. These words you hear are not my own; they belong to the Father who sent me."

JOHN 17:3 "Now this is eternal life: that they may know you, the only true God, and Jesus Christ, whom you have sent."

JOHN 17:25-26 "Righteous Father, though the world does not know you, I know you, and they know that you have sent me. [26]I have made you known to them, and will continue to make you known in order that the love you have for me may be in them and that I myself may be in them."

MATTHEW 11:27 "All things have been committed to me by my Father. No one knows the Son except the Father, and no one knows the Father except the Son and those to whom the Son chooses to reveal him."

Light Versus Darkness

JOHN 3:18-21 "Whoever believes in him [Christ] is not condemned, but who-ever does not believe stands condemned already because he has not believed in the name of God's one and only Son. [19]This is the verdict: Light has come into the world, but men loved darkness instead of light because their deeds were evil. [20]Everyone who does evil hates the light, and will not come into the light for fear that his deeds will be exposed. [21]But who-ever lives by the truth comes into the light, so that it may be seen plainly that what he has done has been done through God."

JOHN 8:12 When Jesus spoke again to the people, he said, "I am the light of the world. Whoever follows me will never walk in darkness, but will have the light of life."

JOHN 9:4-5 "As long as it is day, we must do the work of him who sent me. Night is coming, when no one can work. [5]While I am in the world, I am the light of the world."

JOHN 11:9 Jesus answered, "Are there not twelve hours of daylight? A man who walks by day will not stumble, for he sees by this world's light."

JOHN 12:35 Then Jesus told them, "You are going to have the light just a little while longer. Walk while you have the light, before darkness overtakes you. The man who walks in the dark does not know where he is going."

JOHN 12:46 "I have come into the world as a light, so that no one who be-lieves in me should stay in darkness."

MATTHEW 5:14-16 "You are the light of the world. A city on a hill cannot be hidden. [15]Neither do people light a lamp and put it under a bowl. Instead they put it on its stand, and it gives light to everyone in the house. [16]In the same way, let your light shine before men, that they may see your good deeds and praise your Father in heaven."

MATTHEW 6:22-23 "The eye is the lamp of the body. If your eyes are good, your whole body will be full of light. [23]But if your eyes are bad, your whole body will be full of darkness. If then the light within you is darkness, how great is that darkness!"

MARK 4:21-23 He said to them, "Do you bring in a lamp to put it under a bowl or a bed? Instead, don't you put it on its stand? [22]For whatever is hidden is meant to be disclosed, and whatever is concealed is meant to be brought out into the open. [23]If anyone has ears to hear, let him hear."

LUKE 8:16-17 "No one lights a lamp and hides it in a jar or puts it under a bed. Instead, he puts it on a stand, so that those who come in can see the light. [17]For there is nothing hidden that will not be disclosed, and nothing concealed that will not be known or brought out into the open."

LUKE 11:33-36 "No one lights a lamp and puts it in a place where it will be hidden, or under a bowl. Instead he puts it on its stand, so that those who come in may see the light. [34]Your eye is the lamp of your body. When your eyes are good, your whole body also is full of light. But when they are bad, your body also is full of darkness. [35]See to it, then, that the light within you is not darkness. [36]Therefore, if your whole body is full of light, and no part of it dark, it will be completely lighted, as when the light of a lamp shines on you."

Profiting from Religious Duties

JOHN 2:14-16 In the temple courts he found men selling cattle, sheep and doves, and others sitting at tables exchanging money. [15]So he made a whip out of cords, and drove all from the temple area, both sheep and cattle; he scattered the coins of the money changers and overturned their tables. [16]To those who sold doves he said, "Get these out of here! How dare you turn my Father's house into a market!"

MARK 11:15-17 On reaching Jerusalem, Jesus entered the temple area and began driving out those who were buying and selling there. He overturned the tables of the money changers and the benches of those selling doves, [16]and would not allow anyone to carry merchandise through the temple courts. [17]And as he taught them, he said, "Is it not written: 'My house will be called a house of prayer for all nations'? But you have made it 'a den of robbers.' " (See also Matthew 21:12-13; Luke 19:45-46.)

Receiving the Gospel

MATTHEW 10:40-42 "He who receives you receives me, and he who receives me receives the one who sent me. [41]Anyone who receives a prophet because he is a prophet will receive a prophet's reward, and anyone who receives a righteous man because he is a righteous man will receive a righteous man's reward.

[42]And if anyone gives even a cup of cold water to one of these little ones because he is my disciple, I tell you the truth, he will certainly not lose his reward."

MARK 6:8-11 These were his instructions: "Take nothing for the journey except a staff—no bread, no bag, no money in your belts. [9]Wear sandals but not an extra tunic. [10]Whenever you enter a house, stay there until you leave that town. [11]And if any place will not welcome you or listen to you, shake the dust off your feet when you leave, as a testimony against them." (See also Matthew 10:9-15; Luke 9:1-5.)

Rejecting Christ

JOHN 3:18-19 "Whoever believes in him [Christ] is not condemned, but whoever does not believe stands condemned already because he has not believed in the name of God's one and only Son. [19]This is the verdict: Light has come into the world, but men loved darkness instead of light because their deeds were evil."

JOHN 5:39-40 "You diligently study the Scriptures because you think that by them you possess eternal life. These are the Scriptures that testify about me, [40]yet you refuse to come to me to have life."

JOHN 5:43 "I have come in my Father's name, and you do not accept me; but if someone else comes in his own name, you will accept him."

JOHN 12:48-49 "There is a judge for the one who rejects me and does not accept my words; that very word which I spoke will condemn him at the last day. [49]For I did not speak of my own accord,

but the Father who sent me commanded me what to say and how to say it."

MATTHEW 11:16-19 "To what can I compare this generation? They are like children sitting in the marketplaces and calling out to others: [17]'We played the flute for you, and you did not dance; we sang a dirge, and you did not mourn.' [18]For John came neither eating nor drinking, and they say, 'He has a demon.' [19]The Son of Man came eating and drinking, and they say, 'Here is a glutton and a drunkard, a friend of tax collectors and "sinners."' But wisdom is proved right by her actions."

MATTHEW 13:54-57 Coming to his hometown, he began teaching the people in their synagogue, and they were amazed. "Where did this man get this wisdom and these miraculous powers?" they asked. [55]"Isn't this the carpenter's son? Isn't his mother's name Mary, and aren't his brothers James, Joseph, Simon and Judas? [56]Aren't all his sisters with us? Where then did this man get all these things?" [57]And they took offense at him. But Jesus said to them, "Only in his hometown and in his own house is a prophet without honor."

MATTHEW 21:33-40 "Listen to another parable: There was a landowner who planted a vineyard. He put a wall around it, dug a winepress in it and built a watchtower. Then he rented the vineyard to some farmers and went away on a journey. [34]When the harvest time approached, he sent his servants to the tenants to collect his fruit. [35]The tenants seized his servants; they beat one, killed another, and stoned a third. [36]Then he sent other servants to them, more than the first time, and the tenants treated them the same way. [37]Last of all, he sent his son to them. 'They will respect my son,' he said. [38]But when the tenants saw the son, they said to each other, 'This is the heir. Come, let's kill him and take his inheritance.' [39]So they took him and threw him out of the vineyard and killed him. [40]Therefore, when the owner of the vineyard comes, what will he do to those tenants?"

MATTHEW 21:42-44 Jesus said to them, "Have you never read in the Scriptures: 'The stone the builders rejected has become the capstone; the Lord has done this, and it is marvelous in our eyes'? [43]Therefore I tell you that the kingdom of God will be taken away from you and given to a people who will produce its fruit. [44]He who falls on this stone will be broken to pieces, but he on whom it falls will be crushed."

MARK 12:1-11 He then began to speak to them in parables: "A man planted a vineyard. He put a wall around it, dug a pit for the winepress and built a watchtower. Then he rented the vineyard to some farmers and went away on a journey. [2]At harvest time he sent a servant to the tenants to collect from them some of the fruit of the vineyard. [3]But they seized him, beat him and sent him away empty-handed. [4]Then he sent another servant to them; they struck this man on the head and treated him shamefully. [5]He sent still another, and that one they killed. He sent many others; some of them they beat, others they killed. [6]He had one left to send, a son, whom he loved. He sent him last of all, saying, 'They will respect my son.' [7]But the tenants said to one another, 'This is the heir. Come, let's kill him, and the inheritance will be ours.' [8]So they took him and killed him, and threw him out of the vineyard. [9]What then will the owner of the vineyard do? He will come and kill those tenants and give the vineyard to others. [10]Haven't you read this scripture: 'The stone the builders rejected has become the capstone; [11]the Lord has done this, and it is marvelous in our eyes'?"

LUKE 10:13-16 "Woe to you, Korazin! Woe to you, Bethsaida! For if the miracles that were performed in you had been performed in Tyre and Sidon, they would have repented long ago, sitting in sackcloth and ashes. [14]But it will be more bearable for Tyre and Sidon at the judgment than for you. [15]And you, Capernaum, will you be lifted up to the skies? No, you will go down to the depths. [16]He who listens to you listens to me; he who rejects you rejects me; but he who rejects me rejects him who sent me."

LUKE 14:15-24 When one of those at the table with him heard this, he said to Jesus, "Blessed is the man who will eat at the feast in the kingdom of God." [16]Jesus replied: "A certain man was preparing a great banquet and invited many guests. [17]At the time of the banquet he sent his servant to tell those who had been invited, 'Come, for everything is now ready.' [18]But they all alike began to make excuses. The first said, 'I have just bought a field, and I must go and see it. Please excuse me.' [19]"Another said, 'I have just bought five yoke of oxen, and I'm on my way to try them out. Please excuse me.' [20]Still another said, 'I just got married, so I can't come.' [21]The servant came back and reported this to his master. Then the owner of the house became angry and ordered his servant, 'Go out quickly into the streets and alleys of the town and bring in the poor, the crippled, the blind and the lame.' [22]'Sir,' the servant said, 'what you ordered has been done, but there is still room.' [23]Then the master told his servant, 'Go out to the roads and country lanes and make them come in, so that my house will be full. [24]I tell you, not one of those men who were invited will get a taste of my banquet.'"

LUKE 17:25 "But first he must suffer many things and be rejected by this generation."

Rejecting the Gospel

MATTHEW 10:11-15 "Whatever town or village you enter, search for some worthy person there and stay at his house until you leave. [12]As you enter the home, give it your greeting. [13]If the home is deserving, let your peace rest on it; if it is not, let your peace return to you. [14]If anyone will not welcome you or listen to your words, shake the dust off your feet when you leave that home or town. [15]I tell you the truth, it will be more bearable for Sodom and Gomorrah on the day of judgment than for that town."

MATTHEW 10:32-33 "Whoever acknowledges me before men, I will also acknowledge him before my Father in heaven. [33]But whoever disowns me before men, I will disown him before my Father in heaven."

MATTHEW 11:20-24 Then Jesus began to denounce the cities in which most of his miracles had been performed, because they did not repent. [21]"Woe to you, Korazin! Woe to you, Bethsaida! If the miracles that were performed in you had been performed in Tyre and Sidon, they would have repented long ago in sackcloth and ashes. [22]But I tell you, it will be more bearable for Tyre and Sidon on the day of judgment than for you. [23]And you, Capernaum, will you be lifted up to the skies? No, you will go down to the depths. If the miracles that were performed in you had been performed in Sodom, it would have remained to this day. [24]But I tell you that it will be more bearable for Sodom on the day of judgment than for you."

MARK 6:8-11 These were his instructions: "Take nothing for the journey except a staff—no bread, no bag, no money in your belts. [9]Wear sandals but not an extra tunic. [10]Whenever you enter a house, stay there until you leave that town. [11]And if any place will not welcome you or listen to you, shake the dust off your feet when you leave, as a testimony against them." (See also Luke 9:1-5.)

LUKE 12:8-9 "I tell you, whoever acknowledges me before men, the Son of Man will also acknowledge him before the angels of God. [9]But he who disowns me before men will be disowned before the angels of God."

LUKE 14:15-24 When one of those at the table with him heard this, he said to Jesus, "Blessed is the man who will eat at the feast in the kingdom of God." [16]Jesus replied: "A certain man was preparing a great banquet and invited many guests. [17]At the time of the banquet he sent his servant to tell those who had been invited, 'Come, for everything is now ready.' [18]But they all alike began to make excuses. The first said, 'I have just bought a field, and I must go and see it. Please excuse me.' [19]Another said, 'I have just bought five yoke of oxen, and I'm on my way to try them out. Please excuse me.' [20]Still another said, 'I just got married, so I can't come.' [21]The servant came back and reported this to his master. Then the owner of the house became angry and ordered his servant, 'Go out quickly into the streets and alleys of the town and bring in the poor, the crippled, the blind and the lame.' [22]'Sir,' the servant said, 'what you ordered has been done, but there is still room.' [23]Then the master told his servant, 'Go out to the roads and country lanes and make them come in, so that my house will be full. [24]I tell you, not one of those men who were invited will get a taste of my banquet.'"

LUKE 16:19-31 "There was a rich man who was dressed in purple and fine linen and lived in luxury every day. [20]At his gate was laid a beggar named Lazarus, covered with sores [21]and longing to eat what fell from the rich man's table. Even the dogs came and licked his sores. [22]The time came when the beggar died and the angels carried him to Abraham's side. The rich man also died and was buried. [23]In hell, where he was in torment, he looked up and saw Abraham far away, with Lazarus by his side. [24]So he called to him, 'Father Abraham, have pity on me and send Lazarus to dip the tip of his finger in water and cool my tongue, because I am in agony in this fire.' [25]But Abraham replied, 'Son, remember that in your lifetime you received your good things, while Lazarus received bad things, but now he is comforted here and you are in agony. [26]And besides all this, between us and you a great chasm has been fixed, so that those who want to go from here to you cannot, nor can anyone cross over from there to us.' [27]He answered, 'Then I beg you, father, send Lazarus to my father's house, [28]for I have five brothers. Let him warn them, so that they will not also come to this place of torment.' [29]Abraham replied, 'They have Moses and the Prophets; let them listen to them.' [30]'No, father Abraham,' he said, 'but if someone from the dead goes to them, they will repent.' [31]He said to him, 'If they do not listen to Moses and the Prophets, they will not be convinced even if someone rises from the dead.'"

Repentance

MATTHEW 4:17 From that time on Jesus began to preach, "Repent, for the kingdom of heaven is near."

MATTHEW 9:12-13 On hearing this, Jesus said, "It is not the healthy who need a doctor, but the sick. [13]But go and learn what this means: 'I desire mercy, not sacrifice.' For I have not come to call the righteous, but sinners."

MATTHEW 11:20-24 Then Jesus began to denounce the cities in which most of his miracles had been performed, because they did not repent. [21]"Woe to you, Korazin! Woe to you, Bethsaida! If the miracles that were performed in you had been performed in Tyre and Sidon, they would have repented long ago in sackcloth and ashes. ²²But I tell you, it will be more bearable for Tyre and Sidon on the day of judgment than for you. ²³And you, Capernaum, will you be lifted up to the skies? No, you will go down to the depths. If the miracles that were performed in you had been performed in Sodom, it would have remained to this day. ²⁴But I tell you that it will be more bearable for Sodom on the day of judgment than for you."

MATTHEW 12:39-42 He answered, "A wicked and adulterous generation asks for a miraculous sign! But none will be given it except the sign of the prophet Jonah. ⁴⁰For as Jonah was three days and three nights in the belly of a huge fish, so the Son of Man will be three days and three nights in the heart of the earth. ⁴¹The men of Nineveh will stand up at the judgment with this generation and condemn it; for they repented at the preaching of Jonah, and now one greater than Jonah is here. ⁴²The Queen of the South will rise at the judgment with this generation and condemn it; for she came from the ends of the earth to listen to Solomon's wisdom, and now one greater than Solomon is here."

MARK 1:15 "The time has come," he said. "The kingdom of God is near. Repent and believe the good news!"

MARK 2:17 When Jesus heard it, He said to them, "Those who are well have no need of a physician, but those who are sick. I did not come to call the righteous, but sinners, to repentance." (NKJV)

LUKE 5:31-32 Jesus answered them, "It is not the healthy who need a doctor, but the sick. ³²I have not come to call the righteous, but sinners to repentance."

LUKE 11:29-32 As the crowds increased, Jesus said, "This is a wicked generation. It asks for a miraculous sign, but none will be given it except the sign of Jonah. ³⁰For as Jonah was a sign to the Ninevites, so also will the Son of Man be to this generation. ³¹The Queen of the South will rise at the judgment with the men of this generation and condemn them; for she came from the ends of the earth to listen to Solomon's wisdom, and now one greater than Solomon is here. ³²The men of Nineveh will stand up at the judgment with this generation and condemn it; for they repented at the preaching of Jonah, and now one greater than Jonah is here."

LUKE 13:2-5 Jesus answered, "Do you think that these Galileans were worse sinners than all the other Galileans because they suffered this way? ³I tell you, no! But unless you repent, you too will all perish. ⁴Or those eighteen who died when the tower in Siloam fell on them—do you think they were more guilty than all the others living in Jerusalem? ⁵I tell you, no! But unless you repent, you too will all perish."

LUKE 15:4-10 "Suppose one of you has a hundred sheep and loses one of them. Does he not leave the ninety-nine in the open country and go after the lost sheep until he finds it? ⁵And when he finds it, he joyfully puts it on his shoulders ⁶and goes home. Then he calls his friends and neighbors together and says, 'Rejoice with me; I have found my lost sheep.' ⁷I tell you that in the same way there will be more rejoicing in heaven over one sinner who repents than over ninety-nine righteous persons who do not need to repent. [8]Or suppose a woman has ten silver coins and loses one. Does she not light a lamp, sweep the house and search carefully until she finds it? [9]And when she finds it, she calls her friends and neighbors together and says, 'Rejoice with me; I have found my lost coin.' [10]In the same way, I tell you, there is rejoicing in the presence of the angels of God over one sinner who repents."

LUKE 15:11-32 Jesus continued: "There was a man who had two sons. [12]The younger one said to his father, 'Father, give me my share of the estate.' So he divided his property between them. [13]Not long after that, the younger son got together all he had, set off for a distant country and there squandered his wealth in wild living. [14]After he had spent everything, there was a severe famine in that whole country, and he began to be in need. [15]So he went and hired himself out to a citizen of that country, who sent him to his fields to feed pigs. [16]He longed to fill his stomach with the pods that the pigs were eating, but no one gave him anything. [17]When he came to his senses, he said, 'How many of my father's hired men have food to spare, and here I am starving to death! [18]I will set out and go back to my father and say to him: Father, I have sinned against heaven and against you. [19]I am no longer worthy to be called your son; make me like one of your hired men.' [20]So he got up and went to his father. But while he was still a long way off, his father saw him and was filled with compassion

for him; he ran to his son, threw his arms around him and kissed him. [21]The son said to him, 'Father, I have sinned against heaven and against you. I am no longer worthy to be called your son.' [22]But the father said to his servants, 'Quick! Bring the best robe and put it on him. Put a ring on his finger and sandals on his feet. [23]Bring the fattened calf and kill it. Let's have a feast and celebrate. [24]For this son of mine was dead and is alive again; he was lost and is found.' So they began to celebrate. [25]Meanwhile, the older son was in the field. When he came near the house, he heard music and dancing. [26]So he called one of the servants and asked him what was going on. [27]'Your brother has come,' he replied, 'and your father has killed the fattened calf because he has him back safe and sound.' [28]The older brother became angry and refused to go in. So his father went out and pleaded with him. [29]But he answered his father, 'Look! All these years I've been slaving for you and never disobeyed your orders. Yet you never gave me even a young goat so I could celebrate with my friends. [30]But when this son of yours who has squandered your property with prostitutes comes home, you kill the fattened calf for him!' [31]'My son,' the father said, 'you are always with me, and everything I have is yours. [32]But we had to celebrate and be glad, because this brother of yours was dead and is alive again; he was lost and is found.'"

LUKE 16:19-31 "There was a rich man who was dressed in purple and fine linen and lived in luxury every day. [20]At his gate was laid a beggar named Lazarus, covered with sores [21]and longing to eat what fell from the rich man's table. Even the dogs came and licked his sores. [22]The time came when the beggar died and the angels carried him to Abraham's side. The rich man also died and was buried. [23]In hell, where he was in torment, he looked up and saw Abraham far away, with Lazarus by his side. [24]So he called to him, 'Father Abraham, have pity on me and send Lazarus to dip the tip of his finger in water and cool my tongue, because I am in agony in this fire.' [25]But Abraham replied, 'Son, remember that in your lifetime you received your good things, while Lazarus received bad things, but now he is comforted here and you are in agony. [26]And besides all this, between us and you a great chasm has been fixed, so that those who want to go from here to you cannot, nor can anyone cross over from there to us.' [27]He answered, 'Then I beg you, father, send Lazarus to my father's house, [28]for I have five brothers. Let him warn them, so that they will not also come to this place of torment.' [29]Abraham replied, 'They have Moses and the Prophets; let them listen to them.' [30]'No, father Abraham,' he said, 'but if someone from the dead goes to them, they will repent.' [31]He said to him, 'If they do not listen to Moses and the Prophets, they will not be convinced even if someone rises from the dead.'"

LUKE 17:3-6 "So watch yourselves. If your brother sins, rebuke him, and if he repents, forgive him. [4]If he sins against you seven times in a day, and seven times comes back to you and says, 'I repent,' forgive him." [5]The apostles said to the Lord, "Increase our faith!" [6]He replied, "If you have faith as small as a mustard seed, you can say to this mulberry tree, 'Be uprooted and planted in the sea,' and it will obey you."

LUKE 18:10-14 "Two men went up to the temple to pray, one a Pharisee and the other a tax collector. [11]The Pharisee stood up and prayed about himself: 'God, I thank you that I am not like other men—robbers, evildoers, adulterers—or even like this tax collector. [12]I fast twice a week and give a tenth of all I get.' [13]But the tax collector stood at a distance. He would not even look up to heaven, but beat his breast and said, 'God, have mercy on me, a sinner.' [14]I tell you that this man, rather than the other, went home justified before God. For everyone who exalts himself will be humbled, and he who humbles himself will be exalted."

LUKE 23:40-43 But the other criminal [crucified with Jesus] rebuked him [the first criminal]. "Don't you fear God," he said, "since you are under the same sentence? [41]We are punished justly, for we are getting what our deeds deserve. But this man has done nothing wrong." [42]Then he said, "Jesus, remember me when you come into your kingdom." [43]Jesus answered him, "I tell you the truth, today you will be with me in paradise."

LUKE 24:46-47 He told them [the disciples], "This is what is written: The Christ will suffer and rise from the dead on the third day, [47]and repentance and forgiveness of sins will be preached in his name to all nations, beginning at Jerusalem."

REVELATION 2:4-5 "Yet I hold this against you: You have forsaken your first love. [5]Remember the height from which you have fallen! Repent and do the things you did at first. If you do not repent, I will come to you and remove your lampstand from its place."

REVELATION 2:16 "Repent therefore! Otherwise, I will soon come to you and will fight against them with the sword of my mouth."

REVELATION 3:1-3 "To the angel of the church in Sardis write: These are the words of him who holds the seven spirits of God and the seven stars. I know your deeds; you have a reputation of being alive, but you are dead. [2]Wake up! Strengthen what remains and is about to die, for I have not found your deeds complete in the sight of my God. [3]Remember, therefore, what you have received and heard; obey it, and repent. But if you do not wake up, I will come like a thief, and you will not know at what time I will come to you."

REVELATION 3:15-19 "I know your deeds, that you are neither cold nor hot. I wish you were either one or the other! [16]So, because you are lukewarm—neither hot nor cold—I am about to spit you out of my mouth. [17]You say, 'I am rich; I have acquired wealth and do not need a thing.' But you do not realize that you are wretched, pitiful, poor, blind and naked. [18]I counsel you to buy from me gold refined in the fire, so you can become rich; and white clothes to wear, so you can cover your shameful nakedness; and salve to put on your eyes, so you can see. [19]Those whom I love I rebuke and discipline. So be earnest, and repent."

Unbelief and Motives of Unbelievers

JOHN 3:17-20 "For God did not send his Son into the world to condemn the world, but to save the world through him. [18]Whoever believes in him is not condemned, but whoever does not believe stands condemned already because he has not believed in the name of God's one and only Son. [19]This is the verdict: Light has come into the world, but men loved darkness instead of light because their deeds were evil. [20]Everyone who does evil hates the light, and will not come into the light for fear that his deeds will be exposed."

JOHN 4:48 "Unless you people see miraculous signs and wonders," Jesus told him, "you will never believe."

JOHN 5:36-40 "I have testimony weightier than that of John. For the very work that the Father has given me to finish, and which I am doing, testifies that the Father has sent me. [37]And the Father who sent me has himself testified concerning me. You have never heard his voice nor seen his form, [38]nor does his word dwell in you, for you do not believe the one he sent. [39]You diligently study the Scriptures because you think that by them you possess eternal life. These are the Scriptures that testify about me, [40]yet you refuse to come to me to have life."

JOHN 5:46-47 "If you believed Moses, you would believe me, for he wrote about me. [47]But since you do not believe what he wrote, how are you going to believe what I say?"

JOHN 6:26 Jesus answered, "I tell you the truth, you are looking for me, not because you saw miraculous signs but because you ate the loaves and had your fill."

JOHN 6:35-36 Then Jesus declared, "I am the bread of life. He who comes to me will never go hungry, and he who believes in me will never be thirsty. [36]But as I told you, you have seen me and still you do not believe."

JOHN 8:19 Then they asked him, "Where is your father?" "You do not know me or my Father," Jesus replied. "If you knew me, you would know my Father also."

JOHN 8:21, 23-24 Once more Jesus said to them, "I am going away, and you will look for me, and you will die in your sin. Where I go, you cannot come." [23]But he continued, "You are from below; I am from above. You are of this world; I am not of this world. [24]I told you that you would die in your sins; if you do not believe that I am the one I claim to be, you will indeed die in your sins."

JOHN 10:25-27 Jesus answered, "I did tell you, but you do not believe. The miracles I do in my Father's name speak for me, [26]but you do not believe because you are not my sheep. [27]My sheep listen to my voice; I know them, and they follow me."

JOHN 12:47-48 "As for the person who hears my words but does not keep them, I do not judge him. For I did not come to judge the world, but to save it. [48]There is a judge for the one who rejects me and does not accept my words; that very word which I spoke will condemn him at the last day."

JOHN 15:20-21 "Remember the words I spoke to you: 'No servant is greater than his master.' If they persecuted me, they will persecute you also. If they obeyed my teaching, they will obey yours also. [21]They will treat you this way because of my name, for they do not know the One who sent me."

JOHN 16:2-3 "They will put you out of the synagogue; in fact, a time is coming when anyone who kills you will think he is offering a service to God. [3]They will do such things because they have not known the Father or me."

MATTHEW 14:29-31 "Come," he said. Then Peter got down out of the boat, walked on the water and came toward Jesus. [30]But when he saw the wind, he was afraid and, beginning to sink, cried out, "Lord, save me!" [31]Immediately Jesus reached out his hand and caught him. "You of little faith," he said, "why did you doubt?"

MATTHEW 17:17 "O unbelieving and perverse generation," Jesus replied, "how long shall I stay with you? How long shall I put up with you? Bring the boy here to me."

MATTHEW 17:19-20 Then the disciples came to Jesus privately and said, "Why could we not cast it [a demon] out?" [20]So Jesus said to them, "Because of your unbelief; for assuredly, I say to you, if you have faith as a mustard seed, you will say to this mountain, 'Move from here to there,' and it will move; and nothing will be impossible for you." (NKJV)

MATTHEW 21:28-32 "What do you think? There was a man who had two sons. He went to the first and said, 'Son, go and work today in the vineyard.' [29]'I will not,' he answered, but later he changed his mind and went. [30]Then the father went to the other son and said the same thing. He answered, 'I will, sir,' but he did not go. [31]Which of the two did what his father wanted?" "The first," they answered. Jesus said to them, "I tell you the truth, the tax collectors and the prostitutes are entering the kingdom of God ahead of you. [32]For John came to you to show you the way of righteousness, and you did not believe him, but the tax collectors and the prostitutes did. And even after you saw this, you did not repent and believe him."

MARK 4:37-40 A furious squall came up, and the waves broke over the boat, so that it was nearly swamped. [38]Jesus was in the stern, sleeping on a cushion. The disciples woke him and said to him, "Teacher, don't you care if we drown?" [39]He got up, rebuked the wind and said to the waves, "Quiet! Be still!" Then the wind died down and it was completely calm. [40]He said to his disciples, "Why are you so afraid? Do you still have no faith?"

MARK 6:4-6 Jesus said to them, "Only in his hometown, among his relatives and in his own house is a prophet without honor." [5]He could not do any miracles there, except lay his hands on a few sick people and heal them. [6]And he was amazed at their lack of faith. Then Jesus went around teaching from village to village.

MARK 6:49-51 ...when they [the disciples] saw him [Jesus] walking on the lake, they thought he was a ghost. They cried out, [50]because they all saw him and were terrified. Immediately he spoke to them and said, "Take courage! It is I. Don't be afraid." [51]Then he climbed into

the boat with them, and the wind died down. They were completely amazed.

MARK 16:14-16 Later Jesus appeared to the Eleven as they were eating; he rebuked them for their lack of faith and their stubborn refusal to believe those who had seen him after he had risen. [15]He said to them, "Go into all the world and preach the good news to all creation. [16]Whoever believes and is baptized will be saved, but whoever does not believe will be condemned."[xvii]

LUKE 8:24-25 The disciples went and woke him, saying, "Master, Master, we're going to drown!" He got up and rebuked the wind and the raging waters; the storm subsided, and all was calm. [25]"Where is your faith?" he asked his disciples. In fear and amazement they asked one another, "Who is this? He commands even the winds and the water, and they obey him."

LUKE 9:41 "O unbelieving and perverse generation," Jesus replied, "how long shall I stay with you and put up with you? Bring your son here."

LUKE 12:22-28 Then Jesus said to his disciples: "Therefore I tell you, do not worry about your life, what you will eat; or about your body, what you will wear. [23]Life is more than food, and the body more than clothes. [24]Consider the ravens: They do not sow or reap, they have no storeroom or barn; yet God feeds them. And how much more valuable you are than birds! [25]Who of you by worrying can add a single hour to his life? [26]Since you cannot do this very little thing, why do you worry about the rest? [27]Consider how the lilies grow. They do not labor or spin. Yet I tell you, not even Solomon in all his splendor was dressed like one of these. [28]If that is how God clothes the grass of the field, which is here today, and tomorrow is thrown into the fire, how much more will he clothe you, O you of little faith!"

LUKE 17:3-6 "So watch yourselves. If your brother sins, rebuke him, and if he repents, forgive him. [4]If he sins against you seven times in a day, and seven times comes back to you and says, 'I repent,' forgive him." [5]The apostles said to the Lord, "Increase our faith!" [6]He replied, "If you have faith as small as a mustard seed, you can say to this mulberry tree, 'Be uprooted and planted in the sea,' and it will obey you."

LUKE 24:25-26 He said to them [two people on the road to Emmaus], "How foolish you are, and how slow of heart to believe all that the prophets have spoken! [26]Did not the Christ have to suffer these things and then enter his glory?"

Worship

JOHN 4:22-24 "You Samaritans worship what you do not know; we worship what we do know, for salvation is from the Jews. [23]Yet a time is coming and has now come when the true worshipers will worship the Father in spirit and truth, for they are the kind of worshipers the Father seeks. [24]God is spirit, and his worshipers must worship in spirit and in truth."

MATTHEW 26:6-13 While Jesus was in Bethany in the home of a man known as Simon the Leper, [7]a woman came to him with an alabaster jar of very expensive perfume, which she poured on his head as he was reclining at the table. [8]When the disciples saw this, they were indignant. "Why this waste?" they asked. [9]"This perfume could have been sold at a high price and the money given to the poor." [10]Aware of this, Jesus said to them, "Why are you bothering this woman? She has done a beautiful thing to me. [11]The poor you will always have with you, but you will not always have me. [12]When she poured this perfume on my body, she did it to prepare me for burial. [13]I tell you the truth, wherever this gospel is preached throughout the world, what she has done will also be told, in memory of her." (See also John 12:1-8.)

MARK 14:3-9 While he was in Bethany, reclining at the table in the home of a man known as Simon the Leper, a woman came with an alabaster jar of very expensive perfume, made of pure nard. She broke the jar and poured the perfume on his head. [4]Some of those present were saying indignantly to one another, "Why this waste of perfume? [5]It could have been sold for more than a year's wages and the money given to the poor." And they rebuked her harshly. [6]"Leave her alone," said Jesus. "Why are you bothering her? She has done a beautiful thing to me. [7]The poor you will always have with you, and you can help them any time you want. But you will not always have me. [8]She did what she could. She poured perfume on my body beforehand to prepare for my burial. [9]I tell you the truth, wherever the gospel is preached throughout the world, what she has done will also be told, in memory of her."

LUKE 4:8 Jesus answered, "It is written: 'Worship the Lord your God and serve him only.'" (See also Matthew 4:10.)

9

THE GREATEST WORDS EVER SPOKEN ABOUT PERSONAL RELATIONSHIPS

What Jesus Said About Succeeding with Others

On a scale of one to ten, how would you rate your personal relationships? If you're married, start with your relationship with your spouse. Then rate your relationship with each of your children. How about with your parents and siblings? And the people you work with?

Whenever a relationship isn't everything we want it to be, we are quick to blame it on the other person: "If only he would…" or "If only she didn't…" We've played the game this way ever since childhood. But Jesus shows us that blaming others for our failures is not only offensive to God; it is detrimental to our relationships. While we all want healthier relationships, most of us have a hard time breaking free from our natural inclinations. The words of Christ in this chapter can bring about extraordinary change in every relationship in your life, for the rest of your life.

The Question That Only God Could Answer

This chapter contains the most powerful and important teachings ever recorded on the subject of personal relationships. When Jesus was asked which commandment of God was the greatest, He gave the following answer: "The most important one…is this: 'Hear, O Israel, the Lord our God, the

Lord is one. Love the Lord your God with all your heart and with all your soul and with all your mind and with all your strength.' The second is this: 'Love your neighbor as yourself.' There is no commandment greater than these" (Mark 12:29-31). One point that is often missed when reading this passage is that Jesus' response to the questioner was instantaneous. There was no pause between the man's question and Christ's answer. There was no "That's a good one. Give Me a minute to think about it."

No one other than God had the knowledge or the right to answer this question. And yet Jesus answered it authoritatively and without a second thought. How could He do that? Because He had been united with God the Father for eternity, knowing every thought, every value, and every priority of God. He knew the mind and heart of the Father as completely as the Father knew His.

While we might have expected that loving God with all our heart, soul, mind, and strength would be the greatest commandment, who would have guessed that the second-greatest commandment would be loving our neighbors as ourselves? What about "thou shalt not kill" or "thou shalt not steal"? What about "thou shalt keep the Sabbath day holy"? They are all part of the big ten, and "love your neighbor as yourself" didn't even appear on the tablets of stone. Yet Jesus identified this commandment from Leviticus as second only to loving God.

What does it mean to love my neighbor as myself? How can I possibly love anyone else as much as I automatically care about my own needs and concerns? To do so is contrary to human nature. And once I have determined exactly who my neighbor is, then how am I supposed to love him or her? Jesus answers all these questions in His statements included in this chapter.

Many of His answers run contrary to our natural inclinations and are light-years beyond ordinary human reasoning. For example, Jesus tells us to bless the people who curse us and to do good to people who hate us. And that's just the tip of the iceberg. If we have a conflict with someone, Jesus gives us precise steps to initiate reconciliation and resolve the conflict, even when we are the victims. (Isn't our normal reaction to think, *They started it, and I'm not doing a thing until they say they're sorry*?) Jesus doesn't care who started it; He tells His followers it's *their* responsibility to resolve it, God's way.

And then there is the subject of forgiveness. Jesus commands us to forgive someone as many as four hundred ninety times, for the *same* offense! (See

Matthew 18:22, NKJV.) Even when the disciples heard Him say to forgive "seven times in a day," they pleaded, "Increase our faith!" (Luke 17:4-5). As our heart is changed by the power of Jesus' words, forgiving a person who hurt us and clearly remains in the wrong requires no more effort than forgiving someone who repents.

Prepare for a Life Change

Jesus' revelations on the subject of forgiveness are life shattering, life changing, and life giving. His words are life shattering because He identifies our forgiveness of others as the ultimate evidence of our spiritual birth. If that evidence is not present, then we must conclude that we may not have been born again and that our faith in Christ may be based on a mental exercise rather than saving faith. Jesus repeatedly tells us, "If you do not forgive men their trespasses, neither will your Father forgive your trespasses" (Matthew 6:15, NKJV). And without God's forgiveness, there is no entrance into His kingdom. But Jesus doesn't stop with this revelation. Fortunately for us, He gives an incredible parable that reveals how we can gain a heart that is quick to forgive others. The key is that we gain a clear understanding of how great our offenses against God are. We must understand how hopeless our state is before Him, how miraculous His atoning sacrifice was, and how great a debt of personal sin He has forgiven. When we realize that Jesus paid off our "ten trillion dollar sin-debt" with His suffering and His blood, how can we possibly *not* forgive the "ten cent debts" that others inflict on us? But these are my words. Jesus' words are far more powerful and liberating.

His words on forgiveness are life changing, because as we experience the power of true forgiveness, our hurts, anger, bitterness, and resentment are transformed into peace, joy, contentment, and love. The terrible weight we once shouldered is lifted, freeing us to love others the way He loves us.

His words on forgiveness are life giving, because as we forgive those who have hurt us, we enter into a deeper understanding of God's love and mercy, and we develop a grateful spirit that leads to a more intimate fellowship with Christ. He gives us a "fountain of living water" that really does bring life and refreshment to the deepest part of our being. Our relationship with Him becomes the focal point of our heart, and a once-callous heart toward God and others becomes a tender heart that is easily moved by the promptings of the Holy Spirit. Because our forgiveness of others is God's litmus test of our spiritual birth and the reality of our faith in Christ, few subjects are more important to our walk with God than this one.

In addition to Jesus' wisdom on forgiving others, His words about judging others will change the way you think and how you live. Here again, Jesus' warnings are ominous. While He is just, righteous, and perfect in all His judgments, He reveals that our judgment of others is usually heavily biased. We magnify the faults and mistakes of others as we minimize, excuse, rationalize, justify, and even ignore our own massive failings. Here again, Jesus' guiding light can lead us out of this dead-end path into a course that not only brings us happiness but blesses others with love and encouragement.

We can have better relationships with anyone who crosses our path, but it doesn't happen naturally. Jesus provides both the revelation and the power that free us from our human nature. What may begin as an act of blind obedience—simply doing what Jesus tells us to do—can become a way of life that exalts Christ in every relationship we have. My prayer is that your eyes will be opened to Jesus' wisdom and power and that you will learn to walk in the path that brings true intimacy with God and godly relationships with others.

Anger

MATTHEW 5:21-24 "You have heard that it was said to the people long ago, 'Do not murder, and anyone who murders will be subject to judgment.' 22But I tell you that anyone who is angry with his brother will be subject to judgment. Again, anyone who says to his brother, 'Raca,' is answerable to the Sanhedrin. But anyone who says, 'You fool!' will be in danger of the fire of hell. 23Therefore, if you are offering your gift at the altar and there remember that your brother has something against you, 24leave your gift there in front of the altar. First go and be reconciled to your brother; then come and offer your gift."

Compassion

MATTHEW 5:38-48 "You have heard that it was said, 'Eye for eye, and tooth for tooth.' 39But I tell you, Do not resist an evil person. If someone strikes you on the right cheek, turn to him the other also. 40And if someone wants to sue you and take your tunic, let him have your cloak as well. 41If someone forces you to go one mile, go with him two miles. 42Give to the one who asks you, and do not turn away from the one who wants to borrow from you. 43You have heard that it was said, 'Love your neighbor and hate your enemy.' 44But I tell you: Love your enemies and pray for those who persecute you, 45that you may be sons of your

Father in heaven. He causes his sun to rise on the evil and the good, and sends rain on the righteous and the unrighteous. ⁴⁶If you love those who love you, what reward will you get? Are not even the tax collectors doing that? ⁴⁷And if you greet only your brothers, what are you doing more than others? Do not even pagans do that? ⁴⁸Be perfect, therefore, as your heavenly Father is perfect."

MATTHEW 7:9-12 "Which of you, if his son asks for bread, will give him a stone? ¹⁰Or if he asks for a fish, will give him a snake? ¹¹If you, then, though you are evil, know how to give good gifts to your children, how much more will your Father in heaven give good gifts to those who ask him! ¹²So in everything, do to others what you would have them do to you, for this sums up the Law and the Prophets."

MATTHEW 14:15-20 As evening approached, the disciples came to him and said, "This is a remote place, and it's already getting late. Send the crowds away, so they can go to the villages and buy themselves some food." ¹⁶Jesus replied, "They do not need to go away. You give them something to eat." ¹⁷"We have here only five loaves of bread and two fish," they answered. ¹⁸"Bring them here to me," he said. ¹⁹And he directed the people to sit down on the grass. Taking the five loaves and the two fish and looking up to heaven, he gave thanks and broke the loaves. Then he gave them to the disciples, and the disciples gave them to the people. ²⁰They all ate and were satisfied, and the disciples picked up twelve basketfuls of broken pieces that were left over. (See also Mark 6:35-43; Luke 9:12-17; John 6:5-13.)

MATTHEW 15:32-37 Jesus called his disciples to him and said, "I have compassion for these people; they have already been with me three days and have nothing to eat. I do not want to send them away hungry, or they may collapse on the way." ³³His disciples answered, "Where could we get enough bread in this remote place to feed such a crowd?" ³⁴"How many loaves do you have?" Jesus asked. "Seven," they replied, "and a few small fish." ³⁵He told the crowd to sit down on the ground. ³⁶Then he took the seven loaves and the fish, and when he had given thanks, he broke them and gave them to the disciples, and they in turn to the people. ³⁷They all ate and were satisfied. Afterward the disciples picked up seven basketfuls of broken pieces that were left over.

MATTHEW 20:30-34 Two blind men were sitting by the roadside, and when they heard that Jesus was going by, they shouted, "Lord, Son of David, have mercy on us!" ³¹The crowd rebuked them and told them to be quiet, but they shouted all the louder, "Lord, Son of David, have mercy on us!" ³²Jesus stopped and called them. "What do you want me to do for you?" he asked. ³³"Lord," they answered, "we want our sight." ³⁴Jesus had compassion on them and touched their eyes. Immediately they received their sight and followed him.

MARK 5:18-19 As Jesus was getting into the boat, the man who had been demon-possessed begged to go with him. ¹⁹Jesus did not let him, but said, "Go home to your family and tell them how much the Lord has done for you, and how he has had mercy on you."

MARK 8:1-8 During those days another large crowd gathered. Since they had nothing to eat, Jesus called his disciples to him and said, ²"I have compassion for these people; they have already been with me three days and have nothing to eat. ³If I send them home hungry, they will collapse on the way, because some of them have come a long distance." ⁴His disciples answered, "But where in this remote place can anyone get enough bread to feed them?" ⁵"How many loaves do you have?" Jesus asked. "Seven," they replied. ⁶He told the crowd to sit down on the ground. When he had taken the seven loaves and given thanks, he broke them and gave them to his disciples to set before the people, and they did so. ⁷They had a few small fish as well; he gave thanks for them also and told the disciples to distribute them. ⁸The people ate and were satisfied. Afterward the disciples picked up seven basketfuls of broken pieces that were left over.

LUKE 6:27-36 "But I tell you who hear me: Love your enemies, do good to those who hate you, ²⁸bless those who curse you, pray for those who mistreat you. ²⁹If someone strikes you on one cheek, turn to him the other also. If someone takes your cloak, do not stop him from taking your tunic. ³⁰Give to everyone who asks you, and if anyone takes what belongs to you, do not demand it back. ³¹Do to others as you would have them do to you. ³²If you love those who love you, what credit is that to you? Even 'sinners' love those who love them. ³³And

if you do good to those who are good to you, what credit is that to you? Even 'sinners' do that. ³⁴And if you lend to those from whom you expect repayment, what credit is that to you? Even 'sinners' lend to 'sinners,' expecting to be repaid in full. ³⁵But love your enemies, do good to them, and lend to them without expecting to get anything back. Then your reward will be great, and you will be sons of the Most High, because he is kind to the ungrateful and wicked. ³⁶Be merciful, just as your Father is merciful."

LUKE 7:12-15 As he approached the town gate, a dead person was being carried out—the only son of his mother, and she was a widow. And a large crowd from the town was with her. ¹³When the Lord saw her, his heart went out to her and he said, "Don't cry." ¹⁴Then he went up and touched the coffin, and those carrying it stood still. He said, "Young man, I say to you, get up!" ¹⁵The dead man sat up and began to talk, and Jesus gave him back to his mother.

LUKE 10:29-37 But he [an expert in the law] wanted to justify himself, so he asked Jesus, "And who is my neighbor?" ³⁰In reply Jesus said: "A man was going down from Jerusalem to Jericho, when he fell into the hands of robbers. They stripped him of his clothes, beat him and went away, leaving him half dead. ³¹A priest happened to be going down the same road, and when he saw the man, he passed by on the other side. ³²So too, a Levite, when he came to the place and saw him, passed by on the other side. ³³But a Samaritan, as he traveled, came where the man was; and when he saw him, he took pity on him. ³⁴He went to him and bandaged his wounds, pouring on oil and wine. Then he put the man on his own donkey, took him to an inn and took care of him. ³⁵The next day he took out two silver coins and gave them to the innkeeper. 'Look after him,' he said, 'and when I return, I will reimburse you for any extra expense you may have.' ³⁶Which of these three do you think was a neighbor to the man who fell into the hands of robbers?" ³⁷The expert in the law replied, "The one who had mercy on him." Jesus told him, "Go and do likewise."

LUKE 13:34-35 "O Jerusalem, Jerusalem, you who kill the prophets and stone those sent to you, how often I have longed to gather your children together, as a hen gathers her chicks under her wings, but you were not willing! ³⁵Look, your house is left to you desolate. I tell you, you will not see me again until you say, 'Blessed is he who comes in the name of the Lord.'"

LUKE 19:41-44 As he approached Jerusalem and saw the city, he wept over it ⁴²and said, "If you, even you, had only known on this day what would bring you peace—but now it is hidden from your eyes. ⁴³The days will come upon you when your enemies will build an embankment against you and encircle you and hem you in on every side. ⁴⁴They will dash you to the ground, you and the children within your walls. They will not leave one stone on another, because you did not recognize the time of God's coming to you."

LUKE 23:34 Jesus said, "Father, forgive them, for they do not know what they are doing." And they divided up his clothes by casting lots.

LUKE 23:42-43 Then he [a criminal crucified with Jesus] said, "Jesus, remember me when you come into your kingdom." ⁴³Jesus answered him, "I tell you the truth, today you will be with me in paradise."

Conflict and Lawsuits

JOHN 7:24 "Stop judging by mere appearances, and make a right judgment."

JOHN 8:7 When they kept on questioning him, he straightened up and said to them, "If any one of you is without sin, let him be the first to throw a stone at her."

JOHN 13:34-35 "A new command I give you: Love one another. As I have loved you, so you must love one another. ³⁵By this all men will know that you are my disciples, if you love one another."

MATTHEW 5:3-9 "Blessed are the poor in spirit, for theirs is the kingdom of heaven. ⁴Blessed are those who mourn, for they will be comforted. ⁵Blessed are the meek, for they will inherit the earth. ⁶Blessed are those who hunger and thirst for righteousness, for they will be filled. ⁷Blessed are the merciful, for they will be shown mercy. ⁸Blessed are the pure in heart, for they will see God. ⁹Blessed are the peacemakers, for they will be called sons of God."

MATTHEW 5:21-26 "You have heard that it was said to the people long ago, 'Do not murder, and anyone who murders will be subject to judgment.' ²²But I tell you that anyone who is angry with his brother will be subject to judgment. Again, anyone who says to his brother, 'Raca,' is answerable to the Sanhedrin. But anyone who says, 'You fool!' will be in danger of the fire of hell. [23]Therefore, if you are offering your gift at the altar and there remember that your brother has something against you, [24]leave your gift there in front of the altar. First go and be reconciled to your brother; then come and offer your gift. [25]Settle matters quickly with your adversary who is taking you to court. Do it while you are still with him on the way, or he may hand you over to the judge, and the judge may hand you over to the officer, and you may be thrown into prison. [26]I tell you the truth, you will not get out until you have paid the last penny."

MATTHEW 5:31-32 "It has been said, 'Anyone who divorces his wife must give her a certificate of divorce.' [32]But I tell you that anyone who divorces his wife, except for marital unfaithfulness, causes her to become an adulteress, and anyone who marries the divorced woman commits adultery."

MATTHEW 5:38-48 "You have heard that it was said, 'Eye for eye, and tooth for tooth.' [39]But I tell you, Do not resist an evil person. If someone strikes you on the right cheek, turn to him the other also. [40]And if someone wants to sue you and take your tunic, let him have your cloak as well. [41]If someone forces you to go one mile, go with him two miles. [42]Give to the one who asks you, and do not turn away from the one who wants to borrow from you. [43]You have heard that it was said, 'Love your neighbor and hate

your enemy.' [44]But I tell you: Love your enemies and pray for those who persecute you, [45]that you may be sons of your Father in heaven. He causes his sun to rise on the evil and the good, and sends rain on the righteous and the unrighteous. [46]If you love those who love you, what reward will you get? Are not even the tax collectors doing that? [47]And if you greet only your brothers, what are you doing more than others? Do not even pagans do that? [48]Be perfect, therefore, as your heavenly Father is perfect."

MATTHEW 7:1-5 "Do not judge, or you too will be judged. [2]For in the same way you judge others, you will be judged, and with the measure you use, it will be measured to you. [3]Why do you look at the speck of sawdust in your brother's eye and pay no attention to the plank in your own eye? [4]How can you say to your brother, 'Let me take the speck out of your eye,' when all the time there is a plank in your own eye? [5]You hypocrite, first take the plank out of your own eye, and then you will see clearly to remove the speck from your brother's eye."

MATTHEW 7:12 "So in everything, do to others what you would have them do to you, for this sums up the Law and the Prophets."

MATTHEW 10:34-39 "Do not suppose that I have come to bring peace to the earth. I did not come to bring peace, but a sword. [35]For I have come to turn 'a man against his father, a daughter against her mother, a daughter-in-law against her mother-in-law— [36]a man's enemies will be the members of his own household.' [37]Anyone who loves his father or mother more than me is not worthy of me; anyone who loves his son or daughter more than me is not worthy of me; [38]and anyone who does not take his cross and follow me is not worthy of me. [39]Whoever finds his life will lose it, and whoever loses his life for my sake will find it."

MATTHEW 18:15-17 "If your brother sins against you, go and show him his fault, just between the two of you. If he listens to you, you have won your brother over. [16]But if he will not listen, take one or two others along, so that 'every matter may be established by the testimony of two or three witnesses.' [17]If he refuses to listen to them, tell it to the church; and if he refuses to listen even to the church, treat him as you would a pagan or a tax collector."

MATTHEW 18:21-35 Then Peter came to Him and said, "Lord, how often shall my brother sin against me, and I forgive him? Up to seven times?" [22]Jesus said to him, "I do not say to you, up to seven times, but up to seventy times seven. [23]Therefore the kingdom of heaven is like a certain king who wanted to settle accounts with his servants. [24]And when he had begun to settle accounts, one was brought to him who owed him ten thousand talents. [25]But as he was not able to pay, his master commanded that he be sold, with his wife and children and all that he had, and that payment be made. [26]The servant therefore fell down before him, saying, 'Master, have patience with me, and I will pay you all.' [27]Then the master of that servant was moved with compassion, released him, and forgave him the debt. [28]But that servant went out

and found one of his fellow servants who owed him a hundred denarii; and he laid hands on him and took him by the throat, saying, 'Pay me what you owe!' [29]So his fellow servant fell down at his feet and begged him, saying, 'Have patience with me, and I will pay you all.' [30]And he would not, but went and threw him into prison till he should pay the debt. [31]So when his fellow servants saw what had been done, they were very grieved, and came and told their master all that had been done. [32]Then his master, after he had called him, said to him, 'You wicked servant! I forgave you all that debt because you begged me. [33]Should you not also have had compassion on your fellow servant, just as I had pity on you?' [34]And his master was angry, and delivered him to the torturers until he should pay all that was due to him. [35]So My heavenly Father also will do to you if each of you, from his heart, does not forgive his brother his trespasses." (NKJV)

MARK 11:24-25 "Therefore I tell you, whatever you ask for in prayer, believe that you have received it, and it will be yours. [25]And when you stand praying, if you hold anything against anyone, forgive him, so that your Father in heaven may forgive you your sins."

MARK 12:29-31 "The most important one [commandment]," answered Jesus, "is this: 'Hear, O Israel, the Lord our God, the Lord is one. [30]Love the Lord your God with all your heart and with all your soul and with all your mind and with all your strength.' [31]The second is this: 'Love your neighbor as yourself.' There is no commandment greater than these."

LUKE 6:27-36 "But I tell you who hear me: Love your enemies, do good to those who hate you, ²⁸bless those who curse you, pray for those who mistreat you. ²⁹If someone strikes you on one cheek, turn to him the other also. If someone takes your cloak, do not stop him from taking your tunic. ³⁰Give to everyone who asks you, and if anyone takes what belongs to you, do not demand it back. ³¹Do to others as you would have them do to you. ³²If you love those who love you, what credit is that to you? Even 'sinners' love those who love them. ³³And if you do good to those who are good to you, what credit is that to you? Even 'sinners' do that. ³⁴And if you lend to those from whom you expect repayment, what credit is that to you? Even 'sinners' lend to 'sinners,' expecting to be repaid in full. ³⁵But love your enemies, do good to them, and lend to them without expecting to get anything back. Then your reward will be great, and you will be sons of the Most High, because he is kind to the ungrateful and wicked. ³⁶Be merciful, just as your Father is merciful."

LUKE 6:37-38 "Do not judge, and you will not be judged. Do not condemn, and you will not be condemned. Forgive, and you will be forgiven. ³⁸Give, and it will be given to you. A good measure, pressed down, shaken together and running over, will be poured into your lap. For with the measure you use, it will be measured to you."

LUKE 12:13-15 Someone in the crowd said to him, "Teacher, tell my brother to divide the inheritance with me." ¹⁴Jesus replied, "Man, who appointed me a judge or an arbiter between you?" ¹⁵Then he said to them, "Watch out! Be on your guard against all kinds of greed; a man's life does not consist in the abundance of his possessions."

LUKE 12:54-59 He said to the crowd: "When you see a cloud rising in the west, immediately you say, 'It's going to rain,' and it does. ⁵⁵And when the south wind blows, you say, 'It's going to be hot,' and it is. ⁵⁶Hypocrites! You know how to interpret the appearance of the earth and the sky. How is it that you don't know how to interpret this present time? ⁵⁷Why don't you judge for yourselves what is right? ⁵⁸As you are going with your adversary to the magistrate, try hard to be reconciled to him on the way, or he may drag you off to the judge, and the judge turn you over to the officer, and the officer throw you into prison. ⁵⁹I tell you, you will not get out until you have paid the last penny."

LUKE 17:3-4 "So watch yourselves. If your brother sins, rebuke him, and if he repents, forgive him. ⁴If he sins against you seven times in a day, and seven times comes back to you and says, 'I repent,' forgive him."

Enemies and Adversaries

MATTHEW 5:38-48 "You have heard that it was said, 'Eye for eye, and tooth for tooth.' ³⁹But I tell you, Do not resist an evil person. If someone strikes you on the right cheek, turn to him the other also. ⁴⁰And if someone wants to sue you and take your tunic, let him have your cloak as well. ⁴¹If someone forces you to go one mile, go with him two miles. [42]Give to the one who asks you, and do not turn away from the one who wants to borrow from you. [43]You have heard that it was said, 'Love your neighbor and hate your enemy.' [44]But I tell you: Love your enemies and pray for those who persecute you, [45]that you may be sons of your Father in heaven. He causes his sun to rise on the evil and the good, and sends rain on the righteous and the unrighteous. [46]If you love those who love you, what reward will you get? Are not even the tax collectors doing that? [47]And if you greet only your brothers, what are you doing more than others? Do not even pagans do that? [48]Be perfect, therefore, as your heavenly Father is perfect."

MATTHEW 10:16-23 "I am sending you out like sheep among wolves. Therefore be as shrewd as snakes and as innocent as doves. [17]Be on your guard against men; they will hand you over to the local councils and flog you in their synagogues. [18]On my account you will be brought before governors and kings as witnesses to them and to the Gentiles. [19]But when they arrest you, do not worry about what to say or how to say it. At that time you will be given what to say, [20]for it will not be you speaking, but the Spirit of your Father speaking through you. [21]Brother will betray brother to death, and a father his child; children will rebel against their parents and have them put to death. [22]All men will hate you because of me, but he who stands firm to the end will be saved. [23]When you are persecuted in one place, flee to another. I tell you the truth, you

will not finish going through the cities of Israel before the Son of Man comes."

LUKE 6:27-36 "But I tell you who hear me: Love your enemies, do good to those who hate you, [28]bless those who curse you, pray for those who mistreat you. [29]If someone strikes you on one cheek, turn to him the other also. If someone takes your cloak, do not stop him from taking your tunic. [30]Give to everyone who asks you, and if anyone takes what belongs to you, do not demand it back. [31]Do to others as you would have them do to you. [32]If you love those who love you, what credit is that to you? Even 'sinners' love those who love them. [33]And if you do good to those who are good to you, what credit is that to you? Even 'sinners' do that. [34]And if you lend to those from whom you expect repayment, what credit is that to you? Even 'sinners' lend to 'sinners,' expecting to be repaid in full. [35]But love your enemies, do good to them, and lend to them without expecting to get anything back. Then your reward will be great, and you will be sons of the Most High, because he is kind to the ungrateful and wicked. [36]Be merciful, just as your Father is merciful."

Forgiving Others
(See also pages 142 and 253.)

JOHN 8:3-11 The teachers of the law and the Pharisees brought in a woman caught in adultery. They made her stand before the group [4]and said to Jesus, "Teacher, this woman was caught in the act of adultery. [5]In the Law Moses commanded us to stone such women. Now what do you say?" [6]They were using this question as a trap, in order to have a basis for accusing him. But Jesus bent down and started to write on the ground with his finger. [7]When they kept on questioning him, he straightened up and said to them, "If any one of you is without sin, let him be the first to throw a stone at her." [8]Again he stooped down and wrote on the ground. [9]At this, those who heard began to go away one at a time, the older ones first, until only Jesus was left, with the woman still standing there. [10]Jesus straightened up and asked her, "Woman, where are they? Has no one condemned you?" [11]"No one, sir," she said. "Then neither do I condemn you," Jesus declared. "Go now and leave your life of sin."

MATTHEW 6:9-13 "This, then, is how you should pray: 'Our Father in heaven, hallowed be your name, [10]your kingdom come, your will be done on earth as it is in heaven. [11]Give us today our daily bread. [12]Forgive us our debts, as we also have forgiven our debtors. [13]And lead us not into temptation, but deliver us from the evil one.'"

MATTHEW 6:14-15 "For if you forgive men when they sin against you, your heavenly Father will also forgive you. [15]But if you do not forgive men their sins, your Father will not forgive your sins."

MATTHEW 18:15-17 "If your brother sins against you, go and show him his fault, just between the two of you. If he listens to you, you have won your brother over. [16]But if he will not listen, take one or two others along, so that 'every matter may be established by the testimony of two or three witnesses.' [17]If he

refuses to listen to them, tell it to the church; and if he refuses to listen even to the church, treat him as you would a pagan or a tax collector."

MATTHEW 18:21-35 Then Peter came to Him and said, "Lord, how often shall my brother sin against me, and I forgive him? Up to seven times?" [22]Jesus said to him, "I do not say to you, up to seven times, but up to seventy times seven. [23]Therefore the kingdom of heaven is like a certain king who wanted to settle accounts with his servants. [24]And when he had begun to settle accounts, one was brought to him who owed him ten thousand talents. [25]But as he was not able to pay, his master commanded that he be sold, with his wife and children and all that he had, and that payment be made. [26]The servant therefore fell down before him, saying, 'Master, have patience with me, and I will pay you all.' [27]Then the master of that servant was moved with compassion, released him, and forgave him the debt. [28]But that servant went out and found one of his fellow servants who owed him a hundred denarii; and he laid hands on him and took him by the throat, saying, 'Pay me what you owe!' [29]So his fellow servant fell down at his feet and begged him, saying, 'Have patience with me, and I will pay you all.' [30]And he would not, but went and threw him into prison till he should pay the debt. [31]So when his fellow servants saw what had been done, they were very grieved, and came and told their master all that had been done. [32]Then his master, after he had called him, said to him, 'You wicked servant! I forgave you all that debt because you begged me. [33]Should you not also have had compassion on your fellow servant, just as I had pity on you?' [34]And his master was angry, and delivered him to the torturers until he should pay all that was due to him. [35]So My heavenly Father also will do to you if each of you, from his heart, does not forgive his brother his trespasses." (NKJV)

MARK 11:24-25 "Therefore I tell you, whatever you ask for in prayer, believe that you have received it, and it will be yours. [25]And when you stand praying, if you hold anything against anyone, forgive him, so that your Father in heaven may forgive you your sins."

LUKE 6:37-38 "Do not judge, and you will not be judged. Do not condemn, and you will not be condemned. Forgive, and you will be forgiven. [38]Give, and it will be given to you. A good measure, pressed down, shaken together and running over, will be poured into your lap. For with the measure you use, it will be measured to you."

LUKE 7:41-50 "Two men owed money to a certain moneylender. One owed him five hundred denarii, and the other fifty. [42]Neither of them had the money to pay him back, so he canceled the debts of both. Now which of them will love him more?" [43]Simon replied, "I suppose the one who had the bigger debt canceled." "You have judged correctly," Jesus said. [44]Then he turned toward the woman and said to Simon, "Do you see this woman? I came into your house. You did not give me any water for my feet, but she wet my feet with her tears and wiped them with her hair. [45]You did not give me a kiss, but this woman, from the time I entered, has not stopped kissing my feet. [46]You did not put oil on my head, but she has poured perfume on my feet. [47]Therefore, I tell you, her many sins have been forgiven—for she loved much. But he who has been forgiven little loves little." [48]Then Jesus said to her, "Your sins are forgiven." [49]The other guests began to say among themselves, "Who is this who even forgives sins?" [50]Jesus said to the woman, "Your faith has saved you; go in peace."

LUKE 17:3-6 "So watch yourselves. If your brother sins, rebuke him, and if he repents, forgive him. [4]If he sins against you seven times in a day, and seven times comes back to you and says, 'I repent,' forgive him." [5]The apostles said to the Lord, "Increase our faith!" [6]He replied, "If you have faith as small as a mustard seed, you can say to this mulberry tree, 'Be uprooted and planted in the sea,' and it will obey you."

Judging Others

JOHN 7:24 "Stop judging by mere appearances, and make a right judgment."

JOHN 8:3-11 The teachers of the law and the Pharisees brought in a woman caught in adultery. They made her stand before the group [4]and said to Jesus, "Teacher, this woman was caught in the act of adultery. [5]In the Law Moses commanded us to stone such women. Now what do you say?" [6]They were using this question as a trap, in order to have a basis for accusing him. But Jesus bent down and started to write on the ground with his finger. [7]When they kept on questioning him, he straightened up and said to them, "If any one of you is without sin, let him be the first to throw a stone at her." [8]Again he stooped down and wrote on the ground. [9]At this, those who heard began to go away one at a time, the older ones first, until only Jesus was left, with the woman still standing there. [10]Jesus straightened up and asked her, "Woman, where are they? Has no one condemned you?" [11]"No one, sir," she said. "Then neither do I condemn you," Jesus declared. "Go now and leave your life of sin."

JOHN 8:15-16 "You judge by human standards; I pass judgment on no one. [16]But if I do judge, my decisions are right, because I am not alone. I stand with the Father, who sent me."

MATTHEW 7:1-5 "Do not judge, or you too will be judged. [2]For in the same way you judge others, you will be judged, and with the measure you use, it will be measured to you. [3]Why do you look at the speck of sawdust in your brother's eye and pay no attention to the plank in your own eye? [4]How can you say to your brother, 'Let me take the speck out of your eye,' when all the time there is a plank in your own eye? [5]You hypocrite, first take the plank out of your own eye, and then you will see clearly to remove the speck from your brother's eye."

LUKE 6:37-38 "Do not judge, and you will not be judged. Do not condemn, and you will not be condemned. Forgive, and you will be forgiven. [38]Give, and it will be given to you. A good measure, pressed down, shaken together and running over, will be poured into your lap. For with the measure you use, it will be measured to you."

LUKE 6:41-42 "Why do you look at the speck of sawdust in your brother's eye and pay no attention to the plank in your own eye? [42]How can you say to your brother, 'Brother, let me take the speck out of your eye,' when you yourself fail to see the plank in your own eye? You hypocrite, first take the plank out of your eye, and then you will see clearly to remove the speck from your brother's eye."

Marriage, Divorce, and Remarriage

MATTHEW 5:31-32 "It has been said, 'Anyone who divorces his wife must give her a certificate of divorce.' [32]But I tell you that anyone who divorces his wife, except for marital unfaithfulness, causes her to become an adulteress, and anyone who marries the divorced woman commits adultery."

MATTHEW 10:34-37 "Do not suppose that I have come to bring peace to the earth. I did not come to bring peace, but a sword. [35]For I have come to turn 'a man against his father, a daughter against her mother, a daughter-in-law against her mother-in-law— [36]a man's enemies will be the members of his own household.' [37]Anyone who loves his father or mother more than me is not worthy of me; anyone who loves his son or daughter more than me is not worthy of me."

MATTHEW 19:3-6, 8-12 Some Pharisees came to him to test him. They asked, "Is it lawful for a man to divorce his wife for any and every reason?" [4]"Haven't you read," he replied, "that at the beginning the Creator 'made them male and female,' [5]and said, 'For this reason a man will leave his father and mother and be united to his wife, and the two will become one flesh'? ⁶So they are no longer two, but one. Therefore what God has joined together, let man not separate." ⁸Jesus replied, "Moses permitted you to divorce your wives because your hearts were hard. But it was not this way from the beginning. ⁹I tell you that anyone who divorces his wife, except for marital unfaithfulness, and marries another woman commits adultery." ¹⁰The disciples said to him, "If this is the situation between a husband and wife, it is better not to marry." ¹¹Jesus replied, "Not everyone can accept this word, but only those to whom it has been given. ¹²For some are eunuchs because they were born that way; others were made that way by men; and others have renounced marriage because of the kingdom of heaven. The one who can accept this should accept it."

MARK 10:2-12 Some Pharisees came and tested him by asking, "Is it lawful for a man to divorce his wife?" ³"What did Moses command you?" he replied. ⁴They said, "Moses permitted a man to write a certificate of divorce and send her away." ⁵"It was because your hearts were hard that Moses wrote you this law," Jesus replied. ⁶"But at the beginning of creation God 'made them male and female.' ⁷'For this reason a man will leave his father and mother and be united to his wife, ⁸and the two will become one flesh.' So they are no longer two, but one. ⁹Therefore what God has joined together, let man not separate." ¹⁰When they were in the house again, the disciples asked Jesus about this. ¹¹He answered, "Anyone who divorces his wife

and marries another woman commits adultery against her. ¹²And if she divorces her husband and marries another man, she commits adultery."

MARK 12:24-27 Jesus replied, "Are you not in error because you do not know the Scriptures or the power of God? ²⁵When the dead rise, they will neither marry nor be given in marriage; they will be like the angels in heaven. ²⁶Now about the dead rising—have you not read in the book of Moses, in the account of the bush, how God said to him, 'I am the God of Abraham, the God of Isaac, and the God of Jacob'? ²⁷He is not the God of the dead, but of the living. You are badly mistaken!"

LUKE 14:25-27 Large crowds were traveling with Jesus, and turning to them he said: ²⁶"If anyone comes to me and does not hate his father and mother, his wife and children, his brothers and sisters—yes, even his own life—he cannot be my disciple. ²⁷And anyone who does not carry his cross and follow me cannot be my disciple."

LUKE 16:18 "Anyone who divorces his wife and marries another woman commits adultery, and the man who marries a divorced woman commits adultery."

LUKE 18:29-30 "I tell you the truth," Jesus said to them, "no one who has left home or wife or brothers or parents or children for the sake of the kingdom of God ³⁰will fail to receive many times as much in this age and, in the age to come, eternal life."

LUKE 20:34-38 Jesus replied, "The people of this age marry and are given in marriage. ³⁵But those who are considered worthy of taking part in that age and in the resurrection from the dead will neither marry nor be given in marriage, [36]and they can no longer die; for they are like the angels. They are God's children, since they are children of the resurrection. [37]But in the account of the bush, even Moses showed that the dead rise, for he calls the Lord 'the God of Abraham, and the God of Isaac, and the God of Jacob.' [38]He is not the God of the dead, but of the living, for to him all are alive."

Murder

MATTHEW 5:21-24 "You have heard that it was said to the people long ago, 'Do not murder, and anyone who murders will be subject to judgment.' [22]But I tell you that anyone who is angry with his brother will be subject to judgment. Again, anyone who says to his brother, 'Raca,' is answerable to the Sanhedrin. But anyone who says, 'You fool!' will be in danger of the fire of hell. [23]Therefore, if you are offering your gift at the altar and there remember that your brother has something against you, [24]leave your gift there in front of the altar. First go and be reconciled to your brother; then come and offer your gift."

MATTHEW 15:19-20 "For out of the heart come evil thoughts, murder, adultery, sexual immorality, theft, false testimony, slander. [20]These are what make a man 'unclean'; but eating with unwashed hands does not make him 'unclean.'"

Neighbors

MARK 12:28-31 One of the teachers of the law came and heard them [Jesus and the Sadducees] debating. Noticing that Jesus had given them a good answer, he asked him, "Of all the commandments, which is the most important?" [29]"The most important one," answered Jesus, "is this: 'Hear, O Israel, the Lord our God, the Lord is one. [30]Love the Lord your God with all your heart and with all your soul and with all your mind and with all your strength.' [31]The second is this: 'Love your neighbor as yourself.' There is no commandment greater than these."

LUKE 10:29-37 But he [an expert in the law] wanted to justify himself, so he asked Jesus, "And who is my neighbor?" [30]In reply Jesus said: "A man was going down from Jerusalem to Jericho, when he fell into the hands of robbers. They stripped him of his clothes, beat him and went away, leaving him half dead. [31]A priest happened to be going down the same road, and when he saw the man, he passed by on the other side. [32]So too, a Levite, when he came to the place and saw him, passed by on the other side. [33]But a Samaritan, as he traveled, came where the man was; and when he saw him, he took pity on him. [34]He went to him and bandaged his wounds, pouring on oil and wine. Then he put the man on his own donkey, took him to an inn and took care of him. [35]The next day he took out two silver coins and gave them to the innkeeper. 'Look after him,' he said, 'and when I return, I will reimburse you for any extra expense you may have.' [36]Which of these three do you think was a neighbor to the man who fell into the hands of robbers?" [37]The expert in the law replied,

"The one who had mercy on him." Jesus told him, "Go and do likewise."

Reconciliation

MATTHEW 5:21-24 "You have heard that it was said to the people long ago, 'Do not murder, and anyone who murders will be subject to judgment.' [22]But I tell you that anyone who is angry with his brother will be subject to judgment. Again, anyone who says to his brother, 'Raca,' is answerable to the Sanhedrin. But anyone who says, 'You fool!' will be in danger of the fire of hell. [23]Therefore, if you are offering your gift at the altar and there remember that your brother has something against you, [24]leave your gift there in front of the altar. First go and be reconciled to your brother; then come and offer your gift."

MATTHEW 18:15-17 "If your brother sins against you, go and show him his fault, just between the two of you. If he listens to you, you have won your brother over. [16]But if he will not listen, take one or two others along, so that 'every matter may be established by the testimony of two or three witnesses.' [17]If he refuses to listen to them, tell it to the church; and if he refuses to listen even to the church, treat him as you would a pagan or a tax collector."

MATTHEW 18:21-35 Then Peter came to Him and said, "Lord, how often shall my brother sin against me, and I forgive him? Up to seven times?" [22]Jesus said to him, "I do not say to you, up to seven times, but up to seventy times seven. [23]Therefore the kingdom of heaven is like a certain king who wanted to settle accounts with his servants. [24]And when he had begun to settle accounts, one was brought to him who owed him ten thousand talents. [25]But as he was not able to pay, his master commanded that he be sold, with his wife and children and all that he had, and that payment be made. [26]The servant therefore fell down before him, saying, 'Master, have patience with me, and I will pay you all.' [27]Then the master of that servant was moved with compassion, released him, and forgave him the debt. [28]But that servant went out and found one of his fellow servants who owed him a hundred denarii; and he laid hands on him and took him by the throat, saying, 'Pay me what you owe!' [29]So his fellow servant fell down at his feet and begged him, saying, 'Have patience with me, and I will pay you all.' [30]And he would not, but went and threw him into prison till he should pay the debt. [31]So when his fellow servants saw what had been done, they were very grieved, and came and told their master all that had been done. [32]Then his master, after he had called him, said to him, 'You wicked servant! I forgave you all that debt because you begged me. [33]Should you not also have had compassion on your fellow servant, just as I had pity on you?' [34]And his master was angry, and delivered him to the torturers until he should pay all that was due to him. [35]So My heavenly Father also will do to you if each of you, from his heart, does not forgive his brother his trespasses." (NKJV)

LUKE 17:3-4 "So watch yourselves. If your brother sins, rebuke him, and if he repents, forgive him. [4]If he sins against you seven times in a day, and seven times comes back to you and says, 'I repent,' forgive him."

Sexual Immorality and Adultery

MATTHEW 5:27-29 "You have heard that it was said, 'Do not commit adultery.' [28]But I tell you that anyone who looks at a woman lustfully has already committed adultery with her in his heart. [29]If your right eye causes you to sin, gouge it out and throw it away. It is better for you to lose one part of your body than for your whole body to be thrown into hell."

MATTHEW 5:31-32 "It has been said, 'Anyone who divorces his wife must give her a certificate of divorce.' [32]But I tell you that anyone who divorces his wife, except for marital unfaithfulness, causes her to become an adulteress, and anyone who marries the divorced woman commits adultery."

MATTHEW 15:19-20 "For out of the heart come evil thoughts, murder, adultery, sexual immorality, theft, false testimony, slander. [20]These are what make a man 'unclean'; but eating with unwashed hands does not make him 'unclean.' "

MATTHEW 19:9 "I tell you that anyone who divorces his wife, except for marital unfaithfulness, and marries another woman commits adultery."

MARK 10:11-12 He answered, "Anyone who divorces his wife and marries another woman commits adultery against her. [12]And if she divorces her husband and marries another man, she commits adultery." (See also Luke 16:18.)

Stumbling Blocks

MATTHEW 18:6-7 "But if anyone causes one of these little ones who believe in me to sin, it would be better for him to have a large millstone hung around his neck and to be drowned in the depths of the sea. [7]Woe to the world because of the things that cause people to sin! Such things must come, but woe to the man through whom they come!"

MATTHEW 23:2-4 "The teachers of the law and the Pharisees sit in Moses' seat. [3]So you must obey them and do everything they tell you. But do not do what they do, for they do not practice what they preach. [4]They tie up heavy loads and put them on men's shoulders, but they themselves are not willing to lift a finger to move them."

MATTHEW 23:13, 15 "Woe to you, teachers of the law and Pharisees, you hypocrites! You shut the kingdom of heaven in men's faces. You yourselves do not enter, nor will you let those enter who are trying to. [15]Woe to you, teachers of the law and Pharisees, you hypocrites! You travel over land and sea to win a single convert, and when he becomes one, you make him twice as much a son of hell as you are."

MATTHEW 23:23-35 "Woe to you, teachers of the law and Pharisees, you hypocrites! You give a tenth of your spices—mint, dill and cummin. But you have neglected the more important matters of the law—justice, mercy and faithfulness. You should have practiced the latter, without neglecting the former. [24]You blind guides! You strain out a gnat but swallow a camel. [25]Woe to you, teachers of the law and Pharisees, you hypocrites! You clean the outside of the cup and dish, but inside they are full of greed and self-indulgence. [26]Blind Pharisee! First clean the inside of the cup and dish, and then the outside also will be clean. [27]Woe to you, teachers of the law and Pharisees, you hypocrites! You are like whitewashed tombs, which look beautiful on the outside but on the inside are full of dead men's bones and everything unclean. [28]In the same way, on the outside you appear to people as righteous but on the inside you are full of hypocrisy and wickedness. [29]Woe to you, teachers of the law and Pharisees, you hypocrites! You build tombs for the prophets and decorate the graves of the righteous. [30]And you say, 'If we had lived in the days of our forefathers, we would not have taken part with them in shedding the blood of the prophets.' [31]So you testify against yourselves that you are the descendants of those who murdered the prophets. [32]Fill up, then, the measure of the sin of your forefathers! [33]You snakes! You brood of vipers! How will you escape being condemned to hell? [34]Therefore I am sending you prophets and wise men and teachers. Some of them you will kill and crucify; others you will flog in your synagogues and pursue from town to town. [35]And so upon you will come all the righteous blood that has been shed on earth, from the blood of righteous Abel to the blood of Zechariah son of Berekiah, whom you murdered between the temple and the altar."

MARK 9:41-42 "I tell you the truth, anyone who gives you a cup of water in my name because you belong to Christ will certainly not lose his reward. [42]And if anyone causes one of these little ones who believe in me to sin, it would be better for him to be thrown into the sea with a large millstone tied around his neck."

LUKE 11:52 "Woe to you experts in the law, because you have taken away the key to knowledge. You yourselves have not entered, and you have hindered those who were entering."

Notes

1. Napoleon Bonaparte, cited in Josh McDowell, *Evidence That Demands a Verdict: Historical Evidences for the Christian Faith* (San Bernardino, CA: Here's Life Publishers, 1977), 127.

2. Peter W. Stoner, *Science Speaks* (Chicago: Moody Press, 1963), 109–10. Cited in Josh McDowell, *Evidence That Demands a Verdict* (San Bernardino, CA: Here's Life Publishers, 1977), 167.

3. Most of the Scripture sections in this book begin with verses from the gospel of John, followed by verses from Matthew, Mark, Luke, and sometimes Acts, 1 Corinthians, or Revelation, in that order. I decided to begin the topical sections with verses from John because John's gospel is more direct and more intimate.

4. The earliest manuscripts of the gospel of Mark do not include Mark 16:9-20.

5. Bill Maher, interview by Larry King, on *Larry King Live.*

6. The earliest manuscripts of the gospel of Mark do not include Mark 16:9-20.

7. The earliest manuscripts of the gospel of Mark do not include Mark 16:9-20.

8. The earliest manuscripts of the gospel of Mark do not include Mark 16:9-20.

9. The earliest manuscripts of the gospel of Mark do not include Mark 16:9-20.

10. The earliest manuscripts of the gospel of Mark do not include Mark 16:9-20.

11. The earliest manuscripts of the gospel of Mark do not include Mark 16:9-20.

12. The earliest manuscripts of the gospel of Mark do not include Mark 16:9-20.

13. The earliest manuscripts of the gospel of Mark do not include Mark 16:9-20.

14. The earliest manuscripts of the gospel of Mark do not include Mark 16:9-20.

15. The earliest manuscripts of the gospel of Mark do not include Mark 16:9-20.

16. The earliest manuscripts of the gospel of Mark do not include Mark 16:9-20.

17. The earliest manuscripts of the gospel of Mark do not include Mark 16:9-20.

Scripture Index

Luke

John

SUBJECT INDEX

ABOUT THE AUTHOR

STEVEN K. SCOTT is the best-selling author of *The Greatest Man Who Ever Lived, The Richest Man Who Ever Lived,* and *Simple Steps to Impossible Dreams.* After failing nine jobs in his first six years after college, he learned the laws of life success by studying the book of Proverbs. As a result, Scott and his business partners built more than a dozen multimillion-dollar companies from scratch, achieving billions of dollars in sales. He is the cofounder of Max International, Total Gym Fitness, and The American Telecast Corporation. Scott is a popular international speaker on the subjects of personal and professional achievement and the application of biblical wisdom to every area of life.

www.stevenkscott.com

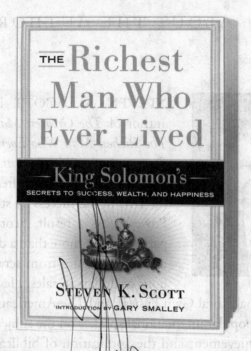